*West Africa under Colonial Rule*

# West Africa
# under Colonial Rule

Michael Crowder

NORTHWESTERN UNIVERSITY PRESS
Evanston, 1968

Library of Congress Catalog Card Number 68–27618

© Michael Crowder 1968

*Printed in Great Britain*

*In memory of*
MOLLY CROWDER

# Contents

# Preface

It is difficult only seven years since the majority of West African countries gained their independence to write a book about West Africa under colonial rule, especially if one is a subject of one of the former colonial powers. How difficult was brought home to me when I gave a lecture on the subject of this book to the officers of the Royal Sierra Leone Military Force. The one British officer present at the lecture stood stiffly to attention during question-time and demanded that I withdrew what he considered my anti-British remarks; by contrast, the African officers for the most part considered my criticisms of colonial rule very tame. It may be a long time before ex-colonial Europe or newly independent Africa will produce a mutually satisfactory account of the colonial period in West African history. Proximity to, and emotional involvement in, this period are not the only obstacles to an objective account of colonial rule in so vast an area as West Africa, comprising as it does thirteen states and one colony. The sheer mass of material to be digested is overwhelming as the end-notes will partially indicate. And this does not include archival sources which, with a few exceptions, I have not been able to consult.

This study, essentially a comparative study of the different impact of French and British colonial rule on West Africans and their reaction to it, is presented as an attempt to synthesise the more important material available on the years 1885–1945. Until more archival material has been worked on by scholars there must be inevitable gaps in our knowledge of the period. Interpretations will be subject to revision once the official dossiers are available. Even were the archives for this period available it would be more than a man's lifetime work to go through all those relating to the political, economic and social history of the twelve countries that are the subject of this study. Two West African states have been omitted: Togo and (Portuguese) Guinea. The latter was not dealt with because of the author's lack of knowledge of Portuguese and the paucity of material available in English and French on it. The former presents a special case of colonial rule, where the colonial powers were subject to some form of international control. Only the brief German period of Togo's history is discussed here and is dependent on French- and English-language sources alone since I do not read German.

Many people have been kind enough to read chapters of the book for me, and I would like to thank them very sincerely for the trouble they have taken on my behalf. I would like to add the customary caveat that none of them is in any way responsible for what follows, especially since one recommended that I spend another two years reading on the subject before going to press. Unfortunately there comes a time in reading for a work of synthesis where one reaches saturation point and can digest no more. I can only hope that the fact that I have reached this point does not become too apparent in the following pages.

Those I would like to thank for reading chapters for me are: John Hargreaves, Thomas Hodgkin, Eldred Jones, John Peterson, Christopher Fyfe, Donal Cruise O'Brien, A. E. Afigbo, Graham Irwin, Shekou Momodu Sesay, Walter Minchinton, J. F. Ade Ajayi, John Lewis, David Foley, David Ross, H. L. Van der Laan, Lalage Bown, John Flint, Richard Rathbone, Jeff Holden, Jamil Abun-Nasr and Robert S. Jordan, John Hunwick, Chris Allen and Bertin Webster.

My work has been greatly facilitated by the helpfulness of the Librarians of the Rhodes House Library, Oxford, the I.F.A.N. Library, Dakar, the International African Institute's Library, London, the Fourah Bay College Library, Freetown, and finally the African Library of the University of Ibadan. Mrs. Elinor Sinette, librarian of the Institute of African Studies, University of Ibadan, and her assistant, Mr. Fola Adediran, were particularly helpful in the preparation of the appendices.

I owe a particular debt of gratitude to La Ray Denzer, who was my indefatigable Research Assistant whilst I was Director of the

Institute of African Studies at Fourah Bay College, University of Sierra Leone. I am also greatly indebted to Rita Cruise O'Brien for her assistance with last-minute research in getting the final manuscript to press. I would also like to thank Dr. J. U. J. Asiegbu for letting me use material from his Cambridge Ph.D. Thesis on *Liberated Africans and British Politics, 1840–1920*; Dr. Gary Spackey for assistance with translations from the French; my agent, Miss Juliet O'Hea, for her encouragement throughout the four years this book has been in preparation; to Professor Vincent Monteil, Director of the Institut Fondamental de l'Afrique Noire, Dakar for all his hospitality while I was in Dakar and for first publishing in the IFAN *Bulletin* a version of Chapter II of Part IV; and to Professor J. Bertin Webster, Mrs. Ariadne Sanford and Mr. Paul Ozanne for help in checking the page proofs. Finally I would like to express my gratitude to Dr. Davidson Nicol, C.M.G., Principal of Fourah Bay College, for providing me with funds for research assistance, and also to my colleagues in the Institute of African Studies for their valuable support to me during the two years I was Director, when most of this book was written.

MICHAEL CROWDER

*Part I*
West Africa and colonial rule

# 1 Introduction

## 1 Colonial or foreign rule

Between 1885 and 1906 most of what is now described geographically as West Africa was formally occupied by four European powers: France, Britain, Germany and Portugal. From it they created a series of colonies all but one of which, Portuguese Guinea, have today become independent states: Mauritania, Senegal, Mali (formerly French Soudan), Guinea, Niger, Ivory Coast, Upper Volta, Dahomey, Togo, Portuguese Guinea, Nigeria, Ghana (formerly Gold Coast), Sierra Leone and the Gambia. The greater part of this area was occupied by force of arms, and where occupation was peaceful it was usually because African leaders, having seen the success with which European-led forces overcame their neighbours, decided resistance would be futile. There were, of course, numerous instances of occupation by peaceful negotiation. Some chiefs signed treaties because at the time an alliance with the Europeans would, in the short run, guarantee their position in the orbit of European trade, others to secure themselves a position in it.[1] But few African leaders desired that political control of their countries should be alienated permanently to the newcomers. It is one of the fictions of colonialism that Africans accepted colonial rule willingly, and in some cases with relief. In fact at least two-thirds of the peoples of West Africa have a history of overt resistance to colonial penetration.

The myth that Africans accepted colonial occupation passively, sometimes even gladly, is easily exploded by the opposition of such states as Dahomey, the Tokolor empire and Ashanti to any form of European penetration other than for purposes of trade; however, it is sufficiently deep-rooted to make it worth while listing the groups of Nigeria, the largest of the countries created by the colonialists, which did actively resist colonial occupation:

The Fulani Empire; Bornu under Rabeh; most of the hill tribes of the Plateau; Abuja; Tiv; the Eastern Ibo; Ibibio; Opobo under Jaja; the Itsekiri under Nana; the Western Ibo; and the Benin empire.

Yorubaland presents a rather special case. It clearly did resist penetration by the British, as evidenced by Lagos, the Egba and Ijebu. But for nearly eighty years Yorubaland had been torn by civil wars and faced with the problem of fending off three powers with ambitions for territorial expansion, namely the Fulani, Dahomey and Britain. When British occupation did take place it was not surprising that it seemed to many Yoruba a welcome respite from a century of strife.

In blunt terms, then, what took place between 1885 and 1906 was the military occupation and subjection of West Africans to an administration they did not want, and whose imposition they often resisted bitterly. The lands so occupied by the European powers were described variously as colonies and protectorates. But these were in fact euphemisms for what were territories under foreign occupation. However, I have resisted titling the present work *West Africa Under Foreign Rule* because the concept of colonial rule and its associated notion of the Protectorate describe a very special case in the history of the occupation of one people by another. The imperial conquests of the nineteenth century were the outcome of a technological revolution that put the industrialised nations of Western Europe in an absolutely commanding position vis-à-vis the rest of the world. Before that time Europe was not markedly in advance technologically of most other parts of the world, and in certain instances was behind.[2] But by the opening of the twentieth century Europe, with America, had achieved a technological supremacy that Africa and the rest of the world, with the exception of Japan, were in no position to challenge. In summary, one of the distinguishing features of early twentieth-century colonial rule was the overwhelming technological superiority of the colonial powers over their colonial subjects. And if Africans seem to have been somewhat passive in their acceptance of the colonial situation once subjected to it, this resulted from a realisation of the uselessness of resisting conquerors so manifestly superior to them technologically. We shall see, however, that as soon as a chink in this armour of technological strength appeared, as it did in French West Africa during the 1914–18 war, Africans were quick to try to overthrow their colonial masters. Their leaders, too, were quick to appreciate that in the long run the colonial master had to be fought with his own weapons; thus we find as a constant theme in nationalist movements the demand for education and in British West Africa a corresponding European suspicion of the educated African, 'the savvy boy' as he was so rudely called as late as the 1950's by the British administrator.

Associated with this technological superiority was another feature of colonial rule that distinguishes it from the ordinary case of foreign occupation. Technological superiority was invariably associated with a feeling of moral and racial superiority. Christian Europe, which had abolished the slave trade, felt itself morally superior to heathen Africa, which seemed to seek every opportunity to continue it. This sense of moral superiority was reinforced by theories of racial superiority which placed the white man at the top of the hierarchy, the black man at the bottom.[3] Thus the European colonial powers found nothing wrong in occupying and ruling lands belonging to African peoples at the same time as they were elevating almost into a natural law the right of national self-determination for the populations of Europe. Indeed it was considered that the subjection of the African to European rule was positively beneficial to him. So the Scramble for Africa, which was triggered off by considerations related to the need to maintain the balance of power in Europe, gained a missionary zeal. For example, the French still describe their bloody conquest of West Africa, with all sincerity, as the establishment of *La paix Française*.[4] Conquerors like Lugard and Archinard, who did not even envisage that a fundamental reorganisation of African society should follow their conquest,[5] nevertheless were fully convinced that the imposition of European rule was of unquestionable benefit to the African. Accordingly, the European occupation of Africa began to be talked of in terms of a 'sacred trust' or 'The White Man's Burden'. The Africans came to be treated very much as children for whom the European powers were happily arrived guardians. But here there was a difference in the approach of different European powers: some believed that the children they watched over could grow up into good Europeans; others believed they were permanently children,[6] or, rather, immutably separate and inferior to the Europeans. One of the most important features of the colonial period in Africa was the assumption by the conqueror of his racial superiority over those he had conquered, an assumption based largely on his manifest technological superiority. In the case of the

Anglo-Saxon, however, this attitude had much deeper roots, going back to Elizabethan times as the work of Philip Mason and Eldred Jones has shown.[7]

Another important aspect of colonial rule that differentiated it from what is normally described as the foreign occupation of one people by another was the fact that the Europeans who went out to administer African colonies did not feel they were foreign in the way the British officer in the British Army of the Rhine (B.A.O.R.) did in Germany after World War II. Since they never questioned their right to be in the colonies, or that the colonies belonged to them, they could not in the circumstances feel themselves foreigners there. They became expatriates, never foreigners. The British in fact maintained the fiction of the Protectorate throughout the colonial period; though the French and the Portuguese were soon treating their colonies as integral parts of the mother country, elaborating such bizarre concepts as the Overseas Provinces of Portugal and Overseas France.

Probably the most important distinction between the colonial empires of the twentieth century and earlier empires was the fact that they could be directly controlled from the metropolis. By the end of the early twentieth century the steamship and tele-communications had brought the metropolis in touch with the colony in a way that never made the European colonial feel totally alienated from his home. This certainly contributed to his feeling that he was not a foreigner but, rather, an expatriate. More important still, the colonial governors came directly under the orders of the metropolis.

The conviction of the European powers that the territories they conquered in the late nineteenth century were not 'occupied territories', or even lands that were essentially foreign, but a special kind of territory which they described as colonies,[8] had an immense impact on the Africans they ruled. So much so that even today many educated Africans still consider it the most important epoch in their history. However, the changes allegedly wrought by the colonial powers, as we shall see, were of far smaller magnitude than the colonial powers, in their self-congratulatory accounts of themselves, liked to believe.

For the above reasons, even though I accept that—looked at in the context of world history—what took place in Africa between 1885 and 1906 was the imposition of foreign rule, I have chosen to retain the word 'colonial' in the title of this book.

## 2 *Colonial rule as a factor for the integration of Africa into the modern world*

It is often forgotten just how short a period of time the colonial occupation of West Africa covered. There are many men alive today who can remember the arrival of the first Europeans in their towns or villages to assume political control either by force of arms or by negotiation with their leaders. The late Sir Milton Margai, first Prime Minister of independent Sierra Leone, was born before the British established their protectorate over Mendeland, his home, in 1896. The Chief of the Hausa quarter of Dakar left Kano on the eve of the fall of Kano to Lugard's forces, so that his only memory of his native city, to which he has never since returned, is one when no white man ruled. As late as 1936, Queen Juliana of Canhabaque in the Bissagos archipelago led her columns against the Portuguese in Guinea before being finally subjected to their rule. With the exception of the coastal enclaves of Senegal, the Gambia, Sierra Leone, the Gold Coast Forts and Lagos, the colonial period in West Africa rarely lasted more than seventy-five years and in many cases it was less than sixty.

More important than the brevity of colonial rule is the fact that it had little impact on the peoples of West Africa. Protectorates were established, but for the most part no radical changes were made in the daily lives of the people.[9] Of course their ultimate rulers had changed: but it took some time before the new rulers could make their presence felt; before they could impose their taxes; introduce health services; build their roads and railways. In many cases the switchover from a subsistence crop economy to one partly producing cash-crops for export, the major revolution in the lives of the peasants, had already taken place before the colonial era.[10] Thus, as Dr. Madden observed in 1841, Eastern Nigeria had adapted itself to the production of palm-oil for the European markets without the stimulus of colonial occupation: 'It is a very singular circumstance, and one deserving of serious consideration, that nearly the whole of this trade has sprung up within the last thirty years, in a place where we have no government agents, forts or settlements.'[11] Even Yorubaland, racked by terrible civil war, had exported comparatively large quantities of cotton before the establishment of the British protectorate. In Senegal peasant groundnut production was undertaken outside the French Protectorate. The Gambia in 1852 exported some £150,000 worth of groundnuts which had been cultivated outside the colony area. By that time, as Newbury points out, it had become 'certain that . . . groundnuts and cotton could be left to the independent African to produce'.[12] Production of these goods was, of course, increased by the introduction of colonial rule, for the imposition of taxes forced those who were not already producing to begin to do so. Furthermore the building of railways and, later, roads, undoubtedly facilitated their export.

A number of new crops, in particular coffee, were introduced only after colonial rule had been imposed. However, cocoa, the most valuable single crop in West Africa, owed its introduction as a cash crop—if not as a plant—to the Ghanaian, Tetteh Quarshie, in 1879,[13] who brought seeds over from Fernando Po. Cocoa had in fact first been introduced to that island by a West Indian-Sierra Leonean, William Pratt, who on settling there 'noted the similarity of the rich soil with that of the West Indian Islands, and he sent for cocoa seeds and started planting cocoa'.[14] Moreover, Africans had shown that they could undertake autonomously, without the stimulus of colonial occupation, a major revolution: that is the change-over from a predominantly subsistence economy to one geared largely to production for the export market. It has been argued elsewhere that Africa contained the seeds of its own modernisation,[15] of which this change-over can be seen as one instance. Admittedly, the changes in agriculture that took place were not a result of the European presence on the coast of West Africa, but what is being suggested is that such change could have taken place without European occupation. Certainly the evidence in West Africa does not invite a conclusion such as Roland Oliver makes with regard to East Africa: 'For the integration of East Africa with the general progress of mankind in the world outside, a drastic simplification of the old political diversity was an inescapable necessity. It was a problem, judging by historical precedent, that only a period of colonial tutelage could solve.'[16] My purpose is to examine how far the colonial powers in any meaningful sense by their 'tutelage' did integrate West Africa into the modern world. It will be shown that to a large extent the administrative system retarded rather than speeded up such integration and that it was African reaction to colonial rule more than anything else that achieved it. It is not until the period following the second world war, when clearly colonial governments in West Africa were guided—albeit involuntarily—by the presence of a vocal group of African critics, that we see any major efforts by them at modernisation of their colonies. Only in this period is there a significant expansion in education and health services; extension of the road and rail system over and above that which was found necessary at the beginning of the colonial period to ensure the export of the primary products which Europe required of Africa; or any significant growth in industry, which in Senegal, Nigeria, Ghana and Ivory Coast has increased a hundredfold since 1955.

Indeed, it will be shown that a great part of the education services provided by the colonial powers were in fact provided by the missionaries,[17] who obviously benefited by the presence of a colonial administration from the point of view of security, but who had been quite prepared to instal themselves in West Africa without such a guarantee of security. For instance, in the Gold Coast the Basel Mission[18] and in Western Nigeria the Yoruba Mission were both opposed to colonial occupation. It was the missionaries in most cases who were responsible for the training of an African élite before colonial occupation took place. Even before the establishment of European protectorates, chiefs and people were seeking education. Chiefs in Sierra Leone were asking for schools twenty years before the establishment of the Protectorate,[19] and most of the important ones had educated clerks.[20] And, in so far as the creation of an African élite can be taken as an indication of the integration of Africa into the modern world, we can see the élite suffering a real setback in the colonial era. Thus in 1875, in Lagos, 'the head of police, the head of posts and telegraphs, head of customs, and the Registrar of the Supreme Court were all Nigerians'.[21] At the same time, an African Bishop headed the Anglican Mission on the Niger. Yet later, in the period of colonial rule, all Africans of their competence were relegated to subordinate positions in Nigeria.[22] In Sierra Leone, where the Creole élite had supplied many senior government officials, including an Acting Chief Justice, an Acting Colonial Secretary and even a Secretary for Native Affairs, it was disinherited after 1900, with the final establishment of the British Protectorate over the hinterland. This is less true of the French-speaking areas, but even there little was done to encourage the formation of an educated élite whereby Africa, through its own people, could be integrated in the modern world.

These are themes that will be developed in the pages that follow. But the essential focus of the book is on the curious experiment undertaken by the European colonial powers at the end of the nineteenth century. Why did they consider it necessary to occupy so vast an area of land about whose riches at the end of the nineteenth century they were no longer optimistic? Could they not have exploited it economically in the very way they were exploiting Latin America, without all the cost of establishing a colonial administration? What were the reactions of Africans to the invasion of their territories by those alien whites who, for the most part, if they were known at all, were known only in their capacity as traders and missionaries? And how radically did these new systems of administration change the indigenous systems of government? How far did colonial occupation produce a social and economic revolution in West Africa? And to what extent did this revolution, if revolution it was, bring Africa into the orbit of the modern world? Finally, what was the nature of African reaction to colonial rule, and how far did the difference between policies of the French and British administration affect these reactions?

### 3 Pre-colonial Africa: the myth and the reality

The European colonial powers, despite the efforts of their explorers, of whom Heinrich Barth is the outstanding example, were for the most part ignorant of the peoples they were subjecting to their rule. Indeed many of them sincerely believed that Africa was a dark continent and that they were bringing the first light of civilisation to a benighted people, lost in primitive barbarity. Thus French textbooks on African history, even to this day, treat France's occupation of West Africa, achieved at the cost of so many lives, as an unqualified blessing for the African. And whilst the British, with a more characteristic reserve, were not so outspoken in praise of themselves, the attitude of the average administrator was that the African was more than fortunate to be placed under his benign rule. The idea of Africa before colonial rule as a primitive and barbarous continent without a history lingers on today, after independence, despite the efforts of the growing body of serious historians of Africa. That it should so linger is an indication of the conviction with which it was held. Thus in 1962 so eminent a historian as Professor Hugh Trevor-Roper could pronounce the much quoted verdict from his august chair at Oxford that 'perhaps in the future there will be some African history to teach. But at the present there is none; there is only the history of the Europeans in Africa. The rest is darkness . . . and darkness is not the subject of history.'[23] Even so distinguished a scholar of Africa as Margery Perham subscribed to this view as late as 1951 when she wrote 'until the very recent penetration of Europe the greater part of the continent was without the wheel, the plough or the transport animal; without stone houses or clothes except skins; without writing and so without history'.[24] It is strange that Perham of all people should have been party to the perpetuation of this view of Africa, for as author of the pioneer work *Native Administration in Nigeria*[25] she knew better than anyone the sophistication of the administrative system of the Fulani empire, founded in the early nineteenth century on the basis of the Habe City States, which appear to date back as far as A.D. 1000. This was a system which was utilised with few modifications by the British in their administration of Northern Nigeria. As disciple and biographer of Lord Lugard she had read his wife's book *A Tropical Dependency*,[26] which is a history of the Western Sudan written shortly after his conquest of the Fulani empire, covering in its five hundred pages nearly a thousand years of history of a people who for the first time were coming under European rule.

The view of Africa as a continent without history gained almost universal currency in the colonial period. Such a view was clearly useful as a justification for the European occupation of Africa, for a people characterised as one without history or culture, indulging in abhorrent practises such as human sacrifice and cannibalism, were clearly in need of European tutelage. Thus the colonial stereotype of the African became that of a people saved from themselves by the benevolence of their colonial rulers. The history of Ghana and Songhai, Oyo and Benin were conveniently forgotten. 'Without us they would be back in the trees', was the philosophy of many Europeans in Africa during the colonial period. Thus when the so-called Mau Mau rebellion broke out in Kenya it was not seen by Europeans as a genuine nationalist movement, based on real griev-ances, but as a reversionary and barbarous movement aimed at turning Kenya into a land of 'darkness and death'.[27] Such an attitude developed despite the historical writings of colonial officials like Richmond Palmer, Maurice Delafosse and Charles Monteil. And it is only within the last decade that it is becoming generally accepted that, in the words of the early Ghanaian national-ist, J. E. Casely-Hayford, 'before even the British came into relations with our people, we were a developed people, having our own institutions, having our own ideas of government'.[28] It is important to insist on this fact, for as will become clear in succeeding chapters the colonial rulers had, right up to the moment of independence, to take into account the cultural sophistication of traditional African societies in most of the decisions they made. The sense of identity of the Ashanti nation, the spiritual power of the Moro Naba of the Mossi, the nature of the traditional administrative system of the Yoruba, the historic role of Islam in the Savannah, all these had to be reckoned with. So it becomes important to appreciate the difference between what Africa was really like and what the newly established colonial administration came to think it was like. Only against this background can the policies of the colonial powers be fully understood. Thus for a time the French, believing that Africans lacked any culture or history worth calling such, were convinced that the only salvation for the African was his assimilation into French 'civilisation'. So persuaded were Europeans of the inferiority of the Negro-African that they invented the Hamitic hypothesis to explain away any Negro achievement.[29] Thus wherever a sophisticated Negro state was found to have existed it was postulated that it was the result of the imposition of the rule of a mythical light-skinned nomadic people, known as the Hamites, over loosely organised sedentary Negroes. These Hamites having learnt how to herd cattle were able to 'herd' people. The essence of this hypothesis was to explain away achievements by Negroes such as the great Sudanic empires which conflicted with the stereotype the European had designed for them. Thus the Ife bronzes *had* to be the work of a non-African, so that even a wandering Roman sculptor was postulated as their creator. Such attitudes die hard, so that even in a recently published history of Africa the genius behind the rise of the Sudanese states such as Ghana, Mali, Songhai, Oyo and Benin is on the slenderest evidence attributed to Egypt, though credit for the transmission of the idea of divine monarchy from Egypt to these states is given to the Negroes themselves.[30] Only now are historians examining the possibility of autonomous inspiration for the growth of these states rather than exclusively external factors.

The portrait of Africa painted by the colonial powers was one of a people who on the eve of occupation were politically decentralised, living in small villages, often naked, dominated by witchcraft, living in terror of their neighbours. The blessings brought them by the colonial administration and its auxiliaries the missionaries were the establishment of security in the form of a central authority that would prevent inter-tribal fighting and free people from the 'bondage' of traditional religion by converting them to that of Christ. Such a stereotype, for which examples on which to base it were not wanting, was an acceptable one for an outside world which could only agree that if Africans did live in such conditions then clearly colonial administration was beneficial to them. Thus E. D. Morel, the champion of the African against the excesses of colonial rule in the Congo, nevertheless did not doubt that colonial rule such as practised by the British was necessary for the African.[31] The missionaries tended to emphasise, even invented, the worst features of African society when they lectured or preached in churches at home, for descriptions of a heroic struggle against the powers of darkness would encourage the parishioner to drop a penny in the collection box for their missions. For the general public an Africa, where law and order reigned, where people lived in large towns and wore clothes, whose élite read and wrote in Arabic script or like the Sierra Leone Creoles, the St. Louisians and the Yorubas of Abeokuta were substantially assimilated, was far less romantic and did not make such an appealing subject for the travel book and later the film. Even today it is 'savage Africa' that still appeals if we are to take seriously travel books such as *Call Africa 999* by John Peer Nugent, correspondent of *Newsweek*.[32] Once it came to be realised that Africa was not in fact all primitive jungle, the need for colonial rule would become less obvious, the role of the missionary less necessary.

This European stereotype of Africa was based on the acephalous society, whose people were organised into independent villages of rarely more than two hundred inhabitants, and had no administrative or judicial institutions. But because of the romantic European mind these peoples were more fascinating than those who had attained a more complex form of political administration. And because even scholarly studies of African societies by anthropologists were predominantly concerned in the colonial period with such societies, the latter began to appear to be the rule rather than the exception that they were in West Africa. The preoccupation of anthropologists with segmentary or 'primitive' societies in Africa rather than those of more complex structure does much to explain the unpopularity of that discipline among Africans today. Anthropologists became, in the eyes of the nationalist leaders, agents of those who held the view that the African was incapable of self-government.[33]

The truth, of course, is that West Africa had long been accustomed to centralised states, many of them covering much larger areas than the colonies the Europeans carved out of West Africa at the end of the nineteenth century. A comparison of the African states on the eve of the scramble for Africa with those created by the European is instructive. (See map.) So too is a similar comparison with the states of West Africa at the beginning of the sixteenth century. Within the framework of these states, whether they were located in the savannah or the forest, Africans had been able to achieve two things of which many European administrators believed they had been traditionally incapable. First they had organised centralised governments with the necessary ancillaries of a strong bureaucracy and judicial system, and above all they had provided security for

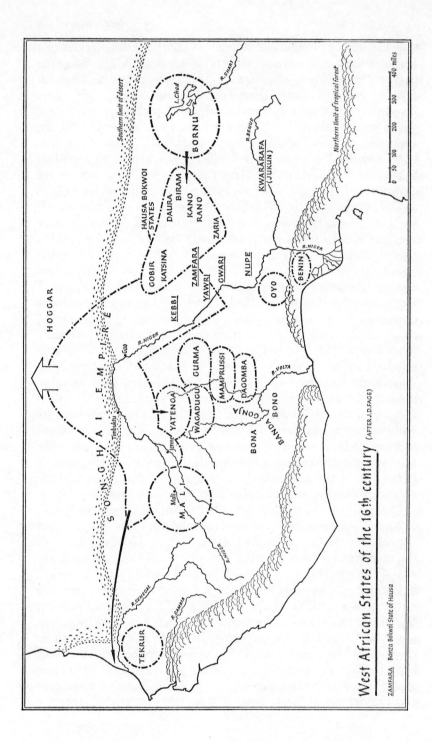

# West African States of the 16th century (AFTER J.D.FAGE)

ZAMFARA  Bonza Bokwoi State of Hausa

HOGGAR

Southern limit of desert

L.Chad

BORNU

R.SHARI

HAUSA BOKWOI
STATES

DAURA

BIRAM

KANO
RANO

ZARIA

GOBIR

KATSINA

ZAMFARA

GWARI

YAWRI

KEBBI

S·O·N·G·H·A·I  E·M·P·I·R·E

Gao

R.NIGER

Timbuktu

Jenne

Mali

M·A·L·I

R.NIGER

YATENGA

WAGADUGU

GURMA

MAMPRUSSI

DAGOMBA

GONJA

BONA

BANDA

BONO

R.VOLTA

NUPE

OYO

BENIN

R.NIGER

KWARARAFA
(JUKUN)

R.BENUE

Northern limit of tropical forest

R.SENEGAL

R.GAMBIA

TEKRUR

0  50  100  200  300  400 miles

their peoples. Thus we might cite in this context the oft-quoted passage written in the fourteenth century by the Arab traveller, Ibn Batuta, who was not entirely free from the prejudices against the Negro held many centuries later by the European. What follows was written of the great Mali empire in the early fourteenth century by a man who, we must remember, had travelled extensively in the Middle East, India and China. 'The Negroes possess some admirable qualities. They are seldom unjust, and have a greater abhorrence of injustice than any other people. There is complete security in their country. Neither traveller nor inhabitant in it has anything to fear from robbers or men of violence. They do not confiscate the property of any white man (Arab) who dies in their country, even if it be uncounted wealth. On the contrary, they give it into the charge of some trustworthy person among the whites, until the rightful heir takes possession of it.'[34]

The British explorers Clapperton and Lander during the Yoruba Civil Wars were able to travel safely from Badagry to Sokoto in the early nineteenth century. Much of the insecurity of which Europeans write in West Africa and which they like to think was its dominant characteristic was a direct result of the slave trade, or a result of the European penetration of Africa. Even the abolition of the slave trade contributed to insecurity, for it suddenly deprived peoples of their main source of foreign exchange and left them often in a precarious economic position.

The second achievement of the early African empires was to bring together into one political unit peoples of diverse ethnic groups. One of the main concerns of British administration was with the problem of inter-ethnic hostility. The system of indirect rule very often was designed to shield one ethnic group from another so as to avoid conflict, because it was believed that ethnocentricity was a dominant feature of pre-colonial society. But whereas it is true that many wars that took place before the period of colonial rule were inter-ethnic wars, there is also considerable evidence for the other view, that of different ethnic groups participating in the same state organisation: Mali, Songhai, the Sokoto Caliphate, Bornu, the empire of El Hajj Omar, and the Oyo empire are cases in point. The French, much less preoccupied with the problems of ethnicity, seem to have left a colonial legacy in which tribalism has not been such a dominant factor.

It is not the aim of this book to prove that pre-European Africa had cultures of great complexity and sophistication. This has been done effectively at the popular level by Basil Davidson in *Old Africa*

*Rediscovered* and by Roland Oliver in his reply to Trevor-Roper's attack.[35] It is only to emphasise the difference between the coloniser's conception of African history and the reality. Refutation of the view that Africa had no history has always been an essential element in African nationalist thought: thus we see that the African past provided an important inspiration for such precursors of modern nationalism as Edward Blyden and J. E. Casely-Hayford, evidence of which can be seen in Blyden's *Christianity, Islam and the Negro Race* (1887) and Hayford's *Ethiopia Unbound* (1911). Early newspapers in the Gold Coast, Sierra Leone and Nigeria gave considerable space to the early history of Africa, maintaining that knowledge of the past was necessary for pride of race. There are extreme reactions such as those of Cheick Anta Diop, in which he tries to prove that the Egyptians were Wolofs, and consequently that European civilisation owes its origins to the Negro.[36] Dr. Nnamdi Azikiwe, First President of Nigeria, continued the journalistic pattern when he wrote a long series of portraits of famous Negroes of the past whilst editor of *Africa Morning Post* in Accra. More recently, J. C. de Graft Johnson published *African Glory*[37] which is essentially an account of the achievements of the Sudanese empires.

During the colonial period, then, there was amongst the colonisers a prevailing view that Africa had no history worth calling such, a view they handed on successfully in their educational programme to many Africans; an African reaction which at times tended to over-emphasise the achievements of pre-colonial Africa; and behind these two views the reality of a continent which, since the time Julius Caesar invaded the countries of the dominant colonial powers in West Africa, had in fact produced a history rich and varied, with moments of glory, and moments of disgrace, similar to that of any other part of the world. But like the rest of the world, at the end of the nineteenth century, Africa found itself in a situation where Europe had outstripped it technologically to such a point that it could no longer resist European occupation. Even so, it is worth remembering that the Ashanti nation had defeated the British soundly in 1824 and again, though much less decisively, in 1863–4, and that Samory held the French at bay for fifteen years. The essential point to be brought out from this discussion then is that the European administrator was not dealing with a *tabula rasa*, but with an Africa whose past impinged on his day to day decisions. However, his attitude that the African was a man without history added fuel to the nationalist reaction against colonial rule, and contributed to the ideas of Pan-Africanism, Negritude and the African Personality, or the search for a cultural self-identity on the part of the African, which is a dominant theme of the history of the colonial period.

## 4 *The periodisation of colonial rule*

Of the four colonial powers that were to occupy West Africa, three, Portugal, France, and Britain, had already been installed on the coast for the whole of the nineteenth century. But prior to 1885 only one had openly demonstrated interest in colonial expansion into the interior of West Africa, and that was France, and even then her government was divided over the issue of colonial involvement in Tropical Africa. The British Government right up to the eve of the Berlin Conference of 1884–5 had been opposed to increasing its limited colonial obligations in Africa. Before 1884 Germany had shown no official interest in Tropical Africa, and Bismarck clearly regarded colonies as useful only in so far as they helped him in the delicate task of maintaining the 'Balance of Power' in Europe; he certainly did not wish colonies in any way to prove a financial burden on his government. Only Portugal, which, as far as West Africa was concerned, had but a tentative foothold on the coastline of modern Portuguese Guinea, was from a governmental point of view whole-heartedly in favour of colonial occupation of Africa and the expansion of her interests. The only drawback to such an intention on Portugal's part was the lack of the wherewithal to achieve these aims. On the eve of the Berlin Conference, which will be discussed in greater detail in the next chapter, the three most important colonial powers in West Africa, Britain, Germany and France, were *officially* opposed to colonial expansion in West Africa or any other part of Tropical Africa, though the last power had important forces, both within government and without, pressuring for rapid colonial expansion. Portugal, whatever her ambitions in West Africa, was too weak to assert them both there and in Southern Africa where she had her major interest. This weakness on the part of the first European power that made contact with West Africa is amply brought out by the diminutive portion of that part of the continent which she finally secured for herself. Although by 1885 the Scramble for Africa was well under way, as we shall see in the next chapter, the Berlin Conference of that year is a significant landmark in the history of colonial rule in West Africa. It was the year in which, however reluctantly, Britain and Germany were forced to change their attitude to the acquisition of colonies in Tropical Africa. It also helped to consolidate that powerful body of opinion in France that was in favour

c

of colonial expansion. And it also forced Portugal to assert, in so far as her limited military resources could permit, her rights to the area around Portuguese Guinea.

In a formal sense the Berlin Conference, even if it was merely giving international recognition to a situation that with hindsight we can see was already well developed, marks the beginning of the colonial era in West Africa. Prior to that date the Europeans, with the exception of France in Senegal, had limited their colonial commitments to small enclaves on the coast from which they could secure their trading interests and from time to time interfere in the politics of the interior when these interests were threatened. This period, an understanding of which is essential to an appreciation of the decision made by the European powers at the Berlin Conference that they should occupy Africa, is what might be called the proto-colonial period and begins effectively at the turn of the nineteenth century with the abolition of the slave trade. Though 1885 marks the beginning of the colonial era in West Africa in the sense that it was in that year that the colonial powers formally committed themselves to colonial occupation, in many ways 1900, the date chosen by Jean Suret-Canale for the opening of the colonial period,[38] is preferable, for it is not until that date that most of West Africa came effectively under colonial administration. Nevertheless the period 1885–1900, which is the period of conquest, was so critical in its influence on the patterns and character of administration laid down by the European conquerors that I have preferred to mark the opening of the colonial era with the year 1885. Nineteen-sixty is the terminal date for the colonial period, even though Ghana and Guinea were independent before then, Sierra Leone and Gambia were not independent by that time, and Portuguese Guinea is still subjected to Portuguese colonial rule. Nevertheless 1960 is the year when all the other nations of West Africa gained their independence and it seems a satisfactory date to mark the effective end of colonial rule in West Africa. However, Suret-Canale chooses 1945 as his terminal date for the colonial era. Here there is considerable justification for such a dating, since the end of the Second World War also marked the beginning of the decolonisation process in West Africa. However, it will be argued that the process began in earnest the moment the Second World War broke out, for the impact of this war on both French and English-speaking West Africans was such that decolonisation became inevitable. As far as Africans were concerned, in both French and English-speaking West Africa it proved the watershed in their political and economic development that was the prelude to their independence. I have thus adopted the following periodisation for colonial rule in West Africa:

A. 1880–1885   = *Proto-Colonial Period*
B. 1885–1945   = *Colonial Era*
subdivided thus:
  (*i*) 1885–1900   = Period of Conquest and Occupation
  (*ii*) 1900–1919   = Period of pacification and elaboration of systems of administration
  (*iii*) 1919–1939   = Period of Colonial Rule Proper
  (*iv*) 1939–1945   = The Watershed between Colonial Rule and Decolonisation
C. 1945–1960   = *Decolonisation*

This book will be concerned with the Colonial Era, that is the background to the fifteen years of decolonisation in which thirteen colonies in West Africa became independent states. But states which were heavily marked by their respective French and British experiences.

# Notes

1 Thus it has been argued that Sultan Umoru of Sokoto (1881–91), when signing the treaty with the Niger Company, which the latter claimed as the basis for its sovereignty over the Fulani empire, considered that he was merely granting the company a monopoly of European trade in return for which he was given an annual payment, by way of tribute, of sixty million cowries (£3,780). See Arthur N. Cook, *British Enterprise on the Niger*, New York, 1943, p. 155.

2 See Peter Worsley, *The Third World*, London, 1964, pp. 1–20; and William H. McNeill, *The Rise of the West*, Chicago, 1963.

3 See Philip D. Curtin, *The Image of Africa*, Madison, 1964.

4 For instance J. Richard-Molard *Afrique Occidentale Française*, Paris, 1956, Chapter III, pp. 141–5.

5 See *Annual Reports for Northern Nigeria*, 1900–1; 1901; 1902; 1903; 1904; 1905. Lugard, *Political Memoranda* (Revision of Instructions to Political Officers on Subjects chiefly political and administrative; 1913–18), Lagos, 1919 and *The Dual Mandate in British Tropical Africa*, Lagos, 1922. Also Archinard's report on the campaign of 1890–1, partially reproduced in Jacques Méniaud, *Les Pionniers du Soudan*, Paris, 1931, Vol. II.

6 Thus in 1924 Lord Leverhulme at a dinner in honour of the Governor of Nigeria, Sir Hugh Clifford, said: 'I am certain that the West African races have to be treated very much as one would treat children when they are immature and under-developed. . . . Now the organising ability is the particular trait and characteristic of the white man. . . . I say this with my little experience, that the African native will be happier, produce the best, and live under conditions of prosperity when his labour is directed and organised by his white brother who has all these million years' start ahead of him.' *West Africa*, July 26th, 1924.

7 See Philip Mason, *Prospero's Magic*, London, 1962, and Eldred Jones, *Othello's Countrymen*, London, 1965, from which it is clear Anglo-Saxon racial prejudice is not a by-product of colonialism.

8 Of course in West Africa they were not colonies in the true sense, since no members of the mother country settled there on a permanent basis. Even in Ivory Coast and Senegal, where there were settlers, they always retired to France. There were only a handful who made Senegal or Ivory Coast their home as the British settlers did in Kenya or Rhodesia. Britons were not allowed to own land at all in any of the British West African Protectorates, and though in the nineteenth century they had been able to own land in the Colony areas, further acquisition became impossible in the twentieth century.

9 As late as 1958 many ethnic groups in West Africa were still living very much as they did on the eve of the European occupation. Thus

the Cabrai of Northern Togo and Ghana, the Somba of Dahomey, the Ibo of Abakaliki still lived entirely naked. It is only as a result of pressure by Independent African Governments that they are now clothing themselves, that is, becoming integrated into the modern world! Much more worrying than nudity, a subject on which the African élite was sensitive because of the way it was used to discredit their demands for Independence, was the terrible poverty of many of these groups after sixty years of colonial rule. The author visited Somba country in 1958, where many of the people, still mostly unclothed, were unsure where their next meal would come from. See Michael Crowder, *Pagans and Politicians*, London, 1959, p. 124.

10 Henri Brunschwig, *L'Avènement de l'Afrique*, Paris, 1963, speculates that Africa was just about to produce something new at the very time she was occupied by the Europeans. Thus he asks whether Samory and Rabeh might not have been the grave-diggers of the old African cultures upon the ruins of which they may have been about to build new modern states that could have dealt with the Western world. One example, which comes to mind, that would back up this hypothesis, is Jaja of Opobo, who clearly understood the advantages of Western technology, and even sent his son to school in Europe.

11 Cited in C. W. Newbury, *British Policy towards West Africa: Select Documents 1786–1874*, London, 1965, p. 112.

12 *Ibid.*, p. 98.

13 David Kimble, *A Political History of Ghana, 1850–1928*, London, 1963, p. 33, in particular, n. 5.

14 Robert Wellesley Cole, *Kossoh Town Boy*, London, 1960, pp. 23–4.

15 Brunschwig, *L'Avènement*, has put forward cogent arguments to suggest that Africa was, as he puts it, *en voie de s'occidentaliser*.

16 *History of East Africa*, ed. Roland Oliver and Gervase Mathew, Vol. I, London, 1963, 'Epilogue' by Roland Oliver, p. 456.

17 As far as British West Africa is concerned a notable exception was Sir Gordon Guggisberg, Governor of the then Gold Coast, who clearly saw the importance of higher education to the modernisation of Africa and clearly also believed that Africans could be agents of this process.

18 The Basel Mission, mostly concentrated in the Eastern Region of the Gold Coast, pursued an educational policy which was geared to produce self-sufficient African farmers and artisans. The curriculum of its schools was a practical one emphasising the techniques of agriculture, carpentry, weaving, and, after 1855, the rudiments of trade and industry. Consequently, the mission was able to maintain its own trading companies and certain industrial enterprises all of which were manned by African staff. Thus colonial occupation would seem superfluous to them. See M. J. Marshall, *Christianity and Nationalism in Ghana*, unpublished M.A. thesis, University of Ghana, 1965, pp. 17–21.

19 For this information I am grateful to Professor John Peterson.
20 *Chalmers Report* (Parliamentary Papers 1899, LX Report . . . on . . . the Insurrection in the Sierra Leone Protectorate).
21 J. F. Ade Ajayi, *Milestones in Nigeria History*, Ibadan, 1962, p. 24.
22 There were rare exceptions in the early stages of colonial rule: i.e. Eric Moore, Henry Carr and Sir Kitoye Ajasa.
23 Hugh Trevor-Roper, 'The Rise of Christian Europe', *The Listener*, 28th November, 1963.
24 Margery Perham, 'The British Problem in Africa', *Foreign Affairs*, July 1951, reprinted in Oxford University Institute of Colonial Studies Reprint Series, no. 2, p. 2.
25 Margery Perham, *Native Administration in Nigeria*, London, 1957.
26 Lady Lugard, *A Tropical Dependency*, London, 1905.
27 Carl Rosberg and John Nottingham, *The Myth of Mau Mau*, New York, 1967.
28 Cited by Basil Davidson with E. K. Buah and J. F. Ade Ajayi, *The Growth of African Civilisation: History of West Africa 1000–1800*, London, 1965, p. 285.
29 W. St. Clair Drake in 'The Responsibility of Men of Culture for Destroying the "Hamitic Myth" ', *Présence Africaine*, No. 24–5 (Feb.–May 1959), pp. 228–43.
30 Roland Oliver and J. D. Fage, *A Short History of Africa*, London, 1963.
31 E. D. Morel, *Nigeria: Its Peoples and Problems*, London, 1912.
32 John Peer Nugent, *Call Africa 999*, New York, 1965. See review by Clyde Sanger in *Africa Report*, December 1965, p. 37.
33 See opening address of Osagyefo Dr. Kwame Nkrumah to the First International Congress of Africanists. Lalage Bown and Michael Crowder, *Proceedings of the International Congress of Africanists*, p. 8.
34 Ibn Batuta, *Travels in Asia and Africa, 1325–54*, trans. H. A. R. Gibb, London, 1929. Compare this with Richard-Molard's statement on the establishment of French administration: 'For the first time in its history, West Africa was about to know security.' *Afrique Occidentale Française*, p. 145.
35 Basil Davidson, *Old Africa Rediscovered*, London, 1960. Roland Oliver, *African History for the Outside World*, London, 1964.
36 Cheick Anta Diop, *Nations Nègres et Culture*, Paris, 1959.
37 J. C. de Graft Johnson, *African Glory*, London, 1954.
38 Jean Suret-Canale *L'Afrique Noire Vol. II: L'ère coloniale, 1900–1945*, Paris, 1964.

# 2 The origins of European imperialism and the rise of militant Islam

*1 The origins of European interest in the West African hinterland, 1800–50*

Before the abolition of the slave trade by Denmark in 1802 and Britain in 1807, the various European settlements of the West African Coast had been almost exclusively concerned with obtaining slaves for the plantations of the New World. The French carried on trade in gum arabic from their posts on the Senegal river; gold was exported from the European forts on the Gold Coast; and various other commodities such as ivory, hides and beeswax were shipped from other settlements. These were but secondary to the main aim of trade with the West Coast: human cargo. Such European settlements as existed were but tentative footholds on the coastline, even when they were fortified; and in the case of the Niger Delta states, Europeans were not allowed to live on land and had to carry on their operations from hulks moored off-shore. Only the French had really penetrated inland any distance, setting up trading posts several hundred miles up the river Senegal, though British traders were active on the Gambia river. All in all the Europeans had established but forty-three fortified stations on the West Coast, of which thirty-one were situated along the two-hundred-mile-long coastline known as the Gold Coast[1]. The nations involved had been France, Britain, the Netherlands, Denmark, Portugal and Brandenburg.

At the time of the British abolition of the slave trade, of the future colonial powers in West Africa France had concentrated her main interests in the Senegal and Upper Guinea coastline. Britain had conducted most of her trade much further down the Coast, along the Bights of Benin and Biafra, and on the Gold Coast where she possessed a number of forts. She did, however, have a long-standing interest in the Gambia, whilst in 1787 she had settled freed slaves in what is today Freetown, Sierra Leone. The Portuguese possessed forts in Cacheu and Bissau in modern Portuguese Guinea.

Only a fractional portion of the coastline had been alienated or leased to their future colonial masters by the Africans at the opening of the nineteenth century. There had been no need for any other arrangement, since the only real interest of European traders at this time was the purchase of slaves and sufficient supplies were available without the necessity of trading inland. The coastal Africans themselves would anyway have resisted any such move, being jealous of their monopoly of the middleman role in the trade; and Europeans had long since learnt that the briefer their stay on the 'Fever Coast' the better for their health. Even if they could have overcome African opposition to penetration, they would have had difficulty in surviving the all-pervading 'fever'[2] of which they did not know the cause but from which their compatriots in forts like that on James Island in the Gambia had died like the proverbial flies. The risk of death, and the adequacy of the supply of slaves made penetration inland both undesirable and unnecessary.

This relationship between Europe and West Africa was to be radically altered at the turn of the eighteenth century. Even before the abolition of the slave trade by Britain in 1807 there had been a growth in interest in that country in the possibilities of establishing a different type of trade relationship with West Africa. Thus in his first report to the African Association founded in 1788 to explore the interior of Africa, Henry Beaufoy, the Secretary, hoped that 'the people of the inland regions of Africa may soon be united with Europe in that great bond of commercial fellowship, which the mutual wants and the different productions of other continents have happily established'.[3] And soon after the report of Major Houghton, the third explorer sent out by the Association, 'to ascertain the course and if possible the rise and termination of that mysterious river', the Niger, had been received, the Committee decided that a British Consul should be established in the Kingdom of Bambuk on the River Gambia. For though Houghton never returned, so glowing were his reports of the lands through which he travelled—'gold, ivory, wax, and slaves, may at all times be had here for the most trifling articles; and a trade, the profit of which would be upwards of eight hundred per cent can be carried on at Fattatenda without the least trouble'[4]—that these together with other data collected on the commercial prospects of the hinterland of West Africa persuaded the Association that there were serious prospects for what later became known as 'legitimate commerce' between Africa and Britain. In 1793 a certain Mr. Willis was in fact appointed British Consul in Bambuk, a post he never actually took up.

The significance of these early moves on the part of the African Association to promote, among other things, commerce with the interior of Africa on a basis other than the slave trade is that they were clearly made independently of the humanitarians who, after the abolition of the slave trade, came increasingly to argue in favour of the promotion of 'legitimate commerce' between Europe and Africa as the only satisfactory remedy for the slave trade. The truth was that England as the first industrial nation of Europe was looking for out-lets for her manufactured goods wherever she could find them, and the tales of the hinterland of Africa gave good hope that there would be found a flourishing market of 'countries new to the fabrics of England, and probably inhabited by more than a hundred millions of people, [which] may be gradually opened to her trade'.[5]

The growing interest of Britain in Tropical Africa had its parallels in France, later to become Britain's greatest rival for the acquisition of colonies in Tropical Africa. Thus in 1802 the *Société de l'Afrique intérieure et de Découvertes* was founded. But until the 1840's France, with the exception of her small and unsuccessful venture in the European colonisation of the Senegal under Louis XVIII, neither expressed the same interest in that part of the continent nor exercised the same influence on it as Britain. France lagging far behind her island neighbour in industrialisation—she did not really become an industrial nation until the 1840's—did not have the same pressing needs as Britain for tropical African products and markets. By the end of the eighteenth century Britain had already industrialised the manufacture of textiles, which would have a ready sale in Africa. So though the African Association was primarily scientific in its aims —seven of its twelve founding members were Fellows of the Royal Society—the commercial possibilities of Africa were never far behind its botanical and geographical interests,[6] the importance of which as motives for the exploration of Africa have been well under-lined by Boahen.[7] In this connexion it is important to emphasise that in its early years, that is the years before the abolition of the slave trade, the African Association, despite the fact that a number of its leading members were humanitarians, did not concern itself with the abolition of the slave trade. It certainly did not consider its recommendations with regard to the promotion of commerce as in any way connected with the abolition of the slave trade.

The importance of the British abolition of the slave trade in 1807 was twofold as far as the future involvement of Britain in West Africa was concerned. In the first place, to ensure that the slave trade was discontinued not only by her own nationals but also by those of other countries, Britain, where diplomatic pressures failed, had to use her dominant position as a naval power to prevent by force other nations carrying on the slave trade on the West Coast. Even though Britain prior to Abolition had been the largest carrier of slaves, there were enough other countries willing to take over her erstwhile role, and sufficient demand for slaves to justify their risking the gauntlet of the Anti-Slavery patrol which anyway rescued less than ten per cent of the slaves shipped to the New World after Abolition. It soon became clear that preventive action against the carriers of slaves was not on its own enough; the source of supply had to be controlled. Thus we find the British naval squadron increasingly interfering in the internal politics of the kingdoms of the Slave Coast and the Bights of Benin and Biafra to try and cut off the source of supply to the traders. In the second place, once the humanitarians had advanced their remedy of the Bible and the Plough as the cure for the slave trade, we find the government giving them their support. The humanitarians believed that effectively to abolish the slave trade one would have not only to seize the carriers and blockade the ports of their supply, but cut the coastal middle-men off from their source of slaves. It was argued that if the Africans of the interior could be given alternative means of earning exchange with which to buy the European imports they desired, other than by selling their fellow men, then the slave trade could be remedied.[8] Thus Africans were to be simultaneously converted to Christianity and encouraged to grow tropical agricultural produce such as cotton which Britain needed. This coincided with official British interest in promoting trade with Africa as well as the desire to ensure the complete cessation of the slave trade.

Why was Britain, formerly the greatest carrier of slaves, so anxious to ensure Abolition not only by her own nationals but by those of other countries? After all other countries also interdicted their nationals from trading in slaves, but none of them, with the exception of France and the United States and they only in a desultory manner, took prophylactic action such as Britain did to prevent not only their own ships but those of other nations carrying slaves. Indeed the French even permitted a camouflaged form of slave trading, with the protection of the very Marine which was meant to suppress it, by recruiting 'engagés' for her West Indian possessions.[9] Whilst in Britain there were certainly solid humanitarian motives for both Abolition and the expenditure incurred on the Anti-Slavery Patrol, the underlying motives for both were economic.

We have seen that interest in establishing commercial relations with the interior of West Africa had preceded the abolition of the slave trade and was not imbued with humanitarian motives. Government, which had shown an interest in the activities of the African Association in the exploration of Africa before 1805, took them over after that date independently of its later decision to abolish the slave trade. Not until well after the discovery of the mouth of the Niger by the Lander brothers in 1830 did the idea become general that the commercial exploitation of the interior would also prove a remedy for the slave trade by providing the African with an alternative means of gaining foreign currency. It had of course been a dominant theme in the founding of Sierra Leone from the early days, and for instance was elaborated by the Sierra Leone Missionary Butscher as early as 1812.[10] But even though Clapperton in negotiating commercial relations between Britain and Sokoto requested Sultan Bello to abolish the slave trade,[11] any reading of the books of the explorers sent out by government shows that at that time the opening up of commerce with the interior of Africa rather than abolition was the main object of their mission.

If the commercial motive behind Britain's exploration of the interior can be established as uppermost, it is more difficult to argue that humanitarian considerations were dominant in her attempts to enforce abolition on other nations. Britain's commercial interest in West Africa was a dual one: first the exploration of new outlets for her manufactured goods; second the securing of a commodity, palm-oil, produced on the West Coast that was vital to her industrial expansion. The first was undertaken through the exploration of the interior and the subsequent financing of expeditions such as those sent up the Niger in 1832, 1841 and 1854. The second, the securing of adequate supplies of palm-oil, which was essential as a lubricant for industrial machinery, for candles, and making soap, which now had become all the more necessary for a nation notoriously averse to washing because of the dirt produced by industry, was achieved by the Anti-Slavery Patrol. Britain had a third, and initially more important, commercial reason for suppressing the slave trade. Her West Indian colonists, deprived of further imports of slave labour, could only compete with neighbouring islands under the rule of other colonial powers, if these too were denied imports of slave labour.

The case of the Niger Delta is particularly instructive in this respect: here, in the main supply area of palm-oil, the coastal states could not be persuaded to trade in this commodity whilst the slave trade remained the more lucrative.[12] Thus the small Anti-Slavery Patrol, which at the height of its strength on the West Coast consisted of no more than twenty ships and 1,000 men, tended to concentrate its activities in those areas such as the Niger Delta where it was essential to secure legitimate trade for the British. This is quite understandable, when one remembers that the very British traders who had been involved in the slave trade were now forced to look to the palm-oil trade as a substitute, and that the British government had to protect their trade to compensate for the loss of their role in the slave trade which became more lucrative than ever during the first half of the nineteenth century.

So much has been written about the humanitarian motives behind the Abolitionist movement and the activities of the Anti-Slavery Patrol, which, it has been estimated, cost the British government some £15,000,000,[13] that one is constrained to ask why governments, as parsimonious as the British governments of the nineteenth century, were prepared to undertake so vast an expenditure. Humanitarian motives could hardly have been dominant in a ruling class that tolerated conditions of industrial labour[14] which made life on the American cotton plantations almost a paradise by comparison, and which passed Factory Acts with such reluctance. Clearly, as far as Britain was concerned money spent on the Anti-Slavery Patrol was worth while in so far as it permitted the import to Britain of commodities such as palm-oil which were essential to her industry and the export to Africa of her manufactures.

If the British government was prepared to assist traders and later missionaries in their efforts to trade with the interior and to implement the policy of Bible and Plough, it was certainly most reluctant about involving itself in any colonial enterprise on the Coast other than that of Sierra Leone. Blockade and bombard, these it was prepared to do, but not to administer African peoples. This dichotomy between Britain's willingness to interfere with local politics and her reluctance to accept what her officials on the spot so often felt were the obvious consequences of assuming any kind of responsibility over the parts of West Africa in which her nationals were interested, is fundamental to the understanding of Britain's relations with West Africa right up to the eve of the Scramble. And indeed long after.

Thus Britain, after 1885, resorted in some cases to the old device of the Chartered Company to avoid direct responsibility for the possessions she had acquired in Africa.

Britain's only colonial obligations in West Africa before 1850 were in Sierra Leone, the Gold Coast Forts and the Gambia, and her attitude to all of these but Sierra Leone, which was necessary as a settlement for the recaptives taken from ships apprehended by the Anti-Slavery Patrol, amply demonstrates this reluctance to involve herself directly in the administration of African peoples wherever this could be avoided.

Sierra Leone, which had been established by the humanitarians as a settlement for indigent Negroes in London, was taken over as a Crown Colony in 1808 by the British Government, that is a year after Abolition. The immediate reason for the take-over was the fact that the Company which had been formed to run the Colony by the humanitarians was insolvent. However with its excellent harbour, and a settlement already established, it could serve as an ideal base from which the Anti-Slavery Patrol could carry on its operations. Captured ships were brought to Freetown and tried before the Vice-Admiralty Court and when condemned auctioned off. The slaves on board were freed and settled in the Colony, where they were ministered to by Christian missionaries and formed the core of the first English-educated élite in West Africa. Because of its crucial role in Britain's suppression of the slave trade, there was ultimately never any question of the British Government abandoning its colonial obligations in Sierra Leone, though it was seemingly considered in the 1820's. This was however not the case with the Gold Coast Forts and the Gambia.

It was a cardinal principle of British colonial policy during the nineteenth century that colonies should pay for themselves, and that grants-in-aid by the mother country to the colonies should be avoided at all costs. This explains the reluctance of the British Government to extend her territorial interests in West Africa, where self-supporting colonies were a chimera. Nevertheless in 1821, as a result of the pressure of the Ashanti on the Gold Coast Forts and their immediate hinterland, and the inability of the British Company of Merchants administering them both to deal with the threat of Ashanti invasion and secure the abolition of the slave trade in the area, the forts had to be taken over by the Crown, and placed under the authority of the Governor of Sierra Leone. The 1816 Parliamentary Committee that considered the problem of the Gold Coast Forts, as Ward puts it, 'refrained from recommending that the Gold Coast Forts should be abandoned altogether, merely because, inadequate as they were, they were better than no base at all'.[15]

In 1821 Sir Charles MacCarthy, who had been Governor of Sierra Leone since 1815, was named Governor of all the British West African possessions, including the Gold Coast Forts. Like so many officials on the spot, he saw the solution to his problems in territorial expansion, and tried to weld the coastal Fanti tribes and the Danish and British forts into an alliance to stave off the Ashanti who were determined to gain direct access to the coast. In 1824 he personally led a force against the Ashanti which was defeated, while he himself was killed in the battle. This disastrous setback confirmed British hostility to any extension of her administrative commitments in West Africa. Though Ashanti was subsequently defeated, a successor of MacCarthy, Sir Neil Campbell, was given instructions in 1827 that there should be no further extension of British territory in West Africa and above all no alliances should be made such as those with the Fanti which would involve Britain in wars with other African states. Moreover the British officials and the garrison of the Gold Coast Forts were to be withdrawn, and the administration of the Forts was to be handed over to the Company of Merchants, which, under the energetic leadership of George Maclean, consolidated British trade interests there. The importance of the British decision in the Gold Coast is that it provides a striking example of the reluctance of the British Government to involve itself in colonial undertakings in West Africa. In the event it did resume control of the forts in 1843, because of attacks on Maclean's administration by his enemies.

The British were inspired by two motives in establishing a settlement on St. Mary's Island at the mouth of the Gambia. First, a new base had to be found for the British merchants who had been trading from Saint Louis and Gorée, which had been taken over from the French during the wars with Britain that followed on the French Revolution, but were handed back to the French in 1817. Second, it was felt necessary to station a garrison at the mouth of the Gambia river, because of the extensive slave trade along it. However, this settlement at the mouth of the Gambia was just as much a subject of parliamentary investigations as the Gold Coast Forts, and once again demonstrated Britain's horror of colonial involvement in West Africa in the first half of the nineteenth century.

This was not the case with the French, who actually tried to set up a European colony on the Cape Verde peninsula, opposite Gorée, after the Treaty of Paris had concluded the Napoleonic wars. This experiment was a failure, so France diverted her attention to Saint Louis, her ancient base at the head of the Senegal river. Here again several attempts at European agricultural settlement were made, but all failed and France abandoned her policy of agricultural settlement in the area. Saint Louis was maintained as a non-settler colony serving as a base for the gum trade on the river Senegal and as a garrison town.

Before the appointment of Faidherbe as Governor of Senegal in 1854, French interest in tropical, as distinct from North Africa (where of course she had recently occupied Algeria), was very marginal. Bouët-Willaumez had made a number of treaties with chiefs on the Ivory Coast as a result of which trading posts were established in Assini and Grand Bassam in 1843. The Old French post at Ouidah in Dahomey was also reopened. But France in the first fifty years of the nineteenth century did not have anything like the influence on West Africa that Great Britain did. After the failure of her colonisation schemes, her activities were limited to trade, though the Governors of Senegal occasionally tangled with the rulers on the banks of the Senegal. But since France did not play an active role in the suppression of the slave trade, nor in the exploration of the interior, her influence was, compared to that of Britain, marginal before the arrival of Faidherbe. It was this soldier-governor who was in effect to lay down the basis of France's empire in Africa and in so doing he came up against the most potent force in West Africa at the time: militant Islam.

## 2 Islam as a counterforce to European penetration

The Europeans in their penetration and conquest of West Africa were to come up against the resistance of large and powerful states such as Ashanti and Dahomey, but their resistance was unco-ordinated and did not stem from any common motive other than the desire to preserve their individual independence. However, those states of the Western Sudan which had been swept by the new spirit of Islamic reform of the nineteenth century resisted European penetration not only to maintain their independence but to preserve their states from the infidel invader. In so doing their resistance was inspired not only by the desire to retain their political and territorial integrity but also by deep religious motives. On occasions different Islamic states joined common cause against the Christian Europeans. And just as the great Muslim reformer Usman dan Fodio had cavalry from the Senegalese Futa fighting alongside him against the Habe-Hausa monarchs of Northern Nigeria in his successful *jihad* at the beginning of the nineteenth century, so his descendant, Sultan Attahiru, in his last stand against the British, was joined by the ruler of Djolof, defeated by the French in Senegal, who had trekked eastwards to assist his brother in Islam against the British. In these states the desire to preserve political integrity was joined with an ideological commitment to maintain their countries for Islam.

The nineteenth-century history of West Africa can be seen as the conflict of two imperialisms: African-Muslim and European-Christian. The most important difference between the two was that the former was indigenous and the latter expatriate; the former had already covered most of the Western Sudan, the latter was just beginning to manifest itself in the region of Senegambia. Both were inspired by the conviction that they had a moral right to impose their religion and civilisation on the pagan African, if necessary by force. The first open clash of these two expansionist movements that dominated nineteenth-century West African history was at Medina in 1857 when the French, under Faidherbe, pursuing a policy of expansion along the Senegal river valley, came up against the forces of Al Hajj Umar, the Tijaniyya reformer, seeking to establish control over his homeland, the Senegalese Futa. After a long siege of the French fort at Medina, which was the frontier post of their penetration into the Western Sudan, Al Hajj Umar retreated, his forces defeated. Though he attacked the French post of Matam in 1859, and continued to harass the French on the Senegal, particularly through anti-Christian propaganda among the Negro and Moorish Muslims who lived along the banks of the river, he diverted his attention to the east, whilst the French for their part did not pursue expansion beyond Medina until the 1880's. Thus there was established an effective *modus vivendi* between the two imperialisms, and they did not come into open conflict again until the last two decades of the century, when the 'Scramble for Africa' began in earnest.

The movement for Islamic reform that swept the Western Sudan can, in the eighteenth and nineteenth centuries, be traced back to the collapse of the Songhai empire at the end of the sixteenth century at the hands of the Moroccan army. Sudanese spears were no match for Moroccan muskets, and the largest of the empires of the Sudan disintegrated into its component parts. Islam, the imperial religion, was largely superseded by the religions of the rulers of the component states. Muslims, now on the defensive without imperial authority to back them, became increasingly conscious of the need for reform and talked more and more in terms of *jihad* or holy war against the infidel as the means to achieve it. This movement had its precursor as far back as the eleventh century when the Almoravids conquered the empire of Ghana in 1076 in an attempt to establish a truly Islamic state in the Western Sudan. More important from the point of view of intellectual impact was the early sixteenth-century Islamic reformer, Al-Maghili, who influenced and advised such rulers as the Askia Mohammed I of Songhai, and the Kings of Kano and Katsina, summarising his views on the true functions of Islamic rulers in the so-called *The Obligations of Princes*.[16] However, as far as the peaceful spread of Islamic ideas, especially those of a reformist nature, were concerned, the collapse of Songhai marked a watershed in the history of Islam in the Western Sudan. It heralded what for Islam were the dark ages of West African history, that is the seventeenth and eighteenth centuries, when the slave trade on the Coast began in earnest and without check, and when the great Sudanese empires of the five preceding centuries had been dismembered. The *Tarikh-es-Sudan*, written admittedly from the Muslim point of view, recorded that as the result of the collapse of Songhai: 'Security gave way to danger, wealth to poverty, distress and calamities and violence succeeded tranquillity; in every place there was plundering and was spared neither life nor property nor persons. Disorder was general and spread everywhere, rising to the highest degree of intensity.'[17] This insecurity was to have particularly dramatic consequences for the Muslim communities of the Western Sudan, who had found themselves a privileged élite in the great empires and states of the Sudan such as Mali, Songhai, the Hausa city-states and Bornu. Now, for the most part they lived in states whose rulers did not owe even nominal allegiance to Islam, and where, though their talents were often exploited, their influence was feared. The origin of the great Muslim empires of the nineteenth century can only be understood in the context of the adverse change in the position of the Muslim communities in most parts of the Western Sudan after 1600.

Before 1600 Islam had percolated through the Western Sudan by means of the trans-Sahara caravan routes. Brought by the Arab and Berber traders, it was adopted in many cases by the Negro merchants with whom they traded. Muslims, because they were literate, were useful in the bureaucracies of the large Sudanese empires, and soon came to assume a role very similar to that of clerics in the courts of Europe in mediaeval times. Muslims were not only welcomed in the courts of the kings and emperors of the Sudanese states, but acquired such influence that Islam came

D

increasingly to assume the role of an imperial cult. Nevertheless Muslims did experience times of persecution as under Sonni Ali (*c.* 1464–92), the founder of the Songhai empire, and times of great influence as under his successor Askia the Great (1493–1528). What is striking is that prior to 1600 Muslims enjoyed an important, and for the most part secure, role in the administrative and commercial structure of the great Sudanese states. They helped with diplomatic correspondence, finance, administration of taxes, justice and were even used as tutors of royal children. They were not on the whole particularly zealous in their proselytisation of the peoples among whom they lived, though even before the *jihads* the Arab traders, through the converts they had made all along the Southern Sahara littoral, had a far greater cultural influence on West Africa than ever the Christian traders of the Atlantic Coast had.

After 1600, the majority of the rulers of the Western Sudan were by Muslim definition 'pagans', though, even so, like the Bambara kings of Ségou and Kaarta, they kept Muslims in their courts to perform the same services as the ostensibly Muslim kings of the great empires had required of them. Nevertheless in avowedly 'pagan' courts, the position of the Muslim was much less secure. Itinerant Muslim traders like the Dyula in towns all over the Western Sudan, and even in the forest zones, had little guarantee of their safety. They did however form a sort of series of Rotary Clubs, receiving news of their brother Muslims in other parts of the Western Sudan from fellow traders, keeping in touch with developments in the wider Islamic world. But they came increasingly to be regarded with suspicion by the rulers whom they served and the people among whom they lived. They were subjected to taxes which they considered illegal and were pressed into wars with fellow Muslims, against both of which they protested. In certain states there was a genuine fear of Islamic 'magic'. The blame was far from being all on the side of the 'pagan' rulers. The Muslim advisers to rulers often interfered more than was politic in the running of the affairs of state. And as their communities grew, so their demands for special rights and privileges increased. Thus to many rulers they appeared as a dangerous and coherent minority élite with political ambitions and fear of them resulted in sporadic and often vicious persecution. The insecurity of their position in these states, as compared with the influence they held in the earlier empires, led many Muslims to think about the possibility of establishing states in which they would no longer owe allegiance to 'pagan' overlords, and where law, taxation and government would be based on the early Caliphate. The only way to achieve this dream, which was given added fuel by prophesies about the coming of a great *Mujaddid*[18] or reformer, who would become Caliph of the Western Sudan towards the end of the eighteenth century, seemed to be the *jihad* or Holy War against their 'pagan' overlords.

Whilst there were many other motives for the successions of *jihads* of the eighteenth and nineteenth centuries—desire for power, ethnic considerations, material gain—the continuous thread was religious reform. In the eighteenth century the only major state where the Muslims were secure was Bornu. The Hausa kings, for instance, had to accommodate adherence to Islam with their obligations to the indigenous religion of the subjects over whom they ruled. Furthermore, since the rule of many of the 'pagan' kings was oppressive both to Muslim and pagan subjects alike, religious and social reform were often linked, particularly since Islam as a religion recognises no separation of Church and State. In these circumstances there was a great deal of thought given to reform by Muslims in the eighteenth century. 'The revival of primitive religion and the prevention of deviations from orthodoxy were', as H. F. C. Smith emphasises, 'for the Sokoto *jihad* the basis of the whole movement.'[19] And in the circumstances of the time this thought soon gave way to action. The earliest movements to effect religious reform took place in the far West of the Sudan, first in the hills of the Futa Djallon (1725) and then in Futa Toro (1775). Their main significance was as precursors of the great empire-building *jihads* of the nineteenth century: those of Usman dan Fodio in Northern Nigeria; Sheik Hamidou in Macina; and Al Hajj Umar in the Futa Toro. These two early *jihads* had as their aim the overthrow of pagan ruling groups and the establishment of theocratic states regulated by the laws of Islam, in which they were much more successful than has often been supposed.

The same motives that led to the declaration of the *jihads* in the Futa Toro and Futa Jallon were present in the *jihad* of Usman dan Fodio, who for long had been tolerated, despite his demands for reform, by the Sarki of Gobir, which had become the most important of the Hausa states by the end of the eighteenth century. However tolerance gave way to persecution as the demands for reform seemed increasingly to threaten the power of the Habe rulers, since such demands received support not only from the Fulani Muslims but also from the Hausa peasantry who were over-burdened by taxes. When persecution became pronounced, Usman, who had for some time considered the possibility that he might have to launch a Holy

War, decided to declare a *jihad* against not only the ruler of Gobir, in whose court he had enjoyed great prestige, but also against the other Habe kings.[20] The *jihad* cannot be explained simply in terms of religious and social reform—like all great revolutionary movements there were many other contributory factors. But reform was the dominant aim of Usman and the inspiration for the war, even if booty and temporal power became uppermost in the minds of some of his followers.

According to Muslim theologians *Jihad*, or Holy War against the infidel, was justified on two counts. First, a Muslim ruler could demand that his subjects go to war against the infidel in order to convert him. Secondly, it was legitimate for Muslims living under a heathen ruler to wage war against him so as to establish a truly Islamic state. This was the justification for Usman dan Fodio's ultimatum to the Hausa kings that they should abandon their laxity in tolerating 'pagan' practices among their peoples, and indeed in their own conduct as 'soi-disant' Muslims. That we find them attacking Muslims can be explained by the strictness of interpretation given by reformers to the nature of the true believer and the infidel. Thus these reformers undertook wars of expansion, sanctioned by their religion, in order to extend over the 'pagan' peoples of West Africa the true way of Islam. The states they created in the process were, as the map opposite shows, impressive in their size, especially when compared with those established by the European powers.

If we are to understand the militant Islamic imperialism of the nineteenth century, we must accept the overriding role Islamic reform played in them. This becomes clear from the *jihad* of Sheikh Hamidou of Macina. Indeed Sheikh Hamidou had participated in the early stages of Usman's *jihad*, and at the beginning of his own *iihad* he had even sought a flag from Usman, though in the event his *iihad* lost its connexion with that of Northern Nigeria. Sheikh Hamidou defeated the 'Muslim' ruler of Macina despite the help given the latter by the pagan ruler of the powerful Bambara kingdom of Ségou and established a large state that stretched along the Niger from Djenne to Timbuktu. His state has been described as the most genuinely Islamic in West Africa, basing itself with great success on the Caliphate. The state was finally conquered and taken over by Al Hajj Umar in 1862.

From the point of view of this study Al Hajj Umar is the most interesting of the *mujihaddin*: his was the first of the movements for Islamic reform in the Western Sudan, with its concomitant attempt

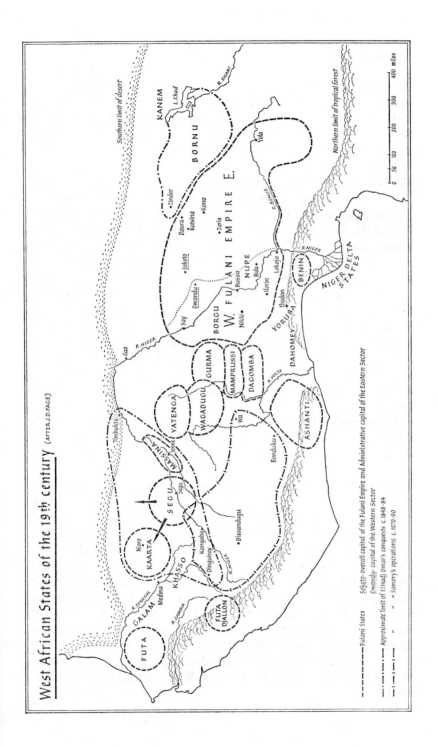

## West African States of the 19th century (AFTER J.D.FAGE)

Southern limit of desert

KANEM

L.Chad

R.SHARI

BORNU

Zinder

Daura · Katsina

Kano

· Zaria

·Sokoto

Gwandu

Busso·

Bida

NUPE

Ilorin

W. FULANI EMPIRE E.

Say

BORGU

Nikki·

Ibadan

Yola

R.BENUE

Lokoja

R.NIGER

BENIN

NIGER DELTA STATES

YORUBA

DAHOMEY

Northern limit of tropical forest

Goo

R.NIGER

GURMA

WAGADUGU

MAMPRUSSI

DAGOMBA

R.VOLTA

Timbuktu

YATENGA

MASSINA

Hamda

Wa

SEGU

Segu

Bonduku

ASHANTI

Nioro

KAARTA

Bissandugu

KHASSO

Kangaba

Dinguiray

R.NIGER

Medina

R.SENEGAL

FUTA

GALAM

R.GAMBIA

FUTA DJALLON

0   50  100   200   300   400 miles

————— Fulani States

Sokoto - overall capital of the Fulani Empire and Administrative capital of the Western Sector

Gwandu- capital of the Eastern Sector

—··—··— Approximate limit of El Hadj Omar's conquests c.1848-84

—·—·—·—    "      "    Samory's operations c.1870-90

to create a new theocratic state, that came into open conflict with European imperialist ambitions in West Africa.

Umar Said Tall was born in 1794 in the Futa Toro, where, a generation before, his people, the Tukolor, closely related to the Fulani, had revolted against their pagan overlords and established a theocratic state. Like Usman dan Fodio he was a scholar, and one of his early teachers, Sheikh Abdul Karim from the Futa Jallon, initiated him into a recently founded order, the Tijaniyya, which was spreading its influence into the Western Sudan from North Africa via Mauretania. The founder of the order, Ahmad al-Tijani, claimed to have had direct communication with the Prophet. The success of the order appears to have been based on two major characteristics: first of all, though like all Sufi orders it was hierarchical in structure, it was much more egalitarian than its major rival in West Africa, the Qadariyya, in that all its followers, no matter what their grade, could have direct access to their spiritual leader. Al Hajj Umar gave the promise of power and sainthood to a much broader based following than the exclusive Qadariyya. Secondly the founder of the order had made it clear that any member who abandoned it for another order would be considered no better than an infidel. Thus the order was a tightly knit one, with control of its members that has a parallel in the Christian faith with the Roman Catholic Church. Finally Tijaniyya had the appeal of the new in a part of Africa which was experiencing rapid change.

Umar made his pilgrimage to Mecca in 1826, passing through Macina whose ruler entrusted his grandson to his care. Whilst in Mecca, which he reached in 1828, he was appointed a *muqaddam* of the order by the Tijaniyya *Khalifa* for the Hejaz, though later he was to claim that he had in fact been appointed *Khalifa* for the Western Sudan. He did not return to West Africa until 1833. He first stopped in Bornu where he married a daughter of the Shehu, and then passed on to Sokoto, where likewise he married a daughter of Sultan Bello, who became mother of his successor, Ahmadou. He spent altogether five years in Sokoto and took part in the various wars in which Bello was at that time engaged to consolidate the vast empire created by his father's *jihad*. Indeed so close were his relations with Bello that it has even been asserted that the latter nominated him as his successor as Sultan of Sokoto. Whether or not this was the case, the close relations Umar established with the courts of Macina, Bornu and Sokoto as well as with Futa Jallon, illustrated what has been described as 'the underlying unity of West African Islam'[21] at that time.

The years that Umar spent in Sokoto were 'decisive in shaping his attitude towards the pagans and those Muslims in the Sudan whose religion he could question'.[22] There in Sokoto he was imbued with the spirit of the *jihad* by Sultan Bello, and read and discussed his justifications for it, particularly where it concerned waging war against self-avowed Muslims who were nevertheless lax in the profession of their faith. Umar was himself, however, not to embark on his own great and bloody *jihad* until 1852, even though for some years before that time he had engaged non-Muslim kings in war from his fortress in Dinguiraye in modern Guinea to which he had been forced to emigrate in 1849. After leaving Sokoto he had made his way slowly back towards his homeland, eventually seeking the hospitality of the Almamy of the Futa Jallon. He was received by the ruling Almamy in 1840 with considerable suspicion; however the latter died in that same year and his successor allowed Umar to establish a Tijaniyya colony within his territory at Diagakou. However, increasing concern at the reformist nature of his preachings led to his expulsion.

At Dinguiray he established a base where he could not only initiate his followers into the Tijaniyya order, but also train them in the art of warfare in preparation for the *jihad* that it seems clear he had been determined to launch before the receipt of his divine revelation on 6th September 1852. In this God commanded him to conquer all those who refused to accept his call to accept Islam. Initially his conquests were directed eastwards into Bambara territory where the majority of the inhabitants were pagan. To begin with he showed no signs that he would direct his *jihad* westwards towards his homeland of Futa Toro, where he would come into open conflict with French interests on the Senegal river. He had in fact been in touch with the French in 1847 and had succeeded in persuading them that he had no unfavourable intentions as far as they were concerned, and that he would not attempt to hinder trade on the Senegal. Indeed he had asked them to supply him with arms, a request which was refused.[23] Nevertheless it seems clear that he planned from the start to include Futa Toro in his future empire, and sought French aid for this very purpose.

However after his successful conquest of the Bambara kingdom of Kaarta in 1854, Al Hajj Umar appeared to the newly appointed Governor of the Senegal, Faidherbe, who had his own expansionist aims, as a definite threat to French interests. Faidherbe was already concerned by the impediment to trade presented by the Moors of Trarza and in 1855 he undertook a three-year-long but successful war against them. It became increasingly clear, however, that Umar was deeply hostile to the French. In 1855 he wrote a letter to the Muslim inhabitants of St. Louis declaring, 'From now on I will make use of force and I will not cease until peace is demanded from me by your tyrant [the French Governor]'.[24] Many Muslims left St. Louis to join his forces, including craftsmen who were to aid in the building of his forts and in the manufacture of his guns. Whilst he was prepared to deal with the French as traders, he was not prepared to allow them to establish themselves on African soil nor to patrol the river Senegal with warships. He would trade with them but only on payment of *jizya*, or tribute levied against non-Muslims under Muslim rule.[25]

The French fort at Medina was built by Faidherbe in September 1855 as a direct result of his fears that Al Hajj Umar was strong enough and had sufficient followers to call up a general revolt against the French. In establishing the fort, Faidherbe was to employ tactics that were frequently used by Europeans in their penetration of Africa. He gained permission of the Muslim ruler of Khasso to build the fort in his territory in return for French protection which this ruler, if he were to maintain control of his state, needed badly, for Al Hajj Umar was championing the claim of his brother to Khasso. It seems that Faidherbe hoped that the establishment of this fort would persuade Al Hajj Umar to accept French presence on the Senegal as a *fait accompli* and that he would agree to live with it, continuing this expansion towards the east. However, Al Hajj Umar could never accept French domination of his homeland, and moreover knew that he would have the support of many people at that time under French protection, though many others, who were not Muslim, having seen the way he had treated the 'pagan' Bambara of Kaarta, would resist any attempt at his domination. Early in 1857, then, he attacked Medina, and very nearly succeeded in taking it. Paul Holle, the *métis* commander of the fort, just managed to hold out until a relief column under Faidherbe arrived and repelled Umar's forces, which on Faidherbe's own admission fought with incredible bravery and tenacity. This was a major setback for Umar, but he continued to harass the French and was successful in his attempts to hinder trade on the river. In April 1859 he again attacked the French, this time in their fort at Matam, but was again successfully repulsed by Paul Holle. It was clear to the French that their trading interests on the river Senegal could only be secured by destroying Guémou, the base from which Al Hajj Umar launched his attacks on them and issued forth his anti-Christian propaganda. An expeditionary force was sent against Guémou in October, destroying it on the 25th.

'The fall of Guémou and the inability of the Hajj firmly to establish his position on the Senegal forced him to seek his fortunes on the Niger instead', writes Jamil Abun-Nasr.[26] Thus 1859 marks a turning point in the history of Islamic imperialism in the Western Sudan. In its first open conflict with the Europeans it had been checked, though not overcome. Indeed Umar even considered negotiating with the French a demarcation of their respective territorial interests. And in 1860 there was a preliminary demarcation agreed between Faidherbe and Umar's emissary.[27] In the event Al Hajj Umar never did accept French presence as a permanent phenomenon, but was too engaged in the establishment of his empire to the east to do more than spread anti-French propaganda in the Senegal river valley, and to attempt to prevent commercial contact between the Niger region he controlled and the 'infidel' traders. In 1862, Jauréguiberry, who succeeded Faidherbe as Governor in 1861, wrote to Paris with great concern about the anti-French activities of Al Hajj Umar in the Senegal. His followers even stopped caravans on their way to the French trading station at Bakel, and in Al Hajj Umar's homeland of the Futo Toro, Jauréguiberry reported there was talk of war with the French.

Vast numbers of men, women and children from Futa Toro migrated to Kaarta and Ségou to join Al Hajj Umar, often under fire from the French forts, showing how strong was his influence over his followers.[28]

Faidherbe returned to Senegal in 1863, by which time Al Hajj Umar had created a vast empire stretching from the French outpost of Médina to Timbuktu. Faidherbe was still hopeful of formalising the preliminary demarcation of 1860 and a young French officer, Mage, was sent out to Al Hajj Umar as 'ambassador' to cement these preliminary agreements, even though for Faidherbe it meant accepting the imposition of customs duties on French traders in the fortified trading posts he hoped to construct as far as Bamako on the Niger. 'That Faidherbe should be willing', as Hargreaves observes, 'to consider co-operation on such terms is a tribute to Umar's success in creating a state.'[29]

A year later Al Hajj Umar was killed in battle. However Faidherbe did not push his frontiers beyond those agreed by implication between himself and Al Hajj Umar in 1859, and this was to mark the easternmost limit of French expansion for the next fifteen years. And when they did push into the lands conquered by Al Hajj Umar, they were to meet with the same resistance from his successors.

Al Hajj Umar came near to creating a state that would have covered much of the territory of the old Songhai empire. Indeed had it not been for the early expansionist policies of the French, a great deal more of West Africa would have come under his rule. Without their presence, he might well have overcome the hostility both of established Muslim rulers and of the pagan peoples of his empire.

# Notes

1 See A. W. Lawrence, *Trade Castles and Forts of West Africa*, London, 1963.

2 Curtin, *The Image of Africa*, Appendix 'Mortality in West Africa'.

3 *Proceedings of the African Association for Promoting the Discovery of the Interior Parts of Africa*, London, 1810, I, p. 258.

4 *Ibid.*, I, p. 320.

5 *Ibid.*, I, p. 202.

6 For a full discussion of the complexity and relative importance of the various motivating factors behind the African Association see Adu Boahen, 'The African Association, 1788–1805', *Transactions of the Historical Society of Ghana*, V. 1, 1961.

7 A. Adu Boahen, *Britain, the Sahara and the Western Sudan*, 1788–1861, Oxford, 1964.

8 T. Fowell Buxton, *The African Slave Trade and its Remedy*, London, 1839.

9 Jean Suret-Canale, *Afrique Noire Occidentale et Centrale* (hereafter referred to as *Afrique Noire I*), Paris, 1961, p. 196.

10 I am grateful to Professor John Peterson for this reference: CMS: CAE/E2/115, Journal of Reverend Wilhelm Klein, 3rd October to 12th January 1812, entry for 6th January 1812.

11 D. Denham, H. Clapperton and W. Oudney, *Narrative of Travels and Discoveries in Northern and Central Africa, in the years 1822 and 1822*, London, 1826, 'Captain Clapperton's Narrative', pp. 81–3.

12 See K. Onwuka Dike, *Trade and Politics in the Niger Delta*, London, 1959.

13 Daniel P. Mannix with Malcolm Cowley, *Black Cargoes: A History of the Atlantic Slave Trade*, London, 1963, p. 214.

14 Cl. Jean Suret-Canale *Afrique Noire I*, p. 179: 'les industriels anglais, qui réduisaient en cette première moitié du siècle leurs ouvriers à un état de misère, d'épuisement et de dégradation inimaginables, condamnèrent au nom de l'humanité l'abomination de l'ésclavage; c'est autant de désintéressement que les industriels de New York et de Boston, au milieu du siècle, soutinrent la campagne abolitionniste, jusqu'à l'écrasement du Sud ésclavagiste.'

15 W. E. F. Ward, *A History of the Gold Coast*, London, 1948, p. 167.

16 Translated from the Arabic by T. H. Baldwin as *The Obligations of Princes*, Beirut, 1932.

17 Cited in E. W. Bovill, *The Golden Trade of the Moors*, London, 1958, p. 166.

18 In Islamic theology a *Mujaddid* is expected at the beginning of each Muslim century, i.e. in 1786, when Usman dan Fodio was beginning his preachings. Dan Fodio himself had Mahdist expectations, see 'Sifohin Shehu: An Autobiography and Character Study of 'Uthman

B. Fūdī in Verse', *Research Bulletin of the Centre of Arabic Documentation*, Ibadan, II, 1, January 1966, pp. 8–9.

19 H. F. C. Smith, 'A neglected theme in West African History: the Islamic Revolution of the Nineteenth Century', *Journal of the Historical Society of Nigeria*, II, 2, 1961, p. 77.

20 See F. H. El Mazri, 'The Life of Usman dan Fodio before the *Jihad*', *Journal of the Historical Society of Nigeria*, II, 4, pp. 435–48. For a contrary view of Dan Fodio's ideas on the *Jihad* see Marilyn Waldman Robertson, 'The Fulani *Jihad*: a Reassessment', *J.A.H.* VI, 3, pp. 33–356 in which she argues he resorted to *jihad* only when it became inevitable, having preferred to preach reform from within the state.

21 J. D. Hargreaves, *Prelude to the Partition of West Africa*, London, 1963, p. 10.

22 Jamil Abun-Nasr, *The Tijaniyya: A Sufi Order in the Modern World*, London, 1965, p. 109.

23 Vincent Monteil, *L'Islam Noir*, Paris, 1964, p. 89.

24 P. Cultru, *Histoire du Sénégal du Xve siècle à 1870*, Paris, 1910, p. 337. Source *Annuaire Sénégalais*.

25 John Ralph Willis, 'Review of Jamil Abun-Nasr, *The Tijanniyya . . .*' in *Research Bulletin of the Centre of Arabic Documentation*, University of Ibadan, II, 1, January 1966, p. 44.

26 Abun-Nasr, *Tijanniyya*, p. 119.

27 Hargreaves, *Prelude*, p. 103.

28 *Annales du Sénégal*. February 1857, p. 124. I am grateful to Mr. Jeffrey Holden for this reference.

29 *Ibid.*, p. 122.

# 3 Background to the Scramble

*1 The location of European interests in West Africa 1850–80*

A comparison of a map of European colonial possessions in West Africa in 1850 with one of 1880 shows very little change in their extent, with the notable exception of Senegal where Faidherbe's expansionist policy had brought almost a third of the modern state under French control between 1854 and 1865.

In 1850 Britain's interests were limited to Bathurst on St. Mary's island at the mouth of the river Gambia; Freetown and its peninsula; and the Gold Coast Forts. Over and above these colonial possessions, Britain had in return for military protection, usually against the Ashanti, contracted special relationships known as 'Bonds' with a number of states on the Gold Coast. Under these Britain could intervene in the administration of justice in these states, where capital punishment was involved, but not their government. In 1874 these states were annexed by Britain, creating her first major colony in West Africa. Further down the coast in the Niger Delta region, a Consul for the Bights of Benin and Biafra interfered frequently in the affairs of the palm-oil exporting states in the interests of both British commerce and the suppression of the slave trade, but there was no attempt to acquire a territorial base from which he could operate. The French had, by West African standards in the 1850's, a major colony in Senegal based on Saint Louis at the mouth of the river Senegal along which she maintained a number of trading posts. She was also established on the island of Gorée off the Cape Verde

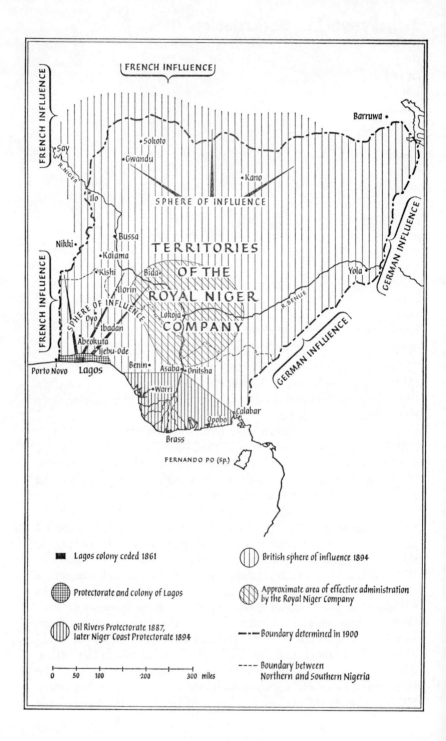

FRENCH INFLUENCE

FRENCH INFLUENCE

FRENCH INFLUENCE

Barruwa •

GERMAN INFLUENCE

GERMAN INFLUENCE

Say

R. NIGER

•Sokoto

•Gwandu

•Kano

SPHERE OF INFLUENCE

Ilo

TERRITORIES

OF THE

ROYAL NIGER

COMPANY

Nikki

•Bussa

•Kaiama

•Kishi

Bida•

Ilorin

Oyo•

SPHERE OF INFLUENCE

•Lokoja

R. BENUE

Yola•

Ibadan

Abeokuta

Ijebu-Ode

Porto Novo  Lagos

Benin •

Asaba• •Onitsha

•Warri

Brass

Opobo •Calabar

FERNANDO PO (Sp.)

▨ Lagos colony ceded 1861

⬤ British sphere of influence 1894

⬤ Protectorate and colony of Lagos

⬤ Approximate area of effective administration by the Royal Niger Company

⬤ Oil Rivers Protectorate 1887, later Niger Coast Protectorate 1894

—·—· Boundary determined in 1900

- - - - Boundary between Northern and Southern Nigeria

0    50    100         200         300  miles

peninsula; Albreda on the Gambia; the Boké region of Guinea, and the posts of Assinie, Grand Bassam and Dabou on the Ivory Coast. In 1850 the Dutch still owned a number of forts on the Gold Coast, but these were later handed over to the British, and the Netherlands ceased to have colonial interest in West Africa. The Danes had ceded their forts to the British in 1850. Portugal held the tiny fort of São João Batista da Ajuda at Ouidah and more important, forts at Cacheu and Bissau in what is still Portuguese Guinea. By 1880, apart from French expansion in Senegal, the situation had changed very little, though in the decade that followed the map of West Africa was to be radically altered.

The thirty years between 1850 and 1880, despite the lack of activity of the colonial powers in West Africa, are of interest because they help to explain why France and Britain obtained their colonies where they did. For though Britain and France in this period had negligible influence on West Africa as a whole as compared with Al Hajj Umar, his predecessors, and contemporaries, there were forces at work for both nations which were extending their influence in many of those parts of West Africa that they were subsequently to occupy. What follows, then, will not in any way be an attempt to describe the extremely complex events that preceded the so-called Scramble for West Africa. This has been done brilliantly elsewhere.[1] Rather it will try to highlight certain trends in the growth of French and British involvement in West Africa during this period, whether this was official, commercial or evangelical, that had significant bearing on the future partition of West Africa.

Throughout this period the British Government, and indeed the Parliament to which it was responsible, maintained a deep-seated hostility towards colonial ventures in West Africa. Only Palmerston and Russell actively backed the expansion and protection of British trade in this region. When Palmerston acquired Lagos for the Crown in 1861, it was described by the Colonial Office which had to take charge of it as 'that deadly gift from the Foreign Office'.[2] Ranged beside the Colonial Office in opposition to such enterprise was the increasingly tight-fisted Treasury, which kept an eagle eye on any gubernatorial venture on the West Coast that might involve it in an increase of expenditure, even if the motive were the protection of British trading interests. Palmerston and Russell had been strong in their advocacy of government support for British nationals in West Africa, but as Hargreaves points out by 1865 both their careers were coming to an end, and that was of course the year when the Parliamentary Select Committee recommended the abandonment of all

Britain's West Coast commitments except Sierra Leone. The pre-
dominant view at the Colonial Office is summed up in the words of
Sir Fredric Rogers, its Permanent Under Secretary from 1860–71:
'expensive and troublesome'.[3] They were seen as useful neither for
the prosecution of the abolition of the slave trade nor for the advancement of British trade.

It is essential to point out here that Britain's hostility towards the
acquisition of colonies in West Africa did not mean she was unwilling
to help advance her trading interests there. Before the Committee
of 1865, Government had helped finance the Niger expeditions of
1841 and 1854, and had been responsible for the great exploration
of Hausaland and the Western Sudan undertaken by Barth, from
which it was hoped to find the means of tapping the supposed vast
commercial potential of that area. The 1854 expedition, led by
Baikie, on which the use of quinine as a prophylactic and cure for
the 'fevers' of Africa was discovered, led to the establishment of a
trading settlement at Lokoja. And though this was not officially a
British Colony, Baikie presided over it with semi-official consular
status. Government supported Macgregor Laird's trading expeditions up the Niger from 1857 until his death. However, after 1865
Government was notably more reluctant to take action on behalf
of her traders, inclining to the view that high risks brought high
profits and that the merchants should look after themselves.[4] Anyway, in the scheme of world diplomacy, in which Britain as the most
powerful imperial nation in the world at the time was more involved
than any other nation, West Africa did not enjoy great prominence
in the thoughts of the Cabinet except with regard to the abolition
of the slave trade.

The British traders on the Coast on the whole agreed with
Government policy: though they were quick to call for the gunboat,
they were reluctant that their activities should be subject to permanent British administration, for this would involve them in paying
dues on their exports to maintain such administration. In this
attitude they were joined, for different reasons, by the missionaries,
who resented government interference and whose guiding principle
was to help the Africans to help themselves through conversion to
the Christian way of life as it was conceived by Victorian England.
They were also seeking the establishment of small self-governing
states, for example like Abeokuta, with emphasis on the 'native
agent'.[5] Thus the three main arms of British influence in West Africa
before the Berlin Conference of 1884–5—government, trader and
evangelist—were agreed on one point: territorial expansion in West

Africa was neither desirable nor necessary. The only divergence from this general policy came from the administrator on the spot, who, faced with the realities of the problems of administering a West African colony, often found, like a Glover in Lagos or a Kennedy in Freetown, that a policy of non-interference in the affairs of the people surrounding the colony he was meant to govern incompatible with effective administration. And though unauthorised expansion was undertaken by local administrators, this was negligible compared with the increase in the interests of the British traders and missionaries in the West African hinterland in the years preceding the Berlin Conference. And it is to them, particularly the former, that we must look for the basis of Britain's occupation of West Africa outside the small enclaves she already possessed.

Britain, apart from the acquisition of Lagos, had, despite its avowed policy, extended its territorial interests in West Africa, but these were in very small size. A full-scale and successful invasion of Ashanti in 1874 did not result in any imposition of British rule or even informal control over that nation. However, the 'Bond' states were declared part of the new Gold Coast colony, which was separated for administrative purposes from Sierra Leone. As Kimble puts it, 'the Ashanti campaign had forced a general realisation of the extent to which Britain was committed on the coast'.[6] The choice was between 'complete annexation or total abandonment'.[7] Complete annexation, however much it might go against the grain, seemed inevitable if Britain were to continue to trade on that part of the coast: nevertheless in the debate on the question in the House of Commons there was an important minority advocating withdrawal. Further down the coast the island colony of Lagos expanded on to the mainland, westwards to Badagry.

The interests of British traders before 1880 were concentrated mainly in the Niger Delta region and along the river Niger, where the palm-oil trade, which together with groundnuts was the only major produce of West Africa of interest to Europe at that time, was the chief attraction. In these parts, traders had in effect preceded missionaries, and were of much greater importance as far as the Africans were concerned. In the Lagos hinterland, missionaries had been at the vanguard of British penetration, but trade, which the missionaries themselves sought to encourage, was of considerable size, though it was frequently impeded by the long-drawn-out civil wars that had followed on the collapse of the Oyo empire in the early part of the nineteenth century. British customs officials were also interested in the area west of Badagry, particularly Cotonou and Porto

E

Novo, which were rival 'independent' ports to Lagos where traders had to pay irksome duties on imports and exports for the maintenance of colonial administration. But here they came up against French interests, and their conflict was the cause of protracted disputes and negotiations between the British and French governments. The other major area in which Britain had trading interests was the Gold Coast, but beyond the Colony, as we have seen, they were impeded by the powerful Ashanti nation. However, it has been argued by Ivor Wilks that British traders were in fact hurt more by their government's policy of supporting the coastal states against Ashanti, which was anxious to open up trade, but on its own terms.[8] Nevertheless the existence of the colony, and the rich trade of the hinterland, indicated this as a natural sphere for British expansion once the European occupation of Africa became inevitable after the Berlin Conference. Again in Sierra Leone British or rather Creole traders had been active in opening up commerce with the hinterland of the Colony, and in so doing there had again been differences with the French over the river Mellacourie region. Bathurst had become an important trading town. Here British, French and Gambian traders were handling over 10,000 tons of groundnuts a year for export to Europe.[9] Though French traders were very active in this area— indeed the bulk of the groundnut crop was exported to France— Britain maintained its hold over the colony, gaining treaty rights over Albreda, where France had once been active. British traders were in fact handling a larger bulk of trade than the French, so that the Gambia river became a natural area for British expansion when this became inevitable.

The only area where British traders had penetrated deeply into the African hinterland and had become deeply involved in local politics was in what later became Nigeria; and it is significant that Britain's largest colony on the West Coast should have been the one where her traders were most active and bears out the contention that, for Britain at least in the West African case, flag followed trade. Indeed the fact that Britain was able to claim the lands of the Niger Delta and its hinterland at the Berlin Conference was due to the activities of Sir George Taubman Goldie, who, foreseeing the dangers of a future Scramble for Africa, in which he considered the Niger region one of the most valuable prizes, welded together his British competitors into a formidable national monopoly to fight off his French rivals. He further took the initiative of signing treaties with local chiefs giving his company exclusive trading rights with them. These treaties were to involve even the distant Sokoto Caliphate.

To the west of the Niger, missionaries in Yorubaland had claimed for British churches this unhappy area plunged in seemingly interminable civil war. From their bases at Abeokuta and Ibadan, they had proclaimed an evangelical empire that was as important in guiding Britain to territorial acquisition in that region as Goldie's trading in the Niger. Whereas in Yorubaland traders had followed evangelists, and were in turn followed by the flag, in the Niger the traders were followed by the missionaries, the Anglican sect of which established a diocese of the Niger under an African Bishop, Samuel Ajayi Crowther.

By 1880, then, Britain's formal commitments in West Africa were very small with the exception of the Gold Coast. Her informal commitments were large only in the Niger region and Yorubaland, and significantly produced her only large colony in West Africa. Any informal commitments traders and missionaries would have liked to make in the hinterland of the Gold Coast Colony were blocked by the Ashanti. Nevertheless Britain's relationship with that nation, though hostile, was symbiotic, so that when the Scramble came, it was natural that Ashanti should come under her sway, and produce from the small colony of Gold Coast a sizeable unit, which in the event turned out also to be very rich. The restricted trading empires of Gambia and Sierra Leone reflected themselves in the smallness of both colonies. In Sierra Leone, flag followed trade too. In this case it was not British traders, but African traders from the Colony, who were British subjects, who acted as a pressure group on Government to occupy the hinterland.

The British Government, reluctant to the last to extend her hegemony over West Africa, ended up by following the interests her private citizens had established for her. The reverse was the case with the French.

The consistency of policy towards the question of colonial expansion of nineteenth-century British Administrations is not to be found among their French counterparts. Indeed it seems that attitudes were almost as varied as the régimes by which that country was governed. Nevertheless on the eve of the Berlin Conference and at the time when French forces were pushing rapidly into the heart of the Western Sudan, France was as anxious as Britain to limit her colonial commitments in West Africa. Indeed a number of French administrations had shared Britain's monolithic distaste for colonial enterprise on the West Coast.[10] But unlike Britain they did not have a Treasury, backed up by the Colonial Office itself, which speedily put a damp cloth on any new colonial venture. Rather they were subjected to strong contrary pressures, the chief of which was their own Marine, which with the Army had, since the defeat of their country at the hands of the British, been seeking to compensate for their humiliation by extending France's empire overseas. This tendency was exacerbated by the defeat they suffered at the hands of the Prussians in 1870. At times the Marine, whose Ministry had responsibility for the colonies, and Army served under administrations that were favourable to their colonial ambitions, and were able to pursue expansion unchecked. Those administrations that found colonies essentially a nuisance could not abandon those already acquired, because of the strength of the interests supporting their maintenance, and often had difficulty in staving off demands for new colonies.

Perhaps too much has been made of the colonies as a compensation for national humiliation, but it certainly serves to explain why France in West Africa acquired tracts of land that were little more than, if not actually, desert, and why even in the early conquest of Senegal Faidherbe took for France the least commercially interesting parts of that region. Whereas for Britain traders largely demarcated her future empire in West Africa, sailors, bizarrely seeking on land the dominion they could not hold over the high seas, traced out the main lines of the future French West Africa. However, so bald an explanation does not take into account the important role of French traders in the acquisition of France's West African empire.

France never had such pressing needs for colonies as Britain did. Her economy was largely self-sufficient. She had no surplus or hungry population to export overseas. She only became an industrial nation in the 1840's, and her need for outlets for her manufactured goods were never as pressing as for Britain. Nor could any desire for colonies be explained by surplus capital seeking new fields for operation. Nor, too, was she interested in acquiring bases for the suppression of the slave trade, as Britain did, for France never showed herself an enthusiastic abolitionist. She did however have traders on the Coast who had been established there since the era of the slave trade, and they naturally sought to find alternative commodities in which to trade. Thus along the Senegal river a desultory trade in gum kept St. Louis and the *éscales* in business. It was not until the 1840's when France's industrial revolution got underway, that her need for vegetable oils became important, and the 1850's saw a great expansion of trading activity on the West Coast of Africa by the French. Thus as Hargreaves points out it was the Marseilles trader, Régis Aîné, who was largely responsible for the hoisting of the French flag at posts on the Ivory Coast and at Ouidah in Dahomey. Again Régis Ainé persuaded the French to establish a protectorate over Porto Novo in 1863 'with the sole purpose of securing for Régis's substantial imports of spirits an entry into Yorubaland free of the heavy duties levied at Lagos'.[11] And here we begin to see that the role of the French trader vis-à-vis his government was not dissimilar to that of his British counterpart. French protection would be invoked if it could serve the useful purpose of gaining the trader commercial advantage. But for the most part French traders preferred like the British to live outside the direct influence of a French colonial administration, though they were happy to call on French force to help them in dispute with Africans. The expeditions against the Moors of Trarza were designed originally to relieve French traders from the crippling taxes that were being imposed on their gum exports. The subsequent subjugation of the area to French protection was the design of the military. French traders in West Africa were as pragmatic as the British: they sought the political situation that brought them most profits. Thus at times they would trade under British protection, at times French. For the most part they preferred African control. But they were quick to put pressure on France for support if they saw dangers of British official encroachment on their domain, as in the case of Britain's trade expansion westward from Lagos during the 1860's and 1870's. In the period from 1850 to 1880, apart from the area conquered by Faidherbe between 1854 and 1865, French trading interests were concentrated in the region immediately north of the Gambia, to its south as far as Sierra Leone, in the Dahomey region and to a lesser extent along the Ivory Coast. These were all eventually to become French colonies, and to a large degree they owed their existence as such to the fact they had initially been identified as of commercial importance by traders. Another area in which French traders interested themselves in the 1870's was the Niger Delta, which hitherto had been the exclusive preserve of the British. To a certain extent their late arrival in this region is explained by the preference of the French for groundnut oil to palm-oil as a base for the manufacture of soap. But as French demands for oil increased this distinction became less important. More pressing a reason was that in the seventies France could rival Britain in manufactures required by the African, and, like Goldie, the French traders saw the Niger as a highway to commerce with the interior.

If the French coastal colonies were largely the result of long-standing French trading activities in that region, the Western

Sudanese colonies of Senegal, Soudan (Mali), Upper Volta and Niger were the result of the desire for imperial expansion for its own sake on the part of the Marine. The precursor of this empire was Faidherbe. This is not of course to say the French military were not as anxious to secure the coastal colonies for France as they were the interior. But it was only in the interior, and in Senegal under Faidherbe, that the soldiers had the initiative. The coastal colonies of Guinea, Ivory Coast and Dahomey were under civilian control and credit for their acquisition must be shared with the traders who were able to give France after the Berlin Conference the necessary claims to established interests in those areas.

Faidherbe was, as we have already pointed out, called in to deal with the threat to French trade on the Senegal by the Moors. He did not content himself with merely demonstrating to them that they could ill afford to risk further military expeditions by the French, but proceeded to establish a French protectorate over this area though not over the Trarzas of the left bank. This too was his method in dealing with Al Hajj Umar so that by the time he left Senegal in 1865 after his second governorship, he had brought a third of modern Senegal under French control, and established a fully fledged colonial capital at St. Louis and sanctioned the founding of Dakar. Yet then, and today, the greater part of the area of Senegal he brought under control was the least interesting from the commercial point of view. As Suret-Canale has pointed out, more than half of France's groundnuts came from the Rivières du Sud. Most of Gambia's groundnut export found its way to France too. Faidherbe in fact considered that the gum and indigo trade were the more important.[12] He was also convinced that the most important markets lay in the Western Sudan, so that his colony pointed like an arrow in that direction, whilst the French trader's 'empire' went at a right angle to it, south from St. Louis towards Sierra Leone. Faidherbe was Governor at a time when France was ruled by a man who sought the renaissance of France's lost glory in the creation of a new empire. He was not particularly concerned about the expense of creating that empire, so long as he could be Emperor in fact as well as name. This suited the Marine well, and thus a colony was acquired for Senegal whose cost of administration compared with its economic viability would have rendered the British Colonial Office and the Treasury hysterical.

The subsequent defeat of Napoleon III's army by the Prussians, and his replacement by a Republican government which was not inspired by the ideal of imperial conquest, did not fundamentally alter the situation. The new governments, whilst not interested in colonies, had to be permissive in their attitude both to the ones they had inherited and the possibility of the acquisition of new ones, for the motivation of the navy and army for compensation for the loss of national prestige was now greater than ever. Considerable pressure was placed on the government by the Ministry of Marine to undertake colonial ventures, and the Marine itself was one of the main instruments in rousing jingoism among the French public. It thus acquiesced in these pressures, only trying to restrain activities that might bring it into conflict with the British, for *perfide Albion* was now replaced by the Germans as France's major enemy. This attitude was reciprocated by the British. Hence Salisbury's main preoccupation, when Lagos occupied the village of Kétenou, was its possible effect on Anglo-French relationships.[13]

In summary, then, before 1880 Britain was able to maintain a monolithic policy towards colonial enterprise in West Africa, whether the administration was Tory or Liberal, because all were agreed that colonies were in that part of the world economically unrewarding. Even when French administrations were persuaded of the validity of such reasoning, there were powerful forces that made the maintenance of a similar policy impracticable so that where Britain's map of West Africa showed her with few colonial commitments over and above those she already had in 1850, France had expanded her territory and was poised for further expansion that Britain was reluctant to contemplate right up to 1900.

In the perspective of West African history, even France had made little impact on the indigenous peoples before 1880 except through her traders. The situation was radically to change in the next four years which culminated in the Berlin Conference of 1884–5, whereby European powers sought *not* to divide Africa amongst themselves, but to seek ways in which they could limit colonial acquisitions, because all, including France, saw them as an economic burden they would prefer to forgo. But the Berlin Conference, far from limiting the Scramble, gave international acknowledgement to its actuality.

## 2 *The beginnings of the Scramble 1880–5*

In a pithy comment on the dramatic change in European attitudes to Africa in the half decade from 1880 to 1885 Lord Salisbury remarked: 'When I left the Foreign Office in 1880 nobody thought about Africa. When I returned to it in 1885 the nations of Europe were almost quarrelling with each other as to the various portions of Africa they could obtain.'[14] Indeed in 1880 there still seemed no pressing reason why any European government should consider the occupation of any portion of Tropical Africa as either politically desirable or economically profitable. Any increases in trade that might be likely to occur as a result of such occupation still seemed sure to be offset both by political repercussions on the chanceries of Europe and by the expenses that would be involved in imposing on, and maintaining over, Africans an administration which for the most part they were quite unwilling to accept. Even France, imperially inclined in North Africa and South East Asia, was still diffident in Tropical Africa. As European powers saw it at the time Tropical Africa offered little inducement to occupation. European colonisation was clearly impossible; the products Europe required, which were anyway very limited in range, were exported without the need for more than the occasional despatch of a gunboat to ensure continuation of trade when terms were disputed between Africans and Europeans. Finally, at least in West Africa, the slave trade could not be induced as an argument in favour of occupation, for the export of slaves had ceased. Nevertheless the question of the widespread existence of domestic slavery caused considerable concern. The abolition of the slave trade and the promotion of legitimate trade had not abolished or even diminished slavery in West Africa. Those who were formerly exported to the New World as slaves were now employed in the production or porterage of the palm-oil and groundnuts European traders now required in place of slaves. Thus the 1865 Parliamentary *Report*, while it advocated the withdrawal of Britain from her West Coast settlements, called for the elimination of domestic slavery. Even in Angola, the importance of the slave trade had diminished as a result of Portugal's effective as distinct from formal abolition of the slave trade by the middle of the century. Leopold of the Belgians was of course to make great play of the continuation of the Arab slave trade from the Congo to the East of Africa as a justification for his occupation of the former.

How then can we account for the spectacular change of attitude on the part of the European powers between 1880 and 1885, so that within twenty years the whole of Tropical Africa, with the exception of Ethiopia and Liberia, was brought under European rule? The answer to this belongs as much to the history of Europe as of Africa. The Scramble of the European powers for Africa raises two questions of importance for the history of the colonial period in West Africa. The first, why it took place when it did, has been the subject of much scholarship in recent years,[15] and some consensus is being reached as to the question of what triggered it off. But the second question—why it took place at all—is still far from being answered, if we do not accept the Leninist-Hobson thesis of the occupation being a function of Europe's imperative need for an outlet for her surplus capital as the unique explanation. In our present state of knowledge it is impossible to provide a satisfactory overall answer as to why Europe occupied Africa. Beyond such obvious basic considerations already discussed, such as the vastly superior technological and economic position Europe had gained relative to Africa which gave her the potential of occupation if trading interests or national pride in relation either to other European powers or to African states were threatened, it is difficult at this stage to point to more than general patterns in the motives that seem to have lain behind occupation.

Although in 1880 European governments saw little reason for occupying Tropical Africa, there were strong pressures at work in favour of such action. First of all ignorance of West Africa had led traders and non-traders to suppose that it was a far more important market for their goods than it eventually turned out to be. The Congo and the Niger assumed much greater importance in their minds as highways to the interior markets than events subsequently justified. Industrialists and traders in Europe *were* looking for outlets for their surplus capital. Africa, still the Dark Continent as far as Europe was concerned, held forth promise of rich opportunities. What little was known was highly suggestive of commercial possibilities. Barth's account of his travels in the Western Sudan, for instance, gave confidence to traders that there would be rich rewards in the Sokoto Caliphate. Explorers like Stanley ventured into the Congo basin to assess, among other things, the commercial potential of the region. Capitalists naturally asked themselves whether railways could do for Africa what they were doing for the Americas and Australia. Already in Senegal two railways were being traced out by government, one to connect the Senegal with the Niger, and another to link St. Louis with Dakar, which was strongly supported by commercial interests. But capital investment on the scale of a railway had to be protected whether it was privately or publicly financed, witness the change in relations between the French and the Tokolor empire from one of co-existence to occupation once the railway had been planned to extend into the latter's territory.[16] Finally, though it may have appeared that the necessary raw materials were forthcoming from Africa without the need for intervention over and above the occasional visit of the gunboat, indications on the Niger were that the growing competition for markets between traders of the same nationality, and between French, British and to a lesser extent the Germans, was forcing European merchants to seek new markets inland where prices were more favourable to them, for those on the coast had been forced up by competition. Inland, they came up against the African middlemen who naturally resented this intrusion into their hitherto unchallenged monopoly. Resentment led to conflict, and in such cases the European traders were quick to call on their own governments for protection. Such appeals were in themselves a prelude to occupation. Faidherbe had been appointed largely at the suggestion of St. Louis traders who were confident that he would take a strong line with the Moors.[17] In the Niger Delta Taubman Goldie was arguing unsuccessfully with the British Government that they should give his Company a Charter whereby it would assume administrative control on behalf of the British Government of a large area of modern Nigeria.

If administrators on the spot, and in some cases missionaries and traders, were coming round to the view that the occupation of African soil was the only way in which the progress of their trading and evangelising could be ensured, the Governments in Europe were either overtly unsympathetic or not really interested. There were exceptions, like Jules Ferry, who actively supported the expansionist policies advocated by the men on the spot and who asked the French Chamber of Deputies on 12th November 1884: 'Is it not clear that, for all the great powers of modern Europe, since their industrial power commenced, there is posed an immense and difficult problem, which is the basis of industrial life, the very condition of existence—*the question of "markets"*? Have you not seen the great industrial nations one by one arrive at a colonial policy? And can we say that this colonial policy is a lunacy for modern nations? Not at all, *Messieurs*, this policy is, for all of us, a necessity like the "market" itself.'[18]

Another spur to occupation was also economic in nature: the fear of Protectionism. If governments were reluctant to occupy Tropical Africa, they were even more reluctant to see any part of it fall to a power that espoused protectionism. Britain and Germany both feared the protectionist trend in French Colonial as distinct from domestic policy, though as Newbury points out the French in West Africa were just as worried about the protectionist aspects of Britain's 'Free Trade' in her coastal colonies.[19] Both Britain and Germany were determined to ensure that the Congo and Niger remained open to Free Trade, while the French, if they could not gain control of these two rivers, were also anxious that they should remain open to all comers.

Colonies and empire became increasingly popular subjects in the major powers of Europe.[20] Interest in them was manifested not only among the commercial classes, who were directly interested in overseas trade, but also among the literate middle classes generally. To commercial motives for the acquisition of colonies, they added those of national glory and 'humanitarianism'. Theories of the racial superiority of the white man coupled with the explorers' and missionaries' tales of the backward condition of Africa, increased support for the occupation of Africa and its subjection to the 'benefit' of European rule. Thus Jules Ferry told the French Chamber: 'It must be said openly that the superior races, in effect, have a right vis-à-vis the inferior races' to which M. Jules Margne replied, 'You dare to say that in a country where the rights of man were declared.'[21] In the Europe of the 1880's the views of Ferry rather than Margne were prevailing, and it was thus easier for governments, even when they were not being demanded to do so, to undertake colonial ventures.

There were, then, substantial pressures of European governments to begin the Scramble for Africa, but they were not strong enough in the early 1880's to force their hand. It is at this point that we have to ask why the Scramble did take place when it did. Here we have to look at the changing political positions and attitudes of the powers which eventually occupied West Africa, and how these influenced each other.

In the 1880's, of the four powers which occupied West Africa, only Portugal was really colonially ambitious in Tropical Africa. France, despite the substantial advances already made in the Senegal region, was still by and large officially hostile to any major extension of her commitments in this area. Britain rejected any prospect of colonial acquisition that would not pay for itself. Germany, under Bismarck, was very reluctant to engage in colonial enterprise of any sort, though again there were pressures on the government to change its attitude, in particular from traders.

These powers, with the exception of Portugal, may have been reluctant to undertake colonial ventures in Tropical Africa, and Portugal anyway was in no position economically or politically to do so at that time. But this was not the view they held of each other. Britain's intentions may have been innocent—from the point of view of her fellow European powers she was the largest imperial power of the day, and there was no reason for them to suppose that, isolated in Europe, she would not seek further expansion abroad, even in Tropical Africa. France, too, may have balked at such expansion, but a country with a history of colonial ventures such as she had in the past fifty years, and which was already active in Senegal, had to be regarded with suspicion as to any move she might make. Germany was an unknown factor as far as colonial expansion was concerned. But nevertheless so great was her power that she could not be discounted in this field. Only Portugal could be looked on with any degree of confidence, unless of course one of the other powers sought alliance with her to further its ambitions in Africa. Thus whilst both Britain and France were reluctant to expand their commitments in Tropical Africa, they watched any move on the part of the other with suspicion. Germany, interested in maintaining the Balance of Power in Europe, was concerned as to how such moves might affect this balance.

The Scramble for Africa took place when it did because the mutual suspicions of the interested European powers of each other's intentions had reached such a pitch that none of them was willing to hold off the undesirable for fear their own interests might be pre-empted by another. However reluctant France may have been officially to involve herself in this Scramble, once committed, the strong political and economic pressures for occupation became dominant.

In France the political pressures for expansion in Africa were almost as strong as the economic. Such expansion was seen increasingly as a means to compensate for the humiliating defeat she had suffered at the hands of the Germans in 1871. Bismarck, himself, was anxious to encourage such an approach to take the mind of France off the loss of Alsace-Lorraine. In France itself, however, there was division between those who sought expansion elsewhere and those who felt France would be better occupied recovering the 'lost provinces'. This is well illustrated by the exchange between Ferry and Déroulède, an ardent 'continentalist'.

'You will end by making me think you prefer Alsace-Lorraine to France. Must we hypnotise ourselves with the lost provinces, and should we not take compensations elsewhere?' asked Ferry, to which Déroulède replied, 'That is just the point. I have lost two children and you offer me twenty domestics.'[22]

Those in France who favoured colonial expansion were given a great boost by Britain's unilateral occupation of Egypt, where Anglo-French control had broken down. In the first place British action there weakened the traditional co-operation between the two governments.[23] It also aroused the indignation of the French public, already increasingly coming to see Britain as the enemy presiding over a mighty and expanding empire, rather than Germany. The occupation of Egypt by Britain supplied the climate in which the French government did not have much alternative to accepting the Makoko treaties in 1882 whereby the explorer de Brazza had acquired for France territory on the Congo.[24] These treaties, it is clear, as much as anything else precipitated the Scramble, though they certainly did not cause it. They made the European powers face the realities of a situation that had been developing over the past three years.

Portugal was the power most directly affected by the Makoko treaties, since she laid claim to the whole Congo area. Britain feared that if France were to establish herself on the Congo, she would preclude other powers from 'free trade' on the river. Germany, too, was concerned to maintain freedom of trade there. In the background, Leopold of the Belgians, unsupported by his own country, was anxious to establish a colony in the Congo for his country under the guise of his International Association. The French ratification of the Makoko treaties threatened his own projected colony, for the Congo river was to be its lifeline. Thus a series of treaties ratified by a reluctant government under the pressure of public opinion and the press were to lead inevitably to a conference of European powers at Berlin whereby the conditions of occupation of the African Coasts and maintainance of freedom of trade on the Congo and Niger were to be determined. And yet, as *The Times* wrote, 'Never has a government submitted to parliamentary ratification a treaty of the reality of which it knew so little'.[25]

Britain responded to the French action by negotiating with Portugal a treaty which would acknowledge Portugal's claims over the Congo mouth in return for a guarantee of freedom of trade on the river, which would be assured by an International Commission. Portugal refused to accept an international commission and insisted on a simple commission limited to Britain and herself. The limited nature of this commission helped build the image of Britain as a power with dangerous ambitions in the Congo area. Indeed Portugal was so fearful of her long-standing ally, whose national David Livingstone had after all explored territory to which Portugal laid claim, and had criticised severely her administration, that at one time she tried to conclude this treaty with France.

The other major participant was Germany under its Chancellor, Bismarck, who felt that 'for Germany to acquire colonies would be like a poverty stricken Polish nobleman providing himself with silks and sables when he needed shirts'.[26] His main concern was preventing any other power in Europe from gaining ascendancy in Africa.

Thus the British occupation of Egypt had persuaded him to drop his antagonism to colonial ventures in Africa and to give support to his nationals' expansionist ambitions of German traders in Togo, Cameroun and South West Africa. This change of heart[27] can be seen both as a response to the changing international situation —Bismarck was particularly alarmed by the nature of Anglo-Portuguese negotiations—and to pressures of German traders. But for Bismarck, colonies in Africa were not of interest in themselves, but pawns in a European game in which some of the players had moved the board to Africa. This intervention on the part of powerful Germany aggravated the situation even more. International opposition to the Anglo-Portuguese treaty increased; it was presented as a sinister conspiracy to keep powers other than Britain and Portugal off the Congo, particularly by Leopold II who became chief lobbyist against it. This, together with British intervention in Egypt, provided a diplomatic situation in which Bismarck was able to call European powers to the Conference table in Berlin. There they would discuss the terms by which henceforth they were to acquire territory in Africa and how freedom of trade could be maintained in the Congo basin and freedom of navigation on the Congo and Niger rivers.

That it took place when it did is explained by the Makoko treaties. What is certain is that the economic factors outlined earlier would have 'en tout état de cause, un peu plus tôt, ou un peu plus tard, déclenché le mouvement'.[28] The European countries felt they needed Africa's supposed wealth, and unable to agree among themselves to leave it open to free trade by all, and not trusting their capital investments to African governments, all had to grab their own portions, large or small.

### 3 The Berlin Conference

The Berlin West Africa Conference of 1884–5 gave international recognition to a situation that already existed. Rather than initiating the Scramble for Africa, it tried to bring some form of discipline to a situation that looked as though it might rapidly get out of hand. That the Scramble had already begun in earnest was brought out clearly at the Conference when the various powers put forward their claims to territory. France had already begun the eastward march across the Sudan and Bamako had fallen to her forces in 1882. Her territories of the Senegal were now linked with the Niger. At the other end of that river, Goldie, with the assent of Britain, had amassed treaties in the Niger Delta and its hinterland and as far north as Sokoto and Gwandu, the twin capitals of the Sokoto Caliphate. Germany had laid claim to Cameroun, and Togo, and Joseph Flegel had similarly drawn up treaties with the Fulani rulers. France had undertaken treaty-making in the Niger Delta and had already established herself on the Dahomey Coast.

The Conference, which met from November 13th 1884 to February 26th 1885, included every major power in Europe. Also present were the Ottoman empire, the U.S.A. and Leopold's still shadowy International African Association. The main question for discussion by the Conference was: how to draw up formalities for the effective occupation of the coast of Africa.[29] It is interesting that the purpose of the conference was to consider only the occupation of the coasts of Africa, though the Act that emanated from the discussions became the basis for the occupation of any part of Africa. It laid down that a power wanting to claim African lands should inform the other signatory powers 'in order to enable them, if need be, to make good any claims of their own'.[30] However, to be valid such claims should be supported by effective occupation. Freedom of navigation was to be maintained on the Niger and the Congo, though no provision was made to secure it: and in the event there was freedom of trade on neither river. There was also to be freedom of trade in the Congo basin: monopoly resulted.

The rules agreed upon, the various participants began to play the game with differing degrees of enthusiasm, and for different stakes. As far as West Africa was concerned, it was rather like a game of Monopoly, with France and Britain the only two serious contestants, Britain relying for her success on Park Lane and Mayfair, Whitechapel and the Old Kent Road, whilst France bought up anything she could lay her hands on that hadn't been taken by Portugal or Germany.

Thus at the conference tables of Berlin, with no African present, the rules for the partition of West Africa into units that were to become the basis of its modern nation states were determined though the guidelines had already been set by the activities of European traders, missionaries and administrators in the eighty-odd years since abolition. Looking back on the colonial period, we may ponder the fact that probably the most enduring mark left by Europe on Africa has been the creation of new political units, which, though they took much more account of ethnic, religious and geographical factors than is usually supposed, completely changed the map of Africa. In West Africa these units have, almost unaltered, formed the basis of the new independent states.[31]

# Notes

1 Hargreaves, *Prelude*.
2 Ronald Robinson and John Gallagher with Alice Denny, *Africa and the Victorians: The Official Mind of Imperialism*, London, 1961, p. 36.
3 Hargreaves, *Prelude*, p. 39.
4 *Ibid.*, p. 33.
5 See J. F. Ade Ajayi, *Christian Missions and the Making of Nigeria*, London, 1965.
6 David Kimble, *A Political History of Ghana 1850–1928*, London, 1963, p. 273.
7 *Ibid.*, p. 273, citing a minute from the Parliamentary Under-Secretary of the Colonial Office, J. Lowther, dated 20th April 1874.
8 Ivor Wilks, 'The Northern factor in Ashanti History: Begho and the Mande', *J.A.H.*, II, 1, 1961, pp. 25–34.
9 Harry A. Gailey, *A History of the Gambia*, London, 1965, p. 72. By 1889, they had reached nearly 20,000 tons.
10 For this account of French colonial policy from 1850–80 I have relied heavily on Hargreaves, *Prelude*, and Henri Brunschwig, *Mythes et Réalités de l'Impérialisme Colonial Français 1871–1914*, Paris, 1960.
11 J. D. Hargreaves, 'Towards a History of the Partition of Africa', *J.A.H.*, I, 1, 1960, p. 102.
12 Suret-Canale, *Afrique Noire I*, p. 182.
13 Hargreaves, *Prelude*, p. 99.
14 Quoted by Jan Stengers from Lady G. Cecil's *Life of Robert, Marquis of Salisbury*, Vol. IV, London, 1932, p. 310, in 'The Partition of Africa —I: L'Impérialisme colonial de la fin du XIXᵉ siècle: mythe ou réalité', *J.A.H.*, III, 3, 1962, p. 471.
15 *Ibid.*, pp. 469–491; Robinson and Gallagher, *Africa and the Victorians*; Hargreaves, *Prelude*; C. W. Newbury, 'The Scramble for Africa: Victorians, Republicans and the Partition of West Africa', III, *J.A.H.*, 1962, pp. 493–501; Henri Brunschwig, 'Les origines du Partage de l'Afrique Occidentale', *J.A.H.*, V, 1, 1964, pp. 121–5.
16 J. D. Hargreaves, 'The Tokolor Empire of Ségou and its Relations with the French', *Boston University Papers on Africa*, Vol. II, African History, ed. J. Butler (Boston, 1966), pp. 138–9.
17 André Villard, *Histoire du Sénégal*, Dakar, 1943, pp. 90–4.
18 Quoted by Stephen H. Roberts, *The History of French Colonial Policy, 1870–1925*, 2nd edition, London, 1963, p. 15.
19 C. W. Newbury, 'Victorians, Republicans and Africans', N.B. In 1878 Germany adopted a protectionist tariff, but as Henri Brunschwig points out in *L'Expansion allemande outre-mer du XVème siècle à nos jours*, Paris, 1957, p. 99, contrary to the opinion of many this did not concern colonial expansion.

F

20 See Carlton J. Hayes, *A Generation of Materialism, 1871–1900,* New York, 1941, pp. 216–33, for a useful summary of the development of the forces favourable to imperial expansion in Europe before 1885.

21 *Débats parlementaires: séance de la Chambre des Deputés,* 28 Juillet, 1885, p. 1062.

22 Quoted by C. P. Gooch in *Franco–German Relations, 1871–1914,* London, 1913, p. 21.

23 Hargreaves, *Prelude,* p. 283.

24 See Stengers, 'Partition of Africa', and Brunschwig, 'Les Origines du Partage'.

25 *The Times,* 30 November 1882, quoted in Stengers, 'Partition of Africa', p. 475.

26 Quoted by W. O. Henderson, *Studies in German Colonial History,* London, 1962, p. 3.

27 Herbert von Bismarck ascribed his father's change of heart to his fear of the pro-English influence of the Crown Prince's wife, who was a daughter of Queen Victoria: 'When we entered upon a colonial policy, we had to reckon with a long reign of the Crown Prince. During this reign English influence would have been dominant. To prevent this we had to embark on a colonial policy, because it was popular and conveniently adapted to bring us into conflict with England at any given time.' Quoted by A. J. Hanna, *European Rule in Africa,* London, 1961, p. 8.

28 Stengers, 'Partition of Africa', p. 490.

29 S. E. Crowe, *The Berlin West Africa Conference, 1884–85,* London, 1942, pt. 1, chap. II.

30 *Ibid.,* p. 90.

31 See Saadia Touval, 'Treaties, borders and the partition of Africa', *J.A.H.,* VII, 2, 1966, pp. 279–93.

*Part II*
The European occupation of West Africa

# 1 The French conquest of the Western Sudan

## 1 *The nature of colonial occupation*

At the Berlin Conference the gun was fired for the start of a race for which two of the participants, France and Britain, had already been in training. The French had already shown themselves impatient of the treaty-making process and quick to resort to the armed column. The British, anxious not to involve themselves in the heavy costs of military expeditions, had fallen back on them only when they seemed unavoidable. Even treaties were made reluctantly because of the long-term financial involvements these might incur. Thus it was left to a trader like Goldie, who as head of a company had no authority to use armed force, to make treaties of his own with grudging British consent. The experience of the years before the Berlin Conference was reflected in the subsequent pattern of occupation of West Africa by France and Britain, and affected profoundly the type and nature of the lands they acquired. France's occupation of West Africa was much more of a military exercise than Britain's. On the Upper Niger the military had virtual autonomy of action, so that it is not surprising that a military approach to the occupation of the Western Sudan should have been the order of the day: quantity of land rather than quality seemed the more important. As Brunschwig has shown, the conquest of West Africa offered great opportunities for promotion[1] and honours for the military. Anyway, 'Soldiers, accustomed to giving orders, were ill-adapted by temperament to peace negotiations', as Soleillet remarked in his *Voyage à*

*Ségou*,[2] an account of his own attempts at peace negotiations with Ahmadou, ruler of the Tokolor empire. For the military a general law operated: the more land acquired, the greater the number of administrators needed. France, nevertheless, was guided by an over-all strategy: to link her coastal footholds with her acquisitions in the Western Sudan and to occupy the Niger as far as a point that would give her a port on the stretch navigable to the sea. The parsimony of Britain with regard to the acquisition of colonies persisted through-out the decade following the Berlin Conference. It was only with the appointment of Joseph Chamberlain as Secretary of State for the Colonies in 1895 that a forward policy for Africa was pursued, and military occupation was seen as a valid alternative to treaty negotia-tion. Until then requests for armed intervention by both adminis-trator and trader on the spot invariably met with a negative response. By 1895 Britain had occupied very little land beyond that which she possessed in 1885. Ashanti was not occupied until 1896, Northern Ghana not occupied until 1897, Yorubaland until after 1895, Benin until 1897, and Northern Nigeria until after 1900. France on the other hand had mapped out and occupied well over half of her future empire in West Africa by 1895. Fear of French or German occupa-tion of areas which Britain considered fell within her influence was a dominant factor in her decision to occupy them by force if necessary. But even though Chamberlain was prepared to sanction force, he was careful to keep a restraining hand on the soldier on the spot, so that where the French military often dictated policy to their govern-ment, the British military often chafed at a bit held tight by hands three thousand miles away.

The areas Britain claimed were those in which her traders had been active, or saw future profit. Thus where with France the flag tended to precede trade, with Britain trade preceded the flag, or directed where the flag should be flown, with the result that Britain gained the smaller but richer part of West Africa, while France, as Salisbury acidly commented, gained a lot of sand in which its cockerel could use its spurs.[3] However, on the French coastal colonies of Dahomey, Ivory Coast and Guinea, traders showed the way to military occupation. And in these colonies the military never played such a dominant role as they did in the conquest of the Western Sudan. However, because the military did play such a dominant role in the French occupation of West Africa, many more traditional states were destroyed than in British West Africa. For even when British occupation was by conquest, the funds available to the armed column were so slender, as in the case of Lugard's invasion of Northern Nigeria, that wherever possible an early peace was sought and attempts were made to rule through the indigenous authority. As we shall see, this was to be reflected in the pattern of local administration that emerged in the years after the conquest. This is of course to generalise broadly, and there are many exceptions which will become apparent in subsequent pages. But these general trends are important for an understanding of the differences that did emerge between French and English-speaking West Africa.

One common theme in both the British and French conquest of West Africa was the conviction that this conquest was morally right, and that the invaders were bringing light to 'the heart of darkness'. Like the conquistadors in Mexico and Peru, there was never any question about the morality of their action, even when it came to the sacking of Benin and Ashanti, and the looting of the national treasures of these states. In the French conquest of West Africa, in which many African lives were lost, the military imposed on the Africans in the name of their 'civilising mission' a system of government that was often much harsher than those it replaced. The belief of the military in the blessings occupation brought to Africans was well summed up by Commandant Legrand in a speech before Monsieur André Lebon, Minister of Colonies, at the inauguration of the Faidherbe bridge at St. Louis on 17th October 1897. 'It has now been accomplished, though at first slowly, then with an almost feverish haste. Was it because of a real need for conquest, because of a mad pursuit of glory and domination? Not at all: because of attacks on our trading posts by people still unaware that we do not intend to enslave them but wish to increase their well-being whilst improving our own.'[4] The conviction that there was nothing wrong in the occupation of Africa and that the African would indeed benefit from it, is the principal unifying theme in the French and British subjugation of West Africa.

If we can draw distinctions between the approaches of France and Britain towards the occupation of West Africa, distinctions between the various motives for resistance to, or co-operation with, the invaders on the part of the Africans are much more difficult to make. At present research into this question has not been undertaken on a sufficiently large scale to do more than to suggest anything other than very broad categories for the classification of the reasons for resistance and co-operation.[5]

In looking at West African society at the end of the nineteenth century we can start from the premise that each political unit, ranging from the small autonomous village to the centralised state, valued its independence and would guard it jealously wherever it could from infringement either by white man or stranger African. Non-Muslim societies, in particular, would regard the imposition of alien rule, whether African or European, as destructive of the whole fabric of their society, of its very integrity where political authority was inseparable from religious authority and where society consisted not only of the living but the dead and the yet to be born. Nowhere has this been brought out more poignantly than in Chinua Achebe's *Things Fall Apart*.[6]

For Muslim societies of West Africa the imposition of white rule meant submission to the infidel which was intolerable to any good Muslim and helps to explain the ferocity of resistance of many Muslim leaders in the Western Sudan to the French advance when the odds were so clearly weighted against them. Lugard, in his occupation of Northern Nigeria, only retained the loyalty of the Emirs after the conquest, many of whom were ready for re-assertion of their independence in 1906, because he deliberately abstained from any interference with their religious authority, and only placed the minimum of limitations on their political authority.

However much African states may have valued their independence, many had long experience of alienation of their authority to other African groups. This was particularly true of the peoples of the Western Sudan where the great Sudanese empires ranging from Mali to that of Al Hajj Umar had succeeded in imposing their rule over a multiplicity of ethnic groups. Even on the coast, empires like those of the Oyo Yoruba and the Ashanti had extended their rule over peoples of different ethnic groups. Occupation by strangers was nothing new. What remains to be discovered by future research is whether Africans saw a categorical difference between occupation by stranger Africans and occupation by white men. For the present one may hazard the guess that many of them did not, for this will help explain why so many African states made treaties of protection with the Europeans against their neighbours. The states of the upper Senegal in the 1850's, for instance, saw the French as potentially less oppressive alien rulers than Al Hajj Umar. Sikasso, again, made alliance with the French against Samory, but clearly valued its own independence so greatly that when the French actually tried to assert the rights they claimed to have gained by this alliance, it joined forces with Samory against them. The Fanti, for instance, preferred loose association with Britain to domination by the Ashanti. But again, as the Fanti Confederacy shows, their desire for independence of any 'foreigner' was uppermost.[7] That so many

African groups, when faced with the prospect of imminent alienation of their authority to European or African, chose the European, may be explained by the fact that much more was known about the European by African peoples than is commonly supposed. News travels quickly in West Africa, and groups threatened with invasion knew quite a lot about both the military potential of the European and the nature of his rule. Thus many groups preferred the apparently lighter burden of French rule to that of Samory. Many, too, capitulated before the European without resistance because they had already seen the extent of his military power and recognised the futility of resistance. The speedy conquest of the Fulani empire by Lugard depended to a large extent on his initial successes which persuaded others that conquest was inevitable. This, too, clearly explains the capitulation of Ashanti without a fight in 1896 when they had already once defeated the British, and put up strong resistance on a second occasion. Many African leaders had the same feeling of inevitability about European occupation as that great warrior, Lobengula of Mashonaland, for whom the British were like 'a chameleon stalking a fly'. As Philip Mason puts it so succinctly: 'he was like a hooked salmon, trying to take out as much line as he could whenever the chance came'.[8]

Another important motive for acceptance of European rule on a voluntary basis was the peace it would bring in areas that had been troubled by wars for, in cases, the past fifty years. This was particularly true of Yorubaland and the river Gambia. Thus the King of Kishi, on the northern frontiers of Yorubaland, told Lugard that 'the British have put the country to right in various directions and done great good, and now he suddenly hears that these same White men are on their way to his own town, and will set the country to rights. Already he says that the people [Borgus] who are troubling him have run away.'[9]

Another important motive for collaboration with the Europeans was the desire to obtain access to European goods. This was clearly a more important factor for those groups which had used slaves as a basis for exchange for European goods and who, with the cessation of the slave trade could not, like the peoples of the Niger Delta, find a substitute such as palm-oil. Brunschwig has suggested that desire for such contact, even at the price of alienation of sovereignty, was most pronounced among such societies.[10] Lugard was clearly aware of the attraction of European trade. On his race against the French to secure a treaty with the King of Nikki, supposed overlord of Borgu, he was told that the king refused to see him. To this he replied, 'I could not waste time here . . . Nikki was not the only place in Africa, and, if the King did not send to me the day after tomorrow, I would march in another direction and it would be his loss not ours, and his country would lose the benefit of trade and development.'[11] The king did receive him and his nominees signed a treaty. The hope that European 'protection', even rule, would bring increased economic prosperity, was for instance demonstrated as late as 1910, when a faction of Cape Palmas Greboes begged for a British protectorate. This they considered would be financially more advantageous than Liberian rule, with its customs duties and its taxes imposed on labourers taking service on British ships.[12]

The European must have presented himself to Africans other than those from the coast, who by now knew him well, as an immensely complex and bewildering being. He possessed technological superiority and was fired with a missionary zeal that compared only with that of the *mujihaddin*. It was also difficult to assess the extent and nature of his power. He came from overseas. The small pioneer party could be defeated—but could those who had sent it? For example what was Samory to make of the accounts of Paris brought back to him by his son who had witnessed from the Presidential Dais the 14th July parade in which General Boulanger had captured the heart of Paris. Furthermore the African ruler was presented with not just one potential European enemy, but several. Thus Sokoto signed treaties with both British and Germans. Lobengula, in Southern Africa, signed treaties with four: Imperial Germany, Portugal, Britain and Transvaal. Lacking intelligence organisations whereby they could assess the real strength of their European enemies, most African chiefs were easy prey. Where intelligence services were used, as in the case of Samory, resistance was kept up for fifteen years. Some other Africans tried to gain time by playing one power off against the other. But the lack of adaptability of most African societies to the new political-military situation led to their easy defeat. Thus the Fulani of Sokoto never learned that cavalry could not charge a square of soldiers with repeater rifles and maxim guns at each corner.

In assessing the nature of African resistance at the end of the nineteenth century we tend to think, as the textbooks tell us, of the resistance of large kingdoms. If the odds seemed overwhelming to them, how much greater did they seem to the smaller states. Finally, we must beware of using the signing of a treaty as an indicator of willingness to accept European colonial rule. Many chiefs did not understand what the treaties meant or were deliberately misled as to their nature.[13] This is clear from the fact that the same chief would sign treaties with several powers. Many thought that such treaties would herald the opening up of trade with the Europeans. Others signed them as the easiest way to get the white man to go away, and when he did come back, resisted him.

## 2 *Securing the Senegalese base*

'The French Union', wrote Alfred Jacobson, Counsellor of the Assembly established for it after the Second World War, 'was constituted on the fringes of the policies of its parliament and its government, by means of individual acts of explorers, soldiers and pioneers. That is probably why the territories administered by France are far from being the richest. . . .'[14]

Nowhere was this more true than of French West Africa, where vast tracts of land, much of it with little economic potential, if any, were acquired by the ambitions of men on the spot. Thus Archinard appears to have been motivated solely by ambition for promotion in his decision to attack the Tokolor fortress of Koundiam in February 1889 without the permission of the French government. Not receiving his expected promotion for this success, he then proceeded to occupy the Tokolor capital of Ségou, again without authorisation, and thus 'committed France to the forcible destruction of the Tokolor state'.[15] Indeed, the French occupation of the colonies of the Western Sudan—Mali (Soudan), Upper Volta, Niger, Mauritania and parts of Guinea—was primarily a military one and very little of it was acquired by treaty. The soldiers, with autonomy of command on the Upper Niger, for the most part determined what should be acquired for France and were more disposed to conquest than treaty-making even if possibilities of promotion were not at stake. Furthermore, they tended to think in terms of square *kilométrege* of land acquired rather than its quality as a sign of success. Such a policy had little economic rationale[16] and was generally at odds with the wishes of Paris and St. Louis. Nevertheless there were those who made money out of the exercise. These vast new territories had to be administered and men found to administer them. In an age before the motor car was a practicable form of transport, railways were the surest. So railways had to be built; telegraph lines had to be erected to link the new administrative posts with those already established; the new administrative posts had to be built, supplied and furnished. There was thus a whole group of businessmen who could benefit from expansion even into the most uninviting lands and often they actively encouraged such expansion, even though it would never profit France herself.[17] Those responsible for the building of the Senegal–Niger railway made great profits from a project whose estimated cost went up each year so that after five years only 54 kilometres of railway had been laid and 110 kilometres of rough road bed completed, at the cost of 260,000 francs per kilometre.[18] It was the taxpayer, not private enterprise, who footed the bill each time the project was seen to be more costly than originally anticipated, but it was private enterprise which benefited.

The instability of French governments in this period gave the military and those who profited from the expansion into the Western Sudan a great advantage over those in Parliament who, as General Mangin put it, felt that it was a desert 'where nothing can be grown except the decorations that flourish on the uniforms of officers impatient for promotion . . . the evacuation of the occupied areas is frequently brought up; every change of government brings forth a declaration in which the head of the new cabinet closes the temple of Janus, ends the era of conquest, and declares that a new period has begun by realising the profits of a colonial domain which cannot be expanded indefinitely'.[19]

The difficulty of controlling the army's efforts whether in West Africa or elsewhere is easier to understand when one realises that between 1882 and 1899 France had twenty-one changes in the holders of the office of Under Secretary of State (later Minister) for Colonies. The longest in power was Eugène Étienne who held the post for five years from 1887 to 1892, with an interruption of two months. Étienne, while opposed to the autonomy of the military on the Niger, worked in favour of colonial expansion in a period when reaction to it was greatest. The Makoko treaties had received public acclaim in 1882 but disillusionment followed in 1885 when the disastrous defeat of the French forces in Indo-China had resulted in the downfall of *Ferry le Traître*, as the crowds called him. It was Ferry, more than anyone, who had been responsible for the creation of the French empire, but even he had been dubious about the West African adventure and had, after his success in Tunisia, ordered a halt to military conquest in the Western Sudan.[20]

Étienne curtailed the independence of the military by personally directing the resumption of the advance into the Sudan. 'If you drop a line from the Tunisian border past Lake Chad to the Congo', he observed, 'you can say that most of the territories between that line and the sea, excepting Morocco and the English, German and Portuguese coastal possessions hidden in the immense circumference, are either French or are destined to enter within the French sphere of influence. We have there a vast and immense domain which is ours to colonise and to make fruitful; and I think that, at this time, taking into account the world-wide movement of expansion, at the same time as foreign markets are closing against us, and we ourselves are thinking of our own market, I think, I repeat, that it is wise to look to the future and reserve to French commerce and industry those outlets which are opened to her in the colonies and by the colonies.'[21]

Deputies may have criticised the fact that four-fifths of the colonial budget were devoted to military expenditure, or suggested that funds would be better invested in the metropolis, but lacking the authority of a stable government to control the soldiers, who anyway had the backing of the ministries of the marine and colonies, if not always of their own ministers, the conquest proceeded often without authorisation to acquire for France one million eight hundred thousand square miles of land, inhabited at the time by probably less than eleven million people.

Only by understanding the vital political role played by the soldiers in the decisions as to what lands should be occupied by France can we understand why she spent such effort in acquiring quantity of land rather than quality. If the driving force behind the French conquest of West Africa was the acquisition of as much territory as possible, there was one important limitation imposed on this objective: the fear of an entanglement with a rival power like Britain or Germany which might lead to war. The French had always to consider whether some small advantage in Africa was worth risking a continental engagement in Europe. The Niger did in fact very nearly become a *casus belli* between Britain and France,[22] for the latter had, in her rapid expansion, two specific goals: to gain a foothold on the navigable stretch of the Niger, and to gain control of as much of its upper reaches as possible. The upper reaches were not claimed by any other power, and were easily accessible to France from her Senegalese base. The lower reaches, however, were claimed by Britain, who despite the free navigation agreement of the Berlin Conference was anxious, through the agency of Goldie's Royal Niger Company, to prevent France from gaining access to a port on the navigable stretch below the Bussa rapids, which the latter could easily occupy from her Dahomean base. But both France and Britain claimed to have treaty rights over Bussa, which became, because of its strategic position, the only place in which France went as far as to risk war with Britain. Finally there were those in France who viewed their African empire as one that would stretch from the Mediterranean to the Atlantic and be lapped by the Indian Ocean. Thus, the coastal enclaves of Guinea and Dahomey were vital to her trans-Saharan ambitions, the acquisition of the Chad basin to her trans-continental dream. Within such broad strategical limits, almost any military decision could be justified.

In 1882 work started finally on the construction of the Dakar–St. Louis line for which funds had been voted by the law of 5th February 1880. The same law also provided for the line that would link Medina with the Niger and enable France seriously to exploit the supposed economic potential of the Sudan. It was clear by this time that those who were behind the Senegal–Niger railway project were determined to overcome any African opposition to their plans.[23] It was also clear that a project such as a railway would 'almost certainly require France to exercise a more direct influence in the Tokolor empire than Ahmadou would willingly concede'.[24] And in the same year a column crossed the Niger for the first time, in order to attack the forces of the Almamy Samory who was himself bent on expanding his own empire towards this part of the Niger and was becoming aware of the threat the French presented to his ambitions. The following year Colonel Borgnis-Desbordes established a post at Bamako, future capital of the colony of the Sudan. But for further expansion along the Niger to be effective the Senegal base had to be secure. This it was not. The Damel of Cayor, despite an earlier alliance with the French, was in deep opposition to their plans for construction of a railway through his lands to open up the area to groundnut production. Thus the same man who had sought common cause with the French in 1875 to stave off the Tokolor Marabout, Ahmadou Cheikou, whose *jihad* threatened the Colony of Senegal and his own Cayor, was to wage war on them when they themselves appeared to threaten his independence. As Faidherbe was to remark, later, of the defeat of Ahmadou Cheikou: 'Lat Dior gave us his complete support in that campaign; but it must not be forgotten that his own interests were at stake'.[25]

Lat Dior saw very clearly that the railway would herald the end of his sovereignty. He had written in 1877 to Governor Brière de l'Isle, who had greatly expanded the colony of Senegal during his governorship and founded the port of Dakar: 'Rest assured that if, today, you build a railway . . . you will take away my country from me and strip me of all I possess.'[26] Though Lat Dior did, in fact, sign a treaty to permit the building of the railway, he later repudiated it vehemently, realising that such a railway with its attendant trading posts would result in his losing his independence. He resorted to armed opposition to the French who sent a column against him and imposed Amady N'Gone Fall of Cayor as its new Damel. However, the new Damel was unable to control Cayor into which Lat Dior made frequent forays, and was replaced by Samba Laobé Fall in 1883. Lat Dior's decision to oppose the railway was quite justified, for Colonel Wendling, head of the Cayor military column, had written to the Governor: 'All the chiefs understand that the decisive moment has come when the railway will make us absolute masters of them and when the commerce of Europe will be open to all instead of being, as it is today, the monopoly of a small number.'[27]

Lat Dior, dispossessed of his country, carried on an incessant war against the French, realising like Samory (and Mao Tse Tung and the Vietcong later) that the easiest way to deal with a force armed with superior equipment was by guerilla warfare. Before his final battle with the French at N'Dékété in 1886, he had the satisfaction of seeing his usurping nephew Samba Laobé Fall turn on his patrons in 1885, the same year as the railway was completed. Samba Laobé, to the chagrin of the French, attacked the Bourba Djollof, who, though at the time on friendly terms with the French, had given asylum to Lat Dior. The Bourba Djollof then obtained French protection, and the French sent a delegation to Samba Laobé to persuade him to cease hostilities. In the course of the interview, Samba Laobé was killed by the leader of the French delegation, Captain Spitzer, 'in self-defence' according to the official version, deliberately (execution) according to *Le Réveil du Sénégal*.[28] The following year a protectorate was declared by the French over Cayor.

Lat Dior was far from being the only major challenge to the French in Senegal. Despite his temporary alliance with the French, the Bourba Djollof, Ali Bouri, was hostile to them and attempted unsuccessfully to link up with Samory.[29] His country was occupied only in 1890 by a column led by the St. Louisien, Dodds, but he himself escaped to join forces with the Tokolor against the French and later with Sokoto against the British. A much more serious threat to the French came from Mahmadou Lamine. He was a Soninke Marabout who in 1886 had proclaimed himself Mahdi at Sénédoubou, near Medina, capital of Bondou, whose ruler had denied Lamine's claim. Mahmadou Lamine's ambition was to re-establish a great Sarakole empire, and his first move was to attack the French fort at Bakel, from which he was repulsed after a long siege. He then invaded Bondou and killed its ruler and went on to attack the French posts at Sénédoubou, which was successfully defended by Yaro

Coumba, an African lieutenant of the French forces. Undaunted, he tried to cut French communications between Bakel and Kayes. Gallieni, commander of the Upper Senegal, was ordered to deal with him, but it took several campaigns before he could break his power. He was finally defeated in his fortified camp near Tambacounda, in the Upper Gambia, on 8th December 1887, and killed the next day by Casamance warriors. Gallieni, victorious, distributed Mahmadou Lamine's wives to his soldiers and had his son, Souaïbou, only eighteen years old, shot.[30]

The most unexpected consequence of this victory for the French was to give them control of the Upper Gambia and much of the Casamance as well as to establish liaison between Bakel and Kayes.[31]

The death of Mahmadou Lamine marked the end of effective resistance to French rule in Senegal. The resistance of this Moslem empire builder was, however, but a foretaste of what they were to encounter in their conquest of Ahmadou, successor of Al Hajj Umar and Samory, who was constructing a formidable empire based on the hinterland of Guinea and the southern parts of modern Mali.

## 3 The conquest of the Tokolor empire

By the time her Senegalese base was secure, France was already inextricably involved with Ahmadou and Samory. The campaigns against them are too many and complex to relate here in detail. We shall be concerned only with the broad outlines, particularly as they show the nature of and reasons for their resistance to French penetration.

Ahmadou Sekou, son of Al Hajj Umar, had succeeded to the vast empire created by his father in 1862, ruling it from his capital at Ségou. He was a scholarly man, forward-looking, anxious to develop trade between his country and its neighbours, in particular the French in Senegal, but also the British in the Gambia and Sierra Leone. Relatives ruled the major provinces of the empire: the most important of these were his brother Aguibou, who ruled Dinguiraye in the south, and Tijani, his cousin, who ruled Macina. Ahmadou, then, was overlord of the whole length of the Niger from the frontier of French penetration, Bamako, to Timbuktu, which was still dominated by the Tuareg. His authority over his brothers and relations who acted as governors was maintained by the fact that he had been explicitly recognised as heir by his father.[32] Nevertheless, his authority over them was not strong at the time of French penetration, but he had felt secure enough to declare himself

Commander of the Faithful in 1874. It was certainly never as weak as it has often been depicted. Though Tijani had brought Macina once more under Tokolor rule, and Ahmadou himself had quelled dissident Bambara subjects, his empire had definite problems: Samory's ambitions extended towards the Niger; Ahmadou's brothers were jealous of his position and many of the peoples who had been brought into the empire by Al Hajj Umar's conquests would seek the first opportunity to regain their independence. Tijani at Macina had never paid homage to Ahmadou as his over-lord, for instance, and the Bambara still carried on resistance from Bélédougou, though Ahmadou had control of their former states of Ségou and Kaarta. Thus when Gallieni arrived in 1880 to obtain a treaty from him to permit the building of the railway connecting the Senegal with the Niger, his first instinct was to stall. He had enough troubles as it was without adding the French to them. Gallieni demanded not only a French protectorate over Ahmadou's terri-tories on the left bank of the Niger, but also that the Niger be opened to French traders to the exclusion of all other foreigners, which would eliminate the middleman role over the export trade of his empire enjoyed by his own subjects. Ahmadou kept Gallieni waiting for ten months, at Niango, some thirty-five miles from his capital, but he was forced to a decision by the French occupation of Kita, well within his territory. Ahmadou refused to accept a pro-tectorate, and only accorded the French the position of most favoured nation as far as trade in his lands was concerned. The French, for their part, agreed never to conquer any land belonging to the Tokolor. The Treaty of Niango, as it was called, was never rati-fied by the French Governor of Senegal, despite the mission sent by Ahmadou to St. Louis in October 1881 to obtain ratification. Furthermore, its text in French differed from the Arabic text.[33] Ahmadou repudiated French pretensions that the treaty gave them a protectorate over any of his lands, claiming that it was only a treaty of trade.[34] At the time he was able to do this with relative impunity for the French were already over-committed as far as colonial adventures were concerned, both in the international con-text and in West Africa itself. In 1882 France had occupied Tunisia and was already embroiled in Indo-China and had become com-mitted in the Congo as a result of the Makoko treaties. Her colony of Senegal, as we have seen, was at that time far from secure. In such circumstances she was unwilling to 'let herself be drawn into great efforts in the Sudan', as Brunschwig has put it.[35]

Ahmadou's repudiation of the treaty was nevertheless to invite

G

eventual retaliation, for the railway, on which work was started in 1881, could only be justified from the French point of view if they could tap in complete security the resources of the Niger bend. And though French official policy was to halt further commitments in the Sudan, as Delafosse pointed out: 'as far as colonial expansion is concerned, the metropolitan authorities propose, but local circumstances dispose.'[36] Thus in January 1883 Borgnis-Desbordes took Bamako which was essential to the railway line as the first part of the Niger it would reach. Laying the foundation stone of the fort at Bamako, Borgnis-Desbordes made it clear that as far as the men on the spot were concerned the conquest of the Sudan had begun: 'We will fire an eleven-gun salute in honour of our flag, flying for the first time and for always, on the banks of the Niger. The noise made by our little cannons will not reach beyond the mountains which lie before us, yet, and you can be certain of this, their echo will be heard beyond the Senegal.'[37]

Much as Ahmadou was hesitant to grapple with the French because of his own internal problems, the construction of the railway line, undertaken by Moroccan and Chinese labourers for whom the death-toll was extremely high, gave him considerable cause for concern. It separated his northern and southern territories. Already the French had occupied part of his territory without negotiation. Sitting in Ségou, he could take little comfort from the fact that in France there was increasing hostility to the Sudanese venture. The Chamber refused credits for the railway in 1883 and after the downfall of Jules Ferry in 1885 consideration was given to complete withdrawal from the Sudan. But the Berlin Act and the ambitions of the men on the spot meant that the eventual occupation and destruction of Ahmadou's empire was inevitable. Thus this attempt, as Hargreaves has put it, 'to create a new type of African Moslem state— one that would transcend ethnic quarrels, draw through trade on the technology of the European world, and utilise the skills of Africans, whose experience or training might be relevant to this aim'[38] was cut short.

As far as the French were concerned, Samory appeared a more immediate problem. His 'Sofas', as the regular infantry of his army were called, were already active in the area in which the railway was being built. In 1881 they had attacked Kita but had been repulsed across the Niger, south towards Siguiri. In 1883 Borgnis-Desbordes fended off a large Sofa attack but he was not authorised to pursue them. In 1885 Samory forced the French to abandon their post at Nafadié and, to conserve French honour and reputation in the area, an expedition was led against him, even though the French were not at this stage anxious to involve themselves deeply with Samory. And on the whole, nor was Samory prepared to take on the French in a full-scale war. It must be remembered that his empire was of recent creation—1870–1875—and that he was as intent on its extension towards the East, in particular the prosperous trading state of Sikasso, as towards the Niger. So by the treaty drawn up as a result of the defeat of his army after the Nafadié incident, he agreed to send his son Karamoko[39] to France as a hostage for his good faith. And a year later, by the Treaty of Bissandougou, he agreed to the establishment of a French post at Siguiri and the occupation by the French of the left bank of the Niger and Tinkisso rivers as far as Niamina. By it the zones of expansion of France and Samory were delimited, and a vague protectorate established by France over his states, though it was a nominal protectorate that they were only able to assume by force of arms. But under the terms of the Berlin convention it did give the French a claim to his empire and also to much of the hinterland of the British colony of Sierra Leone.[40] This was particularly valuable to the French since both the Governor of Sierra Leone and the Creole traders of Freetown were trying to persuade the British government to establish a protectorate over Samory's empire. Samory himself flirted with the idea of submitting his empire to a British protectorate. He certainly denied that he had accepted a French protectorate.

Just as the treaty of Medina had limited Al Hajj Umar's westward expansion, Samory's own westward expansion was now limited and he therefore directed most of his efforts eastwards, trying to take Sikasso, which proved unassailable after a sixteen months' siege. However, its king, Tièba, fearing a return of Samory, signed a treaty of protection with the French as the lesser of two evils.

The Berlin Act made the acquisition of a firm treaty of protectorate with Ahmadou the most urgent. He, himself, anticipating the French advance on Ségou, had moved to Nioro, having earlier complained to the French commandant at Bamako: 'You have burst into our lands without any authorisation, with no right, and without any respect for the treaties which bound us.'[41]

Effectively, by 1886, when Gallieni took over command of the 'Haute Fleuve' (Upper Niger) Ahmadou's kingdom was divided into four clear sections owing varying degrees of allegiance to him. He himself now ruled Kaarta from Nioro; his son, Madani, Ségou; his cousin, Tijani, Macina; and his brother, Agiubou, Dinguiraye. In 1886 Gallieni managed to obtain a protectorate from Aguibou; the following year from Ahmadou, for whom it was a temporary blessing since it allowed him to divert his attention towards Samory, whose activities on the southern borders of his empire were becoming increasingly worrying to him.

In 1888 Archinard succeeded Gallieni as Commandant of the Haute Fleuve. Archinard was a man ambitious for promotion who saw conquest as a sure way to its achievement. He also believed that there was no prospect of assuming protection of Ahmadou's empire by peaceful means and decided, therefore, on its destruction. After attacks by Ahmadou's forces in 1888 on villages near Kayes and Medina, Archinard tried to negotiate for peace with Ahmadou, to which Ahmadou replied that he had nothing about which to negotiate. Thereafter Archinard was confirmed in his opinion. He attacked Aguibou, who had, despite his earlier treaty with the French, considered an alliance with Samory, and subjected this section of the Tokolor empire to France. Thereafter, as Delafosse put it, 'this son of Al Hajj Umar was never to break his perfect loyalty to us'.[42] Archinard then occupied Koundiam, and in April 1890 Ségou, from which Madani had moved to join his father at Nioro. However, Ahmadou's grandson, who had been left behind, was sent by Archinard to Paris, where he was entered in a lycée from which he went on to Saint-Cyr. This little experiment in assimilation ended shortly afterwards with his death.[43] These two attacks were not authorised, but Archinard justified them in his report for 1890–1, recording that Ahmadou had given the following orders to his people: 'on pain of death no inhabitant of the right bank of the river will sell to the French or furnish any *tirailleur* any goods of any sort. The roads to Koniakry, Bafoulabé and Badumbe are closed. No Moorish caravan will sell gum at the [French] trading posts. The people of Kaarta settled on the left of the Senegal must cross back to the right bank under penalty of confiscation of their goods.'

To which Archinard added acidly: 'It is not here on the spot that one forms an opinion favourable to the maintenance of Ahmadou.'[44] He was repeating the opinion Gallieni had formed a decade before: 'The confidence of Ahmadou, as long as he reigns on the banks of the Niger, will remain an impassable barrier between us and the rest of the Soudan.'[45]

Unfortunately, though well aware of the danger he was in, Ahmadou would not make common cause with Samory, who before the fall of Ségou had suggested an alliance between their two empires. He was cold-shouldered: 'The son of Al Hajj Umar could not, without lowering himself, accept an alliance with, or the assistance of, an adventurer.'[46]

In Ségou Archinard installed in Madani's place Mari Diara, the heir to the Bambara dynasty which had been overthrown by Al Hajj Umar, but far from proving the puppet Archinard hoped he would he tried to assert his independence by plotting to kill the French Resident. Forewarned of this plan, the Resident had him shot. He was replaced by a member of the Kaarta Bambara dynasty who was to prove very unpopular with his subjects. From Ségou, Archinard marched on towards Nioro, Ahmadou's capital, but met serious resistance on the way at Oussebougou, a Tokolor stronghold. In the attack he was assisted by the Bambara whose 'independence' he had restored. In the face of difficulties he accused them of cowardice, and told them: 'It is for you alone that I have come here, for Ouessebougou does not bother the French; you told me that I would only have to make a breach in the walls with my cannons and you would pass . . .'[47] As it was, Archinard, who had every interest in conquering this Toucouleur stronghold, met some of the fiercest resistance of the whole of his career. Even women took up swords against the invaders[48] and the chief, Bandiougou Diara, 'blew himself up inside his stronghold rather than surrender'.[49] Archinard's forces were harried from many points and attacks were made on French posts right up to Kayes and Bakel. Only in January 1891 did he take Nioro, finding that Ahmadou had left the ill-defended capital for Macina. His escape to the eastern parts of his empire was facilitated by the strong diversionary tactics of forces led by Ali Bouri, Bourba Djollof, who had joined forces with him since fleeing from Senegal.[50]

Archinard was prevented from following through his victory over Ahmadou by the disturbed conditions in Ségou, and the declaration of open hostilities with Samory. The new Bambara king, Bodian, was far from acceptable to all sections of Ségou and provoked revolt, encouraged quite naturally by Ahmadou's supporters. A separate principality was carved out of Ségou based on Sansanding. A Senegalese clerk in the Posts and Telegraphs, Mademba, was made its *fama* or ruler, foreshadowing the French policy of using those known to be loyal to the régime as chiefs whether or not they had any legitimate claim. Delafosse wrote of him later: 'The *fama* Mademba was to become legendary throughout the Soudan for his absolute loyalty, his political acumen and his hospitality towards Europeans.'[51]

But for Ahmadou it was only a matter of time before the end came.

In Macina he was received in triumph despite the initial opposition of his titular vassal, Mohammadou Mounirou, who was as unused as his predecessor to taking orders from Ahmadou and considered himself effectively independent.[52] Mounirou's council rejected his proposal to fight Ahmadou, paying tribute to the immense prestige the latter still enjoyed in his empire.[53] From Macina, Ahmadou, less proud now, attempted an alliance with Samory and Tièba of Sikasso. But it was too late and in 1893 the French, aided by Aguibou, his own brother, finally defeated Ahmadou at Kori-Kori. His own inclination was to fight on to the bitter end, but he was persuaded that there was nothing degrading about flight (*hijra*) since the Prophet had done this. He left his empire's borders; yet, as his cousin and companion Mohammadou Tall recorded, 'all who accompanied him remarked that the respect that was due to him continued to be shown to him by all the princes and chiefs among whom he sojourned'.[54] A man of remarkable resources, he succeeded in creating a small kingdom for himself at Dounge and spent three years as its ruler, from 1895 to 1898. It was the arrival of the Hourst mission, foreshadowing the coming of French columns, that decided him to continue his onward trek to the East. Before he reached Sokoto, he died. Mohammadou Tall recorded that, on hearing of his death, Sultan Abdurahman of Sokoto cried: 'God has taken away a fine relation. He was the only support that I had in the world'.[55] Ahmadou was succeeded as Khalif by Mohammadou Bassirou. The Sultan of Sokoto gave Bassirou and his followers a village called Dar-es-Salaam in which to settle. In recognition he and his followers aided Sokoto in its fight against the British, who delivered him up to the French in Niger where he was interned.

### 4 The Seven Years' War with Samory

Only in his extremity had Ahmadou contacted Samory for support and one can only speculate on how different the story of colonial conquest would have been if Samory, Ahmadou and the Sultan of Sokoto had, throughout, joined in holy alliance against the Christian invader.

Samory had sized up the virtues of such an alliance. After his defeat at Sikasso he said, in his despatch through the unsuccessful embassy to Ahmadou for a treaty of alliance: 'If you continue to make war on your own, the whites will have no trouble in defeating you. I have already undergone the experience in trying my strength against them. Let us therefore unite. You will hit the French from the North, I will harass them in the South, and we will certainly manage to get rid of them.'[56]

In 1891 war broke out again between Samory and the French, each accusing the other of violation of the Treaty of Bissandougou. The rights and wrongs are of little consequence since it was clear that nothing would halt the French conquest. From then until 1898 it was war to the bitter end, culminating in the French siege of Sikasso, whose new king, Ba Bemba, came out in favour of Samory, realising that the French were now the greater threat to his independence. After the fall of this great fortified city of some seven to eight kilometres in circumference and with some forty thousand inhabitants, protected by great walls, Samory had lost. In all, he had fought thirteen major engagements with the French and had moved his empire a distance of some six hundred kilometres in the process. He displayed the same combination of military and administrative genius as Napoleon. Péroz, his great admirer, quite rightly called him the 'Bonaparte of the Soudan'.[57]

The most striking facet of Samory's military genius was his adaptability to the changing situation. First and foremost he realised the prime importance of maintaining his source of supplies of arms, ammunition and horses. Secondly, he brought the art of strategic withdrawal to near-perfection. And, thirdly, so brilliant was his organisation of men that he could move his sizeable army with surprising rapidity. Finally, he had an excellent intelligence system so that he had good knowedge of French intentions. The combination of his strategic retreats to areas outside French control, together with his maintenance of supplies of modern weapons, were largely responsible for his ability to hold out against the French for so long.[58]

Not only Péroz recognised his military genius. General Baratier wrote of Samory: 'It is not an exaggeration to say that he showed himself superior to all the Negro chiefs who were our adversaries on the African continent. He was the only one who gave proof of those qualities characteristic of a chief of a people, a strategist and even a politician . . . an outstanding leader of men, possessing audacity, energy, the ability to follow up an advantage and plan in advance, and above all an irrepressible tenacity which could not be destroyed.'[59]

Once the French decided to go on the offensive against Samory, he fell back on the plan that was to make their conquest so difficult. One part of his army fought the French, another part conquered new lands to the East into which he could withdraw when the French could no longer be held. Then the lands which the French were about to occupy were 'scorched'. This involved a fantastic administrative ability, for not only was an army on the move, but a whole empire. Yet during all this time Samory managed to keep his constantly moving empire under firm control. Of course the peoples into whose lands he moved suffered terribly, and it is this that accounts for the many gruesome accounts, often exaggerated, given by the French, of the devastations made by Samory. In these accounts, it is rarely mentioned that the initial cause was the French themselves, since they were forcing him to move his army and people so rapidly eastwards and to the south. Samory tried everything to keep his empire. He even sought British protection from the government in Freetown. Trying to play off British and French, he told Governor Hay he no longer accepted his treaties with France. Hay was anxious to extend such protection, but London was unwilling. As far as the French were concerned, Freetown was a major thorn in their flesh in dealing with Samory, for it was from here that he gained most of his arms, albeit, as Hay pointed out, mainly from French shopkeepers.[60] He even demanded peace with the French in the hopes that they would agree to terms, whereby he would remain effective ruler of his empire. But, inexorably, the French moved eastwards and they could not be staved off even by his alliance with Ba Bemba of Sikasso, who had declared at the time of the Morrison mission, sent by Audéoud to arrange for the establishment of a French garrison in the capital: 'I will never give up a scrap of the land of my ancestors to anyone whoever he may be. What they are asking of me can only be had after my death.'[61]

By the time the French attacked Sikasso, Samory had nowhere to manoeuvre. In 1896 the British had occupied Ashanti, with which he had opened tentative negotiations for an alliance. The British had declared a Protectorate over Sierra Leone in 1896 and he could no longer obtain supplies of arms from them. The French could harass him from the Ivory Coast. To the North the French had occupied the Tokolor empire. Their conquest of Sikasso in 1898 blocked any hope of northward expansion. Samory was as good as defeated.

Samory was captured and exiled shortly after the fall of Sikasso: but he was still looking for new supplies of arms. He is the most interesting of all the resisters of colonial penetration for in him we can see the sort of leader who might well have achieved modernisation of his own state, independent of European control. That he had the ability and the instinct is clear from his military tactics, his organisation of trade and his spectacular administration of his constantly moving empire. He had his own 'arms factory' to supplement his supply of European rifles from Freetown. General Baratier estimated he had some three to four hundred men engaged on making arms.[62] He even successfully sent one of his blacksmiths to obtain employment in the arms factory of St. Louis, to learn the latest techniques of the French. Péroz, when he went to Bissandougou to seek a change in the original treaty of Keniéba Kouba with Samory, remarked on the superb and well-laid-out agriculture of an area of some 200 square kilometres on which thousands of workers were engaged.[63] Certainly if Samory had not had to face the French, there is every indication that he had the organising genius and sufficient control of this people to have created a state responsive to the needs of the approaching Twentieth Century.

# Notes

1 Henri Brunschwig, *Mythes et Réalités de l'Impérialisme Colonial Française, 1871-1914*, Paris, 1960, pp. 163-70.
2 P. Soleillet, *Voyage à Ségou*, Paris, 1887, p. 379.
3 Brunschwig, *Mythes et Réalités*, p. 108.
4 Cited in Auguste Terrier and Charles Mourey, *L'Expansion Française et la Formation Territoriale*, Paris, 1910, pp. 352-3.
5 For a brief but stimulating discussion of the problems of assessing the nature of, and reasons for, reaction to colonial occupation see Tekena N. Tamuno, 'Some Aspects of Nigerian Reaction to the Imposition of British Rule', *Journal of the Historical Society of Nigeria*, III, 2, December 1965, pp. 271-94.
6 Chinua Achebe, *Things Fall Apart*, London, 1958.
7 Francis Agbodeka, 'The Fanti Confederacy, 1865-69', *Transactions of the Historical Society of Ghana*, VII, 1964, p. 105.
8 Philip Mason, *The Birth of a Dilemma: The Conquest and Settlement of Rhodesia*, London, 1958, p. 105 and p. 175.
9 *The Diaries of Lord Lugard*, edited by Margery Perham and Mary Bull, London, 1963, Vol. IV, p. 139.
10 Henri Brunschwig, *L'Avènement de l'Afrique*, Paris, 1963, pp. 98-104.
11 Lugard, *Diaries*, Vol. IV, p. 167.
12 Nathanièl R. Richardson, *Liberia's Past and Present*, London, 1959, pp. 31-2 and pp. 181-2.
13 Thus Governor Hill, in 1861, obtained the cession of land from Bai Kanta of Koya by telling him it was 'leased', whereas on the Treaty on which he put his mark it was declared ceded to Britain. Christopher Fyfe, *A History of Sierra Leone*, London, 1962, p. 310.
14 In various authors, *La France d'Outre-Mer: sa situation actuelle*, Paris, 1953, Part IV, 'L'Afrique Occidentale', p. 80.
15 J. D. Hargreaves, *West Africa: the Former French States*, Englewood Cliffs, New Jersey, 1967, p. 102.
16 S. H. Roberts, *French Colonial Policy*, p. 304: 'Whatever economic motives there may have been in the beginning were soon thrust into the background and did not re-appear until the conquest was effected.'
17 Brunschwig, *Mythes et Réalités*, pp. 157-63.
18 Thomas J. Power, *Jules Ferry and the Renaissance of French Imperialism*, New York, 1944, pp. 80-2. Also R. Godfernaux, *Chemins de fer Coloniaux*, Paris, 1911.
19 Preface to P. L. Monteil, *Souvenirs vécus, quelques feuillets de l'Histoire Coloniale, les Rivalités Internationales*, Paris, 1924, cited by Desiré-Vuillemin, *Mauritanie*, p. 84.
20 See Hanotaux, *Histoire des Colonies Françaises*, Vol. IV, p. 178.
21 Roberts, *French Colonial Policy*, p. 21.

22 Robinson and Gallagher, *Africa and the Victorians*, p. 405. Chamberlain 'was determined to resist the French push toward the Lower Niger from the West, "even at the cost of war" '.

23 Jean Suret-Canale, *Afrique Noire I*, Paris, 1961, p. 214.

24 J. D. Hargreaves, 'The Tokolor Empire of Ségou and its relations with the French', *Boston University Papers on African History*, II, Jeffrey Butler, ed., Boston, 1966, p. 138.

25 Général Faidherbe, *Le Sénégal*, Paris, 1889, p. 443.

26 Cited by Vincent Monteil, 'Lat Dior, Damel du Kayor (1842–1886) et l'Islamisation des Wolofs', *Archives de Sociologie des Réligions*, XVI, 1963, p. 95.

27 *Ibid.*, p. 95.

28 *Ibid.*, p. 92.

29 André Villard, *Histoire du Sénégal*, Dakar, 1943, p. 143.

30 Suret-Canale, *Afrique Noire I*, p. 222.

31 J. Jaunet and J. Barry, *Histoire de l'AOF*, Paris, 1949, 3rd edition, p. 96.

32 J. S. Trimingham, *A History of Islam in West Africa*, London, 1962, p. 184.

33 Maurice Delafosse in Hanotaux, *Histoire des Colonies Françaises*, IV, p. 176.

34 His position was thus similar to that of the Sultan of Sokoto: see footnote 1, p. 20.

35 Henri Brunschwig, *La Colonisation Française du Pacte Colonial à l'Union Française*, Paris, 1949, p. 113.

36 Delafosse in Hanotaux, *Histoire des Colonies Françaises*, IV, p. 178.

37 *Ibid.*, p. 179.

38 Hargreaves, 'The Tokolor Empire of Ségou', p. 129.

39 It is not in fact clear whether Karamoko was his son or a slave.

40 Brunschwig, *La Colonisation Française*, p. 113. Also Christopher Fyfe, *A History of Sierra Leone*, Oxford, 1962, p. 474.

41 Cited by Suret-Canale, *Afrique Noire I*, p. 221.

42 Delafosse in Hanotaux, *Histoire des Colonies Françaises*, IV, p. 185.

43 Jaunet and Barry, *Histoire de l'AOF*, p. 113.

44 Terrier and Mourey, *L'expansion française*, p. 169.

45 *Ibid.*, p. 170.

46 Auguste Canu, *La Pétaudière Coloniale*, Paris, 1894, p. 161.

47 Lieutenant Gatelet, *Histoire de la Conquête du Soudan Français 1878–1899*, Paris, 1901, p. 153.

48 Jaunet and Barry, *Histoire de l'AOF*, p. 113.

49 Delafosse in Hanotaux, *Histoire des Colonies Françaises*, IV, p. 185.

50 *Ibid.*, p. 188.

51 *Ibid.*, p. 191.

52 Bendaoud Mademba, 'La dernière étape d'un conquérant (odyssée des dernières années de Sultan Ahmadou de Ségou racontée par son

cousin et compagnon d'infortune Mahammadou Hassimou Tall)' trans. from the Bambara in *Bulletin du Comité d'Études Historiques et Scientifiques de l'Afrique Occidentale Française*, 3, July–September, 1921, p. 473.

53 *Ibid.*, p. 474.

54 *Ibid.*, p. 476.

55 *Ibid.*, p. 478–9.

56 Amadou Kouroubari, 'Histoire de l'Imam Samori', translated from Maurice Delafosse's *Éssai de Manuel Pratique de la Langue Mande ou Mandingue*.

57 Marie Étienne Péroz, *Au Niger-récits de campagne (1891–2)*, Paris, 1894, and *l'Empire de l'Almamy Emir Samory*, Besançon, 1888.

58 Martin Legassick, 'Firearms, Horses and Samorian Army Organisation in 1870–1898', *Journal of African History*, VII, I, 1966, pp. 95–115.

59 Lt. Col. Baratier, *A Travers l'Afrique*, Paris, 1912. I am grateful to Mr. Tom Cassilly for drawing my attention to this quotation; the translation is his.

60 Fyfe, *A History of Sierra Leone*, p. 499. Also Legassick, 'Firearms, Horses and Samorian Army Organisations', and Terrier and Maurey, *L'expansion française*, p. 171. N.B.: The British finally agreed to forbid the supply of arms by Public Order No. 86 of September 1893, whereby no firearms or ammunition were to be supplied to Sofas.

61 Suret-Canale, *Afrique Noire I*, p. 237.

62 Baratier, *A Travers l'Afrique*, Paris, 1912, p. 66.

63 Péroz, *Au Niger*, p. 169.

# 2 The completion of the French occupation of West Africa

## 1 Securing the Guinea hinterland

The lands wrested by the French from Samory and Ahmadou together with the Senegalese conquests represented over half of what was to become French West Africa. This conquest ranks amongst the most difficult undertaken by France in the acquisition of her colonial empire. But force was necessary for the occupation of the rest of French West Africa.

The defeat of Ahmadou and Samory gave France a dominating position in the Western Sudan. But these lands, to be of commercial interest, had to be linked with France's coastal trading posts established in Guinea, Ivory Coast and Dahomey.

France's trading posts on the Guinea coast had been established from Senegal. Their natural hinterland consisted of parts of Samory's empire and the Imamate of Futa Jallon which had remained independent of Samory. The most important stretches of the Guinea coastline had been occupied by France before 1882 by means of treaties with local rulers. A Convention, unratified by the French Chamber, but observed by both parties, divided spheres of influence between the French in Guinea and the British in Sierra Leone. To the north lay the Portuguese with whom a treaty was signed in 1886, settling the frontiers between the two Guineas. The only other problem as far as France's control of the coastline was concerned was Germany's annexation of the Dabreka region in December 1884 where German trading posts had been established since 1881. The following year Dr. Nachtigal also annexed Correa for Germany. However, by the Convention of 24th December 1885 Germany gave up her pretensions to these parts of Guinea, acknowledging France's claims over them.

Both the French in Senegal and the British in Freetown had shown interest in the Futa Jallon. As early as 1794 Mathew Winterbottom had left Freetown, then ruled by the Sierra Leone Company, to try and open up trade relations with Fouta Djallon. In 1872, the great Negro educator and educational philosopher, Edward Blyden, had visited Timbo, the capital of Futa Jallon, and signed a treaty with the Almamy, and fearing French designs had suggested on his return that the British set up a consular agency there.[1] In 1881 Gouldsbury, Administrator of the Gambia, at the request of Rowe, Governor of Sierra Leone and of the British West African Settlements, who was becoming increasingly concerned at the possibility of the French cutting off his hinterland, signed a treaty of trade and friendship with Almany Ibrahima Suri. But Gouldsbury's report on trade prospects in the Futa Jallon were far from enthusiastic.[2] British action stimulated the French to action and Dr. Bayol, Governor of the Rivières du Sud, obtained treaties which he insisted now excluded any claims Britain might have had, since he had obtained the signature of Ibrahima Suri, as well as that of the alternate Almamy. (The position of Almamy rotated between two families every two years.) Whatever the rights and wrongs of Bayol's claims, the treaties were accepted in Paris and the Futa Jallon became acknowledged as being under French influence. However, French occupation of the kingdom was not effective until 1896. Before 1890, the area remained peaceful under the loose protectorate imposed by France which allowed the Almamies the greatest freedom of action and until 1888 gave them subsidies in return for their co-operation. Though a renegotiated treaty of that year abolished the subsidies causing considerable concern to the chiefs, they in fact continued to be paid. However, in 1890, the French decided to formalise their protectorate which was now recognised by the British through the 1889 Anglo-French convention, by establishing a resident at Timbo. But this met with strong objections from the people. At the same time civil war broke out over the succession to the Imamate. The French initially backed Bokar Biro, and paid him the subsidy, but as soon as it became clear that he would not serve French interests, and indeed seemed to be in league with Samory, they switched their support to his rival, Oumarou Bademba. Profiting from the civil war in the country, they sent in a column to annexe the Futa

Jallon. Oumarou Bademba was installed as Almamy, by the grace of the French as distinct from God, and was forced to sign a treaty which placed the country completely under French control, for though the Almamy was still to be elected it was only with French sanction that the successful candidate could take office. France, too, was to be allowed to instal military and civil posts wherever she wished. Oumarou Bademba signed these treaties reluctantly and was forced off the throne a few months later on the grounds that he, too, was in league with Samory. Thereafter the French proceeded to the deliberate dismemberment of the Imamate,[3] which did not however come fully under their control until the taking of Labé in 1900. The authority of the Almamy was reduced by creating constituent chieftaincies as units independent of him. Only his title distinguished him from his former fiefs. 'Divide in order to rule', concluded the *Report* on the situation in Guinea in 1898, 'is the only policy to be followed in Futa Jallon.'[4]

With Futa Jallon subjugated and Samory conquered, the French had secured a hinterland that would make her colony of Guinea viable economically.

## 2 *The occupation of Mossi*

The occupation of the hinterland of the Ivory Coast was largely the result of the great journey of exploration and treaty-making made by Binger in 1887 which, among other things, finally exploded the myth of the mountains of Kong which had haunted the imagination of European geographers for so many years. France already had claims to the coastline since Bouët-Willaumez signed treaties with chiefs at Grand Bassam in 1842, placing it under French protection so that it could serve as a French base and naval staging post between the newly established Libreville—France's lesser Freetown —and Gorée. Following his establishment of French protection a few French firms, and one British firm, had set themselves up in Grand Bassam and neighbouring ports. The presence of these firms did not go unresisted and Bouët-Willaumez's successor, Baudin, had to undertake a number of 'punitive' expeditions against neighbouring peoples culminating in the construction of a fort at Dabou in 1853. From then until the passage of the Berlin Act there was little extension of French activity on that part of the coast, for France's major preoccupation was still with the Western Sudan.

The Berlin Act stimulated the French to action in this area once more, particularly because of the presence of the British in the neighbouring Gold Coast Colony. Binger therefore set off on his remarkable journey of treaty-making to secure the hinterland of the Ivory Coast for France. The biggest prize was the great Mossi empire based on Ouagadougou. Its ruler, the Moro Naba Sanum, had already received a German from Togoland, Von Krause, who was the first European to enter Ouagadougou.[5] He categorically refused to accept French protection. He accused Binger of disrespect, a charge which Binger denied in revealing terms: 'I feel that a white man travelling in this country, whoever he may be, should not prostrate himself before a black king, however powerful he may be. It is necessary that a white man should inspire respect and consideration wherever he goes; for if the Europeans should ever come here, they should come as masters, as the superior class of the society, and not have to bow their heads before indigenous chiefs to whom they are definitely superior in all respects.'[6]

Binger then had to turn back towards Kong, where he had already been successful in making a treaty of protection and where he met his countryman, Treich-Laplène, who had been making treaties with the rulers west of Kumasi to forestall any attempt at expansion into the area by the British from the Gold Coast. Their two expeditions determined France to extend her empire over what are now Ivory Coast and Upper Volta.

Whilst much of this area was brought under French administration by simple treaty-making, especially those areas vital for the security of French hegemony against her colonial rivals, great areas of the Ivory Coast resisted French penetration right up till the eve of World War I[7] (see page 109), while the Mossi of Ouagadougou, as distinct from their cousins of Yatenga, did all they could to stave off French occupation.

In 1890, when a new French expedition under Crozat arrived in Ouagadougou, it found that Moro Naba Sanum had been succeeded by his brother and rival, Boukary Koutou, who was as adamant as his predecessor in his desire to retain his independence. Thereafter Mossi was to be the subject of visits by missions from the Germans in Togo and the British in Gold Coast but it was the French who cast the most avid eyes on the empire. Moro Naba Wobogo, the name Boukary Koutou assumed on accession, was being advised, Crozat reported, in the following terms: 'The white men always act in the same way. . . . One of them always comes and if he is well received, they come in large numbers; where they establish themselves there are no more black rulers. It is their rule.'[8] Such advice echoed the comment of Major Toutée on the Scramble as 'a process of expropriation employed against Negro states imprudent enough to show hospitality to a white traveller'.[9]

In 1891, the Moro Naba refused even to receive Monteil on his expedition to Chad, but in 1894 he signed a treaty with the British negotiated by George Ekem Ferguson, a Fanti in the employ of the Gold Coast Colony government. The French challenged the validity of the treaty. Again, in 1895, when Captain Destenave, Resident of Bandiagara, who was charged with obtaining treaties from all the rulers of the Niger bend not already under French protection, arrived at Ouagadougou, his demands were rejected in clairvoyant terms by the Moro Naba: 'I know that the whites wish to kill me in order to take my country, and yet you claim that they will help me to organise my country. But I find my country good just as it is. I have no need of them. I know what is necessary for me and what I want: I have my own merchants: also, consider yourself fortunate that I do not order your head to be cut off. Go away now, and, above all, never come back.'[10]

Return the white man did. In 1896, becoming increasingly nervous about the presence of the British in the area, the French finally decided to occupy Mossi by force. A column took and sacked Ouagadougou and Moro Naba Wabogo retreated to reconsolidate his forces, shortly afterwards launching an unsuccessful attack on his capital. Voulet, head of the French column, then placed a brother of Wabogo on the throne, but he died shortly afterwards in suspicious circumstances, at least as the French saw it.[11] Moro Naba Wabogo kept up his resistance to the French, who now placed another of his brothers, Moro Naba Sighiri, on the throne. Sighiri signed a treaty of protection with the French while Wabogo, in desperation, sought to revive the Ferguson treaty of 1894 and persuade the British to take over his country and restore him to the throne. In this he was nearly successful, for a Gold Coast force actually accompanied him to a town twenty-five miles from Ougadougou where they were met by the French who flourished the treaty of protection they had signed with Sighiri.[12] Thereafter Mossi became subject to the French, who proceeded to debase as far as possible the central authority of the Moro Naba, and to exploit his people as a source of forced labour and conscripts for their armies in a way that fully justified Wabogo's apprehensions. Mossi was to prove a godsend to the French as a reservoir of labour which was vital in their exploitation of the resources of the rich but sparsely populated Ivory Coast.

H

Control of Mossi meant that the French could now link their colony of Dahomey with that of the Sudan. In their occupation of that country they had brushed with the British; in their occupation of Dahomey they had very nearly come into armed conflict.

## 3 The conquest of Dahomey

Differences between the French on the one hand and Germans, Portuguese and British on the other had been settled amicably on the Guinea Coast, but on the Slave Coast, as the stretch of coast between Lagos and Accra was known, the seeds of armed conflict were sown. France had comparatively long-standing trading interests in this area as did Britain, Portugal and Brazil.[13] In 1851 Bouët-Willaumez had signed a treaty of friendship and commerce with Gezo, King of Dahomey, and in 1863 a French Protectorate had been proclaimed over the coastal kingdom of Porto Novo only to be abandoned in 1868. In that same year the French made a treaty with Gezo's successor, Glele, by which Cotonou, as far as they were concerned, was ceded to them, but it seems clear that Glele viewed it merely as an agreement by which French traders were allowed to establish themselves there, since they had to pay 'tribute' and had to recognise the authority of his representatives. Again in 1878 the French made a treaty with the Yevogan, the Dahomean minister in charge of relations with the European traders, by which they understood Cotonou to have been ceded to them. The Dahomeans on the other hand understood it as a treaty of friendship and trade. Because of this misunderstanding they did not view the installation of a French Resident there in 1879 as a threat to their sovereignty, but rather as a means of increasing their much-needed trade with the Europeans.[14] In 1883 France proclaimed a protectorate once again over Porto Novo, this time at the request of its King, Toffa, who seems to have had a variety of reasons for making such a move. Client-king of Dahomey, he had hitherto had to respect this relationship because of its value in the face of threats from his neighbouring Yoruba states, who were equally enemies of Dahomey. Now this threat was not so great that he could not afford to start asserting his independence. Nearby, the British, with whom Porto Novo had never had very happy relations, were threatening. The protectorate was also being solicited by Catholic missionaries.[15]

France next placed protectorates over Grand Popo, Agoué, Anecho (Petit Popo) and Porto Seguro, though the last two of these ports were eventually handed over to Germany in return for German recognition of French rights over stretches of the Guinea coast to which Germany had laid claim.

French activity on this part of the Coast caused considerable alarm to the British at Lagos who regarded Yorubaland, still in a state of apparently interminable civil war, as their sphere of influence, though the French, too, feared that the British had designs to link Lagos with the Gold Coast.[16] Furthermore, the French activities in the Niger Delta, where Britain had already established a consulate, and on the lower Niger where British trading firms were dominant, threatened another traditional sphere of British influence. In 1887, the French sent a mission to Abeokuta, long a stronghold of British missionaries, and attempted to negotiate the construction of a railway from Abeokuta to French Porto Novo, which if successful would have deprived Lagos of its commercial hinterland. It was also feared that the French intended making a treaty with the Alafin of Oyo, and this prompted the Lagos Governor to forestall them with a treaty of friendship with that monarch in 1888.

In 1889 a French lieutenant, Mizon, sailed up the Niger and Benue, theoretically open to ships of all nations, trying to make a treaty with Yola which would, through its river port of Jimeta, have given France a port on the navigable stretch of the Benue right down through the Niger confluence to the sea. He was unsuccessful, but was able to make a treaty three years later. Mizon's actions exacerbated hostilities between France and Britain in this area, hostilities which had been assuaged somewhat by the Anglo-French Convention which delimited French and British spheres of influence on the Slave Coast. A boundary was drawn 100 miles inland between Lagos and Porto Novo, but an area of indefinition was left between the end of that boundary and the line drawn from Say, in modern Niger, to Barruwa on Lake Chad, which was supposed to mark the southernmost limit of French expansion. This area of indefinition, comprising the important kingdom of Borgu, was a crucial one, for if the French could penetrate far enough east to a point below the Bussa rapids, then she could secure a port on the navigable stretch of the Niger. This was the setting for the famous race to Nikki between Decoeur for the French, and Lugard for the British Royal Niger Company, in 1894, subsequent to which France and Britain very nearly came to war.

In the meantime France had conquered the ancient kingdom of Dahomey which blocked her ambitions to link her coastal foothold with her Niger possessions and, indeed, her hope for a foothold on the navigable stretch of the Niger, for any access to Borgu was by way of Dahomey as far as France was concerned.

The first power to lay claim to Dahomey was Portugal by virtue of a treaty made by Juliano da Souza, Brazilian Chacha[17] (controller of Dahomey's trade with Europeans) of the Dahomean kings at Ouidah. It has been asserted that the Chacha had no right to make such a treaty, and it was thus that Glele was able to repudiate it. As Ross shows,[18] Glele was quite happy about the treaty-making activities of his Chacha, Juliano, who played a skilful diplomatic role in persuading each party that they enjoyed different advantages as a result of the treaty they had signed. The Portuguese believed that they had obtained a Protectorate: the Dahomeans a valuable ally in the increasingly complex diplomatic tangle into which they were being thrust. Furthermore, there were commercial advantages to the treaty in that arrangements were made for the export of indentured labour to São Thomé. In the event the treaty was abandoned, after an unsuccessful Portuguese mission to Glele in 1887 to confirm it. 'All that the Dahomeans had gained by their association with Portugal', Ross comments, 'was to encourage the French to think Dahomey ripe for protection.'[19] As de Beekmann, French representative in Porto Novo, wrote to the Governor of Senegal in March 1899, 'if France does not make a treaty with the king of Dahomey, the Germans will be installed there in very little time'.[20] De Beckman, on sending envoys to Glele to seek the possibilities of a protectorate, received a firm rebuff: '. . . he would never abandon his rights over Cotonou, even in exchange for a rent, that the Yevogan and Cabaceros who had signed the treaty of 1868 and 1878 were mad (avaient la tête tranchée) and that he, Glele, would not recognise treaties which he had never signed and requested me to make known his words to the French chief . . .'[21]

As a result of the Anglo-French Convention of 1889, the Yoruba kingdom of Ketu[22] came under the French sphere of influence. Despite its earlier subordinate relationship to Dahomey it had, since the 1880's, become increasingly independent—though it frequently allied with Dahomey against rival Yoruba states. By the 1880's the Dahomeans had clearly decided that Ketu was more of a potential enemy than a friend, and in 1885 they finally sacked its capital city. Captives were either exported to São Thomé as indentured labour or used as slaves on the Dahomean palm-oil plantations.[23] The Dahomeans continued to make incursions into Ketu and other lands in both the French and British spheres of influence, to obtain slaves for its modern oil plantations which, like Old Calabar, it had developed in order to have a substitute for slaves to exchange for European goods. However, some slaves were still exported to the Congo, São Thomé and Cameroons, from the Dahomean port of Ouidah.[24] Others were used for ritual sacrifice.

The Governor of the Rivières de Sud, Dr. Bayol, tried to negotiate for cessation of these expeditions with Glele, who refused to see him. Shortly after, Glele died. He was succeeded by his son, Behanzin, who chose as his heraldic sign the shark, indicating that he had no intention of abandoning his claim to his seaports.[25]

Behanzin declared himself Suzerain of Porto Novo and declared, also, that Cotonou was still his. He invaded his long-standing enemy, the Egba, to obtain slaves for sacrifice for the funeral of his father: his Yevogan took Frenchmen hostages at Ouidah and sent them to his capital as a reprisal for the arrest, the month before, of Dahomean authorities at Cotonou who had been given up to Dahomey's now bitter enemy, Toffa of Porto Novo.[26] Behanzin then attacked Cotonou on the 4th March and was only repulsed with heavy losses to the French, though the losses to Dahomey were even greater. In late April his army moved against Porto Novo, but was held off after a long battle at Atchoupa. Both sides decided to retreat. The French, with the forces then at their disposition, were in no position to deal with Behanzin: the latter needed a breathing space. So on 3rd October 1890, a treaty was drawn up whereby French protection was recognised together with France's right to occupy indefinitely Cotonou in return for an annual 'compensation' of 20,000 francs, though it was clear from this treaty that there was no cessation of Behanzin's sovereignty over Cotonou.[27]

An interesting side-light on the first clash between the French and Behanzin was the Egba embassy to Victor Ballot, the French Governor requesting an alliance in their proposed march on Abomey. Ballot was inclined to go to the proposed rendezvous at Lako to discuss the question; but Governor Bayol told him that he could not 'authorise him to undertake a journey into a country depending on the colony of Lagos'.[28]

It was only a matter of time before the French and Behanzin came to a real trial of strength. Among the French there was a party in favour of the opportunity to 'distinguish themselves in a march on Abomey'.[29] There was the fear that another power might make a treaty with Dahomey before them. Most important of all, Behanzin's acquisition of arms through German sources and his continued slave raiding, and even slave exporting, gave them the pretext they needed. We must not forget, either, that under French protection, King

Toffa of Porto Novo was continually sending insulting messages to Behanzin who wrote, on 2nd January 1892, that but for the French he would long ago have invaded Porto Novo because of Toffa's insults.[30]

By 1892, however, the French had made up their minds to occupy the kingdom. Étienne, supported by the 'groupe colonial'[31] (which had been formed in the Chamber of Deputies in 1890) obtained the necessary credits. Commandant Audéoud had, in his mission of early 1891, reconnoitred the country so that any military commander had sufficient information to plan his campaign. The pretext for a war which had already been decided on was Behanzin's incursion, in March, into territory which the French claimed depended on Porto Novo and which he claimed was his. That Behanzin was aware of what was in store was made clear in his letter to Victor Ballot about these villages which, anyway, if they did rightly depend on Porto Novo, were not guaranteed by the Treaty of 1890 since France refused to ratify this, and there is no record of the 20,000 francs having been paid to Behanzin. On 10th April he wrote: 'I have just been informed that the French government has declared war on Dahomey and that the matter was decided by the Chamber of France. I warn you that you may start war on all the positions you wish and that I myself will do the same, but I advise you that if one of our villages is touched by the fire of your cannons, I will march directly and smash Porto Novo . . .' He concluded: 'I would like to know how many independent villages of France have been destroyed by me, King of Dahomey. Be good enough to remain quiet, carry on your commerce at Porto Novo, and like that we will remain at peace with each other as before. If you wish war, I am ready. I will not end it even if it lasts a hundred years and kills 20,000 of my men . . .'[32]

But nothing could stave off French determination on war. General Dodds, with Senegalese *tirailleurs* and porters supplied by Toffa (who now saw his chance to help put down his erstwhile overlord and rival), arrived at Cotonou in May. After five hard-fought engagements, he finally defeated the Dahomey army and occupied the capital, Abomey. Dodds at first tried to negotiate a Protectorate with Behanzin whereby the latter would remain its ruler. Much more patient than his colleagues in the Western Sudan, Dodds continued to negotiate for a treaty for a year.[33] But Behanzin remained implacably hostile to the French, who then sought him out on the grounds that alive and free he would constitute a continued threat to their authority. He finally surrendered and was deported to Martinique and, later, to Algeria where he died in 1906.

His brother treated with the French and succeeded to the throne as Agoliagbo in 1894, but he ruled over a much reduced empire, for the French, following as they did in Guinea a policy of divide and rule, gave 'independence' to its component states. He suffered the fate of many others who negotiated with the French in this manner, and was exiled to Gabon in 1900 for (assuming the Protectorate gave him greater freedom than, clearly, the French intended) he showed himself, as two Dahomean authors curiously put it: 'arrogant towards the French residents and committed abuses of his powers over those he administered'.[34]

Given the comparatively small size of the empire, it proved the most difficult of all French conquests. Dodds used three thousand troops and took nearly five months to subject Dahomey whose cannon, for instance, were so efficient that the French members of the column believed they were operated by Germans—unwilling to concede such skill to Negroes.[35] No doubt resistance would have been greater had Dahomey not been going through an economic crisis, brought on both by the loss of external exchange through the suppression of the slave trade, and the domination of the coastal trade by Toffa, under French protection. This situation was exacerbated by the fact that the Dahomeans had deep military commitments in the Yoruba civil wars which occupied their attention as much as threats from Europeans on the Coast. The very difficulty of the conquest, given the complexity of Behanzin's military commitments, is a tribute to the efficiency of the military organisation of his empire.

Nearly all the French who met Behanzin recorded favourable opinions of him.[36] Under his leadership, and with his understanding of international diplomacy, Dahomey, with its agricultural plantations and superbly disciplined army, raises the question of whether it could have modernised itself without European occupation. After all, as early as 1851, Commander Frederick Forbes, who visited the kingdom in 1849–50 and had long experience of China, though critical of their 'indolence', wrote of the Dahomeans: 'In agricultural pursuits they are advanced in knowledge. . . . In short, in the small portions that are under cultivation they rival the Chinese.'[37]

Behanzin's final appeal to the world to save his kingdom from the French was made to a morality which, alas for him, the nations of Europe often vaunted but rarely practised. 'I make this appeal to the great and educated nations of the world so that they will not allow a great power like France, possessing the most destructive of modern arms, to trample underfoot and exterminate a people which has done nothing to her and whose only crime is to be ignorant and weak.

'I make this appeal to the philanthropy and Christian humanity of the great civilised nations.'[38]

### 4 The occupation of Niger

The conquest of Dahomey allowed France to look northwards to the Niger and to the possibility of gaining a port on the stretch of the Niger navigable to the sea. The key to this ambition was Borgu in whose territory lay the Bussa rapids, at the head of this navigable stretch. The British had a treaty with the king of Bussa who styled himself 'Lord of all Borgu'. But the French claimed that Nikki was in fact the overlord of Bussa,[39] so they planned to obtain a treaty with that king on the grounds that it would invalidate the British treaty with Bussa. Captain Decoeur left Marseilles for Dahomey to obtain this treaty. To avoid any possibility that a French Treaty with Nikki might invalidate his own with Bussa, Goldie decided he must get a treaty with Nikki himself. He therefore arranged for Captain Lugard, already famous as an officer of empire for his services in Uganda, to get to Nikki before Decoeur did. Lugard left Liverpool for the Royal Niger Company's headquarters at Akassa. Though the distance from there to Nikki was longer, he had the advantage of being able to cover most of the journey by river steamer, while Captain Decoeur had to take his party overland (see map).

In the event Lugard did arrive at Nikki before Decoeur and obtained a treaty signed not by the King himself, but by the Imam Abdullah and the Head Butcher who did so in the name of the late king of Nikki.[40] Decoeur arrived with his party of Senegalese *tirailleurs* five days after Lugard had left and 'persuaded' the King to sign, in person, a treaty of protection with France.[41] The French rejected the validity of Lugard's treaty and, in January 1895, Victor Ballot reached Nikki with the express intention of getting the King of Nikki to repudiate his treaty with Britain. A dangerous situation was now created on this section of the Niger, with France determined to secure a river port, the Company equally determined to prevent it, but without the armed forces to do so. The race to Nikki was repeated between France and Germany, in Fada N'Gourma, the hinterland of Dahomey and Togo. Indeed, such were the dangers of international competition for this whole area that the three powers decided to negotiate: it was as well, for British and French forces seemed likely to clash in Borgu, France having signed treaties with, and occupied, states that Britain considered properly hers. In fact they very nearly did come to blows in Borgu in the early months of 1898, with French and British forces facing each other with uneasy fingers on the trigger while their respective foreign ministers negotiated the Anglo-French Treaty of 14th June 1898. This, together with the Franco-German Treaty of the preceding July, settled the occupation of the contested areas. The latter Treaty settled the Togo–Dahomey boundary, confirming Gourma, Mossi and Gouronsi as French, but giving the important trading town of Sansanne Mango (to which the French had pretensions) to the Germans. The former Treaty gave Bussa to Britain, thus depriving France of her navigable stretch of the Niger but giving her the contested Nikki.

To complete her Sudanese conquest, France had to push beyond the boundaries of Ahmadou's empire to Timbuktu which, despite René Caillié's dismal impression of it,[42] had continued to seduce the minds of her soldiers, and then on to Lake Chad where her Equatorial, West and North African empires would be joined. Archinard's experiment in reinstating the heirs to the Bambara dynasty of Ségou were unsuccessful, and eventually it was placed under direct rule. However, the French attempted to rule indirectly in Macina by placing Aguibou, Ahmadou's treacherous brother, on the throne. He ruled this section of the empire from Bandiagara, but despite French support he was loathed by the mass of his subjects, in particular the Tokolor, who could not forgive him for abandoning resistance to the French. He abdicated in 1902 and no replacement was made for him.

The French moved from Macina up the river to Timbuktu where they met with stiff opposition from the Tuareg, overlords of the city. Here, the French hoped that the hostility between the indigenous inhabitants and their Tuareg masters would work to their advantage.[43] Their attack on the city was one of the most inept in the French conquest. Lt. Boiteux, commandant of the Niger flotilla based on Mopti, left Mopti without authorisation and without any show of hostility from Timbuktu to justify it, to occupy the city.[44] After entering it on the 16th December 1893, with an apparently joyful reception by the inhabitants, his flotilla, moored at Kabara, the port of Timbuktu, which itself lies several miles inland from the river, was attacked by Tuaregs. Though they were repulsed, they succeeded in wiping out the supporting column led by Aube. The same fate awaited Aube's avenger, Colonel Bonnier. And it was not until Joffre, later the great Marshal Joffre, entered Timbuktu on 9th February 1894 that the city finally came under French rule, though it was many years before the surrounding Tuareg tribes were subjected. Many of them, like the Ouilliminden, presented a continuous problem for French administration right up to World War I,[45] which they seized as an occasion to revolt. Garrisons were only established at the major towns of Gao and Tillabery in 1900. Timbuktu itself remained a military territory until World War I.

By 1897, with Timbuktu under French control and with Mossi and Dahomey conquered, the French could now look towards Chad. What was to become the Colony of Niger had been first reconnoitred for the French by Captain Monteil in 1891, where he made treaties with Dori and Liptougou and reached the Lake Chad area by way of the Fulani empire.[46] But France was unable to take advantage of his initiative. However, in 1897 the move towards Lake Chad began. In 1897 Say fell to the French and in 1898, Cazemajou, a young captain of considerable colonial experience,[47] was received by the Sultan of Zinder. His instructions from the Minister of Colonies were to reach Chad but he was to abstain from all 'diplomatic activity which could have as a consequence the creation of difficulties with England'. He was to avoid entering those lands 'which rightfully belong to the kingdom of Sokoto'.[48] One of his goals was to contact Rabeh, the recent conqueror of Bornu who had come down from the Sudan.[49] Before reaching Zinder, he obtained a treaty with Kebbi, the long-standing enemy of Sokoto. In Zinder, the Sultan—persuaded by his advisers of the dangers of receiving the French—agreed to his murder. Cazemajou's party, under the leadership of a Senegalese sergeant, Samba Traoré, managed to escape from Zinder and bring the news of Cazemajou's death to Say. A column was then organised under Captain Voulet, with Lt. Chanoine as second in command, to occupy Zinder and push on to Lake Chad where it was to meet up with two other expeditionary forces, one from Algeria, the other from Congo.

The Voulet-Chanoine column was bedevilled from the start by troubles. Voulet and Chanoine permitted pillaging and cruelties on a scale that exceeded anything yet witnessed on the French conquest of West Africa and which were reported in France by Lt. Péteau, who was sent back by Voulet as a result of dissension between the two. Lt.-Col. Klobb was therefore sent to take over command from Voulet, who assassinated him. This led to the mutiny of the *tirailleurs* who placed themselves under the authority of Lt. Pallier, the next most senior officer. When Voulet tried to assert his command they murdered both him and Chanoine. The scandal of Voulet's and Chanoine's leadership has been fully described by Suret-Canale[50] and is the worst instance of the method of conquest by promise of booty and plunder so often used by the French.[51]

Under its new leader, Lt. Pallier, the column occupied Tessoua and conquered Zinder, whose Sultan, Ahmadou, was killed in battle. A new Sultan, eighteen years old, was installed by the French to rule, characteristically, over a much reduced territory.[52] By this time morale among the troops was so low that Pallier decided to return, leaving behind loyal troops at Zinder to the command of Lt. Joalland, who led them on to Lake Chad. By the end of October he had reached Nguigmi, the eastward limit of French West Africa, and in February met up with the Algerian column. The Equatorial column did not reach the rendezvous until April, for they had been held up by Rabeh, with whom the French had earlier tried to make a treaty. But, though it was the French who killed him, his conquest properly belongs to the history of British occupation, for Bornu fell to their rule.

The Algerian column had brought Agades, the most important city of the Niger desert, under French protection, but it did not effectively come under French rule until it was occupied by force in 1906. Indeed, France's hold on the Military Territory of the Niger was tenuous until after the First World War, for like their cousins in the Sudan, the Tuareg of Niger were amongst the most bitter and stubborn of France's opponents.

### 5 France and Morocco in Mauretania

Despite their long-standing though far from happy relationship with the French, the Moors of Mauretania were among the last peoples of West Africa to be subjected to French rule. Occupation began only in 1902 and at first, under the skilful direction of Coppolani, was achieved by negotiation. But his murder by Moors in 1905 provoked the French into occupying the territory by force. It was not until 1958 that 'the most notable of the Reguebat Souaad, Ahmed O. Hammadi, made his submission to French troops'.[53]

Until 1900 France had been preoccupied with her eastward march to Lake Chad. Now she was able to look north to Mauretania, a country to which Morocco also laid claim. The Emirs of Trarza, who dominated the North Bank, had, since their defeat by Faidherbe, lived in peace with their Senegalese neighbours. In 1902, however, Emir Ahmed Saloum (who had been recognised as such by the

French) found that most of his subjects had given their support to his rival for the Emirate, his cousin Ould Sidi Mohammed Fall. As Mme. Desirée-Vuillemin remarks: 'It is besides a remarkable fact about the Berberised Arabs, that it suffices that one of their chiefs makes an alliance with the Christian, thus finding a force from which he can gain support, for many of his partisans to go over to the enemy, now assured that the latter will not be sufficiently strong to impose his authority on them. Still, it was at least in the apparent interest of the French government to favour one candidate in order to know to whom they could turn in cases of plundering and to assure themselves of a clientèle in this anarchic country.'[54]

The disturbed character of Trarza was but a pale reflection of that of more Northern parts. Here, however, overtures had been made to the Sultan of Morocco to bring peace to the area and the rumour was current that he was 'going to ask the faithful to cease their quarrels so that they could unite against the French',[55] who had been considerably weakened by the recent and disastrous yellow fever epidemic in St. Louis. The Governor-General at St. Louis, Roume, was in a difficult position, for the conquest of Mauretania was no mean undertaking, which the metropolitan government might well reject, particularly as there seemed little of economic value in this desert land. Yet the Moors, inspired by the apparent inaction of the French, were now raiding across the river into Senegal itself.

Roume's first move was to send a mission to Trarza, which bolstered up Ahmed Saloum's authority and secured the submission of his rival. But peace was short-lived and in December 1902, Coppolani, a Corsican who had spent most of his life in Algeria, was placed in charge of achieving a settlement in Mauretania. His knowledge of Islam helped him to play on the deeply complex tribal and sectarian hostilities of the Mauretanians to secure French protection over much of Mauretania without bloodshed. He had written a massive work on Islam in 1897,[56] and already had experience of negotiation with Muslim desert tribes in the north-western Sudan in 1898 and 1899, bringing many of them into peaceful submission.

By 26th October 1904, such had been Coppolani's success that he was created Commissioner of the new civil territory of Mauretania, comprising Trarza, Sehout el Ma, Brakna, Kroufa, Boutilimit, Nouakchott and Aleg. It was his attempt to bring about the submission of Tagant and Adrar that resulted in his assassination. The Emir of Trarza was determined that he would never come under French rule. When, therefore, Coppolani passed through Tagant

the Emir, in collaboration with the Marabout Ma el Ainine, instigated his death. The Emir then invaded Tagant and besieged the
French garrison at Tidjikja which was subsequently relieved.
At this stage Morocco entered the war, demanding that the French
quit Tagant and laying siege to Tidjika. The Moroccan force was
eventually driven off, but Morocco only ceased to be a threat to
French ambitions with the accession of Moulay Hafid to the Sherifian
throne in place of Abd el Aziz. Since Moulay Hafid owed his throne
partly to French support, he had to discontinue Morocco's intervention in this sphere of French influence.

From 1905 to 1910 the French were engaged in the occupation
of Tagant and Adrar. It was an extremely arduous task, for in those
parts the desert was very mountainous. The forces of the Emir were
well organised and used their knowledge of the country to advantage
in guerilla attacks. Between July and December 1908, the French
were subjected to 125 attacks[57] from the disciples of the Marabout
Ma el Ainine, who had declared a *jihad* against the French *and* the
Emir. Nevertheless by 1910 most of modern Mauretania had been
brought under French rule. But for many years the French had to
conduct regular expeditions against those who remained irrevocably
hostile to their rule. Thus, as late as 1927 Port Étienne was raided and
the majority of the Reguebat were not subjugated until 1933.

Economically Mauretania was of little interest to the French.
Politically it secured France's northern frontier in Senegal, and after
her occupation of Morocco provided another territorial link between
her North and West African empires. Morocco still claims Mauretania is hers. Under French rule Mauretania did not even have its
own capital. Until its independence it was governed from St.
Louis, the capital of Senegal.

## 6 The 'pacification' of the Ivory Coast

The only other area which had not been brought under some form
of French rule by 1900 was the interior of the Ivory Coast. Gabriel
Angoulvant, who became Governor in 1908, wrote in his book *La
Pacification de la Côte d'Ivoire* that in 1893 'The Ivory Coast belonged
to us, but only in the eyes of foreign powers'.[58] The situation had
not much changed when he assumed the Governorship. The frontiers
had been delimited with Liberia and the British colony of the Gold
Coast, but France's control over many of the peoples of the interior
was either tenuous or non-existent. Commercially the Colony gave
no indication of its future wealth. In 1905 only twenty-nine tons of

coffee were exported and cocoa, which had proved so successful in the neighbouring Gold Coast, had only taken on to the extent of six tons in 1920.[59] Angoulvant came to the Ivory Coast determined to make it commercially viable, and therefore determined to bring those peoples who had accepted French protection under the realities of French rule: that being the payment of taxation which would stimulate them to produce for export. His predecessors had followed the policy of 'la conquête pacifique', which Angoulvant considered immoral since it placed the burden of paying the taxes for the upkeep of administration of the whole colony exclusively on those tribes who had submitted to French rule.[60] He argued that only a full-scale military conquest could reduce the Ivory Coast to a state where 'it could be firmly administered and developed'.[61] Angoulvant managed to persuade Governor-General William Ponty that such a policy was the only one that could be adopted, and Ponty gave it his sanction in his opening speech to the Conseil du Gouvernement on 21st June 1909.[62]

Angoulvant was the arch-paternalist, as his instructions to his Commandants de Cercle, quoted by himself, show: 'It is necessary to establish a permanent contact between us and the native and to make him appreciate by example and with advice that we are inspired by the principles of humanity from which he has been chosen to be the first to derive both moral and material benefit. The fact that his character is indifferent to our good works must not discourage us; whether he likes it or not, the influence of our efforts and of our action is being exerted. . . . If we should seem not to be taking into account from the very first the desires of the native, it is important that we follow without weakness the only way susceptible of bringing us to our goal. One must make no mistake about it: the desires of these natives are essentially unproductive, and opposed to all progress.'[63]

The principles of humanity by which Angoulvant, if not the French, was guided were, to say the least, unique. 'That some natives should be killed in the struggle is inevitable, and even desirable, otherwise the victory would be of no consequence in the future because the battle will have been fought without peril . . . to destroy a village is of no significance, so quickly are these agglomerations rebuilt . . . but the destruction of materials, when they are inevitable, should only be visited on annual crops, and never at all on trees of slow growth. . . .'[64]

Angoulvant's pacification was barely completed by the opening of hostilities in Europe in 1914 when, as we shall see, the peoples who had resisted French occupation so stubbornly were to understand the full nature of the principles of 'humanity'. The troops used to conquer them were withdrawn for the European Front and the new subjects of France were also required to provide soldiers for that far off war and, to obtain them, on Angoulvant's own evidence, the French had to undertake 'une chasse à l'homme'.[65]

Chiefs who had led their people against the French were deported, 'the natives were disarmed; others were interned; war fines were imposed on various tribes amounting to more than 700,000 francs between 1910 and 1912. In order to keep the natives under control the government regrouped the native villages.'[66]

The territory was finally 'pacified' by 1917, and it is an interesting commentary on the brevity of colonial rule in West Africa that Houphouët Boigny, President of Ivory Coast, was already four years old before his own people, the Baoulé, were finally 'pacified' by the French.[67]

The military conquest of French West Africa was achieved at great expenditure of human life, the destruction of many towns and villages, the break-up of traditional systems of government, and the movement of populations, but most of all it was achieved against stubborn resistance of the Africans themselves, both those of the Savannah and the Forest. By 1900, when most of French West Africa had been brought under administrative control, there were 8,400 troops of occupation supported by a budget of 12,677,000 francs.[68] Of these, the great majority were African, and we must not forget that the European conquest of West Africa, whether by French or British, was largely effected through African troops and porters. As far as the French were concerned the major work of destruction had been completed by 1900, and it was time to start the work of reconstruction. In some areas, especially in the Senegal and Sudan, the basis of the administrative framework of the colonial era was already being laid. But not until the end of the First World War had France finally settled on a system of colonial administration that compromised between metropolitan theory and local reality.

# Notes

1 Fyfe, *Sierra Leone*, p. 392.
2 Hargreaves, *Prelude*, pp. 267–71.
3 See Jean Suret-Canale, 'La Guinée dans le système colonial', *Présence Africaine*, no. 29, pp. 13–15.
4 *Rapport de l'ensemble sur la situation générale de la Guinée française en 1898*, p. 81, cited by Jean Suret-Canale, 'La fin de la chefferie en Guinée', *J.A.H.*, VII, 3, 1966, p. 467.
5 Elliot P. Skinner, *The Mossi of the Upper Volta: the Political Development of a Sudanese People*, Stanford, U.S.A., 1964, p. 142.
6 Louis Binger, *Du Niger au Golfe de Guinée par les pays Kong et le Mossi, 1887–1889*, Paris, 1892, I, p. 467, cited and trans. in Skinner *Mossi*, p. 143.
7 F. J. Amon d'Aby, *La Côte d'Ivoire dans la Cité Africaine*, Paris, 1951, pp. 26–9.
8 Cited and translated by Skinner, *Mossi*, p. 145, from Dr. Crozer, 'Rapport sur une Mission au Mossi (1890)', *Journal Officiel de la République Française* (5–9 Oct. 1891).
9 Major Toutée, *Dahomé–Niger–Touareg*, Paris, p. vi.
10 *Histoire Militaire de l'AOF*, Paris, 1931, p. 457.
11 Skinner, *Mossi*, p. 151.
12 *Ibid.*, p. 152.
13 See C. W. Newbury, *The Western Slave Coast and its Rulers*, Oxford, 1961.
14 I am very grateful to Mr. David Ross, who is writing a thesis on the subject of Dahomey's relations with the French and other European powers in the nineteenth century, for advice on, and valuable criticisms of, this section.
15 Robert Cornevin, *Histoire du Dahomey*, Paris, 1962, p. 294.
16 Report of Colonel Dorat of 26th July 1884, cited in Cornevin, *ibid.*, p. 295.
17 Chacha was a specially created office given to Francesco Felix de Souza, a Brazilian slave trader, in return for his aid to Ghézo in the 1818 revolution which placed the latter on the throne. It gave de Souza, and his successors, of which Juliano was the fifth, trading privileges, 'and placed him in charge, subject only to the King, of Dahomeyan trading relations with all Europeans'. David A. Ross, 'The career of Domingo Martinez in the Bight of Benin, 1833–64', *J.A.H.*, VI, 1, 1965, p. 79.
18 Ross, thesis, *op. cit.*
19 *Ibid.*
20 De Beckmann, French Representative, to Governor of Senegal, 6th March 1889, in Robert Cornevin, 'Les Divers episodes de la lutte contre le royaume d'Abomey, 1887–1894', *Revue Française d'Histoire d'Outre-Mer*, XLVII, 1960, 2nd Quarter, p. 165.

21 *Ibid.*
22 For the history of Ketu see Geoffrey Parrinder, *The Story of Ketu*, Ibadan, 1959.
23 Ross, thesis, *op. cit.*
24 Newbury, *The Western Slave Coast*, p. 130, footnote 4.
25 Cornevin, 'Les divers épisodes', p. 171-2.
26 Suret-Canale, *Afrique Noire I*, p. 249.
27 The text of this treaty is reproduced in Cornevin, *Histoire du Dahomey*, pp. 332-3.
28 Cornevin, 'Les divers épisodes', p. 173.
29 Newbury, *The Western Slave Coast*, p. 173.
30 *Ibid.*, p. 132.
31 For an account of the 'groupe colonial', see Henri Brunschwig, 'Le Parti Coloniale Français', *Revue Française d'Histoire d'Outre-Mer*, XLVI, 1959, First Quarter, pp. 49-83.
32 Letter of Behanzin to Victor Ballot of 10th April 1892, cited in Cornevin, *Histoire du Dahomey*, p. 340.
33 C. W. Newbury, 'A Note on the Abomey Protectorate', *Africa*, XXIX, 2, April, 1959, p. 148.
34 A. Akindélé et C. Aguessy, *Le Dahomey*, Paris, 1955, p. 30.
35 Suret-Canale, *Afrique Noire I*, p. 252.
36 For instance one of the hostages taken to Abomey recorded his admiration for Behanzin. Dodds was quick to recognise the skill of his Dahomeyan opposing number, the head of the Dahomeyan army, after he had acknowledged defeat and abandoned Behanzin. All were horrified by the role of human sacrifice in the Dahomeyan religion, but few were of the opinion of Edward Fon, *Le Dahomey*, Paris, 1895, p. 53: 'Il faut se rappeler que nous avons affaire içi à des peuples sauvages qui ne connaissent pas encore aujourd'hui aucune de ces conventions nombreuses, dont l'ensemble porte de nous de civilisation'.
37 Frederick E. Forbes, *Dahomey and the Dahomeans: Being the Journals of Two Missions to the King of Dahomey, and Residence at his Capital in the Years 1849 and 1850*, London, 1851, Vol. I, p. 30.
38 Cited in Cornevin, *Histoire du Togo*, p. 350, from the *Bulletin du Comité de l'Afrique Française*, April 1893, p. 6.
39 See J. Lombard, 'Un système politique traditionnel de type féodal: les Bariba du Nord-Dahomey. Aperçu sur l'organisation sociale et le pouvoir central', *Bulletin de l'IFAN*, T.XIX, ser. B. nos. 3-4, 1957, pp. 464-506.
40 For a full account of the race to Nikki, called, elegantly, the Nikki steeplechase by French newspapers, see *The Diaries of Lord Lugard*, Vol. IV, *op. cit.*, and Margery Perham's biography of Lugard, *Lugard: The Years of Adventure, 1855-1898*, London, 1956.

I

41 J. E. Flint, *Sir George Goldie and the Making of Nigeria*, London, 1960, pp. 225–6.

42 Rene Caillié, *Travels Through Central Africa to Timbuctoo and Across the Great Desert to Morocco, Performed in the years 1824–1828*, London, 1830, Vol. II, p. 49.

43 Le Capitaine Granderye, 'Notes et Souvenirs sur l'Occupation de Timbuctou', *Revue d'Histoire des Colonies*. Introduction by editor.

44 *Ibid.*, Granderye's text, p. 113.

45 Delafosse in Hanotaux, *Histoire des Colonies Françaises*, IV, pp. 330–2.

46 Lt.-Col. Monteil, *De Saint-Louis à Tripoli par le lac Tchad*, Paris, 1896.

47 Le Commandant Chailley, 'La Mission du Haut Soudan et le drame de Zinder', *Bulletin de l'Institut Français d'Afrique Noire*, Serie B, Sciences Humaines, T.XVI, 3 and 4, 1954, Juillet–Octobre, 1954, pp. 244–8.

48 *Ibid.*, p. 250.

49 *Ibid.*, p. 250.

50 Suret-Canale, *Afrique Noire I*, pp. 261–9: Voulet's and Chanoine's crimes included, apart from murdering their superior: sacking the town of Sansanne Haoussa, already under French control: taking inhabitants of captured villages as 'captifs'; killing twenty-five women and numbers of children, as an example to the population who had wounded some of their *tirailleurs*; requesting soldiers to bring the hands cut off corpses as proof of the fact they had killed the enemy; sacking of Birnin N'Koni, a town of 10,000 inhabitants many of whom, women and children, were massacred, etc.

51 See *ibid.*, 'Les méthodes de guerre', pp. 237–47: excesses of the French campaign enumerated by Suret-Canale from French sources to offset the 'bloody' picture drawn of the opponents of the French conquest such as Samory include: (1) Payment of African soldiers with 'captifs'. To obtain these, villages had to be destroyed and in the process many were killed. 'It appears that every week the auxiliaries demand prisoners before moving on.' Letter from Lt. Meynier, dated 8 August, 1899, Timbuctou, cited by P. Vigné d'Octon, *La Gloire du Sabre*, Paris, 1900 (JS-C, p. 239). (2) Unnecessary pillage: thus a French officer described the conquest of Sikasso, cited in Vigné d'Octon, *op. cit.* (JS-C, p. 240), 'The order is given to pillage. Everything taken is killed. All the prisoners—about 4,000 of them—are herded together. Each European is given a woman of his own choice. . . . Children and those that get tired (en route) are killed by blows dealt with a rifle butt or are run through with a bayonet. . . .' (3) Increase in the number of slaves as a result of the system of payment: Jean Rhodes, 'C'est par centaines, par milliers, que nos colonnes incessantes augmentent aussi les nombres des esclaves' (JS-C, p. 245). (4) Use of forced labour for porterage by men who never saw their villages again (JS-C, p. 246).

52 Edmond Séré de Rivières, *Histoire du Niger*, Paris, 1965, p. 222.

53 Desirée-Veiullemin, *Mauritanie*, p. 89.
54 *Ibid.*, p. 103.
55 *Ibid.*, p. 104.
56 O. Depont et X. Coppolani, *Les Confréries Religieuses Musulmanes*, Algiers, 1897.
57 Geographical Handbook Series: *French West Africa*, Vol. II, 'The Colonies', London, Naval Intelligence Division, 1943, p. 331.
58 G. Angoulvant, *La Pacification de la Côte d'Ivoire 1908–1915: Méthodes et Résultats*, Paris, 1916.
59 Amon d'Aby, *La Côte d'Ivoire*, p. 76.
60 Angoulvant, *La Pacification de la Côte d'Ivoire*, p. 26.
61 *Ibid.*, p. 27.
62 *Ibid.*, p. 47.
63 Instructions of 26 November, 1908, in *ibid.*, pp. 61–3.
64 *Ibid.*, p. 194.
65 National Archives of Senegal, Série D. 4, D. 45. Recruitement Indigène. Exécution: comptes rendus des colonies: 1915–1916. Folio 85. Angoulvant to Governor-General, Bingerville, 18th December, 1915: 'Recruitement de 50,000 hommes en A.O.F.', p. 30.
66 R. L. Buell, *The Native Problem in Africa*, New York, 1928, I, p. 918.
67 Aristide Zollberg, *One Party Government in the Ivory Coast*, Princeton, New Jersey, 1964, p. 18.
68 Général Maurice Abadie, *La Défense des Colonies*, Paris, 1937, p. 212.

# 3  The British occupation of Nigeria

## 1 Britain and Company administration

In 1885, the year of the Berlin General Act, Britain still was only in effective occupation of the small island colony of Lagos and a narrow strip of the adjacent mainland. Goldie's National African Company and the British Consul for the Oil Rivers had made a series of treaties that gave Britain claims either directly or through the agency of the Company to all the lands bordering the Niger up to its confluence with the Benue. In certain instances both Company and Consul had tried to negotiate treaties with the same chief.[1] Britain could claim informal sway over Yorubaland because of her long-standing evangelical and commercial relations with it. In the Cameroons Britain had been forestalled by Germany, so that the eastward limit of her territorial claims on the Nigerian coast was Calabar where the Church of Scotland mission had been active since 1846.

The hinterland of the Niger–Benue confluence, most of which was covered by the great Sokoto Caliphate, had been secured on paper by treaties made with the Sultan of Sokoto, its spiritual overlord, and the Emir of Gwandu, overlord of its Western sector. French ambitions on the lower Niger had been successfully thwarted by Goldie, whose ruthless price war with the two French companies established there had driven them out of business before the Berlin Conference. The French had now limited their aims to securing a port on the stretch of the Niger that was navigable to the sea.

From 1885 to 1890, apart from the establishment of the administration of the National African Company by the terms of the Charter granted it in 1886 by the British Government under its new name, the Royal Niger Company, Britain administered a 'paper protectorate' over the lands to which it laid claim. Her attitude was summed up aptly by the newly appointed Vice-Consul of the Oil Rivers Protectorate: '... our policy may for the present chiefly assume a negative character. So long as we keep other European nations out, we need not be in a hurry to go in.'[2] Indeed apart from the area administered by the Company, and this too constituted very much a 'paper' régime, British authority over the Oil Rivers Protectorate, which theoretically stretched from east of Lagos to Calabar, differed very little from the hegemony she had exercised with the aid of gunboats and consuls in the sixties and seventies. The treaties with the chiefs of the Oil Rivers acknowledged their internal sovereignty. Even the title of the administrator of the Protectorate was Consul rather than Governor, a fact that caused its holder, Hewett, considerable annoyance.[3]

The Royal Niger Company territories were bound to the south by the Oil Rivers Protectorate (see map on page 46) though a thin strip of land linked its administrative headquarters at Asaba with its sea-port at Akassa. For Britain the advantage of the Charter granted to Goldie was that it avoided expenditure of government money on administering territory which she wished to prevent coming under the control of any other European power. For Goldie it permitted him to exercise *de facto* monopoly of trade on the Niger, since though monopoly as such was forbidden by the Charter, with administrative control of the territory it was easy to secure commercial control.

The Company set up a rudimentary administration over its territories and a string of trading posts on the Niger. It set up a High Court at Asaba backed up by a constabulary consisting of three European officers and 150 African men.[4] Otherwise the existing trading organisation was used as an administrative system. The Company was primarily concerned with maintaining its monopoly of trade against its rivals, and of securing profits for its shareholders, so it was hardly to be expected that it would establish an elaborate administration or indeed spend much on extending effective control over territories to which it laid claim unless trade dictated it, or threat of foreign pre-emption necessitated it. Only foreign threat moved it to translate paper control into effective control.

The Company's monopoly over the Niger trade, and the dues it collected from other traders on the river to defray the cost of its administration, were resented by the Liverpool as well as the African traders of the Oil Rivers Protectorate. The Liverpool traders had for the most part to content themselves with lobbying against the Company in Britain; though the trade war below Onitsha from 1888–92 was resolved by Goldie's offer of a directorship on the Royal Niger Company to the African Association Ltd. There was no open attack on the Company by the African traders until the Brass raid on Akassa in 1896. More serious was the threat of foreign criticism. Thus in 1887 a German trader, Jacob Hoenigsberg, who had hitherto had friendly relations with the Company, tried to test the Company's control over the Emir of Nupe by informing him that the Company not only levied duties on traders with his kingdom, but also claimed a protectorate over it. The Emir rejected both the Company's pretension to his country and its right to raise duties. In the end Goldie had to fall back on his treaty with Gwandu, Nupe's overlord, to claim theoretical control of the emirate, which he was in no position to subject to his authority. Thus he was able to continue to raise duties on Europeans who used the river to trade with Nupe while Hoenigsberg was deported. But the whole affair embarrassed the British Government considerably, for the German foreign office protested vigorously against the treatment of Hoenigsberg: with no result, however, other than to indicate to Britain that by delegating its authority to a Chartered Company it could not escape international responsibility for its actions—as later became only too clear when the French tried to obtain a foothold in the Company's claimed territories. The German rightly felt that 'a clerk and a warehouse did not constitute a true administration' and could certainly not be construed as effective occupation.[5] In 1889 a French lieutenant, Mizon, was attacked by local tribesmen as he sailed up the Niger to make a treaty with the Emir of Yola, on the Benue. The French accused the Company of instigating the attack. Mizon did not in fact secure the treaty but returned two years later, with Foreign Office approval, and much to the chagrin of Goldie obtained a treaty with the Emir of Muri, also on the Benue. However, fortunately for Goldie, this treaty was not followed up with any attempt at occupation. But it was on this basis that Goldie maintained his control over the Company's territories until 1899, when Britain, having been brought near to war with France over her hostilities with the Company, decided to assume direct responsibility for any further situations of this nature that might arise. She had also been subject to heavy pressure by critics of the Company's monopolistic practices.

## 2 The Niger Delta

The first major clash between Britain and an African state under her protection occurred in the Oil Rivers Protectorate. The diplomatic background to the incident is very complex and has been treated in detail by several authors,[6] but need not concern us too much here. The interest of Jaja's struggle with Britain is for the present purpose two-fold: first, Jaja, ruler of a small but rich state, was clearly in the process of modernising it independently of European rule; secondly his deposal by Consul Johnston shows that though the Government at home was willing to maintain a 'paper protectorate', the man on the spot was, apart from his own personal inclinations, subject to pressures to formalise control. In 1884 Jaja had negotiated a treaty with Consul Hewett similar to that made with many other chiefs of the Niger Delta, but deliberately excluded from it the clauses permitting freedom of trade and freedom of religion contained in the prototype treaty. Jaja had founded his kingdom in 1869, when he led fourteen of the eighteen constituent houses of the ancient kingdom of Bonny to a new site where he could control its traditional sources of supply of palm-oil.[7] Jaja was by origin an Ibo slave, who had become acculturated into Bonny society so successfully that with his great intelligence and driving ambition he was able to found what many contemporary visitors agreed was one of the best administered states on the West Coast. He had outstanding commercial acumen and a keen understanding of the value of Western technological achievements for the development of his state. Thus he sent one of his sons to a Glasgow school, set up a secular school in his capital, lived in a European-style house, as did his chiefs, and boasted of the fact to Lord Granville 'to show you that the West Coast of Africa is not quite so uncivilised as generally inferred at home'.[8] He had a well-trained army with modern equipment. But as Ayandele has shown, his modernising tendencies were selective:[9] he would on no account allow Christian missionaries into his state, fully aware that their preaching would herald the destruction of his authority. He rightly appreciated that the missionary was intent on undermining the very fabric of traditional African society, on which his authority depended. In this he was at one with the traders who regarded missionaries as disturbers of the *status quo*.[10] Thus Bonny was divided between traditionalist chiefs and the devoutly Christian king George Pepple I, whose attempts to introduce radical modern techniques[11] and policies led to constant instability and civil war. In the last resort he was propped up on the throne by the British

Consul and the pro-missionary faction, becoming merely a member of the new system of government designed by Johnston for Bonny and over which Johnston himself presided. When he died in 1888 no one, as Anene has put it, 'bothered to recognise his heir, Prince William Pepple, because the office of king had ceased to have any significance in Johnston's new order'.[12]

Jaja's misfortune was to make opponents of consul, trader and missionary. Neither Hewett nor Johnston liked him. The missionaries, as Ayandele has shown, were his implacable opponents because of his exclusionist policies, and though elsewhere they may have resented any attempt at control of states in which they were permitted to be active by local rulers, where they could not gain access by consent they were prepared to lobby government for assistance in gaining it, if necessary by force. Many of the traders who had previously supported Jaja turned against him because of his tight monopoly of trade along his rivers and in particular his refusal to allow them any access of his hinterland markets. Legally Jaja was perfectly entitled to levy duties on British traders in his state under the terms of his treaty, which excluded the freedom of trade clause. He had in fact sought clarification in writing that his treaty of protection meant only that Britain wanted to protect him from foreign aggression and would not interfere with his internal government. But traders who saw potential profits eluding them were only too prepared to put pressure on the Consul to break this treaty. So after a series of incidents between Jaja and the traders, including a complete stoppage of trade on the river until one British firm agreed to trade on Jaja's terms, Consul Johnston, without authority from his home government, and certainly without legality, found the occasion he wanted to settle the issue. He forbad Jaja, who was shipping oil direct to England, to continue levying duties on English traders on the grounds that his direct shipment of oil, without duties, was unfair competition. As a result Jaja sent an embassy to London to protest to the Secretary of State. Johnston then threatened Jaja with gunboats if he did not agree to trade on his terms. Jaja acceded under this threat, but further stoppages of the trade brought Johnston to Opobo on H.M.S. *Goshawk* to bring Jaja to heel. He had in the meantime sought permission from London to deport Jaja, though this was never given.[13] Johnston invited Jaja to meet him on board ship, but the latter refused, fearing for his safety, but finally went under a safe-conduct guarantee given in these terms: 'I hereby assure you that whether you accept or reject my proposals tomorrow no restraint whatever will be put on you . . . you will be free to go as soon as you have heard the message of the Government.'[14] Once on board Jaja was given the alternative of submission for trial or leaving the ship, in which case he would be considered to be at war. Left no real choice, he was despatched to Accra for trial for blocking the highway of trade. Apart from being one of the shabbiest incidents in the history of Britain's relations with West Africa—Salisbury said of his 'deportation': 'In other places it would be called kidnapping'[15]—Johnston's action pointed to the fiction that Britain's protectorate over these states was one under which their internal sovereignty was guaranteed. Indeed Johnston, who had little respect for the traditional forms of government of the Delta states, pursued a policy of replacing them by 'Governing Councils' of his own design, in which the British Consul rather than the King was executive head. These, though they did not work very successfully, were instituted in Old Calabar, New Calabar and Brass, Opobo and Bonny. None of these states, including Opobo, which had lost its king, was in a position to resist the forward policy of the Acting Consul, which had not been approved by the Foreign Office. Indeed the Foreign Office was so disquieted by the whole trend of events in both the Oil Rivers and the Niger Company territories that they sent out a Special Commissioner, Major Claude Macdonald, in 1889 to make a report on the situation there. In the event his reports were not published, though we can see today that his approach to British rule was that the wishes and needs of the African should be of chief consideration.[16]

In 1891 the extent to which Britain had been involved in the administration of the Protectorate by her representative on the spot was recognised in the up-grading of his title from Consul to Commissioner and Consul-General. Macdonald was appointed first Commissioner of the Protectorate, which was re-named the Niger Coast Protectorate in 1893. True to the character of his earlier report, he pursued a policy of peaceful penetration, and only in 1894, when his deputy Ralph Moor was in command, did Britain resume an aggressive policy towards one of the chiefs under her 'protection'. Nana, Governor of the Benin River, an Itsekiri trader with strong Urhobo connexions, controlled the trade of the Benin River and its tributary the Ethiope River with a similar degree of firmness to that with which Jaja had controlled his river-based state.[17] Once again he came up against the resentment of British merchants anxious to break his efficient monopoly of trade to their own profit.[18] Nana, like Jaja, was a modernising chief, with immense commercial ability. He had won the praise of Johnston,[19] and the loyalty of those under his command, including his trading 'boys', as his triumphant return from exile years later demonstrated, though one of the pretexts for his overthrow was his use of these 'boys' as slaves. The main pretext for his overthrow, however, was his 'stoppages of trade' on the river, though as Ikime has shown this was as much rumour spread by rival chiefs who had been put out of business by Nana's greater commercial skills.[20] British traders, and the administration as represented by Moor, resented the fact that he was acknowledged by the people of Benin River and Warri as the only real authority in the area and, as Moor declared, it 'had become necessary to convince them to the contrary'.[21] This Moor effectively achieved, after provoking a situation in which hostilities became inevitable, by the use of an armed force. This had great difficulty in taking Nana's capital at Ebrohimi, where he had ingeniously dug a canal, unfortunately uncompleted, through which he intended to evacuate his people to another site. Nana himself escaped but gave himself up to the British Governor at Lagos, who handed him over to the Commissioner of the Niger Coast Protectorate, by whom he was tried and deported to Gold Coast. The arms found at Ebrohimi by the British raiding force included 106 cannon, 445 blunderbusses, 640 dane-guns, 10 revolvers, 1,640 kegs of gunpowder, and 2,500 rounds of machine gun ammunition.[22]

Once again it had become clear that British trade and administration were not prepared to tolerate the original concept of protectorate. Nana is significant in Nigerian history, not only as a hero of the resistance to Colonial Rule, but as a leader who was clearly in the process of modernising his state under his own authority. As George Neville, who knew him both on the Benin River and in the Gold Coast in exile, wrote in 1915: 'A great organiser, there was no one to take his place; and although loyally accepting and acting on the conditions of his release it is with pain and sorrow that he now views the country (which he so wisely governed) in the occupation of those who do little or nothing to develop it.'[23]

One of the interesting facets of the Nana episode is the patience with which Moor had to construct a sufficiently convincing case against Nana to persuade the Foreign Office to allow him to send the military against him. This contrasts dramatically with the French situation, where the Metropolis constantly had to accept military *faits accomplis* in their penetration of the Western Sudan, when, if asked for permission, it would certainly in many cases have refused.

The most spectacular expedition undertaken by the Niger Coast Protectorate was against the great empire of Benin, which, in contrast to Nana's trading empire, had withdrawn into isolation from the outside world.[24] Efforts at bringing it effectively into the sphere of British influence had failed, despite the treaty of protection signed in 1892, which theoretically opened trade between Benin and British traders. Britain was given the occasion to subject Benin to control in 1897 when, in a renewed attempt to bring Benin under British trading influence and to abolish the human sacrifices known to be practised on a large scale in that empire, Acting Consul-General Phillips set off to negotiate with the Oba. Phillips, only newly arrived on the Coast, was from the start an advocate of the occupation of Benin and the overthrow of its Oba, but did not receive sanction from London for his plans for a military expedition, largely because of lack of available troops.[25]

At the time the Oba was celebrating the great Ague festival, the occasion of rededication of the Bini to their king when no stranger should be seen by him.[26] Though Phillips had gone to the trouble to inform the Oba, Ovenramwen, of his impending visit, he did not wait before setting out to receive a reply as to its convenience. He and his party were massacred en route, when he was met by the Ologbosere, who brought him a message that he should not come to Benin at that time. The murder of Phillips, five other Englishmen and some Africans with the party brought down on Benin the full wrath of the British. A 'punitive' expedition of 1,500 was sent that same year, the town fired, the great treasures* looted. Benin put up feeble resistance: the Oba seems to have lost all initiative in the face of the invader, no doubt knowing full well of the fate of his neighbour Nana. The human sacrifices that were witnessed, and probably exaggerated by the invaders,[27] were a desperate appeal to the gods to stave off what man could not.

### 3 Britain and Yorubaland

With the conquest of Benin Britain was master of the whole coastline of her Protectorate. The peoples of the hinterland—the Ibo, Ibibio and Cross River tribes—were not finally 'pacified' until the end of the First World War. Meanwhile Britain had been active

---

*The Benin bronzes were not, however, recognised as great treasures at the time. The British Museum considered them of no value because they exhibited no trace of any European artistic influence.

in extending her influence over the Yoruba hinterland of her Lagos Colony in the face of French threats to her largely missionary- and trade-based hegemony there.

Since the 1840's missionaries of the British Church Missionary Society, the British Methodist Mission and the Southern American Baptist Mission had been active among the Yoruba.[28] The only major towns where the missionaries were unable to establish themselves were Ilorin, which had become the southern outpost of the Sokoto Caliphate and Ijebu. Though Ijebu had become a powerful middleman in the legitimate trade between the coast and the hinterland, it remained implacably hostile to the penetration of missionary influence, rightly seeing it as destructive of the traditional organisation of Ijebu society. Missionaries were not all European, but included a large number of Sierra Leoneans, known as *Saro*, who, after their Christian education in Freetown, were desirous of returning to the homeland, from which they had been taken as potential slaves, to spread the gospel.[29] At this time Yorubaland was involved in civil war, which signalled the rapid decline of the authority of the Oyo empire over its component states and the consequent emergence of new power centres, in particular Abeokuta, Ibadan, and Ijebu. This divided state of Yoruba politics meant that in most cases missionaries were able to latch on to one faction in each Yoruba state for the support of their enterprise. They came to be valued for the introduction to Western technology they provided and the stimulation of commerce they pursued, hoping that by increasing trade in the natural products of the country they could rid it of the curse of the commerce in its human beings and bring about a 'sunrise in the tropics'. But whilst Yoruba rulers accepted the missionaries, and were prepared to use them even in their defence against neighbours as the Egba did in the 1851 war against Dahomey, they were in no sense willing to alienate their sovereignty. After the British occupation of Lagos, which had been partly due to missionary pressure, the states of the interior became increasingly suspicious of the missionary role. As the first Governor of the new Colony, Brand, remarked in 1862 in a despatch: 'This Government is, in fact, an object of suspicion and mistrust to all the surrounding country . . . the general fear is that the territory of Lagos will gradually extend itself until it swallows up all the neighbouring states.'[30] The forward policies of his successor, Glover, confirmed such fears, and the expulsion of the missionaries from Abeokuta in 1867 was in large measure a reaction to the fear that missionaries were in the vanguard of British occupation, which Glover's aggressive policies, including the defeat of the Egba at Ikorodu in 1865, must have seemed to have portended.

The missionaries themselves, whether European or African, in fact aimed at modernising the states in which they worked independent of British control, though they, like the Yoruba states themselves, were prepared to use British assistance from Lagos when the occasion warranted it. Indeed the missionaries identified to such an extent with the states in which they worked that the C.M.S. in Ibadan and the C.M.S. in Abeokuta produced propaganda in favour of their respective participants in the Ijaye war.[31]

By the time of the Berlin conference, despite occasional setbacks, the missionaries had established a firm position in Yorubaland, and more important still, produced as a result of their 'native agency' policy a substantial educated élite with modernising tendencies. Though their views on the matter differed substantially, they, no less than the rulers, were anxious to preserve African control over their own affairs. Indeed missionaries were often the first to attack any encroachment on the hinterland by the Lagos Colony government, particularly at the time of Glover's aggressive policy towards Abeokuta. The missionaries, at least up until the seventies, fondly hoped that they could become both the agents of peace in strife-torn Yorubaland and the progenitors of several modernised, independent, and self-sufficient Christian nation-states. However, by the eighties it became increasingly clear that nothing short of outside intervention could bring an end to these terrible wars in which not only Yoruba, but also the powerful Fulani from the North and Dahomey from the West, were involved. For British missionaries and the educated Africans, steeped in Victorian Christianity, only Britain could fit this role. They feared the French who were at hand on the Dahomey coast, and who, as we have seen, did in fact offer themselves as 'protectors'.

The ease with which Britain was able to establish her protectorate over Yorubaland, even though she did it reluctantly and late in the day because of the costs that might be involved, and largely because of the impending French threat to pre-empt her, is explained both by the groundwork in favour of Britain, laid by the missionaries both European and African, and by the fragmented state of the country. As far as Britain was concerned a Protectorate had become increasingly desirable because the frequent stoppages of trade, which had so frustrated Glover, had a deleterious effect on the revenues of the Colony of Lagos. It is significant however that in trying to bring peace to the area the Lagos Government used not

British mediators in 1886, but two Christian Yoruba, Rev. Samuel Johnson, author of the monumental *History of the Yorubas*, and the Rev. G. Phillips. That they were able to arrange a cease fire between the warring parties of the day was striking enough; that it failed on account of the intransigence of Muslim Ilorin was a portent of the difficulties Britain would have in establishing her hegemony over the Sokoto Caliphate. When peace-making missions which had gained the support of most interior rulers had failed, and after the French had tried to make treaties with those whom it was felt should come under British protection if any, Governor Carter, who assumed office in 1890, decided to bring peace to the interior once and for all. This he did on his remarkable trek of 1893, on which he succeeded, with opposition only from Ibadan, in bringing the whole of Yorubaland under British protection. Ibadan, the most powerful state of the interior, which had led the resistance against the Fulani, objected to the stationing of a Resident in its capital, but agreed to protection in August on securing assurances from the Governor that there would be no interference in its government, assurances which were to be important for future disputes with the administration.

That Carter's trek was such a success depended to no small extent on the speed with which Carter had subjected Ijebu to his will in the punitive expedition he sent against it in May 1892. Ijebu made a particularly good target for a demonstration of British power as far as Carter, who was in favour of a forward policy in Yorubaland, was concerned.[32] At the time both Egba and Ijebu were blocking the roads to Lagos. But Egba was already under British missionary influence, and had been delimited by the Anglo-French agreement of 1890 as falling within the British sphere of influence. Its internal divisions were such that it seemed likely that it could not long resist the inevitable. Ijebu was a more delectable target, particularly as far as the missionaries were concerned, for the Ijebu had stoutly resisted their attempts at penetration, a fact which occasioned the missionaries, as Ayandele has shown, to pressure Carter to gain them access by force since peaceful penetration had been unsuccessful. Carter, apart from being persuaded of a forward policy, lent a sympathetic ear to the missionaries, for he believed in the value of missionary enterprise in Africa. Ijebu, though it chose to retain its traditional religion intact, even going so far as to refuse the resettlement of Christian Ijebu re-captives from Sierra Leone on its land, had taken advantage of the opening up of legitimate trade between the interior and the coast, and had a well-developed capital at Ijebu-Ode. It seemed to be prospering as much as those states that had accepted missionaries. The pretext for British occupation was an alleged insult offered to Acting Governor Denton by the Ijebu on his visit there in 1891. Despite peace negotiations between the Ijebu and the Lagos Government under Carter, it was clear from the moment of his arrival that he was intent on breaking the power of this state that not only hindered trade but was an obstacle to the extension of British 'civilisation'.

In a short expedition, which met with resistance on its way, British forces reached Ijebu-Ode to find it deserted by the Awujale. Thus the one power in Yorubaland that had tried to preserve the integrity of traditional Yoruba society and yet take advantage of the opportunities provided by modern trade, was destroyed and from the point of view of a Christian African it was seen thus:

'To the vast majority of the common people it was like the opening of a prison door: and no one who witnessed the patient, long-suffering and toiling mass of humanity that week by week stream to and from the coast with their produce could refrain from heaving a sigh of gratification on the magnitude of the beneficial results of the short sharp conflict.'[33]

This would have been more fair as a comment on the results of the general peace established by Carter's trek, for the Ijebu were not alone in contributing to a political situation that could have led an African with great pride in his race to make such a comment. They were guilty because they alone had resisted Christian penetration, not because they had blocked the roads—all the Yoruba states either deliberately or through war had done this.

## 4 The Royal Niger Company and the completion of the British occupation of Southern Nigeria

The Royal Niger Company, largely interested in trade, had not had to pursue an aggressive military policy in the lands it claimed in Southern Nigeria, apart from occasional bombardments of those hostile to its commercial policies. The Niger Coast Protectorate had to deal with the only one major threat to the Company's administration, that of the traders of Brass, in 1895, since though they attacked Akassa, their city state lay within its territory. Living outside Company territories, the Brass traders were treated by the Company as foreigners, a bizarre concept, since they were meant to 'enjoy' British protection. As such they had to pay a fee of £50 for a licence to trade in the Company's territories and £10 for each Company station they traded in. Furthermore trade in spirits incurred an extra £100 a year so that, as the Commissioner appointed to investigate the disturbances reported later, 'trade in the Delta' was 'impossible'.[34] Their attack on the Company's port of Akassa, undertaken in sheer frustration, led to destruction of their capital, Nembe, after fierce resistance on the part of the Brass warriors. It had, however, one happy result in that it drew attention to the illegal monopoly the Company was exercising on the Niger, and was thus one of the contributory factors to the revocation of its charter at the end of 1899.

The Company's main problem in asserting its authority on its northern frontiers lay with the French, as we have already seen, and with the Emirates of Nupe and Ilorin, whose determination to maintain their sovereignty in matters political and commercial led not only to their conquest but to that of Northern Nigeria as a whole.

When, in 1900, the Royal Niger Company's territories south of Idah were integrated with the Niger Coast Protectorate, to form the Protectorate of Southern Nigeria, there were vast areas of the new British administrative entity that had no experience of British administration. These included most of the Ibo, the tribes of the Cross River, the Western Ibo and the peoples north of Benin. The Royal Niger Company had done little to extend its authority over the Ibo in its territories, except where they directly interfered with trade. According to local traditions, cited by Anene, those Ibo who came within the Company's influence bitterly resented it, but their transfer to the new Protectorate government made no difference: they were in principle hostile to alien rule.[35]

The subjugation of these groups to British authority took many years, and involved maintaining 'punitive' columns on a standing basis. Control was extended in some parts village by village, and in the forest areas and swamplands the crudely armed villager had the advantage over his technological superior. In deciding on a policy of conquest, there were the usual arguments about the cost of expeditions, and whether the people concerned could not be brought under British rule peacefully. Those who advocated force found a more sympathetic ear in the Colonial Office after 1895, when Joseph Chamberlain became Colonial Secretary. His view was that: 'You cannot have omelettes without breaking eggs; you cannot destroy the practices of barbarism, of slavery, of superstition which for centuries have desolated the interior of Africa, without the use of force...'[36] He sanctioned the military occupation of Benin and Ashanti. The new phase of militarism which his appointment initiated had its most serious consequences for Nigeria, since the whole of the North and much of the East still remained unoccupied. The North was still threatened by French expansion eastwards along the Niger.

Whether or not Chamberlain had been appointed, force would have had to be used on the peoples of the East, for there was no other way in which these peoples could be made to accept British rule. As the British found to their cost, it was much easier to conquer a great state like Ashanti, Benin or Sokoto than decentralised peoples who may have had cultural unity, but politically were fiercely independent of each other. Thus the 'pacification' of the Ivory Coast was just as hard a task as the conquest of Ahmadou's empire.

There is not room in a book of this sort to detail the numerous expeditions that were sent out to bring the Ibo, Ibibio, Urhobo and many other tribes of Southern Nigeria under British rule.[37] But the destruction of the Aro Chukwu oracle is worthy of note, for it ended one of the most curious and ingenious political systems ever devised by Africans; furthermore 'in the minds of the Protectorate administration . . . the one remaining obstacle to the consolidation of Imperial rule was the Aro'.[38]

Though the Ibo were technically a decentralised people, each village being an authority unto itself, trade, initially in slaves, and later in palm-oil had been carried on through Iboland to the coast under the aegis of the Aro Ibo, possessors of the supreme oracle of Iboland, whose powers extended themselves not only over most Ibo but over the Ibibio and the non-Ibo trading states of the Niger Delta. Using the religious sanction of the oracle, the Aro were able to trade with complete security through Iboland to the coast. The profits of the trade allowed them to purchase arms to reinforce their spiritual authority. Despite earlier hopes for a peaceful settlement, the bitter resentment of the Aro against the imposition of British rule, especially the embargoes they imposed on trade with the foreigner, decided the British on military action. A column, which met with surprisingly little resistance, entered Aro on 24th December 1901 Some of the Aro chiefs were hanged, and the site of the Oracle was destroyed. The British were masters of Southern Nigeria, even though some groups continued to resist them for more than a decade.

## 5 The Royal Niger Company and Northern Nigeria

The occupation of Southern Nigeria was considerably more complex than that of the North. In the South occupation had been effected by conquest and diplomacy, under three agencies: the Royal Niger

K

Company, the Lagos Colony, dependent on the Colonial Office, and the Niger Coast Protectorate, dependent on the Foreign Office. The occupation of the North was by straight conquest, and, though it had its origins in the Royal Niger Company's reluctant decision to extend its real frontiers northwards, was largely achieved by the British Government itself.

Three factors made it imperative for Goldie to occupy effectively the Emirates lying immediately to the North with which he had treaties: first there was the ever-present danger of the French gaining a foothold on the navigable stretch of the Niger; second, two Emirates on his northern frontier, Nupe and Ilorin, were becoming increasingly hostile to his commercial ambitions; and third, Ilorin was proving a continual nuisance to the Lagos administration's newly won peace in Yorubaland.

We have already seen the prophylactic action Goldie took against French designs on the Niger, which were staved off by negotiation between the Foreign Office and the Quai d'Orsay. Nupe, by virtue of a verbal understanding with Britain in 1871, when the latter hoped to save money by acknowledging organised 'native' states as the protectors of their own subjects, continued to consider itself protector of the British rather than vice versa. The Nupe were disquieted by the presence of Christian missionaries at Lokoja and Egga, jurisdiction over which was always a matter for dispute between Nupe and the Niger Company. Hoenigsberg had brought to the fore the problems of the exact nature of the relationship between the Company and Nupe. The latter was clearly unwilling to sacrifice its sovereignty to the Company, but exacerbated the problem by slave-raiding into Company and Lagos Protectorate territories. For these reasons and with the principle of 'effective occupation' always in the background, it became clear to Goldie he would one day have to invade Nupe. He wished to stave off that day until he could gain sufficient force to make victory certain.

Ilorin, where the Company had little trade, was a much more aggravating problem than Nupe for it brought him into conflict with the Colonial Office and the Lagos Government. He had viewed with considerable anger the Foreign Office giving permission to the Lagos Government to negotiate with Ilorin in its attempts to bring peace to Yorubaland. Once Yorubaland was under Lagos protection, and the Emir of Ilorin continued his raids into what was now British territory, the pressures from the Lagos Government to be allowed to take over Ilorin and restore it to Yoruba as distinct from Sokoto control were becoming more persistent.

The rivalry between the various British 'protecting' agencies is one of the more bizarre aspects of the occupation of West Africa. Lugard had made treaties with Kishi and Shaki on the race to Nikki, only to learn from Captain Bower, the first British Resident of Ibadan, whom he met between Ejigbo and Ikirun, that 'these belong to us'.[39] Actually Lugard became good friends with Bower, who, 'like the typical British officer has no idea of kowtowing to the natives',[40] and they were able amicably to delimit the frontier between Ilorin and the Lagos Protectorate. But continued raids by Ilorin into Lagos territory, and the fear that if he did nothing about it, Lagos would occupy Ilorin, forced Goldie's hand. Carter had in fact put up concrete proposals for such action in 1896, suggesting he rely on traditional hatred of Ibadan for Ilorin, and use Ibadan troops.[41]

Goldie set off with his troops apparently confident of victory. But as Flint remarks 'victory was not certain, the Nupe people had a powerful military organisation, were superior in manpower, and their weapons, though inferior, were not to be despised'. Furthermore, for the Company, already under severe attack in Britain, 'defeat would mean the end of the company both as a financial organisation and a political régime'.[42] Nupe, as the rest of the Sokoto Caliphate would be, was defeated because they failed to realise that head-on cavalry charges against rapid-firing rifles, artillery and maxim guns was the worst military strategy possible. But for this error, Goldie might well have been defeated, for on many occasions the battle seemed nearly lost. As it was Goldie shelled the city and brought Nupe to subjection. A new Emir, likely to be disposed favourably to the Company, was installed, and the southern half of Nupe was ceded to the Company. Goldie could not, as Flint points out, administer the rest of the Emirate directly, because it would have cost him too much, and for this reason he used the indigenous administration as his agency of government. 'From this situation was created in embryo the system of indirect rule which Lugard was later to establish as the characteristic type of administration in Northern Nigeria, a system which in the twentieth century was to become the dominant trait of British policy in tropical Africa.'[43] Ilorin made the same tactical errors as Nupe, and was equally soundly defeated, but though it was crushed, Goldie did not attempt to set up any administration over it, or even depose its Emir.

Once Nupe and Ilorin, marcher Emirates of the Sokoto Caliphate, had been conquered the stage was set for the eventual occupation of the rest of Northern Nigeria. But this was not to be undertaken by the Royal Niger Company, for the ensuing crisis between the French and the Company on the Niger led to Britain accepting direct responsibility for 'effective occupation'.

## 6  Lugard's conquest of the North

With the dissolution of the administrative authority of the Royal Niger Company in 1899 and its assumption by the British Colonial office on 1st January 1900, Lugard was appointed High Commissioner of the Protectorate of Northern Nigeria, which consisted of the Company's sphere of influence in the North. Sphere of influence is about all it could be described as, for in reality when Lugard hoisted the Union Jack at Lokoja on 1st January 1900, it comprised effectively only a small strip of territory based on Lokoja. 'A colonial governor', as Margery Perham has written, 'can seldom have been appointed to a territory so much of which had never been viewed by himself or any other European.'[44] Goldie's incipient system of indirect rule failed in Nupe and the deposed Emir overthrew his puppet successor. Ilorin, though it had accepted British sovereignty, was not under any effective administrative control. To the North of Nupe and Ilorin lay the rest of the vast Sokoto Caliphate, with enormous military resources at its disposal. Lugard, moreover, had an annual recurrent budget for 1900 of a mere £85,938 for his administration which covered everything from Posts and Telegraphs to printing (£520).[45] A special Parliamentary grant of £200,000 was made to cover military expenditure. Bravely Lugard declared on that 1st January to the British population of Lokoja, some fifty souls: 'We are charged to hold in peace and good order this vast Territory, no mean part of that Empire. Whatever may betide elsewhere, we have a charge to fulfil.'[46]

It became increasingly clear to Lugard that peaceful administration could only be established by war, for he soon realised that the Emirs were implacably hostile to alien rule. The Sokoto empire, however, did not cover all Nigeria. Within the 'paper protectorate' lay Bornu, now controlled by Rabeh, who, influenced by Mahdist ideas, given time might have proved one of the more efficient administrators that ancient empire had seen. He had already proved himself a military genius with modern arms at his disposal. There were the peoples of the Plateau who had not come under the rule of either Bornu or Sokoto, but whose opposition to 'foreigners' was amply shown in the past by their fierce resistance to the Fulani invaders.

Any idea of a full-scale war against the Sokoto Caliphate had to be ruled out by Lugard soon after his appointment, for he had to release his troops for the Ashanti campaign and they did not return until the following December. It was only in January 1901 that he was able to send a force against the Emir of Kontagora, who had devastated large areas of his Emirate in search of slaves for the markets of the North. Twenty-seven months later Lugard entered Sokoto, with the whole of the Caliphate under his control, as well as Bornu and parts of the 'pagan' areas.

Lugard could possibly have negotiated the occupation of Northern Nigeria by treaty, though the hostility of the Emirs towards the 'infidel' invader does not suggest that such a policy would have been very fruitful. Lugard, however, despite his limited military resources, took the offensive for he was concerned to acquire title to rule Northern Nigeria by conquest. He tended to scorn treaties and the informal gradualism of earlier years. Where the French were unable to control their military, the British Colonial Office restrained Lugard. But, like his French counterparts, he was able to present his desk-bound masters in Whitehall with military *faits accomplis*, for he could always use urgency of decision and poor communications as justification.

Lugard was sensitive about the role of the military in civil administration and in 1902 he felt it necessary to justify the appointment of military officers as Civil Residents: 'It is indeed a characteristic of the British officer that when in civil employ his rule is often marked by less "militarism" than that of the civilian, and he is more opposed to punitive expeditions.'[47]

For his conquest of Northern Nigeria Lugard banked on the prevailing analysis of the situation in the Caliphate: that the Hausa population would welcome the British subjection of their Fulani overlords.[48] As it happened, the Caliphate fell to Lugard's tiny forces because it never succeeded in co-ordinating the resistance of its constituent emirates nor in adapting its traditional military strategies to those of the invader. Nupe and Ilorin fought Goldie separately as did the other emirates Lugard. Each victory for Lugard was a tragic 'Charge of the Light Brigade' for the Fulani. The will to resist was there, the military acumen lacking. And in this the great Muslim empire of Sokoto demonstrated how conservative it was compared with the Muslim states that resisted the French.

At its foundation in the first decade of the nineteenth century, the Fulani empire was the most modern state in West Africa. By the end of the nineteenth century it looked positively archaic beside those of Samory or Ahmadou. It was the absence of a modernising tendency in the empire, demonstrated by its repeated resort to traditional military techniques, that brought its downfall. Thus had the Emirs of Nupe and Kontagora had military intelligence of the calibre of Samory's, they would have realised that a combined attack on Lugard's headquarters at Jebba, when he had to release his troops to the Ashanti campaign, would have resulted in its obliteration. Each major battle—Kontagora (1901); Yola (1901); Kano (1903); Sokoto (1903)—was the same story. Head on cavalry charges at maxim guns, and failure to effect strategic retreats from towns that were being shelled. Some Emirs, notably Nupe and Bauchi, offered no resistance at all but fled, convinced of the inevitability of defeat. One, Zaria, even connived with the British, but was deposed for his pains.

The Fulani resistance is not of interest from the point of view of its efficiency, or rather lack thereof, but its nature. For the British always took their easy submission as an indication not only of the fact that the invaders were welcome but that the Caliphate was in a state of decay. In fact this was not so. The prevailing picture of the Caliphate on the eve of its defeat was one in which Sokoto had lost authority over its constituent Emirates. The evidence, however, does not support this theory. The Waziri or vizier of Sokoto was collecting tribute from the dependent Emirates right up till the eve of British occupation. The Sultan of Sokoto's recognition of the new successor of a provincial Emirate was still necessary; and thus, at the death of Lawal, Lamido of Adamawa, the most distant of Sokoto's provinces, the two candidates for succession journeyed to the imperial court to present their claims to the Sultan.[49] Traditional allegiance to Sokoto was openly acknowledged by the provinces even as they were defeated by the British. Zubeiru, Lamido of Adamawa, wrote to Sokoto after the fall of his capital, Yola, to Lugard's forces: 'I will not be double-faced towards you and the Christians. My allegiance is to you by Allah and the Prophet and after you to the Imam Mahdi. I shall not follow the unbelievers even if my towns are captured. The Prophet declared that he who joins his abode with the unbeliever or dwells with him, is among them.'[50] So too the Emir of Kano wrote to his overlord: 'I have found no more useful plan for all Moslems and for us and you, than as I wrote in my letter which my messenger brought to you, that we leave this country all of us... that is my clear conviction ... as these dogs have surrounded us and threaten to overcome us.'[51] Some provinces did co-operate with the British, but these were the exception not the rule. Zaria treated with the British for political reasons: the Emir was in imminent danger of deposition by Sokoto, and the defeated Emirs of Kontagora and Nupe, who continued their resistance to British penetration, were raiding into his territories.

Britain had invaded an empire ruled by Muslims who were profoundly attached to their faith and determined to act, in both peace and war, as its precepts demanded. The Sultan of Sokoto wrote in a letter to Lugard in c. May 1902: 'Between us and you there are no dealings except as between Mussulmans and Unbelievers . . . War, as God Almighty has enjoined on us.' Lugard chose to consider this as a declaration of war and subsequently conquered Sokoto and installed a new Sultan.

The rulers of the Sokoto Caliphate did not reconcile themselves easily to conquest: the Muslim faith presented a further alternative should war fail: *hijra*, flight from the infidel. More important still, from its inception the Sokoto Caliphate had anticipated the coming of the Mahdi. According to Muslim tradition the Prophet had said that he would be followed by an Imam of God, the Imam al-Mahdi, who would fill the earth with justice and equity. Many of the followers of Usman dan Fodio had believed him to be the Mahdi, but he had denied this.[52] His son Muhammad Bello told the Shehu's followers that he had said that 'this *Jihad* will not end, by God's permission, until it gets to the Mahdi'.[53] Furthermore it was believed that as a result of a prophesy made by Usman dan Fodio, revealed by his daughter Mariam, and his son, Abubakar Atiku, there would be a time when the faithful would be called upon to undertake the *hijra*.[54] The coming of the infidel Europeans coincided with the rise and fall of the Sudanese Mahdi, defeated by British troops in 1898. He had demanded recognition by the Shehu of Bornu, as well as the Sultan of Sokoto, both of whom rejected the demand, though in Sokoto he gained an important following. By the time of the British conquest the need to flee from the infidel, and the recognition that the chaotic conditions which had to precede the arrival of the Mahdi were present, led the Emir of Kano, in his letter already cited, to claim that the present troubles were the necessary, prophesied prelude to such a flight to the East.[55]

Soon after Lugard's conquest of Sokoto, the deposed Sultan called the faithful to follow him to the East; the response he received confounded earlier diagnoses of a peasantry eagerly awaiting liberation from the Fulani yoke, as not only chiefs but also ordinary people gathered around him. The British, perceiving what a profound effect the exodus was having on the peasantry, decided it was necessary to send an expedition to track down him and his followers.[56] They finally encountered the fleeing Sultan at Burmi where, in a hard-fought engagement, the former Sultan and his followers were finally defeated, and the Sultan himself killed. The battle marked the climax of British occupation in Hausaland and the large number of Fulani dignitaries present, with their followers, reveal just how widespread was the belief in the *hijra*.[57] Led by Mai Wurno, the Sultan's son, some 25,000 people continued their trek east to the Sudan and settled on the Blue Nile.[58]

Lugard realised just how delicate the problem of imposing the rule of the 'infidel' on this Muslim population was. Despite the fact that, as Ayandele has shown,[59] he initially favoured Christian penetration of the North, indeed thought it would be a definite asset, he agreed to exclude them from his territories for fear of offending the Emirs. It was in fact the light hand of his administration which involved minimal interference with the Emirs' powers, except for the abolition of the slave trade as distinct from slavery itself and reform of the prison system, that saved him in 1906 when his troops were tied down in occupying the Tiv country. In Satiru, a town only fourteen miles from Sokoto, a religious revolt against the British inflicted the first defeat on Lugard's forces. The Emir of Gwandu, overlord of the Western Sector of the Empire, and the Emir of Hadeija wavered on the side of the rebel forces, but because the new Sultan of Sokoto remained 'loyal' to Lugard, there was no general uprising and these two emirs were deposed. Major Burdon, who knew his Northern Nigeria very well, wrote later, 'had he [the Sultan] shown the slightest indecision, I have no doubt that the bulk of the "talakawa" [peasantry] would at once have joined the enemy'.[60] Thereafter British rule over the Caliphate was secure, but as we shall see in subsequent chapters it relied on maintaining almost intact the traditional system of administration.

Miss Perham has pointed to the impatience of the critics of imperialism 'of all opposing arguments'[61] to European control, and we must not forget that the extension of British sovereignty did bring to an end one of the banes of the Caliphate—the dependence of the marcher Emirates on slave-raiding as a source of income. Unfortunately the British have tended to overplay the role of slave-raiding in the Caliphate and to take Nagwamatse, Emir of Kontagora, who really did devastate vast regions in his slave hunts, as typical of Fulani. That it was bitterly resented by their inhabitants is brought out clearly in the remarkable memoirs of Baba of Karo.[62] The resentment of the Hausa (Habe) against their

Fulani overlords is brought out by her too: 'When the Europeans came the Habe [Hausa] saw that if you worked for them they paid you for it, they didn't just say, like the Fulani, "Commoner, give me this! Commoner, bring me that!" Yes, the Habe wanted them; they saw no harm in them.' It must be admitted that there were many Hausa who did initially welcome the coming of the British. But if we are to understand the subsequent history of British colonial rule over the Fulani emirs, and indeed Nigerian politics today, we must appreciate that its administrative structure remained strong enough to perpetuate their power. Their religious and administrative hold over the people, including the Hausa, was so strong that, shorn of patent abuses such as slavery, they remained not only a force with which the British had to come to terms, but one which was dominant in the history of British colonial rule. The only alternative would have been to smash them entirely as Goldie had once suggested: '. . . if England can spare the force and the money to smash the Central Sudan into an amorphous condition and then re-organise it on a new basis, I raise no objection. It may be the best policy. But it must be deliberately planned and systematically carried out and not by spasmodic efforts.'[64] Like the French, Goldie saw that with these Moslem rulers it was all or nothing. The French chose all, the British, as later critics were to point out, almost nothing. In so opting, far from integrating the Fulani emirates with the modern technological world, Britain partially blocked their entry into it.

The apparent passivity with which the Fulani-Hausa accepted British over-rule lay not only in the reasons given above, but also in the element of fatalism inherent in the Moslem religion. The Sardauna of Sokoto, scion of Dan Fodio's family, was to write later in 1962: 'Whatever the rights and wrongs of the attack on Kano and Sokoto may be, the British were fulfilling the will of God.'[65]

Two years before the occupation of Sokoto, the French had brought Bornu into subjection for the British. By the 1898 Anglo-French Convention, the ancient empire of Bornu, newly conquered by Rabeh, lay largely within the British sphere of influence but straddled both the German and French spheres. The French, who had at one time considered negotiating a treaty with Rabeh, were in fact the instruments of the downfall of his newly created state. Rabeh had swept into Bornu from the Egyptian Sudan where he had worked with its Governor of Darfur, Zubeir Pasha, who had been deposed and imprisoned by Cairo. Escaping his master's fate, Rabeh took his army westwards, conquering Bagarimi and finally the great Empire of Bornu in 1893. He destroyed the Bornu capital at Kuka and established a new one at Dikwa. His occupation of Bornu was done in the name of the Mahdi, though Rabeh refused to correspond with him. However, his soldiers wore the Mahdist uniform and carried the Mahdist flag.[66] It involved great devastations of land, the selling of many people into captivity, but in the short years he ruled from Dikwa he was in the process of stream-lining the administration of the state.[67] To complete this work he had little time, for in 1899 he came into conflict with the French, attacking one of their posts in Bagarimi, and engaging them at Kouni in an indecisive battle.

Shortly afterwards Rabeh came up against the three Chad columns in April 1900. Having access to arms only by way of Egypt, he was hard put to fight the combined columns and was killed in battle. His son Fad-el-Allah escaped with 3,000 followers into what was effectively the British sphere of influence in Bornu. This created an embarrassing situation for Lugard, since the French might well complain at further attacks on them by Fad-el-Allah, now based on theoretically British territory. Furthermore, Fad-el-Allah had asked for British protection, but the High Commissioner, 'believing strongly that co-operation and mutual assistance between Europeans was of vital importance in Africa, was naturally unwilling to accept overtures from a man who had been a moment before in conflict with a friendly European power'.[68] However, Lugard's Resident on the Upper Benue had given Fad-el-Allah reason to hope that he might be given such protection, which his father had told him to seek as he lay dying in battle. Lugard therefore sent a mission to Fad-el-Allah, and the officer returned with a report entirely in favour of recognising Fad-el-Allah as Emir of Bornu. However, the French settled matters by launching an attack on him 150 miles into British territory, apparently in reprisal for a brush with his forces in their sphere of influence.

The French, after the defeat of Rabeh, had restored the heir of the defeated Kanemi dynasty of Bornu. After they had killed Fad-el-Allah they demanded 80,000 dollars from the restored Kanemi ruler in return for killing both his rival and his rival's son. When the British arrived to take over Bornu, only 6,500 dollars remained to be paid. The British promised to recognise him on the throne provided he did not pay the rest of this sum to the French.

British access to Bornu, which now submitted peacefully to alien rule, had been blocked by a Mahdi, Jibrella of Gombe, an old man of some seventy years, whose heroic and fanatical resistance to their forces was recognised by them in the honourable exile into which they sent him.

The phenomenon of Mahdism was to cause concern to both the British and French colonial administrations during the early years of their rule. For not only had Mahdist expectations been aroused in the Niger–Chad region from the East. The head of the powerful Senussi confraternity in North Africa, while he explicitly rejected claims that he was the Mahdi, was greatly feared by the French for his supposed militancy and his influence over Muslims across the desert in the Western Sudan.

The conquest of Sokoto and the occupation of Bornu of the French left the British masters of most of Northern Nigeria. However, as in the Southern Nigerian Protectorate, it took them many years before they could subdue the smaller groups, many of whom, from the fastnesses of the Plateau, did not come under effective British occupation until after the First World War, and many of whom were little affected by British administration.

# Notes

1 J. E. Flint, *Sir George Goldie and the Making of Nigeria*, London, 1960, p. 60.

2 Cited by J. C. Anene, *Southern Nigeria in Transition 1884–1906, Theory and Practice in a Colonial Protectorate*, Cambridge, 1965, p. 72.

3 *Ibid.*, p. 74.

4 Flint, *Goldie*, p. 93.

5 *Ibid.*, p. 117.

6 Notably Roland Oliver, *Sir Harry Johnston and the Scramble for Africa*, London, pp. 107–18. Anene, *Southern Nigeria*, pp. 73–91.

7 For the background to the dispute that led to Jaja's secession from Bonny see Dike, *Trade and Politics*, Chapter X, and G. I. Jones, *The Trading States of the Oil Rivers*, London, 1963, pp. 128–32.

8 Cited by E. A. Ayandele, *The Missionary Impact on Modern Nigeria, 1842–1914, A Political and Social Analysis*, London, 1966, pp. 80–1.

9 *Ibid.*, pp. 75–83.

10 *Ibid.*, p. 82.

11 George Pepple was a friend of the Lord Mayor of London; was 'admired for his erudition and after dinner speeches' in Britain; took holidays in Madeira; read the London *Times*; regularly, 'smokes cigarettes, scents his handkerchiefs with the newest essence, dilates on the acting of Ellen Terry and Irving, and criticises the comic operas of Gilbert and Sullivan' (according to Johnston); was a Sunday school-teacher and member of the Finance Committee of the Niger Mission. In *ibid.*, pp. 77–9.

12 Anene, *Southern Nigeria*, p. 94.

13 Johnston however received what he considered an affirmative reply to his telegram, but this appears to have been a reply to an earlier one. See Oliver, *Sir Harry Johnston*, pp. 113–15.

14 See Sir Alan Burns, *History of Nigeria*, London, 1956, p. 149, for the full text of the letter.

15 Anene, *Southern Nigeria*, p. 91.

16 Flint, *Goldie*, p. 129. See also Anene, *Southern Nigeria*, p. 177: 'It was his [Macdonald's] conviction that British rule had but one justification —the improvement of the social and material conditions of the ruled.'

17 There is a very useful summary of Nana's career by Obaro Ikime, 'Nana Olumu: Governor of the Benin River', *Tarikh*, I, 2, pp. 39–50. See also P. C. Lloyd, 'The Itsekiri in the 19th century: an outline Social History', *J.A.H.*, IV, 2, 1963, pp. 222–3, for the background of Nana's rise to power.

18 Anene, *Southern Nigeria*, p. 154, cites the letter a British trader on the Rivers sent to his employees in which he abuses Nana and adds

tellingly: 'I shan't be sorry when his power is completely broken. We will have much better trade and more profitable too.'

19 Sir Harry Johnston, *The Story of My Life*, London, 1923, pp. 212–13.

20 Ikime, 'Nana Olumu', p. 47.

21 Anene, *Southern Nigeria*, p. 157.

22 Ikime, 'Nana Olumu', p. 41.

23 George W. Neville, 'Nanna Oluma of Benin', *Journal of the African Society*, LIV, XIV, Jan. 1915, p. 167.

24 Thomas Hodgkin, *Nigerian Perspectives*, London, 1960, p. 48.

25 Anene, *Southern Nigeria*, p. 190.

26 See Edun Akenzua, 'The British Occupation of Benin', *Nigeria Magazine*, No. 59, 1960. Akenzua is a son of the present Oba.

27 See for example: H. Ling Roth, *Great Benin—its Customs, Art and Horrors*, London, 1903; Alan Boisragon, *The Benin Massacre*, London, 1897, and R. H. Bacon, *Benin, The City of Blood*, London, 1897.

28 See J. F. Ade Ajayi, *Christian Missions in Nigeria 1841–1871: The Making of an Educated Élite*, London, 1965.

29 See Jean Herskovits Kopytoff, *A Preface to Modern Nigeria: The 'Sierra Leonians' in Yoruba, 1830–1890*, Madison, Wisconsin, 1965.

30 Cited in Ayandele, *Missionary Impact*, p. 13.

31 Ajayi, *Christian Missions*, p. 397.

32 I have revised my earlier views of the politics of the Ijebu expedition (see my *The Story of Nigeria*, London, 1965, revised edition) in the light of Ayandele's very perceptive account, *Missionary Impact*, pp. 54–68.

33 Samuel Johnson, *The History of the Yorubas*, Lagos, 1937, p. 623.

34 Cited in Burns, *Nigeria*, p. 157–8.

35 Anene, *Southern Nigeria*, p. 216.

36 Quoted in *ibid.*, p. 217.

37 See A. Haywood and F. A. S. Clarke, *The History of the Royal West African Frontier Force*, London, 1964, for a list of the main campaigns: North East Benin, March–May, 1901; Irua, 1904; Onitsha Hinterland, 1904–5; Nun River, Eket, Mkpani, 1903; Okpoto, 1903–4; Northern Ibibio, the Asaba Hinterland and Kwale, Jan.–April, 1904; Kwale, Oct.–Nov., 1905; Bende Onitsha, Oct. 1905–April, 1906; Owa near Agbor, 1906; Niger-Cross River, 1908–9; Ogwashi-Uku, 1909–10, etc.

38 J. C. Anene, 'The Protectorate Government of Southern Nigeria and the Aros, 1900–1902', *Journal of the Historical Society of Nigeria*, I, 1, December 1956, p. 21.

39 Lugard, *Diaries*, IV, p. 250.

40 *Ibid.*, p. 250.

41 Flint, *Goldie*, p. 239.

42 *Ibid.*, p. 243.

43 *Ibid.*, pp. 253–4.

44 Margery Perham, *Lugard: The Years of Authority*, Vol. II, London, 1960, p. 27.

45 Sir Charles Orr, *The Making of Northern Nigeria*, 2nd edition, London, 1965, p. 77.

46 Cited by Perham, *Lugard*, II, p. 26.

47 *Annual Report* for Northern Nigeria, 1902, para. 77.

48 Burns, *Nigeria*, p. 182.

49 A. H. M. Kirk Greene, *Adamawa Past and Present*, London, 1958, p. 140.

50 Cited from H. F. Backwell, *The Occupation of Hausaland*, Lagos, 1927, by Thomas Hodgkin, *Nigerian Perspectives*, London, 1960, p. 322.

51 *Ibid.*, p. 323.

52 Saburi Biobaku and Muhammad Al-Hajj, 'The Sudanese Mahdiyya and the Niger Chad Region', in *Islam in Tropical Africa*, I. M. Lewis, ed., London, 1966, pp. 427–8.

53 Cited in *ibid.*, p. 428.

54 D. J. Muffett, *Concerning Brave Captains*, London, 1964, pp. 143–212.

55 Hodgkin, *Nigerian Perspectives*, p. 323.

56 *Annual Report*, 1903.

57 Present were the following: the Sultan of Sokoto and his sons; Emir Bashir of the Melle Fulani; Alfa Hashim, a Tijani leader; Abu Bakr, Emir of Nupe; Bello, brother of the Emir of Kontagora; Ahmadu, Emir of Misau; and the Magaji of Keffi. See Saburi Biobaku and Muhammad Al-Hajj, 'The Sudanese Mahdiyya', p. 436.

58 Burns, *Nigeria*, p. 187, in his usual disparaging way said the ex-Sultan's command for *Hijra* was obeyed 'only by a mob of unarmed peasants and some women'!!

59 Ayandele, *Missionary Impact*, Chapter IV: 'The Crescent and the Cross in Northern Nigeria, 1900–1914', in particular pp. 128–32.

60 Cited in Perham, *Lugard*, II, p. 258. This observation hardly concurs with the general British view developed later, and reflected by Burns, *Nigeria*, p. 187, 'The people were delighted with the overthrow of their old oppressors'.

61 *Ibid.*, p. 44.

62 Mary Smith, *Baba of Karo: A Woman of the Moslem Hausa*, London, 1954.

63 *Ibid.*, p. 67.

64 Perham, *Lugard*, II, p. 88.

65 Sir Ahmadu Bello, the Sardauna of Sokoto, *My Life*, Cambridge, 1962, p. 19.

66 Biobaku and Al-Hajj, 'The Sudanese Mahdiyya', p. 434.

67 Gentil in his book, *La chute de l'empire de Rabeh*, asserted that he was illiterate. 'Yet', as A. D. H. Bivar has asked, 'are we seriously to believe that the communications and government of Rabeh depended entirely on word of mouth?' See A. D. H. Bivar, 'Rabih ibn Fadlullah—The Autograph of a Despot', *Nigeria Magazine*, No. 68, March 1961, in which he shows that it is almost certain that he was literate.

68 Orr, *The Making of Northern Nigeria*, p. 104.

# 4 The British occupation of the Gold Coast, Sierra Leone and the Gambia

## 1 The conquest of Ashanti

By 1885 the largest area controlled by Britain on the West Coast of Africa was her colony of the Gold Coast. This consisted of her own forts, those she had acquired from the Danes and the Dutch, together with the chiefdoms that formed their immediate hinterland. These had been annexed in 1874 immediately after the defeat of the Ashanti in that year, and gave Britain complete control of all coastal outlets for Ashanti trade.

Throughout the nineteenth century British relations with Ashanti had intermittently deteriorated. Looked at from the Coast, Ashanti, with her control of most of what is modern Ghana, appeared to be an expansionist power, seeking to extend its control over Fanti and indeed to subject British and other Coastal traders to its will. The Ashanti, however, from their inland capital at Kumasi, were more intent on preserving the integrity of their large empire built up in the eighteenth century, and in retaining control of their access to the vital coastal trade whereby they gained their foreign exchange not only for arms but also for acquiring a wide variety of European consumer goods. From the British view, the Ashanti invasions on neighbouring states were the work of a bloodthirsty empire which menaced their own existence. Chiefs of some of these neighbouring states, including tributaries of Ashanti, encouraged this view because they wished to use the British as agents in securing their independence from Ashanti or because they were harbouring rebels against

Ashanti authority. Britain, not wishing to assist Ashanti consolidation of the southern coastal extremity of its empire and circumscribed by its commitments to many Fanti states, had chosen to encourage the coastal states in their bid for, or maintenance of, their independence. In part, Britain feared that its own trading position on the coast would be prejudiced by the presence of a more powerful Ashanti there. She preferred a policy of divide and free trade rather than risk a possible African monopoly by Ashanti,[1] though at times the alternative policy of trying to come to agreement with a strong Ashanti could seem attractive.

British protection of the coastal peoples was a source of constant irritation to Ashanti. Apart from blocking their direct access to the coast, and preventing their export of slaves, it provided a refuge for those trying to escape Ashanti authority. One such instance was the refusal of Governor Pine in 1863 to send back a subject of the Asantahene who had violated the state monopoly of gold which was fundamental to the economic organisation of the empire.[2] Despite lengthy negotiations between Pine and Ashanti emissaries and the further assurance that the fugitive would be given a fair trial, Governor Pine refused his extradition, even though he recognised that this act would remove the 'greatest obstacle in the way of amicable relations between us and Ashantee'.[3] Nevertheless it appears that such exchange of prisoners was not only customary but also agreed to by treaty: Bowdich had signed a treaty with the king of Ashanti on 7th September 1817, in which it was stated that 'in case of any crime of magnitude, he [the Governor-in-Chief] will send the offender to the king, to be dealt with according to the laws of his country'.[4] Maclean followed this policy which was well-known to other European powers on the coast: Colonel Nagtglas, former Governor of the Dutch possessions, wrote that 'there is an agreement in existence between the local British Government and the King of Ashanti, either oral or in writing, that on both sides runaway prisoners from crime should be delivered'.[5] Pine's refusal to give up the offender provided the *casus belli* for the 1864 war between Britain and Ashanti. The situation was further aggravated by the seizure of some Ashanti traders by British-protected Fanti.

Although Britain was not interested in extending her authority over Ashanti, her fort administrators on the coast could not restrain themselves from interference in Ashanti's internal affairs. Only the year before the 1863–4 war, trade between the British on the Coast and Ashanti had been at its most flourishing and relations were friendly: 'The Ashantis arrived on the coast daily, bringing gold, ivory and

L

other produce'.[6] Pine's failure to respect both the Ashanti legal system and Britain's own treaty agreements precipitated a war that led to a disastrous defeat for Britain and which, as we have seen, was a major motive for the 1865 Select Committee's recommendation that Britain withdraw from the West Coast.

The cause of the war of 1873–4 was similar to that of 1863–4: a dispute over sovereignty. The Dutch transferred their forts to the British in 1872, among them Elmina, over which Ashanti claimed sovereignty. The Dutch subsequently produced what appears to have been a false document giving themselves rights over Elmina, and the British with obvious self-interest accepted it as genuine. Elmina was Ashanti's one secure outlet to the sea and under the Dutch had been friendly to Ashanti. The prospect of its coming under British protection, a situation in which the Fanti protected states would conceivably goad the British to further hostility against Ashanti, was very serious. Indeed the people living around Elmina hoped to come under Ashanti rather than British rule. Protracted negotiations between Ashanti and the British failed and the Ashanti army invaded the Protectorate. Britain retaliated in an all-out effort to avenge her defeat of 1863. Sir Garnet Wolseley at the head of British forces, which included some sent by Jaja of Opobo, crushed the Ashanti. For one British officer the importance of this victory was that: 'The name of England will now be respected on the Coast—the superiority of her soldiers acknowledged; and I do not think we shall be troubled during the present generation with any more Ashantee invasions of the Protectorate.'[7]

The British victory over the Ashanti was not however followed up by the establishment of a protectorate. In the first place the economic motives for its occupation were not pressing. Now that Britain controlled all the coastal outlets, and had annxed the coastal states, Ashanti could only interfere in this area at the risk of another military expedition against it. Secondly the cost of administering Ashanti would be high for a home administration that was hostile to extending British commitments beyond what was absolutely necessary. The Ashanti had fought valiantly against superior weapons and their permanent occupation would certainly have involved posting sizeable forces in Kumasi. The British officials on the spot were however fearful that Ashanti left to itself would attack again and were anxious to break its monopoly of trade with its northern neighbours.[8] The people of the Colony were even more critical of British reticence. The *Gold Coast Times* in 1877 maintained that 'never was a greater mistake made than when Sir Garnet Wolseley left the

Ashanti Kingdom to itself, satisfied with his paper treaty and his few ounces of Gold Dust'.[9]

For students of modern nationalism, the coastal peoples would appear to be the villains advocating the occupation of Ashanti by Britain and aiding in its subjugation. The Fanti contributed troops to the 1874 campaign although their ability as soldiers was not highly thought of by British officers, one of whom went so far as to describe them as the 'greatest cowards in the world'.[10]

It must be remembered however that one of the results of the British conquest of Ashanti had been the annexation of the coastal peoples to the crown. Their willingness to fight for the British against the Ashanti was the result of their own fear that if the Ashanti were unchecked they would be the sufferers. The coastal peoples had in fact tried their best to secure their independence from both the British and Ashanti.

In the mid 1860's, the Fanti, together with the Ga, attempted to develop two political units—the Accra Confederacy and the Fanti Confederacy—which were to be the precursors of nationalist activities in the Gold Coast. By this time these peoples had long been exposed to European education and technology in the form of both fort and mission-schools, the first notable one being that established by Philip Quaque in 1766 at Cape Coast Castle. By the time of the Scramble the Accra and Cape Coast trained élites, with those in St. Louis, Freetown, and Abeokuta, represented the most educated groups of Africans on the Coast and were beginning to supply the corps of teachers, ministers, commercial and administrative clerks necessary for the maintenance of the coastal establishments. The two confederacies were formed by these educated elements, working with the traditional rulers, with the aim of setting up a series of independent governments which would unite for military, social and economic purposes. Even before their establishment, there had been a period when rulers in the eastern and western regions had chosen to ignore their British overlords, who complained that in some instances the traditional rulers behaved as if there were no Europeans present. Thus King John Aggery refused to go to Cape Coast Castle when summoned there by the British Governor, Colonel Conran, who had received a letter from him threatening that there would be rebellion on the Gold Coast if the British did not recognise that his people preferred their own laws to those of the British. Tartly Aggery added that 'he was the King of Cape Coast but did not know who Colonel Conran was'.[11] Similar statements and actions came from the rulers in Jamestown, Christianborg, and Dutch Accra. The interchange of Dutch and British territory presented an opportunity which the peoples of each region seized as the lever by which they might pry European nations off the coast. Under the cover that they wished Britain to negotiate with Holland for the purchase of former Dutch settlements, the Fanti leaders hoped that by bringing all of these settlements within the Protectorate, their combined strength would be such as to compel the British to withdraw. Indeed for a very brief time the Fanti succeeded in this venture. Thus the establishment of the Fanti Confederacy was as much anti-European as it was anti-Ashanti. For their part the Ashanti were anxious to test the military strength of the new Confederacy.

In their constitutional thinking the Fanti and Ga leaders were greatly influenced by James Africanus Horton, the brilliant Sierra Leonean Surgeon-Major in the British Army, who had sought in his book, *West African Countries and Peoples*,[12] to point out how traditional systems of government could be utilised in the formation of new political units. Published in 1868, it tried to follow up with concrete proposals the recommendation by the 1865 Select Committee that Africans in the British West African Settlements should be self-governing. Some scholars, all too eager to see in the Confederacies symptoms of modern nationalism or the division of the educated élite from the traditional élite, have tended to overlook the fact that the Confederacies were very much traditional in nature at the same time as they sought to incorporate the best of the Western techno-logical world which by now impinged so closely on their daily lives. The Constitution of the Fanti Confederacy provided roles for both the traditional and educated élites. The Constitutional head of the Confederacy was to be a King-President. A Representative Assembly was to be composed of two members from each participating state, one of whom had to be a chief, one a Western-educated man. Members of the Executive Council were to be elected by a National Assembly of Kings and leading chiefs which would also confirm the proceedings of the Representative Assembly. Officers of the Executive Council were actually elected.[13]

The Confederacy placed great emphasis on modernisation, in particular on roads, useful for both trade and war, schools, agri-culture, industry and the exploitation of mineral resources.[14]

This experiment in self-government by a people whom the British had come to think of as being under their informal control did not please the administrators of the Gold Coast. Indeed Ussher and Salmon did all they could to thwart it, by trying to play on differences between chiefs and educated Africans, and between chiefs of different participating states. In 1871 Salmon had members of the Executive Council arrested on a charge of treason and this, together with quarrels between various factions in the Confederacy, so weakened it that by the time of the British decision to annex the coastal states, it was in no position to resist.

By their victory of 1874 the British had effectively destroyed Ashanti as a military power and its empire began to break up. It lost control of northern vassal states like Gonja and Dagomba. And by the Fomena treaty it had signed with the British after defeat it had had to recognise the independence of its southern vassal states beyond the Pra river.

British officials on the spot continued to press the home government to take over Ashanti. But Captain Lonsdale's recommendation for occupation in 1883 was derided by Kimberley who dismissed it as 'the usual recommendation, white men to take care of black men and all will be well'.[15]

Ashanti however did not represent a real threat to the Colony for it was weakened by internal dissension leading to five years of civil war from 1883 to 1888. But in 1888 Prempeh I became Asantanhene and successfully re-consolidated some of Ashanti's lost power. Indeed such was his success that the British, already keeping a wary eye on French activities on Ashanti's western borders, tried to persuade him to accept British protection. This Prempeh turned down in a letter to Governor Brandford Griffith.

'The suggestion that Ashanti in its present state should come and enjoy the protection of Her Majesty the Queen and Empress of India I may say this is a matter of a very serious consideration and which I am happy to say that we have arrived at this conclusion, that my kingdom of Ashanti will never commit itself to any such policy; Ashanti must remain independent as of old, at the same time to be friendly with all white men.'[16]

In 1894 Acting Governor Hodgson requested London for permission to occupy Ashanti. But this was rejected by Lord Ripon on the grounds of the burden it would entail. 'I do not desire to annex Ashanti in name or in fact and thereby greatly to increase the responsibilities of the Gold Coast Government.'[17]

Prempeh, intent on maintaining Ashanti's independence, recognised the threat the Governors in the Colony represented to his independence and even sent an Embassy to London, which was cavalierly treated both in the Colony and in Westminster. In a desperate measure his representatives tried to interest a syndicate in developing the kingdom and even offered to give it partial powers of administration.[18]

Prempeh also tried to secure an alliance with Samory, now driven by the French to the western borders of Ashanti. The British, whose request to send a Resident to Kumasi in 1894 had been turned down by Prempeh who feared this would lead to a British Protectorate, warned Samory off. Governor Maxwell wrote to him to say the British were about to make war on the King of Kumasi 'because he had broken his agreement and has been rebellious'. Samory should not allow his followers 'to come to Ashanti for Ashanti is English territory'.[19] Samory did not pursue the matter since with the French pressing him hard he did not wish to alienate the British.

Until 1895 London had been more sympathetic to Ashanti than the British officials on the spot.[20] With Chamberlain at the desk in the Colonial Office, advocates of occupation at last received a sympathetic hearing. For once the Governor and the Colonial Office were in accord. A full-scale military expedition was planned because Ashanti power had revived to such an extent that it was felt necessary to crush it completely. Thus Prempeh's last-minute offer of negotiation, insured by the despatch of hostages, was rejected. The British column marched on a deserted Kumasi, which like Benin was sacked and the royal treasures sent to Britain. £175,000 was demanded as indemnity from Prempeh, and on his being unable to pay he was deported to Sierra Leone along with the Queen Mother and other senior chiefs. Ashanti had offered no resistance, partly in the hopes of negotiating an honourable settlement, partly because it was well aware of the forces against which it was pitted. Britain was now, it appeared, master of Ashanti. But, as we shall see, in designing a system of government for it, the greatest tact would have to be used.

Ashanti under British control, the way lay open to the North. Britain was able to bring under effective administration the states with which George Ekem Ferguson had signed treaties before the French and Germans did. These states accepted British rule with little opposition, since most of them had already been smashed by Samory, and had not the power or the will to resist.[21]

## 2  The occupation of the Sierra Leone hinterland

The Colony of Sierra Leone, an experiment in the application of the ideals of the European 'Enlightenment', had almost collapsed in its early years because of the wide gap between the rational suppositions of its founder, Granville Sharp, and the realities of life on a peninsula with the heaviest rainfall on the West Coast.[22] But, as we have seen, the establishment of Freetown as the base for the activities of the Anti-Slavery Patrol and as the place of resettlement for the slaves it freed, made Sierra Leone the one Colony on the Coast which Britain could ill afford to abandon. Indeed its functions gave it a natural tendency to expand, for the small area of land acquired by Granville Sharp for the original settlers could not contain all the re-captives brought in by the Navy, for the land was poor for farming and there were limited opportunities for wage labour. The British Government nevertheless was as reluctant to see territorial expansion in Sierra Leone as elsewhere along the Coast, and the Colony remained small right up to the eve of the Scramble. The Colony had to depend primarily on the role of Freetown as a port and on the trade it generated with the hinterland. The agents of this trade were not so much the Europeans as the 'Creoles', the term by which the descendants of the mixed community of settlers and re-captives became known. Thus the Colony established a trading empire in its hinterland whose maintenance was backed up by military force, for if Governors were not allowed to acquire territory, they were prepared to interfere in the affairs of their neighbours in the interests of the security of the Colony and its trade. Thus the Colony, though it remained small in territorial terms, grew large in terms of its influence over the hinterland.

Not even fear of the French allowed the Governors to extend boundaries. Thus in 1845 when William Fergusson, the first British Governor of African descent,[23] proposed to place the groundnut-producing areas to the North under British protection in the face of French presence there, the Home Government refused him permission. He did, however, make treaties of friendship with the chiefs in this area for the groundnut crop was worth some £20,000 a year to Sierra Leone by this time. But, when it looked as though the French might occupy Bendu on Sherbro Island in 1861, Governor Hill was allowed to make part of Sherbro a Protectorate. This protectorate had been solicited by Thomas Stephen Caulker, a trading chief of part European descent who was established at Shenge on the mainland, but claimed overlordship of Bendu. The French were now believed to be threatening to occupy the area in support of their traders settled there since the fifties, but Caulker preferred government by Britain to France. Given this open preference Hill used the occasion to sign treaties with a number of other chiefs so that British Sherbro became much larger than the Home Government had intended. But British Sherbro was British only in name;[24] British rule in Bendu, for instance, 'was represented by a police sergeant and the flag'.[25]

The only other extension of formal British control before the Scramble apart from the Isles de Los and Bulama, both of which were subsequently abandoned, was to bring into a customs union by treaty as many coastal chiefs as possible. For, as with Lagos, if Freetown were to pay for its administration it had to prevent traders using nearby ports to ship their goods and thus avoid the payment of dues which, since the abolition of the House Tax by Governor Pope Hennessy in 1872, remained the main source of income for the colonial government.

In 1882 the French and British agreed that the Scarcies River would mark the northward limits of Sierra Leone, with the result that Sierra Leone was cut off from the valuable groundnut trade. The southern limit was settled with Liberia in 1886 after a somewhat acrimonious dispute in which force was once used on the Mano River.

Whilst the coastline of Sierra Leone had been fixed by 1886, the hinterland did not for the most part have any formal relationship with the British. However, its main access to European goods was by way of Freetown or ports in customs union with Britain. These goods had at first been brought to the hinterland by Creoles, who in turn acted as agents for the export of hinterland produce to the Coast. Many of these Creoles became very rich and the chiefs, particularly in the palm-oil-producing areas of the south, began to see the advantages of entering trade on their own account. Their attempts to extend their influence over strategic trade routes led to what were known as the Trade Wars. Creoles were prompted by these wars to demand the extension of a British Protectorate over the hinterland: thus in 1884 the enterprising and wealthy Creole trader in Sherbro, MacFoy, exasperated by the wars, used his extensive influence over his trading associates in Britain to get Samuel Rowe, already well-known as Governor in Sierra Leone for his belief in a forward policy, re-appointed Governor.[26] However, neither Rowe nor the Colonial Office pursued annexation. The Creoles, hard hit by the depression of the mid 1880's, attributed their difficulties to the Trade Wars rather than to the fall in prices for African produce in the London market, and thus pressed further for annexation.[27]

Britain was not the only power with influence in the hinterland: Samory was extending his empire eastwards in opposition to the French who were already active in Guinea. He had already captured

Falaba in 1883, and was threatening Temne country. However, his dependence on Freetown as a source of supply of arms for use against the French made him accede to Governor Rowe's request to leave Temne country alone in return for maintenance of his supplies. The Governors in Freetown were from their limited territorial base able to influence affairs in the interior in such ways. They sent punitive expeditions against chiefs whose wars interfered with British trade. In 1887 such an expedition against the Yoni was sanctioned after they had killed a number of Creole traders in Senehun, capital of Madam Yoko, who had increased her power by a skilful use of an informal alliance she maintained with Governor Rowe.

Britain changed her policy regarding the extension of control over the hinterland not because of pressure from Creole traders or from the Freetown Government, but because of France. The French by 1890, relentlessly driving Samory south and eastwards, were now dangerously close in terms of British interests to Sierra Leone's hinterland. Should they occupy it, Freetown would be isolated and Freetown was of strategic importance as the only port suitable for coaling British naval vessels on the Coast. But even in this situation, the British would only sanction the making of treaties of exclusive friendship between Britain and the chiefs of the interior. Thus without having to impose a formal administration, France could be kept out. In 1890, therefore, two commissioners, Garrett and Alldridge,[28] were assigned to trek round the country and make treaties with the chiefs by which they would promise not to make treaties with any other European power.

The British were very cautious about making treaties with chiefs with whom the French claimed to have made them. In 1890 when Samory offered to place himself under British Protection, this was refused even though Governor Hay of Sierra Leone was in favour of it, since it would cause difficulties with France, perhaps to the extent of war. As a result in that same year the British and French agreed on the division of their spheres of influence and in fact co-operated in dealing with Samory. This co-operation had a bizarre result for in 1893 the 1st West India Regiment was sent to drive Samory's Sofas out of the British sphere of influence so that the French could deal with them in their own sphere. Ignorant of the British expedition, a French Lieutenant attacked the British forces at Waima, believing them to be Sofas, and paid with his life for his mistake, as did the Inspector-General of the recently created Frontier Force.[29]

The Anglo-French agreement of 1889 left the British with a very small hinterland to her Colony. To maintain peace in the area, part of the Colony police was formed into a new force called the Frontier Police, who were stationed in chiefdoms where the rulers had agreed to accept them. Indeed nearly all of the chiefs visited by Garrett and Alldridge asked to have Frontiers posted in their towns. Governor Hay had given the assurance that the Frontiers were 'forbidden to interfere with their rule'[30] and the chiefs looked on them merely as a force for keeping the peace between them and their rivals. For though they were subject to a British peace-keeping force they had only signed treaties of friendship and were not subject to British jurisdiction.[31]

By the time Britain declared an official Protectorate in 1896, this policy of stationing Frontiers all over the hinterland under British influence had meant the effective establishment of British rule. For though the chiefs had not in fact signed treaties of protection, and the Frontiers were forbidden to interfere with their government, in practice the Frontiers gained a great deal of political power over the chiefs. The declaration of the Protectorate, to which the chiefs for the most part had not consented, merely gave formal recognition to a situation that already existed: Britain was now dominant over the hinterland. The main question for discussion was the nature of the Protectorate. The Creole Secretary for Native Affairs, Parkes, in 1892 had planned a civil administration for a Protectorate in which Creoles would be the District Commissioners but this was turned down by the Colonial Office when it was realised that the proposal involved educated Africans administering 'Protected peoples'.[32] In 1894 Cardew became Governor, and presaged the decline of the political influence of the Creole by insisting on the judicial separation of Protectorate from Colony, and administration of the former by Europeans, not Africans.

Between 1890 and 1896 there had been little opposition to the extension of British influence over the hinterland. Nor was there any open opposition to the proclamation of the Protectorate. However Governor Cardew's decision to raise revenue to pay for the administration of the Protectorate by the imposition of a tax of 10s. on houses with four rooms and of 5s. on those with less led to a severe uprising. The Hut Tax War, as the rising came to be known, was complex in motive and was not limited to a particular ethnic group.[33] In so far as the tax itself was concerned, the chiefs who resisted its payment did so because such a tax appeared to them as payment of rent to the administration for their houses, thus implying that they were no longer their own.[34] It also brought home to them that the

Protectorate Government was not merely to be the stabilising, peace-keeping agency that they had anticipated when agreeing to accept the stationing of Frontiers in their territories. It was a government determined to rule them, even though the majority of them had never signed treaties that alienated their sovereignty to the British. The Hut Tax Wars, apart from the reaction to the tax itself, were above all the result, as Governor Cardew admitted to Chamberlain, of the people's 'desire for independence and for a reversion to the old order of things . . . They are sick of the supremacy of the white man as asserted by the District Commissioners and the Frontier Police.'[35] Loss of authority by the chiefs, in particular the alienation of their judicial powers to the District Commissioners, abuses, often flagrant, by the Frontier Police, the abolition of the internal slave trade, and interference by both missionaries and officials in traditional custom, provoked the Protectorate into a bitter war to regain its independence.

In the South the Mende reaction to the new tax and to the British presence was particularly violent. All that seemed to be connected with British authority was attacked and expatriate missionaries and Africans who wore European clothes, particularly Creoles, were massacred. In the North the Temne, led by Bai Bureh of Kasseh, a small chiefdom on the Lower Scarcies, fought the British for nearly nine months before their leader was captured. The Temne uprising was not marked by the same hostility to manifestations of Western influence as that of the Mende. Only one missionary, the Principal of Fourah Bay College, was killed by Bai Bureh's war-boys, and Bai Bureh appears genuinely to have regretted this act. Nevertheless he and the Temne were fighting a war, not just against particular aspects of the new colonial régime, but to regain their independence. In a brilliant campaign, in which he opposed vastly superior forces from the point of view of weapons, through skilful use of guerilla warfare Bai Bureh gave the British one of the hardest battles they had to fight in their occupation of West Africa.[36]

After the risings of both Temne and Mende had been put down, often with a savagery that matched the worst excesses of the French conquest, in particular the systematic burning of towns and villages, Bai Bureh was given honourable exile. But a large number of participants in the Mende uprising were hanged. Despite strong criticism of Cardew in the report of the Commission of Enquiry conducted by Sir David Chalmers, the tax was retained on the grounds that there was no other source of revenue to pay for the administration and development of the Protectorate.

## 3 *The acquisition of a River Colony*

Of the four British Colonies on the West Coast of Africa, the Gambia
was the one occupied with least enthusiasm despite its long-standing
associations with Britain.[37] The French controlled the natural
hinterland of the British sea-port of Bathurst on the mouth of the
River Gambia which was navigable to ocean-going ships for two
hundred miles. Britain had access only to narrow strips of territory
on either side of the river which in any case had been in a state of
civil war ever since the fifties. The Gambia defied absolutely the
canon that a British colony should pay for its own administration.
The best that could have been hoped for was an exchange with the
French. Indeed in 1866 negotiations, not the first, had been opened
for cession of the Colony to France in exchange for her posts on the
Ivory Coast and later for her posts on the Gabon coast. In 1869
Kennedy, Governor of the British West African Settlements, sent
in a report after a ten-day visit to Bathurst strongly favouring this
exchange. However there was strong opposition from Britain's
African subjects of Bathurst, who in a 500-strong petition protested
against 'a course to which from their knowledge of French institutions in the Senegal they were exceedingly adverse'.[38] Tamanu
Bojang, King of neighbouring Kombo, wrote to Queen Victoria:
'Your Majesty is aware that it was war that compelled me to give
up part of my territory to your people, I now beg, that should you
desire to transfer your settlements to another person, I would rather
you return my territory back to me as an act of friendship.'[39]
Gambians were given backing in Britain by commercial interests
and the Royal Colonial Institute. However, within the Inner
Councils of Government, Lord Carnarvon was anxious to effect a
change if good terms could be gained from the French. Support for
retaining the Gambia prevailed and in 1873 a junior minister stated
that 'no abandonment of territory would ... be permitted by
Parliament, or sanctioned by public opinion'. Nevertheless, Carnarvon went ahead with his proposal and upon the outbreak of war
amongst the inhabitants up-river in 1875 told the Foreign Office
that this 'grave complication affords an additional reason for pushing
forward without unnecessary delay the negotiations with France'.[40]
The matter ended in 1876 when the French withdrew their offer to
cede all their territory on the Ivory Coast, but not before the House
of Lords had shown definite hostility to the proposed exchange.

Britain was stuck with Bathurst, and the small area of land around
it, which together formed the Colony. But she did nothing about

acquiring a hinterland that would ensure that it could pay for itself. Apart from the inbuilt reluctance of the British Government to extend its responsibilities anywhere in Africa until Chamberlain became Colonial Secretary, extension of British influence along the Gambia would require military intervention. Like Senegal, the Gambia was in the throes of war between the supporters of militant Islam and the traditional rulers who refused to become Muslim. The wars along the Gambia River were known as the Soninke-Marabout wars. They began in the 1850's and had as one of their main battle-fields the Kombo kingdom, which as we have seen was immediately adjacent to the British Colony at Bathurst. The Soninke were the traditional ruling group of the area. Most of them practised traditional religion but when they happened to be believers their practice of of Islam was lax by the standards being set by the reformers, known as the Marabouts. No one Marabout, however, was able to impose his will on all the chiefdoms of the river and unite them into a new state like those of the Western Sudan which had proved such an obstacle to European penetration. However, Fode Kabba of Kombo, who inherited the authority of one of the early Marabout leaders, Ma Ba, after the latter's defeat by the King of Saloum in a war started after he had proclaimed himself the Mahdi, came very near to doing so in the forty years that he was active on the river. The Soninke-Marabout wars were bound to involve the British for the fighting in Kombo threatened the security of Bathurst, and the British Governors had frequently to intervene, though their policy was one of strict neutrality. Governor D'Arcy (1859–66) became so involved in punitive expeditions to ensure the security of the Colony that he strongly advocated a Protectorate over the warring peoples. Indeed he had received petitions and requests from Soninke and Marabouts alike for such a course. But these were dismissed after receiving only brief attention from the British Government, and instead the policy of exchange was pursued with France.

In 1880 the Administrator of the Gambia, Gouldsbury, was sent by Governor Rowe to obtain information concerning the commercial potential of the river and to open friendly relations with chiefs. After a most difficult journey Gouldsbury produced a pessimistic report in which he maintained that it would be too costly to promote trade on the river since the major portion of its profitable hinterland was occupied by the French. 'I fear the return would not be much more substantial than that of the scheme known as the South Sea Bubble' was his acid comment.[41]

Until 1887 the French acknowledged Britain as having a sphere of influence over the banks of the Gambia. But in that year France occupied some towns on the river itself in the course of assisting the King of Sine Saloum, who was under their hegemony, to drive off an attack by the Marabout Said Matti, son of Ma Ba. The arrival of the French on the river itself prompted reactions both in Bathurst and Westminster: Sir Samuel Rowe, up from Sierra Leone, made urgent treaties with chiefs along the river. These were agreed to with relief by many chiefs, who saw British protection as the only possible opening for long-term peace and as the surest way of securing themselves from attacks by Marabouts, since the latter were afraid to attack British protected chiefs. Even Marabouts signed for they were now fighting among themselves. Britain asked France to withdraw from the river, and this was negotiated in the general Anglo-French boundary agreements of 1889. Its boundaries were to be 'delimited by arcs of circles centred upon significant points along the river'.[42]

It was not until 1891, however, that Britain set about effective occupation of the strip of land rarely more than fourteen miles wide that straddled the River Gambia for two hundred miles inland. By this time the area had suffered nearly forty years of war. Many Soninke chiefdoms had disappeared. There was no unity among the Marabouts, who were competing with each other for supremacy. To increase the misery of the area, Fula from the Futa Jallon and Bondou had raided it in the eighties. The Fula from Bondou were under French protection, and their chief Bakari Sardu had received French education and held the Legion of Honour.[43] But French protection did not prevent him raiding unoccupied territory.

When the British finally occupied the river, only two Marabouts were in a position to offer serious resistance to the British: Fode Kabba and Fode Silla. In the context of the European Conquest of West Africa as a whole, the British task was easy. After stubborn resistance Fode Silla was defeated in 1894. Fode Kabba, one of the first Marabouts to raise the cry of *Jihad* in the fifties, continued resistance right up to 1900, slipping in and out of French territory to harass the British.

The people of the Gambia, like Yorubaland, for the most part welcomed the respite Britain gave her from over forty years of civil war, during which a great number of the Soninke chiefdoms had been completely destroyed, without being replaced by new political institutions. Few Marabouts had been able to establish their authority for sufficiently long to construct a system of government based on Muslim law in order to replace institutions they had overthrown in the name of Islam. The result was that in many parts of the Gambia the British administration found a political vacuum with few established institutions on which they could build.

## 4 Conclusion

Superior weapons, a skilful manipulation of hostilities between African states or the internal divisions within them, enabled the Europeans to conquer West Africa with small forces and with comparative ease. For the most part Africans were cut off from sources of supply of modern European weapons and even had they been available lacked instructors to teach them how to use them. Too often they met the invaders with the same military tactics they used against each other. Cavalry charges, hails of arrows or spears, and hand-to-hand fighting were no use against repeater rifles and Maxim guns. The great mud walls that would withstand a six-month siege by an African army crumbled before the European artillery. Too little use was made by Africans of their superior knowledge of the terrain on which they were fighting. Only few leaders like Bai Bureh and Samory knew that the only way to deal with superior forces was to use guerilla tactics. The hardest to conquer were often not the great states with regular armies, but people like those of the southern Ivory Coast and the Eastern States of Nigeria where invasion was resisted village by village.

But given the lack of unity in West Africa at the time, and the technological inferiority of the African armies, the Africans defended their independence with much greater vigour than has often been allowed. True some welcomed the European, but the general picture was of a people who fiercely resisted the invader with the few means at their disposal.

# Notes

1 For Ashanti see: D. Kimble, *A Political History of Ghana: 1850–1928*, London, 1963; W. Tordoff, *Ashanti Under the Prempehs: 1888–1935*, London, 1965; W. W. Claridge, *A History of the Gold Coast and Ashanti*, 2 vols., London, 1915, reprinted 1964; C. C. Reindorf, *The History of Gold Coast and Asante*, Basel, Switzerland, 1895; and I. Wilks, 'Ashanti Government in the 19th Century', unpublished paper.

2 Wilks, 'Ashanti Government in the 19th Century', pp. 19–32.

3 Claridge, *Gold Coast and Ashanti*, I, p. 504.

4 Reindorf, *Gold Coast and Asante*, p. 163.

5 Claridge, *Gold Coast and Ashanti*, I, pp. 507–8.

6 *Ibid.*, p. 502.

7 An Officer, *Jottings en route to Coomassie*, Accra, 1964, p. 70.

8 Kimble, *Ghana*, p. 276.

9 *Ibid.*, p. 275.

10 *Jottings en route to Coomassie*, p. 70.

11 F. Agbodeka, 'The Fanti Confederacy, 1865–9', *Transactions of the Historical Society of Ghana*, Vol. VII, 1964, p. 88.

12 J. A. B. Horton, *West African Countries and Peoples*, London, 1868.

13 J. A. Webster and A. A. Boahen, *The Growth of African Civilization: The Revolutionary Years. West Africa since 1800*, London, 1967, p. 222.

14 Claridge, *Gold Coast and Ashanti*, I, p. 617.

15 Kimble, *Ghana*, p. 277.

16 Tordoff, *Ashanti Under the Prempehs*, pp. 43–4.

17 Kimble, *Ghana*, p. 282.

18 *Ibid.*, p. 292.

19 William Tordoff, 'A Note on the Relations between Samory and King Prempeh I of Ashanti', *Ghana Notes and Queries*, 3, September 1961, p. 7.

20 William Tordoff, 'Brandford Griffiths' Offer of British Protection to Ashanti (1891)', *Trans. Hist. Soc. Ghana*, VI, 1962, p. 36.

21 Jack Goody, 'Introduction', *Ashanti and the Northwest*, Research Review, Supplement No. I—Ashanti Research Project, Legon: Institute of African Studies, 1965, pp. 65–78.

22 John Peterson, 'The Enlightenment and the Foundation of Freetown', unpublished paper delivered at the Institute of African Studies, Fourah Bay College, 9th November, 1966.

23 Fyfe, *Sierra Leone*, p. 229, and *A Short History of Sierra Leone*, p. 71.

24 Fyfe, *Short History of Sierra Leone*, p. 97.

25 Fyfe, *Sierra Leone*, p. 312.

26 *Ibid.*, pp. 449–50.

27 *Ibid.*, p. 451.

28 Alldridge wrote an account of his treaty-making: T. J. Alldridge, *The Sherbro and its Hinterland*, London, 1901.

29 For accounts of this odd drama of the conquest see: Yves Person, 'L'aventure de Porèkeré et le drame de Waima', *Cahiers d'Études*

*Africaines*, 11, 18, 1965, pp. 248–316; P. Savin d'Orford, 'New Light on the Origin of the Waima Affair', *Sierra Leone Studies*, New Series, No. 11, Dec. 1958, pp. 128–35; and M. C. F. Easmon, 'A Note on the Waima Incident', *Sierra Leone Studies*, New Series, No. 18, Jan. 1966, pp. 59–61.
30 Fyfe, *Sierra Leone*, p. 487.
31 *Ibid.*, p. 488.
32 *Ibid.*, pp. 516–17.
33 See J. D. Hargreaves, 'The Establishment of the Sierra Leone Protectorate and the Insurrection of 1898', *Cambridge Historical Journal*, XII, 1, 1956, pp. 56–80.
34 Fyfe, *A Short History of Sierra Leone*, p. 139.
35 PRO/CO/267/438, Cardew to Chamberlain, 28 May 1898. That the chiefs were anxious to regain their independence was confirmed by the District Commissioners of Karene and Ronietta. See Sierra Leone Archives/CMP 102 Enc. 98, D.C. (Karene) to Col. Sec., 10 Aug. 1898, and SLA/CMP 102 Enc. 98, D.C. (Ronietta) to Col. Sec., 4 Aug. 1898.
36 For a detailed account of Bai Bureh's war see Michael Crowder and LaRay Denzer, 'Bai Bureh and the 1898 Sierra Leone Hut Tax War', in Robert I. Rotberg and Ali A. Mazrui, ed., *The Tradition of Protest in Tropical Africa* (forthcoming).
37 For a good summary of the British presence in Gambia since the reign of Henry VIII, see Barry N. Floyd, 'Gambia: a Case Study of the Role of Historical Accident in Political Geography', *Bull. of the Sierra Leone Geog. Ass.*, No. 10, 1966.
38 J. M. Gray, *History of the Gambia*, London, 1940, p. 437.
39 *Ibid.*, pp. 437–8.
40 *Ibid.*, p. 441.
41 *Ibid.*, p. 459.
42 Floyd, 'Gambia: a Case Study of the Role of Historical Accident in Political Geography'.
43 Gray, *History of the Gambia*, p. 447.

M

*Part III*
The establishment of colonial rule

# 1 Administration in theory and practice

## 1 The problems of colonial administration

Little time was left to colonial conquistadors of West Africa to consider the advantages and disadvantages of the systems of administration they decided to impose on the peoples whose lands they had occupied. In the first place they were largely ignorant of the nature of the societies they were about to govern; in the second place they were usually preoccupied with the next stage of the conquest. Even where they did have time to ponder the merits of a particular system of administration, there was little chance that they would remain in a specific area long enough to see it put into practice.

The administrations imposed by the occupying powers were necessarily *ad hoc* and greatly influenced by the personality of the man imposing them and the circumstances under which a particular area was occupied—by conquest or treaty. More important still was the character of the society to be governed: different techniques had to be employed to govern the large centralised state, the small independent village and the desert nomad tribe. So by 1906, with the Soko Caliphate finally subjugated, and most of the rest of West Africa under European rule, there was to be found a bewildering variety of administrations. Such heterogeneity naturally offended the Cartesian French, and even upset the tidy mind of the Empirical Briton. There was, furthermore, growing concern among the European colonial powers over the whole question of colonial responsibility: how could African peoples be governed so that both they and the colonial power would benefit from it? It must not be forgotten that during this period a searchlight was turned on the African colonies because of the scandals in King Leopold's Congo and there was increasing concern with the 'Native Question'. Thus E. D. Morel, one of Leopold's most ardent critics, also visited Nigeria in 1912[1] to see how that Colony was administered, and he was received by the colonial authorities as though he were a General conducting an annual inspection.

During the early years of colonial rule there was considerable debate as to what type of colonial rule was desirable for Tropical Africa. This debate became most involved in France and has been summarised in a number of useful studies.[2] The British debate was more restricted in character, and somewhat one-sided, since nearly all agreed that indirect rule, or the government of Africans through their own institutions, was desirable. The 'Native Question' was never publicly debated as it was in France and Germany, and the best statement of the underlying philosophy of the system of government adopted by Britain as its guideline for the administration of African peoples was made by Lord Lugard in his *Dual Mandate in Tropical Africa*.[3]

## 2 Trends in colonial policy

From these debates, and from the practical experiences of the administrators on the spot, there emerged three dominant trends in colonial policy in West Africa which were to be characteristic of the period of colonial rule from 1918–39. The first major trend in colonial policy as practised in West Africa was that of *assimilation* or that body of colonial theory which advocated identity between the colony and the mother country, though the nature of this identity varied from one exposition to another. The second was that of *indirect rule*, or that body of theory which held that there could be no identity between such divergent cultures as those of Europe and Africa and that as a consequence the metropolitan power should rule its African subjects through their own institutions, since these were clearly the ones best suited to them. The third body of theory was one that resulted from dilemma. It could not accept assimilation as a realistic policy for the administration of peoples as culturally different as the African from the European; nor did it consider traditional institutions a suitable basis for the administration of colonies which were to be exploited to the mutual benefit of the indigenous inhabitant and the metropolitan power. Thus a *paterna-*

*listic* approach to administration was advocated whereby indigenous society would be re-organised by the metropolitan power, so that the exploitative aims of colonialism could be achieved to the advantage of both coloniser and colonised. This policy is usually described as association, but because association is so closely linked with French colonial rule, it is best described as paternalism.[4] This term usefully describes German administration in Togo and British administration of those African societies which did not have chiefs, or were very small in size.

Over and above these three trends there was one system of administration advocated for the government of African peoples that arose from the profound reluctance of two of the colonial powers to involve themselves in colonial enterprise at all: Company Rule. Both Britain and Germany used the formula of the Chartered Company for the government of large parts of the African empire. As far as West Africa was concerned this solution was used only in Nigeria, and there it was abandoned in 1899.[5] The Charter Company is an interesting device, for it showed clearly the underlying economic motive for the occupation of Africa and the desirability of administering African colonies, at least from the European point of view, so that they would be commercially viable.

## 3 Assimilation

Assimilation theories fell into two main groups: those which advocated personal assimilation of the administered peoples; and those which, though they discarded personal assimilation as unrealistic, advocated administrative, political or economic identity between the mother country and the colony.

Theories of personal assimilation asserted that all men were equal irrespective of their racial origin or cultural background, there being no differences between men that education could not eliminate. Thus the illiterate African peasant was just as worthy of citizenship as the illiterate French peasant. It followed then that the African colonial subject could be treated as a Frenchmen with all his rights and duties.

The main conflict between the various theories of personal assimilation that were put forward by writers on colonial administration occurred between those who believed in the *actual* equality of all men here and now, and those who believed in the *potential* equality of all men. So, we find both French and Portuguese, overwhelmed in practice by the economic and cultural obstacles to a successful application of a whole-hearted policy of personal assimilation, and yet reluctant to abandon the universalist approach to human society that is part of their heritage, turning to what can best be described as a *gradualist* or *selective* assimilation policy. Thus, they argued that all men could be equal given the right opportunities, but were *not* equal here and now. Consequently, the African had to prove himself worthy of assimilation by demonstrating to the authorities that he had the attributes of citizenship, attributes which were determined by the colonial power. France in her early assimilationist experiment in Senegal practised a policy of *immediate assimilation* which she then abandoned, on taking control of the Senegalese hinterland, for a *selective assimilation* policy.[6] Similarly, Britain, when she occupied the Protectorate of Sierra Leone, abandoned her experiment in the assimilation of the re-captive slaves settled in the Colony.

Non-personal theories of assimilation fell into three main groups. The first concerned the administrative identity between the colonies and the mother country. For administrative purposes no distinction was made between the metropolis and the colonies: Algeria and the Antilles could therefore be considered Overseas Departments, or the colonies could be collectively described as *France Outre-Mer*. Administrative assimilation was used to describe anything from the high degree of centralisation of the administration of the French empire on Paris to the setting up of French-style local government institutions in the colonies.[7]

The second form of non-personal assimilation advocated was that of political assimilation of the overseas territories with the Metropolis. The colonies should send representatives to the Metropolitan political institutions of France after the war, but never on the basis of parity of representation in proportion to the population with the Mother Country.

The last category of non-personal assimilation was that which advocated the integration of the economies of the overseas territories with that of the Metropolis.

## 4 Indirect rule

Both with regard to the status of the individual African and with regard to the relationship of the colony to the Metropolitan power, Indirect Rule was the antithesis of assimilation. Indirect rule was inspired by the belief that the European and the African were culturally distinct though not necessarily unequal, and that the institutions of government most suited to the latter were those which he had devised for himself. Therefore, the European colonial powers should govern their African subjects through their own political institutions. Here it is very necessary to emphasise that indirect rule, at least in theory, did not mean government of African peoples through their chiefs. In practice indirect rule laid heavy emphasis on the role of the chief in the government of African peoples, even for those peoples who traditionally did not have political as distinct from religious leaders.

The use of indigenous political institutions for the purposes of local government was contingent on certain modifications to these institutions. These modifications fell into two categories: modifications of aspects of traditional government that were repugnant to European ideas of what constituted good government; and modifications that were designed to ensure the achievement of the main purpose of colonial rule, the exploitation of the colonised country. Examples of the former would be the abolition of human sacrifice or the abandonment of certain methods of treating criminals. Examples of the latter would be the introduction of taxes, designed to stimulate production of cash crops for export.

Indirect Rule as conceived by Lord Lugard was to be a dynamic system of local government.[8] The indigenous political institutions, under the guidance of the resident European political officer, would be continually developing into more efficient units of administration, responding to and adapting themselves to the new situations created by colonial rule. However, many of Lugard's successors followed a policy of minimal interference in the process of local government, preferring to let the traditional political institutions develop along their own lines rather than along lines laid down or suggested by the European administrator. In its extreme forms such a policy came close to a Protectorate or 'Native States' policy, whilst that of Lugard, in its extreme forms, came close to Paternalism. Lugard's policy can be characterised as *Interventionist* Indirect Rule, that of his successors, *Non-interventionist Rule*.[9]

## 5 Paternalism

Critics of policies of Assimilation fell into two main groups; those who argued that such a policy was from both a practical and an economic point of view impossible of application, and those who claimed that the African was unassimilable.

To take the first set of criticisms. A full-scale policy of assimilation implied that those assimilated would have access to the same rights as those by whom they were assimilated, *i.e.* social services, etc. This was economically impossible for either of the would-be assimilationist countries, France or Portugal, to undertake. Furthermore, from a purely practical point of view how did one assimilate desert nomads or pygmy hunters? It was argued that if assimilation were to be followed at all, then it would have to be on a limited scale. Therefore a separate policy would have to be devised for those not being immediately assimilated. Furthermore, a full-scale policy of assimilation would mean that both France and Portugal would be politically dominated by the peoples they were assimilating, since in both cases the colonial population was greater than that of the metropolis.

The second major corpus of criticism directed against personal assimilation involved the belief that Africans were racially distinct from Europeans; some argued this in terms of biology, asserting that the African was irremediably inferior and therefore could not be assimilated. Most of those who talked in terms of culture insisted that even though the African *qua* human being was equal to the European he was culturally separate and could not be assimilated to an alien culture.

Whatever the approach of the critics of assimilation, there remained the problem of how to administer the mass of non-assimilated colonial subjects. In a number of cases, a policy of indirect rule was advocated. But the idea of ruling through indigenous institutions raised a number of objections, particularly among the French. Arguments against the use of traditional institutions ranged from those who believed that Africans had not really succeeded in evolving political institutions worth calling such, to those who believed that to use these institutions without radical reorganisation would present serious difficulties for the colonial administration. Firstly there was such a great variety of these institutions, particularly with respect to the extent of territory they governed. Secondly these institutions were clearly not adapted to the functions they would have to fulfil in the colonial system whose express object was the exploitation of the territory for the mutual benefit of its inhabitants and the mother country. It was argued that the exploitation of the resources of these colonies by the metropolis would teach the indigenous inhabitants the moral obligation to work and, apart from this benefit, he would be made aware of new wants, which he could satisfy with the money he earned from his labour. The achievement of this ideal did not seem to lie through the use of seemingly archaic Muslim administrations or councils of elders with authority over as few as five hundred people. The best solution to this problem would of course have been direct administration, but this was impossible, for to employ sufficient Frenchmen to institute such a system of administration would have been prohibitively expensive, and there were not enough Europeanised Africans to take their place. Therefore African society would have to be radically reorganised to meet the exploitative requirements of the colonial authorities, and for want of Frenchmen or educated Africans, traditional chiefs would be used in a new role, as agents of the administration, substitutes for the above. This was the system of administration that has been called *Association*, but which is here described as *Paternalism*.

Before examining the administrations of France and Britain in practice, it is suggested that British administration was during the period under study predominantly one of indirect rule, undecided as between interventionist and non-interventionist systems. However, where African society did not lend itself well to application of this policy, there was a tendency to adopt a policy of paternalism very similar to that of the French. At no stage in this period did Britain pursue a policy of assimilation though her rule had strong assimilationist features in the form of missionary education and the legal systems of the colonies as distinct from the protectorates. These were, however, both legacies of the nineteenth century. French administration in this period was paternalist, leavened with a slight application of a selective assimilation policy. Exceptions to this generalisation were Senegal, where the full-scale policy of personal assimilation that had been introduced in the *Quatre Communes* was maintained; and the case of certain powerful chiefs, where France was obliged to administer their populations by means of indirect rule of the Lugardian interventionist type. France, like Britain in her original conquest of West Africa, frequently was forced as a matter of immediate expediency to use the political institutions of the people she conquered as the means to administering them.[10] The difference between France and Britain in colonial administration seems to be that, where Britain gloried in this expedient, and erected it into a whole philosophy of colonial government, France abandoned it wherever she could. Germany was unequivocally paternalist in Togo, until her expulsion in 1914. It was described as her model colony, in which she coupled economic exploitation with social welfare on a scale not achieved in any other West African colony in the period in which she ruled it.

Neither Britain nor France adopted any one of these 'native policies' as her *official* policy nor did their Governors or administrators establish any one policy as paramount. The complexity of Africa defied the application of any single system of administration, but in so far as the colonial period proper is concerned France had a dominant tendency towards Assimilation, Britain towards Indirect Rule. The virtues of different native policies, however, continued to be the subject of debate and study until the Second World War, when both countries had to change their pre-occupation with the problems of 'Native Administration', which were essentially those of local government, to the demands of African nationalists for participation in the running of the central administration of their colony-countries.

# Notes

1 His largely favourable account is given in E. D. Morel, *Nigeria: Its Peoples and Problems*, London, 1911.
2 See for instance: Raymond F. Betts, *Assimilation and Association in French Colonial Theory 1890–1914*, New York, 1961; Hubert Deschamps, *Méthodes et doctrines coloniales de la France*, Paris, 1953; M. D. Lewis, 'The Assimilation Theory in French Colonial Policy', *Comparative Studies in Society and History*, IV, 2, January 1962, pp. 129–53.
3 Lord Lugard, *The Dual Mandate in British Tropical Africa*, Edinburgh, 1922. See also his *Political Memoranda*, Lagos, 1918.
4 See Thomas Hodgkin and Ruth Schachter, 'French-speaking West Africa in Transition', *International Conciliation*, No. 528, May 1960, p. 391.
5 For a good study of it see Flint, *Goldie*.
6 See Michael Crowder, *Senegal—A Study of French Assimilation Policy* (Revised Edition), London, 1967.
7 See Lewis, 'The Assimilation Theory'.
8 In this section I have relied heavily on the various works of Margery Perham on colonial administration in Nigeria and on the important paper by Mary Bull in *Essays in Imperial Government*, ed. Kenneth Robinson, Frederick Madden, Oxford, 1963, entitled 'Indirect Rule in Northern Nigeria: 1906–1911'.
9 For the terms 'Interventionist' and 'Non-interventionist', I am indebted to a discussion with Professor Robert Griffeth.
10 See Martin Klein, 'Chiefship in Sine-Saloum (Senegal), 1887–1914', paper presented to the annual meeting of the African Studies Association, October 22, 1964, Chicago.

# 2 The administration of French West Africa

## 1 The establishment of the Government-General

After a tour of French West Africa in 1918 and 1919, Henri Cosnier wrote:

'The most obvious characteristic of our colonial administration is the instability at every stage of both men and matters. . . . In the Colonies lieutenant-governors succeed each other with a disconcerting rapidity, each one bringing his own ideas and his methods of administration and colonisation . . . each Commandant de Cercle has his own policy, his chiefs, his projects for roads and agricultural development. This all passes before the eyes of the native like a kaleidoscope of which each new image is accompanied by additional burdens and tribulations.'[1]

Severe as they were, these criticisms came not from the pen of an embittered anti-colonialist but one who had for long been a colonial civil servant, later a deputy, and was at the time of writing a Senator and member of the Higher Council for Agriculture. They formed part of a letter to the President of the French Republic enclosing a detailed report on the agricultural and commercial potential of West Africa in which he severely criticised the lack of economic development that had taken place in French West Africa, pointing out that in 1913, the year before the outbreak of World War I, of France's imports of 3,358 million francs, only 288 came from the colonies.[2] He further accused French traders of being 'preoccupied with getting, by any means, the maximum immediate

benefits and of being disinterested in the organisation of production'.[3] And added 'one is a little ashamed when one visits
the British and German colonies, of our inferiority vis-à-vis our
neighbours'.[4]

The first two decades of French administration of West Africa
had far from realised the great hopes of its economic potential
expressed by the advocates of colonial expansion: the explorers, the
colonial visionary Jules Ferry, or pressure groups such as *le Comité
de l'Afrique française* and *l'Union Coloniale Française* which formed
what became known as *le Parti Colonial*.[5] The achievements of the
French administration did not justify the near panegyrics of the
period that were written not only by many contemporaries but
even more recent chroniclers of 'l'œuvre française en Afrique
noire'.

Before examining the achievements and failures of the French
administration in West Africa it may be appropriate to suggest the
main causes to which the state of affairs described by Cosnier can be
attributed. Throughout the years before he wrote his report the
administration was harassed by the need to continue the work of
'pacification'. As we have already seen, parts of Ivory Coast, Niger,
Sudan, and Mauretania were not conquered until as late as 1914.
And the Great World War gave an opportunity for revolt to many
peoples only recently subjugated. There seems never to have been
in the early years of colonial rule a sense of strong central direction
in the administration of the eight colonies, so that actual formulation
of policy lay with the *Commandant de cercle* rather than the Lieutenant-
Governors and the Governor-General who were meant to be
responsible for it. Whilst there was no generally accepted 'native
policy', partly because of the lack of ability of the central powers to
impose their wills effectively on their subordinates and partly because
of the failure of any one of the advocates of assimilation, association
(paternalism) or indirect rule, to make his particular policy prevail,
there nevertheless emerged a general approach to the government of
the peoples of West Africa: the replacement of the traditional chiefs
by a new group who it was felt would be loyal to the French; and
the break-up of traditional political units into smaller units, or the
amalgamation of disparate smaller units into large groups so that
there was some uniformity in the political units to be administered. This led to considerable social dislocation and certainly
did not create the stable society that alone could produce the
goods that could render France's 'œuvre civilisatrice' a profitable
one.

The economic development of the country, apart from the intensive capital programme of the first decade, lacked foresight. The external capital necessary to stimulate production on the scale anticipated by the advocates of colonial rule was forthcoming neither from the administration nor from the commercial houses, whose main aim seems to have been the maximum return for the least input, even if this would reduce long-run profits by exhausting the resources on which these depended. What capital was raised was done so at the expense of the new African taxpayer who was also subjected to compulsory labour for the administration, obligatory cultivation of crops, and in certain instances was forced to work on European concessions.

Any plans for improvement of the colony which the administrator may have had, either economic or social, were severely hampered by the lack of capital funds. Africa itself was not sufficiently developed to provide such funds; without them it could not develop. And since the Metropole was not forthcoming, it necessarily stagnated. Finally, particularly comparing French West Africa with Nigeria or Ghana, one has to remember its vast area, much of which, though inhabited, often densely as in the case of Upper Volta, offered no known sources of development or exploitation.

Until 1895 the administration of the territories being so rapidly acquired by France in West Africa was *ad hoc* and haphazard. Before 1891 the whole of French expansion theoretically depended on Senegal. But the military administration of Archinard in the Sudan was in practice run independently of St. Louis. The colonies of Guinea, Ivory Coast and the Rivières du Sud, jointly administered by Senegal, were given autonomy between 1891 and 1893. There were a number of pressing reasons why the tendency to separate development should be arrested. It was clear that all the colonies would form one contiguous block once the penetration of the Sudan was complete. The hinterland colonies would have to use the coastal colonies as the outlets for their exports. Co-operation between coastal and hinterland colonies was therefore essential. The rivalry between different colonies in what was in effect to be one land mass of French colonial property led the Ministry of Colonies, created in 1894, to see that it could exercise greater control over them by bringing them into a group under the authority of a representative of the Republic on the spot directing a Government-General of the French West African colonies.

The military in each colony were undertaking campaigns without sanction from Paris, and Governors of neighbouring territories squabbled with each other. The Governor of Senegal attacked villages in the Fouta Djallon which came under the Governor of Guinea's sphere of influence; and the Governor of Sudan failed to send any help to Colonel Monteil in his expedition against Samory's forces in the Kong region, complaining that he had not been consulted.[6] Chautemps, Minister of Colonies, told the Senate that the Government-General was, among other things, designed to put an end to an anarchic situation whereby 'the violations of frontiers which sometimes happen in Europe never give occasion for diplomatic correspondence as complicated and impassioned as those that are produced in these circumstances between the governors of neighbouring colonies'.[7]

The separatist tendency of preceding years was nominally brought to an end by the establishment of a loose federation in which the Governor-General and Commander-in-Chief administered Senegal directly, and represented the Republic in Sudan, Guinea and Ivory Coast. Dahomey was left out of this federation, over which the Governor-General had little power other than 'the high political and military direction'.[8] However, Sudan was made directly responsible to the Governor-General, Chaudié, but under the energetic and independent leadership of Colonel de Trentinian it remained effectively independent. As a consequence it was dismembered in 1899 and apportioned to the coastal colonies including Dahomey, which was brought into the federation. The Governor-General laid down firmly with his Lieutenant-Governors that in future any military initiative within the Federation must emanate from him.

Though the authority of the Governor-General was strengthened by this new decree he still lacked the key to federal power: financial and legislative control over the colonies he was meant to govern. Senegal alone felt his authority since he was also its Governor. Between 1902 and 1904 his position was strengthened by decrees which gave him greater control over the local administrative services and made the Governor-Generalship more than a mere appendage of the Governorship of Senegal. The seat of the Government-General was transferred from St. Louis to Dakar, and a separate Lieutenant-Governor was left in charge of Senegal at St. Louis. The Governor-General also had direct control of those parts of Sudan that had not been allocated to the coastal colonies. The reconstructed federation consisted of five colonies, Senegal, Haut-Senegal et Niger, Guinea, Ivory Coast and Dahomey together with

N

the Civil Territory of Mauretania.* The Governor-General was given greatly increased powers. He had the sole right of communication with the Minister of Colonies, which meant that the Lieutenant-Governors in theory could take no major initiative without passing through his office. The entire civil service of the federation was nominated by him with the exception of the Lieutenant-Governors, the Secretaries-General of Governments, magistrates and the directors of local services, who were appointed by Paris. He had direct control of four vital technical services: Agriculture, Posts and Telegraphs, Public Works and Sanitary Services, which of course included the Medical services. Most important of all he controlled customs. He thus had in his hands the necessary powers to construct a strong federation where common policies on roads, all forms of inter-territorial communications, agriculture and medical services could be initiated by him. To enforce his authority he had a Council of Government which consisted of the Army Commander, Naval Commander, the Secretary-General of the Government-General and the four Lieutenant-Governors of the colonies, his representative in Mauretania and the chiefs of the four federal technical services. On this council the only elected representative who sat by right was the President of the Conseil-Général of Senegal. Another elected member of this Council was designated by the Lieutenant-Governor

* The French West African Federation was reorganised on several occasions after its foundation in 1895, thus:

CONSTITUENT TERRITORIES OF FRENCH WEST AFRICA, 1895–1958

1895   Senegal, Sudan, Guinea, Ivory Coast (Dahomey not included).

1899   Senegal and Upper-Senegal-Niger, Guinea, Ivory Coast, Dahomey, and Military Territories (Dahomey included). Sudan dismembered, the largest part going to Senegal which administered it as Haut-Senegal-Niger, small parts going to Guinea, Ivory Coast and Dahomey which absorbed them into their own colony).

1902   Senegal, Senegambie-Niger, Guinea, Ivory Coast, Dahomey and Military Territories (Senegambie-Niger established as a colony from part of Senegal and Upper-Senegal and Niger).

1904   Senegal, Sudan, Guinea, Ivory Coast, Dahomey plus the Civil Territory of Mauretania and the Military Territories of the Chad-Niger region (Sudan reconstituted roughly as it was in 1895).

1920   Upper Volta created from parts of Niger, Sudan and Ivory Coast. Includes the Mossi area.

1932   Upper Volta dismembered and shared between her three neighbours.

1947   Upper Volta recreated.

of Senegal. These two could be either African or European. African representation was secured by nomination of one of the notables on the administrative council of the colonies, but since these were nominated by the Lieutenant-Governors in the first instance they did not have much independence of view.

The Council of Government had a deliberative role only and did not legislate for the Federation. Legislation was usually made by decree of the Minister of Colonies, promulgated by the Governor-General. However, if it wished to, the Chamber of Deputies could legislate for French West Africa. The only way in which the colonies could circumvent the powers of the Governor-General was through the Superior Council of Colonies in Paris to which each colony sent a delegate. Most important of all the Deputy of Senegal was on this Council, but if he had protests to make, he could reach a wider audience through the Chamber. The potential nuisance value of the Deputy for the Four Communes of Senegal was considerable and it was for this reason that the administration took such pains to cultivate the good will of Blaise Diagne (Deputy 1914–34) and his successor Galandou Diouf (1934–40).

The chief weapon of control possessed by the Governor-General over the colonies was the creation of an independent budget which would draw money from the colonies and re-distribute it. And this was in fact the key to the new status of the Governor-General. He was seen primarily as the agent for the rational development of the group of colonies. Political questions, in so far as they did not affect the group, were left for the most part to the individual colonies. But the problem of exploiting their resources lay in his hands.[9] Thus Governor-General William Ponty in his seven-year régime (1908–15) devoted himself almost entirely to economic development.[10] The increased power of the Government-General can be measured by comparing the Federal budget of 17,148,000 francs in 1908 with that of only 4,584,000 francs for Senegal, which in 1895, as the richest of the colonies, had provided from its own budget for the upkeep of the new Government-General.[11] The Governor-General was also the only authority in the Federation permitted to raise public loans, and between 1903 and 1908 Governor-General Roume raised three loans totalling over 140 million francs, primarily devoted to public works such as railways and ports.[12] Justice was in the last resort a federal matter. The army, too, was organised at the federal level, and military operations such as those conducted in Ivory Coast and Mauretania had to be sanctioned by the Governor-General.

## 2 *The Government-General and the Colonies after 1904*

From as early as 1904, the Government-General of French West Africa became a strong centralising force, and to understand both the anger expressed by French-speaking Africans at its dismemberment in 1956 by the *Loi Cadre*, and the strong links maintained between the French-speaking states of West Africa today, we must appreciate that for over fifty years this vast area was shaped by Dakar rather than by the governments of the colonies themselves. Administrators, those who, as we shall see, made the most direct impact on the African, were not attached to individual territories, but could be, and were, moved between the component parts of the federation. This was in strong contrast to the Nigerian Federation, where administrators by and large remained within the group of provinces to which they were initially appointed. Under the system of *rouage* introduced by Governor-General Carde in 1924 to prevent corruption, no administrative official could serve two consecutive tours in the same colony.[13]

Between 1895 and 1945 the power of the Governor-General vis-à-vis his Lieutenant-Governors increased dramatically. Indeed Governor-General Brévié, feeling that too much of the internal affairs of the constituent colonies came under Dakar's scrutiny, tried to decentralise his administration. But as Lord Hailey remarked, 'the five years of M. Brévié's term as Governor-General were not sufficient to provide evidence of any considerable reaction against the tradition of centralisation'.[14] In 1937, Brévié's successor again tried to initiate a policy which would ensure 'the beginnings of broad administrative deconcentration generating fruitful initiatives and increased responsibilities. It is vital that the heads of the colonies govern in their territories.'[15] Accordingly Lieutenant-Governors were redesignated Governors. Even so, real power still lay with the Governor-General, controlling as he did the main source of revenue for the federation, and acting as the sole channel for communication with Paris. Attempts at decentralisation were finally baulked by the advent of the Vichy Government which confided almost total political control of French West Africa to Governor-General Boisson.

Nevertheless in the early days the Governor-General, arrayed as he was with a vast body of powers, had in practice to leave much of his power in the hands of the Lieutenant-Governors on the spot. With responsibility for a sizeable bureaucracy in Dakar, and unable to travel in the colonies frequently because of the poor communications that existed at the time, he had to trust their judgment in all but the most important political decisions. Similarly, the Lieutenant-Governors, bogged down with paper work and restricted in their ability to travel, were very much dependent on the administrator on the spot, and so it is that in the early years of the federation, as Cosnier diagnosed, the most important agent of the 'mission civilisatrice' was the *Commandant de cercle*. Both in French and British West Africa the early years of colonial rule were concerned more with the substructure than the superstructure of the administration. A grand decree could emanate from Dakar, be promulgated by the Lieutenant-Governor of the Colony, but it was the *Commandant de cercle* who put it into effect. And if he chose to interpret it differently from its intention there was little that could be done about it. Coupled with this was the rapid changeover in administrative staff at all levels.[16]

The colonies themselves were administered by Lieutenant-Governors, advised by a *Conseil d'Administration* composed of the Secretary-General of the colony, the delegate of the colony to the Superior Council of Colonies, the Procureur of the Republic, the local military commander, a delegate elected by the Chamber of Commerce, and one elected by the Africultural Section, together with three African notables elected by a special electoral college. Only in Senegal, where a *Conseil-Général* had been established in 1879 on the lines of the *Conseils-Généraux* of France, was there any democratic check on the powers of the Lieutenant-Governor, who also had to contend with the presence of a Deputy elected by the African 'citoyens' and the French living in the Four Communes of Dakar, Rufisque, Gorée and St. Louis. Though the Senegalese Conseil-Général did not have legislative powers, it could reject the budget. Its deliberations on the policy of the Governor were followed closely by the better educated among those who elected its members. There was a very lively press which reported its activities. A measure of its nuisance value to the French administration was the ardour with which the latter pursued the disfranchisement of citoyens. And, having failed in that, their cunning attempts at emasculating it by enlarging its scope to cover the protectorate, but having the latter represented by chiefs who were entirely dependent on them. The Lieutenant-Governors had beneath them diverse services ranging from education to the printing departments, some of which, like agriculture and posts and telecommunications, were dependent on Dakar. The colonies were divided into cercles, roughly equal in size, or population, and these were in turn divided into

'Subdivisions'. The *Commandants de cercle* and the *Chefs de subdivisions* were almost exclusively French.[17]

At a purely administrative level the French made a major impact on the population by their abolition of slavery and their introduction of forced labour and taxation to ensure people worked; by their restructuring of the institution of chieftancy so that the chiefs became effectively subaltern members of the colonial administration; and by their imposition of a French system of administrative justice to the exclusion of 'native law'. This administrative system had taken shape by 1920 and did not change in any fundamental sense until the reforms introduced during the Constituent assemblies of the Fourth Republic. Tentative reforms introduced by the Popular Front Government were halted by the establishment of the Vichy régime in 1940.

## 3 Slavery, forced labour and taxation

By the time of French occupation the problem of slavery was almost exclusively an internal one: the European slave trade had long since ceased; a few slaves still trickled across the desert through which a substantial trade in other goods was carried on until the end of the nineteenth century.[18] Within French West Africa slavery took two major forms. There were the domestic slaves, many of whom were by 'caste' of this status, and in contrast with the European form of chattel slavery enjoyed rights as well as duties. Many had risen to places of high political power in traditional African society. Then there were slaves bought and sold on the internal market primarily for agricultural labour. The French administration committed itself in principle to the abolition of both forms of slavery. The latter was more easily abolished since at least its open form, on recognised markets, could be suppressed. The French, of course, in their conquest had hardly set a good precedent for the newly declared policy of abolishing slavery, for one of the rewards for their African soldiery had been the taking of 'captifs' from conquered villages.

The whole problem of slavery, both the internal trade and the domestic form, could not be ignored, for there were strong humanitarian pressures for its abolition. The French Anti-Slavery Society had supported the explorers of the late nineteenth century and crowned the conquerors in the name of the humanitarian work they were doing in making possible the end of slavery in Africa.[19] But in practice the administration in its early years, for political reasons, did not take any measures to abolish slavery: thus only in 1901 did a circular go out from Governor-General Ponty abolishing the right of pursuit of slaves by their masters.

During the year 1904, however, a general enquiry on slavery in French West Africa was undertaken. The question was precipitated by a dramatic case of slave-trafficking in Senegal involving the son of a former Damel of Cayor.[20] Diéry Fall, as he was called, had admitted to receiving three slaves from a cousin and to having sold one of them. The Commandant de Cercle, Prempain, sentenced him to a fine of 100 francs and two weeks' imprisonment. Diéry Fall, of noble caste and convinced that there was nothing wrong in what he had done since it did not conflict with traditional practice, was deeply shocked by the short term of imprisonment inflicted on him. Seizing a revolver he wounded two guards and tried to escape. In the ensuing fracas a French official, called Chautemps, who was assistant in the Native Affairs Department, was shot. The fact that he was the son of the former Minister of Colonies, Félix Chautemps (1895), naturally gave great publicity to the question of slavery in the French press. It hastened the issuing of the decree of 1905 punishing by two to five years' imprisonment, and a fine of 500–5,000 francs, anybody who had concluded 'an agreement having as its object the alienation of the liberty of a third party'. This decree also suppressed domestic slavery though no measures were taken to enforce this. The political reasons for such tardy action in abolishing even the slave trade was the complexity of the political implications of such an issue. First of all the French, as we shall see, used a system of forced labour in their occupation of West Africa which was tantamount to African domestic slavery. Secondly they had used 'captifs' as a reward for their African troops, and could hardly withdraw them overnight. Thirdly, so many of the slaves in French West Africa were 'captifs' as distinct from domestic slaves that it was feared social dislocation of enormous proportions would ensue. Finally the question of the domestic slave, born to the role, as distinct from subjected to it, was a problem the administrators found difficult to tackle in the early years of colonial rule. Thus the abolition of slavery, the supposed humanitarian goal of the conquest, was slow of realisation both because of the complexity of the problem and because the administration did not have clean hands in the matter. The 1905 decree only abolished future slaving transactions, and those already enslaved, or slave by status, were not affected by it. It was estimated by the administration that at least two million inhabitants were 'non-libre', the euphemism, as Suret-Canale puts it, which the administration used to avoid 'the protestations which were aroused by using the actual term'.[21] In 1908 African agents of the administration were required to liberate their 'captifs'. By the outbreak of World War I, the slave trade had gone under cover. 'Captifs' enslaved before the 1905 decree could leave their masters when they wished under the terms of an earlier circular that owners had no right of pursuit. The administration became more conscientious in procuring the release of 'captifs' as it established itself on the ground. Indeed it followed a conscious policy of both making owners of *captifs* work and of breaking the power of chiefs. Thus prior to the First World War the Mossi chiefs lost much of the economic basis of their power because the administration 'abolished slavery and serfdom, and discouraged the various *corvées* performed by the people for their chiefs . . .'.[22]

The problem of domestic slavery was one that could not be so easily solved, for it was built into traditional social structures and was, as we have pointed out, of a very different category from that of the 'captif'. Its disappearance was largely a function of the changing social situation brought about by the colonisers, which gave new job opportunities, and allowed greater social mobility. For once a domestic slave decided to quit the family that owned him traditionally, the master could not reclaim him. However, he continued to have the social status of slave.

Slave labour for African masters was replaced by forced labour for the new French masters. The most serious form the new system took was in the cynically named 'villages de liberté'.[23] The creation of these villages was the consequence of the desperate need of the military administration for labour: the French found the lands they conquered had not the vast populations earlier explorers had estimated. 'West Africa was a country without Negroes.'[24]

The 'villages de liberté' were created by Gallieni in 1887. In them were settled the 'captifs' released as a result of the French conquest. As Mlle. Bouche puts it, 'for Gallieni and Archinard the "villages de liberté" were an excellent palliative to the shortage of labour'.[25] The villages were established not on the most favourable sites for economic development but where they were most needed by the new administration: on the supply lines of the conquerors and at the new administrative posts.[26] Anyone leaving a 'village de liberté' could be pursued and on recapture be imprisoned for one month.[27] The inhabitants were used as labourers and carriers, and so bad were their conditions of labour that many preferred to leave the 'villages de liberté' and find an African owner to work for.[28] The 'villages de liberté' were for the most part abandoned by 1904 but as late as

1908 they were created in Agades and Nguigmi in Niger. They represent one of the most reprehensible episodes of colonial rule, in which the need for labour was disguised by declarations that by re-settling the freed 'captifs' in these villages the humanitarian work of abolishing slavery would be furthered.

Under French colonial rule all Africans who were not French citizens, which meant all but a handful living for the most part in the 'Quatre Communes' of Senegal, were classified as *sujets* and were obliged to undertake labour for the administration. This took two main forms. First there was a tax in labour known as *prestation*. Each adult was liable to 12 days' labour, redeemable at 1–3 francs a day. Then there was compulsory labour in return for payment. The most common use of labour was on roads and work on 'les champs administratifs' to increase agricultural production. Cosnier in his report to the President of the French Republic demanded that: 'they no more impose obligatory administrative cultivation of crops which lead to so many misunderstandings and which are at the same time a heavy burden for the cultivator and the most detestable form of vulgarisation'.[29] However, in certain areas labour was requisitioned for commercial companies, as in the Ivory Coast, or for the construction of railways, and other public works. Able-bodied men were also subject to conscription into the French army and during the First World War vast numbers were sent to the European front (see pp. 259–66). Not until 1946 was the hated *corvée*, protest against which had been a motive factor of the French Revolution, abolished. And its existence makes the pretentious declarations of the conqueror look very hollow in retrospect: 'On all this territory', wrote Lt. Gatelet in 1901 of the conquests of Borgnis-Desbordes, 'our flag has been carried forward victoriously and the Negro populations, ill-treated for many years by all the adventurers and bandits of this part of Africa, accept with joy our suzerainty.'[30]

The attitude of René Mercier in his book *Le Travail Obligatoire dans les Colonies Africaines*, published shortly after the International Labour Conference at Geneva in 1930 where Blaise Diagne, Deputy of Senegal, and Under Secretary of State for Colonies, defended France's forced labour,[31] was to dominate French thought until 1946: 'a single method appeared capable in certain cases of overcoming the inertia of the natives: the use of constraint, forced labour'.[32]

As early as 1901 a report was made to the French Minister of Commerce in these terms:

'The black does not like work and is totally unaccustomed to the idea of saving; he does not realise that idleness keeps him in a state of absolute economic inferiority. It is therefore necessary to use the institutions by which he is ruled, in this case slavery, to improve his circumstances and afterwards gently lead him into an apprentice-ship of freedom. Scorning work, the black is not aware that, for us, work ennobles a man's character: it is necessary therefore to pass through an intermediate stage before giving him freedom such as we understand it.'[33]

Such attitudes were based on a profound ignorance of how hard the African, often under-nourished and debilitated by a wide range of diseases since his youth, really worked. As Robert Delavignette put it in 1931: 'We have found that the real barriers were not the men but famine and disease, agents of the climate. In Africa we indict the men and their laziness. We forget the sky and the climate.'[34] It was only a more enlightened administration in the post 1939–45 war years that saw that improvement of the living conditions of the African alone would enable him to work to the exaggerated capacity the French arbitrarily assessed of him.

Direct taxation, like forced labour, was seen not only as an instru-ment of servicing the administration but also as the means of forcing Africans to increase production of crops which were needed by Europe. Prior to the imposition of European administration Africans maintained a balance between their production of subsistence crops and crops that would enable them to earn money to purchase imported goods. Under the French colonial system, taxation was imposed at such a level that the farmer had to grow, in many areas, cash crops in order to be able to pay his taxes. In areas that did not produce cash crops in great quantity, particularly in parts of Sudan and what is now Upper Volta, in order to pay these taxes men had to sell the only other commodity they had available to them: their labour. Thus taxation forced farmers in Sudan to migrate seasonally to Senegal to work on the groundnut fields. A great exodus from Upper Volta to the cocoa plantations and timber undertakings in the Ivory Coast was brought about both by the compulsion of taxation and by administrative conscription. France was in Africa, by her own admission, as much for supposed humanitarian reasons as to exploit its economic resources. And taxation, as M. Duchêne put it in his report to the International Colonial Congress of 1900, properly applied, could ensure this. 'The idea that seems the best for achieving the employment of native labour, would be to impose on the blacks relatively high taxes . . . and in default of payment they would incur a sentence of forced labour.'[35]

The use of direct taxation, traditionally applied in Muslim areas but an innovation in most other parts, to stimulate economic activity had unexpected consequences, by forcing the African to seek employment in the British territories. There pay was higher and conditions of service better. This accounts for the great Mossi migration to the cocoa fields and gold mines of the Gold Coast.

Sadly reflecting on the supposed benefits introduced by the white man, Félix Chautemps, former Minister of Colonies, wrote in 1913: 'We must admit, however, that this *eminent* civilisation appears only under the aspect of an infernal and refined savagery to our subjects; they will need some time to understand that we rob them and kill them to teach them to live an increasingly human life . . .' and 'the native submits. But in his eyes we came, officials and traders alike, to live at his expense; we levy a tithe on his goods under the pretext of humanity. We upset his institutions and in the guise of justice we contravene his customs—the native does not like us; he is afraid of us.'[36]

## 4 *The Chiefs*

The agents for the collection of the taxes imposed by the French administration were the chiefs. They were also responsible for raising forced labour for work on the roads, railways and even European plantations and for providing carriers for the administration and for ensuring the forced cultivation of certain cash crops. These new functions were largely responsible for the changeover of the position of the chief from the symbol of the collective unity of his people to the most hated member of that community. The chiefs abused their traditional authority in raising taxes and labour not only for the French but also for themselves. The administration turned a blind eye to this, provided chiefs served their interests loyally. For thus they could continue to pay these agents of the administration a pittance for their services, and be rid of them whenever they were dissatisfied with them on charges of extortion.

The French administration transformed traditional chiefs, even those who had signed agreements of protection, from a position of tributary ruler to that of agent of the administration, and installed a new set of chiefs: the French Commandant de Cercle. As Van Vollenhoven wrote in his circular of 15th August 1917, advocating a more thoughtful use of traditional chiefs as the agents of administration: 'The Commandant de Cercle alone gives orders; only he is responsible. The native chief is only an auxiliary instrument . . .

they have no power of their own of any kind, for there are not two authorities in the *cercle*: French authority and native authority; there is only one. . . . The native chief never speaks, never acts in his own name, but always in the name of the *Commandant de Cercle* and by formal or tacit delegation from the latter.'[37] Thus when the French Commandant de Cercle flew the Tricolor on his car in Ségou it was a symbol of his absolute authority over the former capital of Ahmadou: when the British Resident flew the Union Jack on his car in Sokoto it symbolised as much his quasi-diplomatic position in relation to the conquered Sultan, as his authority over him as agent of the conqueror.

To understand the persistence with which French administration debased the power of the chief we have to take into account the strong centralising tendency in France's metropolitan administration and in particular its dislike of delegating power to local government authorities. Most of the French administrators who came out to French West Africa were Republicans, and distrusted monarchy and aristocracy in principle. We must also look to the way in which colonial rule was imposed in French West Africa: by military conquest followed by military administration. When the military were replaced by civilian administrators the latter were inheritors of an administrative infra-structure that was essentially military in conception. Sole authority was vested in the Commandant de Cercle, who, like the Colonel of a Battalion, had jurisdiction over, if he did not carry out, all fields of administration, including the technical services.[38] The civilian administrator continued to require that the 'natives' salute him, and to enforce his authority he had a para-military force at his disposal in the form of the *gardes de cercle*. These guards obtained great power in the community both because of their police function and because they were frequently used as inter-mediaries between the administrator and the chiefs. Making it their business to know the corruption the chiefs were forced to indulge in to supplement their meagre salaries, they could threaten exposure unless adequately recompensed. They thus served as another, if unintended, check on the chief's authority.

Just as the French army was organised in a neat hierarchy, where there was no duality of command, but a logical chain of authority from the highest to the lowest, so 'the administrative structures introduced (by the military) into Africa were even more than those created by Napoleon in the mother country, based on the hierarchical pyramid of the army'.[39] Thus the chief became 'un sorte de sous-officier, fonctionnarisé sinon militarisé'.[40] The chiefs themselves were grouped into a hierarchy: *chefs supérieurs de province*; *chefs de cantons*; *chefs de villages*. But above them were what Robert Delavignette has called 'les vrais chefs de l'empire', the Commandants de Cercle.[41] Significantly the Commandant, who corresponded roughly in status to the British Resident, was also known as a 'Chef de Circonscription', while his subordinate, equivalent to the British District Officer, was known as the 'Chef de Subdivision'. And these new European chiefs did not appreciate autonomous action on the part of their subaltern chiefs, and so we see a deliberate whittling away by the French administration of all possibility of independent initiative on the part of the chief. Whilst in British West Africa the chief, for the most part, merely had to learn what sort of things upset the British District Officer—like slavery, cruel punishments—and then carry on very much as an independent ruler, the hierarchised French African chief had clear instructions, issued in circulars, as to just what he was allowed to do and had to do.

From the beginning of the conquest there were those who hoped that a system of indirect rule might be applied in French West Africa. Dodds on conquering Behanzin made a declaration very similar to that of Lugard on the conquest of Sokoto where he promised that the traditional integrity of the conquered people would be respected: 'Nothing will be changed in the customs or institutions of the country, whose tradition will be respected. The chiefs who submit in good faith to our protectorate will remain in power; and they will retain the dignities appertaining to it.'[42] But within a few years the ancient kingdom of Dahomey had been dismembered and its ruling dynasty reduced to nonenities. The kings of Dahomey ceased to exist officially, never being recognised by the French in the way the Emperor of Mossi was. The royal palace of Abomey became a museum of I.F.A.N., a curiosity for the tourist. If the French had hoped to use the chiefs as protected rulers, as Lyautey had in Morocco and in parts of Indo-China, they were up against two obstacles: first, by their conquest they had destroyed or deposed the large majority of the great natural rulers; secondly the temperament of the military administrator and his civil successor did not lend itself easily to a sharing of authority with an African chief.

As Governor-General Brévié told his Council of Government in December 1930: '... the most eminent among them [the chiefs] were wiped out as a result of the conquest. Peace-time has devoured an even greater number still, for we could not be content with the imperfect services that they were able to offer us. We have exacted perfection from the start. Only those who, by luck, have had little contact with the representatives of authority, have remained.'[43]

Many Commandants were like Lieutenant Chaudron in Senegal 'who was continually slapping fines on village or canton chiefs for disobeying orders or for being slow in carrying them out. In one month (one chief) received three fines totalling 120 francs, including one for letting his animals stray onto the road'.[44] Village chiefs in particular suffered from the authoritarian disposition of the Commandant, frequently being arrested, imprisoned and beaten for failing in their administrative duties. As Van Vollenhoven told administrators: '(you) should realise that the chiefs would be more respected by the people if they were better treated by us'[45] and 'If in this Colony chiefs are rarely decorated, by contrast they are frequently punished'.[46]

The chiefs, depending on the size of the areas they supervised, became the sergeant-majors, sergeants and corporals[47] of the new régime, and any failure to carry out the duties assigned them, many of which never came within their traditional competence, met with punishment or dismissal. Because the new role of the chiefs differed so greatly from their traditional role, and because literacy in French was deemed essential for their proper functioning in the system, not only did the administrators choose as chiefs those from the ruling lineage who spoke French and were known to be loyal to France, but often they imposed men without any traditional right to rule. These included clerks, old soldiers, and in some instances even personal servants of administrators.[48] Chiefs ruled without the advice of the council which by tradition they would normally have had to consult. However in the thirties two reforms were introduced on paper. Administrators were instructed to appoint as chiefs those who were by tradition entitled to the position. They were also to set up advisory councils in accordance with tradition which the chiefs could consult. In practice, the councils never got off the ground, and 'according to tradition as far as possible' was sufficiently broad a prescription for the administrator, who was anyway arbiter of what tradition was, to continue appointing his own nominee.

Where great rulers defeated in the conquest by the French had been replaced by more pliable ones, the latter soon found themselves ruling over greatly reduced kingdoms, for French policy was to divide these up the better to rule them. Thus in the Fouta Djallon, policy was 'the progressive suppression of the chiefs and the parcelling out of their authority'.[49] Zinder and Mossi were both broken up, and the chiefs initially acceptable to the French were deposed. In 1904 the Sultanate of Zinder, already reduced in size, was suppressed and divided into three provinces each under a dignitary of the court. It was not restored until 1923.[50] Few chiefs ruled territories which corresponded to pre-colonial political units. Apart from wishing to break the power of large chiefdoms by dividing them up, the French tried to impose administrative uniformity throughout West Africa by tailoring all chiefdoms to the same size. The basic unit became the Cantonal chiefdom, inspired by the Malinké model[51] the French found in Guinea and the Sudan.* Large chiefdoms were therefore broken down into cantons, while where there were series of small chiefs ruling areas much smaller than cantons, these were grouped together under a French-created cantonal chief with no roots in tradition. The cantonal chiefs had under them *chefs de villages*. In certain cases where great chiefdoms were broken up into cantons, the special position of the chiefs whose lands had been thus divided was recognised by the title 'Chief supérieur'. But the administration was anxious not to have any more intermediaries between themselves and the people than absolutely necessary.[52] In 1906 in Guinea it was even seriously suggested that the power of the great chiefs should so be broken that the village became the administrative entity.[53]

In the case of a chief like the Emperor of the Mossi his special spiritual position had to be recognised even if his administrative powers were reduced to those of a cantonal chief. The alternating Almamys of the Fouta Djallon were both reduced to the state of cantonal chiefs. They continued to hold the title of Almamy, and were given larger salaries than other cantonal chiefs, but effectively they had no more power than them. They were even removed from their former capitals of Timbo and Ditinn, to Dabola and Mamou respectively.[54]

The chiefs in French West Africa soon bore little resemblance to those who had been conquered at the end of the nineteenth century. Where they were of traditional ruling lineages, they were chosen by the administrator, not by the traditional electoral process which gave sanction for their authority. Among non-Muslim societies the chief had religious functions that depended on his being the properly selected candidate. Imposed candidates gave rise to the phenomenon of straw chiefs, or chiefs elected in secret by traditional methods to carry out their proper religious functions.[55] L. V. Thomas gives a good account of the impact of the new administrative system on the animist Diola: 'Another factor in the rapid deformation of the

* It also corresponded to the Napoleonic canton.

colonial situation has been the diminution of the authority of the fetish-kings, whose religious powers we have alone conserved. Administrative control has passed entirely into the hand of the Commandant de Cercle and to the Chef de Subdivision while the village and canton chiefs, simple agents of the administration, are chosen, no longer according to fetishist tradition but because of their knowledge of French (old soldiers, graduates of schools, etc. . . .).'[56]

Even 'native justice', one of the main means by which the chief could maintain his authority over his people, was reorganised completely by the French. The chiefs lost all jurisdiction in criminal cases but were allowed a small role in the settlement of civil disputes. In place of the many different systems of justice that prevailed in West Africa before their arrival, the French introduced a uniform system for the whole region. For Frenchmen and Africans who were French citizens French justice applied. For the vast mass of subjects, what the French called inappositely 'native justice' applied. This system had almost no roots in traditional justice. For criminal cases there was a *tribunal de premier degré* presided over by an administrator aided by two African assessors in each subdivision. Above it was the *tribunal criminel* at the headquarters of the *cercle* over which the Commandant presided aided by two European and African assessors. Only in civil cases did an African ever preside, and that was only at the level of the *tribunal de premier degré*. But this African was not necessarily the chief, being defined only as a *notable*. Thus while the whole system of 'native justice' in British West Africa depended both on the chief as a judge and on the customary law of the local people, in French West Africa a system without roots in African law, and in which the chief played no role, was introduced. However, it seems that the chiefs, despite the fact that they were forbidden by law to judge criminal cases, settled disputes of a criminal character. For as Hailey points out, in French West Africa in 1934, with an estimated population of fourteen-and-a-half million, only 9,266 criminal cases came before the *tribunaux indigènes* whereas in Nigeria, with a population estimated at twenty million, in the same year over 126,000 criminal cases were tried.[57]

One explanation for this large discrepancy would be the existence alongside the *tribunaux indigènes* of a system of administrative justice known as the *indigénat*. Under this the French administrator could arrest and imprison an African *sujet* for up to fifteen days or impose a fine on him without bringing him to trial. Nor was there any right of appeal. Later the duration of the term of imprisonment was reduced to five days. But there was nothing to stop an administrator immediately imprisoning the same man when he was let out. Even village chiefs were subject to the *indigénat*, and it was only by the Decree of 1924 that chiefs superior in rank to the village chief were exempted from the régime of the *indigénat*.[58] Along with forced labour the *indigénat* was the aspect of colonial rule most hated by the African subject. For political activities, by a Decree of 21st November 1904, under the *indigénat* up to ten years' imprisonment could be given for 'insurrection, grave political disturbances, acts likely to compromise public security and not falling under the application of ordinary penal law'. The only safeguard was that in such instances the Minister of the Colonies had to be informed.[59]

An administrative régime was introduced into French West Africa that was as authoritarian as any African system of government it replaced. To the sparse corps of French administrators—only five to six French administrators and agents of ancillary services were ever in the Cercle de Ouagadougou, comprising 1½ million Mossi, between 1900–1919[60]—were attributed vast powers against which the African had no appeal. It was not Anglo-Saxon prejudice that prompted Sir John Harris's bitter comment in 1912: 'None but Frenchmen should go to the colonies of "Liberty, Equality and Fraternity", for there is little Liberty, less Equality, and no Fraternity in the French colonies for white or black.'[61] The same comments are implicit in Van Vollenhoven's circular and openly voiced by Cosnier: 'By making hired men of the traditional chiefs, the only ones having and actually being able to have authority, in order to replace them by servants and native interpreters we have dug an abyss between the administration and the administered, suppressed a natural organisation, which could have been improved, to replace it by a scatter of puppets who have no control over the native.'[62] Remarking earlier of the all pervading authority of the administrator over the African he concluded: 'Passive obedience has never been a factor for progress.'[63]

Thus the chief in French West Africa progressively lost his traditional authority while his new functions of taxation, recruiting of forced labour and troops and checking on anti-French movements within his area of supervision, together with the authoritarian way in which he was treated by the Commandant, transformed him from the embodiment of the collective will of the community into an agent of some of the most hated aspects of French colonial rule.

While the chiefs were able to preserve their position in the independent states of English-speaking West Africa, in the French-

o

speaking states they count for nothing today. As a class they have been abolished completely in Guinea. Even in Niger, where some of the greater chiefs survived the colonial period, they count for very little in comparison with their cousins in Northern Nigeria. French rule had so deformed the role of chieftaincy in the eyes of the people that *Réveil*, organ of French West Africa's largest political party, the Rassemblement Démocratique Africain, could write in 1949: 'Right up to recent times, the African chief has been the Commandant de Cercle's domestic . . . fiercely oppressed, he oppressed.'[64]

# Notes

1 Henri Cosnier, *L'Ouest Africain Français: ses resources agricoles—son organisation économique*, Paris, 1921, pp. viii–ix.
2 *Ibid.*, p. xvi.
3 *Ibid.*, p. xix.
4 *Ibid.*, p. xx.
5 For an account of the aims of the groups and individuals forming *le parti colonial* see Henri Brunschwig, 'Le Parti Colonial Français', *Revue Française d'Histoire d'Outre-Mer*, XLVI, I, 1959, pp. 49–83.
6 For a detailed account of the circumstances of the creation of the Government-General and its subsequent consolidation see C. W. Newbury, 'The Formation of the Government-General in French West Africa', *J.A.H.*, I, 1, 1960, pp. 111–28.
7 *Ibid.*, pp. 114–15.
8 *Le Gouvernement-Général en A.O.F.* Notice publiée par le Gouvernement-Général a l'occasion de l'exposition franco-brittanique à Londres. M. G. François, ed., N.D., p. 4.
9 Roberts, *A History of French Policy*, p. 308.
10 Delafosse in Hanotaux, *Histoire des Colonies françaises*, 'A.O.F. 1904–1930', p. 350.
11 Newbury, 'The Formation of the Government-General', p. 118.
12 *Le Gouvernement-Général en A.O.F.*, pp. 18–19, where full details of the loans and the works to which they were allocated are given.
13 Lord Hailey, *An African Survey*, London, 1939, p. 237.
14 *Ibid.*, p. 240.
15 'Discours prononcé par le Gouverneur-Général de l'A.O.F. à l'ouverture de la session du Conseil de Gouvernement', Dakar, November 1937, p. 9.
16 For example from 1904–18 the Dahomey had seven governors: Liotard (–1906); Marchal (1906–1908); Peuvergne (1908–1909); Malan (1909–1911); Mewhardt (1911–1912); Noufflard (1912–1917); Fourn (1917–). Cornevin, *Dahomey*, p. 413.
17 For instance, Abdoulaye Diaw, a clerk in the French administration of Senegal, had been frequently acting administrator in Sine Saloum, and was named Resident in Eastern Saloum in 1896; see Martin Klein, *Sine Saloum 1847–1914: The Traditional States and the French Conquest*, Ph.D. thesis, Chicago, 1964, p. 238.
18 C. W. Newbury, 'North African and Western Sudan Trade in the Nineteenth Century: a Re-Evaluation', *J.A.H.*, VII, 2, 1966, pp. 233–46.
19 Suret-Canale, *Afrique Noire II*, p. 81.
20 See M'Baye Guèye, 'L'affaire Chautemps (Avril 1904) et la suppression de l'ésclavage de case au Sénégal', *Bulletin de l'I.F.A.N.*, T.XXVII, sér. B, nos. 3–4, 1965.
21 Suret-Canale, *Afrique Noire II*, p. 87.

22 Skinner, *Mossi*, pp. 159–60.
23 See Denise Bouche, 'Les villages de liberté en A.O.F.', *Bulletin de l'I.F.A.N.*, T.XI, sér. B, nos. 3–4, 1949, and T.XII, 1, 1950.
24 Roberts, *A History of French Policy*, p. 311.
25 Bouche, Part I, pp. 536–7.
26 *Ibid.*, I, p. 537.
27 *Ibid.*, II, p. 158.
28 *Ibid.*, II, p. 180.
29 Cosnier, *L'Ouest Africain Français*, p. xxi.
30 Lieutenant Gatelet, *Histoire de la Conquête du Soudan Français (1878–1899)*, Paris, 1901, p. 51.
31 See Charles Cros, *La parole est à M. Blaise Diagne, premier homme d'Etat africain*, Paris, 1961, pp. 113–33.
32 René Mercier, *Le travail obligatoire dans les Colonies africaines*, Paris, 1933, p. 10.
33 Report of Aspe Florimond to the Minister of Commerce on *L'organisation économique de la Côte occidentale française: Liberté; règlementation*, Paris, 1901, p. 7, cited in Eugène Lestideau, *La question de la main-d'œuvre dans les colonies françaises et specialement dans celles de l'Afrique occidentale française*, Rennes, 1907, p. 80.
34 Robert Delavignette, *Afrique Occidentale Française*, Paris, 1931, p. 19.
35 Report of M. Duchêne cited in Lestideau, *La question de la main-d'œuvre dans les colonies*, p. 81.
36 Félix Chautemps, 'Politique indigène', in *L'Afrique Occidentale Française*, various authors, Paris, 1913, pp. 45–7. See also, Maurice Delafosse's remarks in *Afrique Française*, 1922, p. 271, where he says: 'Many of them are coming to regret the tyranny of an El Hajj Umar or a Samori, which was more capricious, undoubtedly, but the caprices of which had less general importance and were marked by greater intervals of calm than our own exactions.'
37 Governor-General Joost van Vollenhoven, 'Circulaire au sujet des chefs indigènes', Dakar, 15th August 1917, reprinted in *Une Âme de Chef: Le Gouverneur J. van Vollenhoven*, Paris, 1920, p. 207.
38 Suret-Canale, *Afrique Noire II*, p. 95.
39 'Le Problème des Chefferies en Afrique Noire Française', *La Documentation Française* (Notes et Études Documentaires), No. 2508, 10th February 1959, p. 7.
40 *Ibid.*, p. 7.
41 Robert Delavignette, *Les vrais chefs de l'empire*, Paris, 1939.
42 Cited in Cornevin, 'Les divers épisodes', p. 194.
43 Cited in Delavignette, *Afrique Occidentale Française*, p. 189.
44 Martin Klein, *Sine-Saloum 1847–1914*, pp. 242–3.
45 *Une Âme de Chef*, p. 203.
46 *Ibid.*, p. 205.
47 'Le problème des chefferies', p. 8.

48 Suret-Canale, *Afrique Noire II*, p. 408, cites the example of a Governor-General ordering the Lieutenant-Governor of Guinea to make his former steward a Chef de Canton, an order the latter did not dare refuse, even though he feared that trouble would ensue, which it did.

49 *Overall report on the general situation in French Guinea in 1906*, Conakry, 1907, cited in Jean Suret-Canale, 'Guinea Under the Colonial System', *Présence Africaine*, No. 29 (English ed.).

50 Edmond Séré de Rivières, *Histoire du Niger*, Paris, 1965, p. 222.

51 Jean Suret-Canale, 'La fin de la chefferie en Guinée', *J.A.H.*, VII, 1966, 3, p. 462.

52 J. Brévié, *Circulaires sur la politique et l'administration indigènes en A.O.F.*, 1932, cited in Hailey, *African Survey*, 1938, p. 547.

53 *1906 Report for Guinea*, cited by Suret-Canale in 'La fin de la Chefferie en Guinée', p. 467.

54 *Ibid.*, p. 468.

55 See Robert Delavignette, *Freedom and Authority in French West Africa*, London, 1950, and Geoffrey Gorer, *Africa Dances*, London, 1935.

56 L. V. Thomas, *Les Diola*, Dakar, 1959, Vol. I, p. 323.

57 Hailey, *African Survey*, 1939, p. 29.

58 Buell, *Native Problem*, I, p. 1017.

59 *Le Gouvernement-Général en l'A.O.F.*, p. 25.

60 Robert Delavignette, *Afrique Occidentale Française*, Paris, 1931, p. 68.

61 John H. Harris, *Dawn in Darkest Africa*, London, 1912, p. 97.

62 Cosnier, *Report*, p. 164.

63 *Ibid.*, p. xiv.

64 Cited in Suret-Canale, 'La fin de la Chefferie en Guinée', p. 476.

# 3 British administration in West Africa

## 1 The conservation of African society

British methods of colonial rule in West Africa did not receive such trenchant criticisms as those of the French either from its own nationals or from those of other colonial powers. Its main critics were the growing Western educated élite of the coastal towns, who published in their newspapers what were often savage attacks on British policy. Cosnier in his survey of French policy looked admiringly at the economic progress made in Gold Coast compared with the Ivory Coast.[1]

But though the British system of administration was generally lighter in touch than that of the French, it was hardly free from reproach. It permitted forced labour, imposed taxation that was often difficult for the peasant to pay, and was slow to get rid of slavery. In adopting a system of indirect rule it buttressed up the authoritarian aspect of the power of chiefs who frequently abused it in a way they could rarely have done in traditional society without deposition. Most important of all, far from providing the initiative for innovation in African society, it became the chief agency for the conservation of its more traditional elements. Anyway it provided far too few administrators to have any serious educative impact on its colonial subjects. In 1925 there were only 200 administrators in Nigeria for a population then estimated at twenty million, or one administrator for every 100,000 people.[2] And this does not take into account those on leave or sick, probably about a third. The

French by contrast had 526 administrators in 1922 for a population estimated at fifteen million.[3]

The British administrator kept aloof from the people he was meant to be protecting. He was like a headmaster of a public school who left the discipline of the boys to the Senior Prefect and only interfered with it if abuse of power became too flagrant or if there was no suitable person to appoint as Prefect. This aloofness was the dominant characteristic of British colonial administration: epitomised in the organisation of passenger accommodation on the liners plying between Liverpool and the Coast: 'between the upper and lower deck a ladder is fixed, down which the white man may go whenever desire prompts him, but up which neither coloured nor quadroon may climb.'[4] The traditional ruler never asked to be allowed to climb up that ladder; indeed, found that the less contact he had with the administrator, the better. The administrator, his bungalow carefully sited well away from the 'native' town, on top of a hill, or hummock if that was all the local geography provided, hauled down the Union Jack at 6 p.m., and, pink gin in hand, recreated this upper deck on dry land. Unfortunately missionary education and the more liberal policies of the nineteenth-century colonial governments, which even allowed Africans to sit on Legislative Councils, had produced an élite anxious to climb the ladder to the upper deck. To the administration this educated African was 'a worse evil than the primitive savage'.[5] And while the Acting Governor-General of French West Africa in a circular of 1st October 1916 stressed the need for the increase of the educated African élite to fill posts in the administration,[6] the British had instituted a system whereby Africans could not occupy posts normally held by Europeans. Thus for long African doctors with better degrees than their European counterparts could not gain admission to the medical service and when they were admitted it was to a separate grade. The reason, according to Harris, was that 'white men, and more particularly women, would refuse to receive treatment at the hands of coloured medical men'.[7] And we must remember that the medical service was as much, if not more, concerned with the health of the European as the African.

The educated élite was disinherited under the new British system of colonial rule in favour of the traditional chiefs, who were not encouraged to speak the language of the coloniser, nor imbibe Western culture. Rather it was hoped they would not be contaminated by it. Lugard summed up the more enlightened approach of his fellow countrymen in his *The Dual Mandate in British Tropical Africa.*

'Here, then, is the true conception of the inter-relation of colour: complete uniformity in ideals, absolute equality in the paths of knowledge and culture, equal opportunity for those who strive, equal admiration for those who achieve; in matters social and racial a separate path, each pursuing his own inherited traditions, preserving his own race purity and race-pride; equality in things spiritual, agreed divergence in the physical and material.'[8]

The emphasis on the traditional ruler rather than the educated élite as the means for administering Africa was to have a profound impact on the nature of African nationalism in British West Africa, and the character of the countries they inherited on independence. Preservation of traditional chiefs, repositories of tribal custom, emphasised ethnicity; exclusion of the educated African from participation in government led to his demanding that participation much more loudly than his French counterpart, who was more quickly absorbed into the administration where he was available— which was not often.

The aloofness of the administrator from the African was repeated in his relations with those of his fellow-countrymen engaged in commerce. A rigid social distinction developed between government and commerce, the latter being considered socially inferior. The administrator became increasingly isolated from the realities of the peoples he administered and the commerce which alone could provide for their development. As Harris remarked: 'our officials would do well to remember . . . that the natives and the merchants together pay their salaries and pensions'.[9]

This isolation was reinforced by the fact that British administrators, unlike their French counterparts, were not moved from colony to colony, or even within Northern Nigeria from the Holy North to the 'pagan' Middle Belt.[10] The administrator, thus isolated, far from being the agent for integration into the modern world, became increasingly a dam to prevent the flood-waters of change engulfing the societies of which he was 'protector'. This tendency, which was most marked in Northern Nigeria, was to be roundly criticised by the Governor of Nigeria, Sir Donald Cameron, in 1934 in his memorandum on *The Principles of Native Administration and their Application*.[11] He attacked the approach that 'the Moslem Administrations should be sheltered as far as possible from contact with the world',[12] and cited with approval a 'student of Native Administration' who was 'at times disturbed by the widespread emphasis on the importance of preserving as much as possible of indigenous African life and custom'.[13]

His sad comment on the Nigerian situation—'I doubt sometimes whether we have done a great deal to impress on the minds of the Native Authorities concerned that the amelioration of the social and economic conditions of the people is one of the primary duties of an Administration'[14]—is one that could be made generally of British administration in West Africa.

Fortunately there were strong forces that countered the conservative tendencies of the administration. Missionary education and the development of important cash crops and mining, introduced Africans to the modern world and built a basis for a nationalist movement whose goals were the social and economic improvement of their peoples, so often neglected by the Administration. The very real extent to which these were frustrated rather than encouraged is brought out well in John Wilson's account of indirect rule in West Africa:

'. . . British Colonial Administration as it had developed was hierarchical and vertically structured. The officers in the field were organised departmentally, each responsible to the officer above him in the hierarchy, and such departmental integration as there was took place at the top of the hierarchy. Teamwork at the point of contact in the field among, say, education, health, agriculture, and other social development personnel was at best informal, sporadic, and by no means a matter of priority. By the same token there was division between government and mission on one hand and between government and commerce on the other, and, in any case, mission and commerce tended to be themselves vertically structured and hierarchical. All this makes for only the poorest integration and teamwork at the point of impact upon the population with serious lack of personal and team responsibility at that level with its sickening concomitant—frustration by red tape . . .' [Worse still] '. . . comparatively slow progress was accepted as the normal speed of development which gave the impression that time was on the side of development and that slow flowering was essential to soundness of growth.'[15]

## 2 *The political organisation of British West Africa*

In 1900 Britain had six dependencies on the West Coast of Africa: Gambia, Sierra Leone, the Gold Coast and three Nigerian colonies— the Lagos Colony and Protectorate (Yorubaland); the Southern Nigeria Protectorate which was formed in 1900 from the Niger Coast Protectorate and the Southern parts of the Royal Niger Company's territories; and the yet shadowy Northern Nigerian Protectorate. In 1906 Lagos was integrated with the Southern Nigerian Protectorate, and in 1914 the South and the North were amalgamated to form the single colony of Nigeria. Though during the nineteenth century a single administration for the small West African settlements was formed, there was never any question of such an arrangement being continued for the government of the much larger hinterlands that had been acquired for them as a result of the Scramble. The problem of running a federal administration for four colonies each separated from its neighbour by French territory, and each of different size, set aside any question of a joint administration such as that of French West Africa. Even contiguous colonies such as Northern and Southern Nigeria were amalgamated with reluctance under the force of economic circumstances. The North showed a continuous budgetary deficit which was supported by a grant-in-aid from the U.K. government. The South, vastly more prosperous, and at the time allocating £70,000 to the North a year in respect of customs dues on Northern goods passing through its ports, had sufficient surplus to cover the Northern deficit. It could thus save the British taxpayer's pocket and realise the principle that British colonies should pay for their own administration. There was also the urgent need to rationalise the railway systems of the two colonies. Antagonism to amalgamation came from both Northern and Southern officials 'nurtured within their own separate traditions'.[16] Lugard took this into account by joining the two colonies in a federation that would allow for as little contact between the two components as possible. His heart in the North, disliking the South, and fearing its impact on the former, he rejected suggestions by Governor Temple of the North for the division of that colony into three provinces.[17] This would have broken the monolithic structure of the North and avoided much of Nigeria's troubles in the search for a satisfactory independence constitution. Thus North and South, though united, continued in their separatist tradition.

Until the Second World War there was very little communication between the four administrations of British West Africa. The nineteenth-century concept of a united British West Africa was kept alive by the educated élite whose early political activities had a pan-West African focus. By the mid-1930's the 'advantages of a closer relationship between the four British West African colonies, and the appointment of a Governor-General for the whole' was apparently being 'repeatedly advocated'.[18] They culminated in the Conference of West African Governors held just before the outbreak of war, which was the occasion for the appointment of a Minister Resident for West Africa, a super-Governor-General.

Each of the four British territories was divided into colony and protectorate. The colony represented the lands acquired before the Scramble; the protectorate the large hinterlands acquired after it. The African inhabitants of the colonies were British subjects; those of the protectorates were 'protected persons' with no right of entry to Britain without special authorisation of the British government. In each of the nineteenth-century colonies Legislative Councils had been established in accordance with contemporary colonial policy that those who paid taxes should have some representation in the decision-making process of the government. Thus British traders, and a few Africans, were nominated to sit with the officials on these councils. In the Gold Coast the first African was appointed as early as 1850, though some sources give the date as late as 1889.[19] In Sierra Leone two Creole merchants were appointed to the newly formed Legislative Council (1863) while a Creole, Charles Heddle,* had sat on the old Governor's Council. Thereafter Creoles were represented on the Council, the most distinguished and articulate being Sir Samuel Lewis, who often opposed government policy, on the grounds that his class of members were not appointed 'only to say "yes" to every clause of a Bill, and register by their votes the will of the Secretary of State'.[20] Governors were supposed to appoint African members who represented the élite of the community and not just place-men. Thus before some seats in the Legislative Council of the Gold Coast became elective in 1925, a nominated member like Hutton Mills used his position to attack the Forest Bill of 1911.[21] Sapara Williams opposed the Seditions Offences Bill in the Lagos Legislative Council in 1909.[22] Though nominated African members criticised often, not much notice was taken of their opinion, and their presence on the Legislative Councils did not circumscribe the authority of the Governors, as the Conseil-Général did in Senegal, but rather proved a nuisance value. The frustration of the nominated Africans at their impotence was one of the factors behind demands for reform of the Legislative Councils by the National Congress of British West Africa. Most Governors sympathised with Lord Lugard's view 'that the interests of a large native population shall not be subject to the will of a small Euro-peanised class or of a small minority of Europeanised natives who have nothing in common with them and whose interests are often

* His father was an European doctor, his mother an African.

opposed to them'.[23] Lugard put his convictions into practice when he amalgamated Northern and Southern Nigeria. The Lagos Colony Legislative Council had in 1906 extended its competence over the whole of Southern Nigeria.[24] Lugard restricted it once more to Lagos, replacing it by an unwieldy thirty-six man Nigerian Council, with an official majority of twenty-three. Seven Europeans were nominated to represent commerce and shipping and industry, and six Africans—two emirs from the North, the Alafin of Oyo, and one each from Lagos, Calabar and Benin-Warri—to represent the inhabitants of the country. It was purely advisory and was to meet but once a year. In 1923, however, the Legislative Council for Southern Nigeria was restored. The North continued to have laws made for it by Proclamation of the Governor.

The Legislative Councils of Sierra Leone and the Gambia, which did not have an African member until 1913–, had competence over their hinterlands. In the Gold Coast only the Colony came under the Council's competence. The Northern Territories and Ashanti were ruled by Proclamation.

On major matters of policy it was rare for the Legislative Council to oppose the Governor, since its majority was composed of officials. Certainly the African minority could never hope to enlist any official support when they opposed the Governor's policy. In this sense the Legislative Council was only of nuisance value politically to the Governor. And in recognition of this fact Africans wishing to make protest sent delegations to London or despatched petitions direct to the Secretary of State.

On the whole the British Colonial Governor on the West Coast had more independence of action than his French counterpart. Lieutenant-Governors were all subject to the authority of the Governor-General of French West Africa. And in a sense the Governor of the Gambia had more opportunity for initiative than the Governor-General of French West Africa. In the first place, he could originate legislation, though even after he had given it his assent the Crown reserved the right to disallow it. Certain classes of Bills had under Royal Instructions to be assented by the Crown. But otherwise 'what may be described as purely domestic legislation (was) almost invariably left to the local Legislative Councils'.[25] Legislation by the Imperial Parliament for colonies was undertaken very rarely. This contrasts very strongly with French West Africa where all legislation emanated from France, usually in the form of a decree by the Head of State, which did not have to be approved by the Chamber of Deputies. The Head of State being a formal position, it meant in effect legislation by his ministers and in this case by the Minister of Colonies.[26] Thus the Governor-General had to request legislation by the Minister of Colonies, whereas the Governor of the Gambia legislated, and hoped no one in the Colonial Office would object. Since the Colonial Office was concerned with a host of territories in a vast empire, the Gambia figured very low on the priorities of an extremely small department in which even by 1930 few officials 'had even seen a colony, still less a colony on which they are daily called upon to advise the Secretary of State. This fact alone', wrote W. Ormsby-Gore in 1930, 'accounts for the comparatively slender amount of interference or control which the Colonial Office in Downing Street seeks to exercise over colonial governments. As one Colonial Office official once put it to me, "the chief duty of the Colonial Office is to select the best man available for any particular job, and send him out to do it, and back him up".'[27]

The Governors of the British West African colonies, assisted by Executive Councils composed of officials who were primarily heads of the technical departments, were thus extremely powerful beings with few internal or external checks to their authority. But, like their French counterparts, in the early years of establishing colonial rule, they were desk-bound, busy running a growing bureaucracy, drawing up plans for development, hampered by poor communications. And, as in French West Africa, the man who really represented British administration was the District Officer or District Commissioner—the titles were variously used—in the four West African colonies. The Governor in Nigeria had under him the two Lieutenant-Governors (sometimes Commissioners) who in turn had their own bureaucracy to manage, leaving administration to the Residents of the provinces. Even the Residents, powerful though they were, could be thwarted by their District Officers with minds for independent action, as Joyce Cary shows so clearly in his novel about Borgu, *An American Visitor*, set just before the First World War. His District Officer Bewsher, intent on settling a dangerous local dispute in his own manner, rather than that of his Resident, happily named Alabaster, resorted to the 'old trick of the district officer at war with his Resident' by disappearing 'into the most inaccessible parts of his domain' where telegrams could not reach him.[28]

An examination of Britain's system of local administration in her four West African colonies, with particular reference to the abolition of slavery, the use of forced labour, direct taxation, and the relation of British justice to traditional judicial systems, and of the British

District Officer to the traditional chief will show that the former had much less impact on traditional society than his French counterpart. There were of course exceptions, particularly among people without centralised forms of government, as the career of Cary's Bewsher shows.

## 3 Taxation, forced labour and slavery

Like the French, the British saw as one of the main aims of their occupation the expansion of the market economy, both to pay for the cost of their newly established colonial governments and to provide produce needed by the metropolis. If, as we argue, the system of administration imposed by the British hampered rather than helped its expansion, this does not take away from the fact that increase of productivity on the part of the African was one of Britain's main goals. Such an increase would provide revenue either through export or import dues, or through the ability of the producers to support direct taxation. Inversely, taxation, as in French West Africa, could be used as the stimulus to productivity. Lugard, like most other British administrators of this period, was an inheritor of the Victorian belief in the virtue of work: 'direct taxation is a moral benefit to the people by stimulating industry and production',[29] he wrote in 1906, adding that 'there is no civilised State in the world where direct taxation has not been found to be a necessity, and African communities which aspire to be regarded as civilised must share the common burden of civilisation'.[30]

Lugard saw taxation as a triple-edged weapon: as a stimulus to production, as a source of revenue for the support of the colonial administration—'it marks the recognition by the community of the protecting Power'[31]—and finally as the basis for the development of his system of indirect rule which meant the modernisation of traditional institutions through their own agency. Without income from taxation they could not provide for development, let alone the payment of officials on a regular basis.[32] 'Without a tax there can be no treasury, and without a treasury no eventual measure of self-rule.'[33]

Not all British Governors took such a sophisticated view of the role of taxation. Governor Cardew of Sierra Leone in imposing the hut tax on the Protectorate did so primarily because he saw no other way of covering the costs of administration and development. We have seen with what disastrous results.

For Lugard the imposition of tax in Northern Nigeria emirates was to be easy, for direct taxation had been a feature of Fulani and the earlier Habe administrations. It had also been a feature of the government of Bornu. But wherever proposals for direct taxation were put forward for peoples not accustomed to it, the Colonial Office remembered Sierra Leone. In Gold Coast direct taxation was not introduced until 1936, and then only gradually after an unsuccessful attempt in 1932.[34] In 1897 the Governor of the Gold Coast introduced proposals for direct taxation on houses, but these were abandoned not only because of the effect of the Sierra Leone Hut Tax Wars, but also because of Colonial Office memories of the strong protests that had taken place against increases in customs duties in 1874, 1877 and more recently in 1892. Looking further back, there was the memory of the unsuccessful attempt to impose a poll-tax in the Colony between 1852 and 1861, which had led to the Christianborg rebellion of 1854.[35] Fortunately for the administration it gained sufficient revenue from indirect taxation on the buoyant cocoa crop and to a lesser extent gold mining and the sizeable imports which earnings from these sources made possible. In the Gambia a tax on Yards—'a collection of one or more huts and their lands originally held by a kindred group'[36]—was imposed by an Ordinance of 1895, but was difficult of collection in the early years, yielding only £3,168 in 1904[37] and it was not until the 1935 Ordinance that the Tax became regularised. It was never a major source of income for the administration, which depended both on grants-in-aid from the Home Government and on duties on the groundnut crop and the imports generated by income from it.

Only with Lugard's assumption of the Governor-Generalship of the two Nigerias in 1912 did plans materialise for the introduction of direct taxation into Southern Nigeria. Given his views on the desirability of taxing Africans it was not surprising that one of his first actions should have been to send his trusted lieutenant of Northern Nigerian days, Richmond Palmer, on a tour of Southern Nigeria to make recommendations about the introduction of taxation. Palmer proposed that a start should be made with Benin, Oyo and Abeokuta,[38] which until 1914 had remained a semi-independent enclave of Southern Nigeria. Benin presented no problem, since it had been completely subjugated and the new Oba, Eweka II, son of the defeated and exiled Ovenramwen, had only acceded to the throne in 1914, and was dependent for his installation on British goodwill. In Oyo, where the Alafin had never collected direct taxes, the decision to make him and his 'district heads' collect taxes led to riots in the dependent town of Iseyin in 1916. These were speedily put down despite the absence of Nigerian troops on the East African Campaign. Abeokuta, which had lost its autonomy as a protected state in 1914 owing to internal dissensions which forced the Alake, its ruler, and the British Commissioner to call on troops from Lagos, reacted with equal violence. Taxation was maintained, but only as a result of use of force for which Lugard was blamed by Eric Moore,* the African lawyer and friend of Lugard who headed the Commission of Enquiry.[39] In the East and other parts of the West direct taxation was not introduced until after the First World War, with the exception of the Niger Delta where direct taxation had traditionally been levied by the Heads of Houses. In those areas the effects were disastrous for the Administration.

In West Africa, the British, like the French, had recourse to forced labour as an alternative means to taxation of making the African work for the new goals of development they had set for him. Thus in the Gambia able-bodied males had to labour on public works projects—including acting as carriers for the administration—on penalty of six months' imprisonment or a fine. In Southern Nigeria all able-bodied males between fifteen and fifty, and females between fifteen and forty, were liable for labour for road-making and similar work up to six days a quarter.[40] Though the British were anxious to abolish forced labour—Lugard saw the introduction of taxation as 'the corollary of the abolition, however gradual, of forced labour'[41] —as late as 1920 the Secretary of State for the Colonies issued a despatch in which he put a ceiling of sixty days a year on forced labour for Government.[42] However, in British West Africa forced labour never reached the excesses of the French-speaking territories: there was no compulsory culture of crops or recruitment for commercial companies. But nevertheless it was an important factor in the development of West Africa. The railways in Nigeria, for instance, depended on compulsory labour. In 1925, 38% of the 12,500 labourers on railway construction in the North were 'political' labour recruited forcibly by chiefs.[43] As Buell pointed out, this 'political' labour, though paid, did not receive the going market rate for labour.[44]

For the most part forced labour was administered by 'native authorities', since it was the native authorities who were responsible for the maintenance of roads and most other local public works. Since the labour was directly recruited by the British administration only in cases like the railways or where native authorities were so

* Moore was one of the rare members of the African élite who managed to survive the general trend of the times of excluding Africans from the inner sanctum of power.

rudimentary that the administrative officer was in fact the executive of the authority, it tended not to be so obvious a feature of administration. Indirectly administered for the most part, it was not so apparent to the outside world as the *corvée* in French West Africa. The British effectively formalised the traditional powers of many chiefs to use compulsory labour by their subjects. In some cases they regulated it so that it was not work personally done for the chief but for the native authority. In Sierra Leone the chiefs were even allowed to use forced labour as they had done before the imposition of the Protectorate. However, in 1932 the Forced Labour Ordinance limited the obligation of any one man to his chief to thirty days' labour a year, and stipulated that he should never be required to work more than six days in a week.[45] Even after independence chiefs were still raising forced labour legally.

The apparent initiative for recruitment of forced labour came for the most part from the chief, whether or not he was constituted as a native authority in the Lugardian sense. Whereas in French West Africa the initiative came from the French administrator, the recruitment by the chief. The distinction may be a fine one, but in large chiefdoms it left the administrators' hands, Pilate-like, clean. Also it allowed for abuses by the native authorities, a most notable one being the magnificent manor-style rest house built by forced labour in Iseyin for the Alafin of Oyo, but used mainly by the British Resident and his friends. A chief could also send to work enemies, and therefore, when considered in terms of a labour tax, it was inequitably distributed, and certainly never hit the well-to-do sections of the community.

Forced labour was used in the Gold Coast in the same manner as Nigeria, but chiefs, not constituted as native authorities until after the 1930's, were paid in respect of the labour they supplied. One of the problems in discussing forced labour in British West Africa is that by calling it 'political labour', one could deny that forced labour had ever been used, as Sir Gordon Guggisberg did in 1926, stating categorically, 'I can find no record of forced labour in the Gold Coast in the present century.'[46] Buell adds a snide note that Governor Hodgson in 1901 had reported that Africans had complained about 'the compulsory supply of carriers'.[47] However, whereas the French standardised it as a general obligation, the British used it only when voluntary labour was not forthcoming. By 1946, when forced labour was at last abolished in French West Africa, it had ceased to be of significance in most parts of British West Africa.

Slavery as a legal status was abolished throughout British West

P

Africa as soon as occupation became effective. Thus Lugard had passed a proclamation against slavery in the first year of his assumption of duty in Northern Nigeria. In his speech approving Sultan Attahiru's appointment a few days after the conquest of Sokoto he declared 'Buying and selling slaves and enslaving people are forbidden.'[48] However, fearful of the consequences of the immediate and compulsory freeing of those already enslaved, he was careful in his anti-slavery proclamation to insist that only those slaves who applied to become free from their masters would become free. This approach he was later to call 'permissive freedom', that is the initiative lay with the slave rather than the law.[49] Similarly in the Gold Coast in 1874 when Captain Strachan, the Governor, had abolished slavery in the Colony, he was careful to make it clear that existing slaves were not being forced to leave their masters.[50] And again the initiative was left to the slave. In Sierra Leone, even before the proclamation of the Protectorate in 1896, it had been accepted that a slave seeking release from his status had but to hold on to a British flagstaff at a Frontiers' post.[51] However, it was only in 1927 that the Legal Status of slavery was abolished in Sierra Leone. This followed an international outcry against the decision of the Sierra Leone Supreme Court freeing two slave-owners who had been convicted 'for conspiracy and assault in the recapture of runaway slaves'.[52] The reason was that the status of slavery had not been abolished in the Protectorate through oversight of the Legislature. An embarrassed British delegate, Sir Edward Hilton Young, told the Sixth Committee of the League of Nations that 'steps were being taken by urgent measures as quickly as possible to remedy the law of the Sierra Leone Protectorate in regard to slavery'.[53] In the Gambia neither the 1894 Slave Trade Abolition Ordinance nor the 1906 Ordinance abolished the status of slavery. The slave, however, was permitted to ransom himself at £10 and the death of a master meant the freedom of the slave.[54] So fearful were the Government of the social consequences of outright abolition that it preferred to hope that 'the adoption by the Commissioner of a strong moral attitude against slavery would eventually cause the practice to wither away'.[55] The 1894 Ordinance did however permit the Governor to emancipate individuals or districts at his discretion. The transfer of slaves from master to master was forbidden by the 1906 Ordinance. But as late as 1930 the Gambia Government had found it necessary to pass an *Affirmation of Slavery Ordinance*, though by that time social change had created conditions in which most slaves were able to undertake labour independent of their masters.

## 4 *Types of British Administration*

In strong contrast with French West Africa, 'native administration' in British West Africa took on a bewildering variety of forms, the response of the empirical approach of the British to the wide range of differences in the institutions of the people they governed. However, by the 1930's there had emerged a dominant pattern, that of indirection of command, or the use of an indigenous political agency for local government. This did not mean that indirect rule had become the common feature of native administration in West Africa. For indirect rule, as it generally came to be understood, implied the government of the African peoples through their traditional political institutions, shorn of those features that conflicted with British concepts of civilised behaviour, the exaction of direct taxes and the establishment of regularised treasuries. Modernisation was to come from within, stimulated by advice from the British administrator. In this context the use of an indigenous agency for government did not mean that indirect rule was being practised. At the one extreme there was the practice of letting traditional chiefs govern their subjects as though they were under a protectorate in the nineteenth-century sense, so that having agreed to abolish certain customs they were internally autonomous, leaving to the British protector control of external relations and jurisdiction over its own subjects. That is, in parts of British West Africa there emerged a Native States' policy similar to that of India. At the other extreme there was the attempt to discover chiefs where none existed, or to give executive functions to chiefs without traditional political authority. In these instances the British chief came close to fulfilling the same role as the French chef *administratif*. But for the British administrator the objective was different. He did not wish to incorporate these chiefs into the administrative hierarchy as subalterns to whom he could give orders, but to delegate to them the problems of local government. It was only because such chiefs had little traditional power that administrators were forced into the French position of giving them direct orders rather than advising them what to do. Advice is the key word in the pattern of relationship between the British administrator and the native authority, who in the early years was usually a chief.

There seems to have been a general temperamental disposition among British District Officers to assume the role of adviser to chiefs rather than to give them direct orders. Thus the British administration usually did not summon chiefs from outlying districts to his office for orders, as his French counterpart generally did, thereby wasting much of their time,[56] but visited them in their parishes. He called on the chief of his own headquarters town, rather than vice versa. We must, however, note that advice shaded into command when dealing with the smaller chief, and also that advice given by an overlord is very near to being a command. However, the fact that it was given in the form of advice meant the possibility of discussion. A green Assistant District Officer often found that in a dispute with a well-established chief the latter, not himself, gained the support of the District Officer or Resident. As Molly Mahood has written in her study of Joyce Cary, an Administrative Officer of interventionist inclinations: 'The patience and tolerance which were required of a political officer working under the system of indirect rule, even in a division where the Emirs had such restricted powers as they had in Borgu, are shown in Cary's handling of one case of corruption. . . . The Emir of Kaiama agreed with Cary over the teacups that the chief in question, who was despotic and stupid, should be publicly tried and, if found guilty, deposed. The Resident acquiesced. The trial was a full-dress one. . . . The chief not only confessed to extortion but to quite a few other crimes that Cary had not known about. Cary gave his judgment that the Sarkin was unfitted to be a chief, and asked the Emir for his opinion. The Emir, who had received a number of confidential visits between the tea-party and the trial, promptly said he thought the Sarkin ought to be given another chance. "The whole assembly looked at me," Cary wrote later. "I felt like a fool and probably looked like a fool. But I was obliged to say 'in that case O will remain chief'." '[57]

This temperamental disposition to assume the role of adviser was fortified by the pressure of shortage of funds and staff. It was impossible to provide enough staff or funds for direct administration, and the use of native agencies was not only to be cheaper, but would be least disruptive of the social order. The British, being anti-assimilationist and empirical in spirit, did not, like the French, wish to restructure the countries they administered, only to reform them gradually. Thus chiefdoms were not broken up, except in the obvious case of Ashanti; administrators for the most part respected the traditional system of electing rulers, though they kept note of desirable candidates, so that where there was no clear traditional choice they could exert pressure in favour of their candidate.

The chiefs—or indigenous agencies—were responsible for a wide variety of tasks, which varied from one area to another. Essentially public works and administration at the local level was left in their hands. But in contrast to the French the British tried to make it seem that these tasks were being performed by the native authorities for themselves rather than for their foreign masters. The object of 'native administration' was training for local self-government. That it also furthered the interests of the administration was of course not coincidental, for this system of local administration, which was not paid for and undertook necessary local development, was very advantageous. In more highly organised states, the chiefs, though deprived of their armies, maintained their own police force, so that even the task of keeping of the peace devolved on native authorities.

British policy of using indigenous political institutions as the agents of colonial government, and of converting these into Lugardian native authorities, proved exceedingly difficult. And though by the end of the period we are studying attempts had been made to introduce indirect rule in all four West African colonies, the results were far from uniformly successful. Nor was the pattern of local government that emerged uniform. Rather, in contrast to the French system, it was highly heterogeneous. For this reason it is impossible to do more than study a few examples that are typical of the main successes and failures of British administration in West Africa. Their study is important for two main reasons. First, it was through the native administrations that the majority of Africans felt the political impact of colonial rule. Secondly, indirect rule became a *bête noire* of the nationalists. They resented the way the British strengthened the powers of the chief vis-à-vis other political forces in the native administrations. But they were even more concerned at the way the British conceived eventual self-government not in terms of democratically elected representation in a central parliament, but through delegation by the native authorities of representatives, usually chiefs, to a central political organism. Indirect rule seemed designed to exclude the educated élite from an effective national role, and was therefore seen as an agency of reaction against the forces of modernisation which colonial exploitation had stimulated. Rattray put the dilemma neatly with regard to the Gold Coast:

'In introducing indirect rule into this country, we would therefore appear to be encouraging on the one hand an institution which draws its inspiration and validity from the indigenous religious beliefs, while on the other hand we are destroying the very foundation upon which the structure we are striving to perpetuate stands. Its shell and outward form might remain, but it would seem too much to expect that its vital energy could survive such a process.'[58]

# Notes

1 Cosnier, *L'ouest africain français*, though he was not uncritical of British colonial policy, see pp. 169–75.

2 *The Times*, 2nd June 1925.

3 *Annuaire du Gouvernement-Général de l'A.O.F.*, Paris, 1922, pp. 1027–36.

4 Harris, *Dawn in Darkest Africa*, p. 123.

5 *Ibid.*, p. 107.

6 Gouvernement-Général de l'A.O.F.: *Textes rélatifs à la formation et la réorganisation des cadres indigènes en A.O.F.*, Gorée, 1916.

7 Harris, *Dawn in Darkest Africa*, p. 110.

8 Lugard, *The Dual Mandate*, p. 5.

9 Harris, *Dawn in Darkest Africa*.

10 This was not so true of the Gold Coast, as Kimble has pointed out, *Ghana*, p. 328: 'Officials were neither so physically remote from one another, nor so emotionally partisan where their own regions were concerned, as seems to have been the case in Nigeria.'

11 Sir Donald Cameron, *The Principles of Native Administration and their Application*, Lagos, 1934.

12 *Ibid.*, p. 13.

13 *Ibid.*, p. 12.

14 *Ibid.*, p. 14.

15 John Wilson, *Education and Changing West African Culture*, New York, 1963, pp. 8–9.

16 Perham, *Lugard II*, p. 411.

17 *Ibid.*, p. 414. E. D. Morel had also suggested that the amalgamated Nigeria be divided into four states, Morel, *Nigeria*, p. 204 for map. Chapter XIX for detailed discussion.

18 *The Times*, 28th December 1936, and *The Colonial Empire in 1937–38: Statement to Accompany the Estimates for the Colonial and Middle Eastern Services*, Cmd. 5760, London, 1938, p. 64.

19 David Apter, *Ghana in Transition* (Revised Edition of *The Gold Coast in Transition*), New York, 1963, p. 136.

20 Cited in Hargreaves, *Sir Samuel Lewis*, p. 35, from Sierra Leone Legislative Council Debates, 11th June 1898.

21 Kimble, *Ghana*, pp. 364–5.

22 Coleman, *Nigeria*, p. 181.

23 *Report by Sir F. D. Lugard on the Amalgamation of Northern and Southern Administration, 1912–19* (1919), Cmd. 468, p. 19.

24 T. Olawale Elias, *Groundworks of Nigerian Law*, London, 1954, p. 165. Wheare, *Nigerian Legislative Council*, p. 29, wrongly asserts that 'The

Council's competence was throughout its history confined to the Colony.'

25 Hailey, *African Survey* (Revised, 1956), p. 287. Lugard, having removed the Legislative Council's competence for the whole of Nigeria, legislated directly through his Executive Council, subject only to a delay of two months between publication and enactment to allow time for review in England by the Colonial Office. Perham, *Lugard II*, p. 417.

26 Suret-Canale, *Afrique Noire II*, pp. 93–4.

27 W. Ormsby-Gore, *Comparative Methods of Colonial Administration*, Chatham House Pamphlet, London, 1930, pp. 10–11.

28 Joyce Cary, *An American Visitor*, Carfax Edition, London, 1952, pp. 100–1.

29 Sir Frederick Lugard, *Revision of Instructions to Political Officers on Subjects Chiefly Political and Administrative*, London, 1919, known as the *Political Memoranda* issued in 1906. Memo No. 5, 'Taxation', para. 4.

30 *Ibid.*, para. 6.

31 Lugard, *Dual Mandate*, p. 218.

32 *Ibid.*, p. 201.

33 *Ibid.*, p. 219.

34 Lord Hailey, *Native Administration in the British African Territories*, Part III, *West Africa: Nigeria, the Gold Coast, Sierra Leone, Gambia*, London, 1951, p. 204.

35 See Kimble, *Ghana*, pp. 168–91 and 306–15.

36 Hailey, *Native Administration*, III, p. 334.

37 Gailey, *Gambia*, p. 118.

38 This report was not published but exists in typescript as 'Reports on a Tour in the Southern Provinces in 1914 by H. R. Palmer', cited in Perham, *Lugard II*, p. 444, from the Lugard Papers.

39 For a useful account of this whole affair see Margery Perham's chapter, 'Indirect Rule and Western Obscurity', in *Lugard II*, pp. 438–56.

40 Harris, *Dawn in Darkest Africa*, pp. 149–50.

41 Lugard, *Political Memoranda*, Memo 5, para. 5.

42 Hailey, *African Survey*, p. 1366.

43 Buell, *Native Problem*, I, p. 658.

44 *Ibid.*, p. 724.

45 Hailey, *Native Administration*, III, p. 305.

46 Sir Gordon Guggisberg, *The Gold Coast: A Review of the Events of 1920–26 and the Prospects of 1927–28*, Accra, 1927, p. 85.

47 Cited in Buell, *Native Problem*, I, p. 828.

48 *Annual Report for Northern Nigeria*, 1902, Appendix III, p. 105.

49 Lugard, *Dual Mandate*, p. 369.

50  Ward, *Ghana*, p. 394.
51  Fyfe, *Sierra Leone*, pp. 114–15.
52  *The Times*, 27th August 1927.
53  *The Times*, 12th September 1927.
54  Gray, *History of the Gambia*, p. 476.
55  Gailey, *Gambia*, from Annual Report for the Gambia of 1896.
56  Cosnier, *L'ouest africain français*.
57  Cited in Mahood, *Cary*, p. 51.
58  R. S. Rattray, *Ashanti Law and Constitution*, London, 1929, p. ix.

# 4 Indirect rule in practice

## 1 Indirect rule: interventionist or non-interventionist

Indirect rule in British West Africa took two forms: interventionist and non-interventionist. As Lugard conceived it indirect rule was a system of colonial administration which not only relied on the indigenous authorities for local government but was constantly goading them to improvement. The agent for its improvement was the British political officer; the means to it, those funds derived from taxation which were not rendered to the sovereign power. 'The policy of the Government was that these Chiefs should govern their people, not as independent, but as dependent rulers. The orders of the Government are not conveyed to the people through them, but emanate from them in accordance, where necessary, with instructions received through the Resident. While they themselves are controlled by Government in policy and matters of importance, their people are controlled in accordance with that policy by themselves. A political officer would consider it as irregular to issue direct orders to an individual native, or even a village head, as a General commanding a division would to a private soldier, except through his commanding officers.'[1]

Again, 'The Resident acts as a sympathetic adviser to the native chief, being careful not to interfere so as to lower his prestige, or cause him to lose interest in his work. *His advice on matters of general policy must be followed, but the native ruler issues his instructions to his subordinate Chiefs and district-heads—not as the orders of the Resident but as his own*'[2] (italics mine).

The key difference between Lugard's system of indirect rule and the non-interventionist type was how the Resident interpreted his role as adviser. In Lugard's conception it was an active role; his successors in Northern Nigeria tended increasingly to look on it as a passive one. Lugard saw advice as actively stimulating change; his successors in the North, Girouard and Bell, preferred to let the Emirs administer themselves provided they did not incur them in trouble.[3] Lugard, for instance, wanted to include the Emirs' budgets in the General Budget of amalgamated Nigeria and was bitterly opposed in this by Governor Temple, who believed indirect rule meant minimal interference on the part of the British Government. Subjection of the Emirs' budget to central control would inevitably lessen their autonomy.[4] As it was they were already subjected to scrutiny and approval by the Northern Administration, thanks to the energy of Lugard's disciple, Richmond Palmer, who established the *Beit-el-Mal*, a system of Native Treasuries, for the Emirates. This put the Emirs' income and expenditure on a theoretically sound accounting basis which could be checked by the Resident. Though not an introduction of Lugard's, the institution of regulated treasuries for each Native Authority, and the payment of a regular salary to its chief and members, became fundamental to the idea of Indirect Rule as expounded by him in the *Dual Mandate* and practised in other British colonies.

Whether Indirect Rule was interventionist or non-interventionist, it involved a considerable initial change in the position of the Emir. He now acted as tax-gatherer for the Government. It is true that the people were accustomed to taxation by the Emirs. But now the various taxes were consolidated into one main tax which was assessed by the British political officer. 'The taxes are raised in the name of the native ruler and by his agents, but he surrenders the fixed proportion to Government, and the expenditure of the portion assigned to the Native Administration, from which fixed salaries to all native officials are paid, is subject to the advice of the Resident, and the ultimate control of the Governor.'[5] The more important rulers retained up to 70% of the taxes they collected. The Sultan of Sokoto, in recognition of his special position, retained 75%. Between 1926 and 1929 there was even dispute as to whether they should render up the total sum or just the sum to be given to the Government, since by rendering the whole sum they would recognise that the return of their portion was a concession of the administration, not a right.[6]

The Emir, apart from collecting taxes for the new administration, an activity which could be held to correspond to his earlier payment of tribute to Sokoto, now had a fixed salary, and had to budget for his administration. He still controlled his legal system, shorn of repugnant punishments, though up to the late 1920's public execution by a particularly unpleasant kind of beheading still took place.[7] The Emir's courts, many of which retained the right to impose the death sentence, were only subject in certain cases to appeal to the Governor.[8] His prisons were inspected by the District Officers. He maintained his own police force. His election was by traditional methods, subject to confirmation by the administration, which sometimes made known its preference. But he could no longer be deposed by traditional methods, though the British administration had the power to depose him. Since deposition of the more important Emirs was much less frequent than in the Sokoto period, the Emirs' powers consequently increased vis-à-vis other groups in the Emirate. Councils, which under Sokoto could appeal against their Emir's misrule, were often not officially recognised as part of the machinery of the native authority. In the inter-war years most Emirs were recognised as sole native authorities. British reluctance to depose Emirs except in extreme and obvious cases of misrule,[9] coupled with their increasing reluctance to intervene in the internal administration of the native authorities of the Emirates, meant that the Emirs became increasingly autocratic. However, the extent of their autocracy was limited by the genuine fear the Emirs had of exceeding their powers as defined by Islamic law. With little motive for innovation, and little outside interference, the Emirates became something very much like Protected Native States. The Northern Nigerian Emirates in the inter-war period became the classic example of non-interventionist indirect rule.

This development was quite contrary to Lugard's intentions. However, in 1912, when he became Governor-General of Nigeria, he was still so enthused by the apparent success of indirect rule in Northern Nigeria that he determined to introduce it to the Southern Provinces, in particular Benin and Yorubaland. The Yoruba Obas in the years before Lugard became Governor-General had been very much in the relation of protected states to the British on the declaration of the Southern Nigerian protectorate in 1900. The Residents had little more than consular powers.[10] It was not until 1904 that the Yoruba states of Ibadan, Oyo and Ife agreed that British courts should have jurisdiction over cases concerning non-natives and over disputes between their inhabitants and non-natives. In 1908 Ijebu-Ode, which was the only conquered Yoruba state, made a similar concession. Only in 1903 were Yoruba states, with the exception of Ibadan and the still nominally independent Abeokuta (Egba), persuaded to drop tolls levied on traders, including Europeans. Though the Secretary of State ordered Ibadan to drop tolls, such was its protest that it was permitted to continue to levy them, though through European officials, for several years more. Only a rudimentary European administrative superstructure emerged before Lugard's decision in 1916 to form the Yoruba Obas into 'Native Authorities' on the Northern pattern. The skeleton administrative staff supervised courts where cases involving British justice were tried, and watched that agreements for the abolition of slave-trading, human sacrifice and repugnant forms of punishment were observed. The Central Native Council and the Native Councils for the Provinces and Districts, which had mainly judicial functions, consisted of the local British administrator and members nominated by the Governor, and dealt with cases concerning British justice. Here again the touch of British rule was at first light.

In Yorubaland Lugard made the mistake of equating the position of the Yoruba Oba with that of the Northern Emir. He did not take into account that as a result of the Civil Wars of the nineteenth century and the growth of a missionary-educated élite, Yoruba political structure had undergone radical changes. It was assumed that Oyo still retained its pre-eminent position in Yorubaland so that it was given authority over areas like Ibadan which not only considered themselves independent, but had saved Oyo from being overrun by the Fulani. The fact that educated Africans, particularly in Abeokuta, now played an important part in the Government, was ignored. The most important error was to think that Obas could be expected to collect direct taxation, which had never been imposed traditionally. Not surprisingly, as we have already seen, riots followed and these had to be put down with troops. Thereafter the system of indirect rule went to all intents and purposes unchallenged, though it was much resented by the educated élite who found themselves excluded from the process of government of their own states. The British, particularly in Abeokuta, thus halted a modernising process by forcing the Yoruba back on a more traditionalist system, which they mistakenly considered to be the true system of Yoruba government. As a result, the Obas increased their personal executive powers. However, even where they were appointed as sole executive authorities they were unable to acquire the autocratic powers of the Northern Emirs. The traditional division of power among many different groups in Yoruba society was vigorous enough to survive the buttressing up of the position of one source of authority by the British.

Ibadan continued to resent being brought under Oyo's jurisdiction and, after a long series of protests, was given a separate native authority by Cameron in 1934. But thereafter they continued to guard jealously against any suggestion that they depended on Oyo.[11]

The greatest British virtue in the art of government, it has often been said, is their empirical approach to problems. Here in Yoruba-land, and elsewhere in West Africa, they became victims of a theory about government. Whatever the circumstances, indirect rule was held up as the panacea for 'native' administration. Worse still, in actual practice the theory buttressed up the more autocratic elements of African society, and tended to militate against modernising tendencies.[12]

We have seen how shocked Cameron was at the reactionary aspects of indirect rule. Thus he chided Nigerian administrators for 'drifting into a habit of mind that a feudal aristocracy of this kind (i.e. the Northern Emirates) is the be-all and end-all of Indirect Administration',[13] and urged a more modern approach to the development of local government in Nigeria. He sought to broaden the experience of the Emirs by sending them to England, where, however, their visits to the London Zoo seem always to have been the most important event, judging by the prominence *The Times* gave to them.[14] He arranged for the Resident to sit in on the Councils of the Oba of Benin and the Alake of Abeokuta, still in their role as advisers, but, he hoped, more interventionist ones. He also introduced educated Africans into a number of Councils. But even his energies failed to modernise what had in practice become a highly conservative system of administering Africans.

## 2 *Laissez-faire*

Indirect rule in the Nigerian sense was not introduced to the Gold Coast and Sierra Leone until the 1930's. Until then the British administration pursued a policy of laissez-faire. In the Gold Coast, indirect rule was introduced to buttress up the authority of the Colony states, in Sierra Leone to bring the chiefdoms under some form of control.

In the Gold Coast by the terms of the Native Jurisdiction Ordin-ance of 1874, when the Colony was estabished, the relation between the Protecting Power and the Colony Chiefs was formalised as one of minimal interference on the part of the former in the affairs of the latter. From 1874 until the reforms of 1927 the Colony Chiefs managed to retain a degree of internal autonomy that could not be changed because of the nineteenth-century tradition that they were 'independent authorities over whom control could only be secured by their individual agreement'.[15] By the Ordinance, which was not put into force until 1883, they were able to enact byelaws 'with the concurrence of their Chiefs, Headmen and others who by Native Customary Law were Councillors of their Stools'. Similarly Head Chiefs and Chiefs could form Native Tribunals to try breaches of bye-laws and judge civil and criminal cases of a minor character. Appeal against the court could be made to the Secretary of Native Affairs who could then refer the case to a Divisional Court. The importance of the Chief being the source of bye-laws was a negative one: he would not introduce laws that the administration might feel necessary, but which would be unpopular with his people. No provision was made in such circumstances for the administration to enact such bye-laws as they felt desirable but which the chiefs would not pass.

There was no taxation of the people of the Colony, so that the chiefs did not have either to assume a new role as collectors of direct taxation, nor, since taxation was assumed to be, as Lugard put it, a recognition of the sovereignty of the protecting power, did they have in this way to recognise the position of the British. The chiefs continued to claim that their jurisdiction was inherent and not derived from the British. They governed their chiefdoms by the customary methods of collecting tribute and by the sale of lands belonging to the chiefdom (Stool Lands). Fines and court fees were another source of revenue. And since there was no supervision of the Native Tribunals by the administration there was ample scope for abuse which was readily seized upon.

The Colony Chiefs were thus apparently minimally circumscribed in their government of their peoples. Even the Chief's Ordinance of 1904 which 'empowered the Governor to confirm the election and installation of a Chief . . . was only intended to render the position of a Chief unassailable in law; it did not enable the Government to maintain that a Chief can exercise no legal powers till formally recognised as a Native Authority'.[16]

The main reduction in the chief's powers was the limitation on his judicial competence. The British-controlled courts tried major criminal cases, and stopped certain classes of crime from being punished. Thus in 1899 the Omanhene of Larteh complained to the District Commissioner that one of the sons of his predecessor in office 'had had connection with two of his father's wives', a particularly abhorrent form of incest in his eyes. But the District Commissioner replied that 'illicit intercourse with a married woman is not a criminal offence according to traditional law . . . I am to add that Government should not be troubled with these frivolous complaints'. It is unlikely, as Brokensha comments, that this culprit, or those who committed similar offences, went unpunished.[17] However, as Mensah Sarbah pointed out, the circumscription of the chief's judicial competence, and the introduction of District Commissioners' courts, reduced their status for 'in the African mind, leadership carried with it the administration of justice'.[18]

Whilst it became British policy 'to see the authority of the chiefs supported by all Government officers, and the chiefs and their principal advisers taken into the confidence of the Government',[19] the chiefs in fact lost power in the early years of colonial rule. Their authority was challenged by the young men, especially the educated ones, who resented the judicial authority of 'illiterate' chiefs. Chiefs found themselves rivalled by men who had grown wealthy as a result of the cocoa boom. They found their sub-chiefs demanding independence. Most serious of all, when they did try to assert their authority, they were de-stooled in accordance with custom. As the Commissioner of the Colony's Western Province wrote gloomily: 'Everywhere is to be found a spirit of impatience and intolerance among the younger men. The latter, with a mere smattering of education, resent and impede the authority of the Chiefs and elder men, few of whom can either read or write.' He noted with concern the frequent de-stoolment of 'strong chiefs'.[20]

Attempts to introduce indirect rule into the Colony were primarily concerned with strengthening the authority of the chiefs. The 1922 Native Jurisdiction Ordinance tried to regularise the Native Tribunals, making them dependent on the Administration. It was attacked by the educated élite because lawyers would be excluded from the Provincial Commissioners' Courts in which appeals from Native Tribunals would be heard, and because they resented Government interference with indigenous institutions. By pointing out to the chiefs the implication of the Ordinance that the chiefs' authority would now depend on the British, rather than the people, they persuaded a sufficient number to oppose it so that it was in fact dropped. However, the position of the chiefs was successfully fortified by the 1925 Constitution and the 1927 Native Administration Ordinance. Under the Constitution six Colony Chiefs, elected by Provincial Councils established for the purpose in each of the three provinces of the Colony, would sit in Legislative Council. They therefore outnumbered the three members elected directly by the urban voters of Accra, Cape Coast and Sekondi two to one. Thereby they 'gained a prominence at the national level quite out of keeping with their traditional limits'.[21] The 1927 Native Administration Ordinance strengthened the chiefs against de-stoolment by their subjects and against attempts by their sub-chiefs to declare their independence. The Provincial Councils, hitherto essentially electoral colleges, were vested with judicial and administrative authority and later met in combined strength as the Joint Provincial Council which rivalled the Legislative Council as a fulcrum of power.

Whilst the administration thus strengthened the position of the chiefs and the native states, it was only in 1936 that a serious effort was made to introduce the system of indirect rule as practised in Northern Nigeria. Provision was made for the creation of treasuries for the States and some were actually started. But there was no provision that the funds in the treasury should be accounted for or subjected to scrutiny by the administration.[22] In 1939 a law was finally passed by which States could be compelled to set up Treasuries and by which their estimates would be subject to administrative approval. Finally in 1944 the Native Authority and Native Courts Ordinances were passed, establishing indirect rule in the Colony for the first time. Direct taxation in the form of an annual rate was imposed for the first time by the chiefs, in place of their traditional levies. But in contrast to Northern Nigeria, no portion of the sum raised through the Annual Rate was paid to the central government.

In his report of 1898 on the Hut Tax Riots in Sierra Leone, Sir David Chalmers recommended that the only possible form of government in the Protectorate was through the chiefs themselves, who should be responsible for keeping law and order. He also recommended the abolition of the tax. However, this was retained. Responsibility for its collection was delegated to the chiefs along with their other local government duties. It was not until 1937 that Native Treasuries were introduced into the chiefdoms, and this meant that in practice the Protectorate Government in its early years was a compromise between indirect rule and a policy of laissez-faire. Traditionally the power of individual chiefs, whether Mende or Temne, over their peoples was extensive, so there was no great difficulty in their assuming the functions of executive authorities at the local government level. Most chiefdoms—with the notable exception of those who had been wiped out in the Hut Tax Wars— had signed treaties with the British, and as late as 1949 £1,305 was set aside in the Sierra Leone Budget for payment to the chiefs in respect of these treaties.[23] Except in cases concerning the most serious of crimes such as witchcraft, slave-raiding or trading, murder and rape, the chiefs retained judical control of their people. As the chiefs had to hand over the totality of the Hut Tax to the government, they relied on income from traditional sources such as tribute in kind and services from their people which was paid to the Chiefdom Council. The Administration had the ultimate right of deposing chiefs, but the process was extremely complicated and rarely resorted to.[24] The chiefs were under no obligation to the Colonial Government to undertake any functions other than the maintenance of law and order and the collection of the Hut Tax. The Protectorate Ordinance of 1896 and the Ordinances enacted between 1901 and 1905 did not require any development of local government, and meant that no significant advance would be made in this sphere for fifty years.[25] Each chiefdom remained substantially a Native State. There were some 200 such states, as each chiefdom was relatively small and there had never been any traditionally larger unit of centralisation. The District Commissioners, numbering only five, had very little control over them in the early years; a situation augmented by lack of good communications. The only really effective check to their government was the Court Messengers. Initially these were purely messengers of the administration, but after 1901, when the Frontiers were integrated into the purely military West African Frontier Force, they took over the former's police duties and formed a liaison between the District Commissioner and the chiefs. Theirs was a position of great potential power, and many of them were quick to exploit the situation, for they were closer to the people than the chief and could extort suitable compensation from the latter by threatening to expose any malpractices to the District Commissioner. So great was the power of this office that one Court Messenger refused to take on the chieftaincy of a new chiefdom established by a District Officer because he considered himself better off where he was.[26] Apart from the Court Messengers the checks on chiefly powers came from traditional rather than British-inspired sources, although there were politico-social changes set in motion by the fact that British administration gave the sub-chiefs greater powers than they had exercised in traditional society. Thus a chief's activities were circumscribed by the need to placate sub-chiefs and other traditional factions, in particular the Poro, a secret society with considerable religious, social, and economic authority.

Q

It was only with the introduction of Lugardian-style indirect rule that the chiefs were brought under more effective control by the administration. Their political activities were watched more carefully by the colonial government, restrictions were placed on their travel outside their chiefdoms and their financial affairs more closely scrutinised[27] than had been possible under the old laissez-faire system.

### 3 Imposed chiefs

Where the British could not find chiefs in a society, they tended to impose them. In the Gambia such an imposition was not alien, for chiefs with executive powers had existed, but in many areas had been wiped out during the Soninke-Marabout wars. In parts of Northern Ghana clan elders whose authority was primarily religious were attributed executive powers alien to their societies. In Eastern Nigeria, with few exceptions, the establishment of chiefs was entirely foreign, for power in matters both religious and secular was shared in the community. In each case the British did what they could to find someone with traditional authority of some kind to act as intermediary between their inadequately staffed administrative service and the people. In contrast to the French, they did take pains to discover people with some semblance of traditional authority to be chiefs. They rarely imposed chiefs of a different ethnic group on a people. That people without any real claim to traditional authority so often became chiefs was largely due to the ignorance of the administration about the nature of African society. So in Eastern Nigeria the British often acted in a very French manner in appointing warrant chiefs, as Hailey has noted: 'The warrants were sometimes given to people in return for services rendered to the Government, and there was inevitably a tendency to appoint persons of intelligence with some understanding of European ways, so that the more pushing men tended to gain warrants although they may have had no hereditary or customary status.'[28] Nevertheless, even in the East the administration was by and large anxious to appoint those with real claims to authority.

In Gambia the administration confirmed in their position the *Mansa* (the traditional chiefs) where they still existed; where they had been destroyed they sought out likely candidates. In other areas they appointed the apparent rulers of the area if they were favourable to the British. The people did not seem to resent the appointment of chiefs in this manner since there was no revolt against their authority. All chiefs were responsible to the Travelling Commissioner, who assumed a much greater executive role than his counterparts in most other parts of British West Africa. Under the 1894 Protectorate Ordinance the Administrator could withdraw powers from the head man or head chief and appoint successors to those who were deceased or temporarily incapacitated.[29] The Travelling Commissioners not only advised the chiefs but, under Section 13 of the Ordinance, it was stipulated that chiefs shall 'obey all orders given by the Commissioner for the order and general management of the district'.[30] However, it must be remembered that there were only two Travelling Commissioners in the early years, so that the chiefs were not interfered with much. When the Commissioner was absent from their districts, head chiefs presided over their own courts and sat on all matters of customary law 'not repugnant to natural justice or incompatible with any ordinance of the Colony which applies to the Protected Territories'. The chiefs were also responsible for the upkeep of roads and the collection of the Yard Tax. They even had their own police force known as 'badge messengers'.

These chiefs were so successful that in 1933 Sir Richmond Palmer, now Gambia's Governor, felt able to introduce the Native Authority system in the Gambia. Native Authorities were set up, usually consisting of a single chief, empowered to issue Orders enforceable through Native Tribunals and also to make Rules, subject to the Governor's approval for 'the peace, good order and welfare of those within their jurisdiction'.[31] Not until 1945, however, were Native Treasuries established for each Native Authority, which could then finance its activities from a new local rate called the District Tax.

The imposed chiefs of the Gambia were a success because the institution of chieftaincy had deep roots in Gambian tradition. In Eastern Nigeria they were a disastrous failure, having for the most part no such roots. The British, faced by a situation in which there were no readily apparent political authorities through whom they could govern, established courts on which sat 'chiefs' whom they themselves designated and to whom they issued warrants confirming their appointment. These chiefs and the native courts superseded the traditional popular assemblies as the means of local government.[32] The Warrant Chiefs rarely corresponded to those who in precolonial times held authority among their fellow men, and tended to be those who were able to force themselves on the British administrator as leaders of their people, or those whom the people, seeing that the British were determined to nominate chiefs over them, put forward as candidates. 'Native Courts' on which they sat in principle were presided over by a British political officer, and meted out justice and issued rules, with the sanction of the Governor.

The British political officers in practice rarely presided over the courts because they were so few in number and had so many other duties. Under Lugard they ceased to preside altogether.[33] This led to many abuses of power on the part of most of the Warrant Chiefs,[34] who were particularly resented among the Ibo not only because they were an alien institution but because of the way they exploited their people in the absence of proper supervision by the British. In particular the court clerks and court messengers were able to gain power from this lack of control, for it was they who were responsible for the running of the courts. The Clerk was the only official who sat permanently. He issued every summons without reference to the Warrant Chiefs, ordered arrests, was responsible for the court messengers, was in charge of prisoners and conveyed instructions from the District Officer to the Warrant Chiefs. 'In other words', as the Secretary of Native Affairs reported in 1922, 'we are administering these provinces through a junior political service composed of semi-educated Africans, who in many cases are alien to the people they control.'[35]

This report had been made for Governor Clifford because of concern at the way the East was being administered. But despite its sharply critical tone nothing was done to introduce a change. It was only after the introduction of taxation that the people, through their wide-scale revolts against the authorities, forced the Government to reconsider their whole administrative policy in the East. Direct taxation was introduced for all adult males in the form of a poll tax of $2\frac{1}{2}\%$ of their annual income. The main object of this was apparently not to raise revenue for the central government, but to strengthen the Warrant Chief system by the establishment of Native Treasuries.[36] The Warrant Chiefs were charged with the unpopular task of assessing the income of each adult male. Taxation was introduced at a particularly unfortunate time, for prices for palm-oil were low, and in any case for a people with very small cash income presented considerable hardship.[37] Rumours spread that women were also to be taxed and this sparked off riots in large areas of the East, during which police fired on one crowd and killed thirty-two people. The first commission of enquiry was largely concerned with exonerating the officials concerned in the shooting. The second commission of enquiry, on which two Africans sat, considered the causes of the riots, and traced them not only to discontent with taxation but 'the widespread discontent at the persecution, extortion and corruption practised by the so-called Warrant Chiefs or Native Court Members'.[38] Accordingly, Cameron, the new Governor, ordered an examination by Government anthropologists and District Officers of the social structure of the peoples of the East. By 1935 some 200 reports were submitted and in consequence ' "a very great variety of units of Native Authority" were recognised which only in a few instances consisted of a traditional Chief or Chief in Council . . . and for the most part consisted of Group or Clan Councils or Village Councils'.[39] Indirect Rule, not through a chief, but through the indigenous political authority, was introduced.

This policy had its complications. Among the Yakö of Umor, for instance, the Native Court and the Warrant Chiefs had become so institutionalised that when the British Government sought in the early thirties to discover what the 'real' system of indigenous government had been, Forde, who was working among them at the time, reported that 'their own suggestions almost all concerned modifications in the Court . . . (and) . . . few could envisage a new Council which would exercise administrative functions in the village'.[40] Prior to the British occupation, 'indigenous government in Umor was effected through loosely co-ordinated deliberations, judicial decisions, and executive acts of self-perpetuating spirit cult associations, the ritual powers and moral authority of which were in some cases buttressed up by physical coercion of recalcitrants'.[41] The institution of the Native Courts system meant that Umor had to provide Warrant Chiefs to sit on it. The Administrator actually appointed them, but since he desired to appoint someone apparently with authority among the people, he accepted their choice. Far from putting forward those with any traditional position in Umor society the people, so Forde was informed, put forward 'prosperous and generous men who were good speakers and had a reputation in their ward for shrewdness and courage (and were likely to deal effectively with Administration)'.[42] Here then we have a situation in which people in a traditional African society responded to the imposition of centralised executive authority on them by choosing from among themselves those who seemed most fitted for the role. The mistake the British were to make in the thirties, at the apparent failure of the Warrant Chief system, was to try to discover an idealised, pre-colonial structure of government which had been irrevocably changed by twenty years and upwards of colonial rule.

In the end the British were at a loss to find an appropriate native system and introduced, of all things, their own system of local government.

## 4 Direct administration

In newly created townships like Kaduna, capital of Northern Nigeria, the Africans came under the direct rule of the administration. In the capitals of the former colonies rule was effectively direct, and based on English rather than African models. In so far as Africans had a say in the government of the Colony towns it was through the Legislative Councils, except in Freetown which had an English-style City Council headed by a Mayor, who was usually African.

The other important areas in which Britain ruled directly in this period were Ashanti and Benin. The latter presented little problem since it had been effectively conquered by the British in 1896, and its Oba, who was absolutely pivotal to its traditional politico-religious life, deported. The vacuum of power was filled by the British Administrator. The Administrator became effectively Oba until the accession of Ovenramwen's heir Eweka II in 1914, soon after which Benin was constituted into a Native Authority by Lugard.

In Ashanti[43] the British attempted to establish a system of near direct rule after the arrest, deposition, and subsequent removal to Cape Coast of the Asantehene, Prempeh I. While having declared Ashanti a protectorate, they had not yet formulated any clear-cut plan for instituting an administrative system other than appointing a Resident. The first Resident, Captain Maxwell, was appointed in 1896 as the Chief Civil and Military Officer of the Crown and possessed authority to exercise all ordinary civil and criminal jurisdiction. He was not to interfere in the ordinary administration of an Oman-hene (chief of one of the constituent states of the Ashanti Con-federacy) and his chiefs except in the usual instances of practices the British thought repugnant. Each state was treated separately, and was responsible for the arrangement of its own affairs and for the establishment of courts. This meant that the imperial structure at whose centre had previously been Kumasi was broken. It was the original intention of the British that their Resident would assume the powers and prerogatives of the Asantehene, but they were never able to work this out successfully. Their general policy became to isolate Kumasi from its surrounding states and reduce its authority to being merely one amongst the other states of the dissolved Confederacy.

The initial preoccupation of the administration was to raise revenue in Ashanti to recoup the cost of the 1896 expedition and the establishment of the new British administration. Several means were considered and finally a plan was formulated by Resident Stewart, and accepted by Governor Hodgson, for the collection of payments called 'interest on the debt'. Each Omanhene was to be responsible for its collection in a customary manner in his own district, for which he would receive 10% of the amount. Caution in its presentation to the chiefs had been urged, since Stewart was well aware that British administration was not popular in Ashanti, so that any attempt to collect revenue, whatever it was called, would be risky. The garrison at Kumasi was also extremely weak. However, Governor Hodgson ignored these warnings and not only informed the collected chiefs at Kumasi of the scheme but also demanded that they give up to him the Golden Stool, the soul of the Ashanti nation. This silly, and to the Ashanti sacrilegious, demand, coupled with the sending out of search parties for its recovery through a very unstable population sensitive to any rumour, sparked off the Ashanti uprising of 1900. The Governor was besieged in Kumasi fort and only after fierce fighting was Ashanti crushed. The Golden Stool remained hidden from the British, who formally annexed Ashanti to the British Crown.[44] Prempeh was exiled to Sierra Leone so that he could not provide a focal point for resurgent Ashanti nationalism. But as *The Times* wrote on the restoration of the Asantehene, Prempeh II, to his throne in 1935, 'In spite of the policy of disintegration adopted and gradually imposed by the British Government after the rebellion of 1900, the people of Ashanti had always remained a nation.'[45]

The British tried first to isolate Kumasi from the other states of the confederacy. Kumasi chiefs were told that they were not to interfere in any matters outside Kumasi Division. Kumasi was made one compact unit, thus fundamentally altering its status during the days of the confederacy when it had villages under direct rule scattered throughout the whole of Ashanti.

Recognising that the Kumasi chiefs would be reluctant to accept such permanent curtailment of their authority, the Government did offer some appeasement by encouraging the clan heads to form a Council which was to assist the Chief Commissioner in dealing with Kumasi affairs in the absence of a Kumasihene. But they were not to have any power over other head chiefs and were not to deal with criminal cases. This was regularised in 1905 when the Council of Chiefs was created. Its main functions were to settle matters relating to the town of Kumasi and matters dealing with stool lands and property.

Ashanti was divided into four districts each of which had its own commissioner. Over these four commissioners was a Chief Commissioner. The Chief Commissioner in the immediate post-war period had wide discretionary powers. He could make, amend, revoke rules and regulations on a number of specified subjects including such unrelated things as sanitation, regulation of sale of firearms and ammunition, and fisheries. He had wide judicial powers and could try cases without a jury. The prisoner appeared before him undefended, since solicitors and barristers of the Supreme Court were prohibited from practising in Ashanti or appearing in Ashanti courts. He could order the sentence to be imposed before submitting the notes on evidence to the Governor. In cases of the death penalty and heavy sentences of imprisonment there was an obvious danger when the officer in charge might very well have no legal training. Concern over this in both Gold Coast and London resulted in it being obligatory for the Commissioner to wait until the Governor had reviewed the notes of evidence before carrying out the more serious sentences.

Kumasi and Ashanti, deprived of their ruler, came under the direct rule of the Chief Commissioner who was effectively both Asantehene and Kumasihene. Nevertheless Britain was feeling her way towards a system of indirect rule in Ashanti.[46] Each constituent state of Ashanti, except Kumasi, was ruled by its Omanhene, who nevertheless was closely supervised by the British District Commissioner. It was however hoped that these states would become the units of local government in Ashanti. Not all the Amanhene were those elected by tradition: the British appointed a number who they thought would be favourable to their rule. As far as Britain was concerned the Ashanti Confederacy was permanently dissolved. To this end they continued to claim the 'lost' Golden Stool.

Whereas the French had been successful in dismembering Dahomey and Fouta Djallon, the British were unable to quell the strong feeling of Ashanti nationalism, focused round the Golden Stool and the exiled Prempeh, now far away in the Seychelles.

When Guggisberg became Governor of the Gold Coast in 1919 he was anxious to institute indirect rule throughout the territory. With regard to Ashanti, as Tordoff points out, it was above all 'essential that Kumasi Division should have a head if the government policy of indirect rule involving the setting up of tribunals and stool treasuries, and eventually the imposition of a direct system of taxation, was to have a chance of success'.

From 1921, when the Government gave up all claims to the Golden Stool, which was found in 1920, up till 1935 the British followed a policy of restoring Ashanti to its former status. Backed by the research and advice of Captain R. S. Rattray, Government anthropologist, they cautiously reconstructed Ashanti. Prempeh was allowed to return from exile to Kumasi in 1924 as plain Mr. Prempeh. In 1926 he was installed Kumasihene, thus bringing to an end Britain's direct rule of Kumasi. In 1935, his successor, Prempeh II, was installed as Asantehene and the Ashanti Confederacy Council was made supreme native authority for Ashanti. As the Governor said at the time of the installation, 'Monarchy was the most ancient and enduring system, and ensured the unity of the British Empire'.[47] It certainly had endured in Ashanti. Those chiefs whom the British had promoted contrary to tradition, both within Kumasi and in the Confederacy as a whole, were reduced in status in 1926 and 1935 respectively. Chief Commissioner Newlands, who had insisted that direct taxation was essential to indirect rule, found his recommendation that a regular annual levy be raised rejected at the first sitting of the Confederacy Council because it was contrary to Customary Law.[48] The British, quite unlike the French, actually bothered to put together a state they had once destroyed.

## 5 *French and British administration contrasted*

Local administration in British West Africa was one of extreme diversity responding to the diversity of African society itself. In this it contrasts dramatically with that of the French. Nevertheless in this diversity we can see a general tendency towards indirection in administration in all four colonies: if it was possible to administer through the agency of a traditional authority, British inclination was to do so, and to leave that authority to carry on its government with as few restrictions as possible. Taxation, where it had not been traditionally a function of the rulers, proved to be the greatest innovation in local administration, though as we have seen it was not universally applied in British West Africa. The major agencies for change in traditional society and in the powers of the traditional authority itself were not the political officers but the Central Government departments with their plans for development, and the commercial houses that followed their railways and roads. On the other hand the French administrator, as we have seen, was directly charged with problems of economic development, down to the question of increasing the cotton crop through his *champs administratifs*. In British West Africa we find the political officer almost more than the chief acting as an agent for conserving traditional society against the change and modernisation which the technical departments of the Central Government pursued. Lugard saw indirect rule as a dynamic process, in which traditional society would be constantly adapting itself to innovation, as indeed it had through the centuries even before the European came. But indirect rule, in its heyday in the inter-war period, tended to try and discover the exact (and of course mythical) constitution of individual African societies and govern through it, as though African societies were static organisations with a fixed system of government that never altered. A great number of African societies had been constantly responding to the changing economic and political situations produced by the rise and fall of the great states of the savannah and the forest. Those that escaped these influences were for the most part those that were least touched by colonial rule, or those that had nothing to offer in the way of exchange to their neighbours or to the European newcomers.

It has been said that the British, though they thought they were governing through traditional systems, were not in fact doing so. Apart from the fact that they modified traditional political institutions to suit their own needs, these institutions now depended legally on them for recognition. They also assigned unaccustomed tasks to what they termed 'native authorities'. This is of course true. But, in the first place, many of the chiefs whom the British subjected to their authority had been previously subjected to the authority of an alien African state. Here we have to ask whether there is a categorical difference between the subjection of, say, Yoruba Ilorin to the Fulani or Dagomba to Ashanti and their subjection to the British. Furthermore, to suggest that the introduction of new tasks for African 'native authorities' destroyed their traditional integrity,[49] seems to presuppose that innovation was foreign to African society whether it was internally generated or imposed from outside. This is not supported by African history. Change as we have seen had been a dominant theme in nineteenth-century West Africa.

It has also been suggested that since the British, even where their policy was one of laissez-faire, nevertheless restructured African society, the difference between British and French administration was only one of degree. But the difference was surely more profound. Where the French dismissed traditional society as irrelevant to their aims, and only used it where absolutely necessary, the British sought to preserve what their very presence had and was changing. Of course the railway, the road and the telegraph were bound to change African society as much as the development of the slave trade in the seventeenth and eighteenth centuries, and the introduction of cash crops in the nineteenth century had done. But only if we appreciate the very different approach to African society on the part of the British and French, can we understand the very different courses their political development has taken both during the struggle for independence and since. Where chiefs have become largely irrelevant in French-speaking West Africa, they play in English-speaking West Africa, despite prognostications to the contrary,[50] a very important role. How else, but through the study of the importance the British laid on the existence of chiefs as a criterion for the respectability of an African society, can we understand why Eastern Nigeria should, at the very time that Sekou Touré was abolishing the institution of chieftaincy in his country, set up a House of Chiefs for a region in which, as we have seen, before colonial times there had been almost none? .

The British did not destroy the basis of chieftaincy as the French did. They restructured and modified it, but fundamentally it remained the same. Thus the all-African commission set up in 1948 to make proposals for the new constitution of the Gold Coast rejected the view of the Englishman, Watson, who in his earlier report said the chiefs no longer had a place in society. And this commission contained members of the educated élite which had constantly attacked indirect rule for giving too much power to the chiefs. They concluded:

'Contrary to the view expressed in the Watson Report, we believe that there is still a place for the Chief in a new constitutional set-up. Certain aspects of chieftaincy may well undergo changes consistent with modern development, but the central core of the institution remains. Indeed, it is upon the ability of the chiefs to adapt themselves to rapidly changing situations that their future will depend. We are convinced that they have this ability. . . . The whole institution of chieftaincy is so closely bound up with the life of our communities that its disappearance would spell disaster. Chiefs and what they symbolise in our society are so vital that the subject of their future must be approached with greatest caution.'[51]

# Notes

1 *Amalgamation Report*, pp. 14–15.
2 Lugard, *Dual Mandate*, p. 200 (italics mine).
3 See Mary Bull, 'Indirect Rule in Northern Nigeria, 1906–11', in Kenneth Robinson and Frederick Madden, ed., *Essays in Imperial Government Presented to Margery Perham*, Oxford, 1963.
4 Michael Crowder, *The Story of Nigeria* (Revised Edition), London, 1966, p. 246.
5 *Amalgamation Report*, p. 15.
6 Hailey, *Native Administration*, III, p. 7.
7 Stanhope White, *Dan Bona: The Memoirs of a Nigerian Official*, London, 1966, p. 96.
8 This was the subject of strong criticisms by Sir William Nevill M. Geary, the lawyer, in a series of letters to *The Times* arguing 'is it fair to the subjects under British protection that in capital cases they should have anything short of British justice?' *The Times*, 3rd August 1932.
9 British reluctance to depose the Emirs is brought out well by the abdication of Muhammadu, Sultan of Sokoto in 1931. When it became clear that the Sultan was involved deeply in corruption and was losing popularity with his people, the British rather than depose him engineered his abdication. As Dr. Shiels, Under-Secretary for Colonies, replied in a question put by Ormsby-Gore: 'At the time when he abdicated, inquiry was also being made into the following charges: issue of compulsory loans at usurious rates. ... He shocked and offended his subjects and Mohammedans generally by his dealing with sorcerers. ... His successor has been chosen by the traditional electorate and approved by the Acting Governor.' *The Times*, 16th September 1937. The ex-Sultan was struck off the roll of the Order of St. Michael and St. George of which he was Companion!
10 Hailey, *Native Administration*, III, p. 204.
11 *The Petition of the Ibadan Native Authority and the Chiefs of Ibadan Towns to the Right Honourable the Secretary of State for the Colonies*, 1936.
12 See J. B. Webster and A. A. Boahen, *The Growth of African Civilisation: The Revolutionary Years in West Africa since 1800*, London, 1967, Chapter 17: 'West Africans and Indirect Rule', pp. 257–68.
13 Cameron, *Principles of Native Administration*, p. 13.
14 *The Times*, 25th June 1934.
15 Hailey, *Native Administration*, III, p. 201.
16 *Ibid.*, p. 202.
17 David W. Brokensha, *Social Change at Larteh, Ghana*, Oxford, 1966, pp. 134–5.
18 Cited in Kimble, *Ghana*, from J. Mensah Sarbah, *Fanti National Constitution*, London, 1906, pp. 124 and 134.
19 Sir Hugh Clifford (1913) cited in Kimble, *ibid.* p. 469.
20 Cited in *ibid.*, p. 472.

21 Apter, *Ghana*, p. 122.

22 Hailey, *Native Administration*, III, p. 204.

23 *Ibid.*, p. 229.

24 An example of this was one Madam Humonya who moved her head-quarters to Kenema where the British District Officer was stationed; thus, making the town a chiefdom headquarters as well as a district and provincial capital. Unfortunately, her reign was an inauspicious inauguration of the new capital. In 1918 an inquiry was held by His Excellency, Governor R. J. Wilkinson. At that time Madam Humonya was found guilty of (1) failing to appoint a speaker, preferring to rely on privately chosen counsellors; (2) selecting section chiefs without consulting the people of their sections; (3) employing too many chiefdom police and a clerk unwanted by the people. The crux of the palaver was the use of forced labour on her farms. She required the five chiefdom sections to send one hundred men and one hundred women each to Kenema to work for her. While they worked, the home villages had to provide their food. When women became pregnant they were kept at work until time for confinement. Men were often punished for misdemeanors such as gambling by being sent to prison for months or by being put in stocks. Because of her despotism and cruelty, Madam Humonya is still considered to be the worst chief in chiefdom history and many people vow that they will never support another woman for chief. The outcome of the inquiry was that the private counsellors were banished; a speaker and five new section chiefs were elected by the people; Madam Humonya was ordered to accept a tax of rice in lieu of the 'state farms'; stocking and improper punishments were banned; and twenty-five police and a clerk were dismissed. Madam Humonya, however, was not deposed. From Dick Simpson, 'A Preliminary Political History of the Kenema Area', *Sierra Leone Studies*, No. 21, pp. 58–9.

25 K. Little, *The Mende of Sierra Leone*, London, 1956, p. 206.

26 Simpson, 'Kenema'.

27 Kilson, *Sierra Leone*, p. 147.

28 Hailey, *Native Administration*, III, p. 158.

29 Gailey, *Gambia*, p. 117.

30 *Ibid.*, p. 121.

31 Hailey, *Native Administration*, III, p. 336.

32 A. E. Afigbo, 'Revolution and Reaction in Eastern Nigeria: 1900–1929', *J.H.S.N.*, III, 3, December 1966, p. 541.

33 *Report on the Eastern Provinces by the Secretary of Native Affairs*, Lagos, 1922, p. 5.

34 For detailed information see A. E. Afigbo, 'Herbert Richmond Palmer and Indirect Rule in Eastern Nigeria, 1915–1928', *J.H.S.N.*, Vol. III (December 1965), pp. 295–312.

35 *Report on the Eastern Provinces*, p. 5.

36 Afigbo, 'Revolution and Reaction', p. 542.
37 *Ibid.*, p. 551; also G. I. Jones, 'From Direct to Indirect Rule in Eastern Nigeria', *Odu*, II, 2, January 1966, p. 79.
38 *Report of the Commission of Inquiry appointed to inquire into the Disturbances in the Calabar and Owerri Provinces, December 1929*, Nigeria Legislative Council Sessional Paper No. 28 of 1930, p. 94.
39 Hailey, *Native Administration*, III, p. 160.
40 Daryll Forde, *Yakö Studies*, London, 1964, p. 199.
41 *Ibid.*, p. 189.
42 *Ibid.*, p. 192.
43 This information is based largely on W. Tordoff, *Ashanti Under the Prempehs*, London, 1966.
44 Sir William Brandford Griffith was responsible for Ashanti's annexation rather than its continuance as a Protectorate. Joseph Chamberlain opposed him on this issue on the grounds that Ashanti would breed trouble in the future, and cited the case of Sierra Leone where the natives were forcibly resisting the hut tax. Griffith, however, stood his ground saying the Gold Coast Colony had already cost much in blood and treasure. Obituary of Sir William Brandford Griffith, *The Times*, 9th January 1939.
45 *The Times*, 23rd February 1935.
46 Tordoff, *Ashanti under the Prempehs*, p. 151.
47 *The Times*, 1st February 1935.
48 Tordoff, *Ashanti under the Prempehs*, p. 356.
49 L. P. Mair, *Native Policies in Africa*, London, 1936, p. 124.
50 L. P. Mair, 'African Chiefs Today', *Africa*, XXVIII, 3rd July 1958, p. 205.
51 Colonial No. 24 Gold Coast *Report to His Excellency the Governor by the Committee on Constitutional Reform*, 1949, p. 7 and p. 9.

*Part IV*
The Germans and West Africa

# 1 Togo, the model colony

At the Versailles Peace Conference, and in the Press of Colonial Powers with greedy eyes on Germany's overseas empire, a campaign of vilification of Germany's record as a Colonial power was carried out with such effect that Germany stood condemned as morally unfit to govern 'native' peoples. Louis Herbert Grey, Secretary to the Colonial Division at the Versailles Peace Conference, summed it up when he wrote: 'Germany's procedure in her colonies had been open to grave criticism, and that on moral grounds, as well as for political reasons her retention of them could scarcely be justified.'[1] The British Foreign Office, largely using evidence brought before the German Parliament and Courts, condemned German colonisation generally, and 'although no specially scandalous outrages have been brought to light' it wrote of Togo, 'there is plenty of evidence of maladministration and oppression of natives. Forced labour and flogging in particular have been as common in Togoland as in any of the German colonies. . . .'[2] Camille Fidel in a book designed to prove France's worthiness as inheritor of Germany's colonies matched his wartime allies in his attack on the German Colonial record: 'In effect, in peace time, the Germans practised in their overseas possessions the barbaric destruction of tribes which they exploited cruelly; the appropriation of land; forced labour; flogging erected into a method of government (without mentioning the monstrous crimes of officials without scruples who imposed a

R

permanent blot on the honour of Germany); and the innumerable revolts provoked by their odious brutality were steeped in blood . . . etc., etc.'[3] Fidel, like his Belgian and British counterparts, conveniently forgot that many of the crimes of which they accused Germany —flogging, forced labour, bloody suppression of rebellion, militarisation of Africans—were practised by themselves, as Dr. Schnee, former German Colonial Minister, was to point out.[4] Fidel had apparently forgotten that in 1908 he had written a book on German Colonies in which he had made mention of none of their crimes— indeed he had shown himself impressed by the German achievement.[5] Yet most of the crimes which were to be used to such good effect as evidence against Germany's fitness to administer colonies in 1918 had been committed before 1907, when Dernburg became first Colonial Secretary of Germany, and undertook a policy of reform of the colonial abuses which had been denounced in far more vicious terms by the Germans themselves in the Reichstag.[6] Thus the Socialists declared 'that the fruits of German Colonial Policy were "murder, robbery, syphilis and the curse of liquor" and that the colonies were more for experimentation with new rifles than for the introduction of civilisation'.[7]

Indeed, up to 1914 both France and Britain cast admiring eyes on Togo, which the Germans called their model colony. Britain, as Schnee remarked bitterly, had even been prepared to sign treaties with Germany to share Portugal's colonies between them on the grounds that Portugal was incapable of administering them.[8] The first president of independent Togo, Sylvanus Olympio, who had been a factor of the United Africa Company under the German régime, declared that Germany was 'the first country to bring us the benefits of modern life; she opened up the first roads, laid down our railways, and brought the first remedies of science to sickness and epidemics which were decimating our people; she built our first schools and carried us into the main stream of world affairs'.[9] At the Independence celebrations, one of the most rousing welcomes was given to a former German Governor of Togo, the Grand Duke of Mecklenburg. The German record, in Togo at least, was one that not only stood comparison with the French and British record in West Africa before the war, but indeed showed up the deficiencies in their own development policies. In education, health and development Germany had an impressive record in the fourteen years in which she had effective control of the narrow finger of territory only 52 kilometres wide at the coast and stretching 600 kilometres into the hinterland. The occupation of the southern parts had been achieved largely by treaty, or threat of military action; in the North the resistance of the Konkomba and the Cabrai was put down with the thoroughness of French columns. But right from the beginning the Germans set about the exploitation and development of their very unpromising enclave in West Africa. Here we shall be concerned only with what they achieved in comparison with their French and British neighbours. And even in the eyes of a British writer in 1918, the achievement seemed considerable: 'In the thirty years that the country had been under German administration, a stable government had been established, the hinterland had been opened up, three railways and many excellent roads had been built, slavery had been abolished and inter-tribal warfare discouraged, and a number of experimental plantations had been farmed. The Government, by its energetic policy, had developed the resources of the country, established trade and commerce on sound lines, and made considerable progress towards the betterment and prosperity of the people.'[10] Lugard, when he visited Douala in Kamerun in 1915, wrote to his wife: 'We have much to learn from these Germans.'[11]

Between 1903 and 1913 Germany increased the revenue of Togo from 1,132,000 marks to 3,384,000 marks.[12] Initially the main source of revenue was from customs duties, 88% in 1903, but by 1913 these accounted for only 52% and direct taxes (702,000 marks) and profits from the railways and port (305,000) were becoming important. The 1914 budget for the Togo was estimated at 4,174,341 marks, of which 43% was devoted to the cost of the administration.[13] 40% of the budget was set aside for Economic Affairs, of which nearly half was taken up on interest and repayment of loans. Agriculture however accounted for less than 3%. Only 7% of the budget was set aside for social services, and most of this was for health. Government spent very little on education, leaving this mostly in the hands of the missions.

Germany intended that her colonies should pay for themselves— indeed Bismarck had hoped they would all be administered by Chartered Companies, thus saving the Reich the cost of administration. By the outbreak of the 1914–18 war Togo was in fact independent of budgetary subsidy from the metropolitan government, and was repaying some of the loans that had been made to her. Germany, unlike France and Britain, did see that colonial occupation entailed obligation to give her colonies aid. Henderson estimates that colonial budget deficits cost Germany over £50 million from 1884–1914, and only Togo and Samoa in 1914 were not receiving subsidies.[14] Correspondingly she took much more seriously the prevailing colonial philosophy that the colonies should be exploited for their own good and for that of the metropolitan power. Thus in the fourteen years of effective colonial rule we see the German government taking a much more active role in exploring the possibilities of development in Togo than the French and British did in their West African colonies.

As far as infrastructure was concerned, Germany had by the outbreak of war built and re-built, after its destruction by fire, the wharf at Lomé, the capital. They had laid down a complex railway system of five lines stretching in all over 330 kilometres of country and were planning to extend it to exploit iron ore reserves. The French in their mandate only added 113 kilometres, and the British none. The road system of 755 miles was, in the opinion of the British Consul-General, 'unsurpassed anywhere in West Africa . . . for cheapness and excellence of construction'.[15] European travellers from the Gold Coast or Dahomey visiting Togo under German rule frequently expressed wonder at the German roads.

Germany's most striking achievement in Togo, apart from the infrastructure of communications which included an efficient telegraph system, was in the domain of agriculture. The British Consul-General again was witness to this. In his report published in 1910 he wrote: 'Although, as previously stated, Togo does not possess the great natural wealth of some of the neighbouring colonies and protectorates, the German Colonial Government are not only taking full advantage of Togo's resources, but are adding to them today by scientific cultivation, by planting and by experiments.'[16] In 1900 the German Colonial Economic Committee sent a mission to Togo to see whether cotton could be grown there to make Germany independent of foreign sources. An experimental station was set up at Nuatja together with an agricultural training school for Togolese farmers, since Germany's policy in Togo, as distinct from her other African colonies, was to promote agriculture through the peasant farmer and not through the European planter. This did not represent any great virtue on Germany's part, but a realistic assessment that plantations would not for the most part secure the scale of production the indigenous farmer could. Only 26,000 acres of land were alienated to Europeans. The Agricultural College had ninety-nine pupils in 1911 experimenting on a wide variety of crops to see how production could be increased.[17] The German Government invited American Negro agricultural students from the Tuskeegee Institute of Alabama, to come out to Togo and teach farmers improved methods of cotton farming.[18] The Germans also introduced cocoa, rubber and coffee and expanded palm-oil and coconut production. In 1892 they planted 89,400 coffee bushes, 20,900 rubber trees. In 1901 an additional 174,000 coconut palms, 46,000 coffee bushes, and 26,000 rubber trees were planted. In 1909 they tried to promote sisal by planting 135,000 bushes.[19] They undertook reafforestation, particularly with teak trees, which today remain with the coconut palms one of the most striking memorials to their short sojourn there.

By 1912 their intensive agricultural programme, in an area which had before their arrival been only marginally engaged in the production of cash crops for export to Europe, showed dramatic results. Togo exported palm kernels, palm-oil, rubber, cotton, maize, sisal and cocoa, which, as in the Gold Coast, was produced almost entirely on African initiative. The value of exports had risen from £80,834 in 1896 to £497,945 in 1912 and imports had increased from £92,356 to £571,391 in the same period.[20]

The Germans not only interested themselves in export crops. They also experimented with increasing domestic production. For instance they introduced Berkshire boars and selected chickens from Germany and Zebu cattle from Nigeria to improve local stock.[21]

In the context of the problem of dependence on a single export crop from which so many modern West African States suffer, Togo was particularly fortunate, too, that the Germans were interested in experimenting with every possible crop that might be exported. Germany, also, allowed traders from other colonial powers to do business in her colonies and, in fact, while Germany imported 65·2% of Togo's exports in 1912, she provided only 39·6% of her imports.[22]

British and French observers were, at least until the War, nearly without exception admirers of Germany's economic record in Togo, particularly of the Agricultural College and of the assistance and encouragement given by the administration to the peasant farmer.[23] Before they were expelled, the Germans were even proposing to exploit the iron-ore deposits at Bangeli and had built a railway to them for this purpose.

In the field of social services the Germans, through their missions, achieved a remarkably large educational system by the time they left. Hans Vischer, Director of Education for Northern Nigeria, gave a full account of their system in 1915.[24] Three missions, the Methodists, the Bremen and the Catholic (each restricted in their activities to a certain area, since the Germans did not want to show the Togolese that the white man was divided on certain issues), maintained 307 elementary schools, and six high schools, including two seminaries. Government was responsible for only two elementary schools and three high schools including the Agricultural College. Togo, then, on the outbreak of war had a total of 324 schools, with 49 European and 408 African teachers, catering for 13,742 pupils of which 2,279 were girls. 13,347 were at elementary schools, and 395 at high schools of one sort or another, for of the nine high schools, four were technical schools, and two were seminaries.[25] This record compares favourably with French West Africa, which twenty years later had only 59,566 children at school.[26] And as late as 1938 in Senegal, France's oldest colony in the Federation, with an estimated population of 1,800,000, only 17,128 children, taught by 132 European and 337 African teachers, were at school.[27] Comparison with the British Colonies is equally enlightening. Neighbouring cocoa-rich Ghana, with four times the population, had, in 1914, 160 Government and Assisted schools with a total enrolment of 20,246 but an average attendance of only 15,152, and some 217 non-assisted schools with an attendance of 13,500.[28] Southern Nigeria had about 35,000 children at school in 1912,[29] and Northern Nigeria at that time had very few children at all at Western-style schools; and even in 1929 the total number at Native Administration and Mission Schools was only 7,995.

One of the criticisms made of the German education system in Togo was that, like the French, it was essentially assimilationist. 'Natives are taught German history and the names of German emperors, and they can sing German patriotic songs', reported Vischer scathingly.[30] While Calvert wrote, 'the whole aim of their system is to make him [the Togolese] a German as soon as the transformation can be effected'.[31] The Germans, it would appear, believed they could achieve this, for Kuepers, Headmaster of the school at Sokode, assured Miss Gehrts, the actress, that his children make 'far apter and better pupils than do European children of a similar age'.[32]

Togo was not characterised by the colonial abuses that roused such anger in the Reichstag and became the basis for international condemnation of German colonialism in the other German African colonies. The infamous flogging to death administered by Governor Van Horn to a Togolese chief gained a notoriety for the administration it generally did not deserve. The administrative system was based on the grouping as far as possible together of peoples of the same ethnic group into single administrative units. Where chiefs already existed they were confirmed as the agents of the German administration. Where they did not, the Germans created chiefs to govern areas comparable to those ruled by traditional chiefs. These artificial chiefs were recruited from among village heads or loyal employees of the administration. Justice was confided partly to indigenous chiefs, and partly to the German administrators, who sat in judgement with two Togolese assessors. Chiefs could impose fines of up to 50 marks or 100 marks if they were superior-chiefs. The administrator could impose a fine of up to 300 marks, or up to six months in prison. Imprisonment with chains and death could be imposed with the sanction of the Governor. Flogging, in fact, was one of the most common forms of punishment, and private Europeans could bring offending employees to the administration for a 'judicial' whipping. After 1907, with the Dernburg reforms, flogging was strictly regulated; in 1913 some Togolese presented a petition to Colonial Secretary Solf, asking among other things for 'an improvement in the administration of justice . . . and the introduction of codes'.[33] But chiefs in Togo under French rule were later 'to demand the restoration of native courts as they existed under the Germans'.[34]

The Germans took a very authoritarian and paternalist view of their colony. Parts of the North were closed to all Europeans other than the administrators themselves. This ban included missionaries and traders. This decision was made on several grounds: parts of the North were still restive, and it was felt free entry of Europeans might exacerbate old hostilities; missionaries were not permitted in Muslim zones for the same reasons as made Lugard forbid them access to the Nigerian emirates; finally there was the fear that the North was not yet as prepared as the South for European influence, so that it became a sort of 'human reserve'.

Forced labour, as in French and British West Africa, was used for the building and maintenance of roads. Fines could be paid off in labour. Government officials inspected African quarters and if they found them dirty could impose a fine of 20 marks which could be worked off on the roads.[35]

The administrative system of the Germans was no less, and certainly no more harsh, than that of its neighbours. Floggings may not have taken place in Gold Coast, but they did in Northern Nigeria, where, under British protection, even women could be whipped for breaking their marriage vows or for slander. The usual number of lashes was 100.[36]

The most unfair criticism of Germany was that she was militarising her colonies, especially when it came from the French, who sent so many Africans to the European front. (See next section.) In the case of Togo this was a quite ridiculous charge. In 1908 the colony had only a police-force, officered by seven Germans,[37] and the conquest of Togo by a pincer movement of French and British troops from Dahomey and Gold Coast respectively was swift, not only because the land was easily traversed, but because Togo only had a small armed police-force (*Polizeitruppe*), which with European reservists constituted (according to Commandant Maroix, who took part in the campaign), an army of no more than 1,500.[38] Cornevin estimates it was effectively much smaller.[39] In all Germany's colonies there were only 16,079 troops of all kinds of which 5,764 were European.[40] In 1914 France had in West Africa alone 389 officers, 2,182 European troops and 14,785 African troops, making a total of 17,356 effectives. In addition *Tirailleurs Sénégalais* abroad consisted of one battalion in Madagascar, thirteen in Morocco and one in Algeria.[41] The British West African Frontier Force consisted of 45 companies of infantry, 3 companies of mounted infantry, and 3 artillery batteries, and as early as 1901 had consisted of 159 officers and 6,308 other ranks.[42] All this makes a mockery of British and French charges of the Germans militarising their colonies. And the French who recruited, often by force, 134,200 West African troops for their European war[43] were to use them after the war to occupy Germany.[44]

Looking at British and French rule in West Africa during the years in which Germany governed Togo, there is little to support their claims to being more fitted than the Germans to administer African peoples. During the thirties the Permanent Mandates Commission of the League of Nations received many complaints about French administration from the Deutsche Togobund, an organisation of Togolese 'nostalgic for the return of German rule'.[45] As far as Togo was concerned, it was the Germans, and not their French and British successors, who laid down the infra-structure of the country and the basis of its economic prosperity. Even today, after forty years of British and French administration, the landscape of Togo still has a unique German flavour.

# Notes

1 Introduction, *African Questions and the Peace Conference*, New York, 1923, p. xv, cited in Harry R. Rudin, *The Germans in the Cameroons 1884–1914: A Case Study in Modern Imperialism*, London, 1938, p. 11.

2 *German Colonization* (Handbooks prepared under the Direction of the Historical Section of the Foreign Office, N. 36), London, 1919,

3 Camille Fidel, *La Paix Coloniale Française*, Paris, 1918, p. 57.

4 Heinrich Schnee, *German Colonization Past and Future: The Truth about the German Colonies*, London, 1926.

5 Camille Fidel, *Les Colonies Allemandes: Étude Historique et Renseignements Statistiques*, Paris, 1908.

6 W. O. Henderson, *Studies in German Colonial History*, London, 1962, p. 8; and Rudin, *Cameroons*, pp. 147, 149.

7 *Ibid.*, p. 147.

8 Schnee, *German Colonization Past and Future*, p. 66.

9 Speech made at independence, quotation kindly supplied by Dr. B. W. Hodder.

10 Albert F. Calvert, F.C.S., *Togoland*, London, 1918, p. 1. Calvert two years earlier had published a book on *The German African Empire*, London, 1916, in which he had quoted *The Gold Coast Leader* of 12th September 1915: 'The surrender of Togoland has given rise to outbursts of joy and thankfulness among natives throughout the colony. ... The terrible doings of Germans in Togoland ... have become matters of common knowledge. ...'

11 Perham, *Lugard II*, p. 538.

12 L. Péchoux, *Le mandat français sur le Togo*, Paris, 1939, p. 271.

13 Robert Cornevin, *Histoire du Togo*, Paris, 1962, pp. 179–80.

14 Henderson, *Studies in German Colonial History*, p. 34.

15 Cited in Calvert, *Togoland*, p. 27.

16 Diplomatic Consular Reports No. 4528 Annual Series, *Germany: Report on the Trade of Togoland*, edited at the Foreign Office and Board of Trade, London, 1910, p. 11.

17 Calvert, *Togoland*, p. 33.

18 C. P. Groves, *The Planting of Christianity in Africa*, London, 1955, 2nd edition, III, p. 215.

19 Source, Rev. W. A. Crabtree, 'Togoland', in *Journal of the African Society*, XIV, LIV, Jan. 1915, p. 182.

20 *Ibid.*, p. 175.

21 Cornevin, *Togo*, p. 188.

22 *Ibid.*, p. 196.

23 Diplomatic and Consular Reports, *Germany: Report for the year 1913 on the Trade, etc., of German Togoland*. Edited at the Foreign Office and the Board of Trade, London, 1915, p. 4.

24 Hans Vischer, 'Native Education in German Africa', *Journal of the African Society*, LIV, XIV, Jan. 1915.

25  Figures from *ibid.*

26  W. Bryant Mumford and G. St. J. Orde-Brown, *Africans learn to be French: A review of Educational activities in the Seven Federated Colonies of French West Africa, based upon a tour of French West Africa and Algiers undertaken in 1935*, London, n.d., pp. 170–1.

27  *Annuaire statistique de l' Afrique occidentale française 1936–38*, Paris, 1939, pp. 27–8.

28  F. H. Hilliard, *A Short History of Education in British West Africa*, London, 1957, p. 77.

29  *Ibid.*, pp. 129–30.

30  Vischer, 'Native Education in German Africa', p. 124.

31  Calvert, *Togoland*, p. xi.

32  Miss M. Gehrts, *A Camera Actress in the Wilds of Togoland*, London, 1915, p. 289.

33  Mary Evelyn Townsend, *The Rise and Fall of Germany's Colonial Empire*, New York, 1930, p. 280.

34  *Ibid.*, p. 280.

35  Calvert, *Togoland*, p. 29.

36  Heinrich Schnee, citing Sir Hugh Clifford's speech to the Nigerian Council of December 29th, 1920, from *West Africa* of 26th February, 1921, Schnee, *German Colonization Past and Future*, pp. 123–4.

37  Camille Fidel, *Les Colonies Allemandes, op. cit.*, p. 32.

38  Le General Maroix, *Le Togo*, Paris, p. 46.

39  Cornevin, *Togo*, p. 207.

40  Foreign Office, *German Colonization*, p. 135.

41  General Maurice Abadie, *La défense des colonies*, p. 217.

42  A. Haywood and F. A. S. Clarke, *The History of the Royal West African Frontier Force*, London, 1964, p. 89 and p. 37.

43  Abadie, *La défense des colonies*, p. 228.

44  This raised criticism in Great Britain of a racist type, see: *The African World and Cape-Cairo Express*, Saturday, March 17th, 1923. Editorial, p. 251. 'Coloured troops in the Ruhr: It not only furnishes Germany with material for an effective appeal to outside sympathy, but it places men and women of European race under surveillance of a particularly galling character.... And though Germany, in the light of her barbarities during the war, deserves small consideration, reliable reports from the Ruhr testify to general offensive behaviour and in some instances unnecessary brutalities on the part of the coloured French troops... nothing can, in our opinion, justify the militant enforcement of coloured soldiers on an unarmed and conquered white population.' See also former Secretary of State of the German Colonial Office, Dr. W. H. Solf, *Germany's Right to Recover her Colonies*, Berlin, 1919, where he accuses the French of hurling 'the innocent and bewildered children of the desert and the jungle into the hell of European battlefields, where they bled for interests which were not

their own and were taught to slay white men in a white man's land with white men's weapons. This unspeakable abomination against Caucasian civilisation, this betrayal of both the white race and the black, will yet be stigmatised in history as one of the infamies of the age. This violation of immanent (*sic*) laws, ethnological and moral, cannot fail to bring forth its harvest of misery and evil days to come.' pp. 13–14.

45 Claude E. Welch Jr., *Dream of Unity: Pan-Africanism and Political Unification in West Africa*, Ithaca, New York, 1966, p. 58.

# 2 West Africa and the 1914–18 War

## 1 *The Togo and Kamerun campaigns*

Colonial rule brought Europe and Europeans to Africa; it did not bring Africa and Africans to Europe. West Africa, far from being integrated into the wider world, remained largely isolated from it. The first occasion on which it came on to the international stage was during the 1914–18 war. The impact of this war was to be very different for the colonial subjects of France and Britain in West Africa. British West Africa felt the touch of that war but lightly in comparison with French West Africa, for whose people it proved a heavy human and economic burden, and an opportunity for revolt against colonial domination. The Second World War, however, was to bring both French and British West Africa once and for all into the modern world, and heralded their emancipation from colonial rule.

The immediate consequences of the outbreak of war between France and Britain on the one hand, and Germany on the other, was the need to neutralise the German forces in Togo and Kamerun which both had common frontiers with French and British colonies. In each case the Germans were defeated by superior forces, and their colonies were occupied and administered throughout the war not by a joint Anglo-French administration, so that their political unity could have been maintained, but in two parts according to the areas which the French and British forces had conquered respectively. In telegrams of 4th to 5th August, the Acting Governor of Togo, Von

Doering, who realised he could not defend Togo, suggested to the Governors of Dahomey and the Gold Coast and the Governor-General of French West Africa, that Togo be neutralised so that Africans would not witness the spectacle of war between Europeans.[1] Both British and French administrations refused this request. The French and British forces in liaison moved in the next day and conquered Togo in a brief campaign that ended on the 26th August and was notable mainly for the fact that it was the occasion for the first 'British' shot of the whole war to be fired,[2] by a Gold Coast sergeant, Alhaji Grunshi. The Togolese police were apparently armed mainly with rifles used in the Franco-Prussian war of 1870–1.[3] The greater part of Togo fell to the French, the smaller part, including the rich cocoa-bearing areas and the port of Lomé, to the British. In Kamerun, the campaign was much stiffer, partly because the Germans had larger forces at their disposal: 1,200 police (*Polizeitruppe*) officered by thirty Germans, and 1,550 soldiers, officered by 185 Germans.[4] In August the British sent in troops from Gambia, Sierra Leone, Gold Coast and Nigeria to Kamerun across the Nigerian border, whilst two French forces were despatched, one across the French Equatorial African frontier with Kamerun, and one by sea. Belgian colonial troops were also sent from the Congo.

The Kamerun campaign was to last nineteen months. Colonel Zimmerman, in charge of the German forces, though greatly outnumbered by the French and British and attacked on three fronts, was able to contain them until the end of December 1915, when he fled to Spanish Guinea, with the bulk of his forces. The Fort of Mora in the extreme north, under siege since September 1914, only capitulated in February 1916. The African troops on both sides fought with great bravery. By 1915 those of the allies numbered some 13,000. A great number died, particularly in the columns from French Equatorial Africa.[5] Colonel Cunliffe, in command of the British force, wrote of his African soldiers: 'They have been called upon to take part in a great struggle, the rights and wrongs of which they can scarcely have been expected dimly to perceive. They have been through the, to them, extremely novel experience of facing an enemy with modern weapons and led by highly trained officers. Their rations have been scanty, their barefoot marches long and trying, and their fighting at times extremely arduous, yet they have not been found wanting either in discipline, devotion to their officers, or personal courage.'[6]

Like Togo, Kamerun was administratively divided into two by the French and British, the larger half going to the French. The

Allies had concluded secret accords that after the war, if they won, they would divide the German and Turkish empires between them, so that they saw nothing temporary in their occupation of Togo and Kamerun. They did not, of course, at the time envisage that their administration of them would be 'under mandate from an international organisation which would place limitations on the methods by which they would conduct their administration'. From a territorial point of view, the war represented a gain for the British and the French. Politically, as far as the British were concerned in West Africa it had little consequence: for the French it nearly spelled colonial disaster.

## 2 *The war in British West Africa*

In British West Africa the war called forth surprising loyalty from the African population. Even Turkey's participation in the war did not cause unrest among the Muslim populations. In the Gold Coast only in the farthest points of the Northern Territories was there unrest where, as British officials left for the armies 'the impression gained ground that the white man was leaving'.[7] Ashanti even supplied troops for the W.A.F.F. In Nigeria the Muslim Emirs, so recently conquered, did not react to the Turkish entry into war and to pan-Islamic propaganda, even though this was having effect in Niger, immediately to the north. The only revolts against British authority which seemed in any way the result of the war were those of the Kwale Ibo in Asaba division, said to have been aggravated by the Germans and that of the Delta prophet Elijah II. Profiting from the temporary depression in the palm-oil trade which hit the Delta peoples particularly hard, he gained many followers on the grounds that the Germans, in return for the help he said he was giving them, had promised the Delta peoples independence when they had won the war. The revival of the palm-oil trade broke the movement.[8] In Sierra Leone and the Gambia the war called forth no disturbances.

The fact that the Africans in British West Africa did not rise in revolt at a time when their colonial masters were at a disadvantage may be attributed to a number of factors. First of all the hand of British Colonial Rule was comparatively light. Second, the chiefs had found that under the British they had preserved their powers, indeed were consolidating them, so that the risk of revolt, if they did consider it, must have been one that offered little advantage. The educated élite, who in fact supported the war as 'good patriots', had not a mass following whom they could call out to attack the British had they wanted to, and for the most part they believed in the righteousness of the British cause. The British put over an effective propaganda campaign. The main tenor of the attitude of the educated élite is summed up by the speech of Dr. J. K. Randle, an early Nigerian politician, at a meeting in Tinubu Square in Lagos on 4th August 1916. He said: 'The fact must however not be disguised, even here, that in recent years the administration of the Government of this Colony has not given the people entire satisfaction. The people see that the Government is not carried on in their interest. But, however painfully true this is, let us not forget the wider principle that we are citizens of the British Empire.'[9]

Similarly *The Gold Coast Leader* wrote in an editorial in July 1915 that now was 'not the time to ventilate grievances which might prejudice the cause of England or lead her enemies to impugn the solidarity and loyalty of the sons and subject races of the British Empire. We shall play the role of passive spectators with loyalty, determination and devotion in order to qualify for greater trust.'[10] Most important of all was the fact that very few Africans had any idea what the war involved or how far the British were committed. Recruitment of soldiers, in contrast to French West Africa, was on a voluntary basis, and was on a very small scale so that it never produced the social dislocation it did across the border. Only the fall in prices for cash crops had a major impact on the population and even this was limited, for the majority of West Africans had not become entirely dependent on cash crops for their livelihood by this time.

The major problem of the war, as far as the British administration in West Africa was concerned, was economic. There was some initial panic: the Gambia even mistook the H.M.S. *Highflyer* for a German warship, and the tiny port of Bathurst thought it was to be bombarded.[11] Germans, an important trading community in Sierra Leone, Gold Coast and Nigeria, had to be interned and later shipped to England. But after the initial fears of the possibility of actual confrontation with Germany had subsided and victory had been gained in Togo and the Germans contained in the Cameroons, the prime problem was adjustment to the grave economic problems presented by the war. Some indication of how small was the threat to internal security from the Germans is given by the fact that in 1916 the Governor of Sierra Leone solemnly reported to London on Secret Service Expenditure for the year 1915:[12]

| Reproducing photographs of persons wanted | £1 | 4 | 0 |
| Expenses incurred leading to the arrest of a postal official | | 8 | 0 |
| Grant for identification of a person at Bonthe | | 7 | 6 |
| | £1 | 19 | 6 |

The economic problems were indeed grave. Germany had been one of the chief importers of British West African export crops. She purchased 180,000 tons of its palm kernels as against Britain's 36,000. In the Gold Coast half the non-British expatriate community was German, and Germany was second trader to Britain in that Colony. The ban on trade with Germany meant that new markets had to be found in particular for West African cocoa and palm products, especially kernels for crushing and use as cattle cake, an industry which Germany had pioneered. The German occupation of northeast France presented a particular problem for the Gambia, the large bulk of whose groundnuts were exported to the French oil mills, which then re-exported part to the Dutch mills. Only 9% of Gambia's export trade was with Britain in 1912, and in that year there was only one British firm established in Bathurst. The French shipping line ceased to call at Bathurst. There was no means of export, and no means of importing rice, on which Gambian peasants depended. Together these caused a grave economic crisis in the Gambia, only solved by France's realisation of her continued need for Gambian groundnuts and the steep increase in British consumption of them (4%-48% between 1912 and 1916).[13]

The major economic impact of the war on the British West African territories was, as in the Gambia, to increase British trade with them, and to prepare the ground for the great British oligopolies that emerged after the war (see pp. 298-301). Wartime licensing prevented Gold Coast farmers shipping their goods direct, and aided the domination of British importers and exporters, no longer in competition with German rivals.[14] The British houses not only controlled exports, whose price was falling because of lack of shipping space—in Sierra Leone less than half the number of ships passed through Freetown in 1917 as did in 1913[15]—and because of difficulties in obtaining markets for cocoa, but were also the main importers of goods whose price was conversely rising. The Chiefs complained about the situation to the Governor: 'Whilst the Gold Coast produce is taken for almost nothing . . . the prices of European goods have reached such a prohibitive height that one feels most unhappy.' They threatened that if Government did nothing, they would have to take action 'to guard our people against such manifest exploitation of the poor natives' resources'.[16] The Governor responded by permitting licences forfeited by enemy firms to be granted to local producers, a development which evoked great hostility from the European firms, whilst the Chambers of Commerce of Liverpool and London sent delegations to the Colonial Office 'to make allegations against the Gold Coast Government'.[17]

Nigeria fared better than the Gold Coast, for she had as her main exports palm-oil and groundnuts, which, after the initial problems of re-adjustment of the market, secured higher prices, being of much more strategic value in the wartime situation. She also had priority in shipping space. As Sir Charles Lucas commented, 'the Gold Coast had cause to regret that palm-oil and kernels had been so completely supplanted by cocoa',[18] adding that 'every month of the war, as in its later stages it brought growing commercial depression, must have added to the possibilities of unrest'.[19] The Gold Coast suffered in the war in a way that the other three territories did not. Expenditure had to be cut, and the minimal amounts allocated to the Northern Territories were further reduced.[20] Even so the Gold Coast Legislative Council invested £500,000 of its reserve funds 'which might with advantage have been laid out in developing local resources',[21] in the War Loan in London. A further £200,000 was wired to the Imperial Exchequer, and £80,000 raised by local subscription for war and relief funds. Similarly Gambia in 1914 contributed £10,000 from its tiny budget of £122,255 to the Prince of Wales' National Defence Fund, under Colonial Office pressure; in 1917 it contributed another £10,000; and in 1919 £16,000.[22] Perham estimates that Nigeria incurred some £1,400,000 in extra expenditure for the war, including the whole of the cost of the Northern Cameroons Campaign.[23]

In Sierra Leone, new markets were found for her palm-kernels, of which 87% had been purchased by Germany in 1913. Freetown benefited from being the headquarters of the W.A.F.F. and a fortified naval base, so that British military activities in West Africa brought in a great deal of additional revenue. Recruitment of labour carriers for the Kamerun and East African campaigns also brought in additional funds to the country during the period of their training, but robbed it of its best farmers, contributing to the shortage in domestic foodstuffs, and the general inflationary situation this, and the shortage of imported goods, produced.[24]

In all four territories the pattern of the impact of the war was roughly the same as that of Nigeria: initial shock and dislocation;

S

adaptation to new overseas market situations, in particular the replacement of Germany by Britain as chief customer; and then, slump, caused by the acute shortage of shipping through the activities of the German submarines.[25] Fortunately for the Colonial Governments this last period, which could have caused unrest, was cut short by the ending of hostilities on 11th November, 1918.

After the completion of the Kamerun campaign the British Government asked that the 2,000 W.A.F.F. should be used in East Africa. Lugard secured a delay in their despatch to that point on the grounds that without rest and leave the troops might be provoked into rebellion. The troops left Lagos for East Africa in November 1916. Shortly after the French called on Nigerian troops to relieve Zinder, besieged by Tuareg under the influence of Senussi chiefs from Tripolitania who had been preaching Holy War in Niger and Northern Nigeria apparently at German instigation.[26] Lugard was to be thankful that the only revolt in Nigeria after this time took place in June 1918 just after the return of the Nigerian troops from East Africa. The Egba revolt against the introduction of indirect rule might have developed into a very grave problem for the administration if it had taken place before the return of the soldiers. As it was it was put down successfully but at the cost of 500 rebel lives.

In all nearly 30,000 West African troops[27] were used by the British in the war. The return of these soldiers, only 7,200 of which had been employed on the outbreak of war, presented problems of re-habilitation for the administration, and raised speculations as to the disturbing influence they might have.

In Sierra Leone, the problem of resettlement was considerable. The 1921 Census report notes: 'having, through force of circumstances, seen something of the doubtful attractions of civilisation they are at present unwilling to return to their uneventful and peaceful lives . . . in the Protectorate, but prefer to eke out a precarious existence in the crowded capital of the Colony.'[28] Lugard had greater fears for them and wrote to his wife that the African soldier 'also knows how to kill white men, around whom he has been taught to weave a web of sanctity of life. He also knows how to handle bombs and Lewis guns and Maxims—and he has seen the white men budge when he has stood fast. Altogether he has acquired much knowledge which might be put to uncomfortable use some day.'[29] It was, however, another generation of soldiers in Ghana in 1948 who realised Lugard's fears.

The most disappointed group in the war was the educated élite who in pledging their support for the Imperial cause had hoped in return for a more important role in the post-war government of the four British West African colonies. They had hoped for a more effective voice in colonial administration, and representation at the Imperial reconstruction discussions.[30] At the Peace Conference members of the Accra Committee of the National Congress of British West Africa hoped to prevent the return of the former German colonies to Germany.[31] Most important of all they expected that their mature support of Britain in the war would be rewarded by the recognition that Africans were adults and should be treated as such. Thus F. W. Dove, delegate from Sierra Leone to the National Congress, declared:

'... we have passed the days of childhood which have been associated for years past with the blackman. In other words we believe the days have passed when it was commonly supposed that the African is like a child and must be forced against his will. The time has passed when the African peoples should be coerced against their will to do things that are not in accordance with their best interests or for their benefit.'[32] As it was the élite waited until after the Second World War for any meaningful share in the governmental process.

## 3 The war in French West Africa

France had first used West African troops outside their homeland in 1828 when two companies of Wollofs were sent to Madagascar. In 1838 a company was sent from Senegal to French Guiana. Senegalese soldiers fought in the Prussian and Mexican wars, and helped in the conquest of Madagascar, French Equatorial Africa and Morocco. Up till 1910 recruitment of soldiers had been on a voluntary basis. At this time the French were very concerned at the possibility of revolt by their Algerian troops in Algeria. General Mangin in *La Force Noire* suggested that by using West African troops in Algeria rather than Algerian troops, 32,000 French troops could be released to serve on the Franco–German border. 'The result', he wrote, 'would be the creation of an African army, whose camp would be in Algeria, but whose reservoir would be in West Africa.' Furthermore, if war broke out in Europe and 'the struggle were prolonged, our African Forces', he wrote, 'would constitute almost indefinite reserves, the source of which is beyond the reach of the adversary'.[33]

In 1910, Mangin toured West Africa and reported that 40,000 soldiers a year could be recruited. The Senate of France agreed to send Senegalese troops to Algeria. In 1912 by Decree of 17th February the French took the first step towards the creation of a permanent Black Army by introducing obligatory military service for Africans. Under this decree, which was opposed by the Senegalese Deputy Carpot, recruitment by *voie d'appels* for four years was authorised for men between twenty and twenty-eight years old. By this method it was hoped on the outbreak of war to recruit a million men from French West Africa.[34]

The problems raised by this massive ambition nearly plunged French West Africa into chaos during the First World War. First there just were not that number of men of that age available. Secondly, those called up were for the most part reluctant to go, and their families even more reluctant to let them. In some cases reluctance expressed itself in open revolt or flight across the border into neighbouring British West African territories. Thirdly, a policy of taking away from West Africa its able-bodied men conflicted with the other role France had assigned it—that of provisioning beleagured France.

The first full year of recruitment, 1915–16, was limited to 50,000 men. Of these, 23,000 were to be found from Haut-Senegal et Niger (roughly Mali, Upper Volta and Niger). By the end of the year the Governor-General was writing to the Minister of War giving him a sorry tale of resistance to the operation.[35] The Governor of Haut-Senegal-Niger reported that he could not recruit in Mossi until the Koudougou revolt was put down. He also reported that many in the area were leaving the fields and arming themselves.[36] A month later he reported that recruiting had had to be suspended along the Niger from Timbuktu to Gao because of feared resistance.[37] Approval was given for the enlistment of men taken prisoner in the suppression of the Dédougou revolt,[38] and the Governor-General laid it down as policy that, in suppressing subsequent revolts, prisoners would be recruited. Something of the desperation of the Governor of Haut-Senegal-Niger over his task is given by his demand that the doctors be less rigid in their selection and be required to accept men with 'only slight symptoms of goitre or umbilical hernias of small size'.[39] In Guinea the main problem in recruiting was flight across the border into Sierra Leone or Liberia. In Sierra Leone reports of disturbances in Kissi country in French Guinea were sent back to the Secretary of State for Colonies.[40] In Ivory Coast, too, common borders with the Gold Coast and Liberia presented the same problem. But while the Governor of Guinea reported that the recruiting campaign had generally good results,[41] Angoulvant, pacificator of Ivory Coast, was fearful of the consequences of further recruitment, which he described in a fifty-page report as 'a man hunt'.[42] 'I have concluded', he wrote, 'by cautioning that a new effort could not be undertaken without provoking a definite discontent, "a political and economic disturbance"; and without risking spreading among the native masses, who already have before their eyes the spectacle of the British Colonies where recruitment by *appel* is still unknown, the dangerous idea for the future of our rule, that we are not sufficiently strong in Europe to defend ourselves.'[43] He went on to cite reports from individual administrators complaining that only by force could they gain recruits, and that the removal of these able-bodied men was going to be disastrous for the economy. Angoulvant protested bitterly against the despatch of troops from sparsely populated West Africa to the European front, reminding the Governor-General that 'if the inhabitants of French West Africa previously lived in a state of continual war, our mission has consisted precisely in establishing French peace and directing these warlike instincts towards the peaceful work of agriculture and commerce'.[44]

In Dahomey the problems were the same: flight across the border to Nigeria, the need to use force to recruit, the medical unsuitability of many candidates, willing or unwilling, and the threat of revolt. Even self-mutilation to avoid enlistment was reported.[45]

In the event the Governors were only able to recruit 39,798 of their required 50,000. Haut-Senegal-Niger was 9,000 men down on its prescribed 23,000.[46] Of these a tiny proportion were real volunteers.

The French administration tried desperately to secure the co-operation of their British allies in returning deserters and carrying out token recruiting drives along their common borders at the same time as the French were recruiting in the area. British co-operation was half-hearted. In Gold Coast an Ordinance was passed permitting the Commissioner to deport Africans liable to French military service.[47] Lugard repatriated Dahomeans who had crossed into Abeokuta province.[48] In Gambia, where the Travelling Commissioner reported that 'not one of my people will cross the boundary for fear of being caught',[49] the Gambia Company undertook a trek in December 1916 to show force in areas where immigration of deserters had created unrest, and arrested a number of them.[50] The British however refused to undertake wide-scale recruiting, the only way in which they could effectively have discouraged the French Africans from crossing into their territory.

The situation had deteriorated in French West Africa so much by the time Van Vollenhoven became Governor-General in 1917 that he reported to the Minister of Colonies in July that further recruitment was impossible without risking revolt, especially in Haut-Senegal and Niger, and Dahomey. 'To extract from this country yet another few thousand men, we will set it aflame, drench it in blood, and we will ruin it completely.'[51] There had been serious revolts in Haut-Senegal-Niger, Dahomey, Ivory Coast and Guinea. Among the Ouilliminden Tuareg near Timbuktu and the Tuareg of Air, these revolts had amounted to full-scale challenges against French authority. The Tuareg of Air, who besieged Zinder, were, as we have seen, only defeated with the help of Nigerian troops.

It is not surprising that the recruiting campaign caused such violent reaction. Chiefs were told how many people were needed from a particular town or village. If they could, they supplied people of slave status, or without influence in the community. Strangers were seized.[52] Above all the recruiting drive deprived West Africa of its finest farmers, for little recruiting was done in the urban centres, since the administration and commerce did not want to be without their workers.[53] The only urban group that did enlist voluntarily were the 'Citoyens' of the Quatre Communes of Senegal, who had, under the leadership of Blaise Diagne, their deputy, secured their privileged position against French attacks by demanding the duty, readily accepted in the war, to do military service in return for the guarantee of their political privileges. (See pp. 416–18.)

Van Vollenhoven, as his predecessor, was as much concerned about the economy of the country as the problem of recruitment, for the two were inextricably linked, since increased recruitment meant decreased production.

The initial economic impact of the war on French West Africa was very similar to that in British West Africa. Germany had been a major importer from and exporter to French West Africa, where she had a number of trading firms. New markets had to be found for crops previously sold to Germany. Shipping was scarce, and freight rates increased. In French West Africa European company officials and clerks were subject to what Governor-General Clozel described in his speech to the *Conseil du Gouvernement* as a 'mobilisation un peu excessive'.[54] By November 1915, when he made his speech, there had as a result been an 'enormous diminution of revenue' though even so the budget had balanced, and 5,860,000 francs had been given to France for the war effort.[55] For the next year, however, he estimated that they would have to call on French support to the tune of five-and-a-half million francs.[56]

The mobilisation of Europeans in the administration and commerce forced the government to review its policy towards the training of Africans for these posts. Acting Governor General Angoulvant wrote in 1916 to his Lieutenant-Governors about 'the difficulties, daily more grave, which block the recruitment of European staff, the necessity of associating our natives more closely than ever before with our work of colonisation and of ridding the formation of our cadres of local origin of its character of improvisation which it has far too long maintained'.[57] Plans were therefore made to train Africans in a large number of fields hitherto predominantly occupied by Europeans: agricultural supervisors (moniteurs), postal officials, customs officers, mechanics and surveyors of public works. A medical school and an agricultural school were established. The medical school would train African assistant-doctors.[58] This Africanisation was entirely the result of wartime economic expediency. But it was also seen as of long-term benefit since war forced the government to count the cost of employing Europeans in 'subaltern' posts, which could easily be filled by Africans with sufficient training.[59]

By the time Van Vollenhoven became Governor-General the problem of staffing, production and shipment had become acute. But France demanded West Africa's food as well as her men. Not just her cash crops, but also her subsistence crops: sorghum, millet, maize, paddy-rice, yams and beans.[60] He urged the governors and their administrators to encourage the farmer to maximum effort, and to ensure that he knew a good price would be paid for his crop.[61] But Van Vollenhoven found himself in what seemed to him an impossible predicament. At the same time as the Minister of Production (Ravitaillement) demanded food, the Minister of War demanded more troops. On his doorstep the Lieutenant-Governor of Senegal was telling him that further recruitment would be an irreparable disaster, removing the only remaining labour force from the farms.[62]

On top of this, up to three-quarters of the European staff of French companies had been mobilised, and foreign trading companies were profiting from the French predicament. By 1st January they had increased the number of their trading posts from 746 before the war to 857. At the same time many French companies were forced to close shops. Public works had come to a standstill, though in British West Africa they continued, even if slowed down. It was calculated that 61,500 able-bodied men had left French for the British territories. Columns had to be maintained to put down revolts brought about by recruitment: the number of companies stationed in West Africa had been increased from twenty-six to fifty.[63]

Almost at his wit's end as to how to find the men required, the food required, and maintain France's commercial interests against the foreigners and avoid revolt, Van Vollenhoven wrote to the Minister of Colonies at the end of September in the same terms as his letter of July: 'I beg of you, Monsieur le Ministre, not to give the order to go ahead with the new recruitment of black troops.' Repeating his earlier fears in the same words, he warned: 'You will set this land afire, you will ruin it completely, without any gain.'[64]

France, however, was determined to find more troops and by January Van Vollenhoven had resigned himself to it, telling the Minister of Colonies that recruitment could only be effective if neighbouring British West African countries and Portuguese Guinea co-operated by carrying on a counter-recruitment.[65] However, the Government had by 11th January decided that recruitment should be entrusted to one who appeared to be ideal 'to enlighten the natives about the future of their race and their duties towards a tutelary France. He will be able to achieve with success the most intensive collaboration in our war effort of all the African peoples of whose attachment to our country and of whose fidelity to our flag, we are well aware.' He was the African deputy for Senegal, M. Blaise Diagne, who by a Decree of 11th January was appointed High Commissioner for the Republic for the Recruitment of troops in French West and Equatorial Africa. He would have powers equal to those of the Governor-General (article 3) and had the right to demand the communication to himself of any instructions and measures taken by any authority from the Governor-General downwards (article 5).[67] This decision was taken without consulting Van Vollenhoven who arrived in Paris the day the decree was promulgated. On the 17th January, Van Vollenhoven resigned, not in protest against the further recruitment, which he had come to accept as inevitable (though he still drew to the attention of the Minister, as he had done his Conseil de Gouvernement, the dangers of further recruitment), but because he would not share power and have his decisions subject to the scrutiny of another.[68] Van Vollenhoven's admirers present him as the champion of the African who tried to save him from service on the front, and when he could not, resigned his post. His critics say he resigned for racial reasons, since he could not share power with an African. Neither can be substantiated. It is clear Van Vollenhoven had reluctantly accepted the necessity of further recruitment even though he was fearful of division of power at a time when the political situation in the colony was delicate and an intensive recruitment was about to be undertaken.[69] The arrogant young Governor-General, in whose circulars the first person singular appears more frequently than in those of any other man who held his post, was unlikely to share power with anyone, so one cannot attribute his decision directly to the fact that Diagne was an African, even though earlier he had described Africans as 'children'.[70]

Diagne, by contrast, has frequently been the subject of attack for sending his fellow Africans as cannon fodder to the front, for despite Van Vollenhoven's gloomy predictions he recruited all the soldiers that were asked of him without any trouble. In fact Diagne agreed to undertake recruitment, which was going to be pursued anyway, in return for special privileges for those who served, and development programmes for French West Africa as a whole. He gave his reasons publicly for taking on the task in the Chamber of Deputies: 'The first reason was that in fact it was an aid given in tribute of recognition of what France, hitherto, had brought to these peoples. . . . The second was that thus they were gaining the ransom for their liberty in the future.'[71] For those who served there would be relaxation of the indigénat, increased facilities for naturalisation, improved medical facilities, and reservation of jobs for them; generally there would be efforts to ameliorate the standard of living of all Africans. In the letter to the Governors-General of A.O.F. and A.E.F. which the Minister of Colonies wrote describing these proposed reforms, he said that Diagne would make the Africans understand that 'this victory which will save our race will also save theirs; he will assure them, so that they can never henceforth doubt it, that their generous assistance, creates for a grateful France a debt which she will acquit fully one day'.[72] She never did, and wartime promises were forgotten in victory.

The success of Diagne's recruitment[73] was based on showing the Africans that soldiers who had left for the front had returned bemedalled, and promoted, and that some of them had even become officers. This, accompanied by the promises of a brighter future for all, seems to have been the chief factor accounting for his recruiting 63,378 men, that is 23,378 more than the 40,000 required of French West Africa that year.[74] Above all the presence of an African with such power, whilst it put a number of European noses out of joint, was certainly a great boost to African morale. Angoulvant, successor to Van Vollenhoven and a great admirer of Diagne, summed it up thus: 'an evident enthusiasm was raised up in a large number of native "milieux" by the presence of one of them who had achieved a high position in the country. His action certainly had great influence on the decision made by numerous chiefs to enlist or make their relatives enlist in order to give an example to the masses.'[75] Diagne's greatest triumph was in Haut-Senegal-Niger where he was able to recruit even in areas which had previously been dissident.[76]

To back up Diagne's recruiting drive, Angoulvant sent telegrams to all the British governors asking them to send back those who had escaped before, and to deter others by carrying on parallel recruiting drives. In sending them he noted sourly to the Minister of Colonies, 'Up to this year we have obtained but courteous promises without any real or effective follow-up, giving the impression that the Franco-British alliance is not known about in British West Africa.'[77] However, this time he gained better response: Gambia, as we have seen, co-operated. So too did Lugard, in Nigeria, even going so far as to promise a recruiting drive along the Dahomey frontier. Even Monrovia was approached. Sierra Leone said it could not recruit further because of the heavy enlistment of men for the labour corps, but it would agree to expel any fugitives from Guinea.[78]

For French West Africa the impact of the war was tremendous. Counting those already enlisted on the outbreak of war, some 200,000 able-bodied men were removed from a population of only 11,000,000 spread over an area of 1,822,855 square miles. The British colonies, with a combined population of over twice that of French West Africa spread over 482,749 square miles, only recruited 30,000. This meant that even by 1918 over 2% of the population had left West Africa for Europe.

As Ly Abdoulaye in his little book about the use of French Africans as soldiers in the World Wars, in Morocco, Vietnam and Algeria has put it: African troops 'became the instruments of imperialist rivalries and above all of repression in order to conserve the system of exploitation (capitalist) in the colonies and the metropolis'.[79]

But, as we shall see in the last chapter, if their participation in the First World War brought Africans little benefit, this situation was to be reversed in the Second World War, the herald of decolonisation.

# Notes

1 Cornevin, *Histoire du Togo*, p. 208.
2 *The Times*, 25th March 1940.
3 Sir Charles Lucas, *The Gold Coast and the War*, London, 1920, p. 18; Cornevin, *Togo*, p. 207.
4 Rudin, *The Cameroons*, p. 195.
5 J. Suret-Canale, *Afrique Noire II*, pp. 190–1.
6 Cited in Sir Alan Burns, *History of Nigeria*, London, 1958 (5th edition), p. 221, no source given.
7 Lucas, *The Gold Coast and the War*, p. 14.
8 Information supplied by Mr. Robin Horton.
9 Pamphlet published by C.M.S. Bookshop, Lagos, 1916, p. 1.
10 *Gold Coast Leader*, 10th July 1915.
11 P. H. S. Hatton, 'The Gambia, the Colonial Office, and the Opening Month of the First World War', *Journal of African History*, VII, I (1966), p. 128.
12 Sierra Leone National Archives (S.L.N.A.), Governor's Confidential Despatches for 1916.
13 See Hatton, 'Gambia and the First World War'.
14 Kimble, *Ghana*, p. 49.
15 N. A. Cox-George, *Finance and Development in West Africa: The Sierra Leone Experience*, London, 1961, p. 173.
16 Cited in Kimble, *Ghana*, p. 49.
17 *Ibid.*, p. 49.
18 Lucas, *The Gold Coast and the War*, p. 31.
19 *Ibid.*, p. 34.
20 Kimble, *Ghana*, p. 534.
21 Lucas, *The Gold Coast and the War*, p. 31.
22 See Hatton, 'Gambia and the First World War', p. 126; and Gray, *History of the Gambia*, p. 486.
23 Margery Perham, *Lugard: The Years of Authority 1899–1945*, London, 1960, p. 558.
24 Cox-George, *Finance and Development in West Africa*, p. 183.
25 Perham, *Lugard*, II, p. 557.
26 'Les sénoussistes pendant la guerre 1914–18', in *Les troupes coloniales pendant la guerre 1914–1918*, Paris, 1931, pp. 483–98.
27 The figures for the soldiers participating in the war from West Africa are as follows:

|  | Europeans | Africans |
|---|---|---|
| Nigeria Regiment | 1,587 | 13,980 |
| Gold Coast Regiment | 397 | 9,890 |
| Sierra Leone Battalion | 48 | 646 |
| Gambia Company | 20 | 351 |

Sources: *Statistics of the Military Effort in the British Empire during the Great War, 1914–20*, London, 1922, p. 383; cited by Sir Charles Lucas, ed., *The Empire at War*, IV, p. 4, in which he queries the Sierra Leone figure. Clearly the carriers have been forgotten. Lucas, *ibid.*, p. 17, says that 3,500 were recruited in addition to those sent to the Inland Water Transport Service for Mesopotamia. Others, Cox-George, *Finance and Development in West Africa*, p. 182, have put the figure as high as 7,000. Sierra Leone in fact provided the bulk of the carriers for the W.A.F.F. on the ground, according to the Governor, that the 'population of the Protectorate Sierra Leone is better adapted for providing labour battalions than for providing troops of the line. . . .' Governor of Sierra Leone to Governor-General of French West Africa, 30th March 1918, National Archives of Senegal, Series D, 4. D. 75, folio 280.

28 *Sierra Leone: Report of the Census for the year 1921*, London, 1922, p. 5.

29 Cited in Perham, *Lugard II*, p. 549.

30 La Ray Denzer, *The National Congress of British West Africa*, pp. 27–30.

31 *Ibid.*, p. 34.

32 *Memorandum of the National Congress of British West Africa.*

33 For the above see General Mangin, *La Force Noire*, Paris, 1910; Buell, *Native Problem*, II, pp. 4–7; and Abadie, *La Défense des Colonies.*

34 *Ibid.*, p. 217.

35 *National Archives of Senegal* (N.A.S.), Serie D, File 4.D.45, Recrutement indigène: Execution: comptes rendus des colonies: 1915–16. Governor-General to Minister of War, 'Recrutement de tirailleurs en A.C.F.'

36 *Ibid.*, Governor Niger to Governor-General Dakar, 26th November 1915, folio 45.

37 *Ibid.*, Governor Niger to Governor-General Dakar, 19th December 1915, folio 49.

38 *Ibid.*, Governor-General Dakar to Governor Niger, 14th December 1915, folio 56.

39 *Ibid.*, Governor Niger to Governor-General Dakar, 17th October 1915, folio 62.

40 S.L.N.A. Governor's Confidential Despatches, 10th April 1915, enclosing Intelligence Return for the Quarter ending 31st March 1915.

41 N.A.S., Série D, File 4.D.45, Extrait du Rapport Politique de la Guinea, 1st Quarter, 1915, folio 15.

42 *Ibid.*, Lt.-Governor, Ivory Coast to Governor-General, 18th December 1915, folio 85, p. 30.

43 *Ibid.*, p. 4.

44 *Ibid.*, p. 47.

45 *Ibid.*, Lt.-Governor of Dahomey to Governor-General, 2nd September 1915, folio 185.

46 N.A.S., Série D, 4.D.45, Recrutement de 50,000 Tirailleurs Rapport No. 117, 28th January 1916, Governor-General to Minister of Colonies.

47 *Ordinance for Ashanti No. 9, 1915*, 'An Ordinance to provide for the deportation of certain persons liable to French military service, 29th December 1915'.

48 N.A.S., Série D, 4.D.45, 'Recrutement de 50,000 Tirailleurs', cited by Lugard to Governor-General of French West Africa, 27th December 1915.

49 Gambia Archives (G.A.), Colonial Secretary's Office, Confidential Minute Paper, N. 175, 22nd December 1915 (opened): 'Immigration of Natives from French Territory to Escape Military Service', Hopkinson to Colonial Secretary, 22nd December 1915.

50 *Ibid.*, pp. 68, 73, 89.

51 N.A.S., Série D, 4.D.75, Recrutement indigène (1918), Rapport et correspondance du Ministre des Colonies et du Ministre de Guerre. Reprise du Recrutement mission Diagne, 1917–18, Van Vollenhoven to Maginot, July 1917, p. 13.

52 Jérôme et Jean Thiraud, *La Randonnée de Samba Diouf*, Paris, 1919: a novel telling of the 'capture' of a young Senegalese by the chief and people of a village which has to supply five young men to the army.

53 Jean Baptiste Forgeron, *Le Protectorat en Afrique Occidentale et Les Chefs Indigènes*, Bordeaux, 1920, p. 56.

54 *Gouvernement de l'A.O.F. Discours prononcé par M. Clozel, Gouverneur-Général de l'A.O.F. Session Ordinaire de 1915*, Imprimerie du Gouvernement-Général, 1915, p. 4.

55 *Ibid.*, p. 4.

56 *Ibid.*, p. 5.

57 Gouvernement-Général de l'A.O.F. *Textes relatifs à la formation et la réorganisation des cadres indigènes en A.O.F.*, Gorée, 1916. 'Circulaire relative à la formation du personnel des cadres indigènes, Dakar, 1st October, 1916, pp. 3–4.

58 *Ibid.*, p. 16.

59 *Ibid.*, 'Circulaire relative à la réorganisation des cadres des agents indigènes de l'A.O.F.', Dakar, 1st October 1916, pp. 27–8.

60 'Circulaire au sujet du ravittaillement' of June 7th, 1917, in *Une âme de chef: Le Gouverneur-Général Joost van Vollenhoven*, Paris, 1920, p. 122.

61 *Ibid.*, pp. 124–5.

62 N.A.S., Série D, 4.D.73, already cited, folio 13, Lt.-Governor of Senegal to Governor-General A.O.F., Dakar, 25th December 1917, p. 2.

63 N.A.S., Série D, 4.D.73, already cited, 'Projet de Recrutement', pp. 1–8.

64 N.A.S., Série D, 4.D.73, Van Vollenhoven to Minister of Colonies, 29th September 1917.

65  N.A.S., Série D, 4.D.73, already cited, Ministre des Colonies au Président du Conseil, Paris, 12th January 1918.

66  N.A.S., Série D, 4.D.73, Minister of Colonies in Report to President of the French Republic.

67  *Décret portant organisation d'une mission chargée d'intensifier le recrutement*, Paris, 11th January 1918.

68  *Une âme de chef*, allocution prononcée par le Gouverneur-général Van Vollenhoven à la clôture de la session du Conseil du Gouvernement de l'Afrique Occidentale Française (24th December 1917), pp. 264–5, and letter to Minister of Colonies, pp. 265–6.

69  *Ibid.*, p. 266.

70  *Ibid*, 'Circulaire au sujet des chefs indigènes', Dakar, 15th August 1917, p. 191.

71  Quoted by Traoré in *Forces Politiques*, p. 8.

72  N.A.S., Série D, 4.D.73, Minister of Colonies to Governors-General A.O.F. and A.E.F., accompanied by series of decrees dated 11th January instituting some of these reforms.

73  This and the whole subject of recruitment of Africans in French West Africa is the subject of a study being made by the author and Professor G. Wesley Johnson.

74  N.A.S., Série D, 4.D.74, 'Recrutement', Governor-General to Inspector of Colonies (1918—no date).

75  *Ibid.*

76  N.A.S., Série D, 4.D.77, *Recrutement 1918*.

77  N.A.S., Série D, 4.D.75, Correspondence with neighbouring colonies, 3rd file, folio 156.

78  All from N.A.S., Série D, 4.D.75.

79  Abdoulaye Ly, *Mercenaires Noirs: Notes sur une forme d'exploitation des Africains*, Paris, 1957, p. 66.

*Part V*
The colonial economy

# 1 Colonial development and commercial exploitation

## 1 The nature of colonial development

In 1926 Alan McPhee wrote of what he described as *The Economic Revolution in British West Africa* in eulogistic terms: 'English capital has come in and built the railways and constructed the harbours and cleared the channels; it has also introduced new cultures and improved old ones; it has built roads and towns and established markets; it has introduced banks and a convenient currency; it has exploited minerals. More than this, English government has brought peace and security and abolished slavery. The result is an enormous expansion of trade, in which the natives performed their part and reaped their reward.'[1] Cosnier, taking a harder look at the situation in French West Africa eight years earlier, wrote: 'We have left almost nothing for the producer in return for the considerable riches our commerce has gained. Almost nowhere are there any fixed riches.'[2]

Looking back on the early years of colonial rule, indeed the whole period up to the Second World War, Cosnier's account is the more accurate of the two. Only the railways remain as a major legacy of the economic policies of the colonial powers of that period, and they were paid for by taxes imposed on the African himself. In both British and French West Africa economic policy on the part of the newly established governments subordinated African interests to those of the needs of the Metropolis. The railways, and later the tarmac roads, tell the tale most clearly: simple feeders linking areas

T

that produced the crops and minerals Europe needed with the ports on the coast. There was little attempt to develop communications in such a way that the internal as distinct from the export economy of the colonies would be stimulated. So West Africa was subjected to an administrative system whose avowed purposes were to bring the material as well as the spiritual 'benefits' of Europe to the African, but saw these not in terms of the rational development of these colonies in their own interest, but in the interest of the mother country. Thus in the Gambia the peasant produced groundnuts to the exclusion of rice, so that that colony imported rice. The same was true of Senegal. In 1911, for instance, in the Fouta-Djallon, there was a shortage of rice created by the insistence of the Guinea colonial administration on the production of rubber, so that the money earned from the latter was lost in buying rice, normally domestically produced in sufficient quantities, at inflated prices.[3]

Whereas before colonial occupation groundnuts and palm-oil had been produced by the African in a situation where he could balance the comparative advantage of concentration on subsistence crops against growing export crops to exchange for imported goods, the colonial system, primarily through taxation, forced him to concentrate on export crops to the detriment of his subsistence crops. Thus in the Gold Coast, where there was no taxation, but a shortage of labour for the cocoa plantations and gold mines, migrants from the heavily taxed regions of the Upper Volta filled the gap. Seasonal labourers from Sudan worked on the groundnut-producing lands of Senegal and Gambia in order to pay their taxes. Development took place only in those areas that were of interest to the Metropolitan economies, with the result that vast areas of West Africa remained untouched by the colonial régime until the beginning of economic planning in the 1940's, when the colonies were looked at not exclusively in terms of their usefulness to the mother country but as economic entities in themselves. Under colonial rule any economic benefits that may have accrued to the African resulted from accident not design, by-products of the primitive economic system the colonial powers instituted to carry from Africa its raw materials for processing in the factories of Europe, in exchange for a strictly limited range of European manufactures. The principal beneficiaries were the stockholders of the companies importing and processing the raw materials, and those that produced the goods exported to Africa in exchange: assorted cloths, tobacco, alcohol and rice, and of course the materials for the development of the transport system that could facilitate this economic régime.

European governments played a much more dominant role in the economics of their African colonies than they ever did at home. State ownership of the means of production which would have been rejected by an anti-socialist Britain or France if it concerned the Metropolis was never challenged as far as Africa was concerned. Commerce was unwilling to invest anything but short-term capital in West Africa. Thus government had to provide the bulk of capital for long-term investment like railways and ports. Government also made an impact as the agency for law and order in which commerce would thrive. Much too much, however, has been made of this aspect of government's role in the economy by writers of the colonial period such as McPhee. West Africa, as we have shown, was not in the state of disorder colonial apologists liked to suggest it was before the imposition of the colonial régime and was in fact, even in conditions of disorder, as in Yorubaland, supplying Europe with the products she needed without European control. Nevertheless the colonial régime did facilitate economic exchange between regions that had been previously hostile to each other, and by building railways, which it is unlikely they would have done if they did not have control of the countries through which they passed, they did increase opportunities for commercial intercourse dramatically.

The economic impact of the colonial governments in the period up to 1918 was felt most in the following fields: the development of a communications system; the introduction of a portable currency; and in a negative sense, the prevention of the alienation of the land from Africans to Europeans. They failed to take the initiative where it was needed in three important fields: first the regulation of the activities of the expatriate commercial companies and their Lebano-Syrian adjuncts so that these would not be detrimental to the peasant who, with the exception of gold from Ghana, tin from Northern Nigeria and the cocoa, coffee and bananas of the Ivory Coast and Guinea plantations, produced everything on which the economies of the West African colonies were based. Second, they devoted a minimal amount to research into and improvement of the agriculture of West Africa, even though this was the basis of these economies. Finally the 'mission civilisatrice' faded into the background and the educational and social services for the African that an enlightened man like Cosnier saw were essential to economic improvement played a very minor role in government activities.

## 2 *The communications revolution*

If colonial powers can be said in any way to have brought about an economic revolution in West Africa, it was through the construction of railways. Built over uncharted country, through thick forest, over massive hill ranges, and often marked by the grave-stones of workers, they were an immense stimulus to the production of the cash crops which they were designed to evacuate. The Germans in Togo actually named their railways lines after the products they served: Coconut line, cocoa line, cotton line, iron line, and palm-oil line (öl-bahn).[4] Railways were exclusively a feature of colonial rule, and with the exception of two French lines, later bought up by the government, were all publicly financed by loans from the Metropolitan government or from public sources. The Dakar–St. Louis line was started in 1882 and finished three years later. Work on the Senegal–Niger line was started in 1881 and was to become the basis of the Dakar–Niger line completed in 1923. The Guinea railway was begun in 1900, the Ivory Coast railway in 1903, the Dahomey railway from Cotonou to Savé in 1900. Of these the Conakry–Niger railway, was an 'œuvre d'art remarquable, a des rampes de 25 mm. par mètre, des courbes de 120 mètres de rayon, qui sont incompatibles avec un fort rayon'. The Sekondi–Kumasi line in Gold Coast was completed in five years between 1898 and 1903. Work started on the Accra–Kumasi line in 1909 but its completion was delayed by the First World War. The Lagos–Ibadan railway was completed in four years between 1896 and 1900 and extended North to join the Northern Nigerian Railway; though until 1916, with the completion of the Jebba railway bridge over the Niger, trains had to be ferried across the river. Actually, Sir Percy Girouard, Lugard's successor in Northern Nigeria, had built a competing railway from Kano to Baro, lower down the Niger where goods could be shipped by barge to the sea, thus giving the North an independent transport system. But this diversion was not a success, and the Northern and Southern lines were linked and became the principal means of evacuating Northern produce.[5] During the First World War work was begun on the Eastern Railway to the North.

The railways were all single line. Their gauges varied, and were determined both by funds available and the nature of the terrain. The Sierra Leone Railway, begun in 1896, had a gauge of only 2 ft. 6 ins., because of the limited funds available, and 'to prevent any linkage with a future French line'.[6] The railways all proved profitable ventures, even the Sierra Leone railway, which was later to be eclipsed by road transport. The Southern Nigerian line, for instance, was built at the enormous cost of £13,000 a mile compared with only £3,800 for the Northern line, and yet by 1913 was showing a net surplus of over £250,000.[7] The Gold Coast line opened up the expanding cocoa production of the colony. In Ivory Coast, Governor Antonetti was to plead in the early twenties for the extension of his railways northwards to tap the resources of the Sudan: 'all routes which used to lead westward should now be directed to the south . . . of the six million inhabitants of the French Soudan, four million should now be tributary to the Ivory Coast railway . . . this line will link the rather infertile but densely peopled lands of the Upper Volta with those of the lower Ivory Coast which are very fertile, but are underpopulated. In the north there are the hands, in the south the riches. . . . The lower Ivory Coast can take another million men. Only the railway can bring them. . . .'[8] These railways, all directed to the coast, with no links between them, of different gauges, so that a rationalisation of the railway system of West Africa today is impossible, were the work of early governors who saw that 'coloniser c'est transporter'. Like Colonel Cardew, Governor of Sierra Leone, they looked on the construction of the railways as their own pet projects, though we may hope that in inaugurating them they did not have the same ill-fortune as that distinguished personage:

'After having been photographed from a temporary stand in front of the station, His Excellency the Governor made a speech which owing to the noise of the engine was not heard. Mr. Bradford, it was understood, replied. . . . "The Governor and some 10 or 11 guests having seated themselves in an improvised carriage made with seats and attached to the truck engine which Mrs. Cardew drove, the signal to proceed having been given in the usual way, the start was made amid the deafening shouts of a multitude of people. The train proceeded in ordinary speed from the station at the Racecourse in a winding course towards the jetty a distance of about half-a-mile. Here again, a hitch occurred. The car jumped the points and jolted and nearly threw out the occupants. Every possible effort was made to return to the starting point but without success; the engine not having sufficient motive power. The carriage was thereupon detached and its occupants alighted in order to seek solace, each in his or her own hammock or sedan-chair, for the homeward course: The crowd then reluctantly dispersed.'[9]

Since timber was the only source of fuel, deposits of coal existing only in Nigeria, the railways contributed greatly to the rapid deforestation that took place in the early colonial period because of the need to produce cash crops. Ports were built at the termini of the railways and a system of telegraph communications essential to commercial exploitation as well as administrative control spread across the countryside, following the track of the railway. Roads, in those early days, were seen as adjuncts not competitors of the railways, for commercial road transport was not to become feasible in West Africa until the late twenties. They were thus conceived of as feeder roads to the railways. The impact of these roads was never-theless very great, as Joyce Cary's *Mister Johnson*, which is as much a novel about a road as about its African hero, so amply demonstrates. Rudbeck, the administrator, reflects on the completion of his road: the road itself seems to speak to him. 'I'm smashing up the old Fada—I shall change everything and everybody in it. I'm abolishing the old ways, the old ideas, the old law; I am bringing wealth and opportunity for good as well as vice, new powers to men and there-fore new conflicts. I am the revolution. I am giving you plenty of trouble already, you governors, and I am going to give you plenty more. I destroy and I make new. What are you going to do about it? I am your idea, you made me, so I suppose you know.'[10] For the French administrator this dichotomy between development and administration did not exist since the two were never separated in his mind. For his British counterpart, development was essential to raise funds for government, but destroyed the traditional system of government through which he was supposed to rule. It was a con-flict that was never resolved.

## 3 Government and commerce

The greatest hindrance to the expansion of commerce brought about by the railways was the lack of a uniformly accepted portable cur-rency. The only currency that had gained universal acceptance in West Africa was the cowrie, which, valued at 4,000 to the shilling in 1900, was quite impossible as a basis for large-scale commercial trans-actions since the cost of porterage of cowries was quite prohibitive. This had long been accepted by Africans who had established local systems of more portable currencies: Kissy pennies in the Sierra Leone–Guinea area, manillas and certain foreign currencies in the Niger Delta, Maria Theresa dollars in the Chad region, gold dust and the Ounce on the Gold Coast.[11]

Trading was carried on at a sophisticated level of credit in the Niger Delta. At Jarra in what is now Mali, Mungo Park was able to obtain funds from a merchant in respect of a debt he had incurred with an English trader in the Gambia, many hundreds of miles away five years before.[12]

But the installation of colonial government necessitated the introduction of a commonly accepted currency as well as a banking system. The main problem was to gain acceptance not only for coin, but more particularly paper-money. Coin was the more readily accepted, but this was far from practicable. Thus 'a produce buyer had to take large quantities of coin on his buying mission. It was said that a porter could carry a head-load of coin valued at £250. Even at the produce price of 1910, a merchant might need a large number of porters together with suitable escorts'.[13] The issue of this coin was a monopoly of the Bank of West Africa in the British colonies and profits from it accrued to the metropolitan power and not to the colonies in which it circulated. As a result the West African Currency Board was set up as the source of issue of coin. It was also given power to issue notes, which were issued first in 1916, though they were far from popular, and not until after World War II did they overtake coin as a currency.[14] Notes were not made legal tender for Gambia, Sierra Leone and Gold Coast, for the Committee set up in 1912 to consider the whole question of currency in the British West African colonies thought it fair that only when they were generally and willingly accepted should they be made legal tender.[15] However, in 1916 they were made legal tender in Nigeria regardless of this recommendation. In French West Africa the Banque de l'Afrique Occidentale was founded in 1901 by decree and charged with control of all types of banking operations and issue of currency. However, until 1926 it combined the role of a commercial bank and that of a Bank of Issue, and not until then did the French State and the colonies in which it operated have any say in its operations.[16] As in British West Africa, so in French West Africa, notes were slow to be accepted by the African. The common currency was the five-franc piece, carried in sacks by donkey or camel for the merchants trading in the interior.[17]

In West Africa both the French and British Governments made it a matter of policy that there should be no alienation of land to European companies such as took place in French Equatorial Africa and in Kenya and Rhodesia. In British West Africa the policy was rigid: but in French West Africa concessions were granted in Guinea for the establishment of banana plantations and in Ivory Coast for the exploitation of timber and coffee. But these were not significant in comparison with what had taken place in Equatorial Africa and the Congo. By 1912, for instance, 40,000 hectares of forest and 3,290 hectares for other purposes had been alienated to Europeans.[18] An attempt by Lever brothers in 1907 to establish plantations in West Africa was opposed by the colonial governments. And they resisted the intensive propaganda of the Empire Resources Development Committee to the same end in 1917. The African peasant, not the European planter, was to be the basis of the exploitation of West Africa.

In the field of mineral production, however, it did appear 'that direct European control [was] the necessary condition of economic progress'.[19] In the first decade of the twentieth century in the Gold Coast, African chiefs to the distress of the colonial government were granting concessions to mining companies at what were, in relation to their economic value, ridiculously low prices. Attempts to control the 'flourishing trade in concessions' met with wide opposition and the cry was raised that the government was trying to rob the people of their land (see p. 421). The report on the whole question made in 1912 condemned the chiefs whose 'sense of obligation to the tribe ... was frequently obscured by their greed for money'.[20] In Nigeria the Royal Niger Company after the revocation of its charter received in compensation a half share of government mining revenue, derived primarily from the tin mines in Jos, which between 1906 and 1944 totalled two and a quarter million pounds.[21] The tin mines themselves were on land leased from the government in virtue of its assumption of ultimate ownership of land in Northern Nigeria.[22] The coal deposits in the Enugu area were operated by the government and therefore involved no real alienation of the land from the people as distinct from individuals. This distinction was not however appreciated by the African, particularly with regard to the establishment of forest reserves, which from the point of view of the government was done in the best interest of the people, but from the African's point of view involved the acquisition by the alien colonial power of his land. The opposition to the Forest Bill in the Gold Coast in 1910 was the outstanding example of this conflict of views and resulted in a political storm.[23] The question of ownership of land, so fundamental to traditional African society, was, particularly in British West Africa, where Africans had voices in Legislative Councils, to be the frequent cause of political agitation (see pp. 421–24). In French West Africa however a conscious effort was made to persuade Africans to accept the concept of individual ownership, particularly in the towns. By the 1920's former Governor Camille Guy could report that 'the black is adapting to our conception of ownership [propriété]' but added 'it is not yet proved that we have rendered him a service'.[24]

The policy of both French and British colonial governments during the early years of colonial rule towards the expatriate trading companies was predominantly one of laissez-faire. They were, of course, subject to pressures from them, both through the parent companies in the metropolis and in the colonies themselves through the Chambers of Commerce, and in the case of the British colonies the Legislative Councils to which members of the commercial community were nominated. The *Bulletin* of the Comité de l'Afrique Française kept a close watch on government activities, carrying detailed and often critical articles. The *Union Coloniale Française*, a commercial pressure group, founded in 1893, 'followed closely colonial policy and watched over the interests of its adherents'.[25] Apart from their policy concerning land alienation, governments brought little pressure to bear on the trading community. In British West Africa a régime of free trade existed. In French West Africa Senegal and Guinea enjoyed protection, but Ivory Coast and Dahomey, the other outlets for trade in French West Africa, were bound by the Free Trade agreements of the 1898 Anglo-French Convention settling frontiers between French and British West Africa. French West Africa did more trade outside the French empire other than 1906 every year from 1895 to 1906.[26] In 1914 imports from France still trailed behind those from other countries: 53·6 million as against 60 million francs.[27] The French Government came under criticism both for its lack of initiative in stimulating commercial enterprise, and for favouring foreign traders by the abolition of the protective tariff on cloth imports to French West Africa.[28] There were many advocates of a policy of full-scale economic assimilation of the colonies to the mother country. The colonial empire, wrote one author, 'will permit us, if we know how to exploit it, to find on our own national soil all that we need for our existence, and consequently render us independent of foreign countries'. It would not only have economic advantages, he added, 'but also enormous political consequences would result from such a policy from the point of view of the affirmation of our power and prestige in the world'.[29] But his ideas were not to gain currency until after the First World War when the French Government took active interest in 'la mise en valeur des colonies'. In British West Africa the Ten Year Development Plan launched by Sir Gordon Guggisberg for the Gold Coast immediately after the First World War was a notable exception to an otherwise laissez-faire approach.[30]

## 4 Government and agriculture

The laissez-faire attitude of governments towards commerce was unhappily reflected in their approach towards research for development. As Lord Hailey wrote in 1956, 'it is only in relatively recent years that the Colonial Powers have realised the need to provide for a comprehensive system of research into the problems involved in the administration of their African territories'.[31] The intensive programme of research conducted by the Germans in Togo, for example, did not have parallels in French and British West Africa. Expenditure on agriculture in both sets of colonies was perversely low considering that agriculture was the life-blood of all these colonies. France and Britain started a tradition of minimal expenditure on this major revenue-earning sector of the economy which has unfortunately been perpetuated by independent African governments.[32] There were of course exceptions. General de Trentinian, Lieutenant-Governor of Sudan in 1895, experimented with rubber at Kayes, corn at Koulikoro, and established experimental gardens at Khati, Goundam and Siguiri. He also experimented with cotton.[33] But such activities were not reflected in the series of development loans for French West Africa from 1903 to 1914 where no sum was devoted to agriculture. The rise of the cocoa industry in the Gold Coast has been claimed as a 'foster child of the government' which 'apart from careful nursing . . . would have had a stunted development and not the luxuriant growth as has been the case'.[34] Whilst credit must be given to the work of the Gold Coast Government Botanical Station at Aburi, which by 1897 had supplied cocoa and coffee seedlings to hundreds of small plantations and which was visited by many Africans anxious to know how coffee and cocoa was cured,[35] the peasant was the one really responsible for its phenomenal expansion. In 1891 exports were a mere 80 lbs. By 1908 when the Department of Agriculture for the first time admitted that the results obtained were 'highly creditable to the enterprise and industry of the indigenous population' it had reached 13,000 tons.[36] It was certainly not the government which was responsible for the two major social innovations that made the expansion of the cocoa industry in the Gold Coast possible: the changes in the traditional systems of land tenure, and the employment of immigrant free labour.

Indeed as Nowell, Chairman of the Commission on the Marketing of West African Cocoa, reported in 1938, 'its development is phenomenal when it is explained to be the sum of production of small native farms, mostly of one to five acres'.[37] Between 1892 and 1917 the annual average export of cocoa from the Gold Coast had risen from 12 tons to over 118,000 tons, and in Nigeria, where it had been just introduced by a Calabar chief in the same period, it had risen from 32 tons to over 37,000.[38]

The general indolence of colonial governments in affairs agricultural in the early years was a reflection of the general policy that agricultural production was essentially a problem for the African peasant, even if, as in French Africa, he had to be forced into it as for instance with the compulsory production of cocoa in Ivory Coast under Angoulvant's régime. Overall attempts to assist him increase his output through research into more productive varieties of the cash crops were negligible in this period. Agricultural techniques, for the most part, remained just as they were in pre-colonial times.[39] The important French Company C.F.A.O. for instance tried out mechanised cultivation of groundnuts in Senegal in 1921, but it was found that the cost of production would be higher than that for the peasant farmer, since a hired labourer would expect a higher return for his work, even at the low rates prevailing.[40]

It was Cosnier's main complaint that the French West African Government had done nothing to improve agriculture.[41] The same was largely true of the British West African governments. Just as serious was the lack of initiative in the provision of social services, such as education and health facilities, which ultimately would be the main factors for integrating Africa into the modern world.

## 5 Education and health

In 1908 Ponty, Governor-General of French West Africa, recognised the need for educational and health services for the African: 'Everything we do to improve his moral and physical well-being will profit our prestige and culture.'[42] Again in a circular of 1910 he declared: 'After we have formed an élite of young people destined to aid our own efforts, we must occupy ourselves with the education of the whole race and attempt to give the greatest number of our subjects if not assimilation, at least a French imprint.'[43]

Unfortunately government's efforts in the educational field were miniscule in this period. French West Africa did not even benefit as British West Africa did from the initiative of the missionaries, for in 1905 the separation of Church and State in France made it very difficult for the government to assist the missionary schools started by the Catholics in Senegal and Dahomey. By 1918 the only major educational institution founded in French West Africa was the École

Normale William Ponty, which aimed at producing teachers, interpreters, and professional cadres though for a while it trained sons of
chiefs. In 1909, there were only 190 primary schools in French West
Africa with 10,000 pupils. The situation had little changed by the
outbreak of World War I. The instruction given was criticised
severely by Cosnier: 'The vulgarisation of the French tongue, the
discipline of the mind within the best family traditions, the apprent-
iceship to the agricultural life should be the basic pre-occupation
of the village schoolmaster. Knowledge of the rights of man and
of the citizen, notions of French history and geography, and civics
seem to me much less necessary.'[44]

Government activity in the field of education in British West
Africa was little more distinguished. However, there missions had
free reign, with the exception of Northern Nigeria, where permission
had to be gained from the Emir to establish a mission school (see
above, p. 358). Hilliard's comment on early development of secondary education in Sierra Leone as being 'almost entirely due to the
faith and high ideals of the various Christian missions',[45] is as true
of the other three British West African colonies. For the most part
governments in the early period contented themselves with establishing a system of supervision of the standards of the mission and
making grants of assistance to them. These grants were of a very
limited nature, and in 1910 a conference at Cambridge of mission
groups put pressure on colonial governments to take a more active
role in the field of education.[46] Governments had established some
notable schools: Bo school in Sierra Leone in 1905, which was to
become the cornerstone of education in the Protectorate, and the
Katsina College in Northern Nigeria, which fulfilled a similar role
there. But an idea of the small role of these governments in education
can be derived from their annual budgets for education as late as 1929.

ANNUAL BUDGETS FOR EDUCATION, 1929

| | |
|---|---|
| Gambia: | £6,455 |
| Gold Coast: | £218,052 |
| Nigeria: | £304,623 |
| Sierra Leone: | £44,141 |

*Sources: Blue Books for Gambia, Gold Coast, Nigeria and Sierra Leone, 1929*

Yet education was indispensable to development. The commercial
houses and government needed the literate subalterns the schools
produced. The First World War forced realisation of this on the

French (see p. 263) and in 1925 the Advisory Committee on Native Education in the British Tropical African Dependencies reported: 'As a result of the economic development of the British African Dependencies, which has placed larger revenues at the disposal of the Administrations, and on the other hand of the fuller recognition of the principle that the Controlling Power is responsible as trustee for the moral advancement of the native population, the governments of these territories are taking an increasing interest in native education, which up to recent years has been largely left to the Mission Societies.'[47]

One outstanding exception to the limited range of educational opportunities for Africans at home was Fourah Bay College, a Christian institution founded in 1814, which became a training college for teachers and missionaries in 1827. In 1876 it was affiliated to the University of Durham, a development which aroused considerable criticism in Britain. The London *Times* asked whether the next step would be for the University to affiliate itself to the London Zoo.[48] Other than Fourah Bay, Africans seeking higher education before 1918 had to go to Britain or France.

Health services in the early years were largely devoted to the European population. The Yellow Fever Vaccination Scheme in French West Africa for which five-and-a-half million francs were set aside was a direct result of the terrible epidemic that broke out in Senegal in 1900, killing large numbers of Europeans. In Sierra Leone a railway was built from central Freetown to the hills above the city to enable the Europeans to avoid the unhealthy climate and conditions of Freetown. It had the distinction at the time of being 'the steepest non-funicular railway in existence, its maximum gradient being 1 in 22'.[49]

Not until the inter-war years did medical services in either French or British West Africa begin to make anything like a substantial impact on the peoples outside the major towns, though the French medical services, organised by the military, reached a more dispersed section of the population. Missionaries sometimes found physical medicine for Africans a convenient introduction to the application of what they considered spiritual medicine, so that in British West Africa missionaries supplied many of the 'bush' hospitals.

## 6 The European commercial régime

The commercial régime that was to become characteristic of colonial rule did not consolidate itself until the 1920's. Nevertheless in the early years of colonial rule its dominant traits were becoming apparent. Before the establishment of colonial rule, European firms were for the most part content to trade on the coast and rely on African middlemen for the penetration of the interior. There were major exceptions to this: the commercial penetration of the Niger and the Senegal being the obvious ones. With the establishment of colonial rule, and in particular the construction of railways, the European traders became more venturesome, establishing trading posts in centres where hitherto their source of supply of produce, and their means of distribution for their imported goods, was an African trader. To begin with, in the general expansion of trade that took place in the early years of colonial rule, there was room for the African trader despite such competition. But the European traders, with their access to greater capital resources, were soon to edge the African out of business in the main centres of the interior. If the African, accepting local defeat, tried to pioneer new trade frontiers by moving to centres where there was no European trading post, he found himself pre-empted by the arrival of a new and highly competitive rival, the Lebano-Syrian trader, who was increasingly to take over his middleman role between the large European trading company and the peasant producer. Until the world trade depression of 1920 African traders, as middlemen, as retailers and as importers and exporters, managed to survive in the face of European and Levantine competition. Till then in Nigeria and Gold Coast they still held considerable initiative, for in the war, with the expulsion of German firms, they were presented with 'an opportunity they were quick to grasp'.[50] But the extended market established by the colonial powers favoured in the long-run the trader who had the capital resources and connexions with Europe to establish series of trading posts in the interior as centres for purchasing crops and retailing or wholesaling imported goods. No African, not even an R. B. Blaize of Lagos, who had resources estimated at £150,000[51] and who anyway died in 1904, or a *métis* company in Senegal like Dévès, which employed 300 men in 1900,[52] could in the long run compete with European firms, like the United Africa Company in Nigeria, or the Bordeaux houses in Senegal, which had access to capital that was completely beyond the reach of the African.

The trading system established by the European companies under colonial rule was very rudimentary, their main aim being to obtain those products of West Africa—groundnuts, palm-oil, cocoa, coffee, rubber, timber—which the European countries needed in return for a small variety of imported goods. The pioneering of new areas was at first left to the African but by the 1920's he was being rapidly displaced in this role by the Lebano-Syrians. Even in rich Gold Coast as late as 1920 the main demands of the African were reported by a correspondent from Kumasi to be limited to staple commodities '... such as rice, sugar, salt, cotton cloths, pots and pans and beads'.[53] Yet the same correspondent writing from Accra advised British traders to heed the German example and listen to the 'tales innumerable heard first hand in the colony of how the Germans were making headway with their policy of service, no little detail being beneath their consideration and no trouble too great in the pursuit of their aim to deal with a customer as an individual and supply him with exactly what he wanted delivered at his door'.[54] He was also impressed by the fact that German traders had created new demands among the Africans, citing mouth-organs as a specific example. European trade in both British and French West Africa was unambitious, as the annual lists of imports for each set of colonies show. They invested as little capital in the colonies in which they traded as was compatible with making a reasonable profit: theirs was essentially a short-run operation. Concomitantly there was almost no attempt at industrialisation until after the Second World War. The only major industries were the extractive ones: tin at Jos, coal at Enugu and gold in Ashanti. The attempts to process the export crops of Africa on the spot rather than in the metropolis were few: even groundnuts were exported undecorticated. No attempt was made in British West Africa, for instance, to encourage inter-colonial trade. Rice, maize and palm-oil from Nigeria could have been sold in the Gold Coast and Sierra Leone, but only the pressures of the Second World War forced this development.[55] Little was done to give African employees training in the mechanical and managerial skills that would have saved the companies the heavy overheads of bringing out Europeans.

The dominant trend in the development of European trade in West Africa was towards the concentration of power in the hands of a few major commercial houses who created in many parts of West Africa a situation of effective monopoly for themselves. This was achieved by alliances between major businesses operating in the same colony, tacit agreements between potential rivals as to the areas in which they should operate and as to the price that should be paid for crops. In all this the African peasant was the helpless victim, unless, as in the case of the great cocoa hold-up of 1938, he was able to organise himself into a sufficiently strong selling monopoly to counter the buyers' monopoly.

This domination of the market by the great European commercial houses in West Africa was achieved not only through superior capital resources but also because they were able to control the sources of supply of most of the goods the Africans wanted as well as the markets for the crops the African produced as exchange. The really big houses controlled the companies that produced the commodities that the African wanted, the ships that transported them, the shops in which they were sold, the factories in which the cash crops they bought would be processed. The United Africa Company is the obvious example. The most important factor in the achievement of this hegemony was the fact that the credit necessary for the purchasing of the crops was readily made available by the banks to the European companies but was rarely given to the African trader.

The European commercial régime, whose dominant characteristics have been sketched here, will be considered in the next chapter, with special attention as to how the large European companies were able to obtain complete domination of the interior trade of West Africa to the exclusion of those who had controlled it before the conquest: the Africans. The reasons for treating these developments of the pre-World War I years along with those of the inter-war years are several. The most important is, as Hopkins puts it, that the 'full implications of this trend were obscured during the first two decades of the century by the period of prosperity in which African businessmen shared'.[56] It was only in the post-war years that African traders became fully aware that they had been disinherited; that the Lebano-Syrians consolidated their position as middlemen; and that the smaller European firms fell by the wayside to give way to the great monopolies.

The trade boom in which all were to participate in the early years of colonial rule—European, African and Lebanese—was indeed considerable as the following table shows.[57]

TOTAL TRADE: IMPORTS AND EXPORTS

|  | *British West Africa*<br>£ | *French West Africa*<br>£ |
|---|---|---|
| 1895 | 4,682,000 | 3,148,000 |
| 1900 | 7,620,000 | 5,192,000 |
| 1905 | 10,810,000 | 6,120,000 |
| 1910 | 20,826,000 | 11,132,000 |
| 1912 | 25,309,000 | 10,128,000 |

But the boom was very much a function of the new markets that had been opened up to the traders by colonial conquest, and in particular the railways that gave access to them, as a comparison between per capita total trade in 1913 and 1929, the year before the great depression hit West Africa.[58]

|  | *1913* £ | *1929* £ |
|---|---|---|
| Senegal | 4·9 | 6·2 |
| Sudan | ·09 | ·07 |
| Guinea | ·75 | ·65 |
| Ivory Coast | ·91 | 1·0 |
| Dahomey | 1·4 | 1·8 |
| Nigeria | ·87 | 1·4 |
| Gold Coast | 6·9 | 11·6 |
| Sierra Leone | 2·3 | 2·4 |
| Gambia | 10·0 | 8·5 |

U

# Notes

1 Alan McPhee, *The Economic Revolution in British West Africa*, London, 1926, p. 104.
2 Cosnier, *L'ouest africain français*, p. xvi.
3 Suret-Canale, *Afrique Noire II*, p. 68.
4 Cornevin, *Togo*, pp. 192–3.
5 Perham, *Lugard II*, p. 410.
6 R. J. Harrison Church, 'The Evolution of Railways in French and British West Africa', *Compte Rendu du XVIème Congrès International de Géographie, Lisbonne, 1949*, Lisbon, 1952, p. 107.
7 Perham, *Lugard II*, p. 410.
8 Cited by Harrison Church, 'Evolution of Railways', from articles in *L'Afrique Française*, 1921–24.
9 Quoted by J. Ralph Best, *A History of the Sierra Leone Railway, 1899–1949*, typescript, n.d., and no source given for this eye-witness account.
10 Joyce Cary, *Mister Johnson* (Carfax Edition), 1952, pp. 168–9.
11 Marion Johnson is making a study of the West African cowrie currency. See her 'The Ounce in Eighteenth-Century West African Trade' in *Journal of African History*, VII, 2, 1966, pp. 197–214, also G. I. Jones, 'Native and Trade Currencies in Southern Nigeria during the 18th and 19th centuries', *Africa*, XXVIII, 1, 1958; and N. A. Cox-George, *Finance and Development in West Africa—The Sierra Leone Experience*, London, 1961, Chapter 4, 'The Behaviour of Money', for a fascinating account of the 'mosaic of currency' in use in Sierra Leone before the introduction of the West African Currency Board coin and notes.
12 Mungo Park, *Travels in the Interior Districts of Africa*, I, London, 1816, p. 111.
13 J. B. Loynes, *The West African Currency Board, 1912–1962*, London, 1962, p. 6.
14 *Ibid.*, p. 16.
15 *Ibid.*, p. 15.
16 Charles Richon, *La production coloniale et le crédit*, Paris, 1931, pp. 112–13.
17 Suret-Canale, *Afrique II*, p. 28 and p. 79.
18 *Ibid.*, p. 40.
19 *Survey of British Commonwealth Affairs*, Volume II, 'Problems of Economic Policy, 1918–39, Part II' by W. K. Hancock, London, 1942, p. 181.
20 *Report on the Legislation governing the alienation of Native Lands in the Gold Coast and Ashanti*, by H. Conway Belfield, Cmd. 6278 of 1912, cited in Hancock survey, p. 182. In the Colony only 879 out of a total of approximately 24,300 square miles, and in Ashanti 408 out of a total of approximately 24,800 square miles of land had been alienated. See table in Kimble, *Ghana*, p. 367.
21 J. Mars, 'Extra-Territorial Enterprises' in Margery Perham, ed., *Mining and Commerce in Nigeria*, London, 1948, p. 58.

22 Hailey, *African Survey* (Revised), 1956, pp. 734–5.
23 Kimble, *Ghana*, pp. 362–71.
24 Camille Guy, *L'Afrique Occidentale Française*, Paris, 1929, p. 67.
25 Brunschwig, 'Le Parti Colonial', p. 69.
26 Source, *L'Afrique Occidentale Française*, Paris, 1913, p. 80.
27 Constance Southwark, *The French Colonial Venture*, London, 1931, Table III.
28 Francis Mury, 'Notre conception coloniale actuelle: administration et colons', *Le Correspondent*, Paris, 25th February, 1908, pp. 741–66.
29 Camille Fidel, *La Paix Coloniale Française*, Paris, 1918, p. 000.
30 See D. K. Greenstreet, 'The Guggisberg Ten-Year Development Plan', *The Economic Bulletin of Ghana*, VIII, 1, 1964, pp. 18–26.
31 Hailey, *An African Survey* (Revised), 1956, p. 1600.
32 See Rene Dumont, *L'Afrique Noire est mal partie*, Paris, 1962.
33 Lieutenant Gatelet, *Histoire de la conquête du Soudan français* (1874–99), Paris, 1901, p. 491 ff.
34 McPhee, *Economic Revolution*, p. 41.
35 Polly Hill, *The Gold Coast Cocoa Farmer*, London, 1956, p. 103.
36 *Ibid.*, p. 104.
37 *Report of the Commission on the Marketing of West African Cocoa*, London, 1938, Cmd. 5845, p. 16.
38 *Ibid.*, p. 16.
39 Suret-Canale, *Afrique II*, p. 275.
40 *Ibid.*, p. 279.
41 Cosnier, *L'ouest africain français*, p. xix.
42 Speech to Conseil de Gouvernement, 18th Feb. 1908, cited in Terrier and Mourey, *Afrique Occidentale Française*, p. 519.
43 Cited in *ibid.*
44 Cosnier, *L'ouest africain français*, p. xv.
45 F. H. Hilliard, *A Short History of Education in British West Africa*, London, 1956, p. 23.
46 L. Gray Cowan, James O'Connell, and David G. Scanlon, *Education and Nation Building in Africa*, p. 5.
47 *Education Policy in British Tropical Africa*, London, 1925, p. 3.
48 Cited in Hilliard, *A Short History of Education*, p. 30.
49 Best, *Sierra Leone Railway*, p. 4.
50 A. G. Hopkins, 'Economic aspects of political movements in Nigeria and in the Gold Coast, 1918–1939', *Journal of African History*, VII, 1, 1966, p. 135n.
51 A. G. Hopkins, 'R. B. Blaize: Merchant Prince of West Africa', *Tarikh*, I, 2, 1966, p. 73.
52 G. Wesley Johnson, 'Blaise Diagne', 'The Ascendancy of Blaise Diagne and the Beginning of African Politics in Senegal', *Africa*, XXXVI, 3, 1966, p. 240.
53 *The Times* (Trade Supplement), 24th January 1920.

54 *Ibid.*, 31st January 1920.
55 J. Mars, 'Extra-Territorial Enterprises', p. 74.
56 Hopkins, 'Economic aspects of political movements', pp. 134–5.
57 McPhee, *Economic Revolution*, London, 1926, p. 13.
58 Southwark, *The French Colonial Venture*, Appendix C.

# 2 Lebanese and monopolists

## 1 The emergence of the Lebanese trader

The collapse of the post-war boom in 1920 stripped the West African market of its weaker traders and revealed the true nature of its structure: the domination of trade by a half dozen or so European import-export houses. The few African traders who did engage in the import-export trade—and some in Nigeria and Gold Coast had been big—did not have capital resources sufficient to carry them through the slump years of 1921 and 1922 that followed the post-war boom. They were quite unprepared for a fall in export prices to 50% of the 1920 level. They were caught holding large stocks, whose prices fell steeply, and many had to sell out to European firms.[1] As a group they ceased to be significant commercially, though their frustration at failure and their jealousy of the success of the European firms led them to join actively in politics. The retail and middleman trade, in which both Europeans and Africans engaged up to the 1920's, passed increasingly into the hands of their more competitive rivals, the Lebanese, who by this time had spread all over West Africa. The colonial commercial régime, then, was characterised by the almost total lack of participation in it by Africans except as producers.

Given the scale of operations of the large European import-export houses, with their sophisticated network of commercial contacts in Europe, their ability to raise capital, and, more important, raise loans from the European banks to finance the purchase of crops, it is not surprising that they found no African rivals to their position. Much more significant from the point of view of the long-term development of an economy in which Africans could not participate other than as primary producers was the influx of Lebanese at the beginning of the twentieth century. Until their arrival the African had to a large extent controlled the middleman trade. Within two decades he was almost completely removed from it, the major exceptions being in the Gold Coast, and to a lesser extent Western Nigeria where he shared in the buoyant profits of the cocoa crop. The African however retained control of traditional trade. Trade in kola, in dried fish and cattle were still in the hands of Africans. The cattle trade, itself, was one in which large sums of money changed hands, and which involved a sophisticated system of credit.[2] The trans-Saharan trade, however, had become negligible by the 1920's, all the goods brought by that route, in particular salt, being more easily and more cheaply obtained from the coast.

The Lebanese who gained control of the bulk of the retail trade from the Europeans and Africans, and likewise the purchase of the peasant's export crops, first arrived in West Africa at the end of the nineteenth century. Their arrival was all but accidental. Emigrants, leaving poverty stricken villages for a new life in the United States or Brazil, were re-routed from Marseilles to Dakar. Some had insufficient funds to reach the States or Brazil; others could not conform to the strict U.S. Health requirements; some were re-routed because there was no need for travel documents in West Africa;[3] some were re-routed unwittingly. Once there, whatever the reason for their arrival, they decided to stay, for their families had invested in their journey in anticipation of future remittances. So they decided that the 'White Man's Grave' was 'easier to face than their hungry families'.[4] Their initial success was so great that they were soon sending for their compatriots. In French West Africa alone their number increased from 28 in 1897, to 276 in 1900, and 1,110 in 1909. By 1929 there were over three thousand.[5] Attempts to control their immigration were made in both British and French West Africa. In French West Africa, even though they enjoyed the status of French protected persons, each Syrian on landing was obliged to deposit the sum of 4,500 francs, about £36 10s., with the authorities as a guarantee against repatriation expenses.[6] In British West Africa, since they were foreign nationals, control of their entry was much easier.

The Lebanese formed the most important single expatriate group in West Africa other than nationals of the colonial powers. Fulfilling a similar function to them were the Syrians, a much smaller community, which nevertheless has usually been assumed to be the dominant one. The Greeks in Ivory Coast, the Indians in the British West African territories, Tripolitanians in Northern Nigeria all fulfilled similar functions to the Lebanese, though at present no detailed study has been made of them.

Guinea provides the most dramatic example of the rapidity with which the Lebanese were able to take over the retail and produce buying trade from Europeans. In 1898 there were two Lebanese in the Conakry market engaged in the rubber trade. Within six months, by buying rubber at higher prices than the Europeans and thus contenting themselves with smaller profits, they had made French business houses dependent on them. By 1899 there were 150 Lebanese engaged in the trade, by 1904—600.[7] In the same year of 1898 a law was passed forbidding Lebanese to trade in the markets, so they set up small stores, selling a wide variety of goods at lower prices than their European competitors. In a short while they had captured the retail trade from the Europeans.[8]

The Lebanese had a number of advantages over their European competitors, the main one being the comparative lowness of their costs. Coming from an environment much harsher than that of West Africa and fearing to return empty-handed, they were able to, and did, live in conditions that were often more wretched than that of the poorest African in the town where they worked. They were prepared to live in mud-huts, where the European required a European-style house. They were content with much lower profit margins on sales than their rivals. They spent little on themselves, at least in the initial stages of their enterprises, re-investing every bit of profit they could. Their overheads were small. They sent for members of their family to work for them in return for just their food, lodging and clothing and the longer-term prospect of establishing themselves on their own.[9] They worked long hours and did not have the expense of paying for overseas leaves. Furthermore, they had a similar approach to trading as the African, being prepared to bargain for everything, whereas the European came from a predominantly fixed-price economy. When it came to letting customers have credit they were not only more skilful in assessing the reliability of the creditors, since they had a facility for, and did learn, African languages, but were prepared to profit from their loans by usurious rates the European would rarely charge. Some of them were equally prepared to deceive the illiterate African through the use of false weights and measures. They tried wherever possible to ensure that rather than pay the peasant producer for his crop in cash, which he might spend elsewhere, it was exchanged for goods from their stores. During the First World War the Lebanese were not subject to call-up, whereas many French traders, as we have seen, had to leave for the front.[10]

The European trader could not survive such competition. For instance in Thiès in Senegal in 1919 there were 50 European traders and only 11 Lebanese. By 1935 there were only 11 Europeans and 200 Lebanese. In Bambey, also in Senegal, there were 47 Europeans in 1919 and only 4 Lebanese; by 1935 only 20 Europeans and 105 Lebanese.[11]

Being prepared to live at the same economic level as the African was not sufficient to give the Lebanese initiative over him. His advantages lay in the fact that he did not have the same financial obligations as his African rival. The African was bound by his extended family so that profits which would be ploughed back by the Lebanese into his business would have to be spent on a cousin, a wedding, a funeral, a baptismal ceremony. The structure of African society is such that it is impossible for the African to escape his obligations to the extended family, to fail to celebrate the birth of a son in a fitting manner. To be accused of meanness when one is well-off is a humiliation few Africans would care to risk. Where the extended family proved, through its willingness to act as parasite on its prosperous members, a disadvantage to the African business-man, the Lebanese as we have seen turned it to his advantage. In African custom it was impossible to demand that a relative work for you in return for the food you were obliged to give him because of his relationship to you. The Lebanese also felt more secure in employing their own relatives in their shops, the likelihood of being cheated by them being less great. Indeed the pattern of Lebanese emigration was such that single areas of Lebanon sent emigrants to single areas of West Africa. Thus in Senegal most Lebanese came from Tyre, in Mali from Bayt Shabab, in Accra from Tripoli in North Lebanon.[12] In Calabar in Nigeria all the Lebanese came from the same village.[13] Lebanese who had made a success tended to back up relatives during their pioneer days.

The Lebanese not only went into competition with the African in the shop-retail trade, but on the streets as pedlars. Here he was prepared to sell at a lower profit than the African. Even when he was forced off the streets by taxes, his shops sold the same goods as the Dioulas (itinerant Malinke traders) at lower prices and thus killed much of the indigenous pedlar trade, for example, in Guinea.[14]

They outmanœuvred any rival: thus in Sierra Leone the 'respectable Creoles despised them, conceiving them little better than the aborigines and quite as dirty. But customers up-country, tired of the well-known assortments of trade-goods, were attracted by their wares. They would go anywhere, undersell anyone, and slowly began driving less enterprising rivals from the field.'[15]

Enterprise, low-costs, collective support—these alone were not enough to secure them in the position they gained as intermediaries between the European import-export houses and the African producer. The key to their domination of their African rival in the retail and produce trade was capital.

First of all a prosperous Lebanese would give credit to other Lebanese relatives. In Magburaka in Sierra Leone, Khuri in 1965 found 47 Lebanese traders managing some 21 shops, but of these some had very little capital and were attached to richer relatives.[16] In supplying Lebanese shops with goods the large expatriate firms like United Africa Company were very liberal in the credit they allowed their owners. Similarly the banks gave credit to Lebanese to finance purchase of produce where they refused it to Africans, who bitterly resented this discrimination against them.[17] The refusal of most companies and banks to grant credit to Africans killed any possibility of commercial initiative on their part in competition with the Lebanese.

The Lebanese were despised as a community by the Europeans, and hated by Africans as competitors who had taken trade from them they felt should have been theirs. Yet their role in opening up West Africa to increased international trade cannot be exaggerated. Where European firms were too timid, or African businessmen lacked the resources, they pioneered new markets.[18] Thus they went ahead of the new railway lines, establishing themselves in villages through which these would pass and which as a result would become major commercial centres. In a report made in 1930 on British firms' activities in West Africa, Mr. A. W. Hall, of the Senior Trade Commissioner's office in South Africa, praised the commercial initiative of the Lebanese traders. His opinion was that with satisfactory safeguards there was little doubt that they would become increasingly excellent media for the distribution of British goods on the Coast.[19] Yet British officials were generally unfavourable towards, and very suspicious of, the Levantine businessmen, so much so that they were 'largely divorced from this important section of the commercial community'.[20] Although the latter remitted much of their capital to Lebanon, they were nevertheless responsible for a good deal of capital investment in buildings in the towns where they settled. Their large and hideous unarchitected concrete-block houses, with crude concrete verandahs, painted in gaudy colours, dominate the commercial section of nearly every West African town today.

## 2 *The European oligopolies*

Presiding over West Africa's commerce in the inter-war period were six major European trading companies and a number of smaller ones, some independent of the major companies, some allied to them. These companies, together with the European banks which financed their purchases of the African peasant's crops, dominated the import-export trade of West Africa. The United African Company (U.A.C.), formed in 1929 from the Niger Company and the African and Eastern Trading Corporation, was the giant of British West Africa. By the 1940's it accounted for over 40% of the import and export trade of Nigeria. Its main rivals were John Holt's, Paterson Zochonis and the two major companies of French West Africa, S.C.O.A. (Société Commerciale de l'Ouest Africain) and C.F.A.O., (Compagnie Française de l'Afrique Occidentale). U.A.C., too, traded in French West Africa under the name of N.O.S.O.C.O.

The extent of the domination of the import-export trade by these large firms is demonstrated by the fact that as late as 1949 in French West Africa S.C.O.A., C.F.A.O., and N.O.S.O.C.O., imported between them 73% of the sugar sold in Senegal, 66% of the rice imported, and 45% of the flour.[21] In 1937 ten firms in Nigeria reached an agreement whereby they would purchase effectively 90% of Nigeria's cocoa exports. Similarly in Ghana 98% of the cocoa trade was in the hands of thirteen European firms.[22]

Many of the seemingly independent smaller European firms operating in West Africa were bound to the great firms either by financial links at home or by fear. If a small firm tried to go into direct competition with a major firm by offering more competitive prices, it risked a price-war which it, with more slender resources, could never hope to gain. Suret-Canale has shown the large number of Bordeaux firms operating in West Africa which were linked with the mighty S.C.O.A. and equally the number of firms linked with C.F.A.O.[23] The same situation existed in British West Africa where the major companies had interests in a number of the smaller companies.

The emergence of these great companies in the inter-war period was facilitated by a variety of factors. The depressions of 1921 and

1929–35 eliminated most of their rivals. Even without depression conditions the tendency of prices for African crops to fluctuate, often violently, from year to year meant that small concerns without large reserves were hit hard in years of low prices in which their profit margins were small. Their elimination of course meant that a large firm operating exclusively in one area could offer the peasant-producer the price that it considered would make its business worthwhile, rather than the competitive price. During the 1936–7 buying season in Northern Nigeria at Baro, where U.A.C., and Holt's, had a monopoly of trade as well as transport by river and did not try and compete with each other, the opening price for groundnuts was £7 10s. od. a ton, the closing price £3 15s. od., whereas at Kano, where a Tripolitanian buyer, J. Raccah, bought competitively against the major firms, the price was maintained at £7 10s. od.[24]

Given the overheads of the European trading firm outside the maintenance of its trading posts—employment of expatriate staff, construction of quarters for them, payment of leave passages for themselves, their wives and children—the market favoured larger-scale operations. The types of goods imported—cheap cotton cloths, sugar, flour, mass-produced utensils—favoured large-scale buyers in a market where a ½d. difference in price was crucial, since the African peasant had such slender purchasing power. Furthermore, the great trading companies often owned, or were financially allied with, the factories that manufactured the goods they wished to sell on the West African market so that there again they had an advantage over their smaller competitors with no such links. Holt's and U.A.C. both owned their own shipping lines whilst C.F.A.O. and S.C.O.A. both had interests in the Fabre et Fraissinet shipping line. In an undiversified market from the point of view of imports as well as exports the larger-scale operation was favoured. So the great monopolies emerged: and having gained monopolistic control they were in the inter-war period to turn the market to their benefit beyond the normal returns for entrepreneurship.

In the inter-war period the operations of these large companies, and indeed of the smaller ones which followed their lead rather than competed with them, were very unsophisticated. They bought the peasant's export crop for processing in the factories of Europe and sold to him only goods imported from those factories. 'This simple form of export and import trade', as the Leverhulme Trust Commission described it after its tour of West Africa in 1938–9,[25] was an addition to, rather than a part of, the subsistence economy or the internal system of trade in cattle, kola or yams. Singly or collectively these firms created area and even territorial monopolies of the purchase of the export crop; their capital investment was nearly all short term and the profits from it went mainly to their European shareholders; they established industries in West Africa only where it was absolutely essential; they employed high-cost European company officials rather than train lower-cost Africans to replace them; similarly they did little to train their junior African employees; and finally, being untrammelled by government minimum wage laws and trade unions, wherever they exercised a monopoly of the labour market they used it to keep its price down.

The dominant characteristic of the import-export trade in the inter-war years was one of monopoly. Monopoly, if not de facto in an area, was achieved by negotiation between potential rivals, or through fear of the weaker rival to challenge his stronger competitor. At the national level monopolies were established by agreement between firms to follow a common buying policy so that they could maximise profits. Thus the Nowell Commission on the Marketing of West African Cocoa in 1938 revealed a whole range of agreements some of which had been in operation since the beginning of the century, concerning the purchase of West African cash crops. Cocoa, palm-kernels and palm-oil, groundnuts, even cotton and benniseed had all been the objects of such agreements.[26] With regard to cocoa these had even gone as far as pooling of sales as well as purchases in Gold Coast between 1903–17.[27] The cocoa-buying agreements of 1937, which operated in both Gold Coast and Nigeria, allocated to each member an agreed portion of total purchases of cocoa based on their performance in recent years. They also agreed on a common price policy. Resentment on the part of the African middlemen and producers in the Gold Coast was such that there was a complete hold-up in trade (see pp. 476–477) and in Nigeria the Cocoa Pool became the subject of bitter attacks by the nationalists (see p. 477). But for the rest the peasant in French and British West Africa suffered the domination of the prices paid for his crops by the European companies in silence. They resented lowering of prices, and even when these were genuinely the result of falls in the world-market price it was hard to convince them that it was not a conspiracy on the part of the European companies. But it was only in the Gold Coast that the peasants, as we shall see, were able to give effective voice to their resentment. Sir Keith Hancock in his pioneer work on West African trade wrote in 1942: 'The government has the responsibility of basing British rule upon the consent of the governed, and this consent will become forfeit if Africans believe themselves imprisoned in a commercial order which they feel to be unjust and detestable. There is no doubt about their detestation of the pools.'[28]

Colonial governments were well aware of the harmful effects of the monopolies exercised by the expatriate companies. In 1930 the Government of Nigeria wrote in its *Annual Report*: 'The prices of all agricultural export commodities exported from Nigeria have been very low throughout the year. The price agreement entered into between some of the biggest firms was also a factor which tended to depress the export trade, though fortunately, as has repeatedly occurred before, the agreement only lasted a few months.'[29] Nevertheless, in the inter-war period, the expatriate commercial houses were given free reign by the British authorities who, 'apart from the provision by state action of essential public works concentrated their main attention upon the political aspects of their subjects' affairs, leaving the more powerful and penetrating economic forces to operate upon them almost without regulation or understanding'.[30] Just how deleterious to development these monopolies were is illustrated by the merger of the African and Eastern Trade Corporation with the Niger Company in 1929 to form the United African Company. Not only did the sum total of the trade done by the two companies operating independently fall, but following a deliberate contraction of their business many shops and buying stations were closed. Nevertheless, despite the depression, the company from September 1932–8 made profits at the rate of 9% per annum. As Mars points out, part of these profits can be attributed to the streamlining of business resulting from amalgamation, 'but the oligopolistic and oligopsonistic position of the U.A.C., undoubtedly plays a large part in the explanation of that profit'.[31] The British attitude to the monopolistic activities of the import-export firms was one of laissez-faire though in the early 1930's when U.A.C. tried to start trading in subsistence crops, Government asked them to stop because of fierce African opposition to this move.[32] By contrast the French actively supported their import-export firms. The firms, as in British West Africa, could fix their own prices for crops, prices that were often so low that it was barely worth the peasant growing them. Inclination to abandon production of low-return cash crops was countered by the administration's taxation policy coupled with its imposition of obligatory cultivation of certain crops. Thus the companies were assured of the crops they needed, at the prices they determined, partly through the assistance of the administration.

### 3 *Investment and development by commerce*

In British and French West Africa the import-export economy was largely in the hands of the companies. Not until the Second World War did the British West African governments acquire economic advisers, and though the French were more conscious of the role of planning at the Government level, and interfered directly in the market economy in forcing peasants to grow certain crops, the companies had very much a free reign as far as pricing and commercialisation of crops were concerned. Being therefore the major determinants of the economic life of the West African colonies, it was a great disadvantage that their policies were laid down in Liverpool and London, Bordeaux and Marseilles rather than in Dakar and Lagos. It was difficult for boards of directors, many of whose members had never seen the colonies which provided them with their salaries, to be very venturesome in their policy decisions. Indeed, far from being venturesome, they were extremely cautious. Their capital investment reflects this. Very little of it was devoted to production: nearly all of it was tied up in the buildings essential for the conduct of their business. In 1930 Carsaw considered that one of the main causes of stagnation in French Black Africa was the excessive amount of capital invested in commercial operations compared with that invested in the productive sector of the economy, which he estimated at only 26% of the total, or 180 million to 710 million francs.[33] Frankel, in his *Capital Investment in Africa*, showed in 1938 just how little capital had been invested in Tropical Africa in the period 1870–1936, especially in the French areas.[34] French West Africa accounted for only 2·49% of the total invested as against Angola's 2·62% and Gold Coast's 2·89%.[35] Nigeria accounted for 6·15%, Sierra Leone 0·28% and Gambia a mere 0·02%.[36] West Africa together accounted for less than 15% of the total capital, private and public, invested in Tropical Africa of £1,221,686,000, that is a mere £147,156,000 of which French West Africa's share was only £30,426,000. Of this total public and private capital represented roughly half each. Not only was capital investment small, but in a period where the British and French Governments at home took relatively little initiative in public investment, government capital was strikingly high.[37]

This low rate of capital investment was the responsibility of commercial firms, one of whose essential characteristics was short-run planning,[38] and of colonial governments who saw it neither their duty to interfere with the policies of these firms nor to invest funds over and above those derived from the colony itself in its development. Even the funds they raised locally were smaller than they could have been, for the commercial firms had very light tax loads. Not until 1939 was there any taxation of company incomes in Nigeria.[39] The profits of these companies, as of the mines, went almost exclusively to their European shareholders.[40] Perhaps the most scandalous example of expatriation of profits earned in a West African country was the £2·25 million received by the Niger Company, and its successor the U.A.C., between 1906–44, from government mining revenue in compensation for the revocation of the Royal Niger Company's Charter.[41]

Entrepreneurial profits, however derived, for the most part found their way back to Europe rather than being invested locally. The most obvious reflection of this is the almost total lack of industry other than mining industries in West Africa on the outbreak of World War II. In French West Africa there were no mining activities, and indeed almost nothing had been done to see whether there were mineral resources to be exploited.[42] Manufacturing industries were almost negligible: a few palm-oil mills in Dahomey and Ivory Coast and after 1936 a groundnut-oil mill in Senegal, producing 5,000 tons of oil a year, or 3% of the volume of groundnuts exported.[43] By 1939 half the groundnuts in Senegal were decorticated locally. Over and above this there was no significant industrial undertaking in French West Africa. The same was true for British West Africa. Nigeria on the eve of World War II, wrote Mars, 'like other British colonies, has no manufacturing industries worth mentioning. In particular it has no construction goods industries which could produce the capital equipment so badly needed to increase the natural output of the country.'[44] The only important industries in British West Africa were the mines: tin in Northern Nigeria, gold and manganese in Gold Coast, coal in Eastern Nigeria, iron ore and diamonds in Sierra Leone. Significantly these were industries which by their very nature could not be carried out elsewhere. If there was a choice between siting an industry in West Africa or in the metropolitan countries, it was the metropolis which won. The companies trading in West Africa invariably were linked with, or as in the case of Unilever, owned the mills or factories which processed the crops of West Africa.[45] Similarly there was no attempt by these companies to set up industries in West Africa to manufacture some of the goods they imported. U.A.C., dependent on Unilever, could, and did later, set up soap factories in Nigeria and Gold Coast using locally produced oils. But in so doing it competed with Unilever's home soap factories. The prevailing attitude was that of McPhee, that Africa should supply the raw materials for the factories of Europe. Thus in 1926, discussing the development of cotton-growing in Nigeria, he wrote: 'Part of the problem, then, is to divert the supply of cotton from the Nigerian hand-looms to the power-looms of Lancashire.'[46] In one of the few cases where an industry was established in West Africa competitive with a metropolitan industry, restrictions were placed on it when it seemed to threaten the existence of its metropolitan rival. Thus in 1938 French oil extractors had become so alarmed at Senegalese competition that a limit was placed on the amount of oil allowed into France duty free.[47]

If the European companies were not interested in developing Africa's resources, nor establishing industries there, they were even less inclined to develop its manpower. This is the more surprising in view of the cost of employing Europeans to do jobs that could with education and training have been done by Africans. The cost of employing a European in Africa is about four times that of an African. Yet by 1939 there were only a handful of Africans in managerial posts in any of the major companies operating in West Africa. Mighty U.A.C. offered one £300 scholarship for a Ghanaian student, one for a Nigerian student.[48] This was about as far as any company, French or British, went towards encouraging Africans. In French West Africa, however, Europeans were employed in jobs that in British West Africa would have been held by Africans, so that the problem was even more acute there. Even at lower levels there was little provision for the training of Africans in manual skills. What Mars said about Nigeria was generally true for West Africa: 'Nothing is more needed than manual skill in Nigeria, for without it no real progress in civilisation is possible.'[49]

Labour policy in West Africa was however in this period very reactionary. Wages to adult males, the Leverhulme Commission reported in 1943, were as low as 4d. a day in some industries and 1s. 6d. a day was considered a good wage.[50] In Ivory Coast Europeans resisted raising wages for their labourers on the grounds that, the needs of Africans being limited, if their salaries were doubled they would work only half the time.[51] As Schachter-Morgenthau observed, employers in French West Africa had 'little incentive to know personally or care for their workers. The whip and the stick were therefore in current practice. If any of the labourers died, climate or change of surroundings was blamed . . . and if the administrator heard of it, the whole thing cost 300 francs.'[52]

Where monopolistic conditions existed in a given area, the firm, being the sole purchaser of labour, could fix its own price. Even where several companies were established in an area, 'they often have a tacit agreement as to the wages they offer African labour'.[53] Neither in French nor in British West Africa before the Second World War were there any minimum wage laws or regulations concerning the use of labour that *effectively* interfered with the labour policies of the commercial companies, planters or mines, so that they were free to decide rates of pay and the perks they chose to give their employees. It was not until the period of decolonisation that government began actively to interfere in labour policy of private firms. Indeed, the general policy of government was to leave commerce to itself.

x

# Notes

1 J. Mars, 'Extra-Territorial Enterprises', p. 120.
2 Abner Cohen, 'The Social Organisation of Credit in a West African Cattle Market', *Africa*, XXXVI, 1, Jan. 1965, pp. 8–20.
3 R. Bayly Winder, 'The Lebanese in West Africa', *Comparative Studies in Society and History*, IV, 1962, pp. 296–333.
4 Marwan Hanna, 'The Lebanese in West Africa', *West Africa*, 26 April, 1958, p. 393.
5 Jean-Gabriel Desbordes, *L'immigration Libano-Syrienne en Afrique Occidentale Française*, Paris, 1938, p. 9.
6 Department of Overseas Trade, *Economic Conditions in French West Africa (1928–1930)*. Report by H.M. Consul-General in Dakar, London, 1930.
7 Winder, 'The Lebanese in West Africa', p. 298.
8 Suret-Canale, *Afrique II*, pp. 24–5.
9 See J. Bingley, *Mr. Khoury*, London 1952, p. 195.
10 This account is based on J. Mars, 'Extra-Territorial Enterprises', pp. 99–102; Desbordes, 'L'immigration Libano-Syrienne'; Suret-Canale, *Afrique II*, p. 27; Winder, 'The Lebanese in West Africa', p. 307–10.
11 Winder, 'The Lebanese in West Africa', p. 309.
12 Fuad I. Khuri, 'Kinship, Emigration and Trade Partnership among the Lebanese of West Africa', *Africa*, XXXV, 3, p. 65.
13 Warren T. Morrill, 'Socio-Cultural Adaptation in a West African Lebanese Community', *Anthropological Quarterly*, XXXV, 1962, pp. 146–55.
14 Camille Guy, *L'Afrique Occidentale Française*, pp. 74–5.
15 Fyfe, *History of Sierra Leone*, p. 514.
16 Khuri, 'Kinship, etc., among the Lebanese', p. 387.
17 J. Mars, 'Extra-Territorial Enterprises', pp. 101–2.
18 Desbordes, 'L'immigration Libano-Syrienne', p. 127.
19 *The Times*, 14th June 1930.
20 P. T. Bauer, *West African Trade* (Re-issue), London, 1963, p. 149.
21 Suret-Canale, *Afrique II*, p. 213.
22 Hancock, *Survey*, p. 210.
23 Suret-Canale, *Afrique II*, p. 217 and p. 225.
24 Hancock, *Survey*, p. 217.
25 The Leverhulme Trust, *The West African Commission 1938–1939: Technical Reports*, London, 1943, p. 5.
26 *Report of the Commission on the Marketing of West African Cocoa*, London, 1938, Cmd. 5845.
27 *Ibid.*, p. 49.
28 Hancock, *Survey*, pp. 223–4.
29 *Annual Report for Nigeria*, 1930, p. 12.
30 Margery Perham, 'Introduction' to D. Forde and R. Scott, *The Native Economies of Nigeria*, London, 1946, p. 16.

31 Mars, 'Extra-Territorial Enterprises', p. 76.
32 P. T. Bauer, *West African Trade* (Re-issue), London, 1963, p. 392.
33 Michel Carsaw, *Quelques aspects du commerce imperial de la France*, Paris, 1935, p. 147.
34 S. H. Frankel, *Capital Investment in Africa—its Course and Effects*, London, 1938, table, pp. 158-9.
35 *Ibid.*, p. 168. Frankel makes reservations about his calculations for French Africa because of paucity of data.
36 *Ibid.*, table, pp. 160-1.
37 *Ibid.*, p. 169.
38 Mars, 'Extra-Territorial Enterprises', p. 66.
39 Hancock, *Survey*, p. 199, n. 1.
40 See *Report of the Commission on the Marketing of West African Cocoa*, p. 17.
41 Mars, 'Extra-Territorial Enterprises' p. 63.
42 The French, however, complained at this lack of enterprise. In 1926 M. Victor Beauregard in *Front Républicain* drew telling comparisons between British and French West Africa in the field of mineral exploitation. See A. Jean François, *La France et la Mise en valeur des Colonies*, Paris, 1931.
43 Suret-Canale, *Afrique II*, p. 275.
44 Mars, 'Extra-Territorial Enterprises', p. 67.
45 See Suret-Canale, *Afrique II*, p. 240; Mars, *op. cit.*, p. 68.
46 McPhee, *Economic Revolution*, p. 49.
47 R. J. Harrison Church, 'French and British West Africa—Some Contrasts', *West Africa*, 28th February 1953.
48 Mars, 'Extra-Territorial Enterprises', p. 73.
49 *Ibid.*, p. 73.
50 Leverhulme Trust, *Report*, p. 5.
51 Labouret, *Paysans*, p. 231.
52 Ruth Schachter-Morgenthau, *Political Parties in French-speaking West Africa*, Oxford, 1965, p. 4, based on the Report of Inspector of Colonies Maret, Bouaké, 1931.
53 Mars, 'Extra-Territorial Enterprises'.

# 3 Government and economy in the inter-war years

## 1 Government and capital investment

In 1933, at the height of the depression in West Africa, Sir Arnold Hodson, Governor of Sierra Leone, who like his colleagues in other West African colonies had had to take extraordinary measures to protect his colony's economy, told his Legislative Council: 'It is the duty of every African Government, not to provide work for the workless, but so to govern that private enterprise is encouraged to do so; that trade is allowed to grow without hindrance; that business houses are given every facility and encouraged to start new productive works, and that the inhabitants are helped to cultivate and utilise the soil.'[1]

This laissez-faire attitude towards the economy was characteristic of West African colonial administrations in the inter-war period. Their main concern was that their colonies should pay for themselves. Not surprisingly, there was an absence of long-term planning. Development tended to be *ad hoc*, without continuity from one administration to another, without long-term goals or basis in research. Development jostled for priority in the minds of Governors with the problems of native administration and who should be awarded the O.B.E., or Légion d'Honneur. The instability of prices for West African cash crops and the depression years of 1921-3 and 1930-5 made it almost impossible to devise grandiose development plans, especially in the absence of any substantial reserve funds on which to draw.

An attempt at long-term planning was however made for French West Africa in 1921 by Albert Sarraut, who saw in the colonies the source of supply of the raw materials that would furnish French industry with the wherewithal for France's post-war recovery.[2] His ambitious scheme for 'La mise en valeur des colonies françaises', introduced to the Chamber of Deputies in 1921, envisioned for French West Africa alone the expenditure of 497 million francs on railways; 63 on ports; 62 on water supplies; 38 on urban development; and 280 million on a vast irrigation scheme on the Niger.[3] But the economic crisis of that same year killed it. Not until 1936, under the Popular Front government, was another attempt made at planning for French West Africa's overall development, and this too was abandoned. In British West Africa the story was the same. Chamberlain's famous statement that he regarded many of British colonies 'as being in the condition of underdeveloped estates and estates which can never be developed without imperial assistance . . .'[4] evoked no response from his successors as Colonial Secretary. Right up till the Second World War they held that the colonies should pay for their development from their own slender resources and that the British taxpayer had no responsibility in this direction. A remarkable exception to the lack of long-term planning in West Africa, as we have noted, was the Gold Coast under Sir Gordon Guggisberg. Six weeks after his appointment in 1919 he introduced an ambitious £24·6 million ten-year development plan. Even when the 1921 slump intervened he did not abandon it, but re-oriented it in the light of his reduced economic circumstances.

Guggisberg was an engineer by training, and it was thus not surprising that he should devote much of his attention as Governor to railways, roads, bridges and harbours. These he saw as indispensable for the development of the economy to a level at which it could afford the education and the medical services the country so badly needed.[5] His plan covered the development of a deep-water port at Takoradi, the extension of the railway system northwards, though this had to be curtailed because of shortage of finance, the extension of the road system, the improvement of water supplies, and the building of an institution of higher learning at Achimota. The original plan was reduced by half to £12 million in 1922, but in 1927, when economic circumstances were more favourable, it was increased to £16·6 million.[6]

The financing of this plan fell entirely on the Gold Coast. There was no contribution on the part of the metropolitan government. Two loans were raised in London, one of £4 million at 6% in 1920 and one of £4,628,000 at 4½% in 1925. It was another twenty years before the concept of aid to colonies became fully accepted by Britain, another twenty-five by France. In 1924 however the Commission du Commerce et de l'Industrie had proposed that France contribute 50 million francs a year for 20 years to Colonial Development.[7] The contribution by the British taxpayer to the West African territories before 1940 was minimal, with the exception of Nigeria, where before Amalgamation in 1914 the Northern Protectorate had been dependent on a grant-in-aid (see p. 202). The following table from Frankel shows how large was the ratio of loans raised to 'aid' from the British Government.

CAPITAL INVESTMENT BY GOVERNMENT TO 1936[8]

| Country | Loans £000 | Grants in aid £000 | Grants by Colonial Development Fund: loan and free grants £000 | Total £000 |
|---|---|---|---|---|
| Nigeria | 28,813 | 5,737 | 171 | 34,721 |
| Gold Coast | 12,961 | 401 | 100 | 13,462 |
| Sierra Leone | 1,881 | 33 | 540 | 2,454 |
| Gambia | 200 | 9 | 25 | 234 |
| | 43,855 | 6,180 | 836 | 50,871 |

Interest rates on loans raised immediately after the War were high at 4½–6½% compared with 3–3½% before the War. They continued to rise, and the French West African Federation did not take up 17 million francs of the 167 million-franc loan authorised in 1913 because of this.[9] In Nigeria the ratio of debt charges to the total value of domestic exports rose from approximately 7·8% in 1928 to 19·1% in 1934, and the ratio of debt charges to its gross revenue from 13·7% in 1926 to 32·8% in 1934.[10]

FRENCH WEST AFRICAN LOANS ACTUALLY RAISED:

| | |
|---|---|
| 1903 | 65,000,000 at 3% |
| 1907 | 100,000,000 at 3% |
| 1910 | 14,000,000 at 3% |
| 1913 | 25,000,000 at 3½% |
| 1920 | 25,000,000 at 5½% |
| 1922 | 50,000,000 at 5½% |

| 1924 | 50,000,000 at $6\frac{1}{2}\%$ |
|---|---|
| 1931 | 1,570,000,000 |
| and | 120,000,000 |
| 1932 | 60,000,000 |
| 1936 | 187,000,000 |

The amount of capital made available to French West Africa through public loans was very small compared with that of British West Africa, and taking into account the fluctuating value of the franc after 1918 probably did not exceed £15 million. The loans thus raised by the colonial governments were invested mainly in the infrastructure of the colonies. Railways took priority, then ports, trailed by roads, water and electricity supplies, sanitation, health and educational facilities. Agriculture, with the exception of France's major irrigation scheme on the Niger, still took very low priority. It gained no place in Guggisberg's original plan, for instance, and no place in the 1931 Colonial Loan for French West Africa apart from the Niger Dam.[11] Railways dominated the capital budgets of the West African administrations in the inter-war period. Whilst railways in Britain were all privately owned until 1946, and only two out of the seven lines were in state hands in France until the government obtained a 51% interest in the railway system in 1938, in West Africa all but one line was state-owned. The British hoped to interest private enterprise in taking over railways and commissioned Lord Ronaldshay to report on the prospects of gaining its participation in future railroad development. However, he reported that private enterprise would not be willing 'to finance and construct and operate railways unaided by Government in the present stage of Tropical Development of Africa. He also found that it would not be practicable to transfer railways to private ownership.'[12]

In Nigeria the Eastern Railway was extended north to meet with the Western system by 1926. The joint system was extended by 1929 to Gusau and Nguru. In Dahomey the railway was pushed north to Parakou (1933); in Togo north to Blita (1933); in Gold Coast Kumasi was joined with Accra (1923); and a new line pushed into the Central Province to open up new areas to cocoa production and timber exploitation. In Ivory Coast, now 'pacified', the administration was able to realise Governor Antonetti's dreams of linking the Savannah with the Coast (see p. 227) and in 1934 Bobo-Dioulasso was linked with Abidjan. The other major extension in this period was the linking of Dakar with Koulikoro on the Niger when the Dakar–Thiès line was linked with the Senegal–Niger line in 1923.

These lines were built at great cost in terms of lives and suffering and of money. Yet they left vast areas without communications. In 1926 *The Times* criticised the lack of development in Nigeria particularly with regard to its railways and suggested it 'prosecute vigorously a comprehensive scheme of railway construction'.[13] It was equally critical of French plans for a Trans-Saharan railway from Ouagadougou to Oran, which would cost an estimated £17 million and serve primarily military needs.

The construction of further railways was held up by lack of finance, and also by the intervention of a rival system of transport—the motor vehicle. Before the 1914–18 war roads in West Africa were of little significance as a means of transport compared with the railways. Not only was the cost per ton-mile prohibitively higher by lorry than by train, but the heavy lorries then manufactured dug up the laterite surfaces of the roads. In the rainy season these roads were usually impassable to vehicles. Before the War Gold Coast had, according to *The Times*, only 14 touring cars and two lorries.[14] But the introduction of a light-chassis lorry by Ford was to revolutionise transport in the inter-war years, and to stimulate the building of thousands of miles of motorable roads by governments. In 1920 A.O.F. had about 12,500 miles of road, most of which were mere tracks, completely unsuitable for motor-vehicles.[15] By 1940 it had over 62,500 miles of road, of which nearly 17,000 were classified as all-season roads. In Nigeria road building was slow: in 1926 it had only 2,596 miles of roads maintained by the Public Works Department. It was impossible to motor from Lagos to Kaduna, capital of the North, and the road systems of North and South remained entirely unconnected.[16] The situation had improved considerably by 1937, by which time 19,500 miles had been constructed by government or the native authorities, only 8,000 of them all-season roads.

In the Gold Coast under Guggisberg a veritable road revolution took place. It was there, too, that the problem of road-rail competition first came to the fore. Guggisberg pursued an energetic policy of building roads as feeders to the railways which were also being constructed at the same time. Between 1919 and 1927 3,388 miles of new road had been built, and 1,310 reconditioned. Of these 4,688 miles of motorable road, 260 had metal surfaces. Guggisberg was later to be criticised for spending so much money on railways, especially when the capital for them had to be raised at 4½ and 6½%, on the grounds that roads and road transport would have been cheaper. But as Bourret points out he could hardly have been expected to foresee that the cost per ton mile of lorry freight, which stood at 2s. 9d. in the early twenties, as compared with rail at 4d.–

7½d., would fall as low as 3d. ten years later.[17] But as early as 1926 lorries were having no difficulty on the improved roads made under Guggisberg 'in undercutting the Government railway, and Government was faced with the problem of largely financing its own competitor, while having to maintain unremunerative roads in more distant parts of the Colony'.[18] In French West Africa greater care was taken to see that roads did not compete with rail. In Nigeria the roads from North to South did not become competitive except on limited stretches, because the long-haul of low-cost groundnuts by small lorries could never compete with the railway. In Sierra Leone, the narrow gauge railway could not compete against road haulage save with government protection. In 1934 it was found that goods were being shipped from Freetown via Port Loko to join with the road from Port Loko to Makeni, the terminus of the Northern sector of the line. To protect the railway a toll of £2 was levied on all vehicles carrying imported goods to Makeni.[19] The Southern line to Bo and Pendembu was however protected by the lack of a directly competitive road.

By 1940 roads and motor transport had become an integral part of West Africa's economic life. Many lorries were owned by Africans—one of the few enterprises in which they were not eased out entirely by Europeans and Lebanese. The reasons for this were, however, not altogether complimentary, as Mars points out: 'European firms found that they would lose money if they tried to run the bulk of their own transport in the small lorries which the state of the roads permit. Africans buy lorries from companies on the high purchase system and cut their costs by not setting aside depreciation reserves, so that when the lorries are worn out or sold second hand, the owners find themselves sometimes with less capital than they had when they entered the transport industry.'[20]

One of the most distressing features of the road construction policies of the British and French colonial administrations was their lack of consultation in planning, indeed deliberate avoidance of interconnection. The only significant road links between French and British West Africa were the Kano–Maradi road, and the road linking Northern Ghana with Upper Volta.

## 2 Government and agriculture

The European export-import firms did nothing to improve the quality of the cash crops which were vital to their livelihood. This was left entirely to the agricultural departments of the colonial governments. Their resources were so slender that they could do relatively little to help the peasant farmer. All colonial budgets, both capital and recurrent, devoted minute amounts to agriculture. The agricultural departments themselves were short-staffed. In 1920, for instance, Nigeria had only 20 European officials in the Agricultural Department, and their number had only increased to 82 by 1938.[21] Such staff as were recruited lacked specialised training, for the study of tropical African agriculture was still in its infancy. Most of their experience was gained in the field. Hampered by lack of funds, by the vast areas they had to cover, by the difficulty of conversing with the peasant farmer, who was by nature unresponsive to change, it was little wonder that these often devoted men did not have much effect on agricultural practices in West Africa in the inter-war period. It is not surprising then that in a survey of the possibility of establishing secondary industries in West Africa, a writer paying tribute to the hard work of the agricultural officers nevertheless concluded in 1943 'that farming methods and the marketing of agricultural produce are far from satisfactory' and stressed the primary importance of agricultural education.[22] In the inter-war period agricultural officers were concerned primarily with the cash crops for export. Only the Germans had shown real concern with the improvement of the subsistence crops of Africans. Within this limitation, government activity in agriculture was fourfold: research and experiment; education; diversification of crops; and organisation of agricultural co-operatives.

For the long-term, research was undoubtedly the most important aspect of the work of the colonial governments, for its fruits were to have immense impact on agriculture in later decades. The pioneer work of the groundnut research centre in M'Bambey in Senegal, founded in 1913, was to be largely responsible for the great increase in the size of the Senegalese groundnut crop in the years after the Second World War. Unfortunately the number of specialised research stations established in West Africa in the inter-war period was very small. A cacao research station was established at Bingerville in Ivory Coast and a research station primarily concerned with cotton was established in Zaria, Northern Nigeria. Not until 1938, after stern warnings by a visiting agricultural mission two years earlier that the whole cocoa industry was in jeopardy from 'swollen shoot' disease, whose cause was not known, did the Gold Coast government set up a special research station at New Tafo.[23] Research was carried on outside the specialised research stations both by individual agricultural officers and by departments of agriculture in colonies without research stations.

Major research into cotton- and rice-growing was conducted in French West Africa by the *Office du Niger*, established in 1932 to harness the Niger at Sansanding for irrigation of the right bank of the river and its colonisation by peasants from over-populated Upper Volta. The *Office du Niger's* largely unsuccessful colonisation scheme, originally anticipating the resettlement of 1,500,000 Africans, would have been a vast experiment in agriculture resettlement and education. (See p. 321 ff.) Agricultural education such as the Germans had started in Togo was not repeated in the other West African territories. In Sierra Leone an agricultural department plantation was started at Njala in 1912 to which chiefs and farmers were invited to see improved farming techniques such as deep hoeing. A school was established there later, for which a number of agricultural scholarships were available. However, in 1927 the Department of Education wrote in its report that 'so far nothing has been done to justify the qualifying of the word "agricultural" in connection with the name of this school'.[24]

Elsewhere 'education' was largely limited to visits to experimental centres by chiefs and farmers, or 'extension' work by an over-worked agricultural officer, trying in a hurried visit to persuade conservative peasants to make radical changes to their farming techniques.

Though they were far from being successful or of major importance in the inter-war period, the establishment of co-operatives by government was of considerable significance, since they foreshadowed what has become the commonest pattern of agricultural organisation in West Africa today and were in themselves agencies for agricultural education. The advantages of the co-operative to the African peasant were threefold. First, definite arrangements for the conservation of good seed for planting for the next year's crop could be made. Too often the peasant, overwhelmed by debts or caught by an unanticipated fall in the price for his cash crop, sold off his seed reserve. Second, a co-operative, properly formed, could market its own produce rather than leave this in the hands of unscrupulous middlemen or unscrupulous monopolistic arrangements like the infamous 'cocoa pool'. (See p. 300.) Indeed the Nowell Commission recommended as a result of the investigations into the 'cocoa pool' that henceforth the whole marketing of cocoa in the Gold Coast should be re-organised and be handled by co-operatives under government control.[25] Thirdly, through co-operatives peasants could acquire capital to finance the purchase of ploughs and other equipment normally beyond their pocket. In British West Africa the co-operative movement, supervised by the Departments of Agriculture, was only just getting off the ground before the Second World War. In 1931 co-operatives were legalised in the Gold Coast, but by 1938 the 371 cocoa co-operatives that had been established handled only 9,405 tons of cocoa out of a total crop of 137,000 tons.[26] In Nigeria, co-operatives were only legalised in 1935 and were primarily focused on cocoa marketing. By 1939–40 138 societies had handled only 5,872 tons of cocoa out of a total crop of 82,000 tons. In 1938 the Ibibio people of Eastern Nigeria started organising limited liability credit societies in which farmers and traders pooled savings to make loans to those who were credit-worthy.[27] In French West Africa the history of the *Sociétés Indigènes de Prévoyance* (S.I.P.) was a long and not altogether happy one. The original motivation for the foundation of the S.I.P.s was the failure of the peasant to conserve enough seed for his next year's crop, and to protect himself against lean years. As Suret-Canale has convincingly argued, these conditions arose not so much from the African peasant's 'chronic improvidence' as the French thought, but from an economic system where through taxation and coercion he was forced to produce cash crops to the detriment of subsistence crops, where his able-bodied men were taken away for the army or for compulsory labour, and where he was paid prices for his produce lower than their real economic value.[28]

The S.I.P. was born in Sine Saloum where the Commandant de Cercle organised a co-operative whereby seed would be lent at 5% interest repayable in seed. Private traders had been lending at 200–300%. In 1910 the S.I.P.s were recognised by decree, by which time it had been decided to charge a membership fee and to exact 25% interest on seed advanced to the peasant. Though the S.I.P.s were initially organised with African presidents, and voluntary membership, by the decree of 1915 membership became compulsory, a development which, as Mamadou Dia, sometime Premier of Senegal, noted in his book on the co-operative movement in Africa, was fundamentally opposed to the co-operative spirit.[29] In 1923 the African president of the S.I.P. was replaced by the Commandant de Cercle ex-officio. Initially the S.I.P.s were restricted mainly to Senegal, but between 1930 and 1933, during the Depression, they were established throughout French West Africa.

In principle the S.I.P.s had a wide scope: to take all measures contributory to the development of agriculture, animal husbandry, fishing and uncultivated produce, as well as to improve the conditions under which produce was harvested, processed, stocked and marketed. In practice their main functions were the advance of seed and, after 1935, the compulsory stocking of grain supplies. By the decree of January 1935 establishing grain stores under the aegis of the S.I.P., to which peasants had to contribute stocks, everyone other than infants had to supply between 100–150 kilos of grain. Thus a family of ten, as Thompson and Adloff point out, might have to supply between 1,000 and 1,500 kilos of grain, virtually its whole production, on penalty of fine or imprisonment for failure.[30] A measure designed to avoid famine itself created great hardship, and when the grain was distributed much of it had been ruined by poor storing.

Many of the S.I.P.s became rich, and in 1935 a common fund was created in each colony for the S.I.P.s, controlled by the Governor. In 1932 agricultural credit banks, based on credit organisations started in 1926, were established in Sudan and the coastal colonies.

Though the S.I.P.s were well established in French West Africa, they were not true co-operatives, being compulsory and run autocratically by the administration. The peasant had little say in the expenditure of the funds derived from his labour, and very often they were spent to the advantage of the administration rather than himself.[31] However, against such hostile views we have the laudatory one of the British Consul-General in Dakar in 1937 who wrote that 'commercial houses complain that in many cases they [the S.I.P.s] carry their activities into the realm of trading to the detriment of these concerns'.[32] They also provided the agency through which improved seed could be distributed. Selected groundnut seed from the Bambey research station, for instance, was distributed through them.

In British West Africa the Colonial governments staunchly opposed the alienation of land to Europeans. In French West Africa, however, it continued to be permitted. By 1st January 1938 352,968 acres had been conceded to European planters, thus:[33]

|  | Provisional (acres) | Permanent (acres) |
|---|---|---|
| Senegal | 7,744 | 9,956 |
| Sudan | 17,816 | 27,379 |
| Guinea | 38,973 | 18,115 |
| Ivory Coast | 124,017 | 104,195 |
| Dahomey | 1,685 | 3,064 |
| Niger | — | 24 |
| TOTAL | 190,235 | 162,733 |

However, one highly placed Frenchman at least was beginning to have second thoughts about the wisdom of European colonisation. Governor Boisson of Cameroun, who was later Governor-General of French West Africa, told the *Académie des Sciences Coloniales* in February 1938 that European colonisation of our possessions on the West African Coast had reached its fill, and that it should now give way to native colonisation. He himself had already stopped further European colonisation in Cameroun.[34]

In British West Africa Lord Leverhulme, now owner of the Niger Company, attempted to persuade the Nigerian authorities to concede him land for palm-oil plantations along the lines of those he had successfully established in the Congo. As Sir William Lever he had already set up kernel-crushing mills in 1910 at Opobo and Apapa in Nigeria, and at Yonibana in Sierra Leone in 1912. He had made himself a controversial figure in Gold Coast through his successful attempt in 1912–13 to obtain a local monopoly of palm-kernel crushing. It came to nothing because of the failure of the Nigerian and Sierra Leone mills.[35] Lord Leverhulme after a tour of West Africa, during which he received cool response from the Governor of Nigeria, Sir Hugh Clifford, to his demands for concessions, declared to the London Commercial Travellers' Benevolent Society in March, 1925: 'Europe could not exist without the products of the Tropics; equally the people of the tropics could not exist without the organising ability of the white men from Europe and European products.' He delivered a venomous attack on the colonial administration for its 'fatuous policy of preventing the native from selling his freehold land to the white man'. The administration was bureaucratic and 'ostrich-like buried its head in the sand and refused to see the march of progress. Crown Colonies under the policy which prevailed, had become a collection of tin tents. Substantial buildings could only be erected on freehold properties.'[36] Both Governor Clifford and his Chief Secretary assured the people that Lord Leverhulme's views were diametrically opposed to Government policy. However, the argument for plantations became stronger when Sumatra emerged as a rival producing superior palm-oil by cheaper methods. The extent of the threat can be seen from the following table from Hancock comparing Nigerian with Dutch East Indies production.[37]

|  | Yearly average—metric tons | | | |
|  | 1909–13 | 1924–8 | 1930 | 1936 |
|---|---|---|---|---|
| Nigeria | 81,900 | 128,136 | 136,756 | 163,174 |
| Dutch East Indies | Nil | 25,136 | 49,342 | 172,396 |

In 1926 the matter was brought to a close after the Parliamentary Under-Secretary for the Colonies, W. A. Ormsby-Gore, visited West Africa and rejected the setting up of plantations on the grounds that government would have to recruit labour compulsorily for the planters' profit. The House of Commons in July 1926 rejected the idea of plantations and gave their support to the system of indirect rule.[38] However, permission was given for the establishment of nucleus plantations 'as a means of ensuring regular supplies to mills and of educating native producers' following a recommendation in the Ormsby-Gore report. Between 1926 and 1936 14,566 acres were conceded for plantations.[39]

This account has tended to draw a negative picture of government role in agriculture in the inter-war years. Nevertheless within their severe limitations the agricultural departments did make considerable contributions to the improvement of agriculture in the colonies they served. Take Nigeria, for example. American cotton which had proved suitable in Uganda was introduced to Northern Nigeria with success. The poor quality indigenous cotton of Western Nigeria was replaced by an improved local variety selectively bred by the Agricultural Department. Ginger was successfully introduced into Zaria province in 1928–9, and by 1933–4 86 tons were being exported. A new technique of drying benniseed was started in Benue province to replace the wasteful system practised before. The Veterinary Department undertook considerable work in the immunisation of cattle against rinderpest (427,446 in 1934), against blackwater (450,768 in 1934), and against pleuro-pneumonia (54,279 in 1934). Large numbers of inferior bulls were castrated at the request of their owners.[40]

At a time when peasant production of cash crops was expanding at a rapid rate, and forests and woodlands were being cleared ruthlessly and indiscriminately for new farms and plantations, or in other areas to supply Europe with quality timbers or the local railways with fuel, the establishment of Forestry Reserves was of the greatest importance. By 1920 in Nigeria, 10,630 square miles of Reserves had been established and 25% of Benin province alone had been reserved.[41] By that same year 1,758 square miles had been reserved in the Gold Coast.[42] By 1940, in French West Africa some 40 million hectares of forest had been 'protected' by legislation.[43] Thus at the same time as the colonial administrations pursued a policy of increasing production of cash crops, and consequently deforestation, they did at least try to stop it getting completely out of hand. And in the savannah today these reserves are oases of trees in otherwise bare lands.

The main economic activities of both British and French governments during the inter-war period lay in their development of the infrastructure and on a much smaller scale the development of agriculture. Otherwise the commercial companies were paramount in the economy though government did insist on inspecting certain crops for quality before export. They were not hampered by labour laws: in the Gold Coast a labour department was not established until 1938, and in Nigeria till 1939. There were, however, special labour inspectors for the Gold Coast and Nigerian mines. In French West Africa an effective and reasonable labour code was not introduced until 1944. In the inter-war period a code did exist, but there was no provision for labour inspectors, and the minimum wages laid down by it were lower than those prevailing.[44]

The governments did not even have overall control of the currency of their colonies. In French West Africa the issue of currency by the private Banque de l'Afrique Occidentale was confirmed by the law of 29th January 1929, which insisted however on certain restrictions on its issue of credit. It also provided for the participation in the capital of the bank of the French State and the colonies concerned. The French State also reserved the right to nominate the Director-General of the Bank and several of its administrators. The cash in hand also had to correspond to a third of the amount of notes in circulation.[45] In British West Africa the private bank the Bank of British West Africa was banker both to the colonial governments and to the West African Currency Board. Not until the eve of independence were central banks, independent of the commercial banks, established.

## 3 The Great Depression

All the colonial governments possessed an instrument which potentially could bring about radical changes in the economy: taxation. The use of direct taxation as a means not only of raising revenue but also of forcing African peasants to increase their production has already been discussed. Indirect taxation, in particular the imposition of duties on imports and exports, was not only a major source of revenue for the colonial governments, but, as the Great Depression of 1929–32 showed, a means of exercising great influence on the economy.

For the colonial governments in West Africa the Great Depression nearly spelt disaster, dependent as they were for the most part, and in the case of the Gold Coast entirely, on duties on imports and exports for their revenue. Prices for West Africa's main crops dropped catastrophically from between 60% and 70%, not only reducing the value of exports where they were taxed, but also the ability to purchase imports, which were the primary source of customs duties. The great reduction in their revenue forced the colonial governments to intervene actively in the regulation of the economic life of their colonies. In this they foreshadowed their role in the next crisis, the Second World War, after which it became accepted that responsibility for the economy of the colonies lay with government and not with the commercial houses.

In French West Africa a series of measures were taken to protect the economy during the period 1930-5. Special premiums were paid on West African export crops such as coffee, rubber, sisal, manioc, bananas and pineapples. Preference was accorded by France to oleaginous products coming from her West African colonies. Those coming from outside the French empire were subject to special import duties on entering France, and part of the proceeds were paid to the budgets of the colonies.[46]

In 1935, as a further measure of protection, the French Government abrogated provisionally Article 9 of the Anglo-French Convention of 1898 whereby no preferential treatment for French goods was to be given in what was known as the *Convention Zone*, consisting of Ivory Coast and Dahomey. After 1936, a surtax was levied in these two colonies on all foreign imports similar to that levied in the ironically titled *Free Zone* consisting of Senegal, Sudan, Upper Volta, Guinea, Mauretania and Niger.[47]

Apart from these fiscal measures, the French Government undertook a programme of development of the empire which would make it as far as possible internally self-subsistent. The great colonial loan of 1931, of which 1,690 millions was eventually allocated to French West Africa, had this as its main aim. Thus the *Office du Niger* was launched in order to supply France with cotton that otherwise she had to purchase outside the franc zone. The scheme, it was hoped, would not only irrigate over 500,000 hectares for cotton, but nearly the same amount for rice which was the staple diet of the Senegal–Sudan region. It was anticipated, as we have seen, that the scheme would provide re-settlement for nearly 1½ million peasants from impoverished areas like Upper Volta and thus contribute to the increase in the well-being of the African. The scheme was a failure. In the post-war years the *Office* rarely produced more than 4,000 tons of cotton, and 20,000 tons of rice. By 1940 only 12,000 odd Africans

had been re-settled there. Lack of research was the main cause.[48]
The generalisation of the S.I.P.s were also part of the scheme to
increase production in West Africa despite falling prices, and to
make France and her empire self-sufficient. In 1932 Governor-
General Brévié launched a five-year economic development plan
and ordered all administrators 'to follow the path of development
laid down, instead of being allowed to give play to their own pet
ideas which would as often as not be upset by their successors'.[49]
The main aim of this plan was to get away from French West
Africa's dependence on the monoculture of groundnuts by developing other crops.

France's efforts in West Africa to reduce dependence on foreign
trade were rewarded: in 1938 82% of French West Africa's exports
went to the franc zone compared with 66% six years earlier; imports
from the franc zone rose in that same period from 44·5% to 69%.

The French administration also found itself in the unaccustomed
role of coming to the rescue of private enterprise. The depression,
whose effect can be seen from the fall in currency circulation from
1928 to 1935, put many firms out of business.[50]

CURRENCY CIRCULATION: 1928–35

|         | 1928 | 1929 | 1930 | 1931 | 1932 | 1933 | 1934 | 1935 |
|---------|------|------|------|------|------|------|------|------|
| Maximum | 706  | 670  | 583  | 389  | 217  | 192  | 199  | 258  |
| Minimum | 425  | 364  | 319  | 176  | 117  | 103  | 84   | 128  |

In July 1931 a major bank, the Banque Française de l'Afrique, failed,
and but for the quick intervention of the Administration, which
bought up the credits of the depositors and settled dishonoured
cheques by borrowing from the semi-official Banque de l'Afrique
Occidentale, the effects of its failure would have been disastrous.
Again at the end of 1931 the Banque Commerciale Africaine had to
close for six weeks and was only saved by support from the administration and the Banque de l'Afrique Occidentale, which to help
this bank and the administration had to call in all its non-paid up
capital, about three-quarters of its total.[51] The British administrators
were not faced by anything so disastrous as a bank failure. But the
drastic fall in world prices for West African crops called for similar
intervention in the economy.

In the Gold Coast the fall in prices for cocoa from £50 in 1929
to £20 in 1930 was a disaster for an economy so dependent on this
crop. Revenue was derived from export duties on cocoa, from the
railway that carried it, and from the duties on imports bought with

earnings from it. Government's first reaction was to 'associate the Colony with an advertising scheme in collaboration with other cacao-producing colonies and manufacturers ... with a view to stimulating the consumption of cacao'.[52] Nothing came of this, and with a drop in revenue from £4 to £2½ million, Government was forced to resort to fiscal measures and to reduce its expenditure. Import duties were increased in June 1930 from 10%–12½% *ad valorem* on cartridges, gunpowder, beers, matches, potable and perfumed spirits, tobaccos and wines.[53] 200 European and African senior officials were retired, social services and public works were cut, and in 1931 the Governor proposed the levying of an income tax. But in the Legislative Council African opposition to direct taxation, which was by now traditional in the Gold Coast, forced the Government to shelve the proposal.[54] Instead a levy of between 4–10% was made on all official salaries. Despite the fall in world prices for cocoa and all other export crops, and the decrease in production of cocoa, copra, rubber, timber and palm-oil products, the colony survived the depression, though at the cost of a major reduction in public works and much needed officials.

In Nigeria the fall in prices had equally dramatic effects, for though Government imposed direct taxation throughout the Colony, this amounted in 1933–4 to only £808,075 against a total revenue of £6,750,407, including that from the Nigerian railway.[55] The reduction in revenue led to the laying off of senior officials and the cutting back of public works projects as in the Gold Coast. Duties on imported goods were increased in 1932 to 15% *ad valorem* on hardware, earthenware, glassware, furniture, cutlery, musical instruments, and a long list of items were subject to specific rates. As from October 1934 all, with the exception of gin, rum and petrol, were subject to a surtax of 10%. In 1933 excise duty was imposed for the first time on tobacco and cigarettes.[56] There were also export duties on cocoa, palm products and tin. Despite the steep fall in prices for cocoa and groundnuts, production, contrary to the experience in other West African countries, increased substantially, and thus revenue was not so badly affected as if producers had responded to the fall in prices by a curtailment of production.

COCOA[57]

| Year | Average monthly Lagos price per ton | Exported |
|---|---|---|
| 1929–30 | £30 | 51,700 |
| 1930–31 | £18 | 48,700 |

| 1931–32 | £18 | 55,000 |
| 1932–33 | £18 | 68,400 |
| 1933–34 | £15 | 68,400 |

GROUNDNUTS[58]

| Year | Average Price Kano | Tons Exported |
|------|--------------------|---------------|
| 1929–30 | £8 18s. od. | 147,000 |
| 1930–31 | £4 17s. od. | 154,000 |
| 1931–32 | £6 16s. od. | 165,000 |
| 1932–33 | £5 14s. od. | 197,000 |
| 1933–34 | £2 13s. od. | 234,747 |

In face of the depressed prices for tin the Tin Producers' Association asked the Nigerian Government to participate with other tin-producing countries—Bolivia, Malaya and the Dutch East Indies—in a scheme to restrict production, whereby it was hoped the world price level would rise to make tin production profitable. This Government agreed to do.[59]

The Depression hit government schemes to improve palm-oil production without resorting to the establishment of European controlled plantations. The Agricultural Department had introduced a small press by which farmers could extract higher quality oil than by traditional methods. The fall in prices however made it impossible for farmers to invest in the machine.[60]

In Sierra Leone total external trade fell by half between 1929 and 1933. Here again Government was forced to adopt fiscal measures to avert the disastrous consequences of the depression to its revenue. In 1928 the export duty on palm-oil had been increased from 20s. to 30s. per ton. In 1934 it was reduced to a mere 10s., in the hopes of increasing sales. When these where not realised it was increased to 20s. a ton.[61] Import duties were increased by as much as 50% on motor spirits, beers and ales. Public Works programmes were curtailed, officials laid off. A poll-tax of £2 was imposed on non-residents. All British West Africa was affected by Imperial Preference, which ostensibly gave preference to goods produced within the British Commonwealth and Empire. But while West Africa had to forego cheap Japanese textiles in favour of the more expensive products of the Lancashire mills, Britain continued to purchase whale-oil from Norway rather than the more expensive substitute of West African palm-oil. As T. H. Doherty, a Nigerian Negro member complained, 'the subject races, especially those in West Africa, were the greatest sufferers'.[62]

While France initiated a programme of public works to relieve the depression in French West Africa through the Great Empire Loan of 1931, the British equivalent, the Colonial Development Fund, only came into operation when the depression had passed its worst. Thus in Sierra Leone it 'stimulated the revival rather than relieved the depression'.[63] But the funds, which became available only in 1932 and 1933 after the height of the Depression, were very small indeed:

| | |
|---|---|
| Nigeria | £69,024 |
| Gold Coast | £94,018 |
| Sierra Leone | £248,500 |
| Gambia | £7,924 |

But most of the money made available under the C.D.F. was limited to helping governments support their recurrent expenditure. A major exception was the support given by the C.D.F. to the Sierra Leone Development Company to establish its iron-ore mine at Marampa. However, since production did not start until 1933, it did not significantly solve the effects of the Depression.

The colonial governments have been much criticised for the lack of development they undertook in the colonies in the inter-war period. Certainly they were for the most part unambitious and laissez-faire. But account must be taken of the fact that even a coherent, well-conceived plan like that of Guggisberg was hampered by the serious financial difficulties occasioned by the depressions of the inter-war period. Unfortunately the concept of aid to colonies was not accepted by either France or Britain. The furthest they ventured was to establish loans through the Great Empire Loan of 1931, and the Commonwealth Development Fund of 1929.

As a result of the depressions of the inter-war years, government revenue and the value of imports and exports were about the same in 1929 as they were in 1922. (See Appendices F and G.) If income had not risen, the volume of production had, dramatically. When during the Second World War the demand for West Africa's products increased, boom conditions resulted. These continued after the war, and, coupled with the new approach of the metropolitan powers to the question of aid for development, produced the economic revolution which accompanied decolonisation in West Africa.

## 4 Health and the economy

The development of the economy depended intimately on the health services provided by government and voluntary agencies. Those who were not blinded by beliefs about the African's 'inherent laziness' realised that more efficient production both in agriculture and industry must involve preventing and curing the many debilitating diseases to which the African peasant was subjected from youth. Nutrition also was a major consideration. As late as 1944 John Noon in his study of African labour problems reported the 'frequent mention . . . made in the Colonial Reports of West African Territories of Natives found either dead or starving along the migration routes'.[64] Given the crucial relationship of productive efficiency to the improvement of the West African economy, little was done to tackle the root cause of African inefficiency—his health. In criticising the efforts of the colonial governments in the inter-war years, however, one must take into account the lack of knowledge about many tropical diseases, the difficulty in recruiting doctors, and the shortage of funds available. Even so their efforts, particularly in British West Africa, were pathetically small.

In British West Africa the medical services had as their primary consideration the health of the European community. Sir Hugh Clifford, Governor of the Gold Coast, was quite explicit about this in a despatch to his colleague in Sierra Leone, in which he stated that 'his Medical Establishment [was] maintained almost exclusively for the benefit of the European population'.[65] And here we must remember that the health services were paid for by the African taxpayer. Governor Mereweather of Sierra Leone however stated categorically that his own service was not for exclusive use by Europeans.[66] But well-qualified Africans found it difficult to obtain appointments in his Medical Department. In 1916 Dr. J. A. Williams, who gained First Class honours at Edinburgh, applied for appointment, but was not taken on until 1925, and then only for two years on probation.[67] Africans were appointed to a separate Medical Service from the European doctors, so that the most senior African doctor, however well qualified, was junior in rank to the most recently appointed European. By 1938 in Nigeria there were only fourteen African medical officers, and in the Gold Coast only eight.[68]

In French West Africa the position was very different. There were, in 1936, 185 African auxiliary doctors (*médecins africains*). The French argued that the health problem was so enormous and the cost of training a doctor in France so high, that the best solution to the problem would be to train African doctors locally, in Dakar, to a level where they would be able to deal with the majority of diseases which they would be called on daily to diagnose. Better to have a large number of auxiliary doctors able to deal with the common diseases that afflicted the African, than a few, fully qualified, who could deal with rarer diseases as well. Anyway, the auxiliary doctor could always refer difficult cases to the European medical officer. When this system was proposed for Nigeria it was bitterly opposed by the nationalists on the ground that it was merely training Africans as second-class doctors.

Some idea of the limitations of the medical services in British West Africa can be given by the number of beds available in Government Hospitals. In 1936 Nigeria had only 3,503 for Africans, and Gold Coast only 995. Expenditure on health services was minute: Sierra Leone only spent £66,910, Nigeria £387,600 and Gold Coast £312,413. In Nigeria and Gold Coast the number of doctors in Government Service, European and African, was 190. And we must remember that many of these doctors, and a considerable part of these funds, were devoted to the health of the European community.

Much of the treatment of Africans was given in dispensaries rather than hospitals. But these of course did not have doctors. Missions supplemented government efforts. Most of the health services in the Protectorate of Sierra Leone were provided by missions. In Nigeria they maintained 22 African hospitals, 97 dispensaries, 16 leper settlements and 116 maternity and infant welfare centres, treating 216,500 patients. Government hospitals in the same year, 1936, treated 650,209 patients.

In the same year the French West Africa treated the impressive number of 3,113,819 African out-patients. This was achieved through a basically different approach to health problems. As Hailey puts it, 'whereas in the British territories hospitals are regarded mainly as centres for treatment, those in French Africa function largely as the headquarters of field stations, whence curative and preventive medicine is made available in rural areas'.[69]

Indeed the French tackled the battle for health as a military operation: her European medical officers, numbering 180 in 1936, were nearly all members of the army. Each *cercle* had at least one *centre médical* staffed by a European doctor, with dependent dispensaries supervised by African auxiliary doctors. There were only eleven hospitals in the Federation, but 437 ambulances and dispensaries through which qualified medical treatment could be obtained.

The doctors were assisted by health visitors (30 European and 250 African).

Despite these efforts, both in French and British West Africa, the problem of health remained dire right up to the time of independence. The major contribution of the colonial powers was not in their treatment of individuals, but in the research they conducted into tropical diseases in the Institut Pasteur or the London School of Hygiene and Tropical Medicine, and their programmes for the eradication of endemic diseases like yellow fever, sleeping sickness and smallpox. But even today, health remains one of the major problems for the African. In 1961 during a recruiting campaign in Northern Nigeria, army doctors had to reject at sight 380 out of 500 candidates who presented themselves at Bauchi. And of the 12 who passed all other tests for enlistment, only 5 were able to pass the final medical test.[70]

# Notes

1 Sierra Leone Legislative Council Debates, 1933–4, Governor's Address, pp. 5–6, cited by Cox-George, *Finance and Development, West Africa*, p. 296.
2 Albert Sarraut, *La Mise en valeur des colonies françaises*, Paris, 1923, p. 27.
3 Suret-Canale, *Afrique II*, p. 352.
4 *Hansard*, 22nd August 1895.
5 See R. E. Wraith, *Guggisberg*, London, 1967, pp. 99 ff; also Kimble, *Ghana*, pp. 55–8.
6 See table in Kimble, *ibid.*, p. 56.
7 Southwark, *The French Colonial Venture*, p. 55.
8 Frankel, *op. cit.*, p. 171.
9 Naval Intelligence Division, *French West Africa*, I: 'The Federation', London, 1943, p. 348.
10 Frankel, *op. cit.*, p. 181–3.
11 Department of Overseas Trade, *Economic Conditions in French West Africa (1931–1933)*, London, 1934, p. 9.
12 *The Times*, 29th January 1923.
13 *The Times*, 7th April 1926.
14 *The Times*, 1st January 1924.
15 *The Times*, 5th March 1921.
16 *The Times*, 7th April 1926.
17 F. M. Bourret, *Ghana: The Road to Independence 1919–1957*, London, 1960, p. 30.
18 Wraith, *Guggisberg*, p. 117.
19 Best, *The Sierra Leone Railway*, p. 81.
20 Mars, 'Extra-Territorial Enterprises', p. 121.
21 Perham, *The Native Economies of Nigeria*, p. 11.
22 R. W. Stopford, 'Some Problems involved in the Development of Secondary Industries in West Africa', *Africa*, XIV, 4, 1943, pp. 165–6.
23 Bourret, *Ghana*, p. 121.
24 *Education Department Report* (Sierra Leone), 1927, p. 8, cited in Cox-George, *Finance and Development*, p. 210.
25 *Report on the Commission on the Marketing of West African Cocoa*, pp. 511–45.
26 Bourret, *Ghana*, pp. 121–2.
27 *Nigeria Handbook* (Crown Agents for the Government of Nigeria), 2nd Edition, London, 1954, pp. 137–8.
28 Suret-Canale, *Afrique Noire II*, pp. 299–310.
29 Mamadou Dia, *Contribution à l'étude du mouvement co-opératif en Afrique noire*, Paris, 1952, p. 23.
30 Thompson and Adloff, *French West Africa*, p. 356.
31 Suret-Canale, *Afrique Noire II*, pp. 307–9.
32 Department of Overseas Trade, *Report on Economic and Commercial Conditions in French West Africa (1933–36)*, London, 1937, p. 13.

33 Naval Intelligence Bureau, *French West Africa*, Vol. I, p. 311.
34 *Bulletin de Documentation Coloniale*, No. 124, 1–15, Mars, 1938, pp. 2–4.
35 See Kimble, *Ghana*, p. 46.
36 *The Times*, 30th March 1925.
37 Hancock, *Survey*, p. 196.
38 Debate in House of Commons, 29th July 1926, *Hansard*, 198, p. 2,399 ff. See particularly speech of Mr. Snell, who made a strong attack on the plantation system in Africa.
39 Hancock, *Survey*, p. 185.
40 See *Annual Report for Nigeria 1934* for above figures.
41 *Ibid, 1930*, p. 15.
42 *Annual Report for the Gold Coast 1930–31*, p. 11.
43 Thompson and Adloff, *French West Africa*, p. 344.
44 See Buell, *Native Problem*, Vol. I, pp. 30–4.
45 Charles Richon, *La Production Coloniale et le Crédit*, Paris, 1931, p. 113.
46 Suret-Canale, *Afrique Noire II*, pp. 360–3.
47 Department of Overseas Trade, *Report on Economic and Commercial Conditions in French West Africa 1933–36*, London, 1937.
48 See Suret-Canale, *Afrique Noire II*, pp. 354–60; Em. Perrot, 'Ou en est l'A.O.F.?', Chapter II: 'L'aménagement du Niger', in *Travaux des laboratoires de matière médicale et de pharmacie Galénique T XXX*, Année 1939, Paris, 1940, pp. 270–85.
49 *Report on Economic and Trade Conditions in French West Africa (1933–36)*, p. 11.
50 Source, Department of Overseas Trade, *Economic Conditions in French West Africa (1931–33)*, London, 1934, p. 15, and *Report on Economic and Commercial Conditions in French West Africa (1933–36)*, p. 9.
51 *Economic Conditions in French West Africa (1931–33)*.
52 *Annual Report for the Gold Coast 1930–31*, p. 1.
53 *Ibid.*, p. 2.
54 Bourret, *Ghana*, pp. 57–8.
55 *Annual Report for Nigeria 1934*, pp. 91–2. The breakdown of revenue from direct taxation was:

|                                   | £       |
| --------------------------------- | ------- |
| General Tax, Northern Provinces   | 447,223 |
| Cattle Tax, Northern Provinces    | 82,494  |
| General Tax, Southern Provinces   | 240,782 |
| Cattle Tax, Southern Provinces    | 1,248   |
| Income Tax, Colony                | 22,076  |
| Income Tax, Protectorate          | 14,252  |
|                                   |         |
| Total                             | 808,075 |

56 *Annual Report for Nigeria 1934*, p. 93.
57 *Ibid.*, p. 38.

58 *Ibid.*, p. 40.
59 A. N. Cook, *British Enterprise in Nigeria*, 2nd Impression, London, 1964, p. 230.
60 *Ibid.*, p. 234.
61 Cox-George, *Finance and Development in West Africa*, p. 282.
62 Nigerian Leg Co Debates, 12 June 1934, reference supplied by J. Bertin Webster.
63 Cox-George, *Finance and Development*, p. 296.
64 John A. Noon, *Labor Problems of Africa*, Philadelphia, 1944, p. 327.
65 S.L.N.A. Confidential Despatches 1915, Mereweather to Harcourt, 14th April 1915.
66 *Ibid.*
67 S.L.N.A. Confidential Despatches 1916, Secretary of State to Wilkinson, 7th November 1916, and M. C. F. Easmon, 'Sierra Leone Doctors', *Sierra Leone Studies*, N.S., June 1956.
68 Hailey, *African Survey* (1938). Unless otherwise stated all statistics are taken from Hailey.
69 *Ibid.*, p. 1086.
70 Athaji Metteden, 'Recruiting in the North', *Nigeria Magazine*, No. 72, March 1962, p. 17.

*Part VI*
Social change

# 1 Migration and the new towns

## 1 *The colonial situation*

The establishment of colonial rule in West Africa produced what has been described as the colonial situation.[1] As Wallerstein puts it: 'By the term *colonial situation* we simply mean that someone imposes in a given area a new institution, the colonial administration, governed by outsiders who establish new rules which they enforce with a reasonable degree of success. It means that all those who act in the colony must take some account of these rules, and that indeed an increasing amount of each individual's action is oriented to this set of rules rather than to any other set, for example, the tribal set, to which he formerly paid full heed.'[2]

The background to the genesis of the colonial situation has already been described in preceding chapters. During the inter-war period its distinguishing features began to emerge. An understanding of the colonial situation is essential to an understanding of the growth of African national self-consciousness, which was to lead to the rejection of colonial rule. This situation had taken definite shape by the opening of the Second World War.

The impact of European administration led to change in all spheres of African life, though it was limited in the number of people it affected. Colonial occupation grouped peoples into new political units, and facilitated their movement within them, especially towards the new urban centres which were the focus of colonial commerce and administration. Peasants became increasingly involved in the cash crop economy in which the dominant element was no longer the African but the expatriate European and Lebanese trader. Indigenous African religions lost ground to the great monotheistic religions of Islam and Christianity, though they succeeded in imposing some of their personality on these alien religions. An important minority of the population acquired Western education and therefore an understanding, however partial, of the way of life and thought of their colonial masters. Traditional political authority declined in the face of the changes brought about by colonial rule. Finally Africans were brought increasingly into day-to-day contact with the white man, and in the interaction of these two groups we can best see that the colonial situation was essentially one of crisis:[3] behind the placid exterior of the colonial system lay the seeds of its own destruction, seeds it had itself planted. Colonial rule created a new geo-political framework within which Africans had to re-orient their lives. Within the new administrative entities established by the colonial powers, security of movement and trade were established, so that for some peoples the extension of their activities beyond the visible horizon was first made possible. For others, especially the peoples of the savannah, the imposition of colonial rule did not make so much difference, since they had been used to long-distance movement and trade for many centuries. What was important, both for the village that was self-sufficient, and the town that was an international trading mart, was that under colonial rule security of intercourse was guaranteed over the whole of West Africa. While the new administrative divisions of West Africa assumed political significance for the educated élite, the mass of Africans were 'superbly unconcerned with the frontiers established by the European powers' and showed 'a surprising degree of response to economic stimuli'.[4]

## 2 Migration

Opportunities for trade or employment provoked great movements of peoples into areas inhabited by other ethnic groups and across Anglo-French boundaries. In some cases this movement was a purely economic response to opportunities for profit; in others it was stimulated by social considerations, such as the desire to escape from the restricting nature of traditional African society; in yet others it was induced by the policies of the colonial powers.

The movement of Yoruba traders into the markets of Togo, Gold Coast and Upper Volta, the spread of the Ibo from impoverished or over-populated land to the North of Nigeria as traders and clerks, are obvious examples of movement sponsored by predominantly economic motives and facilitated by the imposition of colonial rule. Much of the movement of peoples in West Africa was stimulated by considerations that were as much social as economic. The new administrative and commercial centres of the colonial powers presented many Africans with the opportunity of escaping from situations that they did not wish to tolerate at home. A slave could liberate himself from his obligations to his master, and even hope to forget his inferior status. The authority of the chief and elders could be avoided. A young man with even a rudimentary education could escape the long hours of dull labour on the land and hope to obtain a job as a messenger or clerk in a colonial administrative centre. And, increasingly, as wealth and education became rivals to traditional position as indicators of status, the motives to leave the village for the towns to seek a fortune became stronger. The exodus from the countryside to the towns was one of the most striking of social changes under colonial rule; but it was not as dramatic as the great shifts of population which resulted from the taxation and labour policies of the French.

All Africans were subject to taxation by the French, but since many lived on lands that produced no cash crops and taxation had to be paid in five-franc pieces rather than cowries or kind, the young men were forced to migrate to regions where there was a shortage of labour for the cultivation of cash crops. Thus the Mossi of Upper Volta first began to migrate in search of work because of the taxes demanded in francs after their conquest in 1896.[5] The Mossi sought work in the Gold Coast in the cocoa fields and in the mines, as did Zaberma from Niger and Gao from Sudan, who were again forced by heavy taxation to seek work beyond their own unproductive native soil.[6] These groups also migrated to the Ivory Coast to work on the cocoa plantations there, but they preferred to work in Gold Coast, since they were forced to pay taxes in both the Ivory Coast and their territory of origin, those in the former being even higher than those they had to pay at home.[7] Furthermore, wage rates and conditions of labour, particularly for Europeans, were better in the Gold Coast. In Ivory Coast a decree laid down that labourers on European plantations should be forced to save. Only half their salary would be paid on the spot. The balance would be paid in stamps which could be cashed at the nearest administrative post to the labourer's village. This was a considerable disadvantage since Ivory Coast shops were better stocked and goods were cheaper than in the migrants' homeland.[8] The extent of French African migration to the

z

Gold Coast is borne out by the census figures for 1931 in which 196,282 were recorded.[9]

In Senegal and Gambia the cultivation of the groundnut fields depended on the seasonal labourers from Sudan and Guinea known as *navetanes* who came to earn money to pay their taxes. In 1930 there was an estimated floating population of workers of 70,000 in Senegal and by 1937, 85,000.[10] Some *navetanes* travelled as much as 2,000 kilometres to work on the Senegalese fields. In 1930 vast numbers of labourers from Upper Volta moved into Ivory Coast, Nigeria and Gold Coast in search of work. Labouret estimates that 160,000 alone left for the Gold Coast that year.[11]

Taxation was not the only reason labourers moved from one territory to the other. Forced-labour, conscription, and the exactions of the administrator and the chief all pushed the young peasant to seek work on the fields of other peoples. Avoidance of forced labour seems to have been a strong factor in the migration of Zaberma and Gao to the Gold Coast.[12] Both during the First World War and after it many young men left for British territory to avoid conscription, which was put on a regular basis under the Governor-Generalship of Merlin (1919–23). In 1920 23,000 men were recruited; in 1921 12,000; and in 1922 13,000.[13] Thereafter it continued at an average rate of 10,000 a year, meaning that one in every twenty to twenty-five eligible men were conscripted.[14] During the war, as we have seen, it was estimated that about 61,500 men had left for British territory from French West Africa. Robert Delavignette, administrator and later Governor, estimated that obligatory cultivation of cash crops in Upper Volta was responsible for 100,000 Mossi leaving for the Gold Coast.[15]

Over and above the forced labour the French exacted from the peasants on roads and other public projects in their own regions, they also recruited labour for major projects like the building of railways. Upper Volta in particular was treated as a labour reserve. Between 1921 and 1925 it supplied nearly 49,000 men for the construction of railways in Senegal and Ivory Coast.[16] Between 1921 and 1930 nearly 43,000 were taken to Ivory Coast for timber cutting and work on European plantations.[17] In 1932 the Ivory Coast planters finally got Upper Volta attached to the Ivory Coast so that they would have easier access to labour.[18]

The French administration, beginning with the Villages of Liberty, and continuing through taxation, compulsory cultivation, recruitment and requisitioning of labour, forced hundreds of thousands of the ablest-bodied men of Niger, Sudan, Upper Volta and Guinea to migrate over distances up to 2,000 kilometres.

Very few of the migrants installed themselves permanently in their host countries. The majority were seasonal. The Mossi, the *navetanes* on the Senegambian groundnut fields, the Zaberma and Gao lived in two societies, their own and that of their hosts. Rouch has put it succinctly with regard to the Gao and Zaberma migrant: 'His village on the Niger thus has its counterpart in Ghana and his life may be compared with that of a colonial carrying out a series of tours and leaves, but without abandoning his social or religious milieu.'[19] However, of these seasonal migrants a number would remain in their host country, either attracted by the towns or because they had not enough money to return home.[20] In Ivory Coast, for instance, by 1956 the town of Rubino, named after a murdered French railway stationmaster and essentially a creation of the railway and the expanding cocoa and coffee industries, had a population in which the indigenous Abe were outnumbered 1,350 to 1,043.[21] Many of these immigrants were from other parts of Ivory Coast, as distinct from other French territories.

Whilst much of the labour migration that took place in West Africa was caused by oppressive measures on the part of the colonial régime, it soon became so embedded in the lore of the peoples concerned that it became essentially a voluntary movement. The journey to Ghana has become a tradition among the young men of Western Niger, and the accomplishment adds considerable prestige.[22] Even when forced labour was abolished in Mossi in 1946 the economy of their land had become so inextricably involved with seasonal migration, that the flow of young men to Gold Coast did not cease.[23] Kumasi became a sort of Eldorado for the peoples of Western Niger, Upper Volta and the Sudan, where the money they could not earn on their own poor soil could be gained not only to pay taxes but to buy the merchandise brought in by their colonial rulers.[24] The extent of the 'internationalisation' of Gold Coast as a result of immigration both under administrative pressure and the desire to make money is indicated by the figures for immigrants in 1931.[25]

25 Gambians
2,808 Sierra Leoneans
67,703 Nigerians
196,282 French West Africans
6,812 Liberians
15,586 Unclassified

We have been generally concerned with large-scale migrations which have been reasonably well documented. But we must not forget the great shifts of population that took place within individual colonial territories. In Senegal the Tokolor left their poor homeland in the valley of the river Senegal for Dakar to supplement their incomes.[26] In Nigeria Hausas and other Muslims set up 'Zongos' on the edge of Yoruba towns, dominating the kola and meat trades.[27]

Generally, colonial rule opened up new opportunities for, or forced people to undertake, migration from one part of West Africa to another. This was not a new phenomenon—many cities and towns like Ghana, Gao, Djenne, Timbuktu, Katsina and Kano had for long had stranger quarters.[28] But under colonial rule not only did the scale of movement of peoples increase enormously, but the status of the migrant was altered. No longer was he at the mercy of his hosts, but his position was regulated by the new colonial law. Even in Northern Nigeria, where Emirs and chiefs had wide judicial powers, a Southern Nigerian, Mr. Victor Eluaka, who was flogged in the market-place of Bukuru in 1933 by order of the Alkali for allegedly failing to pay his taxes, managed to bring his grievance before the House of Commons.[29]

## 3 The new towns

The focal point for the changes brought about by the movement of peoples and the impact of the new commercial and administrative régimes was the town. The growth of new towns was one of the most marked developments of the colonial period. Towns had existed before the imposition of colonial rule in the Savannah and Yorubaland: elsewhere they were few and far between. Under colonial rule their number and population grew rapidly. In the Gold Coast towns were a function of the rapid growth of the economy since the beginning of the century, but it was the growth in the number of townships rather than in their size that was most marked by 1931.[30] The towns, which experienced such rapid growth under colonial rule, were varied in origin and character. There were traditional towns like Kano, Ibadan, Kumasi and Ouagadougou which became modern trading and administrative centres. There were old cities of European origin like St. Louis and Freetown, new administrative centres like Kaduna and Niamey which until the final years of colonial rule remained essentially administrative in function, or new towns like Dakar and Conakry which served both as commercial and administrative centres. All towns were characterised by an influx of migrants. In the case of traditional towns like Kano, strangers were forced to live outside the city walls, or as in Ibadan, at least to begin with, in areas that did not belong to the indigenous inhabitants. But for the most part the indigenous inhabitants were swamped by the immigrants. In Dakar by 1953 the indigenous Lebou only formed 15% of the population.[31] By the 1950's Lagos was fast ceasing to be a Yoruba town, and by 1966 the immigrant Ibo and Ibibio were on their way to forming a majority. Generally the new towns were characterised by the high proportion of their expatriate African inhabitants. 90% of the population of Poto-Poto in Brazzaville, for instance, was born outside that suburb.[32] Another striking feature was the large number of young people living in the towns. As much as two-thirds of a city could be composed of people under 30. The city attracted the young, in particular, for without wives and children it was easier for them to leave home to seek their fortune in the cities, where they could escape oppressive features of home life, both colonial and African; where, like the Tokolor in Dakar, they could earn the money to pay taxes their impoverished lands could not produce; or where they could gain cash to pay bride-price, purchase a bicycle or even build a house at home, for wealth in the village was increasingly becoming a rival in status to traditional position. Whatever the motive for coming to the town, the immigrant was much more liable than the migratory agricultural labourer to come up against the forces of European modernisation. Sometimes he would have come specifically to enjoy them in the form of education. Sometimes, like the Tokolor immigrant to that most Europeanised of West African cities, Dakar, he was able to stave off the worst effects of these forces by reproducing an adapted form of his traditional life in the city.[33] But the town with its bars, its prostitutes, its crime, its delinquency, its dedication to the pursuit of personal gain, its over-crowding, its unemployment, fought a strong battle in favour of individualism against the traditional values of communal African society. Nevertheless most of the immigrants tended to link up with fellow immigrants from the same ethnic group, and in some towns particular sections were inhabited by one ethnic group. The traditional sanctions, particularly those of religion, were not here as effective, and immigrants formed themselves into voluntary associations that ranged from loan and mutual benefit societies to those which were to become the basis of political development. The towns were also the residence of the new African educated élite, who found it easier than their less well-educated brethren to cross the barriers of ethnicity. They formed debating and literary societies, where a person's ethnic origin did not matter, and where political questions came increasingly to the fore. The town, then, became a melting pot of ideas in which the immigrant was able to save himself from drowning because of the strong feeling of family and ethnic patriotism which gave him security in the artificial new world of commerce and colonial administration.

The consequences of the great movements of peoples and particularly their concentration in the towns were many. Migrants facilitated the spread of European ideas and knowledge about Europe. Though at the official level there was minimal contact, and even less exchange of ideas and information between the French and British administrations, news of the differences between the two systems of administrations was carried across the borders by these migrants. The new movements of people tended to give *raison d'être* to the arbitrary administrative units created by the colonial powers. The migrant and trader more than any group other than educated élite began to learn what it meant to be a Nigerian or Guinean, for crossing boundaries with customs posts gave physical reality to the new concept. The change in administration as he crossed the border brought home the difference at least between French and British West Africa. Probably most important of all from the political point of view were the voluntary associations formed in the towns, for though often ethnic in origin, and mainly interested in mutual protection and benefit, these associations were soon to become vehicles for protest. The number of people involved in these changes in the inter-war period was, however, limited. The mass of the people were still tied to peasant-farming, and even then many of them did not become significantly involved in the colonial cash economy.

# Notes

1 Georges Balandier, *Sociologie actuelle de l'Afrique noire*, Paris, 1955, pp. 3–36, and Immanuel Wallerstein, *Africa: the Politics of Independence*, New York, 1961, p. 31.
2 Wallerstein, *ibid.*, p. 31.
3 Balandier, *Sociologie actuelle.*
4 Paul-Marc Henry, 'The European Heritage: Approaches to African Development', in C. Grove Haines, ed., *Africa Today*, Baltimore, 1955, pp. 131–2.
5 Elliot P. Skinner, 'Labour Migration and its Relationship to Socio-Cultural Change in Mossi Society', *Africa*, XXX, 4th October 1960, pp. 378–9.
6 Jean Rouch, 'Migrations from French Territories into Ghana—Field Studies', *Africa*, XXVIII, 2, April 1958, p. 158.
7 Henri Labouret, *Paysans d'Afrique Occidentale*, Paris, 1941, pp. 230–1.
8 *Ibid.*, p. 231.
9 A. W. Cardinall, *The Gold Coast*, 1931, Accra, n.d., p. 155.
10 Labouret, *Paysans*, p. 223.
11 Henri Labouret, *La main-d'œuvre dans l' Ouest Africain*, Paris, 1930, pp. 240–50.
12 Rouch, 'Migrations from French Territories', p. 158.
13 Maurice Delafosse in Hanotaux, *Histoire des Colonies Françaises*, IV p. 352.
14 Edouard de Martonne, 'La vérité sur les Tirailleurs Sénégalais', p. 32; source: IFAN—Dakar collection of pamphlets and articles on the army in French West Africa.
15 Robert Delavignette, *Les Vrais Chefs de l'Empire*, Paris, 1939.
16 R. L. Buell, *Native Problem*, Vol. I, p. 1,043.
17 Robert Delavignette, *Freedom and Authority in French West Africa*, London, 1950, p. 113.
18 Immanuel Wallerstein, 'Migration in West Africa: the Political Perspective', in Hilda Kuper, ed., *Urbanization and Migration in West Africa*, Berkeley and Los Angeles, 1965, p. 64.
19 Rouch, 'Migration from French Territories', p. 157.
20 Elliot P. Skinner, 'Labour Migration', p. 375.
21 M. Dupire, 'Planteurs Autochtones et Étrangers en Basse-Côte d'Ivoire Orientale', *Études Éburnéennes*, VIII, 1960, p. 91.
22 Rouch, 'Migration from French Territories', p. 158.
23 Skinner, 'Labour Migration', p. 380.
24 Cardinall, *The Gold Coast*, p. 152.
25 *Ibid.*, p. 155.
26 Abdoulaye Diop, *Societé Toucouleur et Migration*, Dakar, 1965.
27 See, for example, Abner Cohen, 'The Social Organisation of Credit in a West African Cattle Market'.

28 See Elliot P. Skinner, 'Strangers in West African Societies', *Africa*, XXXIII, 4, 1963, pp. 308–9.
29 *The Times*, 15th June 1933.
30 Cardinall, *Gold Coast*, p. 157.
31 P. Mercier, 'Aspects de la societé africaine dans l'agglomération dakaroise: groupes familiaux et unités de voisinage', *L'Agglomeration dakaroise*, Dakar, 1954, p. 16.
32 Georges Balandier, 'Approche Sociologique des "Brazzavilles noires": Étude préliminaire', *Africa*, XXII, 1, 1952, p. 25.
33 See Abdoullaye Diop, *Societé Toucouleur*, esp. Chapter VI, pp. 150–83.

# 2 The economic impact of colonial rule

## 1 The African role in the colonial economy

The economic impact of colonial rule on African society was much less profound than colonial administrators liked to think. The period 1919–39 was one of 'immobilisme' in which what little change there was did not stand comparison with what was taking place in the outside world.[1] The railway systems had for the most part been completed by 1918—only the introduction of the motor vehicle was a significant factor for change in this period. The African found himself the simple producer of raw materials for which Lebanese were the agents of sale and European companies the exporters. Conversely these same companies imported the goods which the African bought, mainly at the shops or through the agencies of Lebanese traders, with the money he earned from the sale of his crop. Only in rare cases did the African survive as an importer, almost never as an exporter, and in neither role was he significant after 1920. Except in the cocoa-producing areas of the Gold Coast and Nigeria, the African was squeezed out of his pre-colonial role of middleman between peasant producer and expatriate exporter by the Lebanese. This meant that the African's role in the colonial economy became almost exclusively that of petty trader and primary producer of cash crops, on his own account or as labourer on the farms of others, African or European, in the case of the few plantations that existed in French West Africa. A small number were employed in mining industries in Ashanti, Jos and Enugu, on the railways and as casual labourers in the urban centres. The income they derived from the colonial economy was for the most part so low that it brought about no significant change in their standard of living. Only cocoa and coffee fetched high enough prices to affect the traditional socio-economic structure of the peoples producing it. The other cash crops, most of which had, like palm products, groundnuts and cotton, been exported before the imposition of colonial rule fetched such low prices that the peasant produced just enough to pay taxes and satisfy his immediate needs for imported cloths, utensils and foodstuffs like sugar. The narrow range of goods in the Lebanese stores was not substantially different from those which the African middleman used as the basis of barter in pre-colonial times.

For the African peasant the growing of cash crops during the colonial period was, except in the cocoa- and coffee-producing areas, primarily geared to paying taxes and supplementing the subsistence economy with imported luxuries. If the price for cash crops was low, his marginal propensity to produce cash crops for sale over and above those necessary for the purposes of paying taxes fell also. For the peasant could provide most of his basic needs from internal sources. Even when the price for crops was high, immense effort was required in labour terms to produce larger quantities. This problem was solved, partially, by the importation of labour from other areas. This migratory labour was available, as we have seen, because of taxes imposed on peoples inhabiting areas on which no cash crops would grow. In certain areas the peasant would involve himself in commitments based on the previous year's price for a crop, and be forced to produce greater quantities of his cash crop in order to meet them if it fell. Where immigrant labour was scarce, he would have to transfer labour from the subsistence crops to the cash crops. In parts of Senegambia this situation, aggravated by the long-standing dependence on imported goods, reached the point where peasants were importing rice which they could grow themselves, and going without food for nearly two months a year, because they had neglected the subsistence economy in favour of the cash crops. Counteracting the propensity of the peasant to abandon cultivation of the cash crop in favour of subsistence crops, was his tendency to incur debts to the Lebanese traders, who were quite aware that indebtedness was one of the only ways over and above taxation which could force him to produce for a low price. The French, however, resorted to the introduction of compulsory production of crops in areas where the peasant would otherwise have refused to grow them because of the low price. Thus, anxious to be independent of cotton supplies from outside the French empire, the administration in French West Africa forced the peasant to produce it under threat of imprisonment if the quality was not good enough or the quantity insufficient.[2] The ease with which people moved out of the cash economy into a purely subsistence economy also related to the dependence their society had built up on imported goods. In Senegal, where by the time of the Depression many families had been involved in the export of groundnuts to Europe for over seventy years, imported cloths, utensils and rice had become part of their way of life. But even they, despite predictions of famine and political upheaval, were able to revert to subsistence production in 1932.[3] Millet, manioc and taro were substituted for imported rice. Home-grown tobacco replaced imported varieties. Honey was gathered in place of sugar, and local soap and perfumes were produced again,[4] thus stimulating the subsistence economy.

The extent of the involvement of the peasant in the cash crop economy was limited by the extent of the colonial transportation system. Vast areas, such as Bornu in Nigeria, remained largely untouched by it because no railway passed through them, and until after the Second World War long-distance road haulage of the low-priced cash crops did not pay. Even the term cash applied to these crops is inappropriate, for in many areas the exchange of 'cash' crop for imported goods was largely by barter. It was the migrant labourer rather than the peasant farmer who became the pioneer of currency as a means of exchange.

Just how little the bulk of the people were affected by the European-dominated import-export economy is brought out by Governor Clifford's report to the Nigerian Council in 1923: 'The vast majority of the indigenous population are still independent of the outside world for all their essential supplies. They can and do spin their own thread, weave their own garments, provide their own foodstuffs, and even, when the necessity arises, forge their own tools, and make their own pottery. For them imports from Europe are still, in the main, luxuries with which, if needs must, they can wholly dispense; and the sole exception to this, in pre-war days, was imported spirits of European manufacture.'[5] And for these latter they had 'illicit' substitutes. Twenty years later, with regard to the whole of British West Africa, the Leverhulme Trust Commission reported that 'all Africans are, to a very large extent, and very many of them wholly, outside the system of money economy which dominates the economic life of Europe and the rest of the world'.[6] The African, encouraged in times of good prices to produce cash crops, and ignorant of the fluidity of prices on the world commodity markets, was easily convinced that he was being robbed and deceived by the whites if they offered him a low price,[7] and refused to continue production unless under pressure of taxation, indebtedness or force.

## 2 The African peasant and new crops

The colonial régime did little to improve growing techniques of low-value export crops: they remained the same as in pre-colonial times. For most peasants the European agricultural officers were an irrelevance. There was of course no attempt to improve the methods of production of subsistence crops, as the Germans had done in Togo. Thus the peasant, whether farming for himself or working on the farms of others, did not gain any new knowledge of agricultural techniques under colonial rule. Even the labourer in European plantations used for the most part his traditional instruments, and stayed there as short a time as possible, learning nothing about improvement.[8] Rather the peasant was allowed to exhaust the land. In Senegal, for instance, large areas, like the Baol, have been reduced to semi-desert by the cultivation of groundnuts. As early as 1925 certain areas of Senegal like Thiès and Diourbel were exhausted and the peasants had to move eastwards, following the railway[9] to earn enough money to pay taxes and buy imported goods.

The colonial administration did nothing to prevent situations such as that in Gambia where rice that could have been grown by the peasant more cheaply was imported and to pay for it he devoted more of his energies in the cultivation of groundnuts. Indeed it favoured the colonial economic system, for French rice exporters in Indo-China could find a market in Senegal. Only when Indo-China became independent of France did France make efforts to develop Senegal's own rice potential. Similarly, Cardinall, commenting on the imports of foodstuffs in Gold Coast in 1930, noted that the country could have produced itself half 'the fresh fish, rice, maize and other meal, beans, salted and fresh meat, edible oils, spices and fresh vegetables (imported), or in other words would have saved 200,000 pounds'.[10]

The only crops that did radically alter the standard of living of their producers were cocoa and coffee in the Gold Coast, Ivory Coast and Western Nigeria. For both these crops the price was consistently sufficiently high for the farmer safely to depend on imported goods in substitution for domestically produced goods. Under the stimulus of a crop whose value increased in the Gold Coast from £4,764,067 in 1921 to £11,229,000 in 1928 on the eve of the Depression, great tracts of new land were opened to cocoa cultivation by immigrant 'rural capitalists' who used the profits from their first crops to purchase further farm land.[11] It has often been thought that the revolutionary aspect of the Gold Coast cocoa industry was the fact that Africans sold land which was supposed to have been communally owned.[12] But as Polly Hill has shown, the sale of land had been common in some areas for fifty years or so before the introduction of cocoa into the Akwapim and Akim-Abuakwa area. What was an innovation was not the idea of sale of land itself but 'the intensity of its application'.[13] In Ivory Coast the Abe found no difficulty in selling land, but the Agni strongly resisted it.[14] The cocoa boom in the Gold Coast and later in the Ivory Coast stimulated migrations of farmers into new lands. Those who could not buy land, worked for the owners. In the case of the Gold Coast two systems of tenant-farmer relation have been described by Hill. The first was that of *abusa*, whereby the labourer was paid one third of the cocoa he plucked for his employing farmer, the second that of *ntotokuano*, whereby the labourer was paid a fixed sum per load for the cocoa he plucked for his employing farmer.[15]

The cocoa industry in Ghana created a rich class of farmers who were able to undertake social innovations at their own initiative, and who showed that the African peasant, if prices were good, did not have to be forced into production. Sir Hugh Clifford was full of praise for him:

'This man, reputed to be lazy by the superficial globe-trotter or the exponent of the damned nigger school, has carved from the virgin forest an enormous clearing, which he has covered with flourishing cocoa farms. Armed with nothing better than an imported axe and machete, and a native-made hoe, he has cut down the forest giant, cleared the tropical undergrowth, and kept it cleared. With no means of animal transport, no railways and few roads, he has conveyed his produce to the sea, rolling it down in casks for miles and carrying it on his own sturdy cranium. Here is a result to make us pause in our estimate of the negro race.'[16] The same was true of the Ivory Coast cocoa industry which grew from a mere 1,000 tons in 1920 to 52,714 tons in 1938, and the coffee industry which grew from 248 tons in 1928 to 14,076 tons in 1938.[17]

Of the peasant-farmers in West Africa, only those producing

cocoa and coffee were significantly involved in the money economy and experienced substantial social change as a result. In Larteh, Akwapim, in Ghana, cocoa-farming and the wealth it brought had 'far-reaching effects on all aspects of economic and social life'.[18] The farmers of Larteh on their own initiative built roads and bridges to link their farms with the government road and the main cocoa-collecting centres. In 1914 they even employed a Swiss engineer to build a wooden bridge, still standing today, for which nine of them and one other subscribed £2,000.[19] Between 1914 and 1930 the people of Akwapim spent at least £30,000 on roads to connect with the government-built road. One such road, built entirely without government assistance, was actually opened in 1926 by the Acting Governor, to whom the chief responsible addressed a request for government assistance with the debt of £2,600 still outstanding to the contractor. The chief, the Benkumhene, also asked that government 'appoint a Town Engineer to lay and carry out the construction of streets and other works of public utility' in Larteh. These demands for development were refused and a warning given against the construction of further roads.[20] As it was, apart from the railway the communications system of the area was built by the local people with little or no assistance and encouragement from government.[21]

Over half Larteh's completed houses in 1963—some 1,000—were built with profits from the cocoa trade before 1910.[22] Apart from investment in communications, housing, education and funerals became the main items of expenditure of the cocoa farmers. Unfortunately, as Field has pointed out, the acquisition of wealth did not mean a necessary improvement in basic standards of living and nutrition, for far too much money was spent on luxuries, and at the same time concentration on cocoa farming led to neglect of subsistence farming.[23] No other group was brought into the money economy in the way the cocoa and coffee farmers were. The migrant labourer depended on currency, but he earned very little, and most of it was taken in taxes and by his family on his return.[24]

## 3 The African labourer

Those employed on the European plantations of the Ivory Coast or Guinea were little affected by their experience. Their terms of labour were seasonal for the most part, and they were not only underpaid, but not given, as we have seen in Ivory Coast, all that they earned in cash. No rural proletariat arose from among the workers on the European plantations. Before 1940 only the railways employed a large number of regular workers, among whom many were, or were trained as, skilled artisans. The only comparable industries to the railways as employers of labour were the mines. But much of the labour on the mines was irregular. In Jos, the tin mines employed for the most part daily paid unskilled and illiterate labour to dig at the faces of the open mines. In the gold mines of Ashanti the main problems were the shortage of labour and its irregularity.[25] And most of those employed were immigrants who intended returning home eventually. In Enugu labourers were press-ganged by unscrupulous chiefs into work on the coal mines in the early years from 1915 till 1922. After that labour flowed freely into the mines so that by 1930 the management, which was a government agency, was able to be selective in the employment policy. The peoples of the area in which the mines were situated tended to be less educated than those from neighbouring divisions, and management deliberately pursued a policy of recruiting illiterate locals rather than their neighbours who were 'relatively more educated and could voice their grievances and were therefore regarded as trouble makers'.[26]

The mines, then, employed a labour force which was either of temporary immigrant nature as in the case of the Gold Coast gold mines, or, where locally recruited as in the case of the Jos and Enugu mines, largely illiterate. Wages on all three mines were low for the ordinary labourer: in the coal mines in 1929 they were about 7d.–1s. 6d. per day;[27] in 1930 in the gold mines they were 1s. a day for unskilled surface labourers and between 1s. 3d. and 1s. 9d. for unskilled underground labourers;[28] on the tin mines in 1s. 6d. per day for unskilled labourers.[29]

The wages for these labourers were too low to alter their standard of living significantly. Before 1940 none of the mine workers had organised themselves into effective trade unions, though wild-cat strikes had taken place before that time. For instance in 1925 pick boys in the Enugu mines downed tools in protest against the failure of management to raise their pay to 1922 levels. They were dismissed.[30] In 1937 after the recovery of the colliery from the Depression, workers undertook considerable but unco-ordinated agitation for an increase in their rates of pay.[31] In September of that year the tub-boys struck when a European overman assaulted one of their fellows.[32] In 1924 there was a strike at Obuasi on the Ashanti goldfields against the introduction of time-clocks.[33] None of these strikes were organised by a union. Indeed until the Second World War trade unions were of no real significance in either British or French West Africa. In the latter they were illegal until the advent of the Popular Front Government in 1937. In the former they were tolerated but not recognised until about the same time. Trade Union Ordinances were passed for Gambia in 1932, Sierra Leone in 1939, Nigeria in 1939 and Gold Coast in 1941. The attitude of the Sierra Leone Government to Trade Unions was not much different from that of the Southern Nigerian Government with respect to employment on the Enugu mines. In 1921 it refused to recognise a union on the grounds that 'a tribal ruler is elected for each tribe in Freetown by the members of the tribe themselves. These tribal rulers are recognised by law and form the intermediaries between the members of the tribe and the government, and it is not possible for the government to deal with or recognise any rival authority introduced by strangers to the colony.'[34] Only some ten trade unions of any importance seem to have been formed and to have survived any length of time in West Africa before 1940. Significantly of these five were African Civil Servants unions, and two were railway workers unions.[35] Civil servants and railway employees formed the only two major coherent groups of workers among whom there was an educated élite in any way capable of organising workers against government. Thus in 1919 daily-paid workers on the Sierra Leone railway went on strike from 15th–22nd July because they had not been paid their 'War Bonus'. The railway was brought to a standstill, and work was only resumed when they were promised payment of their war bonus as soon as possible. Daily paid staff of the Public Works Department also went on strike at the same time.[36] In 1926 the unrecognised Sierra Leone Railway Workers' Union led a strike for improved conditions of service, which led to a slow-down of service. Government took a very tough line against the strikers who returned to work on its terms. The 1926 strike, in contrast to those in 1919, had the active support of the Sierra Leone members of the National Congress of British West Africa.[37]

In French West Africa the railways too were the main focus of strikes. In 1925 railway workers on the Dakar–St. Louis line went on strike, and in the same year Bambara conscripted for work on the Thiès–Kayes line provoked a general strike after three of their leaders were arrested as a result of discontent among them. The troops, many of whom were Bambara, refused to be involved in any action against the strikers and the administration had to release the Bambara leaders to bring an end to the strike.[38]

From a social point of view, then, the impact of the colonial economy was much less than has usually been supposed. Perhaps the most important effect was the ousting and consequent frustration of the African businessman from a share in the profits from the expansion of the economy that took place under colonial rule.

# Notes

1 Suret-Canale, *Afrique Noire II*, p. 199.
2 See Albert Londres, *Terre d'ébène*, Paris, 1929, p. 159.
3 Herbert Ingram Priestly, *France Overseas: A Study in Modern Imperialism*, New York, 1938, p. 279.
4 *Ibid.*, pp. 279–80.
5 *The Times*, 23rd June 1923.
6 The Leverhulme Trust, *The West African Commission 1938–39 Technical Reports*, London, 1943.
7 Pierre Lyautey, *L'Empire colonial français*, Paris, 1931, p. 400.
8 Suret-Canale, *Afrique Noire II*, p. 276.
9 Labouret, *Paysans d'Afrique Occidentale*, p. 223.
10 Cardinall, *Gold Coast*, p. 101.
11 David Brokensha, *Social Change in Larteh, Ghana*, Oxford, 1966, p. 37.
12 Cardinall, *Gold Coast*, p. 84.
13 Polly Hill, 'The Migrant Cocoa Farmers of Southern Ghana', *Africa*, XXXI, 3, 1961, pp. 211–12.
14 Dupire, 'Planteurs Autochtones et Étrangers', p. 228.
15 Polly Hill, *The Gold Coast Cocoa Farmer*, *op. cit.*, p. 8 and p. 25.
16 *The Times*, 2nd June 1925.
17 Aristide Zollberg, *One-Party Government in the Ivory Coast*, Princetown, 1964, p. 24.
18 Brokensha, *Larteh*, p. 35.
19 *Ibid.*, p. 60.
20 *Ibid.*, p. 64.
21 *Ibid.*, p. 60 and p. 61.
22 *Ibid.*, p. 58.
23 M. J. Field, *Search for Security: An Ethno-psychiatric Study of Rural Ghana*, Evanston, 1960, p. 29.
24 Labouret, *Paysans d'Afrique Occidentale*, p. 230–2.
25 Cardinall, *Gold Coast*, p. 244.
26 Agwu Akpala, 'The Background of the Enugu Colliery Shooting Incident in 1949', *Journal of the Historical Society of Nigeria*, III, 2, 1965, p. 340.
27 *Blue Book* (Nigeria), 1929, Section 23, 'Persons in Employment and Average Rates', p. 560.
28 Cardinall, *Gold Coast*, *op. cit.*, p. 245.
29 *Blue Book* (Nigeria), 1930, p. 574.
30 Akpala, 'The Enugu Colliery Shooting Incident', p. 347.
31 *Ibid.*, p. 345.
32 *Ibid.*, p. 347.
33 Kimble, *Ghana*, p. 44.
34 Cited from the Macaulay papers in Ibadan University Library by Imanuel Geiss, 'Some Remarks on the Development of African

Trade Unions', *Journal of the Historical Society of Nigeria*, III, 2, 1965, p. 368.
35 Charles A. Orr, 'Trade Unionism in Colonial Africa', *Journal of Modern African Studies*, IV, 1, pp. 66–7.
36 See Best, *Sierra Leone Railway*, p. 46.
37 *Ibid.*, pp. 58–60.
38 Suret-Canale, *Afrique Noire II*, p. 556.

# 3 Islam and Christianity

## 1 Islam versus Christianity under colonial rule

The monotheistic world religions of Christianity and Islam made great advances in West Africa under colonial rule. Islam, as Froelich has put it, made greater and more profound progress in fifty years of colonial rule than in the thousand years preceding it. In that half century the Muslim population of West Africa doubled.[1] Christian advance was less spectacular, but considering that at the beginning of colonial occupation converts numbered less than fifty thousand, the estimated figure of 2,727,000 by the early fifties is impressive.[2] Both these religions were to have a profound effect on African society in the period of colonial occupation. The Christian impact, because it was so closely linked with that of the occupying powers, particularly in the field of education, has often been given greater emphasis than that of Islam, even though Islam made much greater progress than Christianity. By the early fifties 34% of the population of West Africa was estimated to be Muslim, that is some 20,067,000 as against only 4·5% Christians.[3]

What were the reasons for the rapidity of the spread of Islam and why did not Christianity enjoy the same success? Islam had the initial advantage over Christianity in that it had been much longer established in West Africa. Christian missionary activity did not become significant by comparison until the second half of the nineteenth century. Colonial occupation meant that 'pagan' frontiers which Muslims had long been unable to cross were now open to them. The colonial powers made it impossible for pagans who had resisted Islam for centuries to continue their opposition.[4] The Hausa state of Kebbi at Argungu, which had spent a century staving off forcible conversion by the Fulani, officially became Muslim about 1922.[5] Armed resistance to the presence of Muslims was no longer possible. Islam, too, was not restricted in its spread by the newly imposed colonial frontiers, whereas the Christian missions, which had their bases in Europe, had to gain permission to establish themselves in a particular colony from its administration, and had to organise their missions colony by colony. Islam, too, did not have political associations with imperial Europe as did the Christian missions,[6] though many Muslims were to collaborate with the European administrations. Islam was able to present itself, though an immigrant religion, as an African religion, whereas Christianity always suffered from being 'the white man's religion', and therefore, from a nationalist point of view, the religion of the colonial oppressors. Islam was for the most part propagated by Africans, Christianity by whites. Islam, too, was better adapted to African society. In conversion it did not make the same initial heavy demands as the Christian missionary who sought complete abandonment of the convert's old religion. A man can become a Muslim without needing to understand all the teachings of his new faith. The simple affirmation 'There is no god but God; Mohammed is the apostle of God' is sufficient for a man to be accepted into Islam. By contrast admission into a Christian Church involves arduous teaching and spiritual preparation of the catechist, and conviction on the part of the missionary that the latter has abandoned his old religion completely. As an African priest has asked, why is the Church 'demanding so much from its converts, when according to the New Testament, all that is necessary for Baptism, is the affirmation: "Jesus is Lord"?'[7] That it has demanded so much has cost it many converts. Islam, apart from making conversion fairly easy, did not attack polygamy, even where this involved more than four wives. Christian insistence on monogamy was to prove one of the greatest obstacles to conversion, and a number of separatist African Churches owe their origin in part to the obstinacy of missionaries insisting that even first generation converts abandon all but their senior wife.[8] Where Islam sought out the leader of the community and by converting him hoped to convert all his followers, the Christian missionary, so often European, insisted on individual conversion, and tended to see the chief as the bastion of traditional religion. Bishop Crowther, as an African, realised the advantages of the Muslim-type approach over that of the Christian, and advocated group rather than individual conversion. This, among other things, led to attacks on his episcopate by European colleagues for laxity in supervision and toleration of heathenish practices among his clergy.[9] Islam seems to have had the advantage over Christianity because it was more gradualist in its approach to conversion, as compared with the heavy demands it made later on the faithful. (See pp. 367–8.) It tolerated polygamy and was permissive about magic. Above all it was determined to secure the conversion of the leaders of society.

While Islam presented itself as a fairly united force, and sectarianism was not important (at least in matters of fundamental belief)—members of different sects could worship in the same mosque—the Christian missions reproduced in Africa the whole history of the divided Church in Europe and America. Catholics and Protestants vied for power, and different protestant sects vied among themselves for converts. In Ibadan in 1951 there were nine different European-origin Christian sects and twelve separatist sects.[10] But too much should not be made of these divisions which, as Parrinder remarks, 'are perhaps more apparent to the European than the African. For the latter is accustomed to the sight of a variety of cults, to any of which he may go in time of need.'[11]

In similar vein, it has often but incorrectly been asserted that Islam appealed to the African because it was a more 'simple and easy to understand' religion than Christianity. Even if this were true, it would have no validity, for most African religions are much more complex in structure than either Islam or Christianity.

## 2 The colonial administration and Islam

Islam enjoyed a second great advantage over Christianity in that the colonial governments gave it more active support than they gave the missions. Missionaries were forbidden to enter the Muslim areas of Northern Nigeria unless they had the consent of the Emirs. Having initially supported the idea of missionary penetration of the North, Lugard abandoned it when he saw how strong was the reaction of most Muslim rulers to it.[12] He summed up government attitude to the question of Christian activity in the Emirates thus: '. . . in a matter solely concerned with religion the Government does not feel justified in compelling a Moslem ruler to grant permission which but for Government intervention he would refuse'.[13] If it were a case of converting a 'pagan' to Islam or Christianity, the overwhelming number of British officials considered the social consequences of conversion to Islam preferable to those of conversion to Christianity. 'To the British official or trader in West Africa', wrote Sir Harry Johnston in a review of Lugard's *Dual Mandate*, 'there is little doubt that the Mohammedan Negro, Negroid, Fula, Hausa, Arab or Tuareg is a more likeable, attractive personality than the Christian Negro of Sierra Leone, Liberia, the Gold Coast, or Southern Nigeria. His costume, to begin with, used to seem so much more becoming, climatically suitable, than the extravagant caricature of European dress worn by the Christian Negro of the coastlands. I remember vividly how in my early journeys in West Africa I felt far more respect for the Yorubas in their stately dress than for the Christian or Pagan blacks of Lagos and Egbaland with their preposterous, tall chimney-pot hats, their gaudy Manchester prints, or suits of heavy black coats and trousers and double-breasted waistcoats.'[14] In Northern Nigeria administrators were punished by transfer from the Holy North to the pagan areas.[15] In the Northern Territories of the Gold Coast Chief Commissioner Watherston (1905–9) 'considered Islam a religion "eminently suited to the native" which was helping to spread civilisation, encouraging "a much more decent life" and giving an impetus to trade'.[16] Watherston made life much more difficult for missionaries than Lugard did, even though there were many more 'pagans' than Muslims in the area.

In French West Africa Islam was seen as a problem in a way that it was never in British West Africa. True, in the early years British officials in Northern Nigeria, like their French counterparts, were fearful of an outburst of Mahdism, but once Lugard had secured the co-operation of the Emirs in Northern Nigeria, and the Sultan of Sokoto had shown his loyalty after the 1906 Satiru rising, Islam was seen as the ally rather than the potential enemy. The French, however, had occupied a much larger Muslim empire—in 1900 Gold Coast and Sierra Leone were not heavily Islamised. The chief opposition to her penetration of the Western Sudan had come from Muslim *mujihaddin* or their successors. These had been smashed rather than their co-operation sought. Islam did become for some the enemy, even though Muslim chiefs threatened by the *mujihaddin* had rallied to the French. In the early years of French rule there was considerable discussion of the 'Peril of Islam'. Mangin, Archinard and Mage were all hostile to Islamic expansion.[17] But the fact that Islam was of the greatest political importance in West Africa was recognised by the French in the foundation of the *Service des Affaires Musulmanes et Sahariennes* in Paris in 1900 and the *Service des Affaires*

*Musulmanes* in Dakar in 1906. There was no counterpart in British West Africa, a fact which must be regretted, since there is no British equivalent for the studies made by Robert Arnaud, Le Chatelier and Paul Marty of Islam in West Africa in that period. But the existence of these services did not commit the Governor-General to a pro-Islamic policy. Ponty, who became Governor-General in 1908, favoured a *politique des races* which would 'safeguard non-Moslem peoples from being ruled by French-appointed Moslem chiefs from other groups'.[18] He also discouraged the use of Arabic in official correspondence, since this clearly gave an edge in administration to the literate Moslem. In 1911 Clozel, Governor of Sudan and later Governor-General of French West Africa, advocated the re-inforcement of 'fétichisme' in the face of Islam, and called for the codification of Bambara, Malinke and Bobo traditional law.[19] However, as Gouilly points out, 'The same men who in Bamako or Dakar elaborated directives aimed at warding off the "peril of Islam", in their policy took measures likely to strengthen it.'[20] The so-called dangers of Islam soon came to be seen as grossly exaggerated. And even at the popular level the advantages of co-operation with Muslims was being explored, and the peril of Islam being dismissed: 'Not only does the religion of the Prophet not constitute a threat for us on the black continent, but the obstacles it placed before us at the beginning of the conquest are in the process of disappearing. Islamised Negroes are on the whole gentle people who are grateful for the security which our arms have brought them; they only think of living in peace in the shade of our power.'[21] There emerged in French West Africa a policy which accepted that Islam could be used by the French administration, but which kept a wary eye on Islamic revival movements which might oppose the colonial administration. Administrators came to favour Islam for a number of reasons. Like their Nigerian counterparts they felt it a more dignified religion for the African than 'fétichisme' or Christianity. The anti-clerical strain in the administrator showed itself in favouring Islam 'pour embêter les curés'.[22] At a more practical level Islam was seen as 'a bridge mediating between the narrow particularism of traditional society and the wider impulses and requirements of modern life and economic interests'.[23] The most striking example of this was in the French attitude to the Mouride offshoot of the Qadariyya in Senegal. This movement, founded by Amadou Bamba, on the basis of the reward in heaven for labour on earth and the total dedication of the follower to his religious leader, had initially opposed the French. Amadou Bamba was twice exiled, but his disciples continued to follow his precepts and the French soon found that the Mourides were the greatest producers of groundnuts in the country. By attracting young men and women away from their villages to set up pioneer villages for cultivation of groundnuts, the Mourides became a vital factor in the Senegalese economy, and above all kept the young on the land, so that the French began to give them their support.[24] Even where their expansion into other peoples' lands involved friction the administration was prepared to turn a blind eye.[25]

Islam also provided the administration with literate nominees for positions as chiefs, clerks, non-commissioned officers and *gardes de cercles*. Muslim justice was easier to administer than traditional African law, with all its varieties, so that *cadis* were nominated almost everywhere.[26] Most important of all, the French saw that if they supported those Muslims who appeared to be favourable to them, they could control their vast Muslim domain the more easily. Thus a policy of co-operation with leaders of the Qadariyya and Tijanniyya orders, even to the extent of aiding them against their rivals, was pursued. In the twenties and thirties the French in Sudan supported the Tijanniyya against the Hamallist reformist movement which sought to return to the original character of Tijanniyya. There is no evidence that its leader Cheick Hamallah was anti-French, but his Tijanniya rivals managed to persuade the authorities that he was, and he was thrice exiled between 1925 and 1942 when he died in prison in France.[27] It is however significant that the main support for the radical R.D.A. party in Sudan after 1946 came from Hamallists.[28]

The French built mosques, sent Muslim leaders on pilgrimage, established *medresas* or Franco-Muslim schools and decorated Marabouts in order to secure the loyalty of Islam to France. In this they succeeded remarkably well, and Islam was able to make great inroads among those who had for long resisted conversion, like the Bambara.

## 3 Islam and the colonial situation

But in both French and British West Africa the new colonial situation favoured the spread of Islam irrespective of encouragement by the colonial authorities. In the new towns the 'pagan' immigrants were separated from the priests and circumstances of their own religion, and felt lost men. 'Their traditional tribal religion [could] offer no adequate rationale of life in their new environment.'[29] In such

circumstances they could turn to Islam or Christianity as a substitute
for the religion they had left behind—with few exceptions traditional
African religions were non-missionary and limited to a particular
ethnic group. To enter the Christian Church was much more
difficult than to be accepted into Islam, whose members were only
too ready to welcome newcomers.

Labour migration was another major factor in the Islamisation of
West Africa. Pagan *navetanes* working on the groundnut fields of the
Muslim Wollof were frequently converted. The rapid progress of
Islam among the Mossi was in large part due to the seasonal migration. The 'pagan' labourer would find himself travelling with
Muslims, working with them, usually under a Muslim overseer. On
the road he would have to eat apart from his fellow-Muslims, at
work he found a Muslim overseer tended to favour his co-religionists,
so he returned home having decided not only to become a Muslim
but also to persuade his family to convert.[30]

Military service, too, was another avenue for Islamisation,
particularly in French West Africa where it involved much greater
numbers than in British West Africa. The same need for a substitute
for traditional religion existed in the army as in the towns. Imams
were provided for the soldiers. In 1928 in the transit camp for
*Tirailleurs Sénégalais* in Fréjus, France, the Commandant got the
soldiers to build a mosque modelled on the great mosque at Djenne,
itself built by a French administrator.[31] Non-commissioned officers
tended to be Muslim and anxious to spread their faith. Even the
dress of the soldiers was Muslim in inspiration.

Finally Islam brought prestige to the convert. In the towns, where
the immigrant found most of the community adherents to either
Islam or Christianity, he had to identify with one or the other if he
were to be respected.[32] Particularly for the man of low caste or ser-
vile status, Islam was a means of franchising traditional obstacles to
social progress. Skinner records that in Nobere (Mossi) nearly all
liberated slaves and serfs had become Muslims whilst a man of lowly
status who had gone on the pilgrimage had enough status openly
to challenge the Muslim District Chief.[33]

Islam under colonial rule became a force of conservatism rather
than change, as it had been in the nineteenth century. Reformist
movements such as Hamallism and Senoussism were looked on with
great suspicion by the administrations, who were frightened that
their subjects might be drawn into the Pan-Islamic movements of
the Middle East.[34] Administrators supported established Islam in
the form of Emirs and Marabouts of whose loyalty they were sure,

and saw in them a dam harnessing Western ideas to African society whilst holding back what they considered its disruptive influences. Christianity, which gained only a tenth of the converts Islam did, nevertheless made a much greater impact on African society, for, far from trying to control the flow of ideas from the West, the missionaries positively pumped them into West Africa. The pump was the school, the end product an educated élite and a mass of young men with primary education in the three Rs, discontented with the traditional social structure, despising the occupation of farmer, and anxious to get to the town away from the shackles of their traditional environment. From the mission schools emerged many of the political leaders of modern West Africa, and from these schools, too, emerged the backbone of their support. Only the Pakistani-based Ahmadiyya sect of Islam pursued a policy of modern education alongside conversion. By the 1940's it had, however, only small footholds on the coast in the British colonies.

## 4 Christian missions under colonial rule

Christian missionaries before colonial occupation depended on the goodwill of their hosts, and there were obvious limitations to their ability to challenge the authority of traditional society. But under colonial rule the missionaries had a free hand, in so far as the administration would let them.

The separation of Church and State in France in 1905, however, had consequences for the Catholic missions in West Africa. This robbed them of any possibility of a special status in the colonies. It also meant there would be no official support for their schools as there was for those of both Catholics and Protestants in British West Africa. Government was careful, too, not to give a favoured status to Christian Africans for fear of alienating Muslims.[35] However, in Dahomey and Ivory Coast, where the Catholics had been entrenched before the imposition of colonial rule, they were, in the absence of Muslim rivals, able to gain themselves a privileged position they never could in the Sudanic belt. Suret-Canale, however, shows that the Catholic missions did enjoy considerable privileges if the local administrators were well disposed to them. They were given land in towns, often well situated, so that they owned valuable real estate. They were even allowed to use forced labour, and with their workshops, small industries and farms had become an important economic element in French West Africa by World War II.[36] They insisted, as Father Bouchand put it in his *L'Église en Afrique*

*Noire*, that for their converts 'work itself was as a proof and guarantee of a sincere and lasting conversion',[37] and obtained labour from them in much the same way as the Mouride marabouts did. Bouchand himself accused Catholic missionaries of living in comfort at the expense of the labour of the faithful. School children at missionary schools cultivated crops for the missionary teachers.

The administration was able to control the activity of all missions, Catholic and Protestant, in the inter-war period 'by issuance of decrees forbidding the establishing of any religious group or parochial school, the holding of public meetings, or the making of any tours involving propaganda or money-raising without specific official authorisation'.[38] But the Protestants were particularly hard-hit by the 1923 decree requiring that all missionary teachers hold degrees from French institutions and teach in French, in a native tongue or in Latin a curriculum that had been given administrative approval.[39] This effectively kept Anglo-American Protestantism out of French West Africa.

Administrative measures were not the only limitation to the activity of the Christian missionaries. Where Islam was already established they could make almost no headway; where Islam and Christianity were battling on the same field, Islam won; only in those areas which had been untouched by Islam did Christianity make spectacular headway. Thus in Eastern Nigeria, Dahomey, Ivory Coast, Southern Ghana and Togo Christianity, which preceded Islam, had the field largely to itself. In Sierra Leone, however, the Christian colony of Freetown did not manage to convert its hinterland. Groves attributes the lack of success of the Church in Gambia, Sierra Leone and Liberia as compared with Ghana and Nigeria to the fact that 'in the former the descendants of liberated Africans constituted the main membership of the local churches, without kinship contact with interior tribes—yielding, indeed, to the temptation to regard themselves as superior people—while the Gold Coast and Nigeria churches, with Lagos a possible exception, belonged racially and socially to the peoples around them'.[40] Indeed the separation of identity between missionary and potential convert, whether as between European or Creole on the one hand and 'tribal' African on the other, was one of the major obstacles the Church tried to overcome. The European and 'Europeanised African' missionaries regarded traditional society without understanding and with contempt. They attacked the very foundations of traditional African society, as Ayandele puts it, 'denouncing ordered polygamy in favour of disordered monogamy, producing disrespectful and detribalised children through the mission schools, destroying the high moral principles of indigenous society through denunciation of traditional religion, without an adequate substitute, and transforming the mental outlook of Nigerians in a way that made them imitate European values slavishly, whilst holding in irrational contempt features of traditional culture'.[41] Many Africans reacted against the sweeping and ignorant condemnation of African society made by the European missionaries and many of their Creole colleagues. They reacted, too, against the development away from the nineteenth-century policies of Africanising the missions. From 1900 to 1950 Africans were kept out of the policy-making positions of the missions. The C.M.S. under the Secretaryship of Henry Venn had pursued a policy of handing over control of established missions to Africans. The most notable example of his faith in the ability of the African to govern himself in matters ecclesiastical was the appointment of Crowther as Bishop of West Africa beyond the Queen's dominions.[42] The Church Missionary Society had gone farther than any other mission in the policy of Africanisation, but it was certainly not alone, for because of heavy death toll of Europeans most missions saw that they would have to rely on Africans. But in the twentieth century, with increased medical facilities and under the security of colonial rule, the African was relegated to a subordinate position, just as he was in the colonial administration. Seminaries had, for instance, been set up in Senegal and Dahomey with the object of training African priests. But between 1870 and 1938 there were only three ordinations of Senegalese, and in a shorter period of thirty years in Dahomey a similar number. In Guinea and Sudan before World War II only one African priest was ordained.[43]

## 5 The rise of the African Churches

The reaction of African Christians both to the destructive approach of missionaries towards their own societies and to the relegation of the African to the back-seat was to form break-away churches. In 1891 nine Yoruba Anglicans and Methodists founded an independent 'native African Church', being of the 'opinion that Africa is to be evangelised, and that foreign agencies at work at the present moment, taking into consideration climatic and other influences, cannot grasp the situation. Resolved that a purely Native African Church be founded for the evangelisation and amelioration of our race, to be governed by Africans.'[44] The Church they founded, the

United Native African Church, was orthodox Anglican in its doctrine, with the major exception that it permitted polygamy. The Orthodox Churches, that is those that broke with the parent mission in order to govern themselves, and only made minor changes in their practices, such as permitting polygamy, have been described as African by Dr. Webster (in his *African Churches among the Yoruba*) as distinct from Aladura Churches, which focus around a particular prophet, are syncretistic, and are concerned with faith healing and purification.[45] The African Churches are so-called because they seceded from European missions on the grounds that they wanted self-government, but were not concerned with major changes in doctrine. Balandier has suggested that such churches which were aristocratic and modernist 'to some degree correspond with the early stages of nationalist claims'. The Aladura Churches, which tend to be syncretistic, rely heavily on emotional experience, use African elements such as drumming in their services and 'correspond with the later more radical nationalist action'.[46] In Nigeria and Ghana secessionist churches whether of the orthodox type or prayer-healing, or prophet-leader type, became an important element in the Christian Church. The Orthodox Churches were important as contributors to the growth of national self-consciousness. In Sierra Leone they made no ground because, it has been suggested, as far as Freetown is concerned Christianity had effectively become Creolised and was no longer a missionary religion. Need for the revivalist elements in the prayer-healing churches was met with by voluntary associations closely linked with Orthodox Churches. Finally the immigrant from up-country, finding the majority of his fellows were Muslim, tends to become a Muslim rather than seek out a prayer-healing church.[47] In French West Africa, as we have seen, the possibility of independent action on the part of the African and the controls to which church-activities were submitted made it difficult for independent African Churches to take root. In British West Africa all the African Churches were break-aways from Protestant Churches, and in French West Africa Protestants had very little impact because of the restrictions on their activity. In 1925 the *World Missionary Atlas* gave the number of Protestants in French West Africa as only 666, an underestimate, to be sure, but indicative of the minimal nature of Protestant influence there.[48] It is significant, then, that the only major separatist Church movement in French West Africa was Protestant but inspired not by a French West African but a Liberian. In 1913, William Wade Harris from Cape Palmas, Liberia, arrived in Ivory Coast to preach the Gospel to the 'heathen' as he had been instructed to do in a vision from the Archangel Gabriel in 1910. Already he had been in trouble with the Liberian authorities, and the French looked on his successful evangelisation of Grand Lahou, Abidjan, Bassam and Assinie with concern. The administrator of Lahou had him expelled from his district. But thereafter the government tolerated his activities until some of his followers became involved in diffusing a rumour that the War would force the French to leave. As a result he was expelled from Ivory Coast in April 1915, having made between 60,000 and 100,000 converts.

For the French, the Prophet Harris appeared, after initial concern, as someone they should support, for he preached obedience to the government in a disturbed area, and demanded the destruction of 'fetishes' and of the authority of priests of the traditional religion, whom the French saw as a major source of opposition to them. For the Ivory Coast African, so recently and with such difficulty subjugated to French administration and taxes, the Prophet seems to have fulfilled a great need with his simple message that there was only One God and that all others should be rejected and destroyed. He forbade alcohol but apparently tolerated polygamy. His movement was so successful that in 1923 great numbers of Harrisites were still found to be active in the area of his mission. In 1926 a conservative estimate of 40,000 Harrisite Christians was made.[49]

## 6 Christianity and social change

The Christian missionaries preached not only a new religion but a revolutionary social ethic: that life could be separated into spiritual and secular. They also asked that their converts accept the secular values of European or American Society. Thus to the individualism of the Christian religion was added the individualism of an increasingly materialist industrial West. This accent on the individual, and the notion that life could be compartmented into two spheres of activity, was diametrically opposed to traditional African society where the individual mattered only in relation to the community as a whole, and where life was a total religious experience. Because of this Christianity destroyed the very foundations of African society whereas Islam built upon them. Islam's notion of the spiritual leader with secular authority, its refusal to separate Church and State, its brotherhoods, its requirement that the faithful pray five times a day rather than just on Sunday, together with its more tolerant attitude towards African society made it much less revolutionary in nature. Its prohibition of the consumption of alcohol kept many of its adherents out of bars and dance-halls, vehicles of Western popular culture and of moral laxity.

Christian missionaries, rather than convert the chief, sought out the least privileged of his followers, slaves, social outcasts, and opened up to them avenues of social advancement that were impossible to conceive in traditional society right down to questions of dress, particularly where nudity, total or partial, was concerned. The missionary taught his convert not only the revolutionary doctrine of the equality of all men before God and man but also to look on his own society with contempt. Thus the slave-convert could look on his 'heathen' master as an equal, even with contempt. This notion of equality combined with the individualism of the Christian religion played an important role in the development of African nationalism. For the educated African could argue not only that he was equal to his colonial master, but that the secular and religious premises of the latter's culture demanded that he recognise not only the fundamental equality of the African as a man, but also that he recognise individual achievement when he saw it.

By attacking all that was fundamental to African society—respect for elders, obedience to the chief as the source of the corporate will, the practice of polygamy, marriage payment (which linked the bride's family with the groom)—and by attacking initiation ceremonies which consisted not only of features repugnant to the Christian, but a sound educational programme,[50] the missionaries produced converts for whom 'the difficulties of individual adjustment to a socio-political structure incapable of realising Christian ideals became insuperable'.[51]

Something of the determination of the missionary to cast aside all aspects of traditional society is given by the account of King Prempeh's burial written by the Reverend St. John Evans in *Golden Shore*, the magazine of the Accra Diocesan Association. Prempeh had become a Christian and was a Churchwarden of St. Cyprian's, Kumasi.

'It was imperative to secure a Christian burial for Nana in spite of the multitude of native funeral customs which were to take place.' So Reverend St. John Evans and the braver members of his choir went to the lying in state of the dead king.[52]

'After a few minutes we started a hymn. Africans can at least sing loudly, and we completely drowned all other noises ... when we felt things were getting a little too exciting and hysterical, we started another hymn ... at one time we would be singing, at another various heathen customs would be taking place.'

At considerable risk to his own and his choir's safety, St. John Evans was able by sheer effrontery to get Prempeh buried a Christian at Bantema, the royal mausoleum.[53]

The social ferment that resulted from Christian teachings was to prove one of its major, though unintended, contributions to the growth of nationalism. Many of the leaders of movements demanding greater participation in the governmental process, and later self government and independence, were mission-trained. The educated élite, particularly in British West Africa, was largely a product of the missions. Missionaries contributed in other ways to the growth of national self-consciousness. They produced the first newspapers in Nigeria: *Iwe-Irohin*, founded in 1859 by Henry Townsend of the C.M.S., gave 'news of Church and State from near and far ... educating the growing reading public through didactic essays on history and politics'.[54] Some of the earliest Gold Coast newspapers were produced by the missionaries. The *Gold Coast Methodist* was published in 1855 and the demand, 'reasonable and just', for African representation in the Legislative Council was made in its columns.[55] Where print was not available, the pulpit provided another vehicle for airing grievances and demanding greater African participation in the affairs of their country. The missionaries also contributed greatly to linguistic unification. Not only did they spread the use of English or French as a *lingua franca*, but they also contributed to the standardisation of African languages. Thus T. J. Dennis of the Church Missionary Society devised a 'Union' Ibo for his translation of the Bible, and by 1913 he was able to conclude that the 'so-called Union Ibo, actually spoken by no one division of the tribe [was] gradually proving comprehensible by all'.[54] The New Testament, published in 1909, in Union Ibo was to prove an important vehicle for the unification of dialects. Similarly the orthography of Yoruba devised by the C.M.S. mission at Abeokuta for translation of the Bible and Prayer Book, in which Crowther played a leading part, is substantially used today.[56]

All these were part of the missionaries' educational programme. To them education was fundamental to the propagation of their religion. To government, education was indispensable to the functioning of their administration and of the commercial houses, for they could not afford to employ whites in subaltern posts. Whatever the reasons for which it was made available, Western-style education was to prove the most important single factor for social change in West Africa in the colonial period.

# Notes

1  J. C. Froelich, 'Essai sur les causes et méthodes de l'Islamisation de l'Afrique de l'Ouest du XI<sup>e</sup> au XX<sup>e</sup> siècle', in I. M. Lewis, ed., *Islam in Tropical Africa*, London, 1966, p. 166.

2  J. Spencer Trimingham, *Islam in West Africa: The Report of a Survey*, London, 1953, p. 28.

3  *Ibid.*, p. 28.

4  Froelich, 'Causes et méthodes de l'islamisation', p. 170.

5  Trimingham, *Islam in West Africa: The Report*, p. 19.

6  Thomas Hodgkin, *Nationalism in Colonial Africa*, London, 1956, p. 94.

7  E. W. Fashole-Luke, 'Religion in Freetown', paper presented at the Symposium on Freetown held by the Institute of African Studies, Fourah Bay College, University of Sierra Leone, December 1966.

8  See J. Bertin Webster, *The African Churches among the Yoruba 1888–1922*, Oxford, 1964, Chapter II, 'The Causes of the African Church Movement', pp. 42–91.

9  J. F. Ade Ajayi, *Christian Missions in Nigeria 1841–1891: The Making of an Educated Élite*, London, 1965, pp. 253–4.

10  Geoffrey Parrinder, *Religion in an African city*, London, 1953.

11  *Ibid.*, p. 106.

12  Ayandele, *The Missionary Impact on Modern Nigeria*, pp. 128–30, 142–4 and 150–1.

13  Lugard, *Dual Mandate*, p. 593.

14  *The Times*, 6th March 1922.

15  W. R. Crocker, *Nigeria—a Critique of British Colonial Administration*, London, 1936, p. 54.

16  Kimble, *Ghana*, p. 79.

17  Alphonse Gouilly, *L'Islam dans l'Afrique Occidentale Française*, Paris, 1952, pp. 249–50.

18  Donal Cruise O'Brien, 'Towards an Islamic Policy in French West Africa, 1854–1914', *J.A.H.*, VIII, 2 (1967), p. 314.

19  Instructions of August 1911, cited in J. Brévié, *Islamisme contre naturisme au Soudan Français*, Paris, 1923, p. 257.

20  Gouilly, *L'Islam*, p. 254.

21  'L'Islam est-il un danger pour notre colonisation en Afrique occidentale française?', *A Travers le Monde*, 1912, p. 221.

22  O'Brien, 'Towards an Islamic Policy in French West Africa', p. 307.

23  I. M. Lewis, 'Introduction' to *Islam in Tropical Africa*, p. 80.

24  See Gouilly, *L'Islam*, pp. 118–24.

25  Suret-Canale, *Afrique Noire II*, p. 541.

26  Gouilly, *L'Islam*, p. 257.

27  *Ibid.*, pp. 134 ff.

28  Thomas Hodgkin and Ruth Schachter-Morgenthau, 'Mali' in James Coleman and Carl G. Rosberg, Jr., ed., *Political Parties and National Integration in Tropical Africa*, Berkeley and Los Angeles, 1965, p. 228.

The radical attitude of Hamallism to 'the problems of West African Society, and its militancy in its relations with the authorities, whether French or Muslim, were inherited in a secularised form by the Union Soudanaise—R.D.A.'

29 Michael Banton, *West African City*, London, 1957, p. 135.
30 Elliott P. Skinner, 'Islam in Mossi Society', in *Islam in Tropical Africa*, pp. 361–2.
31 Paul Catrice, 'L'emploi des troupes indigènes et leur séjour en France', *Études: Revue Catholique d'Intérêt Général*, 20 November 1931, p. 406.
32 See Banton, *West African City*, p. 135.
33 Skinner, 'Islam in Mossi', p. 362.
34 See 'L'Islam est-il un danger pour notre colonisation'.
35 Thompson and Adloff, *French West Africa*, p. 580.
36 Suret-Canale, *Afrique Noire II*, p. 450.
37 R. P. Bouchand, *L'Église en Afrique Noire*, Paris, 1958, p. 40, cited by Suret-Canale, *Afrique Noire II*, p. 451.
38 Thompson and Adloff, *French West Africa*, p. 582.
39 *Ibid.*, p. 582.
40 C. P. Groves, *The Planting of Christianity in Africa III (1878–1914)*, London, 1955, p. 209.
41 Ayandele, *The Missionary Impact on Modern Nigeria*, p. 329.
42 See Ajayi, *Christian Missions*, pp. 180 ff.
43 Suret-Canale, *Afrique Noire II, op. cit.*, p. 458.
44 Quoted in Parrinder, *Religion in a West African City*, p. 109.
45 See also Bengt Sundkler, *Bantu Prophets in South Africa*, London, 1961, pp. 53–9, where the distinction is 'Ethiopian' and 'Zionist'.
46 Georges Balandier, 'Messianismes et nationalismes en Afrique Noire', *Cahiers Internationaux de Sociologie*, XIV, 1953, cited in Thomas Hodgkin's excellent chapter on 'Prophets and Priests' in his *Nationalism in Colonial Africa*, pp. 93–114.
47 See Fashole-Luke, 'Religion in Freetown'. His observations are based on H. W. Turner's unpublished Ph.D. thesis, *A Study of an Independent West African Church*, p. 1963 (Melbourne College of Divinity, Australia), p. 46.
48 Buell, *The Native Problem*, Vol. II, p. 68.
49 See B. Holas, *Le séparatisme religieux en Afrique noire*, Paris, 1965, p. 263; C. P. Groves, *The Planting of Christianity in Africa, IV: 1914–1954*, pp. 45–6, 123, 124; Buell, *The Native Problem*, II, pp. 66–8.
50 Groves, *The Planting of Christianity in Africa*, IV, pp. 213–14.
51 Coleman, *Nigeria*, pp. 253–4.
52 Quoted in *The Times*, 15th July, 1931.
53 Ajayi, *Christian Missions*, p. 159.
54 Kimble, *Ghana*, p. 162.
55 Groves, *The Planting of Christianity in Africa*, III, p. 220.
56 Ajayi, *Christian Missions*, p. 128.

# 4 Western Education

## 1 The African background

Though Western education was to prove in its impact the most radical of all the innovations introduced by the colonial powers, education as such was not foreign to African society. In the Western Sudan Koranic education was widespread, and had been established in some parts for many centuries. In non-Muslim areas, whilst reading and writing were unknown, each African society had a system of education designed to enable its children to participate fully in its life; that is if we regard education 'as the whole process by which one generation transmits its culture to the succeeding generation'.[1] Such education, usually culminating in initiation rites, involved a wide range of instruction: education about environment; the practice of agriculture; technical knowledge such as how to build houses, make pots, forge tools, weave baskets; athletic skills such as hunting, fishing, canoeing, swimming; the art of warfare; household management; instruction in the social norms of society, with particular emphasis on religion and government; cultural instruction in dancing and music. In all but the most isolated of societies children would be given instruction in trading which would include understanding not only of barter but also of rates of exchange, since apart from cowries there were many different units of currency in use, particularly on the Coast. With low-value cowries as a basis of the currency, skill in addition was essential for any African trading beyond his own village. Contrary to a generally European held opinion that Africans could not count beyond ten, the Yorubas could count to a million .[2]

Children also acquired considerable linguistic skill and enlarged their vocabularies through listening to folk tales and sagas, proverbs and riddles. Some indication of the richness of African oral literature not only as a means of enriching a child's knowledge of his language, but also as an educational medium, can be obtained from the translations of the literature of certain African peoples recently made available in the Oxford Library of African Literature.[3]

In Muslim societies the educational system varied from recitation of the Koran by heart to instruction in reading and writing in Arabic and elementary mathematics to the intensive education given Usman dan Fodio under a series of noted scholars, most famous of whom was Mallam Jibril of Agades. Dan Fodio's education consisted of the traditional Islamic sciences of Grammar, Law, Exegesis, Theology, Rhetoric and Prosody. All over the Western Sudan there were scholars to whom pupils would attach themselves to gain increased knowledge in the subject in which the teacher had gained fame. The student's diploma was in fact the pedigree of teachers under whom he had studied. A distinguished scholar might well attach himself to a younger man as a pupil if the latter were particularly knowledgeable in a field in which he wished to improve himself. While this intensive education touched only a small section of the society, it was responsible for the vast, still largely unexplored body of Arabic literature that exists in the Western Sudan.[4] Though the bulk of students who passed through the Koranic School did not gain much more from an educational point of view than what Gouilly has called 'L'ingestion mnémo-technique du Livre d'Allah', a small élite emerged who 'read with ease classical Arabic, wrote it fluently and gave witness to a definite culture and science. Negroes of a much greater number than is usually thought know how to comment with great insight and feeling on the most difficult texts of Arab authors, translate them at sight and devote themselves to writing poetry, literature or theology.'[5]

Works by Negro Muslims on philosophy, law, theology, history, and medicine exist all over the Western Sudan. An idea of the importance of Muslim education is given by the fact that Lugard in his *Annual Report* for 1902 for Northern Nigeria suggested building up the existing Muslim schools.[6] In 1945 it was estimated 80,235 children attended traditional Muslim schools in French West Africa.[7] These schools, however, were given no support by the French, even though on the eve of conquest in areas like Bondou and

Futa-Jallon there was hardly a village without its school.[8] The British Government, too, never pursued Lugard's early plans to develop the existing Muslim education system, so that generally Arabic education suffered a set-back under colonial rule since the criterion for success, except for posts with the Native Administrations of Northern Nigeria, became a Western Education. The French made a half-hearted attempt at developing the *medresas* (see p. 361) but these were of little significance except in Mauritania and the emphasis was on the French rather than the Arabic aspect of education.

## 2 *The colonial education system*

Both France and Britain, whether through the agency of the missionaries or directly through their colonial administrations, came to see the introduction of Western education as essential to the prosecution of their exploitation of West Africa. Without Western education there would be no clerks and technicians to fill those roles in the administration and commerce that it was either not profitable or impossible to fill with Europeans. With so limited an objective, it is not surprising that very few children ever got even to primary school under the colonial régime, let alone to secondary school. It is not surprising, also, that governments spent minute percentages of their annual budgets on the education of those whose occupation they had earlier undertaken on the declared grounds that they were going to bring them the fruits of Western civilisation. With rare exceptions, such as Governor Guggisberg of the Gold Coast, the idea of education for its own sake, or as a means for modernising African society, was conspicuously absent in the inter-war period. Even the missionaries had a limited objective: for them education was a means of teaching Africans to read the Bible and of securing them to their faith. There was little thought as to what form of education was desirable for the African; hence their concentration on a literary education to the exclusion of the technical education so desperately needed if any real transformation of the economic well-being of Africans was to be achieved. It was left to African leaders themselves in the era of de-colonisation to insist on the primacy of education as a means to the social and economic transformation of African society into one that could compete with the West on its own terms.

Statistics bear out how small the efforts of the Colonial Governments and missionaries in the field of education were before 1939:

In 1934 in French West Africa there were 265 government village and 13 urban schools, usually with only one teacher, giving students an elementary knowledge of French, and in the more advanced among these schools giving them some instruction in farming and sanitation. Attending these schools were some 22,323 students of whom only 2,301 were girls.[9] Their schools were usually poorly equipped and in Bamako one teacher was in charge of a class of 200.[10] The age groups attending these schools were from six to thirteen years old.

Above the village and urban schools were 75 regional schools with 22,289 students of whom 2,243 were girls. Here the education of students was carried from six to thirteen years old and during the last two years students learnt history, geography and arithmetic. In the main towns there were what was known as urban primary schools, whose curriculum was almost entirely academic, and whose 929 pupils, exclusively boys, hoped 'for employment as clerks in business or government houses, as store-keepers, traders, workmen on the railways or ports'.[11] Alongside these elementary schools were a number of trade and craft schools and adult courses where the level of education was very rudimentary.

Higher education was very restricted. The higher primary schools took in students by competitive examination from the regional schools and sometimes from mission schools. Here there were many European teachers and the level of education was good. Indeed Mumford and St. Orde-Browne, two British officials who visited the school at Bamako, wrote:

'The general impression gained from a visit to the Bamako school was that the institutions were equal in standing and equipment to the best that Europe can produce. Using the term in its biological sense, these schools are the "growing points" of French civilisation in Africa.'[12] But there were only eight such schools with 930 pupils in 1934. These schools had technical sections where artisans for the Posts and Telegraphs, Survey, Public Works, Railways, and Commercial Houses were trained.

Secondary education properly speaking was pathetically inadequate for a population estimated at some eleven million. The Lycée Faidherbe at St. Louis and the École Normale William Ponty in Dakar took in between fifty and eighty boys a year, half of whom became teachers, while the other half went into the professions, in particular medicine, engineering and veterinary services. The level of education here was equal to that of France and nearly all the teachers were French. While courses were taught with reference to

Africa, Mumford and Orde-Brown felt after conversation with the boys that they 'were French in all but the colour of their skin'.[13]

Two professional schools were established in Dakar: the Marine Engineering School, and the Medical School, which trained assistant doctors, dispensers, midwives and district nurses. In 1934 there were fourteen doctors, two dispensers, eleven midwives, ten district nurses and five vets produced by the school. At Bamako there was a Veterinary School from which graduates joined the veterinary service.

In all there were less than six hundred pupils at government secondary and post-secondary schools in French West Africa in 1934. Private schools run by missions did not bolster up the global figures of children at school much over its figure for 1934 of 50,099 students. While statistics for private schools were not reliable, Mumford and Orde-Browne estimated that there were some 74 schools with 9,467 pupils, meaning that still less than 60,000 children were at schools of all kinds in 1934. By 1944 the figure had only risen to 76,000, of whom 57,000 were at government schools and 19,000 at mission schools.[14] Of the individual territories in 1934, the following numbers of children were at government schools: Senegal, 12,367; Mauretania, 436; Sudan, 11,744; Niger, 2,610; Dahomey, 7,077; Ivory Coast, 9,307; and Guinea, 6,558.

British West Africa had comparatively a much better record, though in the context of its population the numbers at school were very small. In Gambia in 1938 only 0·5% of the children of school-going age actually attended school in the Protectorate, though in the Colony it was up to 83% in that year.[15] In the Sierra Leone Protectorate only 9,828 children out of a population of children of school-going age estimated at 330,000 in 1936 actually attended school, though in the Colony some 50% of the children went to school. In Northern Nigeria in 1939 only 25,067 children were at school in a population greater than that of all French West Africa. In Southern Nigeria and Gold Coast the situation was comparatively better: in 1938 in Gold Coast 76,006 children were at school, though few of these were from the Northern Territories, which was very backward educationally. In Southern Nigeria in 1938 some children were at government-assisted or non-assisted schools.

Secondary education in all the British West African territories was sparse, though it compared very favourably indeed with French West Africa. The Gambia alone had four secondary schools, two for boys and two for girls. Sierra Leone had nine, one of which was financed exclusively by government. In Southern Nigeria there were thirty-three in 1938, three of which were owned by government. In Gold Coast that year there were only 3,089 secondary students.

Over and above the secondary schools were three institutions of higher education. Fourah Bay College in Sierra Leone had since 1877 the powers to offer degree courses of the University of Durham in Theology and Arts subjects. It was unfortunately limited by lack of funds, by its religious origins and the archaism and lack of interest of the British university to which it was affiliated. Achimota College in the Gold Coast had by 1938 thirty-two students in its University department pursuing degree courses in arts, sciences, medicine and engineering. In Lagos the Yaba Higher College founded in 1934 had seventy-three students, studying medicine, engineering, agriculture and education. It did not, however, provide full university level degree courses.

British West African governments, with the exception of Northern Nigeria, administered directly a very small section of the school system. Their main educational effort was undertaken through the agency of mission schools which they supported on condition that these schools conformed to their standards. This control was initially weak, being exercised through a single Inspector of Schools supported by a Board of Education. It grew much stronger with the establishment of governmental departments of education under directors. While the Gold Coast appointed its first director of education in 1890, one was not appointed in the Gambia until 1937 and prior to 1930 the Police Magistrate was responsible for the inspection of schools.[16] In Sierra Leone, with its long history of education in the Colony, a director was not appointed until 1911.

In Northern Nigeria, because of the decision to exclude missionaries from the Muslim emirates, the government had to take a much greater role in education and in 1910 Hans Vischer was made its director. Here, again, however, the Northern Nigerian government sought to delegate much of its authority to the Native administrations in conformity with its policy of indirect rule. The support given by all governments to education was very small in relation to its importance for the development of Africa. In 1938 Gold Coast headed the list with £213,000 spent on education, but in that same year the government's overall budget was £3,637,000. Gambia in 1939 spent only £4,106 on assistance to mission schools.

In British West Africa the standards and curricula of the schools were roughly the same, and an elementary or secondary school in West Africa corresponded roughly to its British counterpart. The main difference between West African schools and British schools was that initial instruction was in the vernacular. Apart from this little concession was made to the fact that the students were Africans: they studied English not African history; the constitution of Britain, the geography of Britain, and English literature, etc.

### 3 Philosophies of education under colonial rule

Whilst both Britain and France saw as the basic objective of their educational policies the training of Africans for participation in the colonial economy and administration, they differed substantially in their approach. France in the education of her élite aimed at producing 'French' Africans, whose loyalty to France and indifference to local nationalism would be assured; Britain sought to produce an 'African' African, and was aware she could not 'educate the people of a colony without expecting them to ask for self-government'.[17] The British educational system, being dominated by the missions, naturally had as one of its basic goals the conversion of students to Christianity. But it also laid special emphasis on the virtue of hard work, for the missions in educating the African had, of course, pursued a policy of 'the Bible and the Plough'. Indeed it was one of the complaints of missions that Africans preferred a clerical education to training in manual and industrial skills. Partly this was a result of the higher wages available for clerical jobs, partly a result of the fact that Africans felt that a clerical education had greater prestige in a white man's world.[18]

The French system was much more concerned with persuading children of the virtues of the colonial system and French culture. Thus in a textbook written for village schools concerned with the journey of two young boys, Moussa and Gi-Gla, a European tells them: 'It is always necessary to love those who deserve it and merit it. Difference in race makes little difference. Goodness has nothing to do with colour. It is, on the one hand, an advantage for the native to work for the white man, because the whites are better educated, more advanced in civilisation than the natives, and because, thanks to them, the natives will make more rapid progress, learn better and more quickly, know more things, and become one day really useful men. On the other hand, the blacks will render service to the whites by bringing them the help of their arms, by cultivating the land which will permit them to grow crops for Europeans, and also by fighting for France in the ranks of native troops. *Thus the two races will associate and work together in common prosperity and happiness of all.* You who are intelligent and industrious, my children, always help the whites in their task. This is a duty.'[19]

The emphasis on the virtue of work was a recurring theme in French statements on the goals of education in Africa. Sarraut put it most bluntly: 'To educate the natives is assuredly our duty. . . . But this fundamental duty in addition coincides with our obvious economic, administrative, military and political interests. Education, in effect, has as its first result the amelioration of the value of production by increasing in the mass of native workers the quality of intelligence and the variety of skills: it should in addition pick out and train from among the labouring masses élites of collaborators who, as technical assistants, foremen, employees or clerks will make up for the numerical insufficiency of Europeans and satisfy the growing demands of colonial agricultural, industrial and commercial enterprises.'[20]

Sarraut's philosophy was essentially the one followed by the French in the inter-war years, and they were accordingly careful to gear educational output to demand by administration and commerce for educated Africans. Men like Governor-General Brévié tried to insist that 'however pressing may be the need for economic change and the development of natural resources, our mission in Africa is to bring about a cultural renaissance, a piece of creative work in human material, an association of two races which can be brought about only by a free and wholehearted acceptance of the African by the French'.[21]

The British, less inclined to philosophise, also saw the need for education of Africans for participation in their colonial venture. Thus in Northern Nigeria, after the completion of the conquest it was considered that the education immediately required was one that would train 'intelligent natives . . . for clerkships in Government and other offices . . . to . . . replace the native clerks who have of necessity been drawn hitherto from other West African colonies and possessions, where schools are in existence'.[22] Over and above this the sons of chiefs would be given primary education 'without imbibing ideas of European dress and habits unsuited to their environment', while the masses would be sent to schools where industrial teaching would feature.[23] In Sierra Leone in 1926 the Governor insisted on the primacy of industrial and manual education and sniped at the older secondary schools in Freetown which 'still take a pride in including Latin and Greek in their curriculum, and [where] the B.A. Dunelm is still probably the ambition of most youthful students'.[24]

The concentration on academic rather than the more profitable 'vocational' education caused much concern among colonial governments. Thus one of the objects of sending a soil and plant-life expert on the Phelps-Stokes commission on African education, sponsored by the Advisory Committee on Native Education in British Tropical African Dependencies, established in 1923, was to relate education activities to agricultural possibilities.[25] Together with its purely utilitarian aspects, the British were concerned that the character of education given be adapted to the African situation. Thus the British Government in 1925 issued a statement on its policy towards African education which expressed this concern neatly: 'Education should be adapted to the mentality, aptitudes, occupations and traditions of the various peoples, conserving as far as possible all sound and healthy elements in the fabric of their social life; adapting them where necessary to changed circumstances and progressive ideas, as an agent of natural growth and evolution. Its aim should be to render the individual more efficient in his or her condition of life, whatever it may be, and to promote the advancement of agriculture, the development of native industries, the training of the people in the management of their own affairs, and the inculcation of true ideals of citizenship and service. . . . The first task of education is to raise the standard alike of character and efficiency of the bulk of the people, but provision must also be made for the training of those who as chiefs will occupy positions of exceptional trust and responsibility.'[26] The French, by contrast, were much less concerned to adapt education to the African situation. In West Africa if assimilation was abandoned as a policy, it was still pursued in the educational programme. Thus Ponty in 1910 wrote: 'Once we have trained an élite of young people to aid our efforts, we must occupy ourselves with the education of the whole race and try to give to the greatest possible number of our subjects if not assimilation, at least a French imprint'.[27]

In their educational policy the French did, however, make a great distinction between the élite and the masses. The limited élite were given a full French education; the mass, where they did manage to get to school, were just given a rudimentary education aimed mainly at teaching them the French language. From the beginning the French insisted that the chiefs and all those with whom they came in daily contact speak French. Ponty expressed the hope in 1910 that the French language would be spoken wherever France had extended her empire. In 1924 Governor-General Carde was still insisting on the need to expand the teaching of French so that in the most remote villages there would be, apart from the chief, some Africans who could speak French.[28]

British officials on the other hand were quite prepared to speak to a chief through an interpreter, or directly in his own language, which some of them took pains to learn. Where the French insisted on children being instructed in French from the first day they entered school, the British primary schools taught in the vernacular for the first two years. For the French their language was the means of 'initiation into French civilisation' and since they did not consider African culture had any relevance to the modern world, this civilisation was the only one open for the African élite to adopt. Albert Charton, Inspector-General of Education in French West Africa in the thirties, insisted on an exclusively French education for Negro-Africans since 'Africa is not capable, as are India, China, or the countries of Islam, of evolving a fully formed intellectual culture of her own'.[29] Nevertheless it was Charton who insisted that the African should not become exclusively French, and that he should enrich his acquired French culture with his own. Thus he noted, in citing Governor-General Brévié, 'an intellectual movement is taking form which, deriving its inspiration from the pure French tradition, is dipping deep into the springs of native life'.[30] The government, far from discouraging this attempt by Africans, mainly teachers, to explore their own culture and traditions, offered an annual prize for the best result. Here, then, we find France officially encouraging the movement which became known as *négritude*. Thus the élite, having been thoroughly Gallicised, were encouraged to return to their own sources. Little wonder that the critics of *négritude* feel that its African exponents looked at their culture through an essentially French optic. (See also pp. 445–6.)

## 4 The training of an élite

The élite, whether it was to be French- or African-oriented, became increasingly important to the colonial administrations which, as they expanded their commitments, could only with difficulty cover the high costs of bringing out Europeans to fill the junior posts of their senior administrative and technical services. Apart from the Gold Coast, the response to this problem, which was exacerbated by the General Depression, was haphazard. Guggisberg, energetic and far-sighted, saw education as the 'keystone' to Africa's development and had no hesitation in pursuing a policy of Africanisation of the 'European' civil service. Thus shortly after he assumed duty he set up a Native Civil Service Committee which prepared a draft public statement that: 'The Government desire so to develop the country and so to educate the people that they may gradually replace Europeans in the Higher Appointments. . . . Any Higher Appointment which the Government consider could with no loss of efficiency direct or indirect be held by any African will be thrown open and the vacancy notified in the Government Gazette in addition to the newspapers in England.'[31] Though Africans had been employed in senior posts in the British Colonial Government in West Africa during the nineteenth century, as we have seen they were progressively replaced by Europeans in the first two decades of the twentieth century. Guggisberg's policy, therefore, was far in advance of its time, for it was not until 1950 that it was effectively adopted in the Gold Coast, and 1948 in Nigeria.[32] Guggisberg planned a phased Africanisation which would increase the number of Africans holding senior appointments in the Civil Service from a couple of dozen to 229 out of a total of 558 appointments by 1945–6, so that more than 50% of the Civil Service would be African. As it was he both overestimated the rate at which Africans would be recruited and underestimated the rate of expansion of the Civil Service. To provide these African Civil Servants, Guggisberg founded Achimota School, which was the culmination of his philosophy of education as stated in *The Keystone*: 'Government's duty at present is to lay the foundation of development in every direction, to organise the departmental machinery necessary for dealing with each system, and to provide such European staff as the revenue permits; while at the same time it must prepare, organise, and bring into being the system of schools where Africans can obtain the better and higher education that will fit them to enter the various trades and professions, both in the public service and in private enterprise.'[33] In Nigeria it was only with the appointment of Sir Donald Cameron as Governor in 1931 that serious attention was given to the role of educated Africans in the Government. The founding of Yaba Higher College, which was his work, was a reflection of his government's future policy of employing more Africans in its service. But the training given was to be 'of a university type though not necessarily of a university standard' and none of its courses led to degrees.[34] The object was to train a second-level élite, an auxiliary to, not a substitute for, the expatriate employee of the administration. Miss Perham, who praised Cameron's policy had, however, one major reservation: Africans should not enter the administrative service.[35] This too had been the policy of Guggisberg who feared chiefs would not be willing to accept educated African District or Provincial Commissioners of their own or another tribe.[36] In French West Africa, where the élite was much smaller, no public office was technically closed to it. In 1936 for instance Sir Arnold Hodson, Governor of the Gold Coast, made a tour of French West Africa and was received in Sudan by Félix Éboué, a French Guyanese, who was then acting governor. At Ouahigouya the Commandant de Cercle was M. Dimbour, 'the first African Commissioner I had met on my trip who had gone to much trouble to entertain us. My room had everything I could want in it, even whisky and soda and a tube of English toothpaste.'[37]

The French trained a small élite under a system which stressed the importance of loyalty to France. This élite was absorbed into the colonial system, and was sufficiently small to present no threat to white society. The French were well aware of the dangers a large, unemployed intelligentsia could present to their position.[38] In British West Africa, where the élite was much larger, both because, as we have seen, there were far more educational opportunities available to them, and because it was comparatively more easy under the British régime for them to go abroad for their higher education, the opportunities for employment in the administration were very few. As a generalisation it is fair to say that the French absorbed a carefully controlled élite into their colonial system, while the British frustrated an élite over whose growth it had no control since the educational system was only indirectly administered by it. For an understanding of the attitudes of French and British Africans towards nationalism in the post-war period, this difference is vital.

The emergence of the educated élite was by far the most important consequence of the imposition of colonial rule, for it was this élite that was to take over government from France and Britain. An examination of the list of graduates of the William Ponty School shows that on or just before independence the following graduates were at the head of French-speaking West African governments: Modibo Keita, President of the Republic of Mali; Mamadou Dia, Prime Minister of Senegal; Hubert Maga, President of Dahomey; Ouezzin Coulibaly, Prime Minister of Upper Volta until his death in 1958, just before independence; Félix Houphouët-Boigny, President of Ivory Coast; Djibo Bakary, Prime Minister of Niger until he was forced out by the French in 1958; only Guinea and Mauretania did not have a President or Prime Minister educated at this school.[39] Similarly in Northern Nigeria the Katsina College, now Government College, Zaria, has a school roll that included the

Premier, the Minister of Finance, the Minister of Education, the Federal Prime Minister and three Federal Ministers, the leader of the opposition in the North, the Speaker of the Northern House and the Governor of the Northern Region before the January 1966 military coup.[40]

A major problem is the definition of the educated élite. Educational standards are no use, for the educated élite of Northern Nigeria was far less qualified on paper than that of the South. After independence it can be usefully defined as that group which has taken over those jobs in government, commerce and industry hitherto reserved for Europeans, or the equivalent of these posts in earning power.[41] During the inter-war period it can better be characterised by Nadel's concept of élite as 'a stratum of population which, for whatever reason, can claim a position of superiority and hence a corresponding measure of influence over the fate of a community'.[42] The educated élite had a common identity in that they had all had a Western education and with this education they had the key tool for dealing with the colonial government. As Perham observed in 1936 the educated élite was well aware 'that only by an overseas education can they hope to understand their rulers'.[43] The educated élites of French and British West Africa, whatever their ethnic origin or their religious differences, had a language in common, French and English, adopted Western clothes and customs, and discussed Western ideas, all of which tended to give them a separate identity from their uneducated brothers. Many of the educated élite had risen from humble backgrounds in traditional society to positions of status under the colonial system such as lawyers or doctors, or positions of wealth as merchants. As education, rather than traditional status, began to be seen as the key to success in the white man's world, the demand for it grew, and the position of those already educated became enhanced so that they became the standard-setting group, as Nadel puts it, for the community.[44] The only major exception to this was the traditional chiefs in British West Africa under indirect rule. In Northern Nigeria, particularly, ascribed status remained as important as achieved status right up until after independence.[45] Nevertheless for most West Africans in the inter-war period success through education in the new colonial system, rather than achievement in the traditional system, became the more important. In 1924 *The Times Educational Supplement* remarked on 'the universal demand for better and more education among the Africans of the Gold Coast'.[46] In 1930 the Governor-General of French West Africa, Brévié, in his statement on Educational Policy, declared: 'Everywhere natives in their multitudes are clamouring to be educated. Here, a chief wants a school of his own, so he builds it; or, again, some village or other may offer to bear the cost of fitting out a school; at certain places in the Ivory Coast the villagers pay the teachers out of their own pockets.'[47] To begin with, demands for education were the result of the perception that it provided the only way to success in the colonial situation. Soon it became clear that only through education could Africans gain control of the new administrative structure erected over them by the colonial powers. Chief Essien, elected member for Calabar in the Nigerian Legislative Council, put it clearly in the debate of 8th March 1939: 'Without education it will be impossible for us to get to our destination which is Nigeria's economic independence and Nigeria's political independence.'[48] Only education could enable Africans to step into the shoes of their European overlords, and gain control of the new political and administrative posts established by them. In their report on progress at Achimota issued on the eve of World War II, the Crown Agents for the Colonies wrote of education: 'It is certain that it is coveted as the means by which the young African can obtain that equality with the European which is perhaps the most intense, or at least the most obvious, desire of himself and his compatriots.'[49]

Membership of chiefly families gave way to academic titles in importance. One of the main factors in Azikiwe's rise to the position of leader of the Ibos in Nigeria was his academic success. He was the first among them to gain post-graduate qualifications and to have taught in an American University, Lincoln. In the 1935–6 election for the Deputyship in Senegal, women supporters of Lamine Guèye chanted 'Bachelier ès lettres, professeur, avocat, docteur en droit, magistrat' in support of their candidate who, of all French-speaking Africans, had achieved more academic and professional laurels than anyone. They introduced, as Bakary Traoré has put it, 'the cult of diplomas and the prestige of intellectuals into Senegalese politics'.[50]

Testimony to the importance attached by the élite to education was the protest against its inadequacy both in quality and quantity in Nigeria and Gold Coast.[51] Africans also founded and financed their own primary and secondary schools. They even financed the education of their children at universities overseas so that they could gain the higher education which was not available to them at home.

2C

## 5  Education and change

Not only Africans were concerned about the nature and effects of the education provided. Europeans criticised the excessive attention paid to the literary as distinct from the vocational side of education in the system. Africans on the other hand feared that the substitution of agricultural and vocational education would be a means of subjecting them for always as 'hewers of wood and drawers of water'.[52]

One of the main points of criticism was the method of teaching of the English and French languages in the schools. Apart from being the vehicle of communication among the educated élite, English and French became lingua franca for an ever-increasing number of people, making it possible for men of different ethnic groups to communicate, even if in an Africanised form of the language or 'pidgin'.[53] For the French African child in school the insistence that only French be spoken provided a major culture shock, but it did result in a relatively high standard of French being spoken by those who survived though because of the repetitive nature of the lessons much of what was taught was not understood.[54] Guggisberg remarked in 1925 that the reason English was so 'imperfectly learned' was that it was taught in English and not the vernacular. 'A language cannot be taught to a child by making him repeat by memory certain sounds the meaning of which he does not understand, yet this is a system which has generally prevailed and has laid the foundations of the parrot-like knowledge that is such a strong characteristic of the boys and girls turned out by our primary schools.'[55] However, the Basel mission in the Gold Coast had insisted that the early education of their pupils should be in the vernacular, in this case Ga and Twi.[56] As late as 1963 a French psychologist criticised the use of French rather than the vernacular as the medium of instruction in primary schools in Dakar.[57] In 1908 the Sierra Leonean Bishop, James Johnson, made a plea for the use of Krio, the form of English used by Sierra Leoneans which has been recognised as a language in its own right in schools, on the grounds that it would help children 'understand England's English better and take in English teaching more readily and more intelligently, and with greater appreciation'.[58] However imperfectly learned, both English and French as languages opened up to the African the thought and opinions not only of their fellow men but also of their colonial masters. They could read attacks in newspapers, where publication of these was permitted, on the colonial administration by African leaders judging the colonial governments by French and British ideals of democracy and justice. The differences in standards between the practice of colonial and domestic government were laid bare by appeal to the works of French and British philosophers and political theorists.

Beneath the educated élite was the vast body of men who had been through primary schools, learnt French or English, however imperfectly, and had been taught, whether by assimilationist missionaries in British West Africa or assimilationist lay teachers in French West Africa, to despise their own heritage. They were given a brief glimpse of the Western world but only part of the educational equipment needed to deal with it. Their educational system emphasised individual achievement as against corporate responsibility, the virtue of the clerical and technical career as against the agricultural. The pen, at least as far as status was concerned, was mightier than the matchet. So far from returning to the land and applying new knowledge to the improvement of farming, the primary school children flocked to the urban centres. As recently as 1954, of 1,000 rural Senegalese who received their Primary School Certificates (C.E.P.) only 2% were farmers five years later, while 75% were in the towns.[59] It was this group, with jobs, if they obtained them at all, as junior clerks, messengers, typists, cleaners, storekeepers, mechanics, or labourers, who were to provide the mass support in the towns to which nationalist leaders like Nkrumah, Azikiwe and Sékou Touré appealed.

Education has often been seen as creating a break between Western-oriented and traditional society. Many writers have stressed the apparent antipathy of the educated élite, and even the primary school leavers, to their traditional environment.[60] True, education was the most powerful factor for social change, but as Brokensha insists, it should not be regarded 'as a causal agent working on a passive society'. Nor, too, can it be isolated 'in its effects on culture and society from changes initiated in political, economic or religious institutions'.[61] Here again African society was much more adaptable to change than has commonly been supposed, and while at first many chiefs opposed education, seeing it as a threat to their own traditional position, many adapted to it. Altogether the thesis of a break-down in traditional society in the face of Western education, and Western political, social and economic forces, has been given too much prominence in accounts of the colonial period in West Africa. Thus E. R. J. Hussey, writing in 1940, insisted that 'almost everywhere in West Africa, as a result of European contacts, tribal sanctions have been weakened and there has been a steady growth of individualism which in many ways has made the exercise of authority by tribal leaders somewhat difficult'.[62] More accurate was Meek's assessment of the situation in the same volume: describing the Lala of North-East Nigeria, he wrote that the first administrative officer to visit them without an armed guard did so only in 1930, adding that '. . . they are almost untouched by European influence and are likely to remain so for many years to come. . . . There are many tribes in West Africa who are at the same cultural stage as the Lala.'[63]

In those areas which were touched intimately by Europe— whether through the presence of a school, a trading post or administrative centre, what is surprising is not that traditional society fell apart but that it held together so effectively; that traditional moral obligations to one's family triumphed over Western individualism; that traditional religious beliefs survived alongside and permeated Christianity and Islam; that Chiefs, seeing that the new social system demanded both achieved status as well as ascribed status, particularly from the financial point of view, entered the money economy and sent their children to school. The educated élite itself, though often opposed to the chiefs, nevertheless had feet in both traditional and Western-oriented society. Thus two of Ghana's major political leaders, J. B. Danquah and K. A. Busia, have made very perceptive and sympathetic studies of their own societies.[64] Perhaps the most impressive account of the resilience of traditional society, even in dealing with members of the élite, is Chinua Achebe's *No Longer at Ease*,[65] a sequel to his novel about the impact of the European conquest on an Ibo village in Nigeria.[66] In it his hero, Obi, grandson of the hero of his village's resistance to the European occupation, returns from England to join the government senior service. His tragedy is his failure to reconcile the exigencies of his Western-style office with his traditional obligations, which, try hard as he may, he cannot escape.

Between traditional African society and Western-oriented society there was not dichotomy but a continual process of re-adjustment. This is probably best brought out by Margaret Read in her account of the six stages she notes in the cultural contact between Britain and her African colonial territories in the field of Western-style education.[67] The first stage is one of conservatism, even to the extent of resistance, with regard to the introduction of modern education. The second stage is a gradual acceptance of some of the new ideas and the new ways of living introduced through the schools. This is followed by a third stage, marked by the rejection of certain traditional values and customs. This stage gives way to a fourth in which there is a full acceptance of the opportunities given by the British educational system and the determination of educated Africans to show they are equal to Europeans in intellect and can assimilate *all* their standards. This stage reached, Africans look back selectively at their traditional culture and reinstate it partially. 'It is significant', Read points out, 'that those Africans who led the way in this new process of selectiveness had for the most part achieved a high level of educational parity with Europeans.'[68] The sixth and final stage is the determined effort on the part of the élite to weld Western and African culture, what Read calls a kind of cultural *swaraj* movement. This sixth stage was to be typical of the post-war movements for independence.

# Notes

1 Edwin W. Smith, 'Indigenous Education in Africa', in E. E. Evans-Pritchard, ed., *Essays Presented to C. G. Seligman*, London, 1934, p. 321. For a most useful discussion of the nature of indigenous education, see John Wilson, *Education and Changing West African Culture*, pp. 17–22.

2 Robert G. Armstrong, *Yoruba Numerals*, London, 19—, p. —.

3 See in particular: S. A. Babalola, *The Context and Form of Yoruba Ijala*, Oxford, 1966; H. A. S. Johnston, *A Selection of Hausa Stories*, Oxford, 1967; Ruth Finnegan, *Limba Stories and Story-Telling*, Oxford, 1967.

4 See Ivor Wilks, 'The Growth of Islamic Learning in Ghana', *Journal of the Historical Society of Nigeria*, II, 4, December 1963; W. E. N. Kensdale, 'Field Notes on the Arabic Literature of the Western Sudan', *Journal of the Royal Asiatic Society*, 1955; A. D. H. Bivar and M. Hiskett, 'The Arabic Literature of Nigeria to 1804: a Provisional account', *Bulletin of the School of Oriental and African Studies*, XXV, 1962, pp. 104–38; Thomas Hodgkin, 'The Islamic Literary Education in Ghana', in I. M. Lewis, ed., *Islam in Tropical Africa*, pp. 442–59; Alphonse Gouilly, *L'Islam dans l'Afrique Occidentale Française* Chapter X, 'L'enseignement', pp. 221–8, especially pp. 224–7.

5 Gouilly, *L'Islam*, pp. 223–4.

6 Orr, *The Making of Northern Nigeria*, p. 265.

7 Gouilly, *L'Islam*, p. 221.

8 Suret-Canale, *Afrique Noire II*, p. 461.

9 These and following statistics are taken from W. Bryant Mumford and G. St. J. Orde-Brown, *Africans Learn to be French: A review of Educational Activities in the Seven Federated Colonies of French West Africa based on a tour of French West Africa and Algiers undertaken in 1935*, London, 1936.

10 *Ibid.*, p. 33.

11 *Ibid.*, p. 35.

12 *Ibid.*, p. 44.

13 *Ibid.*, pp. 46–7.

14 Suret-Canale, *Afrique Noire II*, p. 469.

15 Statistics taken from Hilliard, *Education in British West Africa*.

16 *Ibid.*, p. 55.

17 Sir Ivor Jennings, *The Approach to Self-Government*, London, 1956, p. 138.

18 Philip J. Foster, *Education and Social Change in Ghana*, London, 1965, p. 91.

19 L. Sonolet and A. Peres, *Moussa et Gli-gla: Histoire de deux petits Noirs*, Paris, 1919, cited in Buell, *The Native Problem*, II, pp. 62–3.

20 Albert Sarraut, *La Mise en valeur des colonies françaises*, Paris, 1923, p. 95.

21 Statement of Governor-General Jules Brévié, December 1935, cited in Mumford and Orde-Brown, *Africans Learn to be French*, p. 96.

22 Orr, *The Making of Northern Nigeria*, p. 266.

23 *Ibid.*, p. 266.

24 *The Times*, 5th January 1926.

25 *The Times*, 9th January 1924.

26 Advisory Committee on Native Education in the British Tropical African Dependencies, *Education Policy in British Tropical Africa*, London, 1925, p. 4.

27 Circular of 30th August 1910, cited in Terrier and Morey, *The Native Problem*, pp. 522–3.

28 *Circulaire du Gouverneur-Général*, 1st May 1924, cited in Buell, *op. cit.* II, p. 52.

29 Albert Charton, 'The Social Function of Education in French West Africa', in Mumford and Orde-Brown, *Africans Learn to be French*, p. 110–11.

30 No source given, cited by Charton in *ibid.*

31 Cited from *Sessional Paper No. VII* of the Gold Coast Legislative Council, 1920–1, by Kimble in *Ghana*, p. 106.

32 See *Report of the Select Committee of the Legislative Council on the African-isation of the Public Service*, Accra, 1950, and *Report of the Commission appointed by His Excellency the Governor to make recommendations about the recruitment and training of Nigerians for Senior Posts in the Government Service of Nigeria*, Lagos, 1948.

33 Cited in *The Times Educational Supplement*, 21st June 1924.

34 Perham, *Native Administration*, *op. cit.*, p. 361.

35 *Ibid.*, p. 361.

36 Sir Gordon Guggisberg's *The Gold Coast: A Review of Events of 1920–1926 and the Prospects of 1927–1928*, Accra, 1927, p. 254.

37 *The Times*, 15th June 1936.

38 Thompson and Adloff, *French West Africa*, p. 517.

39 See Bergo, 'L'Ecole William Ponty' in *Le Mali*, special number of *Europe–France–Outremer*, No. 368, July 1960, p. 23, where a full list of its distinguished graduates is printed.

40 See Vivian Jones, 'Pioneer of Northern Education', *Nigeria Magazine*, no. 73, June 1962, pp. 29–30.

41 See Michael Crowder, *The Story of Nigeria*, Revised Edition, London, 1966, p. 311.

42 S. F. Nadel, 'The Concept of Social Élites', *International Social Science Bulletin*, Paris, 1956, III, 3, p. 413, and Kimble, *Ghana*, pp. 136–41, where he discusses the whole question of the definition of the élite, especially with reference to the use of the term African middle-class. Kimble favours Nadel's definition.

43 Perham, *Native Administration*, p. 359.

44 Nadel, 'The Concept of Social Élites', p. 417.

45 See Richard L. Sklar and C. S. Whitaker, Jr., 'Nigeria', in *Political Parties and National Integration in Tropical Africa*, 1964, especially pp. 615–19.

46 *The Times Educational Supplement,* 21st June 1924.
47 Cited in Mumford and Orde-Brown, *Africans Learn to be French,* p. 88.
48 Cited in Coleman, *Nigeria,* footnote 33, p. 445.
49 Cited in *The Times,* 18th July 1939.
50 Bakary Traoré, *Forces Politiques,* p. 14.
51 See Coleman, *Nigeria,* pp. 116–19, and Kimble, *Ghana,* pp. 85–7.
52 Coleman, *ibid.,* p. 120.
53 David Hapgood, 'Sub-Saharan Education and Rural Development', in William H. Lewis, ed., *French-Speaking Africa: the Search for Identity,* New York, 1965, p. 122.
54 *Ibid.,* p. 123.
55 Cited from 'Review of Events of the last year' in *The Times Educational Supplement,* 21st February 1925.
56 Foster, *Education and Social Change in Ghana,* p. 88.
57 Hapgood, 'Sub-Saharan Education', p. 123.
58 *Sierra Leone Weekly News,* 22nd February 1908: reference kindly supplied by Dr. Davidson Nicol.
59 Fr. Lebret, et al., *Rapport Général sur les Perspectives et Développement du Sénégal,* I, pp. 1–5 (19), cited in Hapgood, 'Sub-Saharan Education', p. 124.
60 See for instance Margery Perham, *Native Administration in Nigeria,* p. 358, for an account of the alleged alienation of the élite from its background.
61 Brokensha, *Social Change in Larteh,* p. 261.
62 E. R. J. Hussey in C. K. Meek, W. M. Macmillan, E. R. J. Hussey, *Europe and West Africa,* London, 1940, p. 125.
63 *Ibid.,* p. 22.
64 J. B. Danquah, *Gold Coast: Akan Laws and Customs,* London, 1928. K. A. Busia, *The Position of the Chief in the Modern Political System of Ashanti,* London, 1951.
65 Chinua Achebe, *No Longer at Ease,* London, 1960.
66 Chinua Achebe, *Things Fall Apart,* London, 1958.
67 Margaret Read, *Education and Social Change in Tropical Areas,* London, 1955, pp. 105–11.
68 *Ibid.,* p. 110.

# 5 The Colonial European

The colonial situation involved not only the Africans but also the Europeans who came out to administer and exploit them. The middle-class Frenchmen or Englishman was suddenly projected into a social setting where he was an aristocrat both by birth and by income. A white skin was sufficient to set him off from the mass as a member of a privileged minority: his income, so vastly superior to that of all but a very few Africans, meant that he could also live as an aristocrat. Servants were cheap to hire, and a man who never had a servant in his house could now have several. Moreover, he could treat these servants as crypto-slaves, for in colonial society there were far fewer checks to the authoritarian temperament than at home. And if colonial society agreed on nothing else, it agreed that Africans were poor servants, and many a dinner-party has thrived conversationally on nothing more than an exchange of latest unhappy experiences with 'the boys'.[1]

It is essential to appreciate the fact that colonial society was a bourgeois one, acting out an aristocratic way of life abroad, and returning on leave to middle-class suburbs or country cottages in England and France. There were very few who came to the colonies who were aristocrats at home. Indeed it was difficult to recruit any but the indifferent for service in the unpopular posting of West Africa, which was slow to lose its reputation as the White Man's Grave. One reason the British did not recruit administrators by examination for West Africa was because it was thought it would be impossible to obtain sufficient candidates because of its unpopularity.[2]

The motives for joining the colonial service or a commercial company with African connexions were many, but recurring throughout was the desire for a freedom that did not exist in middle-class, industrialised France and Britain. Delavignette reports that those pupils who passed into the *École Nationale de la France d'Outre Mer* always replied to the question 'Why did you want to come here?' with answers that throbbed with the desire for freedom.[3] Robert Heussler tells of the legendary 'Rusty' Buckle in Nigeria who refused promotion in the administration, preferring to be 'sole lord of his inaccessible domain to serving in a more bureaucratic and less individualised post'.[4] When the Governor of Nigeria, Sir Arthur Richards, insisted that promotion to higher posts in the Nigerian Colonial Service would lie only through the Secretariats, some officials asked that it be recorded that they did not wish to be posted to them.[5]

In Africa, however, the European found liberty only if he was sent to a bush station where there were few if no other Europeans. And then it was a liberty with real disadvantages. Not everyone overcame the sense of solitude, the sense of deprivation, when mails were late or telecommunications broke down. In the administrative centres where there were more than three or four Europeans, and especially where there were wives, colonial society created its own hierarchy, albeit the hierarchy of an aristocracy, its own customs and codes. Because it was small, deviation from the norm was difficult. Suret-Canale records the observation on an official's dossier: 'Mixes with the natives. Even receives them at his table. Not cut out for colonial life.'[6]

The French were much more tolerant of their officials having relations with African women than the British. Indeed Dr. Barot in his *Guide Pratique de l'Européen dans l'Afrique Occidentale*, published in 1902, warned that Europeans without their own African women are poorly viewed by their soldiers, employees and domestics who jealously guard their own wives.[7] However, he decreed that Europeans should 'never use domestics for obtaining native women, for it is a role which implies necessities incompatible with good service'. This was of course written at the beginning of the twentieth century. But in 1934 Geoffrey Gorer observed that unmarried Frenchmen took as a matter of course a 'mousse', or young African girl, whose dowry they paid.[8]

Once wives had arrived on the scene in the healthier conditions of the late twenties and thirties, the bachelor, especially in British West Africa, had to be more cautious in his relations with African girls.[9] Some turned to sleeping with youths as more easy to conceal from suspicious and bored European women's eyes; others did so from inclination. Stanhope White tells of the time he and his Resident at Kano destroyed the file of the trial of a European trader for sodomy, a file which contained the trader's allegation that such activity was common among government officials. The man committed suicide after being sentenced to imprisonment.[10]

One activity which was indulged in without disapproval was excess drinking, though *The West African Pocketbook*, compiled by direction of the Secretary of State for the Colonies, warned in bold type: 'Heavy drinkers should not go to West Africa, moderate drinkers should be very moderate there, and total abstainers should remain so.'[11] Gorer, exaggerating of course, even said most Europeans in West Africa could be qualified as drunkards.[12]

Whether French or British, the 'colonial' saw Africa as a special society of which the African was a second-class, if not inherently inferior, member. 'That they had no sovereign rights in their own country', as Joyce Cary noted wryly in his *The Case for African Freedom*, 'was so much a matter of course to Europeans that no one threw any doubt upon it.'[13] Lord Lugard dismissed the question of equality between Europeans and Africans on the grounds that 'however true from a doctrinal point of view, [it] is apt to be misapplied by people in a low stage of development, and interpreted as an abolition of class distinction'.[14] Binger took a similar paternalist view: 'One must act with sweetness but firmness toward the African; one must never forget that nineteen centuries of civilisation separate us from their ignorance and that we must above all be for them educators and protectors.'[15]

The European separated himself physically from the African for health reasons, thus encouraging his mental isolation from him. In *Colonial West Africa* an instruction from the Liverpool School of Tropical Medicine advised: 'It is usually very dangerous, and often deadly, for Europeans to live or sleep in houses occupied, or recently occupied, by natives.'[16] The French tended to move the Africans out of the centre of the towns they occupied or built, the British to establish 'reservations' outside them. In Hill Station, the European reservation in Freetown, no African children were allowed, and each resident had to comply with the Government regulation that only one African sleep on their compound at night.[17] In both cases the colonials became isolated from any intimate contact with the African except through their servants. Thus a long service District Officer in Northern Nigeria could lament the death of his horse Njaro by saying, 'The Hereafter will be a poor place if Njaro, Kamkura and Garuba are not there to greet me on my arrival.' Kamkura and Garuba were his horse-boys.[18] One European sailing to Freetown with an administrator, a missionary and an educated African, wrote that the last wanted 'to fraternise with the European on board as he has done in the Inns of Court, in the hotels or the playing fields of England. But the European has left Britain behind. He is *en route* for Africa and the native of that continent must be kept in his place. . . . The administrator pays the African too little attention, the missionary too much.'[19] With such little contact with the African it is not surprising that European attitudes to them were very strange and had little relation to reality. The majority of Europeans considered the African degenerate, over-sexed, lazy, dirty and intellectually inferior, with no past achievements worth recording as such. For example, Crocker, a Nigerian administrator in the thirties, wrote, 'the first sensation of the European coming into contact with the African is that of smell'.[20] (An African had annotated the Rhodes House copy in the margin 'We feel you stink'.) Crocker again: '. . . the reproductive impulses are active enough among all peoples, but among none do they monopolise interests and energies to the degree they do among the African'.[21] By contrast most Africans are far too polite to comment on what they consider the very unpleasant smell of many Europeans. And one must remember that some Europeans still cling to the metropolitan habit of the weekly bath. So too is the African much more indulgent of the not infrequent sexual lapses or deviations of the European in the Tropics.

E. Beurdeley, of the French Ministry of Colonies, after a tour of West Africa 1913–14, wrote: 'Anyone who has lived for some time in contact with our natives and takes the trouble to observe them, rapidly begins to discover imperfections in them such as the following: they do not know how to appreciate the value of time any more than of distance; they are useless at all kinds of work demanding any appreciation of symmetry; they are incapable of laying out their fields in straight lines; incapable of laying a table cloth evenly on a table; of placing a carpet on the floor parallel to the walls.'[22] In similar vein the European lady in Freetown in the early 1950's deigned to make her own ice-cream for a dinner party because 'You just can't depend on these people at all. I find it's best to get on with things myself.'[23] More emphatic was the view of the Englishman with Gold Coast experience forty years earlier: 'A hereditary indolent subject.'[24]

The British administrators reacted violently to the educated African in a way his French counterpart did not. Even Sir Alan Burns, who was a popular Governor of the Gold Coast, admired by the élite, wrote: 'The African who gets a University degree is hailed by certain journals and individuals as a paragon of learning; the African who gets called to the Bar is referred to in such glowing terms that he might be pardoned for considering himself already an eminent lawyer. The demand that such men should be placed immediately in positions of trust and superiority shows a kind heart (and no doubt earns popularity) but generally argues lack of serious thought.'[25] He even cited Sir Harry Johnston with approval: 'When the youth arrives at puberty there is the tendency towards an arrested development of mind. At this critical period many bright and shining examples fall off into disappointing nullity. As might be imagined, the concentration of their thoughts on sexual intercourse is answerable for this falling away.' To which observation, made in 1897, Sir Alan in 1949 gave the seal of his own experience which 'forces me to agree with this evidence'.[26]

These ignorant and prejudiced observations, without foundation in fact, can be culled *ad nauseam* from colonial writings. They were unfortunately held widely, even by a missionary like Walter Miller who wrote of what he described as 'the mental dishonesty, habitual deceit and apparently ineradicable lying' of the Hausa whom he sought to convert.[27] The educated African being the particular victim of these kind of attacks, it is little wonder that a sense of inferiority was inculcated in him, for he had to live in a society in which the most slatternly European considered herself inalienably superior to him, and in which his defects were the subject of daily conversation. As Richard Oakley, a Nigerian District Officer, wrote in 1938, 'It is this sense of inferiority, so constantly thrown in their faces by unthinking Europeans, that leads to resentment, attempts at self-assertion and agitation among those who have been educated on Western lines...'[28] The constant proclamation of European superiority produced what Sékou Touré has called 'la mentalité coloniale', that is a belief, even among educated Africans, resulting from absorption of this barrage of propaganda, that perhaps the Europeans were right.

For the British the educated African was a gaudy, despised imitator of European ways. For them the 'real' African was the peasant or the traditional chief who, unlike the educated African, did not challenge their supremacy. Thus Guggisberg, in urging the Paramount Chiefs of the Gold Coast to open their councils to the educated Africans, actually said in Legislative Council that he would watch with interest to see, if they did, 'how far the members of the great professions in this country are going to throw in their lot with the real [*sic*] people, that is the people who are ruled by Native Rulers of the country with their State Councils'.[29] The 'real' African had no ambition to enter the world of the British. His reality was of course a chimera.

In the colonial situation, then, the European insisted on bolstering up his new aristocracy by a declaration of inalienable superiority, which made it a closed aristocracy like that of France before the Revolution.

The French, however, were less closed in their aristocracy than the British. More Africans were admitted to positions of actual equality with the French than ever with the British before the Second World War. Francis Rodd commented in an article on French West Africa in *The Times* of 1928 'the British administrator calls his term of service in West Africa "tour", the French refer to theirs as *séjour*. The difference is inherent: it means that we visit the natives as strangers, they live among them as permanent rulers and are of them.'[30]

W. E. Dubois after a visit to Dakar wrote, 'there is nothing here in French West Africa like the open race repulsion, the studied separation that one sees in British West Africa . . . Black France is the most hopeful meeting place of black and white in the world'.[31] This, coming from the pen of the great American Negro Panafricanist, was praise indeed, though much exaggerated if we are to believe Geoffrey Gorer's account of the situation a decade later.[32] Nevertheless it is true to say that the French, while many believed the myths about the Negro, and were as paternalist as the British, had easier personal relations with the educated African. These were, however, always relations of extreme formality, governed by almost excessive politeness. Few Frenchmen ever asked Africans into their homes, either in the inter-war years, or during the years of de-colonisation.[33] And we must remember that the majority of French Africans were anyway *sujets* and therefore legally completely subordinate to the French.

But whether French or British, the white man, though numerically a minority, formed a sociological majority in the African colonies.[34] The maintenance of his domination and prestige in this society in relation to the greater mass of Africans depended on his society being a closed and unattainable one,[35] in which its members proclaimed constantly superiority of pigmentation. This contemptuous superiority produced at first an African élite of Uncle Toms, who were only too grateful for any mark of recognition by this aristocracy of pigmentation. But a later generation succeeded, determined not only to prove their human, but also their racial and cultural, equality with the European. Above all they demanded the right to govern themselves, a right the European with no moral justification had alienated from him. This generation élite was the crisis generation of colonial rule, the bridge between acceptance and rejection, the inspirers of African independence.

# Notes

1 For a hilarious and very perceptive account from the steward's point of view, see Ferdinand Oyono, *Houseboy*, London, 1966.
2 Richard Symonds, *The British and their Successors*, London, 1966, p. 127.
3 Robert Delavignette, *Freedom and Authority in French West Africa*, London, 1950, p. 28.
4 Robert Heussler, *Yesterday's Rulers*, London.
5 White, *Dan Bana*, p. 199.
6 Suret-Canale, *Afrique Noire II*, p. 401.
7 Dr. Barot, *Guide pratique de l'européen dans l'Afrique occidentale*, Paris, 1902, p. 329, and *Ibid.*, p. 325.
8 Geoffrey Gorer, *Africa Dances*, London, 1936, p. 107.
9 See the correspondence in *West Africa*, January 1926, on 'European Wives in West Africa' and the editor's comment: '. . . we must urge most earnestly that whenever it is at all possible the wives of married Europeans working at the Coast should accompany their husbands; and we regard the creation of the people neither European nor African as the supreme racial disloyalty.'
10 White, *Dan Bana*, pp. 166–7.
11 *The West African Pocketbook—A Guide to newly appointed Government Officers*, 2nd Edition, London, 1906.
12 Gorer, *Africa Dances*, p. 130.
13 Joyce Cary, *The Case for African Freedom and other writings on Africa*, Austin, Texas, 1964, p. 15.
14 *Annual Report for Northern Nigeria*, cited in Orr, *The Making of Northern Nigeria*, p. 263.
15 Introduction by Binger to Barot, *Guide Pratique*, p. ix. I am grateful to Mrs. Rita Cruise O'Brien for drawing my attention to the quotations from Barot's book.
16 *Colonial West Africa*, published by *The African World*, London, 1925, p. 121.
17 H. Osman Newland, *Sierra Leone: Its People, Products and Secret Societies*, London, 1916, p. 20.
18 White, *Dan Bana*, p. 58.
19 Newland, *Sierra Leone*, p. 4.
20 W. E. Crocker, *Nigeria—A Critique of Colonial Administration*, London, 1936, p. 202.
21 *Ibid.*, p. 203.
22 E. Beurdeley, *La Justice indigène en Afrique Occidentale Française: Mission d'Etudes*, 1913–14, Paris, 1916, p. 36.
23 Pearce Gervis, *Sierra Leone Story*, London, 1952, p. 16.
24 Louis P. Bowler, *Gold Coast Palaver*, London, 1911, p. 50.
25 Sir Alan Burns, *Colonial Civil Servant*, London, 1949, pp. 68–9.
26 Sir Alan Burns, *Colour Prejudice*, London, 1948, p. 104.

27 Walter Miller, *Yesterday and Tomorrow in Northern Nigeria*, London, 1938, cited in Burns, *Colour Prejudice*.
28 Richard Oakley, *Treks and Palavers*, London, 1938, p. 41.
29 R. E. Wraith, *Guggisberg*, London, 1967, pp. 455–6.
30 *The Times*, 11th July 1928.
31 W. E. Dubois, 'France's Black Citizens in West Africa', *Current History*, 21, No. 4, July 1925, p. 561 and p. 564.
32 Gorer, *Africa Dances*.
33 Mrs. Rita Cruise O'Brien has made a detailed study of the Europeans in Dakar which confirms this. See also my *Senegal: A Study in French Assimilation Policy* (Revised Edition), London, 1967, pp. 81–95.
34 Balandier, *Sociologie actuelle de l'Afrique noire*, pp. 16–17.
35 *Ibid.*, p. 19.

2D

*Part VII*
The beginnings of modern African politics

# 1 The origins of protest

## 1 The nature of early West African politics

By the time of the Pan African Congress in Paris in 1919 and the
National Congress of British West Africa in Accra in 1920, there
had grown up a small but articulate body of Africans which openly
criticised the administrative and economic régime imposed on it
by the colonial powers. This body consisted primarily of the Western-
educated élite which had its origins in the missionary schools
established in pre-colonial times. But it did, particularly in the Gold
Coast, have the support of certain chiefs and others who had not
come under strong Western influences. The ambition of its members
was not to re-establish their pre-colonial independence, but to obtain
representation in, and some control of, the machinery of government of the colonies in which they found themselves. They accepted
the new colonial frontiers as constituting their countries, and did not,
like the traditional nationalists, demand a return to the pre-colonial
status quo. They were the first to identify themselves as Nigerians
rather than Yoruba, Gold Coasters rather than Fanti, Senegalese
rather than Wollof. Their education, basically Western in conception, left them well versed in European history and politics,
and they justified their demands for participation in government and
for economic reforms by appealing to European ideals and experience. In 1931 Dr. F. U. Nanka-Bruce, member of the Gold Coast
Legislative Council for Accra, opposed the introduction of direct
taxation in terms reminiscent of the American Revolution:

'In every country where direct taxation is imposed there must be equal representation. I will only put the proposition: is the government prepared to give the colony full representation and is the government prepared to give control of our finances to the people of this country? If not, it is better that we remain where we are and try to balance our budget in some other way.'[1]

Though the chief distinguishing feature of this group was its Western education, it was certainly not divorced from traditional Africa. Even the Creoles of Sierra Leone, usually referred to contemptuously by their colonial masters as Black Englishmen, despite their respectable middle-class Victorian exterior retained many more links with traditional Africa than even they cared to admit.[2] A very large proportion of the members of the Gold Coast section of the National Congress of British West Africa was connected with the traditional ruling élite.[3] Blaise Diagne in his 1914 campaign for the deputyship of Senegal gained financial support from the important Mouride sect of Muslims.[4] And though the language of Western democratic ideals was the easiest for their colonial opponents to understand, the élite also looked to pre-colonial Africa for justifications for their demands. Thomas Hutton-Mills in his presidential address to the National Congress of British West Africa delegates meeting in Accra stressed:

'. . . It is important to note that each one of these Delegates is an *African* belonging to a *Distinctive African Family* and thereby commanding the right of property and other interests either in his own right or in the right of the family to which he belongs. It follows from this that apart from the fact of the Delegates to the Conference being the natural leaders of the people of their several communities they have in themselves the right to appeal to His Majesty's Government for each constitutional reform as in their judgment are necessary.'[5]

The importance of the influence of European culture and status on the thought and activities of these leaders is too often emphasised to the exclusion of traditional African culture and status, as LaRay Denzer has pointed out.[6]

This educated élite, because of its demands for a greater share in the governmental process, because of its identification of the colonies within which it lived as the 'nation' to which it belonged and owed loyalty, has often been described as nationalist. Yet in British West Africa demands for full independence were not articulated until the return of Azikiwe and Nkrumah from America, that is, effectively, not until the Second World War. In French West Africa no major politician publicly voiced the demand for it until 1958.[7] Indeed, the declaration of Blaise Diagne, the first purely African deputy for Senegal, to the Chamber of Deputies in 1927 was to be typical of the attitude of French African deputies for the next thirty years: 'I, who am of [African] origin, will never accept that you should tell us that the end of French colonisation should be for us an independence in which we would be our sole masters. And for whose profit? For the profit of the first-comer, precisely because we should be ill-prepared to look after ourselves.'[8]

If we accept that a nationalist, as defined by the *Shorter Oxford English Dictionary*, is one who pursues 'a policy of national independence' then the politicians of the inter-war years were not strictly speaking nationalists. Students of African nationalism such as Hodgkin and Kimble prefer a broader definition of nationalism. Thus Hodgkin considers it as covering 'any organisation or group that explicitly asserts the rights, claims and aspirations of a given African society (from the level of the language group to that of Pan Africa) in opposition to European authority, whatever its institutional form and objectives'.[9] Yet this seems to be casting the net too wide, and one agrees with Balandier, whom Hodgkin quotes, that it is 'a kind of misuse of language' to consider as expressions of nationalism 'any form of organisation, however rudimentary, which escapes from the control of the dominant Powers, any protest against a situation of political inferiority, any movement stimulated by local policies of racial discrimination'.[10] Apart from this, it is useful to distinguish that phase of African politics which demanded only an increasing share in the political process and fairer deals for the African, from that phase which actually demanded that the political process be handed over in its entirety to Africans. The first phase can be described as proto-nationalist; the second phase as truly nationalist. In both British and French West Africa the politicians of the inter-war period were by this definition almost exclusively proto-nationalist. After the Second World War in British West Africa the political scene was dominated by true nationalists; but in French West Africa, the political leaders were still proto-nationalists since they did not demand independence from France, but an increasing share in government. This accepted, the rise of nationalism in West Africa cannot be understood except in the context of the broad panorama of activities and reactions which Kimble designates as contributory to the growth of nationalism. These cover opposition to foreign control; the growth in consciousness of belonging to a particular nation, to Africa, or to the Negro race generally; pride in the history, culture and traditional institutions of one's country; the awareness of common political rights and responsibilities; the demand for self-government; and especially all forms of persuasion, agitation and concerted action through which such sentiments are expressed or encouraged.[11]

In French West Africa before 1944 political activity of any sort except in the *Quatre Communes* of Senegal, where representation at the local, colonial and metropolitan level had existed since the 1870's, was made almost impossible by the existence of the *indigénat*. Under this any African who criticised or led campaigns against the administration could be summarily tried and imprisoned. In British West Africa the colonial authorities were more liberal, and Africans did and could voice protest against their colonial governments. Africans were nominated to the Legislative Councils before World War I, and afterwards provision was made for elected representation in Nigeria (1923), Sierra Leone (1924), and Gold Coast (1925), but not in the Gambia until 1946. Before 1920 political activity had been somewhat disjointed, except in Senegal, where Blaise Diagne formed a political party and won the election to the Deputyship against the hitherto dominant mulatto and French interests, and in the Gold Coast where the Aborigines Rights Protection Society had proved a highly efficient organisation, drawing support from both educated and traditional élites for protest against administrative injustices. Growing demands for participation in the colonial government and increasing discontent with the colonial economic régime found its earliest outlet in the National Congress of British West Africa. This marked the prelude to twenty years of political activity in which constitutional opposition was the order of the day.

In Senegal, the only territory in French West Africa where political activity was permitted, Blaise Diagne and his successors also worked within the constitutional limitations imposed on them by the French.

## 2 Extra-African influences

Political activity in the inter-war years was to be influenced by movements among Negroes of the New World. The most famous of these were the Pan African Congresses of W. E. DuBois and Marcus Garvey's Back to Africa scheme. The range and extent of these influences on African politicians were very wide, as George Shepperson has shown;[12] but they have also been exaggerated.

Pan-Africanism has now become one of the most important motive forces in African politics. But the Pan-Africanism of the

1920's was a vague emotional idea which had much greater impact in the New World than Africa. Indeed the idea of a politically united Africa was never actually formulated even at the 1945 Manchester Congress. The Congresses were Pan-African not because they conceived of a politically united Africa, but because they tried to bring together Negroes from Africa and Negroes who had been forcibly removed from Africa in the days of the slave trade to demand a fairer deal from the white men who now dominated their lives. Not until the 1945 Congress was a demand for 'complete and absolute independence' made for the African colonies. And that Congress, as far as political Pan-Africanism is concerned, only went as far as to resolve 'that the artificial divisions and territorial boundaries created by the Imperialist Powers are deliberate steps to obstruct the political unity of the West African peoples'.[13] The Pan African Congresses of the inter-war years echoed the demands of political leaders in West Africa by asking only for progressive participation of the African in his government.[14]

The first Pan African Congress was held in London in 1900 on the initiative of H. Sylvester Williams, the Trinidad barrister. West Africa had only just been subjected to white rule. American Negroes and West Indians, on the other hand, had experienced several centuries of treatment as an inferior race. The Congress was the reaction of only a small section of their educated élite, the majority of whom followed Booker T. Washington and his ideas on educational self help. It was this small section of New World Negroes which was the inspiration of this and the four Pan African Congresses of the 1920's. These Congresses, held in 1919, 1921, 1923 and 1927, called for black solidarity and the rejection of the inferior status imposed on them by the white race. They urged the Negro to take pride in the colour of his skin. They insisted that the Negro had a history and culture of equal value to those of the white before the latter destroyed them. For the West Indian and American Negro, Africa became the spiritual haven where he could salve the wounds inflicted by the white man on his pride.

The 1900 Pan African Congress, as far as the composition of its delegates was concerned, reflected the essentially extra-African inspiration of the movement. The delegates, although three were from West Africa, were mostly British West Indian Negroes. The Congress resolutions were concerned with pointing out the increasing displacement of qualified coloured colonial citizens from positions of responsibility. Thus the Trinidadian lawyer, R. E. Phipps, complained, as the West African press was also at the time complaining, that coloured civil servants were only given the lowest positions where their actions were entirely under the control of white superiors.[15] It was at this meeting that W. E. B. DuBois, then unknown and just beginning his career, made his oft-quoted prediction: 'The problem of the Twentieth Century is the problem of the Colour line.' The Congress did not demand independence for the newly established European colonies, but only more proportionate African participation in social, political, and economic matters. The Pan African movement's only impact on West Africa was made at the end of the 1914–18 War, when DuBois gave it new life by calling a Congress in Paris to draw up resolutions to send to the Paris Peace Conference. He was as much concerned with securing justice for American Negroes, 100,000 of whom had fought in France, as for Africans. DuBois had difficulty at first in gaining permission to hold the Congress in Paris, especially as France was still under martial law. He was however fortunate to enlist the support of the now prestigious Blaise Diagne, 'the ace that I have up my sleeve' as he put it.[16] Diagne gained permission for the Congress to be held from his friend Clemenceau, who said, 'Don't advertise it, but go ahead.'[17] It was Diagne who through his connections was able to foil attempts by President Woodrow Wilson to stop the congress being held.[18]

The Congress when it did meet was far from adventurous in its resolutions. The farthest delegates went was to state: 'The natives of Africa must have the right to participate in the Government as fast as their development permits, in conformity with the principle that Government exists for the natives, and not the natives for the Government. They shall at once be allowed to participate in local and tribal government, according to ancient usage, and this participation shall gradually extend, as education and experience proceed, to the higher offices of states; to the end that, in time, Africa is ruled by consent of the Africans. . . .'[19] In short this was reflecting the whole debate of self-determination of nations, but changing it to meet the colonial situation.

The moderate tenor of the Congress was partly due to Blaise Diagne, who was by now identifying himself with the French Government. He later told Garvey, 'We French natives wish to remain French, since France has given us every liberty.'[20] But it also reflected the moderate temper of the New World Negro élite which sponsored the Congress. DuBois did not become a radical until the thirties.

However Diagne was to prove at the next Congress in 1921 that he was far too moderate for the rest of the delegates. At the Paris session he declared, 'I am a Frenchman first and a Negro afterwards.'[21] They felt he had betrayed the cause by forcing on them a weak resolution on Belgium's colonial policy. Jessé Fausset in her *Impressions* of the Congress lamented that 'Diagne on account of his high position in the French Government had undoubtedly felt called on to assure the Belgian Government that no "radical" step would be taken by the Congress. He sponsored therefore a mild resolution . . . that Negroes were "susceptible" of education and pledging the co-operation of the Pan African Congress with the international movement in Belgium.'[22] After this Diagne broke with the movement and the 1923 meetings in London and Lisbon almost deteriorated into sight-seeing tours, while the 1927 meeting in New York was reduced to seeking support from various Ladies Auxiliaries of important New York Negro Churches. West Africans who attended these meetings did so only because they happened to be in the cities where they were being held at the time. Indeed no English-speaking West African leader of importance attended any of the meetings until the Manchester Congress of 1945. Diagne was the only leader of importance from French West Africa to attend the Conference.

The Pan African Congresses received little coverage in the British West African Press. The 1919 meeting was noted in passing with a brief statement that if British West Africans would not unite and form their own meeting complete with resolutions such as the National Congress of British West Africa, which was in the planning stage in 1918 before DuBois conceived his own meeting, they had only themselves to blame if the colonial powers took the Pan African Congress seriously and made decisions as a result of its misinformed resolutions. The 1921 Congress was denounced by the Gold Coast Press and Garvey's movement was held up as a much more reasonable one.[23] The *Gold Coast Independent* of 1st October 1921, for example, issued the following warning: 'The lesson is obvious. World interests and world politics have so contracted that there is no standing still, no looking back. We must be up and doing or going under. In plain words, if we don't think and act and make representations, others will do all three for us; and if any of our interests are compromised it will be no fault but ours. West Africans will do well to remember that to most of our Afro-American and West Indian friends we are still in the backwoods of civilisation— unlettered, untutored, very much requiring articulation through our brethren on the other side of the Atlantic. And it is perfectly natural, this innocent assumption. They know no better. They have no means of judging. It is for us to enlighten them, to make them realise that nationhood has dawned on the West African horizon, and that we mean to take our free, independent place in the great imperial chain.'[24]

As the Gold Coast Press of the day indicates, African politicians were much more taken with the ideas of Marcus Garvey and his Universal Negro Improvement Association than with the Pan African Congresses.

Marcus Garvey was a Jamaican immigrant to New York, who in 1917 founded the New York division of his Universal Negro Improvement Association (U.N.I.A.), first established by him in Jamaica in 1914. By 1920 it had become a mass movement of spectacular size, even for the United States. In August of that year he told an enormous convention of the Association in Harlem: 'If Europe is for the Europeans, then Africa shall be for the black peoples of the world. . . . The other races have countries of their own and it is time for the 400,000,000 Negroes to claim Africa for themselves.'[25] Later that month, at Carnegie Hall, he declared: 'The Negroes of the world say we are striking homewards towards Africa to make her a big black republic . . . we are coming 400,000,000 strong and we mean to take every square inch of the 12,000,000 square miles of African territory belonging to us by right divine . . . we are out to get what has belonged to us politically, socially, economically, and in every way. And what 15,000,000 of us cannot get we will call 400,000,000 to help us get.'[26]

Garvey's Back to Africa movement, his cry 'Africa for the Africans', his militant call to arms stirred hearts even in remote Northern Nigeria. Joyce Cary recalls that at the time, when he was a District Officer in the North, a horse-boy was arrested by the local Emir and sent to him on a charge of sedition. 'He had been telling the local pagans, wild islanders, that a black king was coming, with a great iron ship full of black soldiers, to drive all the whites out of Africa.'[27] The élite was impressed by Garvey's plans for Negro commerce, for it was they who had been edged out of their entrepreneurial role by the European monopolies and the Lebanese, and the National Congress resolution on commerce called for commercial connections between British West Africans and Garvey's Black Star Line.

As a movement the U.N.I.A. was a failure. Liberia, where he planned to resettle his Negro compatriots, refused to allow him land on which to establish a colony. He lacked assistance from the American Negro educated élite, who were indeed venomously hostile to him. The Black Star Line founded by Garvey who had been proclaimed Provisional President of Africa by the 1920 Convention was designed to open up trade between American and African Negroes. Chaotic administration of funds led to the arrest of Garvey and his imprisonment on a charge of using the mails to defraud. Despite the failure of his movement, its militant demands were to be an inspiration for later African leaders, in particular Nkrumah. As it was the much less successful Pan African Congresses more closely reflected the élitist politics of the inter-war period.

Garvey however did not only influence later mass politicians. Casely-Hayford was to write in his *The Disabilities of Black Folk* that Garvey's movement had done more than any other to focus world attention on Africa's problems.[28] Branches of the U.N.I.A. were founded in Lagos under Patriarch J. G. Campbell, leader of one of the Christian separatist Churches, and Reverends Abiodun and Euba.[29] In the Gold Coast there was a branch formed, but there is very little information concerning it, for the Colonial authorities, who had already demonstrated their hostility to the Back to Africa movement of Chief Alfred Sam in 1914 by tightening up their immigration regulations to keep out 'undesirable' American Negroes,[30] closed its offices and impounded its papers. Even Aggrey, according to his biographer, was the object of suspicion from the Gold Coast C.I.D. for alleged sympathies with Garvey, which seems rather odd in the context of Aggrey's famous statement about the harmony of the black and white keys.[31]

Colonial authorities elsewhere were worried by Garvey's impact. For instance, at a dinner given in honour of President King of Liberia, who had violently opposed Garvey's pretensions and in particular his intention of settling American Negroes in his country, the Governor of Sierra Leone said: 'Lastly, may I say how warmly we in Sierra Leone appreciated your courage and applauded your statesmanship in taking such prompt and vigorous steps to show that Liberia would have nothing to do with any movement having as its avowed object the fomenting of racial feeling of hatred and ill-will. Your Excellency, by slamming the door on spurious patriots from across the Atlantic, men who sought to make Liberia a focus for racial animosity in this Continent, deservedly earn the gratitude not only of every West African Government but of all who have the true welfare of the African at heart.'[32]

Even if Garvey's movement failed, 'his massive propaganda for pride, not shame, in a black skin left an ineradicable mark on African nationalism everywhere, all the criticisms which were made of him by men of his own colour notwithstanding'.[33]

## 3 The Senegal election of 1914

Until well after the Second World War, no African politician attained as high a status within the constitutional frameworks laid down by the colonial governments as Blaise Diagne. In 1914 he was elected Deputy for the *Quatre Communes* of Senegal in the French Chamber of Deputies. By 1918 he had become Commissioner of the Republic for the Recruitment of African Troops with the rank of Governor-General.[34] He even became Under-Secretary of State for the Colonies in 1931, and President of the Chamber's Commission on Colonies.

Senegal had been given a representative institution as early as 1848, when the 'citizens' of St. Louis and Gorée were allowed to elect a Deputy to the French Chamber. This liberal innovation of the Third Republic was abolished by the Second Empire in 1852, and restored by the Third Republic in 1871. A *Conseil-Général*, similar to those of the *départements* of France, was established for the Communes of St. Louis and Gorée in 1879.* In 1872 St. Louis and Gorée were given elected Municipal Councils, which privilege was extended to Rufisque in 1880, and Dakar in 1887, when it was separated administratively from Gorée.

During the nineteenth century these institutions were dominated by French interests despite the presence of a majority of African voters. In 1901 Pierre Mille, a well-known writer on Colonial Affairs, described Senegal as a 'rotten borough' in which Europeans bought up the African votes.[35] Sacks of rice and five-franc pieces flowed freely from the hands of the dominant European commercial community, the Bordeaux merchants, whose pre-eminence was challenged at the turn of the century by the Senegalese *métis*. Members of this group, part-European and part-African in origin, had attained considerable wealth. At first employed as auxiliaries of the Bordeaux merchants, they started trading on their own account and by 1900, one *métis* family, the Devès, had over 300 people in its employment.[36] In 1902, no longer content to take a back seat in managing elections for the Bordeaux firms, they made a successful bid for power. François Carpot, a *métis*, was elected Deputy, and his brother, soon after, President of the Conseil-Général.[37] Carpot was in fact the second *métis* Deputy, the first being Durand-Valentin who sat for two years from 1848–50.

Until 1919 Senegalese politics were dominated by the *métis*. Like

* A *Conseil-Général* had originally been provided for in 1840.

the Bordeaux merchants before them, they were essentially French in outlook, and the Africans were only incidental to their politics as the source of supply of 90% of the votes. However, in 1914 their position was successfully challenged by Blaise Diagne when he defeated eight other candidates, French and *métis*, to become the first Deputy of full African blood. By 1919 Diagne had captured all the most important posts in the representative institutions for the Africans. Diagne's election was of more than symbolic importance: it marked the first time that the Senegalese voters realised that you could do more with a ballot paper than sell it to the highest bidder.

Diagne returned to Senegal after nearly twenty years abroad when there was a great deal of unrest among the electors of the *Quatre Communes*. He, himself, was a disgruntled man who in his service as an officer in the French Colonial Customs Service had frequently quarrelled with his French superiors. Well-educated—he passed out first in his class from the Secondary School at St. Louis—he had travelled widely in the French empire. Never allowed to stay long in any one post because of his readiness 'to defend persecuted comrades or egalitarian ideas',[38] he had seen service in Dahomey, French Congo, Gabon, Réunion, Madagascar and French Guiana. He was very conscious of his colour, particularly after his marriage in 1909 to a French woman. He was 'hypersensitive to the slightest criticism or opinion of Negroes, and gave the impression of a rebellious young man bent on commanding respect from his superiors'.[39]

In Paris in 1913, on leave from Guiana from which he had nearly been expelled for his hostility towards the French merchants, he made speeches and wrote articles about French Colonial Policy. Towards the end of the year he sounded out the possibilities of his being elected Deputy. Though the information sent back was pessimistic he decided to stand, and returned in February.

In Senegal, Diagne, a tall imposing figure, and an eloquent speaker, though rusty in his native Wollof after a long absence, brought new life to Senegalese politics. By welding together the forces of discontent he introduced real issues into the election. He gained the support of an incipient political party, the Young Senegalese, a political forum which had originated from a cultural club called the Aurora, founded in St. Louis in 1910 by young Senegalese clerks and teachers. This group was particularly disgruntled at the differences in benefits gained by Frenchmen of the same grade and the monopolisation of scholarships for further education in France by the *métis*. Its members were to provide articulate and enthusiastic support for Diagne's campaign, especially since they had financial interest in a newspaper, *La Démocratie*, which also gave Diagne its support.[40] Diagne's chief ally in the Young Senegalese was Mody M'Baye, a citizen from St. Louis who had spent most of his time in the protectorate, first as a teacher, then, after his dismissal for insubordination, as a champion of those who had suffered injustices at the hands of the administration. M'Baye was violently anti-French and anti-*métis*, and injected a strong element of racism into a campaign in which the dominant issue became Africans versus the whites and their *métis* allies. A Wollof song current during the campaign was 'If Blaise orders it, we will kill all the whites'; and Carpot, the *métis*, could not believe his ears when he was howled at by a mob of Diagne's supporters.[41]

Another group strongly hostile to the French was the indigenous Lebou inhabitants of Dakar, who had had much of their land expropriated by the French for what they considered unfair compensation. This group was very chauvinistic, resenting the immigration of other ethnic groups to their land, and resistant of French assimilation. Nevertheless Diagne, a Serer by origin, was able to gain the support of their traditional leaders, who controlled the majority of votes in Dakar and neighbouring Rufisque, and who hoped he would secure the return of some of their lost lands.

A major problem for Diagne was finance for his campaign. His leading opponents were of course representatives of rich merchants. Here he was able to use the discontent of the wealthy Mouride community (see pp. 360–361) which still suffered oppression from the administration. Their leader, Amadou Bamba, was no longer in exile, but he was still under house arrest and the French were suspicious of the immense power he had over his growing community. Though they were not electors, the Mourides gave Diagne considerable financial support in the hopes that as Deputy he would be able to protect them from French administrative oppression.

One major issue united all the citizens: the attempt, partially successful, by the French administration to deprive them of their rights. The French had for some years questioned the propriety of citizenship being held by people the majority of whom were illiterate in French, Muslim and often polygamous. Some were fearful of the dangers of a 'native electorate'. Thus in the 1880's *Le Reveil* of St. Louis wrote that the three greatest dangers of the colony were 'yellow fever, clericalism and the native electorate' and warned that if the Africans were allowed to vote 'from conquerors, we will become, we French, we masters of the country by right of conquest and civilisation, . . . humble subjects and tomorrow's slaves'.[42] In 1908 the Lieutenant-Governor had tried to have 1,563 voters struck off the electoral roll on the grounds that since they had not been naturalised as French citizens they could not vote and were not in fact citizens. The Court of Cassation in Paris upheld the view that those concerned were not French citizens but confirmed that they had the right to vote. This meant that the non-naturalised citizens, the *originaires* of the *Quatre Communes*, were, apart from their voting rights, not citizens. If they went to the Protectorate they would be subject to the hated *indigènat*. Also those born to citizen parents outside the *Quatre Communes* would not be considered as eligible to vote. This affected Lamine Guèye, the first Senegalese advocate, born of *originaire* parents in Sudan, who summed up the horror of the citizens at being subjected to the *indigènat*: 'Our fears were more than justified by the spectacle of what happened in the interior of the Colony, where administrators, reviving in certain respects feudal practices, imposed upon the persons of our compatriots of the protectorate acts which are neither human nor French.'[43] Carpot, the *métis* incumbent of the Deputyship, had done nothing to protect their rights, and this accounts in large part for his failure in the 1914 campaign. In 1911 a number of *originaires* doing their military service in metropolitan units of the army in West Africa, and serving under the same conditions as Frenchmen, were discharged. Diagne therefore campaigned for a law for obligatory military service for those living in the *Quatre Communes* without distinction of race or colour. In return he would ensure that the rights of the *originaires* as citizens would be confirmed. To a St. Louis rally he declared, 'They say that you aren't French and that I'm not French. I tell you that we are, that we have the same rights.'[44]

Diagne's was a very sophisticated campaign raising a large number of issues, as Wesley Johnson's admirable and pioneering article on the 1914 election has shown. Thus 'Diagne favoured stopping Senegal's contribution to the federation of French West Africa's budget, since this drained the local treasury; he wanted to create a Colonial Council empowered to vote the budget for the entire group of colonies (which anticipated the *Grand Conseil* of French West Africa created after World War II); finally, he thought the head tax should be abolished, especially in the Four Communes. He drew analogies with the West Indian colonies, which had no such burdens. His experience in travelling the empire reinforced the sophistication of his analogy and argument. He pressed for the

2E

establishment of a medical school in Dakar, patterned after those in Madagascar and Indo-China. He favoured such advanced social legislation as payments for expectant mothers, pensions for older workers, weekly sabbatical rest laws, and the right to organise labour unions. He favoured compensating the Lebou people for their lost lands. He drew from his personal experience and argued that customs should be re-scheduled to favour the small rather than the large businessman. He charged that Bordeaux got special treatment and that . . . those sharks and their agents are bewildered to think the natives will now freely use their votes, and will be joined by many French workers'.[45]

Diagne got the largest number of votes in the election, partly due to the fact that for the first time the secret ballot was being used. But he did not get over the 50% required to secure him the Deputyship. On the second ballot on 10th May he beat his European rival by 175 votes, and Carpot, the incumbent, by 1,942.[46] Diagne kept his promise to his electors and by the Law of 29th September 1916 gained from the French Government the confirmation that 'the natives of the *communes de plein exercice* of Senegal are and remain French citizens subject to military service as provided for by the law of 15th October 1915'. Using France's need for troops in the War, Diagne had been able to extract this at the price of obligatory military service for his voters.

He told the Minister of War in a debate in the Chamber: 'That group which sent me to this Chamber has the right to consider that the mandate which has been given me will not be complete except on condition that you place this group in the same situation as that group of the population which sent you to Parliament. . . . The question is this: if we can be here to legislate, it is because we are French citizens; and, if we are such, we demand the right to serve in the same quality as all French citizens.'[47]

The law was popular with the *originaires* for it secured them the rights of citizens, that is the opening up for them of a full-scale assimilation policy which for the most part they desired. In 1911, even before Diagne was elected, the Conseil-Général had asked through one of its Commissions that voters, without distinction of colour, be called upon to perform obligatory military service.[48] And the 1919 election, which he won by 7,444 votes against Carpot's 1,252, showed clearly the extent of his popularity.

Blaise Diagne had come to power on a radical platform, but one which differed very greatly from that of his English-speaking contemporaries. Whereas they sought increasing autonomy and recognition of the uniqueness of the African situation, he and his supporters, and indeed his opponents, were in the twenties to seek assimilation into the French system. Diagne was to be criticised by his opponents in the twenties not because he was too pro-French, though nationalist students in Paris were indeed critical of the pro-French character of the Pan African Congresses over which Diagne presided,[49] but because his demands for the fruits of assimilation were tempered by personal considerations from the administration and the Bordeaux merchants. (See p. 435.)

## 4 Early protest movements in British West Africa

As a milestone in the political history of English-speaking West Africa the National Congress of British West Africa, which held its first meeting in 1920 at Accra, was of equal significance to the 1914 Senegal election to French West Africa. It brought together delegates from the four British West African colonies and consolidated grievances independently expressed through the agency of diverse organisations into a single petition. It also projected the idea of a West African nationality, albeit an English-speaking one, which would be fostered through the creation of a West African University. It also envisioned the establishment of a West African Dominion, which like Canada, Australia or India could make its voice felt in the Councils of the World, as these three had done at the Peace Conference of 1919. The National Congress of British West Africa was essentially the creation of the educated Africans of the West Coast towns. Some of this élite, mainly among the Nigerians, had grandparents who had been settled in Sierra Leone as liberated Africans during the days of the Anti-Slavery Squadron and who had subsequently emigrated back to their homeland. Many had attended Fourah Bay College for their Higher Education and formed an old-boy network up and down the coast. These contacts were cemented by the regular exchange of news through the lively press which the élite had established by the turn of the century. Sierra Leone papers were read in the Gold Coast and vice versa.

The West Coast élite was far from being divorced from the chiefs and people they claimed to represent. Many were related to royal houses; in disputes between the administration and a chief, they were quick to give their aid and advice to the latter. Eventually the British administration's policy of indirect rule succeeded in creating a barrier between the élite and the chiefs, but it was never as effective as they imagined, for the chiefs themselves soon saw that education was the goal to successful dealing with the administration and sent their children to school. Conversely those responsible for electing chiefs increasingly gave preference to educated candidates for the same reasons. Nor too were chiefs as hostile to the idea of democratic representation as they have often been pictured to be by the Colonial administrators. In 1920, when challenging Crown claims to Lagos land before the Judicial Committee of the Privy Council, Chief Oluwa, who was advised by Herbert Macaulay, the engineer grandson of Bishop Crowther, visited the House of Commons and told *The Times*, 'I wish the Government would extend such a franchise to West Africa.'[50] Even in the bastion of Indirect Rule, Northern Nigeria, Ladipo Solanke, President of the militant West African Students Union, was able to secure the Emir of Kano as one of its patrons.

The National Congress combined in its resolutions the demands and grievances of a large number of groups, individuals and organisations: a thinker like Edward Blyden; political protest such as made by the Aborigines Rights Protection Society of the Gold Coast and the People's Union of Lagos; newspapers such as the *Lagos Weekly Record*, the *Gold Coast Leader*, the *Sierra Leone Weekly News*; independent Church Movements; land grievances of chiefs and people; economic grievances of African merchants squeezed out of the market by European and Lebanese rivals; or lawyers forbidden from practice in the courts of the hinterland.

Edward Blyden, a West Indian who completed his secondary education in Liberia through his copious writings and his contacts up and down the West African coast, was, if anyone could claim the honour, the intellectual precursor of the National Congress of West Africa.[51] First of all he had earlier envisioned a West African empire, though under British control, which would be extended to the interior from the four established colonies. Like many other members of the educated élite he saw the extension of Britain's influence to the interior as a means of securing a wider field for the trade of the coastal colonies. Further, like them, he felt that if West Africa was to be ruled by a European power, better by far that it be Britain than France, which by the 1880's was pursuing rapid expansion across the hinterland of the four British colonies. Blyden did not envisage the British West African empire as a permanent colony, but one which would eventually gain Dominion status as Canada had done. In this approach he anticipated that of the Congress which, as it became clear from discussions members had in London after the Accra session, looked ultimately to self-government.[52] Blyden was also among the pioneers of the idea of a West African University which would provide the trained indigenous élite to run such an empire. Its other champions were James Africanus Horton, the great Sierra Leone doctor, and the volatile and dearly loved little Irish Governor of Sierra Leone, Sir John Pope-Hennessy, who was also Governor of the West African Settlements, and first received Blyden's proposals for such a university.

Blyden also anticipated the growing concern of the educated élite to find a basis in traditional African society for the form of government for their new colonies. At first convinced that only Christian education could provide the means for the development of Africa, Blyden turned to African society, and increasingly Islam, as the source for the ideal African society of the future.

'We must enlist the help of the Europeans', he wrote, anticipating the general approach of the inter-war-years politicians, in particular Casely-Hayford, 'but not to Europeanise ourselves—but to help us form our own needs, to formulate our own ideas, to express our own feelings, to realise our own actions.'[53]

These were very much the views of J. E. Casely-Hayford, the chief architect of the Congress, as expressed in his *Ethiopia Unbound*, who paid tribute to Blyden thus: 'The work of Edward Wilmot Blyden is universal, covering the entire race . . . [He] has sought . . . to reveal everywhere the African unto himself; to fix his attention . . . as to his place in the economy of the world; to point out to him his worth as a race among the races of men; lastly and most important of all, to lead him back unto self-respect.'[54]

In both the Gold Coast and Nigeria early movements of political protest were focussed on land questions. Conflict arose largely over a misconception on the part of the British as to the nature of African land tenure, particularly with regard to waste or unoccupied lands. In West Africa there is no land that does not have an owner, even if the owner is collectively the tribe. Thus, in 1894, when the Gold Coast Government, concerned at the rapid sale of land to expatriate trading companies and timber concessionaires, introduced a Land Bill vesting 'Waste Lands, Forest Lands and Minerals' in the Crown, there was immediate opposition to it. The clause which set aside Waste and Forest Lands 'for the use of the Government' provoked especial hostility,[55] which was encouraged by European vested interests and those involved in the profitable business of land speculation. But the root of the protest was the real horror with which the people of the Colony viewed the prospect of the alienation of their land by the Government. Protest resulted in the drafting of a new bill which in fact exacerbated feelings. The 1897 Land Bill vested in Government administrative rights over all Colony land and implicitly made African rights of ownership subject to Government recognition. Government could grant certificates of ownership but these would be subject to English, not customary, law.

The opposition of chiefs and people provided the educated élite, already concerned about the way bills affecting the future of the country were introduced into Legislative Council without prior public discussion, with an ideal opportunity to mobilise the public behind it. In 1897 the Aborigines Protection Society was formed at Cape Coast to protest against the Bill. Chiefs, people and African religious leaders gave it their support. In 1898 a deputation of three prosperous merchants was sent by the A.R.P.S. to London to protest against the Bill on behalf of the natural rulers, whose fears are best summed up in the words of the petition sent by the King and Chiefs of Eastern Wassaw to the Secretary of State in 1897.

'That the provisions of this Bill have terrified us greatly for that by the passing of a law we and the people whom we represent should lose all our rights as natives of the soil where our lot did cast us.'[56]

The deputation saw Chamberlain, who finally decided to withdraw the Bill. A jubilant A.R.P.S. decided to form itself into a permanent organisation 'for the protection and good-government of the rulers and people of the Gold Coast'.[57] The élite had thus assumed the role of 'watchdogs of colonial rule', as Webster and Boahen have put it.[58] The A.R.P.S. consolidated its success with its sustained and successful attacks on the Forestry Bill of 1910, which they claimed would also alienate African land rights.

These protests, and similar protests in both Gold Coast and Nigeria, were what Coleman has described as being in the nature of 'primary resistance' since 'they were particular responses to particular imperial measures deemed oppressive, rather than fundamental challenges to imperial rule or positive affirmation of the objective of [Nigerian] self-government'.[59] Their method of protest was constitutional. As the *Gold Coast Methodist Times* warned the new-born A.R.P.S., 'To achieve the highest good—the *summum bonum*—in the Gold Coast, we must agitate, but agitate constitutionally.'[60]

Most important of all these movements brought to the fore leaders who were to dominate politics until the thirties. In Ghana the A.R.P.S. included among its most active members J. Mensah Sarbah and J. E. Casely-Hayford. In Lagos the father of Nigerian politics, Herbert Macaulay, came to the fore over a land case. There, too, land provided an issue on which educated élite and traditional rulers could find common cause.

No organisation of the dynamism of the A.R.P.S. was formed in Lagos as a result of early protest movements. Indeed, protest was much more *ad hoc*. In 1895 a mass demonstration forced the Government of Lagos to withdraw a proposed tax measure. In 1901 a Forest Bill was similarly withdrawn. The élite, leading the protest, warned government that there was no such thing as waste land.[61] It was not until 1908, after strong protest against Government attempts to expropriate Lagos land and impose a water rate, which was considered to be a means of taxing the African to give improved facilities to the European,[62] that the People's Union was founded. This was an élite organisation with the same aims as the A.R.P.S.: to defend African rights, and to oppose particular government measures. Despite the popular feeling aroused by these last two issues, the People's Union was a pale shadow of the A.R.P.S., and was never a significant political force, degenerating into a 'conservative wealthy man's club defending the colonial government'.[63]

In 1912, for the first time, the educated Lagos élite and chiefs from the Yoruba hinterland were brought together[64] over the issue of the proposed application of Government control over land rights in the South. The élite sent delegations to awaken the chiefs of the interior to the threat to their rights and a delegation of élite and chiefs from Abeokuta, Ibadan, Ijebu-Ode, Ife and Ilesha was sent to London in 1913. A Lagos Branch of the London Anti-Slavery and Aborigines Protection Society was at the same time formed to watch over Nigerian land interests. The élite feared that this government measure would be a prelude to the alienation of their land to European commercial interests, even though Government declared that its intention was in fact to prevent 'ill-advised alienations and to secure the unearned increment of the land to the community and government'.[65] Exigencies of war and the strength of African feeling shelved the legislation.

Only one politician of importance was thrown up by this protest, which was spear-headed by what the government chose to describe maliciously as 'alien natives', that is Sierra Leonean and other repatriates.[66] He was Herbert Macaulay, who seized on both the Lagos Water Rate and the alienation of Lagos land by the Crown as sticks with which to beat the Nigerian government and rise to political prominence. In 1915 Lugard asked the Eleko or hereditary ruler of Lagos[67] to persuade his people to pay the unpopular water-rate. But the Eleko refused. Foremost among the 'political adventurers' by whom Government alleged he had allowed himself to be exploited in his opposition to the rate[68] was Macaulay, who thus secured himself an alliance in Lagos, at least, with the traditional élite. He consolidated his position by championing the cause of the chiefs and peoples of Lagos against the Lagos High Court ruling that the 1861 cession of Lagos to Britain involved all lands which were not prior to that date privately owned. A test case was brought by Chief Oluwa under Macaulay's guidance against the Nigerian Government before the Judicial Committee of the Privy Council, which ruled in favour of Chief Oluwa. The Nigerian Government, under its new Governor, Sir Hugh Clifford, tried to force the Eleko to disown the right of the petitioners in London to present the case on behalf of the chiefs of Lagos. He was asked to cable Macaulay to return the staff which had been given him as token of his right to speak for the chiefs. His refusal cost him his salary of £300 p.a., and his title as Eleko.[69] But Lagos had secured its land for the future. Government had been ordered to pay £22,500 compensation for land acquired, and Macaulay had become a popular hero.

The most powerful political weapon possessed by the élite was the Press. Through this they were able to bring their grievances to the attention not only of local people, but of members of the élite up and down the coast. Here they were in a more fortunate position than their French West African counterparts who were subjected to strict censorship by government and were hampered by the low literacy rate resulting from French educational policy. Furthermore only French citizens were allowed to run newspapers. The National Congress of British West Africa was to owe much of its success to the fact that the most prominent editors and proprietors were among its membership, thus ensuring strong support during its formative days from the *Gold Coast Leader*, the *Sierra Leone Weekly News* and the *Lagos Weekly Record*, edited by a Liberian, J. P. Jackson, who through the columns of his newspaper had been one of the most persistent critics of the Lagos government. The Press in British West Africa has a long and distinguished history of criticism of Government. As early as 1900, by Kilson's count, the Sierra Leone élite 'had been exposed to 34 newspapers'[70] and by the same year 19 newspapers had been published in Gold Coast.

The Press in West Africa owed much of its development to the missionaries. The first newspapers in Nigeria and some of the earliest newspapers in the Gold Coast were published by them. Henry Townsend, of the C.M.S., edited *Iwe-Irohin*, which first appeared in 1859 with 'didactic essays on history and politics', and contributed 'to the keen interest in journalism and the technical excellence of the many newspapers that began to appear in Lagos in succeeding years'.[71] The *Gold Coast Methodist Times*, edited by Rev. S. R. B. Solomon, who later changed his name to Attoh Ahuma, was to be one of the main vehicles for attack on the Lands Bill.[72] The Churches had another powerful means of expressing disapproval of government, whether they were missionary churches or independent African churches: the pulpit or the Church Hall. African churchmen, even if they belonged to a European church like Solomon, in their sermons spoke to their congregations about all aspects of life. These ranged from educational practice to straight political issues such as the Land Bill. Thus James Johnson, consecrated Assistant Bishop of the Niger Delta in 1900, argued in the *Sierra Leone Weekly News* in favour of using Krio as Yoruba was used in Nigeria as 'a medium of instruction and education and for the teaching and learning of English', since it was 'like every other language in the world, an outcome of the people's own situation . . .'[73] Expatriate missionaries, even after the lines had been clearly drawn between them and the independent or secessionist Churches in the 1900's (see p. 365), protested against certain government measures. Thus Bishop Tugwell of the C.M.S. in Nigeria was forced by the anger of his flock over Lugard's actions with regard to the disturbances in Abeokuta of 1914, which resulted in its loss of independence to protest that these were the result of 'the exasperation of an oppressed people'. He said that only a Commission of Enquiry would satisfy loyal subjects of the Crown.[74]

The independent Churches, whether they were orthodox or syncretic, also served as a model for African self-government, albeit within only one sphere of human activity, but one of immense importance in Africa. James Bertin Webster has shown how the African Churches in Yorubaland were legitimate precursors of the nationalists, not only in their belief in African ability to govern themselves, in this case within the Church, but also through their insistence on the values of traditional African culture.[75] Patriarch J. Campbell of the West African Episcopal Church, which like other African Churches had links up and down the Coast, was leader of the Nigerian delegation to the National Congress of British West Africa. These Churches provided an outlet for the 'pent-up energy of African leadership, which found little outlet in colonial civil life'.[76]

The lack of opportunities for the élite in civil life was a grievance that was so deeply felt that it provided a constant source of fuel for their political activities. Senior posts in the Colonial Civil Service, open to them in the nineteenth century, were now reserved for Europeans. Even in the vital and understaffed medical services, African doctors with perfectly good qualifications were refused appointment. Thus in 1913 Dr. R. A. Savage, Medical Health Officer to the Cape Coast Municipality since 1907, lost his job when his post came under Gold Coast government control. Not surprisingly in the circumstances, he is credited with first suggesting the National Congress.[77] Similarly when the British took over the Egba United Government in 1914, its African medical officer, Dr. Ayodeji Oyejola, lost his post.[78] Africans, excluded for the most part from the administration of the colonies in which they lived, even when they were better qualified than European incumbents, took up professions which they could practice outside government: law, medicine, the Church, or commerce. The missionary churches relegated Africans to auxiliary positions in their hierarchy. Where Crowther had become a bishop in his own right, those who followed him could only aspire to be assistant bishops. Expatriate control of these churches was to be secured, even at the cost of European missionaries denigrating their African fellows in Christ.[79] Law, too, was a difficult profession. In Nigeria, Lugard forbade the appearance of lawyers in Northern courts and as Governor-General extended this exclusion to the South where hitherto they had been permitted. This proved a great financial set-back to many practising lawyers. In Ashanti they were also excluded and in 1924 the *Gold Coast Leader* published the following 'Litany' by Opirim Quansah:

*Priest.* That it may please thee to Order the early *opening up of Ashanti* in British West Africa to the administration of British Law and Justice.

*People.* We beseech thee hear us good Lord. . . .[80]

In business, too, they found themselves ousted by either the European trading companies or the Lebanese. The Sierra Leone delegation, which had already felt the strong pressure of Lebano-Syrian rivalry, got the National Congress of British West Africa to pass a resolution against the Syrians as 'undesirables' and 'a menace to the good Government of the land' and demanded their repatriation.[81] This demand followed violent anti-Syrian riots in Freetown in which it was alleged that they cornered the rice market. Many years later, independent Sierra Leone was to make the sale of rice a monopoly of indigenous traders in a law directed at the Lebanese.

In Nigeria the grievances of African businessmen were particularly acute. They had been supplanted on the Niger by Goldie's monopoly. The Shipping Ring established in 1896 formed a monopoly of shipping space between Nigeria and Europe. Priority for space was given to European merchants, and African merchants, to obtain space, had to pay rates 10% higher than their European rivals.[82] The Nigerian élite found a surprising ally in Lugard as far as commerce was concerned. He was deeply opposed to any form of monopoly, even to the extent of opposing attempts to ensure the exclusion of Germany from trade with Nigeria after the First World War had ended.[83] He told one leading British merchant that he was going to watch the expatriate firms carefully in the African interests.[84]

But in Sierra Leone, Gold Coast and Nigeria, African merchants were fighting a losing battle against their much more highly capitalised, and intensively clannish, European rivals.

## 5 *The National Congress of British West Africa*

The National Congress of British West Africa which gave vent to their grievances was conceived in 1913, but because of the war did not finally meet until 1920. It was supported by almost all the British West African newspapers and their editors were usually in key positions in the Congress. Only the *Gold Coast Nation*, the mouthpiece of the A.R.P.S. which was edited by E. J. P. Brown, one of J. E. Casely-Hayford's opponents, criticised the Congress. Fifty-two delegates from all four colonies of British West Africa met in Accra in March 1920: 6 from Nigeria, 40 from the Gold Coast, 3 from Sierra Leone and 1 from Gambia. They demanded that half of the seats in the Colonial legislative councils be set aside for African members who should be elected by the people. They asked for the establishment of a House of Assembly which would be composed of the Legislative Council plus six elected financial representatives. This House would have the power of taxation and would debate the annual budget. They asked that municipal councils be established for all the major towns, of which four-fifths of the councillors would be elected.

They also demanded reforms in education, commerce, the medical services and the legal system—all of which would give the élite greater opportunities for influential, decision-making positions. In short they put forward the first concrete demands for Africanisation.

Alluding to the Shipping Ring, they specifically welcomed the impending competition that Garvey's Black Star Line would provide to the European lines.

The Congress formed itself into a permanent organisation and sent a delegation to England in 1920 to put forward its recommendations to the Secretary of State for the Colonies. Many groups in England, such as the League of Nations Union, came out in their support, but the Congress had failed to inform the Colonial governors of their intended campaign in England, and once news of their speeches got back to the West African coast, a great deal of alarm spread amongst many important interior chiefs who were just beginning to be included in the machinery of government. Nana Ofori Atta I, most important of those chiefs, so included, gave a speech in Legislative Council against the Congress delegation's activities which proved to be a decisive factor in Guggisberg's denunciation of the delegates as unrepresentative to the Secretary of State. The other governors were equally alarmed; of these, Sir Hugh Clifford, Governor of Nigeria, spoke the most scathingly of the delegates, describing them in a speech before the Legislative Council in Lagos as follows:

'... a self-selected and self-appointed congregation of educated African gentlemen who collectively style themselves the "West African National Conference", ... whose eyes are fixed, not upon their own tribal obligations and the duties to their Natural Rulers which immemorial Custom should impose upon them, but upon political theories evolved by Europeans to fit a wholly different environment, for the government of peoples who have arrived at a wholly different stage of civilisation.'[85]

He went on to attack their claims to represent the illiterate masses; the idea of West African and national unity was pronounced preposterous. His speech illustrates how clearly Britain was coming down in favour of the chiefs as the group which would be trained in self-government. After they returned from England, the heads of the National Congress would never again be able to organise any effective opposition. They spent most of their time, instead, in organising social events geared to help them pay off debts incurred in London.

# Notes

1 Gold Coast Legislative Council, *Debates* (1931), p. 385, cited in Bourret, *Ghana*, p. 57.
2 See John F. Peterson, 'The Sierra Leone Creole: A Further View', Paper read to the Institute of African Studies, Fourah Bay College, Seminar on 'Freetown', December 1966.
3 Denzer, *National Congress of British West Africa*, Table 2, pp. 88–9.
4 Wesley Johnson, 'Blaise Diagne', p. 243.
5 *Memorandum of the Case of the National Congress of British West Africa.*
6 Denzer, *National Congress of British West Africa*, p. 4.
7 Michael Crowder, 'Independence as a goal in French-speaking African Politics, 1944–60', in William H. Lewis, ed., *French-Speaking Africa: The Search for Identity*, New York, 1965, pp. 15–41.
8 Cited in Charles Cros, *La parole est à M. Blaise Diagne, premier homme d'État Africain*, Aubenas, France, 1961, p. 29.
9 Hodgkin, *Nationalism in Colonial Africa*, p. 23. See also the very stimulating chapter on the 'Growth of National Consciousness', in Kimble, *Ghana*, pp. 506–53.
10 Georges Balandier, 'Contribution a l'étude des nationalismes en Afrique Noire', *Zaire*, VIII, 4, April 1954, p. 379.
11 Kimble, *Ghana*, 'Introduction', p. xiv.
12 George Shepperson, 'Notes on Negro American Influences on the Emergence of African Nationalism', *J.A.H.*, I, 2, 1960, pp. 299–312.
13 George Padmore, ed., *History of the Pan-African Congress*, 2nd Edition, London, 1963, p. 55.
14 See the resolutions of the Congress reprinted in *ibid.*
15 *The Times*, 25th July, 1900.
16 W. E. Dubois, *The World and Africa*, Enlarged Edition, New York, 1965, p. 9.
17 *Ibid.*, p. 10.
18 Rayford W. Logan, 'The Historical Aspects of Pan-Africanism, 1900–45', in *Pan-Africanism Reconsidered*, Berkeley and Los Angeles, 1962, p. 44.
19 DuBois, *The World and Africa*, pp. 11–12, where the resolutions are reproduced in part.
20 Cited in Buell, *Native Problem*, II, p. 81.
21 Cited in Logan, 'Historical Aspects of Pan-Africanism', p. 44.
22 Jesse Fausset, 'Impressions of the Second Pan-African Congress', *Crisis*, XXIII, 1, November 1921.
23 I am grateful to Miss LaRay Denzer for supplying the information on which this section is based.
24 The *Gold Coast Independent*, 1st October 1921.
25 Cited in Edmund David Cronon, *Black Moses—the Story of Marcus Garvey and the Universal Negro Improvement Association*, Madison, Wisconsin, 1962.

26  Cited in *ibid.*, p. 66.

27  Cary, *The Case for African Freedom*, p. 20.

28  W. Casely-Hayford, *The Disabilities of Black Folk and their Treatment with an appeal to the Labour Party*, Accra, 1929.

29  Coleman, *Nigeria*, p. 191.

30  Shepperson, 'Notes on Negro American Influence', p. 306.

31  William M. McCartney, *Dr. Aggrey*, London, 1949, p. 57, cited by Coleman, *Nigeria*, p. 455.

32  Cited in Buell, *Native Problem*, II, p. 733.

33  Shepperson, 'Notes on Negro American Influence', p. 303.

34  His appointment was dated 11th January 1918, though a number of authorities date it incorrectly from 1917, e.g. Buell, *Native Problem*, I, p. 955; Morgenthau, *Political Parties in French-Speaking West Africa*, p. 127. H. Deschamps, *Le Sénégal et la Gambie*, Paris, 1964, p. 69, even puts it as early as 1916.

35  Pierre Mille, 'The Black Vote in Senegal', *Journal of the African Society*, I, 1901, pp. 64–79.

36  G. Wesley Johnson, 'Blaise Diagne', p. 240.

37  I. O. Idowu has written a thesis for the University of Ibadan on the rise of the *métis* in Senegalese politics entitled, 'The Conseil-Général in Senegal, 1879–1920', Ibadan, 1966.

38  Wesley Johnson, 'Blaise Diagne', p. 237.

39  *Ibid.*, p. 238.

40  For a study of the Press in this period see Marguerite Boulègur, 'La Presse au Sénégal avant 1939', in *Bulletin d'I.F.A.N.*, T XXVII, ser B, 3–4, 1965, pp. 715–54.

41  Bakary Traoré in Bakary Traoré, Mamadou Lô et Jean Louis Alibert, *Forces Politiques en Afrique Noire*, Paris, 1966, p. 8.

42  Cited in Roger Pasquier, 'Les débuts de la presse au Sénégal', *Cahiers d'Études Africaines*, 7, 1962, p. 482.

43  Cited in Buell, *Native Problem*, I, p. 950.

44  Wesley Johnson, 'Blaise Diagne', pp. 247–8.

45  *Ibid.*, p. 248.

46  Results of the first ballot were:

| Diagne | 1,910 |
|--------|-------|
| Carpot | 671 |
| Heimburger | 668 |
| Marsat | 516 |
| Theveniaut | 408 |
| Patey | 365 |
| Pellerin | 252 |
| Crespin | 71 |

and of the second ballot:

| | |
|---|---|
| Diagne | 2,424 |
| Heimburger | 2,249 |
| Carpot | 472 |
| *Registered voters:* | 8,677 |

47 Cited in Cros, *Blaise Diagne*, p. 77.
48 Buell, *Native Problem*, I, p. 951.
49 See Immanuel Geiss, 'The Development of Pan-Africanism in the Twentieth Century: II', *Afrika*, VII, 6, 1966, p. 7, where he cites the research of Fred Spiegler.
50 *The Times*, 15th July 1920.
51 For a useful discussion of Blyden's role as a precursor of many of the ideas of later African leaders, see Robert W. July, 'Nineteenth Century Negritude: Edward W. Blyden' *Journal of African History*, V, 1, pp. 73–86.
52 Denzer, *The National Congress of British West Africa*, p. 56.
53 E. W. Blyden, *The West African University*, Freetown, 1872, correspondence with Governor Pope-Hennessy.
54 Cited by July in 'Nineteenth Century Negritude', from Casely-Hayford's preface to Blyden's *West Africa before Europe*, pp. i–ii.
55 Kimble, *Ghana*, p. 335.
56 Cited in *ibid.*, p. 347.
57 Preamble to the *Byelaws, Rules and Regulations*, Aborigines Rights Protection Society, Cape Coast, 1907.
58 J. B. Webster and A. A. Boahen, *The Growth of African Civilisation; West Africa since 1800*, London, 1967, p. 293.
59 Coleman, *Nigeria*, p. 178.
60 Cited by Kimble, *Ghana*, p. 343.
61 J. U. J. Asiegbu, *Liberated Africans and British Politics, 1840–1920*, Cambridge Ph.D. Thesis, 1966.
62 Coleman, *Nigeria*, p. 179.
63 Webster and Boahen, *West Africa since 1800*, p. 294.
64 Coleman, *Nigeria*, p. 181.
65 Buell, *Native Problem*, I, p. 771.
66 See Chapter IX, 'Liberated Africans and the Origins of Nigerian Nationalism, 1886–1920', Asiegbu, *Liberated Africans*.
67 In return for a modest pension from Government the ruler of Lagos was persuaded to give up his title as Oba or King and was referred to as Prince.
68 Nigeria, *Annual Report for 1920*.
69 Asiegbu, *Liberated Africans*, p. 453.
70 Kilson, *Sierra Leone*, p. 74.
71 Ajayi, *Missions*, p. 159.
72 Kimble, *Ghana*, pp. 162 and 342.
73 *Sierra Leone Weekly News*, 22nd February 1908. I am grateful to Dr.

Davidson Nicol for this reference. Incidentally, Kimble's assertion that 'J. E. Casely-Hayford was probably the first African—in a letter to the *Weekly News* of 5th May 1908—to criticize publicly the practice of starting children's education in the English Language' is wrong by four months. See Kimble, *Ghana*, p. 514.

74 Perham, *Lugard*, II, p. 595.
75 James Bertin Webster, *The African Churches among the Yoruba, 1888–1922*, Oxford, 1964.
76 *Ibid.*, p. 93.
77 I am grateful to Professor J. Bertin Webster for this information.
78 I am grateful to Professor J. Bertin Webster for this information.
79 Webster, *African Churches*, pp. 191–2.
80 Cited in Tordoff, *Ashanti*, p. 183.
81 *Memorandum of the Case of the National Congress of British West Africa.*
82 Asiegbu, *Liberated Africans*, pp. 431–2.
83 Perham, *Lugard*, II, pp. 567–8.
84 *Ibid.*, p. 576.
85 Coleman, *Nigeria*, p. 193.

# 2 French West African politics, 1919–39

## 1 Politics in the 'Quatre Communes'

As a manifestation of political radicalism, the Senegal election of
1914 was the high water-mark in French West African politics for
the next three decades. In the rest of French West Africa politics
were officially forbidden. M. J. Lemaire, Honorary Governor-
General, wrote in 1913: 'the reason, to my mind, for the happiness
of French West Africa is the absence of politics. They do not vote
in French West Africa. No electoral campaigns to trouble and break-
up the collective life, to divide the population into rival parties, to
over-excite evil passions! . . . the great mass of the indigenous
population remains outside all competition and agitation. It is there
that lies its privilege. And not a small one.'[1] And with regulations
such as were in force in Bouaké in Ivory Coast in 1926, the French
made sure the 'native' was kept well in his place: 'Order regulating
the circulation of natives in the town of Bouaké after 8 p.m. Article
I: Every native circulating after 8 p.m. in the streets of Bouaké must
carry a lamp of a sufficient lighting power to signal his presence.
(15 days plus 100 francs summarily imposed for contravention).'[2]
The African was not without champions, however, as far as his
political ambitions were concerned. Cosnier in 1919 was very
critical of the fact that the Africans had no representation whatsoever
in the councils of government and advised that they should be given
some.[3] There were those who had hoped that Blaise Diagne would
secure it for them, especially after his great recruiting campaign.

They were to be disappointed. Two concessions were made to them which were of little consequence politically. In 1919 a number of towns in French West Africa outside the *Quatre Communes* were given consultative commissions under the terms of the decree of 15th May 1912, which allowed the Governor-General to set up mixed communes in centres which, while 'capable of supporting a municipal organisation, do not contain a large enough European or assimilated population to be created *communes de pleine exercice*'. These 'communes mixtes' were divided into three categories. In each case their Mayor was a French administrator. Africans were nominated to those of the second category, and elected by universal suffrage to those of the third category. Most of the towns were of the first category however, and none of the third. For instance Abidjan was only raised to the second category in 1939 and, because of the war, elections did not take place until 1945.[4] In 1920 four unofficial appointed members were added to the Conseils d'Administration of the constituent colonies of the Federation: two citizens, and two subjects. In 1925 provision was made for these appointed unofficial members to be elected by restricted franchise, and the number of *sujets* was increased to three. The reform applied only to Guinea, Ivory Coast, Sudan and Dahomey. But the powers of these councils were very limited, and they were dominated by the French.

If Diagne had been unable to secure economic and political reforms for the colonies from which he recruited soldiers for France, he had nevertheless excited the imagination of their people. He toured Sudan as a man more important than the Governor-General, and much more important than the local Lieutenant-Governor. It is difficult today to conceive the significance of this reversal of status except to imagine Herbert Macaulay suddenly taking precedence over Lord Lugard. Diagne was well aware of the problem. On arriving in Dakar he wrote to Angoulvant that he would not insist 'on observing strictly the protocol which would have it that I remain in person, in my capacity as Commissioner of the Republic, outside and above the administrative hierarchy, to receive the Governor-General'. He added: 'I will accompany the Governor-General in charge of the two Governments-General to his residence by sitting on his left in his vehicle.'[5] He thus courteously yielded precedence to the Governor-General which should have been his. On his arrival he was met by the senior administrators from the Governor-General downwards as well as the Diplomatic Corps.

On tour he made it clear to the Africans that this status reversal heralded a new era. 'When you return,' he told them, according to a bitter report by 'Un Vieil Africain', 'you will replace the whites in the administration [*sic*]. You will have decorations and you will gain the same salaries as the whites who are here.'[6] Another European, equally unwilling to sign his name, wrote, 'The natives are holding up their heads again: they show on every occasion a detestable attitude with regard to the Europeans.'[7]

The French were clearly worried by Diagne's impact. In Senegal he had Africanised all the representative institutions by 1919, and had been returned to the deputyship. He had behind him a political party, the Republican-Socialist party, with returned veterans as its nucleus.[8] He continued to hold his post as Commissaire-Général until October 1921. The French Government therefore appointed a hard-line Governor-General Merlin, to counter-balance his influence. The powers of the Conseil-Général were deliberately limited in acceding to the old demand that its competence be extended to the interior. The administration, agreeing to this, insisted on having representation from the Protectorate. Instead of representatives, elected by the people, chiefs, elected by fellow chiefs, would represent the Protectorate on a basis of parity with the *citoyens*. There would thus be twenty citizens, neutralised by twenty chiefs, who would always vote for the administration since the administration controlled their appointments. In 1925, however, the administration had to agree to increase the number of citizen seats to twenty-four and reduce the chiefs to sixteen in order to persuade the citizens to pass the budget.

At first Diagne tried to fight the forces of reaction that confronted him, and was certainly considered a radical by the French right up until 1922, when he was already clearly seeking compromise. In 1921 he had helped the Banque de l'Afrique Occidentale retain its privileges as the sole issuer of currency for West Africa by opposing the creation of a State Bank.[9] And in 1923 he signed the famous 'Bordeaux pact' with the Bordeaux merchant houses, whereby he arranged a political truce with them, agreeing to cease his attacks on them in return for their support. Acidly, his rival Carpot wrote: 'The Deputy Blaise Diagne, worshipping what a little while back he would burn, has become the ally of the Bordeaux coffers, the collaborator of what his friends called not so long ago Sharks.'[10]

Unfortunately for the development of Senegalese politics no one of Diagne's stature arose to challenge his policies. In 1924 he was opposed at the election by Paul Deferre, father of Gaston Deferre, who complained on his defeat that the Africans 'voted not for the man, but for the skin'.[11] Lamine Guèye, first French-speaking African to gain a Doctorate of Law, successfully wrested the Mayoralty of St. Louis from Diagne's supporter in 1925, but resigned from it in 1927 to enter the magistrature. There had been some 'maladresse' in the running of St. Louis and Blaise Diagne, seeing this as a way of ridding himself of a rival, persuaded Guèye that, since certain colonial interests wanted him out of the way, he would be well advised to leave the country. Guèye went to the West Indies as a magistrate and Diagne was freed not only from a rival but also his most persistent newspaper critic. Guèye differed in his views from Diagne only in that he advocated a more thorough policy of assimilation. The same is true for the Young Senegalese who broke with Diagne after the war. They wanted, for instance, the extension of full commune status to towns in the Protectorate.

Diagne entrenched himself even further in the colonial system. In 1928 he only defeated Galandou Diouf, his former henchman and now rival, with the aid of French administrative connivance.[12] In 1930 he defended France's forced labour policy at Geneva in the following terms: '. . . at this time when the International Labour Conference is engrossed . . . with the question of forced labour, the presence of the delegate of France in my person is already symbolic; it signifies that my country has intended to show through my presence here what her feelings are. The French Government is in favour of the total suppression of this contemporary form of slavery and enslavement, and you will perhaps be surprised that a man who belongs to one of those races on whom, for four centuries, slavery has weighed heavily, has come here to bring at the same time both the adherence of France and himself, in solidarity with those very races.'[13] Diagne defended France's policies at a time when women, carrying their children on their backs, worked on the *corvée* making up roads in French Congo with their bare hands, since the administration did not provide them with tools. This scandal was well known by 1930, for André Gide had given it wide publicity three years before through his *Voyage au Congo*,[14] which caused a furore in France.

In 1931 Diagne became Under-Secretary of State for Colonies. He held the post in the three Laval Ministries from 27th January 1931 to 20th February 1932. He was acting Minister in 1931 during the absence of Paul Reynaud in Indo-China.[15] He thus showed that an African could reach even the position of deciding policies for his own colony. But the price was complete co-operation with France and the suppression of any demands for a more liberal régime for his fellow men. Nevertheless he did manage during the Depression to negotiate the first subsidies for the Senegalese groundnut crop in return for campaigning for greater production. In 1934, when he died, he had been completely absorbed into the life of Metropolitan France, visiting Senegal rarely. One of the honours noted in the short biography of him in his Personal File in the Archives in Dakar was that he was President of the National Committee for Monuments for Borgnis-Desbordes and Archinard![16] By the time of his death Diagne had succeeded in raising against him a journalistic onslaught which attacked not only him but his two pillars of support: the administration and Bordeaux.[17]

Diagne was succeeded as Deputy by his former lieutenant, and later opponent, Galandou Diouf. Much less articulate than Diagne, he made little contribution to political life in Senegal. He co-operated with the administration and Bordeaux, and in 1935 he supported Alfred Goux, an ambitious European, as Mayor of Dakar against the wishes of his supporters.

The opposition to Diouf and the establishment now focussed around Lamine Guèye, who in 1935 founded the Parti Socialiste Senegalais. Like the Parti Républicain Sénégalais, Diagne's party, which had supported Guèye at the 1936 election against Diouf, it was a party centred very much on its leader. However, in 1936, with the advent of the Popular Front Government, the new S.F.I.O. section in Dakar made an alliance with Guèye's P.S.S. Two years later the P.S.S. integrated itself with the S.F.I.O. and the Federation of Senegal of the S.F.I.O. was founded. Far from following a nationalist cause, Lamine Guèye pursued a policy of further assimilation with France which the integration of his party into the S.F.I.O. symbolised. With his friend, Marius Moutet, as Minister of Colonies and with the nomination by the Popular Front of De Coppet as Governor-General, Lamine Guèye became identified with the administration and its policies. He gained a seat on the Executive of the S.F.I.O. and so was close to those in Government. Guèye hoped to be able to use his position to extend the privileges enjoyed by the citizens to the subjects of the interior.[18] But the Second World War prevented Guèye testing his popularity against Diouf in the next contest for the Deputyship, for Vichy suppressed all representative institutions in Senegal. Nevertheless by 1939 Lamine Guèye's S.F.I.O. had captured St. Louis and had gained seats on the Conseil Colonial. With the more sympathetic administration of the Popular Front he might well have defeated Diouf and replaced a policy of collaboration with Bordeaux by one demanding the full fruits of France's assimilation policy.

## 2 *Protest and politics*

In Senegal in the inter-war years politics were very lively. There were 'riots, demonstrations, strikes, imprisonment of candidates, enormous political rallies and impassioned speeches'.[19] Outside Senegal they were, with the notable exception of Dahomey, very dull. Africans had neither right of assembly nor freedom of speech. Thus political expression was largely confined to protest movements against particular injustices or demands for particular reforms. The formation of political parties as such was forbidden. There was little cause for them to arise. As Coleman has written: 'The really decisive factor—the precipitant in the formation of political parties—has been constitutional reform providing for (i) the devolution by the imperial government of a sufficiently *meaningful* and *attractive* measure of power to induce or provoke their movements into political parties, and (ii) the introduction or refinement of institutions and procedures, such as an electoral system, which would make it technically possible for parties to seek power constitutionally.'[20] Significantly in Dahomey, which apart from Senegal had the largest élite in French West Africa, after the introduction of elections for the African members of the Administrative Council rudimentary political organisations were formed.[21]

Any associations formed before 1937, the year when the Popular Front Government permitted limited freedom of associations to the *sujets*, including the formation of trade unions by those literate in French holding Primary School Certificates, was subject to the approval of the French authorities. Signs of political activities hostile to the administration led quickly to suppression. The same held true of the Press. However, since civil servants in France could openly hold membership of political parties, Africans were sometimes allowed greater freedom than a strict interpretation of the law indicated, if the political opinions of a particular administrator coincided with their own.

What is surprising in the inter-war period is how much political expression was vented by Africans, for the *indigénat* and the laws concerning the Press and liberty of association were very harsh. Applied rigorously, they could lead to exile or imprisonment, a fate that befell several critics of the administration.

Since political parties were not allowed and the only objective which presented itself as a legitimate goal was the election of five Africans to the emasculate Territorial Administrative Council, to trace the origins of African politics in inter-war French West Africa we have to look elsewhere than formal political organisations. Protest movements, voluntary associations and the activities of the élite are our main source for the history of French West African politics in these years. It is a period that has not yet received the attention it deserves from political historians, which hampers any attempt at synthesis from secondary sources.[22]

Protest took many forms in the inter-war period. Tuareg and Mauretanians continued to assert their independence of French control. The French, as we have seen (p. 108), only completed their conquest of Mauretania on the eve of that country's independence. Mauretanians not yet under French 'protection' raided Port Étienne in 1924 and 1927. But in the inter-war period attempts to assert pre-colonial independence were limited to these desert nomads, whom the French found as difficult to control as the Sudanese kingdoms had before them. The most common form of protest was that against the nature of French rule. In Ivory Coast and Upper Volta hundreds of thousands of people abandoned their villages to avoid forced labour. Sometimes whole villages were deserted.[23] In 1934 among the Bobo of Upper Volta a resistance movement known as the *Nana Vo*[24] sprang up to resist the arbitrary requisitioning of food and animals by the chiefs, who were permitted to do this by the French administration.[25] The administration had to use force to suppress the movement. In the Porto Novo commune of Dahomey in 1923 there were riots against the increase in the head-tax from 2·25 francs a person to fifteen francs a man, ten francs a woman, and five francs a child. Taxes on market selling rights and European-style houses were also increased.[26] The riots were so serious that Governor-General Merlin sent in three companies of *tirailleurs* and a machine gun section from Dakar and Togo, and proclaimed a state of siege.[27] There were further riots in 1933 and 1934 in Dahomey against the use of coercion to obtain taxes. In Lomé protests were made in 1933 against an increase in taxes at a time when the Depression was reducing nearly everyone's income. The administration arrested two men, Gartey and Johnson, working respectively for Deutsche Togo Gesellschaft and John Holts, whom it suspected of instigating the demonstration. A crowd of 3,000 rescued the two men from prison. The administration called in troops from Ivory Coast, who sacked two villages in retaliation for the continued demonstrations.[28]

The Dahomean riots of 1923 were not merely a protest against a particular administrative measure. They were the culmination of a large number of grievances as Ballard has shown. Rivalry between two sections of the royal house of Porto Novo was given added fuel by the administration's emasculation of the power of the incumbent king's powers. Added to this was resentment at the new administrative duties imposed on him of tax collection and recruitment of labour and troops through his officials.[29] Schism within the Muslim community and French support for one group against another further added to discontent. On top of this Dahomey was the only French colony with a substantial, politically motivated élite, whose protests had already been countered by administrative measures (see below, pp. 444–5).

Illegal strikes demonstrated workers' discontent with an economic system in which they had no rights of negotiation. Despite the difficulties of organising strikes under the *indigénat* several were held in the inter-war period in Guinea, Senegal, Sudan and Dahomey. (See p. 352.) The most notable strike took place after the legalisation of certain forms of trade unions in 1937. Though a railway workers' union had been formed, the 1938 strike on the Dakar–Niger line was an unofficial one. The strikers at Thiès were protesting against the transfer of one of their fellow workers. Troops were called in, resulting in six dead and thirty wounded.[30] According to ex-Governor-General Annet, Governor-General de Coppet was transferred because of his mishandling of this strike.[31] It was hardly handled in a way that symbolised the ideals of the Popular Front.

Religious movements served as a vehicle of protest and assertion of independence. Hamallism, like Mouridism, was viewed by the French, as we have seen, with great suspicion as a potential threat to the administration. The Mouride Caliph-General exercised a control over the spiritual and economic life of his followers that the French could never rival. Their constant fear was that the Mourides were creating a state within a state, which because of their fanatical devotion to their Caliph could shake French control of Senegal. An ever-increasing amount of the groundnut crop, on which the colony depended for its revenue, was produced by the Mourides. At the same time their control of their faithful was absolute. Eventually the French turned from a policy of oppression to co-operation, accepting that the Mourides were too powerful, and too important economically, for them to break.

The Harrisite movement in Ivory Coast was an assertion of African independence in the religious sphere. Here was the most important of the self-governing African Churches in French West Africa, where otherwise only the *French* Catholic Church had any real freedom of operation.

African protest against their exclusion from participation in the colonial political system took a particularly interesting form in Guinea. Demobilised troops from Kissi, having seen the wider world, were reluctant to return to a subservient role in Kissi society. They tried to replace the chiefs recognised by the administration or to form their own cantons. Riots ensued, and though put down the veterans remained a constant source of opposition in Kissi. They alone dared to treat the Europeans as men and not as beings apart.[32]

## 3 Voluntary associations

To seek the origins of modern political organisations in French West Africa one must look to the voluntary associations. Before 1937 voluntary associations were restricted largely to sporting and cultural associations. If members started discussing politics, the administration was quick to suppress them. For instance in 1937 Mamby Sidibé founded the *Association des Lettrés du Soudan* at Bamako. The administration, finding that politics were being discussed by its members, took the precaution of sending Sidibé, a teacher, to a new post at Bandiagara.[33] Nevertheless it is clear that as early as 1929 the 'Jeunes Turbans' or Young Turks were causing the administration concern. As Georges Hardy wrote in 1929 of the difference between the older and younger generation in Africa: 'The first have experienced European might, and, besides, know that they have not lost much in losing their so-called independence, consisting above all of cruel and impoverished tyrannies. The second have a less complete experience: they are entirely without recognition of good, of which they are ignorant of the real character and origin; they do not fear us, they judge us.'[34] Hardy in 1929, and later Annet reflecting on his Governorship in Dahomey in 1939, recognised the frustration of the youths,[35] who had received primary education which turned them from the land but gave them little future in the colonial administrative and economic system. No child who had been forced to cultivate crops whilst at primary school looked on the agricultural life except with horror.[36] Their main ambition was further education, which they saw as the only way to progress. Apart from William Ponty, which passed out less than 2,000 graduates in the inter-war years,[37] there was no institution of Higher Education to which they could aspire. Education in the Lycée at Dakar or in France was only possible for those living outside the *Quatre Communes* if they had independent means.

This second-level educated élite was to form the backbone of the political parties created after the Second World War. In 1937 the Popular Front Decree of 11th March, permitting the formation of trade unions and professional associations by those with primary education, gave them a modest formal outlet for their grievances. By November 1937, 119 unions had been formed, of which forty-two were Professional Associations.[38] But they were to be short-lived, for the imposition of the Vichy régime on French West Africa brought an end to organised activities of this sort.

The Popular Front Government took a greater interest in voluntary associations. Those that had existed before its advent were devoted to sport, the theatre, old boys' unions, or defence of the interests of a particular ethnic group. The administration recognised that such associations could be used as a forum for political discussion, and decided to harness them to its own ends. Thus in Sudan the administration took an active interest in the formation of sporting associations, and in the organisation of a Veterans' Association. But Frenchmen held the important positions in these associations.[39] In doing this the administration were merely following the advice of Hardy a decade earlier: 'The real remedy is not to leave these "Jeunes Turbans" to themselves even if they are really intolerable.'[40] In 1938 voluntary associations in Sudan were brought together into a union called *La Maison du Peuple* for which the administration provided a building in Bamako. Here again the administration took precautions to keep control over the members of the voluntary associations, and through it disseminated the ideals of the Popular Front Government.[41] The Association of the Friends of the Popular Front Government (A.R.P.) was also allowed to recruit support from non-citizens. The first non-citizen member of its Committee was Modibo Keita, later President of Mali.[42] The A.R.P. also published a newspaper, *Le Soudan*. Many of the members of the A.R.P. and the *Maison du Peuple*, which worked in close concert, were to be members of the first major political party in Mali, the *Union Soudanaise*. In their attempt to bring the educated élite, whether of the first rank like Modibo Keita who had been educated at William Ponty, or the second rank, into a system of voluntary associations whose political ideology they could control, the administration contributed to the increase in, rather than restrained, the political consciousness of Africans. They also provided them unwittingly with a hierarchical structure in which later activists of the *Union Soudanaise* could meet freely and discuss politics, albeit of a pro-government nature. But then the ideology of the Popular Front Government was much closer than that of its predecessors to the views of Africans.

Unfortunately no account of the impact of the Popular Front Government on other French West African territories exists. But if Snyder's account of developments in Sudan reflects a general trend in West Africa we can see that these two years 1937–9 were crucial.

The political importance of voluntary associations, even if they were not greenhouse-forced as they were in those years in Sudan, has been well described by Immanuel Wallerstein: 'Voluntary associations also served as communications networks through which new ideas, even forbidden ideas, could circulate. They often provided excuses for travel and contact; even football has "sociological importance" in that it provided "one of the few inter-territorial meeting-points for Africans" ', and here he is quoting Hodgkin.[43] 'Furthermore, voluntary associations were a proving ground for political leaders, where they demonstrated the support they could garner among a significant segment in the population.'[44]

Most important of all, voluntary associations gave an opportunity of contact between the educated élite of both the first and second ranks. The first rank became the leaders of the political parties of the post Second World War years. But the second rank, those who did not get to William Ponty or the Lycée, provided not only their strongest support but also a bridge between them and the masses.

## 4 The élite and politics

The élite in French West Africa in the inter-war years was tiny. But in the political history of West Africa it was of immense importance for from it were recruited the leaders of the political movement of the post-war years. It consisted primarily of graduates of the William Ponty School. Very few West Africans had managed to get to France for University education. In the first place, outside Senegal and Dahomey there were few families with sufficient means to pay the costs. The French administration made no provision for scholarships. In the second place very few students could even attain the secondary education that was the prerequisite to University entrance. Outside Senegal there were no opportunities for secondary education until after 1945. The French government, as we have seen, was careful that education was strictly controlled to produce an élite of auxiliaries, not rivals. There were 'assistant doctors' and teachers without University degrees. Unlike British West Africa, there was not a class of Africans that complained that it had the degrees to enter the higher ranks of the Civil Service but was excluded on the grounds that it was not European. The few who did get degrees were absorbed by the administration. Thus Lamine Guèye, the lawyer, became a magistrate; Ousmane Socé Diop, a veterinarian, joined the Veterinary Service.

The élite then was not a University trained élite as we shall see part of it was in British West Africa. Nevertheless for French West Africans education was also seen as the key to success in the new white-man-dominated world.

In the inter-war years, there were three interacting stages in the development of the élite. Before William Ponty produced its first graduates it was essentially dominated by Senegalese and Daho-means. William Ponty gave it a West African basis. Partly because it was absorbed in its entirety by the administration, and partly because of the tight control the French exercised over the activities of French West Africans, it rarely challenged the administration. It was too small for clandestine activities to go unnoticed. But the élite had undergone a dose of assimilation, and was at this time much less anti-assimilationist than some scholars have suggested.[45] Reaction to assimilation and nationalist demands were injected into the élite from those of its members who had managed to get to Paris.

The special position of the Senegalese citizens has already been examined. They had had educational opportunities of some sort for nearly a hundred years in St. Louis. They became the subalterns of the French expansion in West Africa in much the same way as the Creoles did in British West Africa. Dahomey had had long-standing trade relations with European powers. Freed slaves, notably Brazil-ians, had returned there to prosper in trade. Most important of all, Catholic missionaries had made Dahomey their main field of evangelisation outside Senegal. This was accompanied by a con-siderable educational programme which continued after the promul-gation of the *Loi Laïque*. Thus Dahomey provided a second source of subalterns for the French administration and they and the Senegalese were to be found up and down the Coast. The Senegalese, of course, were the privileged community, since they were citizens and had much greater freedom. A fascinating instance of the relationship of these two élites is the role of Diagne in early Daho-mean politics. In 1917 Governor Charles Noufflard of Dahomey was retired from Dahomey after a campaign against his administration led by a *métis* lawyer, Germaine Crespin, from Senegal and a Dahomean businessman, Tovalou Quenum. Crespin was related to

Adolphe Crespin of Goré who had been responsible for Diagne's early education. They accused Noufflard of supporting two tyrannical Commandants de Cercle. Diagne, as Deputy, was able to insist on an inquiry into the affair by the Government-General. Similarly Louis Hunankrin, a brilliant Dahomean who had been educated at the École Normale at St. Louis, was supported by Diagne. He had been dismissed from his post as teacher at the Ouidah Government School in 1910 for indiscipline. In 1912 he was sent to jail in Dakar for one year on the grounds that he stole goods from his new employers, C.F.A.O. When he was released he campaigned for Diagne's election in 1914, before returning to Dahomey to set up a branch of the French *Ligue des Droits de l'Homme*. Diagne was to repay his earlier support. In 1918, on his recruitment tour of Dahomey, he secured a safe passage for Hunankrin, who had fled to Nigeria, fearing imprisonment under the *indigénat* for his attacks on Noufflard. Diagne obtained an 'amnesty' for him, and he became one of the 63,000 troops Diagne recruited. However, Diagne arranged an appointment for him in the office in Paris dealing with Colonial Troops. There he was able to continue his anti-colonial activities until he was discharged in 1921 and shipped to Dakar, where he was imprisoned for six months for possession of 'subversive' literature.[46]

Hunankrin was the first of the African élite in Paris to have a direct influence on politics in Africa. In Dahomey he continued from his prison cell to campaign against the government. Though there was no direct evidence of his implication in the 1923 riots, it was considered best to keep him outside Dahomey and he was exiled to Mauritania for ten years.

Senegal, with its free press, was to have a major impact on the élite from the rest of French West Africa. Only in Dahomey was there a press which could in any way compare to that of Senegal. And there it was constantly under threat of suppression by the French. The students at the École Normale William Ponty who came from Sudan, Ivory Coast, Guinea and Niger, where the *indigénat* reigned supreme, were introduced to a new life where candidates abused each other as Communists,[47] where French newspapers circulated freely and where the Senegalese Deputy and his opponents carried on violent wars in the local press, which reached its height when Diouf became Deputy opposed by Lamine Guèye.[48] But the students of William Ponty had an assured future, even if a restricted one, and they were subjected to a strongly assimilationist education. There is little evidence that many of them reacted strongly against this assimilationist policy at the time. Even the growing interest manifested by them in African culture was as much the result of a change in French educational policy as an initiative of their own. At the time Mumford and St. Orde-Browne made their tour of French West African educational institutions in 1934 the French had decided that 'the educated African has to enrich the French culture he receives with a form of culture of his own; he has to effect the fusion of two races'.[49] Governor-General Brévié had earlier remarked with enthusiasm that 'an intellectual movement is taking form which, deriving its inspiration from the pure French tradition, is dipping deep into the springs of native life'.[50] The French even instituted a prize to encourage this essentially negritudinous movement. Charles Béart, a Popular Front appointee as Director of William Ponty, in encouraging Ponty students 'to develop African culture through the use of French forms', was not therefore an innovator, as Schachter-Morgenthau seems to suggest.[51] And 'the preoccupation with African culture—which was their reaction to the assault French education made on African values and customs—[which] they carried into the field of politics after the war',[52] seems to have had a French origin. The first play on an African theme produced by students of William Ponty was *La dernière entrevue de Behanzin et de Bayol*, performed in the 1932–3 session. It was written by some Dahomean students. In 1937 William Ponty students performed two of their African plays in Paris at the Théâtre des Champs Élysées, just after the formation of the Popular Front Government in 1936.[53]

These explorations of the African past and culture represented bold thinking at a time when the entire educational emphasis was on the production of the *évolué*, as Dathorne has put it.[54] However, the élite still seems to have had primarily assimilationist goals. Ouezzin-Coulibaly, who was Beart's director of studies at Ponty, and a leader of the radical *Rassemblement Démocratique Africain* in post-war years, was applying for French citizenship in 1939.[55] In the same year he volunteered for service in the war, writing to the famous French administrator Robert Delavignette in these terms: 'It is up to us to give the example, to bring in our ignorant brothers, who, for the most part, are spontaneous enthusiasts for the defence of France.'[56] It was Ouezzin who wrote the article for *Dakar-Jeunes*, a Vichy publication, entitled 'La magnifique aventure des noires Français: La Colonisation Française vue par un indigène evolué'.[57] Ouezzin-Coulibaly was not an exception. Rather he was typical of his generation of Ponty graduates. He after all founded with Mamadou Konaté, the Sudanese radical of the post-war years, the first French West African trade union, the teachers' union, which grouped together much of the élite in French West Africa.

William Ponty was important not as a hothouse for incipient nationalism, but because it brought together Africans from all the French colonies. In so far as they seem to have been politically oriented, it was to the attainment of better conditions for themselves: equal pay with Europeans and greater opportunities for their further education. Their return to African culture was encouraged if not instigated by the French and was not an initiative of the Popular Front régime. Nor indeed was it discouraged under Vichy, as has been suggested. *Dakar-Jeunes*, the Vichy periodical, carried many articles about African culture written by Africans like Ousmane Soce Diop, Ouezzin-Coulibaly, and Mamadou Dia.[58]

It was in France that open hostility to the colonial system was manifested by the élite. If the élite felt such hostility in French West Africa, it was never expressed openly. But it is not surprising that the élite in French West Africa was restrained in its public criticism of the administration. Apart from the provisions of the *indigénat*, laws were passed in 1927 against the importation of 'subversive' literature, and in 1935 against practically all forms of criticism of authority. Only in France was it possible for any free discussion to take place. And, as we have seen, there were few African students there. But some of them did participate in radical movements such as those who took part in 1936 in the *Comité d'action éthiopienne* with left-wing French students.[59] Alas there is as yet no detailed study of the political activities of French African students in this period.[60]

The influence of Paris on Hunankrin, for instance, was profound. His anti-colonial spirit fed on anarchist and communist doctrine whilst he was in Paris. It was for possession of communist and anarchist papers that he was sentenced to six months' imprisonment on demobilisation in Dakar. He was then shipped to Dahomey where he was sentenced to three years in prison for possessing false identity papers. The real motive for this was of course his wartime activities, now covered by a general amnesty. His contacts with the *Ligue des Droits de l'Homme* while he was in Paris enabled him to obtain publicity for administrative injustices in Dahomey even while he was in prison. Indeed he was able to re-establish his local branch of the *Ligue* since a society legally recognised in France could establish a branch in the colonies.[61]

Before the passage of the 1927 law against the importation of subversive literature, the administration had clearly been worried by its impact. Garvey's *Negro World* had been imported by Hunankrin into Dahomey. And though in 1923 Governor-General Carde said 'Garveyism had disappeared the moment it was born',[62] in 1925 he was complaining that the increasingly close relations between Africa and Europe were bringing in the seeds of tares.[63]

The administration did its best to ensure that Africans who returned from Paris with revolutionary ideas, like Hunankrin, did not have a chance to sow these tares. His exile in Mauritania after the 1923 riots effectively silenced him where prison in Dahomey could not. The same fate awaited Kodjo Tovalou Houenou, who, after founding the *Ligue universelle de défense de la race noire* in Paris in 1924, was incautious enough to return to Africa. Landing in Lomé, he was sent to Dahomey where the authorities were only too happy to place him under house arrest. He had supplied the Dahomean Press with articles, had published an anti-colonial journal in Paris, *Les Continents*, and was in close touch with the Communist Party and Garvey.[64] His *Ligue* was re-established in 1927 as the *Comité de la défense de la race nègre* by Lamine Senghor, a veteran of the 1914–18 war. He was a founder of the *Ligue contre l'impérialisme et l'oppression coloniale* whose inaugural meeting was attended by Mme Sun Yat Sen and Nehru. In 1929 he was arrested and died in prison.[65] His successor was a Sudanese, Kouyate, who published a series of newspapers, all banned in the colonies, *La Voix des Nègres*, *Le Cri Nègre*, and *La Race Nègre*. He was shot by the Nazis during the German occupation of France.[66]

The Paris of the '30's was a curiously interesting city for the Negro, for Africa was very much in vogue. Its art, its dancing, its music were in great demand.[67] Even if the acceptance of the Negro stemmed from a contemporary interest in the exotic, Negro students had a freedom and range of intellectual contact not open to their British West African counterparts in London. French West Indian and African students discussed with each other and with French students the virtues of communism and surrealism. In 1932 *Légitime défense* was launched by Martiniquan students to defend the originality of the Negro race, using communism and surrealism as its tools.[68] Its ideas influenced African students including Senghor.[69] In 1934 Senghor, future President of Senegal who had just become the first African *agregé de l'Université*,[70] together with Aimé Césaire founded *L'Étudiant Noir* in which they launched their concept of *négritude*. 'Their great hope', wrote Guibert, 'was to link Negroes of French nationality or *statut* with their history, with their traditions, and with their languages which express their soul again.'[71] The organisers of *L'Étudiant Noir* included two other Senegalese who became famous as writers, Birago Diop and Ousmane Socé Diop, whose novel *Karim*, published in 1934, is a striking document of the life and dilemma of Senegalese *assimilés*.[72] They differed in their approach to the problem of the Negro from the organisers of *Légitime défense* in that they asserted that cultural renaissance, rather than political revolution, was the more important. They did not deny the importance of political emancipation, but saw it only as an aspect of their cultural emancipation.[73] They rejected Communism while accepting the validity and usefulness of many of Marx's ideas. However, Senghor, though a member of the S.F.I.O., voted Communist in 1936.[74] Aimé Césaire did not join the Party until 1944.

Though Senghor and Césaire believed in the primacy of cultural renaissance, their movement was nevertheless essentially political in that it rejected the French policy of assimilation. It rejected the idea that Africans had no culture of their own. It rejected a policy that assimilated an élite and associated the masses, thus dividing the two. The inspiration for Aimé Césaire's *Cahier d'un retour au pays natal*, published in 1939, was his horror at finding himself being ashamed of a Negro in the same train as himself.[75] This forced him to seek his Negro roots to deny his assimilation by France. Whilst Césaire cried 'Hurrah for those who invented nothing' Senghor, more sure of his roots as an African, was able to develop the more eclectic approach of 'assimiler, non être assimilé'.[76]

Senghor's reaction against assimilation came at a time, as we have seen, when French educational policy was to encourage Africans to look to their past. This makes it no less important, for, after years of assimilation, the élite would look with unaccustomed eyes at the past, and seize on it for inspiration for the future. The élite in British West Africa was familiar with its past, for the British through indirect rule tried to preserve much of it. Senghor, in the post-war years, tried to erect negritude into a political ideology. And most French West African leaders sought inspiration in a traditional Africa for their political ideas in a way the British did not.

Outside France and Senegal political activity was minimal. The strictures against it were such that it became well-nigh impossible. The administration had its eyes everywhere in the person of its chiefs, one of whose duties was to report criticism of the administration. Given such strictures it was clearly very difficult for the élite to make criticisms, even clandestinely, such as the British West Africans were able to do openly both in the Press and in the Legislative Council. There is little evidence, however, that the William Ponty élite did hold radical views in those days. Their general attitude was expressed

2G

in Lamine Guèye and Leopold Sedar Senghor's programme at the elections to the Constituent Assembly of 1945:

'Our programme can be summarised in a very simple formula: a single category of Frenchmen, having exactly the same rights since all are subject to the same duties, including dying for the same country.'[77]

The speeches of those elected to the two constituents confirm this.[78] Some leaders have attempted to present a more radical picture of their past. But as Bakary Traoré says: 'One of the difficult tasks of those who are concerned with African political science, is to distinguish the truth from what is pure propaganda after the event in the "écrits apologétiques" of politicians.'[79]

# Notes

1 Preface to *L'Afrique Occidentale Française* (various authors), Paris, 1913, p. 11.
2 Reproduced in 'Native Affairs in the Ivory Coast and Togoland', *The Gold Coast Review*, II, 2, 1926, July–September.
3 Cosnier, *Report*, p. 162 and p. 165.
4 Amon d'Aby, *La Côte d'Ivoire*, pp. 46–7.
5 N.A.S. Personal File of Blaise Diagne. Diagne to Angoulvant, Dakar, 14th February 1918.
6 'Un Vieil Africain' in *Les Annales Coloniales*, July 1918.
7 'Un Administrateur', *Les Annales Coloniales*, July 1918.
8 Wesley Johnson, 'Blaise Diagne: Master Politician of Senegal', *Tarikh*, I, 2, p. 53.
9 Traoré, *Forces Politiques*, p. 9.
10 *L'A.O.F.*, 1st May 1924, cited by Suret-Canale, *Afrique Noire II*, p. 550.
11 *Ibid.*, 8th May 1924, cited by Suret-Canale, *Afrique Noire II*, p. 551.
12 Johnson, 'Blaise Diagne: Master Politician', p. 54.
13 Cited in Cros, *Blaise Diagne*, pp. 119–20.
14 André Gide, *Voyage au Congo*, Paris, 1929, p. 89.
15 See Joel A. Rogers, *World's Great Men of Color*, New York, 1947, p. 419.
16 N.A.S. Personal File of Blaise Diagne.
17 Boulégur, 'La Presse au Sénégal', p. 719.
18 Schachter-Morgenthau, *Political Parties in French-Speaking West Africa*, p. 132.
19 Wesley Johnson, 'Blaise Diagne: Master Politician', p. 54.
20 James Coleman, 'The Emergence of African Political Parties', in C. Grove Haines, ed., *Africa Today*, pp. 234–5.
21 John Ballard, 'The Porto Novo Incidents of 1923', *Odu*, II, 1, July 1965, p. 53.
22 G. Wesley Johnson is completing a thesis on Senegalese political history from 1900–40; James Spiegler is making a study of African politics in the inter-war period in Paris.
23 Schachter-Morgenthau, *Political Parties in French-Speaking West Africa*, p. 7.
24 *Nana* in Bobo means taking without paying and *Vo* means end.
25 Schachter-Morgenthau, *Political Parties in French-Speaking West Africa*, p. 8, citing an unpublished eye-witness account.
26 See John Ballard's article already cited.
27 *The Times*, 17th March 1923.
28 Suret-Canale, *Afrique Noire II*, pp. 553–5.
29 Ballard, 'The Porto Novo Incidents', p. 57.
30 Suret-Canale, *Afrique Noire II*, p. 558.
31 Armand Annet, *Aux heures troublées de l'Afrique française, 1939–43*, Paris, 1952, p. 17.

32  Yves Person, 'Soixante ans d'évolution en pays Kissi', *Cahiers d'Études Africaines*, I, 1960, p. 106 and p. 90.

33  Gregory Snyder, *One Party Government in Mali*, Newhaven, 1965, p. 13.

34  Georges Hardy, *Nos grands problèmes coloniaux*, Paris, 1929, pp. 203–4.

35  Armand Annet, *Aux heures troublées de l'Afrique française, 1939–43*, pp. 15–16.

36  Schachter-Morgenthau, *Political Parties in French-Speaking West Africa*, p. 12.

37  *Ibid.*, p. 13.

38  Suret-Canale, *Afrique Noire II*, p. 557.

39  Snyder, *Mali*, pp. 23–5.

40  Hardy, *Nos grands problèmes coloniaux*, p. 205.

41  Snyder, *Mali*, p. 28.

42  *Ibid.*, p. 27.

43  Hodgkin, *Nationalism in Colonial Africa*, p. 88.

44  Immanuel Wallerstein, 'Voluntary Associations' in Coleman and Rosberg, *Political Parties and National Integration*, pp. 333–4.

45  Schachter-Morgenthau, *Political Parties in French-Speaking West Africa*, pp. 14–15.

46  The above is based on Ballard, 'The Porto Novo Incidents'.

47  Suret-Canale, *Afrique Noire II*, p. 565.

48  Boulégur, 'La Presse au Sénégal', p. 179.

49  See Albert Charton (Inspector-General of Education in French West Africa), 'The Social Function of Education in French West Africa', in Mumford and Orde-Brown, *Africans Learn to be French*, p. 111.

50  *Ibid.*, p. 111.

51  Schachter-Morgenthau, *Political Parties in French-Speaking West Africa*, p. 14.

52  *Ibid.*, p. 14.

53  O. R. Dathorne, 'Pioneer African Drama: Heroines and the Church', *Bulletin of the Association for African Literature*, 4th March 1966, pp. 19–20.

54  *Ibid.*, p. 20.

55  Robert Delavignette, *L'Afrique Noire française et son destin*, Paris, 1962, p. 89.

56  *Ibid.*, p. 87.

57  *Dakar-Jeunes*, No. 22, 4th June 1942.

58  Schachter-Morgenthau, *Political Parties in French-Speaking West Africa*, pp. 272–3, writes: 'During the Second World War, Vichy tightened the autocratic system again, discouraged African Associations from working on historical subjects. . . .'

59  Lilyan Kesteloot, *Les écrivains noirs de langue française: naissance d'une littérature*, Brussels, 1963, p. 201.

60  Spiegler's study, referred to above, will help fill this important gap in our knowledge.

61 For the above: Ballard, 'The Porto Novo Incidents'.
62 Cited by Suret-Canale, *Afrique Noire II*, p. 561.
63 *Ibid.*, p. 561.
64 *Ibid.*, p. 562.
65 *Ibid.*, p. 562.
66 *Ibid.*, p. 563.
67 See Geoffrey Gorer, *Africa Dances*, London, 1935, p. 3. Sexual attraction seems also to have been important. Feral Benga, Gorer's Senegalese travelling companion, was much distressed in Paris 'that because he was a Negro and a dancer everybody considered that they had a right, if not a duty, to make sexual advances to him'.
68 Kesteloot, *Les écrivains noirs*, pp. 25–6
69 *Ibid*, p. 26, on Senghor's own evidence.
70 Armand Guibert, *Léopold Sédar Senghor*, Paris, 1961, p. 24, writes that this was considered so extraordinary an achievement that on his return to Dakar he was accorded military honours.
71 *Ibid.*, p. 23.
72 Ousmane Socé Diop, *Karim: Roman Sénégalais*, 2nd Edition, Paris, 1948.
73 Kesteloot, *Les écrivains noirs*, p. 92.
74 Guibert, *Senghor*, p. 24.
75 See Peter Guberina's preface to the 1956 edition, Paris, p. 17.
76 *Ibid.*, pp. 68–9. See Kesteloot's comments on this passage, *Les écrivains noirs*, p. 156.
77 Cited by Abdoulaye Ly, *Le Nationalisme dans l'Ouest Africain*, Dakar, 1958. See Traoré, *Forces Politiques*, p. 24.
78 See Michael Crowder, 'Independence as a Goal in French West African Politics, 1944–60', in William H. Lewis, ed., *French-Speaking Africa: The Search for Identity*, New York, 1965.
79 Traoré, *Forces Politiques*, p. 24.

# 3 Politics in British West Africa, 1920–39

## 1 The constitutional framework

Politics in British West Africa during the inter-war years was dominated by the same élite that sponsored the National Congress of British West Africa. The ambition of this élite was increased participation by its members in the government and administration of the country, but it sought to achieve this by constitutional means. It chose to operate within the boundaries established by the new constitutions introduced by the British government for Nigeria, Sierra Leone and the Gold Coast in the early 1920's. Though self-government was the ultimate aim, the immediate goals were to ensure that the educated élite rather than the traditional rulers were looked on by the colonial governments as the basis for future political developments; to increase the pace of Africanisation in government services so that there would be more openings for its members in the administration of the country; to broaden educational opportunities; and to secure opportunities for African businessmen in the colonial economy, which was increasingly dominated by expatriate companies and the Lebanese.

The élite showed little concern for the masses, and as Obafemi Awolowo pointed out in 1947, 'the illiterate masses have little or no confidence in the educated few, for the simple reason that the latter, in their political activities, are completely out of touch with the former'.[1] It was only in the 1930's that political groups began to emerge that tried to broaden the hitherto exclusive politics of West

Africa to gain support from, and show concern for, the common people, and to look for support beyond the limits of the coastal towns to the vast but still largely undeveloped hinterlands. It is in these groups that we can trace the origins of the political parties which after the Second World War secured the support of the masses for their demands for independence. These youth movements were no longer content merely with improving their 'position *within* the colonial system [but] sought to change the whole system into another which would make them masters instead of the British'.[2]

The first of the British West African colonies to be given a new constitution in which provision for elected representation was made was Nigeria in 1922. This replaced Lugard's Nigerian Council which could pass resolutions at its annual meetings, which would, however, only be put into effect if the Governor thought fit. It was a useless body and Sir Hugh Clifford talked contemptuously of 'the dreary and apathetic meetings of the so-called Nigerian Council which always seemed to me a debating society in which nobody would enter debate'.[3] The most important feature of the new constitution was the provision made for the election of four of the Legislative Council members: three from Lagos and one from Calabar. In addition there were to be fifteen unofficial members nominated by the Governor to represent business interests and the various provinces of Southern Nigeria. The nineteen unofficial members were, however, in a minority of seven, for there were twenty-three official members sitting on the Council by virtue of their office, and three nominated by the Governor, who sat as President of the Council with a casting vote and the power of veto.

The new Nigerian Constitution was followed by that of Sierra Leone in 1924. There, the official majority was much smaller. Of the twenty-one members of the Legislative Council, only eleven were officials. However, of the unofficials two represented European business interests, and nearly always the Europeans sided with the official majority in any vote. Of the remaining eight unofficials, three were directly elected by the Colony, and five were nominated by the Governor, two of them being from the Colony, and three Paramount Chiefs from the Protectorate. Its legislative competence included both Protectorate and the Colony.

The most complex of the three new constitutions was that of the Gold Coast, introduced in 1925. It was the only one that provoked sustained opposition. Officials numbered fifteen, unofficials fourteen, including three directly elected members for Accra, Cape Coast and Sekondi. The distinctive feature of the constitution was the provision it made for the election, by specially constituted Provincial Councils, of six unofficial members to represent the Colony. A Council was established for each of the three Provinces of the Colony and was composed of the Omanhene, or head chiefs, of the Province. Each Council then elected two of its members, by definition chiefs, to the Legislative Council. Whereas under the reforms introduced by Clifford in 1916 provision was made for the nomination of three 'educated' members and 'three chiefs' to sit on Legislative Council, the new constitution kept the number of 'educated' representatives the same, though now they were elected, but doubled the number of chiefs who were also now to be elected. This, as we shall see, aroused bitter opposition from the educated élite. Furthermore, the three members for Accra, Cape Coast and Sekondi could only be elected after the Municipal Corporations Ordinance of 1924 had been put into operation. This Ordinance had, however, been solidly opposed in the three towns meant to benefit from it. On the surface a liberal ordinance which provided for an elected majority in the Municipal Corporations to be presided over by an African Mayor as in the Freetown City Council, it angered the people because it entailed the imposition of a direct tax in the form of rates, and did not satisfactorily make provision for the position of the traditional authorities of these towns. The educated élite were highly annoyed that elections to Legislative Council should be dependent on the electors accepting an unpopular local government ordinance. Eventually this provision was withdrawn, but the Government stuck to its ground over the matter of the Provincial Councils.

Because of opposition it was not until 1927 that the new Gold Coast Legislative Council came into operation. The only colony for which no provision was made for directly elected representatives was the Gambia.

These new constitutions remained substantially unchanged until after the Second World War. The only major change was the establishment of a standing Finance Committee for Sierra Leone in 1938 with an African unofficial majority. This was the first time an institution of colonial government in Africa had an African majority.

The new constitutions of Nigeria and Sierra Leone were generally welcomed as a significant step forward by the African élite. The Sierra Leone section of the National Congress of British West Africa was however unhappy about the representation of the Protectorate by Paramount Chiefs rather than commoners, partly because they considered them too closely involved with the colonial administration, partly because they resented the power the chiefs already possessed, without it being reinforced by their participation in the Central Legislature.[4]

It was only in Gold Coast that opposition was strong enough to lead to a delegation of protest to the Secretary of State in 1926, and the subsequent boycott of the municipal elections. Even so, when the constitution was first published J. B. Danquah, later to be leader of the first political party of the Gold Coast, wrote to *West Africa* that 'all things considered, the new Constitution is a splendid advance on the old one, and one can confidently hope that the Governor and his advisers will receive general appreciation for this additional evidence of their desire to lead the Gold Coast people from progress to progress'.[5] However, he did warn that the educated élite might resent the preponderance of chiefs in the new constitution, and hoped that the chiefs could, under the provisions for the Provincial Councils, elect lawyer-politicians as well as chiefs,[6] so that there might be up to six commoners in Legislative Council, as Casely-Hayford hoped.[7] If, in fact, the British had made provision for this, they might have fostered unity between the chiefs and educated commoners, instead of driving a wedge (deliberately as the nationalists saw it) between the two.[8]

The British Government, however, determined to make the constitution work without changing it, though it was agreed to allow the election of municipal members even though the Municipal Corporations Ordinance was not yet in force. However, since time would be needed to amend the Letters Patent to allow for their election without the Municipal Corporations being established,[9] three members were nominated to represent the coastal towns. Casely-Hayford, despite his long-standing membership as a nominated member, refused to accept the offer of a seat. The Executive Committee of the A.R.P.S. tried to ensure that none of their members accepted nomination in these circumstances. 'The issue is one of life and death with us. For if you perpetuate the possibility of the return of dummies to the Legislature, our national independence is gone forever. Probably that is what has been aimed at all the time,' warned the *Gold Coast Leader*, 'so to gag the people that while they have a machinery ostensibly of an advanced type, yet to be truly voiceless in the affairs of their own country.'[10] The A.R.P.S. also persuaded many chiefs of the Central Province not to attend their Provincial Council meeting, though enough did to return their two members. The Western Province, through apathy and hostility to the new councils, did not elect members till 1928, showing that the educated élite still had influence on the chiefs.

In 1927, when the constitution had been amended with regard to the election of the municipal members, the government arranged elections in all three towns. While Sekyi and the bulk of the A.R.P.S. in Cape Coast continued to boycott the elections, Casely-Hayford, Secretary of the A.R.P.S., decided to stand in Accra on the grounds that eventually some educated Africans would, and it might as well be members of the A.R.P.S. for otherwise others would gain seats in the one institution of government in which Africans could make themselves heard. In Cape Coast, despite the boycott, a young lawyer, K. A. Korsah (later Chief Justice of the Gold Coast), who had been elected a member of the Executive Committee of the A.R.P.S. in 1922, stood and was returned unopposed. Opposition was so deep-rooted, however, that the traditional ruler of Cape Coast and Sekyi unsuccessfully tried to stop the election and petitioned against its result. Thereafter Sekyi and the Cape Coast A.R.P.S. remained an intransigent rump, refusing to recognise the legitimacy of the new constitution.

The three constitutions gave the educated élite relatively little room for manœuvre. Though there was considerable freedom of speech in the Legislative Council, the elected members had no actual power. Only when their views coincided with mass opposition outside the walls of the chamber was the colonial government likely to withdraw a bill. Thus in 1934, against the combined opposition of the six elected chiefs and the three elected municipal members, the Waterworks Ordinance and the Criminal Code Amendment Ordinance were passed by the official majority. But the Waterworks Ordinance, which would involve the paying of rates, and the Criminal Code Amendment Ordinance, which effectively meant that the Governor and not the courts decided what was a seditious publication, also met with widespread opposition outside Legislative Council. Petitions were presented to the Secretary of State by the chiefs and by the A.R.P.S.[11] Though they were not withdrawn, the application of the Waterworks Ordinance was delayed until 1938 and the Sedition clause of the Criminal Code Amendment Ordinance was rarely implemented.[12]

The elected representatives in the Legislative Councils had a very narrow base. They represented only a small group in the towns. In Nigeria qualifications for the municipal electors were to be an adult male, who was a British subject or a 'Native of the Protectorate' with residence qualifications, and to have a gross income of £100 per annum. In the Gold Coast both sexes could vote in the elections, provided they occupied a house of a rateable value of £6 per annum. In 1939 this meant an electorate of 7,063 for a combined population of the three towns of 114,003.[13] While the elected representatives were able to, and did, introduce discussion on a wide variety of matters, their actual powers were limited by the impervious official majority which sat opposite them: Government, in both its executive and legislative capacities, ready to block any measure of which it was told the Governor disapproved. As Nana Ayirebi Acquah complained in a Legislative Council debate in the Gold Coast: 'Our impression is that as soon as a measure gets to the Secretary of State and a decision thereon is arrived at, we shall find it very difficult to put up a real fight by making any objections, because we shall, as usual, be beaten down by the prevailing official majority.'[14] Another major limitation on their powers was the short time for which the Legislative Councils sat each year. For instance the Gold Coast Legislative Council never had an opportunity to discuss the Cocoa Hold-up.[15] Government always had the initiative, as the Chief Secretary of Nigeria put it so patronisingly during the Estimates Debate of 1938. 'It is no doubt difficult for unofficial members to study them efficiently for the purpose of criticising them, but you must trust those of us who have been at this game for nearly thirty years not to accept them blindly.'[16]

How much influence the unofficials on Legislative Councils had depended very much on how seriously a Governor took their views. Some saw Legislative Councils as vehicles through which they could sound out African opinion, others, like Sir Shenton Thomas of the Gold Coast (1932–4), saw it as 'a platform for publishing government measures and not an incipient Parliament . . .' He considered that he '. . . had to discover public opinion through other channels as well'.[17] On the other hand the existence of an active press in all three colonies reporting debates to an interested, if limited but vocal, public meant Government had to take account of unofficial opinion in controversial matters. And not only elected unofficials. In Nigeria and Sierra Leone the nominated African members, despite their apparent dependence on Government for their position, were sometimes as outspoken in criticism as the elected members.

Government expected the elected members to be strictly constitutional in their opposition. When it was found that two of the elected members of the Sierra Leone Legislative Council, Bankole-Bright and Beoku-Betts, had assisted and encouraged the railway strikers of 1926, the Colonial Secretary proposed suspending the constitution as far as it provided for elected members. The Governor rejected this extreme reaction but reported to the Secretary of State that 'the events of the last few months have supplied Government with abundant reasons for proceeding at a much slower pace with Africanisation of the service ... and ... they obviously afford unanswerable arguments against any requests for further constitutional developments in the present generation'.[18]

Real power lay squarely with the Governor, who controlled the official majority which was much better disciplined than any political party. Whereas the unofficials had no representatives on his Executive Council, several of the official members of Legislative Council sat on Executive Council. Even Executive Council had limited powers with regard to the Governor. Whilst he was bound to seek its advice, he still retained executive supremacy over his colleagues. So far as their influence on the machinery of government was concerned, the elected members were only of significance in so far as the colonial authorities were prepared to listen to their protests and criticisms. What is significant about them is the way they chose to protest, and the issues about which they protested.

## 2 Élite politics

The members of the educated élite who gained control of the elected seats in the three legislatures were, with rare exceptions, constant in their dedication to the principle of protest only through constitutional channels. They were also strong in their protestations of loyalty to the British empire. It was not difficult for the Government to seduce them with invitations to Governors' garden parties, presentation to H.R.H. the Prince of Wales, or the prospect of an O.B.E. or even, distantly, a knighthood. As members of Legislative Council they were accorded the title of Honourable, and enjoyed one of the few opportunities the African had of sitting with white officials on equal terms. However radical their views may have been on first entering Legislative Council, the majority of members soon became more concerned with prestige than politics. They were effectively bought over by the colonial régime. Even the Nigerian National Democratic Party, leading party in Lagos, which had clashed bitterly with Governor Clifford, addressed his successor in 1925 in these terms: '... we have always endeavoured, in so far as consistent with the ideals of a people labouring in the throes of nation-birth, to co-operate with Government for the purpose of preserving Nigeria not only as an integral part of the Empire, but also as a bright jewel within the imperial panorama . . .'[19] These affirmations of loyalty to the British Crown are a constant theme in the speeches of the élite politicians. In 1922, Casely-Hayford told the delegates to the Freetown Session of the N.C.B.W.A. in his Presidential Address: '. . . notwithstanding any local differences that may exist with the local Administrations, the heart of British West Africa today beats true in loyalty and devotion to the throne and person of His Majesty the King Emperor.'[20] And at the Bathurst Session of 1925 he was talking of the fine and warm reception given by the Governor of the Gambia to a Congress delegation.[21]

The elected members were all professional men or businessmen, the majority being lawyers. Many of them still looked to West Africa as the ultimate focus of their activities, though the fact that the four colonial governments remained separate meant that they concentrated increasingly on local rather than West African issues. In Sierra Leone the elected members were Creoles; in Gold Coast they were indigenous commoners though many had connections with royal houses. In Nigeria, curiously, immigrant Africans dominated politics until 1938. For instance in the 1923 election, of the three Lagos members only one was Nigerian born. The other two were of Gambian and Sierra Leone origin respectively, whilst the member for Calabar was a full-blooded Ghanaian, Ata-Amonu.[22] The Nigerian Youth Movement was later to campaign on the issue of representation of Nigerians by Nigerians in the Legislative Council. Aware that at least one colonial official of importance had publicly commented 'that the electors of Nigeria on the first grant of the franchise have not found it possible to elect members of Nigerian descent to represent them', their slogan was 'Nigeria for the Nigerians'.[23]

In Nigeria the provision for elected members in the new constitution led to the formation of a number of voters' associations, only one of which became recognisable as a political party: the N.N.D.P., founded by Herbert Macaulay, who himself could not stand for election because he had served a prison sentence, owed much of its success to his ceaseless energy, his considerable organising ability, and his 'caustic pen'.[24]

Macaulay, grandson of Bishop Crowther, and an engineer by profession, dominated Nigerian politics until 1938, when the Nigerian Youth Movement won the elections. Even after that his party was returned to power again right up to and including the 1947 elections under the new constitution. Though there were only three seats, the party organisation had to fight more elections than may be imagined. For members held their seats for five years from the date of their individual election, and this meant that between 1923 and 1947 there were eleven elections.

Though the N.N.D.P. had national pretensions, it was primarily a Lagos party, whose activities were consumed by the Eleko question (see p. 423). Its greatest triumph came when in 1931, three years after Macaulay had been imprisoned for six months for publishing a false rumour concerning a plot to blow up the Eleko if he returned to Lagos from exile in Oyo,[25] the Eleko was restored. Despite the N.N.D.P.'s early plans to establish branches elsewhere in the country, it never did, not even in Calabar, where at least there was the stimulus of the prospect of gaining a seat in the Legislative Council. It sometimes tackled issues of nation-wide interest, but this was not the result of a coherent national programme. After 1931, though it retained its electoral control of Lagos, it became increasingly conservative in character. Even so Macaulay, by then an old man, kept in touch with the masses to a much greater extent than other politicians of his generation.

In Sierra Leone the N.C.B.W.A. transformed itself into a political party for the purpose of fighting elections. It had been active in demanding 'popular representation and the elective franchise' and in 1926, as we have seen, two of its elected members had given support to the railway strikers. This was, however, the only occasion on which the N.C.B.W.A. in Sierra Leone joined forces with the common man and thereafter it remained the exclusive organisation[26] it was at its foundation. It made no attempt to reach out to the Protectorate. Its predominantly Creole members and electors were mentally cut off from the Protectorate, many of them looking down on its inhabitants, talking about them with the same disdain many English showed for the Creoles themselves. It was not until 1938, when I. T. A. Wallace Johnson founded his youth league, that new life was injected into Sierra Leone politics.

J. B. Danquah had expressed the hope that the 1925 constitution would herald 'the birth of real party politics in the Gold Coast'.[27] In the event no political parties emerged, even though there were two active organisations of a political nature that might have converted themselves into parties—the A.R.P.S. and the N.C.B.W.A., whose membership overlapped at the time the new constitution was promulgated. The President of N.C.B.W.A., Casely-Hayford, was a Vice-President of the A.R.P.S. After the initial opposition of the A.R.P.S. to the N.C.B.W.A., Casely-Hayford had ousted the former's executive, and effectively captured the A.R.P.S. for his Congress. In 1927, the A.R.P.S. was split in two by the decision of Casely-Hayford to stand for election to the Legislative Council and was in disarray. The N.C.B.W.A., itself, was conceived as a pan-West African organisation, and though it adapted itself in Sierra Leone to the new opportunities that the 1924 constitution presented, it was largely an obsolete organisation in the Gold Coast. Casely-Hayford was so involved in the struggle for leadership in Gold Coast politics that he gave little time to its local organisation.[28] In Nigeria it had effectively folded up, though in 1925 there were reports of attempts to revive it there.[29] Increasingly a social organisation of considerable prestige, it was not geared to being used as a machine for electoral purposes and no attempt was made to resuscitate it to this end. In the 1927 elections in Accra and Sekondi, the A.R.P.S. and N.C.B.W.A. took no part as such: all that happened was the creation of what might most aptly be called Voters' Registration Associations.[30] And from then until the eve of the Second World War no party emerged. The N.C.B.W.A. died in 1930 with Casely-Hayford. The only active branch of the A.R.P.S. had as a matter of policy refused to fight elections under the existing constitution. As Martin Wight commented: 'It is difficult to describe municipal members in terms of policy. In the absence of party organisation, their importance lies in their personal qualities, not what they "stand for".'[31] Indeed the political élite seems to have been dominated by personal and municipal rivalries, and it took major issues to unite them. This feuding was true also of Lagos politics, but in the midst of it the N.N.D.P. was able to act as a party machine. In 1926, at the first bye-election under the constitution, it was able to get elected its candidate, Dr. P. J. A. Caulrick, over his better-known rivals, Messrs. P. J. C. Thomas, A. Alakija and G. D. Agbebi.[32] Certainly personal feuding was the bane of early African politics. As Casely-Hayford told his colleagues of the N.C.B.W.A. just before his death: 'The gods, indeed, must be weary of our ever-lasting wranglings, weary of our vain disputations, weary of our everlasting quarrels, which are a drag upon progress, and which keep from us, as a people, the good that is intended for us.'[33] Casely-Hayford, himself, had indulged in a great deal of wrangling in his time. However in 1929 he had managed to settle his differences with Nana Ofori Atta, the unofficial leader of the chiefs in the Legislative Council, and a member of as long standing as Casely-Hayford. Though they had quarrelled bitterly over the respective roles of chiefs and commoners, this rapprochement laid the basis of a co-operation in the Legislative Council that was of great significance. Thereafter chiefly and municipal members met together before Legislative Council to decide common lines of action, meaning that on important issues Government met a united unofficial African opposition.

Throughout the period under consideration the elected members only infrequently voiced demands for liberalisation of the constitution: their main concern remained to gain a place in the sun for the educated African.

## 3 Grievances of the élite

No other government policy raised such hostility among the educated élite as that of indirect rule. In Nigeria it was the most prominent subject in Legislative Council debates.[34] In the Gold Coast it broke the long-standing alliance between the educated élite and traditional rulers. In Sierra Leone it entrenched the differences between Colony and Protectorate. In all three colonies the educated élite resented Britain's belief that the chiefs were 'the true representatives and spokesmen of the people', and her policy 'that constitutional representation must grow naturally from the indigenous political systems . . .'.[35] Where the élite hoped that constitutional reform would come in the shape of an African majority in Legislative Council based on elected representation, the British Government talked in terms of increased local self-government for Africans through their traditional rulers. To this end the British strengthened the powers of the chiefs, and where necessary protected them against attacks by the educated Africans whose numbers had increased greatly as a result of the imposition of colonial rule. Britain became bizarrely the agent for the conservation and modernisation of African society at one and the same time.

For the educated African indirect rule appeared as a subtle policy designed to frustrate his ambition to take a greater part in the government of his country. He regarded with great suspicion the relationship of the chief to the administrator under the system of indirect rule, and feared that it was a means of setting educated African against chief, another example of the well-tried imperial formula of divide and rule.[36] The classic example of this was the acrimonious battle over the N.C.B.W.A. in which Casely-Hayford called Nana Ofori Atta, who had sided with Guggisberg, a traitor to his face. But the élite did not oppose the native authorities as such, and never called for their abolition. Indeed some of the most ardent champions of the chiefs and traditional systems of government were the educated élite. But they wanted the chiefs and their governments modernised, and provision made for their own participation in these governments. In Western Nigeria, for instance, the educated élite cited Abeokuta as obvious proof that even before British occupation, traditional authorities in co-operation with the educated élite had produced a modernising system of government. Like Lugard, the élite believed that the native authorities could, and should, be open to constant innovation. Traditionally all African states, including the Emirates of Northern Nigeria, had shared power between the ruler and other sections of the community. Under indirect rule the educated élite saw Native Authorities become autocratic bastions of conservatism. As Oyerinde, nominated member for Oyo, complained in the Nigerian Legislative Council, 'there was inadequate representation of the people in the direction and management of the native administration'.[37] The *Gold Coast Leader*, attacking the Native Jurisdiction Ordinance of 1927 for the increased powers it gave the chiefs, wrote fearfully: 'The time is coming when a chief once installed will sit firmly on the neck of the people, like the old man of the sea, and rule them in his own way without any lawful means of getting rid of him.'[38] Traditionally authority in Akan society was decentralised, and the commoners had more control over the decision-making process than in most African societies ruled by chiefs. It was thus particularly galling for the educated élite to see the authority of the chiefs strengthened by the colonial authorities to such an extent that even the traditional sanction of de-stoolment by the people now lost its force, since Government had to uphold it. And as Rattray emphasised, 'Every political officer is familiar with the dictum "the power and the authority of the Paramount Chief must be upheld" '.[39] It was for this reason that the élite were so persistent in their opposition to the various measures introduced by the government to strengthen the chiefs; and the reason they appeared to be champions of tradition and accused the British administration of perverting custom, was that by tradition they, the commoners, had much more influence in the government of the native authorities than they would have under indirect rule. Calls such as those made by Awolowo for the abolition of indirect rule[40] did not imply a demand for an end to chiefs, but to the system of government that had made them unpopular and distorted their role as 'fathers of the people'. As Awolowo admitted: 'Whatever may be the shortcomings of individual chiefs, the fact remains that the masses of the people think the world of the office' and 'Chiefs

2H

will continue to have incalculable sentimental value in Western and Northern Nigeria'.[41]

Only in Sierra Leone would the élite, or at least the educated élite of the Colony, happily have done away with the chiefs. The Creoles, of course, had no chiefs, and for them they represented the major obstacle to progress in the Protectorate, and more particularly to Creole influence there. In the nineteenth century the Creoles had dominated hinterland trade and, when the Protectorate was proclaimed, had hoped that they would be its administrators. But they were excluded from the administration except in subordinate roles, and lost their control of trade. The British pursued a policy of protecting the Protectorate from the Creoles, and 'Creole merchants, business men, petty traders and landowners ... found their activities in the Protectorate subject to the selfish caprice and erratic whim of chiefs and tribal authorities, without much hope of political or legal redress. European and other expatriate entrepreneurs, on the other hand, had the power and authority of the colonial system to serve their interests.'[42] To the Creole, the chiefs represented not only a rival power group but an entirely alien one which they had every reason to resent. Creole tendencies to look down on Protectorate society with contempt were reinforced by the colonial policy of indirect rule. The rising class of educated men in the Protectorate, many of whom had chiefly connections, found themselves unable to penetrate exclusive Creole society. There was no hope of them reaching Legislative Council as Colony representatives, or of making their voice heard through them. There was hope, however, of them gaining influence through the nominated Paramount Chief members, either by becoming their advisers, or by standing for election as Paramount Chiefs, which a growing number did. Thus, as Kilson points out, the position of the chiefs in Legislative Council enabled them to gain control of political development in the Protectorate.[43] It also served to widen the gulf between Colony and Protectorate.

Next to indirect rule, the main preoccupation of the élite was Africanisation of the colonial administration. Educated Africans resented their exclusion from Government Service, especially since in many cases they were as well, if not better, qualified than the Europeans who held posts. They resented the fact that taxes raised directly or indirectly paid for these officials, with all their special allowances. They had never forgotten in the Gold Coast and Sierra Leone, as the *Gold Coast Independent* put it in 1919, that 'every office from that of the Governorship downwards has been held by a black or coloured man. . . . No amount of disparaging their descendants can obliterate the fact.'[44]

Officially Colonial Governments were committed to limited Africanisation. In 1923 Governor Slater of Sierra Leone announced that his Government was making a real attempt to reduce its European staff and appoint Africans to senior posts whenever men qualified by training and character were forthcoming. An African had been appointed Assistant Colonial Secretary and another Assistant Treasurer.[45] In the Gold Coast, as we have seen, Guggisberg introduced a definite plan for phased Africanisation. But in practice Africanisation in all four colonies was very slow, and it took the Great Depression to give any impetus to it. In their newspapers the élite drew constant attention to the slow rate of Africanisation. It was a dominant theme in Legislative Council debates. From the outset the N.N.D.P. had as its policy 'the opening of the magistracy and of the higher branches of the Civil Service to properly qualified Africans and the abolition of the unpopular provincial courts system'.[46] In the Provinces of Nigeria and in large parts of the Gold Coast lawyers, African or European, were not permitted to appear in courts, which were presided over by Administrative Officers without legal qualifications. The growing body of African lawyers was thus excluded from two avenues of employment in the provinces: as advocates and judges.

Africans were not only upset at the slow rate of Africanisation of the Civil Service, but also at the lack of opportunities for them in European commercial companies. Very few Africans gained executive posts in commerce. As the *African Messenger* wrote in August 1925: 'The young European assistant (it is said) is placed in each department in turn, until he is familiar with all sides of his business, while the African lives and dies a book-keeper, storekeeper or Customs clerk.'[47]

African efforts to combat the general distrust Europeans had of their holding executive positions was not helped by the conviction of the Mayor of Freetown and some of his officers on a charge of conspiracy to defraud. The first African-controlled municipal corporation had proved an apparent failure. The Special Commissioner, Sir Charles O'Brien, in his report on the Freetown City Council, did not 'consider that blame for the failure of the Council can fairly be placed upon the shoulders of Africans alone. The institution was not an organic growth. It was forced fully-fledged upon a people who were not ripe for the experience.'[48] The lesson as far as rapid Africanisation was concerned, however, was all too clear.

The élite saw clearly that a successful policy of Africanisation depended on education. The criticisms of government's miniscule education programme were therefore as frequent as those of its slow rate of Africanisation. Kojo Thompson, one of the most outspoken members of the Gold Coast Legislative Council, complained in 1941 that 'if you go through the country you find that the vast majority are illiterates. It is the fault of the Government— a government who has thought it fair in the headquarters of the Empire to provide or insist on compulsory education; but it is deplorable that after so many years' contact with the British Government, in a place like the Gold Coast, there is not one free elementary school.'[49] Without education there would be no hope of self-government or independence, as the nominated member for Ibibio in the Nigerian Legislative Council put it in 1939.[50] Fourteen years earlier, in similar vein, Ladipo Solanke, President of the West African Students' Union, had proposed the establishment of a £1,000,000 Educational Endowment Fund by the N.C.B.W.A.: 'It is only by undertaking, ourselves, the task of educating the masses in West Africa on national lines that our legitimate aspirations for national independence can be achieved in the quickest and most constitutional way.'[51] Despairing of help from the Colonial Government, Africans tried to provide the education they wanted themselves. They set up scholarship funds to send deserving scholars to university in Britain or America. They established and ran their own schools, few of which gained government recognition. In 1936 boys in 'irregular' primary schools in the Gold Coast numbered 14,896 as against 35,778 in 'regular', government-recognised schools.[52] Unfortunately many of these schools merely exploited the desperate desire of young Africans for education. Standards of teaching were often abominably low. But these schools show as dramatically as anything the desire of Africans for modernisation and their determination to achieve it even without the assistance of the colonial government.

Whilst a number of Africans saw that there was a need to provide education that was African-oriented, all were suspicious of attempts by the Colonial Government to change the educational system in case these proved a conspiracy to fob them off with a second-class education. For thus they would become permanent second-class citizens, with second-class diplomas and certificates, making the ultimate Africanisation of the senior civil service even more remote than it already seemed. It was for this reason that there were mass demonstrations in Lagos when it was learnt that Government intended to substitute a Nigerian School Certificate for the Oxford and Cambridge School Certificate. And for the same reason, the Lagos Youth Movement was founded to protest against the inferior diplomas which would be given to students passing out from the new Yaba Higher College. They wanted it, like Fourah Bay College, to give degrees recognised by an English University.

Just as the N.C.B.W.A. had put forward demands for a West African University, so all their successors put education as one of their top priorities. Only thus could they achieve equality with their colonial masters.

The élite had many grievances—racial discrimination, expenditure of funds in the European sections of colonial capitals, lack of development; but what humiliated them most was their almost totally subservient role in the colonial economy. The N.C.B.W.A. had put forward as a priority the promotion of African enterprise. The N.N.D.P., while it did not have a specific economic programme, agreed that improved political status was worth little if Africans had no control over their country's economy. Politicians in Nigeria, Gold Coast and Sierra Leone became involved in commercial ventures designed to break the expatriate stranglehold of their economies. The most remarkable enterprise was that of Tete-Ansa, a Gold Coast entrepreneur who tried to link up West African and American Negro businessmen. His West African Co-operative Producers Ltd. succeeded by 1930 in gaining control of 60% of the cocoa annually exported from West Africa.[53] Among the directors of his company were leading politicians from the Gold Coast and Nigeria. He acquired an English bank and set up its new head-quarters in Lagos and a branch in Accra with the aim of mobilising African savings and making available to African businessmen the credit they were not granted by the European banks. Like his Co-operative Producers Company, its success was brief, and it had to go into voluntary liquidation.[54] But this 'Hero in the Commercial Battle', as Herbert Macaulay called him, set up another bank with Adeniyi-Jones, President of the N.N.D.P., and member of Legislative Council, as its Chairman. He called on farmers and businessmen to 'release yourselves from your economic bondage, always bearing in mind that every independent nation must have its own Economic Freedom and that without your own Banking Institution, which can be recognised abroad, you cannot attain that freedom'.[55] His second bank also failed, but he did set the example for the founding of the National Bank, which later became the Action Group party bank, as the African Continental Bank became that of the National

Council of Nigeria and Cameroons. If nothing else, Tete-Ansa's ventures, combined with the earlier propaganda of Marcus Garvey, served to emphasise that economic independence was as important as political independence.[56]

The élite resented the apparent close co-operation between government and expatriate commerce and the corresponding lack of help given to African businessmen. Beoku-Betts complained in the Sierra Leone Legislative Council that 'there has been no encouragement for us as a people to carry on industries', and cited the case of a concern of which he was a director. Where his Freetown Mineral Waters Company had established itself after a certain amount of difficulty without Government assistance, an expatriate firm, the Freetown Cold Storage Company, had received a subsidy of £10,000.[57] When Africans finally did get control of the purse, they made up for the colonial governments' neglect of African businessmen by providing generous loans to them.

As we have seen, the grievances of the élite were mainly concerned with the betterment of their own position. It was only in the years immediately before the war that the basis of opposition to the colonial régime began to broaden.

## 4 Broadening the political base

In the 1930's a series of youth organisations arose to challenge the established élite. Though many of the members of these organisations were far from young, the word Youth symbolised for them and their supporters the rejection of the jaded ideas and lack of achievement that characterised the incumbent elected legislators. The 'Youth' were concerned with the complete transformation of the colonial system rather than its gradual reform. They pointed to the record sheets of those who sat in Legislative Council as representatives of the people and proclaimed that they had achieved nothing in the way of reform. Rather they had compromised with their colonial masters.

The precursors of these youth organisations were the student movements in London, the most important of which was the West African Students' Movement, led by Ladipo Solanke who, as one reader of *West Africa* declared, 'is perhaps of all contemporary students the one doing most for his race and country'.[58] W.A.S.U. was founded in 1925 after a meeting held at the instigation of Bankole-Bright, then on a visit to London, 'to discuss matters affecting West Africa educationally, commercially, economically and politically, and to co-operate with the National Congress of [British] West Africa'.[59] Solanke, the moving spirit of W.A.S.U. right up to and during the Second World War, was an indefatigable organiser and wrote hundreds of letters to the Press on issues concerning West Africa. In 1927 he published his *United West Africa at the Bar of the Family of Nations* and was always at pains to emphasise the unity of the four West African territories. There were students, organisations representing the individual territories and a Union of Sons of African Descent (U.S.A.D.) which at first challenged the necessity of a new students' union of West African scope. But the pre-eminent position held by Solanke, his energy and the fact that he obtained funds from Marcus Garvey in 1928 for a hostel, made it the most important African student organisation in the inter-war years. Solanke toured West Africa to obtain funds and support for W.A.S.U., and even chiefs like the Emir of Kano, Nana Sir Ofori Atta and the Alake of Abeokuta, whom Solanke personally admired, agreed to become its patrons. Politically it was far more radical than any of the organisations then existing in West Africa itself. Its members came into contact with people like communists and socialists who had radical views on the whole issue of imperialism. Students also came into touch with Negroes from the New World or other parts of Africa and shared their grievances. Thus a student like H. O. Davies, who on his return to Lagos helped to organise the Nigerian Youth Movement, shared rooms with Jomo Kenyatta. W.A.S.U. gained sufficient recognition as a student organisation to be able to persuade not only visiting African legislators but even Colonial Governors to address its members. It had a journal in which it published nationalist articles and kept up demands for the radical policies of reform in West Africa which since Congress days the elected legislators seemed to have forgotten. The students increasingly saw these legislators as an unimaginative bunch of old men who had compromised with the colonial system and offered it no serious challenge.

By the 1930's there was in each of the coastal capitals a quite substantial group of returned students and an increasing number of boys graduating from the secondary schools. In the depressed conditions of the times, it was not surprising that they began to organise themselves to obtain the reforms the incumbent legislators seemed unable or unwilling to.

In 1934, the most successful of these movements, the Nigerian Youth Movement, was founded in Lagos. It grew out of the Lagos Youth Movement and its main leaders were Samuel Akinsanya,

Ernest Ikoli, H. O. Davies and J. C. Vaughn. One of its earliest members was Obafemi Awolowo, later President of the Action Group; and in 1937 it was joined by Nnamdi Azikiwe, who founded the National Council of Nigeria and the Cameroons. His adhesion was significant, for he was an Ibo from Eastern Nigeria joining a predominantly Yoruba organisation. He had great prestige as one of the first of his people to receive a higher education, having studied and lectured in the United States. On his way back to Nigeria he had spent some time as Editor of the *African Morning Post* in Accra, being jailed for, though not finally convicted of, sedition. He was also one of a group of young men who talked in terms of self-government not in the distant future but now. To the N.Y.M. he brought not only Ibo support but also his considerable journalistic talents, publishing the *West African Pilot* which was to become the bane of the colonial administration. The N.Y.M. could claim to be the first truly national party, securing support beyond Lagos and its immediate hinterland. It whipped up considerable popular anger over issues like the Italian rape of Abyssinia and the European Cocoa-Pool, so that unlike the N.N.D.P. it was concerned with issues of more than just Lagos significance. Macaulay and his colleagues, for instance, did not support the 'Hands off Abyssinia' campaign.[60]

In 1938 the N.Y.M. successfully challenged the N.N.D.P. at the polls, winning all three Lagos seats. They painted 'a glorious and enchantingly beautiful future of "a New Nigeria" which fired the imagination of young and old electors'.[61] Azikiwe's *West African Pilot* and Ikoli's *Daily Service* campaigned vigorously for the new-style leadership the N.Y.M. offered the electors. The *Pilot* declared that 'all is not well and that the era of submission, without constitutional opposition and all the concomitants of Uncle Tomism is gone. And that the Nigeria of today and tomorrow must realise that it is part of the Sleeping African Giant who must be awakened from its deep sleep, in order to harness its energy and usher in a New Nigeria.'[62] Whilst it made no bones about the limitations imposed on the power of the elected members of Legislative Council both by the constitution and the presence of the official majority, it promised to watch vigilantly over the problems of relief of unemployment, increased educational opportunities, openings in the Civil Service and elsewhere for Africans, and monopolistic practices such as the European Cocoa-Pool. The tired élite leadership was replaced by a vigorous new élite, actively pursuing social and political reform. Unhappily personal feuds among its leaders brought it to its knees and the N.N.D.P. once more gained control of the elected seats in the Legislative Council. The potentially radical N.Y.M. in its turn was condemned as being parochial and conservative by its post-war nationalist successors.[63]

The Gold Coast Youth Conference organised by J. B. Danquah was not, as its name indicates, a political party but rather an annual congregation of societies, unions and clubs. It was a forum where the politically motivated could discuss 'the Essentials in the Progress and Development of the Country', which was the theme of its first session at Achimota in 1930.[64] Through lack of funds it did not publish the results of its first session and did not meet again until 1938 at Mfantsipim. There it made it clear that it was non-political though the subjects it put forward for discussion were the essence of politics. 'Its main purpose', according to its organisers, was 'to focus the mind of the Youth on the Country's social and economic problems and invite suggestions for solution.' It held further meetings in 1939 at Kumasi and in 1940 in Akropong when it proposed to discuss 'The Problems of our Social and Economic Reconstruction in War and Peace'. Whilst it did not enter the political arena, it brought together the growing number of voluntary associations like debating and literary societies and forced them to think about national issues. It sought co-operation with the chiefs and in one of its earlier publications talked in glowing terms of the success of the Joint Provincial Council. Several important chiefs were its patrons.[65] Its somewhat ponderous and high-minded tone was brought out in its publication *First Steps Towards a National Fund* in 1938: 'Neither integrity, nor ability, nor the spirit for co-operation is wanting in the African. The youth of the country does not believe that these calumnies are true of the African as such, or of the European as such for the matter. Individuals may prove themselves dishonest, incompetent, self-centred and vain not because they are Africans but because they have been so brought up. Heredity alone is not responsible for what an individual turns out to be in society; environment counts for much, and the social milieux, and it is the duty of the country's leaders to improve the environment and the conditions of the social balance in which the growing child must weigh his future possibilities.'[66]

Not a very dynamic organisation, it did, however, present a programme for reform to Sir Arnold Hodson, the Governor, to which he paid no apparent attention. And in 1944 it put forward plans for constitutional change. But it never transformed itself into a political party to challenge the established élite at the polls.

Much more vigorous was I. T. A. Wallace Johnson's West African Youth League (also known as the Sierra Leone Youth League). Wallace Johnson is one of the more colourful figures of the nationalist movement in West Africa. A great traveller and political agitator, he had been to Moscow and joined protest movements in London. A journalist by profession, he had worked in the Gold Coast as well as Freetown. In Accra he had been convicted of sedition on the same charge as Azikiwe for his article 'Is there an African God?' His pen was indefatigable and belligerent, but hardly elegant. Most important of all, he was the first West African leader of consequence openly to advocate Marxist policies. His Youth League, founded in 1938, had as its aim to mobilise urban labour and to bring the people of the Colony and Protectorate together. Its programme, which included constitutional reform, was announced in Wallace Johnson's paper, the *African Standard*. The League's success was dramatic, and both Government and the Creole establishment began to fear it. W. M. MacMillan, in Freetown at the time, gave a vivid account of its impact: 'Night after night the Wilberforce Hall has been crowded to the doors and windows by those assembled to consider and foment grievances, and though the subjects of protests and demonstrations have by no means always been well chosen or well founded, the ventilation of constitutional or labour grievances has begun to bridge the old deep cleavage between the Creoles and the people of the Protectorate.'[67]

So dangerous were Wallace Johnson and his party considered that on the outbreak of war he and his colleagues were interned and the Youth League proscribed, bringing to an end the first, short-lived, radical political organisation of West Africa.

The colonial governments were much more concerned about socialist influences in West Africa than events in the inter-war years justified. J. B. Danquah records that a delegation protesting to the Colonial Secretary of the Gold Coast, Sir Percy Cunliffe-Lister, against the 'Sedition Ordinance' in 1934, were shown samples of Communist literature that had been imported into the Colony.[68] One of the pamphlets produced read: 'Our task is not only to defend the Soviet Union, which is the only friend of and champion of all the oppressed people in the world, but we must be prepared to take advantage of the next war when it breaks out to join up with the armed forces and use the guns which the Imperialists will be forced to put into our hands, as they did in 1914–18, to strike a final and decisive blow for the freedom of the Negro peoples in Africa, the West Indies, and America, and for the emancipation of toiling humanity from the fetters of the capitalist slave system.'[69] Danquah's comment was that 'many of the ideas and phrases in this paragraph are utterly foreign to the political conception of the Gold Coast Paramount Chiefs . . . [and] . . . entirely unknown to them. Soviet interference with the political peace of the Gold Coast people has compelled them to accept an ordinance which unless applied with care will most likely lead to increasing friction, hitherto unknown, between the Government and the people. . . .' Yet a decade earlier Guggisberg had warned Manchester businessmen 'to cut their losses and start trade with other parts of the world' if those sort of radicals should come to power who would say to the African: 'You are men and brothers with us. Some of you are very finely educated. We will give you self-government and see how you can govern yourselves.'[70]

But no such radicals came to power and politically West Africa was surprisingly peaceful. International Communism seems to have influenced only one West African leader of importance. I. T. A. Wallace Johnson was for a time an associate editor of *The Negro Worker*, a communist journal published in Hamburg for Negro sailors. He was a friend of the influential sometime Communist, George Padmore, from the West Indies, whom he met in Moscow. There were, however, disturbances symptomatic of the economic grievances that were to bring the masses increasingly into the political arena. In the cities there was growing unrest as a swelling immigrant population sought a restricted number of jobs at wages that made it only just possible to feed and house their families. This unrest manifested itself in strikes like the Sierra Leone Railway Strike of 1926, the most violent to take place in the inter-war years. Troops had to be called in and strikers and their supporters were fired on. Incipient economic discontent did not manifest itself in the towns alone. The Aba riots, as we have seen, were very much economic in origin: a protest as much against the imposition of taxes at a time of economic hardship as against the system of local administration. Lord Passfield (Sidney Webb) as Colonial Secretary wrote in his despatch on the disturbances to the Acting Governor of Nigeria that: 'The situations with which the various officers were confronted were without precedent, so far as I can judge. I might almost say in the history of the British Empire. Disturbances in which women have taken the foremost, or the only, part are unknown here and elsewhere in the Empire. . . .'[71]

Probably the most curious manifestation of rural discontent was the Haidara Rebellion of 1931. This occurred at a time of falling prices when there was considerable economic hardship for peasant-farmers still subject to the Hut Tax. Haidara was a Marabout of the Senegalese Mouride sect who had entered Northern Sierra Leone from French Guinea. He directed his preaching to the poorer peasants and in a letter to his devotees in Kambia on 10th February 1931, he exhorted them to revolt: 'God sends his messengers without guns or sword staffs or daggers. But he gives them something which is more than a gun or sword but I have the name of God with me, you should look at what is in the air, so you should not fear the European be he French or English as the four corners of the earth are guarded by the Prophet Mohammed. Bai Inga [the local Paramount Chief] and the Government have all fallen. I have also curse everybody who is under the Government. I am also telling you not to pay your House Tax to any Paramount Chief.'[72] On 16th February 1934, Government troops were despatched against Haidara on the grounds that he preached sedition and was exacerbating peasant discontent. Haidara was killed though his followers fought fiercely and had the satisfaction of killing the British force commander. The interest of Haidara's rebellion lies not in his conflict with the British so much as his mobilisation of peasant discontent and his attacks on rich Muslims who did not help their poorer brothers in Islam.[73]

The most spectacular demonstration of rural discontent was the Gold Coast Cocoa Hold-up of 1937. There had been earlier hold-ups, notably that led by John Ayew and his Gold Coast Farmers' Association which he formed just after the First World War to improve the cocoa farmers' bargaining position in relation to the buyers.[74] Ayew also helped organise the 1937 hold-up which successfully thwarted the expatriate cocoa-buyers' price-ring led by the United Africa Company. Chiefs, who regarded the movement with suspicion in its early stages, seeing how solidly their people were behind the stoppage of trade with the commercial companies, gave it the leadership it needed for success. And the prestigious Nana Sir Ofori Atta, still a member of Legislative Council, was to become a popular hero because of his championship of the farmers' cause. In the event the hold-up received almost 100% support from the farmers over a period of nearly seven months and the Nowell Commission appointed to inquire into the whole stoppage of trade had to arrange terms by which they would start selling again. The commission condemned the way expatriate companies arranged among themselves to control the prices paid to farmers so that they could reap the maximum benefits from rises in prices, and the farmers bear the brunt of the falls.[75] The hold-up showed that ordinary peasants, pushed far enough, were capable of organising themselves to fight a seemingly invincible European commercial combination. In victory, they did not forget the role the companies had played in their exploitation and as late as 1947 'Hostility to the United Africa Company [was] deep-seated and widespread, but it [was] found among European officials as well as among Africans. . . .'[76] In Nigeria there was no hold-up, but the Nigerian Youth Movement relentlessly attacked the 'Cocoa Pool' of ten firms controlling 90% of the trade which made a similar agreement with regard to the buying of cocoa as the Ghana one. And farmers remained suspicious of the European companies for a long time after the 'Pool' was broken. The trouble was that farmers in the Gold Coast and Nigeria could not understand the violent fluctuations of prices, which ranged from £122 in 1920 to £18 a ton in 1930 and averaged only £21 in the depression years.[77] As the Nigerian report on the Nowell Commission's findings recorded: 'There is every indication that the farmers of the Western Provinces, if not of Nigeria as a whole, still regard the prices paid for their produce during the boom years as normal and those paid during the more frequent years of depression as abnormal.'[78] What did become clear from the cocoa hold-up in Ghana and the protests and demonstrations in Nigeria was that the peasant could no longer be looked on as a passive producer whose interests were of marginal interest to the state. It so happened that the war provided the ideal opportunity for Government to safeguard his interests by introducing state marketing boards and consequent control over the activities of the exporters. The Nowell Commission also urged Government to put its full weight behind the co-operative movement which would avoid the dependence of the farmer on middlemen who were often dishonest and inefficient.[79]

The masses in the 1930's were still largely inarticulate. Under the system of indirect rule they had no adequate means of communicating their grievances to the administration. If these became greater than they could bear they had to resort to passive resistance or violence. However, during the thirties, there flooded southwards into the coastal towns great numbers of primary school-leavers who resented the strictures of traditional society, and came equally to resent the colonial system since they could not find the jobs to which they felt their elementary education entitled them. These school-leavers were to form the numerous voluntary associations which in Ghana were harnessed by Nkrumah's Convention People's Party and in Nigeria by Azikiwe's N.C.N.C. into great nationalist movements.[80] It was these people who provided the link between the educated leader and the illiterate peasant with grievances he could not articulate on his own, and secured the votes at the elections that gave Africans the chance to govern themselves.

# Notes

1 Obafemi Awolowo, *Path to Nigerian Freedom*, London, 1947, pp. 31–2.
2 K. W. J. Post, 'Nationalist Movements in West Africa', in J. F. Ade Ajayi and Ian Espie, *A Thousand Years of West African History*, Ibadan, 1965, p. 454.
3 Cited in Joan Wheare, *The Nigerian Legislative Council*, London, 1950, p. 30.
4 Kilson, *Sierra Leone*, pp. 128–31.
5 *West Africa*, 2nd January 1926.
6 *Ibid.*
7 *West Africa*, 20th November 1926.
8 *Ibid.*
9 Buell, *Native Problem*, I, p. 841.
10 *Gold Coast Leader*, 22nd May 1926.
11 See *The Humble Petition of the Gold Coast Aborigines Protection Society*, February 1934, reprinted by the Institute of African Studies, University of Ghana, n.d.
12 Bourret, *Ghana*, p. 66.
13 Martin Wight, *The Gold Coast Legislative Council*, London, 1947, p. 44.
14 Cited in *ibid.*, p. 79.
15 *Ibid.*, p. 57.
16 Cited in Wheare, *Nigerian Legislative Council*, p. 166.
17 Wight, *Gold Coast Legislative Council*, p. 61.
18 Cited in Kilson, *Sierra Leone*, p. 121.
19 Address of the N.N.D.P. to Sir Graeme Thompson, 13th November 1925, cited in *West Africa*, 12th December 1925.
20 J. E. Casely-Hayford, *Presidential Address delivered during the Second Session of the National Congress of British West Africa held in Freetown, Sierra Leone, January 1923*, reprinted in Magnus J. Sampson, *West African Leadership*, Ilfracombe, 1949.
21 *Presidential Address delivered during the Third Session of the National Congress of British West Africa, held in Bathurst, Gambia, December 1925*, reprinted in *ibid.*
22 Tekena N. Tamuno, *Nigeria and Elective Representation 1923–1947*, London, 1966, pp. 73–4 and pp. 79–81.
23 *Ibid.*, pp. 75–6.
24 *West Africa*, 14th February 1925.
25 Tamuno, *Nigeria and Elective Representation*, p. 83.
26 Kilson, *Sierra Leone*, p. 104.
27 *West Africa*, 2nd January 1926.
28 Kimble, *Ghana*, p. 399.
29 *West Africa*, 31st January 1925.
30 Kimble, *Ghana*, p. 452, gives details.
31 Wight, *Gold Coast Legislative Council*, p. 72.
32 *West Africa*, 19th June 1926.

33 *Presidential Address delivered during the Fourth Session of the National Congress of British West Africa, held in Lagos, Nigeria, December 1929,* reprinted in Sampson, *West African Leadership.*
34 Wheare, *Nigerian Legislative Council,* p. 149.
35 Wraith, *Guggisberg,* p. 175.
36 See the objections of the Ashanti Freedom Society to the restoration of the Asantahene as recorded by I. T. A. Wallace Johnson in *Restoration of the Ashanti Confederacy,* cited in Tordoff, *Ashanti under the Prempehs,* p. 343.
37 Wheare, *Nigerian Legislative Council,* p. 159.
38 Kimble, *Ghana,* p. 494.
39 Rattray, *Ashanti Law and Constitution,* p. 400.
40 Awolowo, *Path to Nigerian Freedom,* p. 57.
41 *Ibid.,* pp. 65 and 66.
42 Kilson, *Sierra Leone,* p. 135.
43 *Ibid.,* p. 128.
44 Cited in Kimble, *Ghana,* p. 106.
45 *The Times,* 14th December 1923.
46 *Ibid.,* 2nd October 1923.
47 Quoted in *West Africa,* 22nd August 1925.
48 *Ibid.,* 18th December 1926.
49 Cited in Wight, *Gold Coast Legislative Council,* p. 177.
50 Wheare, *Nigerian Legislative Council,* p. 147.
51 Letter to *West Africa,* 25th April 1925.
52 Wilson, *Education and Changing West African Culture,* p. 55.
53 Hopkins, 'Economic Aspects of Political Movements', p. 138.
54 *Ibid.,* p. 139.
55 *Ibid.,* p. 145.
56 See Essien's speech to Legislative Council already cited from Wheare, *Nigerian Legislative Council,* p. 147.
57 Kilson, *Sierra Leone,* pp. 141-2.
58 *West Africa,* 27th June 1927.
59 *Ibid.,* 15th August 1925.
60 Webster and Boahen, *West Africa since 1800,* p. 311.
61 Tamuno, *Nigeria and Elective Representation,* p. 86.
62 *West African Pilot,* 20th October 1938, cited in *ibid.,* pp. 86–7.
63 Webster and Boahen, *West Africa since 1800,* p. 315.
64 Wight, *Gold Coast Legislative Council,* p. 187.
65 Bourret, *Ghana,* p. 69.
66 Cited in Apter, *Ghana,* p. 128.
67 W. M. Macmillan, 'African Development', in *Europe and West Africa,* p. 76.
68 J. B. Danquah, letter to *The Times,* 21st September 1934.
69 Cited in *ibid.*
70 *West Africa,* 9th June 1923.

71  *Despatch from Lord Passfield, Secretary of State for the Colonies to Acting Governor of Nigeria*, Cmd. 3784 of 1931.
72  Cited in B. M. Jusu, 'The Haidara Rebellion of 1931', *Sierra Leone Studies*, N.S. no. 3, December 1954, p. 150.
73  See Kilson, *Sierra Leone*, for an interesting discussion of the significance of the Haidara rebellion, pp. 113–17.
74  Hopkins, 'Economic Aspects of Political Movements'.
75  *Report of the Commission on the Marketing of West African Cocoa*.
76  Wight, *Gold Coast Legislative Council*, p. 173.
77  Bourret, *Ghana*, p. 66
78  *Report of a Commission appointed in Nigeria to examine recommendations by the Commission on the Marketing of West African Cocoa*, Nigeria Sessional Paper, no. 20, 1939, para. 93.
79  *Report of the Commission on the Marketing of West African Cocoa*.
80  See Dennis Austin, *Politics in Ghana 1944–60*, London, 1965, p. 26.

# 4 Prelude to de-colonisation: The Second World War

## 1 Africa in a wider world

The Second World War burst rudely upon the colonial backwater that West Africa had become. It changed the lethargic speed of social, economic and political change into a higher gear from which it was difficult to go into reverse. Most important of all, West African colonies ceased to be the exclusive preserve of the colonial powers. They became indispensable to the war effort of the Allies which included the United States and Russia, both of whom openly questioned their position as dependencies. Even within the colonial governments there were those who questioned the moral foundations of colonialism. When President Roosevelt and Prime Minister Churchill signed the Atlantic Charter, which promised in its third clause 'the right of all peoples to choose the form of government under which they live . . .', the British Colonial Secretary, Oliver Stanley, like his Prime Minister, denied that this applied to African dependencies. However, the British Deputy Prime Minister, Mr. Clement Attlee, told West African students that the Charter applied to all the races of the world, coloured as well as white. 'I look for an ever-increasing measure of self-government in Africa,' he told them, 'and for an ever-rising standard of life for all the peoples of Africa. Out of the horror of war and destruction we shall come to a world of peace, security and social justice, not for one people, nor for one continent, but for all the peoples of all continents of the world.'[1]

Anti-colonial Labour Members of Parliament made their views heard not only from the back-benches but through the influential Fabian Colonial Bureau which kept in close touch with nationalist elements in the colonies. Mr. Reg Sorensen, one of the most outspoken Labour critics of colonialism, assured the West African Students' Union at the beginning of the war: 'Most of all I want to see the time when West Africans will be able to govern themselves. I know that you have some meagre representation in your councils, but still the official mind dominates. It is almost as though, if good, you are invited into the parlour for a piece of cake.'[2]

For the first time colonial freedom was being openly discussed by members of a British party exercising power in the Government. Even so the majority of the members of the coalition National Government remained hostile or indifferent to any rapid emancipation. It was something that would take place in future generations or centuries rather than within the next two decades.

Among the Free French there were also those who questioned the old colonial order. Henri Laurentie, Director of Political Affairs in the Ministry of Overseas France, wrote in 1945: 'We shall have to be resolutely anti-colonialist. We are already so at heart. We must endeavour to be so in fact.' Though he rejected any precipitate decolonisation, he affirmed: 'Colonialism must come to an end, but for the good of all mankind . . . France has been giving very careful consideration to the problem. She only had to turn back to the source of her revolutionary tradition to find the one legitimate solution: liberty and equality for the individual and the nation.'[3] The goal of the Free French since 1941, according to Laurentie, had been a French Union within which each country would be 'morally equal to every other—not excepting the mother country—and free to follow its own bent, while sharing the rights and duties of the same human and social organisation'.[4] This was a far cry from the old formula of *association* of French citizen and African subject.

While the anti-colonialism of the Fabians and the Free French was tentative, that of the Americans and Russians was dogmatic. In the early days of the war, America, ever-conscious of its own successful bid for freedom from colonial subservience, was seized by a strong anti-imperialist sentiment. This was in great part due to genuine concern about America's coming to the rescue of Britain and thereby helping her to maintain her hold on her colonies. *Life* put it bluntly: 'Great Britain had better part with her Empire, for the United States is not prepared to fight in order to enable her to keep it.'[5] The impact of American anti-colonial propaganda was considerable. René Pleven, Commissioner for Colonies in de Gaulle's Algiers Government, wrote later that the widespread propaganda of the Americans concerning the emancipation of colonial peoples, diffused through many different channels, was to have an important impact on colonial peoples.[6] While Churchill denied that the third clause of the Atlantic Charter applied to Britain's colonies, Americans insisted that it did. This had a great impact on both French[7] and British West Africans. A West African correspondent of *The Times* wrote in 1942: 'We West Africans maintain that the Atlantic Charter does apply to us as members of the British Commonwealth of Nations.'[8] In the Sierra Leone Legislative Council, Paramount Chief Caulker expressed the hope that the Government had already drawn up plans to make the country 'what it should be after the war in the spirit of the Atlantic Charter'.[9]

When Russia, the most resolutely anti-colonialist of world powers, broke with Germany and joined the Allies, from being a bogey it suddenly became a respectable ally. Communist theories on colonies could not now be so easily dismissed or suppressed as emanating from an immoral and tyrannical system of government opposed to freedom. In British West Africa, however, Communist ideas seem to have gained little currency. But in French West Africa, with the establishment of the Free French régime, *Groupes d'Études Communistes* (G.E.C.s), Communist Study Groups, were established in Dakar, Abidjan, Cotonou and Bamako, for the Communists were a leading element in the Free French Government. African members of these G.E.C.s studied Russian and French Communist literature and discussed ' "the social, economic, and political situation of each territory" and "a common strategy and tactics for fighting against colonialism within the mass organisation (political, trade union, cultural, etc. . . .) of the territory" '.[10] What was most significant about the G.E.C.s was that they brought members of the élite into contact with a wider world through their discussion groups, conferences, courses and tours.[11]

The need to placate America and Russia meant that Britain and the Free French could no longer consider their colonies an exclusive preserve in which other powers could not poach. The principle of international accountability discussed with regard to Germany's colonies in 1918, and weakly established under the League of Nations Mandate System, was now to be generalised. But West Africa did not enter a wider world just because Americans, Russians and metropolitan radicals were challenging the colonial system. West Africa assumed a vital role in the war effort: she contributed both militarily and economically to victory to such an extent that both Britain and France felt obliged to reward Africans politically, socially and economically. Most important of all, the political, economic and social changes that took place during the war opened new horizons for Africans beyond which lay self-government and independence.

## 2 The military involvement of French West Africa

Throughout the inter-war years, the French had continued to look on Black Africa as a source of recruitment of troops not only for a possible European conflict, but also for the suppression of colonial revolts such as that of the Rif in Morocco in 1925. African troops were cheaper to maintain than European troops[12] and under the colonial system they could be subjected to longer terms of service than French conscripts. Many of these African conscripts served in France and some were trained as under-officers and officers, so that where the officer corps in British West Africa was exclusively European, in French West Africa there was a handful of African officers. Potential officers were trained as under-officers at the *Centre de Perfectionnement des Sous-Officiers Coloniaux* (Centre for Advanced Instruction of Colonial n.c.o.s) at Fréjus after which they became eligible for promotion to second-lieutenant.[13]

On the outbreak of the Second World War the French had at their disposal a large, well-trained source of troops in West Africa. And in the short months before the fall of France to the Germans, 80,000 were embarked for Europe,[14] and another 90,000 mobilised. But the peace terms made between Vichy France and Germany took France out of the war, so that these troops did not see service.

In French West Africa itself the outbreak of war brought forth an apparently enthusiastic response to the demands made on the indigenous population to help save 'la mère-patrie' from the 'Teuton hordes'. Public prayers in Dakar led by the Grand Marabout, El Haji Seydou Nourron Tall, grandson of Al Hajj Umar, were attended by Governor-General Cayla and the Mayor of Dakar, Alfred Goux: 'By Thy names by which Thou appearest in all Thy glory when Thou art enangered against peoples that disregard the rules of Justice and when Thou wouldst chastise them, I beg of Thee to exterminate the Germans, to overthrow them, to repel their artifices.'[15] In Ivory Coast (which then included Upper Volta) Ouezzin-Coulibaly was able to write to Administrator Robert Delavignette not only that mobilisation in Sindou had gone smoothly but that he had 'admired in this bit of the bush the affection which the natives feel for France'.[16] When rumours circulated that France might be capitulating the Lebou collectivity of Dakar asked to be allowed to fight alongside their French and English comrades: 'Preferring death to dishonour, we ask the French Government to utilise overseas children.'[17] And on the fateful days of surrender *Paris-Dakar* published numerous telegrams from all over French West Africa supporting continuation of the war from an African base.[18] The Governor of the Gold Coast reported that he had received a telegram from Abidjan from French ex-servicemen of the Ivory Coast 'supported by all sections of the population' assuring him of their 'unshakeable will to continue to struggle. . . .'[19]

For French West Africa, however, from a military point of view, the war was over when France surrendered. Under Vichy France it was to be neutral territory. Governor-General Cayla seems to have hesitated in the first few days after the establishment of the Vichy régime as to whether to support it or continue the fight. But for the most part the army, navy and administration in French West Africa favoured the Vichy régime. The destruction of the French fleet at Mers-El-Kébir by the British brought many waverers on to the side of Vichy. Again the attack on the *Richelieu* in the port of Dakar by the British on 8th July hardened anti-British attitudes. Nevertheless the administration in French West Africa had to move cautiously, as the newly appointed High Commissioner for Black Africa, Boisson, admitted, because of those elements favourable to the Free French cause.[20]

Governor-General Cayla was transferred to Madagascar, and Boisson, despite his grander title, effectively replaced him as Governor-General of French West Africa, for Equatorial Africa went over to the Free French, led by the Guyanese Governor of Chad, Félix Éboué. Boisson sent Éboué a bitter telegram: 'By your decision you have betrayed the duties with which you were charged. By taking the initiative in handing over to England the territory confided to you, you have by a deliberate and plotted act, broken the cohesion of the Empire.'[21]

In the event Boisson had little difficulty in imposing the Vichy régime on French West Africa. The only senior administrator who continued openly to support de Gaulle was Ernest Louveau, head of Upper Volta, who was eventually imprisoned after a visit to Dakar on which he had hoped to be able to persuade this *mutilé de guerre* to come out in favour of the Free French.[22] It is interesting to speculate whether if Cayla had from the outset decided to support de Gaulle, French West Africa like Equatorial Africa would have gone over to the Free French. Louveau considered that it would. Boisson, however, was convinced that by following a policy of strict neutrality as laid down by the Vichy régime, he was preserving French West Africa from occupation by the Germans or Italians. He had little love for the Germans, having had a leg shot off by them in the First World War.[23]

For French West Africa, then, the establishment of the Vichy régime meant a policy of non-involvement in the conflict. Boisson gained the support of the great majority of European population, both civil and military. A few crossed the frontiers into British territories; a few, including some Africans, carried on resistance within French West Africa itself.

For the majority of Africans the change of régime made little difference. The same Governors and administrators ruled them through the same *indigénat*. Only the *citoyens*, both Senegalese and naturalised, suffered a major setback when their representative institutions were abolished and they were effectively reduced to the status of *sujets*. In one sense the establishment of the Vichy régime was positively beneficial, since its policy of non-involvement brought an end to recruiting for the army.

Despite Boisson's policy of neutrality, French West Africa was brought into the war briefly when the British and Free French bombarded Dakar on 24th–25th September 1940. De Gaulle, completely mis-assessing the sentiments of both the European and African population, anticipated that Dakar, in the face of an attempted landing by his forces, would rally to him. However, Frenchmen had been outraged, Africans puzzled, by the destruction by the British of the French Fleet. Furthermore, de Gaulle was a comparatively unknown figure, whereas Pétain, whose fatherly, mustachioed face stared from every wall emblazoned by the Tricolor, was the Hero of Verdun under whose command many Africans had fought. In the textbooks they read how he had saved France in the First World War; it was not unreasonable to suppose that he was saving it again. And Vichy propaganda certainly did all it could to persuade Africans of this. Pétain had personally visited West Africa to study recruitment of African soldiers in 1925[24] and in a land where so many of the leaders were old soldiers, the Vichy régime was able to call on loyalty to a man they knew rather than a Brigadier-General unknown to them. Finally the successful British blockade of Dakar had deprived Europeans and Africans alike both of imports and of the money they gained from exports.

On 24th September, the beginning of the attempted landing, leaflets exhorting the population to support de Gaulle were dropped over Dakar. Galandou Diouf countered with a statement of loyalty to Vichy: 'Indefectibly rallied around the illustrious Marshal whose portrait adorns all our dwellings and who remains for us the symbol of all that is most noble in France, we mean to remain French. By staying loyal to France, the coloured people are staying loyal to themselves, to their past, to their traditions.'[25] The propaganda bombardment was followed by a real bombardment in which a large number of Africans and Europeans were killed and wounded. The people did not rise up in favour of de Gaulle and his ill-conceived invasion failed miserably, alienating any possible sympathy for him among the large majority of the African population. Indeed de Gaulle, on his first visit to Dakar in 1943, had to have special protection because it was feared that the resentment of those who had lost relatives in the bombardment might lead them to take revenge on him.

Boisson, however, took great care to secure the loyalty of the African population through a barrage of propaganda, praising Pétain and damning the 'Anglo-Saxons', as the British and Americans were called. In September 1942, *Paris-Dakar*, the main newspaper in French West Africa, went so far as to describe the British as the 'enemy' when they invaded Tananarive.[26] The press carried detailed information on the difficulties being experienced in the neighbouring British territories.[27] And propaganda was able to feed on the 'widespread irritation' of the Africans and French at the hardships caused by the British blockade of Dakar.[28] Much of Vichy's propaganda was directed to showing how West Africa and her inhabitants would play a vital role in the Marshal's France. In the special magazine, *Dakar-Jeunes*, such men as Ouezzin-Coulibaly, Mamadou Dia and Ousmane Soce Diop were able to publish articles on African culture as well as Africa's debts to France and her civilisation. The virtues of healthy living and sport—a sort of boy-scout morality—were put forward to the African readers. Its approach was symbolised by the photograph on the cover of the first issue in which a French and an African scout were shaking hands. Another major agent for propaganda and support for the Vichy régime was the *Légion Française des Combattants de l'Afrique Noire*. Curiously, though anti-Jewish, it was not anti-Negro. It appealed to Franco-African unity, and in 1941 held a mass parade of 6,000 African and European *légionnaires*, for which a special brochure was prepared. On the back it bore the information: 'Printed by both European and Native Légionnaires at the Press of the High Commission for French Black

Africa.'[29] Walls were covered with posters seeking the support of the literate population. One demanded resistance to the 'desperate assaults launched by the monstrous alliance of Communism and Gaullism effected under the influence of British gold'.[30] By contrast reception of all British radio services and of any others transmitting 'anti-national propaganda' was forbidden.[31]

While the majority of the population remained indifferent to the issues at stake, persuaded if they had doubts by this barrage of propaganda, some took an active if small part in the Resistance. When de Gaulle bombarded Dakar a number of Europeans were interned and deported, including the Mayor of Dakar, Alfred Goux, the President of the Chamber of Commerce, and the future deputy for Sudan, the West Indian, Silvandre. Five Africans at least were shot for treason. Abdel Kader Diagne and a team of resistants passed information from Senegal to Gambia.[32] While the scale of resistance in West Africa was small, and of little strategic importance since Boisson did effectively maintain French West Africa's neutrality contrary to British apprehensions, the bravery of those, especially Africans, who were willing to risk their lives for a free and honourable France should not go unrecorded.

In November 1942, when the Allies landed in French North Africa, Boisson had to reconsider his position. Admiral Darlan after all was negotiating with the Allies, and on 21st November he decided to support Darlan. On 19th December, after Darlan's assassination, General Giraud, now head of the French in Algiers, came to Dakar and declared: 'Our sole duty is to chase the Germans out of our Empire and liberate the Motherland.'[33] Boisson began to talk of the Allies rather than the 'Anglo-Saxons'.[34] However, as far as the newspapers were concerned General de Gaulle was not mentioned until 23rd April 1943.[35]

Boisson announced French West Africa's new role: 'We must produce. The next groundnut crop in Senegal must in particular be a great success ... I conclude with an equation: Work = Victory = Liberation of the Motherland.'[36] Finally, de Gaulle arrived in Dakar, and with the resignation of Boisson at the end of June 1943 the change-over in French West Africa's role in the war was complete. Though the owner of *Paris-Dakar*, Charles de Bréteuil, praised Boisson in a valete: 'For him, there was one enemy before which he never disarmed: the Boche', de Gaulle had the man who successfully thwarted his landing in Dakar imprisoned. No mention was made of this in the local press at the time. Indeed one of the main difficulties of the new administration was how to explain to the Africans the sudden *volte-face* of the French in West Africa. De Gaulle the enemy was now the saviour of France: but how could they describe Pétain, on whose behalf their predecessors had done such a good propaganda job, as a traitor? So it was explained that they had joined with the Free French to save the Marshal from the Germans, who had made him a prisoner.

Under the Free French West Africa assumed for a second time its role as provisioner of troops and food for an embattled France. Over 100,000 African soldiers, constituting at one time over half the Free French forces, left for the Allied front between 1943 and 1945. Harsh methods were used to step up production of essential crops. But whereas in the First World War Africa's contribution had gone unrewarded, her contribution this time was to herald major social, economic and political reforms.

## 3 The military involvement of British West Africa

British West Africa's contribution of soldiers to the First World War had been very small compared with that of French West Africa. In this war, the position was partially reversed. The strength of the West African Frontier Force was raised from a pre-war level of 8,000 to 146,000.[37] For the first time West African troops were used outside the continent, notably in the Burma campaign. Towards the end of the war, the Duke of Devonshire, who was then Under Secretary of State for the Colonies, declared that West African troops in Burma had performed great feats of arms and that he had been immensely impressed by the success with which the enormous expansion of African forces had been carried out and with the smartness and keenness of the men.[38] In Burma, the African troops became indispensable not only as soldiers better suited to the conditions of jungle warfare than their white comrades, but as carriers who could transport supplies through territory where no vehicles could pass. The ability of the African carrier to move heavy loads over great distances in tropical conditions gave the Allies the initiative they needed over the Japanese. African troops fought in the 'Abyssinia' campaign where they 'acquitted themselves with distinction'.[39] They were also used in Kenya and Italian Somaliland. These soldiers were recruited on a voluntary basis, though since chiefs were used as the agents of recruitment it is difficult to know how voluntary it was. However, Sir Ahmadu Bello, the late Premier of Northern Nigeria, recorded that in Northern Nigeria, which supplied the largest corps of soldiers, 'recruiting was pushed as far as possible, but no pressure was employed'.[40]

As in French West Africa, the outbreak of war called forth protestations of loyalty from many sections of the African population. Substantial sums of money were voted as gifts by the West African Legislative Councils with the support of African members or were raised by subscription from the African and European communities. These gifts totalled £931,127.[41] The Gold Coast had its 'Spitfire Fund' and supported the Gold Coast Bomber and Fighter Squadrons. Nigeria established a 'Win the War Fund'. Interest-free loans were made to the Imperial Government by the four colonies. Savings campaigns raised further funds for the war effort. Herbert Macaulay told Lagos citizens in a radio broadcast plugging Savings: '... Victory for Democracy and the Freedom of Mankind depends on our Contributions, and our Determination and our Loyalty. Lagos, Honour your Cheque: and rally round the Union Jack.'[42]

More important than its contribution of men and funds for the war effort was British West Africa's strategic role. When Italy joined the Germans, the Allies could no longer be sure of the Suez route. The establishment of the Vichy régime in France denied the Allies bases in North Africa. Once Japan entered the war and occupied Britain's Far Eastern colonies, West Africa became of prime importance as a staging base for the Middle and Far East. Freetown, with its deep-water port, held the key to the South Atlantic, once Dakar went Vichy. The loss of Freetown, *The Times* speculated, 'might have meant the loss of the South Atlantic'.[43] President Roosevelt declared that the importance of West Africa as a staging base for American troops and supplies could not be overestimated.[44] This new strategic role of British West Africa led to the development of ports like Lagos, Port Harcourt, Freetown and Takoradi, and to the construction of new, or improvement of existing, airports. Between 1942 and 1943 something like 200 American aeroplanes a day used Accra airport and from the end of 1943 it was for two years under complete American control. Many thousands of American and British troops passed through West Africa on their way to the front. To co-ordinate the new military and economic functions of the four British West African colonies a Minister Resident was appointed for British West Africa with his headquarters at Accra.

Fighting itself was never brought to West Africa, though in 1939, according to *The Times*, the Accra earthquake was mistaken for a German naval bombardment by African troops who were 'ready to march down to the beaches and drive off the impudent Nazi hordes'.[45] The Vichy régime was a constant source of anxiety to the British lest it permit the Germans to use Dakar as a submarine base. There were constant rumours about German activities there. But in the event no shot was fired in West Africa.

The Germans directed their propaganda war at British West Africans, and the British authorites countered by trying to demonstrate to them how well off they were under British rule. In 1940 the Germans broadcast a radio play in which part of the dialogue went: 'A report from Rome states that three Natives in a British Crown Colony were executed because they refused to fight on the Western Front.' Cracks of whip and brutal British laughter. A voice screams in an extremity of terror: 'Me no want fight German. German good man.' English soldier: 'You dare say that! Take that, you black swine. Ha! Ha!' Commentator: 'If the gentlemen in London only knew how eagerly His Majesty's subjects in Nigeria are volunteering.'[46] Germans broadcast that African contributions to the 'Win-the-War Fund' were obtained by force, to which the Sultan of Sokoto replied: 'That is a lie, and I would also like to ask Hitler whether it is by force that we gather in our mosques and schools and offer up prayers from our hearts, day and night, for the success of the British armies and the downfall of His Majesty's enemies.'[47] The vast majority of the Africans were impervious to German propaganda. The élite was well aware of the implications of domination by racist Nazi Germany. What was significant about Germany's propaganda offensive was that for the first time the British were compelled to justify themselves and their rule to their subjects.

Unlike the First World War, this war was fought far beyond West Africa's frontiers. In British West Africa it had none of the drama which the politics of Vichy brought to French West Africa. But it was the occasion of dramatic economic, social and political changes that were the prelude of independence.

## 4 *The economic impact of World War II*

In British West Africa the war was the prelude to a radical restructuring of the economy. For the first time the large expatriate commercial houses were subject to control by the colonial governments. The latter now purchased the cash crops, with the former acting as their agents. Prices for these crops were determined by the Ministry of Supply, and their export was controlled in each territory by a supply board which was in turn directed by a West African Produce Marketing Board. These boards were the forerunners of the post-war marketing boards which placed in the hands of the government the determination of the prices to be paid to the producer in relation to the prevailing world market prices. Less significant were the restrictions placed on imports. Only goods from the British Empire could be imported freely, otherwise licences had to be obtained from the Government. In the short run the big firms, far from suffering from these restrictions, derived considerable benefit from them. For instance when the British Government in November 1939 decided to buy up the whole of the West African cocoa crop, because they feared a collapse in cocoa prices, they chose to use the established firms as their agents, meaning that though their previous monopolistic control of prices was broken, they still formed a buying monopoly. Similarly when all major exports became controlled by government after the loss of the Far East in 1942, licences were given primarily to established firms of good repute, because considerable trust in the loyalty of the firms was involved. This system effectively eliminated newly created and unreliable firms from the export trade and prevented new firms from setting themselves up. The one notable exception to this was A. G. Leventis in the Gold Coast. In particular it made it even more difficult than ever for the African to break into the export trade.[48] Since the only area from which goods could be imported freely was the British Empire, primarily the United Kingdom and India, the large British firms were the principal beneficiaries from this new régime. For 'since Indian goods were very expensive (and) British goods were allocated to British exporters, African and Levantine firms and newcomers had not much chance of obtaining supplies unless British exporters believed them to offer profitable post-war business prospects'.[49] However, the Directors of Supplies did have a deliberate policy of allocating goods to non-European firms.[50] The result, however, was that the large British firms, organised as they were into an Association of West African Merchants, to which 'in some cases even formally, the framing and administration of the most important controls were handed over by the British and West African Governments',[51] consolidated their control of the bulk of the import trade. On the other hand they lost their freedom of deciding how much and what they could import from where. Despite the apparent increase in their stranglehold of the import-export trade, the firms were for the first time subjected to Government control. In the long-term, this was an important departure since the peasant was no longer at the mercy of the firms as far as the determination of prices was concerned: however, in the short-term he derived no benefit, since the Government fixed prices for crops which were 'exceedingly low',[52] and were certainly below the prevailing world prices, so that the peasant substantially subsidised the British war effort. The establishment of the principle of Government as purchaser of export crops and regulator of their price, while it did not benefit the peasant during the war, was the prelude to an important new departure in his life. After the war Government, through statutory marketing boards, continued its role as purchaser and regulator of prices. These Marketing Boards paid prices lower than the prevailing world price when it was high, retaining the difference to boost up the price paid to the peasant when the world market price was low. The peasant was thus protected from the worst excesses of world price fluctuations and monopolistic price agreements among the expatriate firms.

While no place had been provided for the African businessman in the war-time economy, as far as the peasant was concerned a new era in his commercial exploitation was being ushered in. Nevertheless, as far as the prospective African merchant was concerned, Government use of the established firms meant that the pre-war commercial structure was now being officially supported.[53] Suspicion and distrust of the large firms, and in particular the Association of West African Merchants, among the educated African was justifiably very deep. As Julian Huxley wrote in 1944: 'It is probably safe to prophesy that means will be found to bring the great companies within the scope of some system of regulation in which they will assume various social obligations. It is certainly true that if this is not done, discontent will grow.'[54] The Marketing Boards established after the war were Government's attempt to ensure this regulation.

These Boards marked a significant turning point in the history of West African commerce. In the first place they transferred control of marketing the crop from private enterprise to Government. Second their pricing policy cushioned the often violent fluctuations in world prices that had so often confused the peasant-producer in the inter-war years, and brought to him real hardship. Thirdly, by accumulating substantial surpluses, they provided African governments, albeit unintentionally, with a large source of funds with which to prosecute their development programmes. Finally the Marketing Boards were the prelude to the socialisation of Agriculture.[55]

In one field, the retail trade, the large companies were forced to concede to the African. The call-up of expatriate staff for service in the war meant that many of the larger, expatriate-supervised stores had to be closed down. Even some African-supervised stores had to be shut because of lack of supplies with which to stock them. However, many of the African supervisors who thus lost their jobs set themselves up as independent retailers drawing supplies from several different firms.[56]

The loss of Britain's Far Eastern colonies gave West Africa a new importance as a source of supply for raw materials. Not only was there an increase in demand for traditional exports, but also for new or abandoned ones like rubber. The recently exploited iron ore reserves at Marampa in Sierra Leone now replaced traditional European sources. Bauxite was exploited for the first time in the Gold Coast, and a new railway line of forty-six miles built to link the deposits with the existing rail network. In Nigeria tin output was stepped up to compensate for the loss of Malayan tin. To obtain increases in supply, however, forced labour was used. In the House of Commons, Arthur Creech Jones, the future Labour Colonial Secretary, attacked the Government for allowing the use of forced labour in the tin mines, declaring that all progressive opinion in Britain had been greatly shocked and asking what was to be done about the profits and royalties made out of the exploitation of cheap labour for private enterprise.[57] He was told by Harold Macmillan, Under Secretary of State for Colonies, that an Export Production Tax of 100% was being imposed on the Tin Mining Companies. But forced labour was to continue.

A major change in the structure of West Africa's economy, resulting from the war, was the establishment of a whole range of secondary industries to provide goods which were either in short supply from traditional sources or which were impossible to obtain because of the German submarine blockade. Building materials, concrete, furniture, leather goods, preserved fruits, dried fish and meat were now being manufactured on the spot.[58]

The great expansion in the economy that took place in West Africa as a result of war-time demands is indicated by a comparison of the imports and exports for the years 1938 and 1946.

EXTERNAL TRADE: BRITISH WEST AFRICA

(£ million)

| Year | Exports | Imports | Total Trade |
|------|---------|---------|-------------|
| 1938 | 23 | 21 | 44 |
| 1946 | 48 | 38 | 86 |

The Colonial Governments, faced with the problem of both increasing production and controlling imports as well as avoiding inflation, for the first time appointed Economic Advisers to help them in their first essays in economic planning. In 1943 Mr. Noel Hall, formerly Director of the British National Institute of Social and Economic Research, was appointed Development Adviser to the Resident Minister for West Africa. At the same time Mr. Maxwell Fry was appointed as town planning adviser, in view of the rapid growth of the main economic centres during the war. British Trade Unionists were appointed as Labour Advisers. From now on the Colonial Governments were to abandon their *laissez-faire* approach to the economy, and to intervene more and more in a system of economic exploitation with which 'the entire West African population [was] growing more and more dissatisfied'.[59]

In French West Africa the war once again emphasised its role as a source of supply of goods for the metropolis in distress. In August 1939 Léon Cayla was appointed Governor-General with the task of exacting the maximum contribution of men and produce for the war. From the level of the Federation to the *Cercle*, committees were set up to requisition food and conscript men. At a West African level, agreement was reached on economic co-operation between the French and British administrations. In April 1940 Georges Mandel and Malcolm Macdonald, colonial secretaries of France and Britain, concluded arrangements for the common marketing of cocoa and announced that 'as a result of the Paris conference we have decided to set up definite machinery for permanent co-operation at *Home* and in *the colonies*'.[60] Within French West Africa itself priority was to be given to the improvement of roads, tracks, railways, ports and airports. Workmen's camps were to trace out 8,500 kilometres of tracks. And work on the second portion of the Mossi railway was to be started.[61] These ambitious plans as well as the healthy new departure in Anglo-French co-operation had to be abandoned when French West Africa went Vichy. With the blockade of Dakar and other French West African ports by the British the problem became not how to increase production for export but how to survive without imports. These imports included, in particular, rice which had become a staple for wealthier classes of peasants. Not only was the peasant cut off from supplies of imported rice, but he was now unable to earn much for his cash crops, since there was nowhere to export them. Groundnut production, for example, fell from 419,000 tons in 1940 to 199,000 in 1941 and only 114,000 in 1942. Guinean and Sudanese *navetanes* ceased to travel to Senegal to work on the groundnut fields.[62] Cocoa production in Ivory Coast declined even more dramatically from 55,185 tons in 1939 to 542 in 1943,[63] and timber from 42,887 tons in 1939 to nil in 1942.[64]

When French West Africa joined the Allied cause once more, she resumed her traditional role as an exporter of cash crops. However, certain products were in greater demand than others. In Ivory Coast, for example, the administration forced peasants to abandon one cash crop for another more urgently needed by the Allies. This they achieved by two methods. First, most African cocoa and coffee planters were *sujets* and therefore could be compelled to cultivate what the administration wanted. Second their plantations could be legally destroyed on the grounds that they were diseased though the real motive was usually that they were competing in a tight market with European plantations. Third, a premium was paid on all plantations of twenty-five or more contiguous hectares which skilfully included all European plantations but only the fifty largest African ones.[65] Dispossessed planters were then forced into production of alternative crops like rubber and palm-oil. African planters also suffered because priority in recruitment of labour was given to the European planters.

Throughout French West Africa each *cercle* was set a production target and told what goods it was to produce. The Free French considered that France's honour was as much bound up with her material as her military contribution to the Allied cause.[66] Unfortunately in many cases the targets were quite unrealistic: either they set targets which were above the productive capacity of the *cercle* in question or demanded crops that could not be grown there. Richard-Molard cites the case of the *cercle* required to produce so many tons of liana rubber though no liana rubber had ever been grown in the territory.[67] There were many instances of peasants purchasing produce to fulfil their obligation to the administration.[68] Suret-Canale cites a draconian circular sent out to the Chefs de Canton by the Administrator:

'I give you till 31st May latest to complete your supply of millet for the present trade season to S.C.O.A.

On the 15th May, you still had *x* kilos outstanding to deliver.

If you fail to execute this order within the given time limit, you will be put under house arrest in Kissidougou and be subject to such necessary sanctions until the amount to be supplied by your canton is complete.

Kissidougou, 20th May 1945,<br>sgd. Commandant de Cercle.'[69]

Whereas under Vichy the peasant had to subsist largely on his own resources, under the Free French he was subject to ridiculous demands for crops without the possibility of obtaining imported goods in exchange, since these were in short supply and anyway he was not paid the market price for what he was forced to produce.[70]

In Senegal a veritable 'Battle of Groundnuts' was launched by Governor Deschamps. He envisaged raising production from its 1942 level of 114,000, lowest since 1906, to 400,000 tons in 1943. 45,000 *navetanes* were despatched from Guinea and Sudan with the 'co-operation' of the Governors of these two territories. A big propaganda effort was undertaken, but primarily he relied on the efforts of the administrators and chiefs.[71] But actually only 275,000 tons were produced because the administration had over-estimated the cultivable surface available. Worse still, better prices and finer cloth in the Gambia had drained off some of Senegal's output.[72] The following year the crop increased, but as Suret-Canale points out this was not due to economic incentives but to administrative pressures.[73] The war was however advantageous to Senegal in the field of industrialisation. Before the war metropolitan oil refiners ensured that a local Senegalese industry did not in any way rise up to challenge them. However, when war broke out it was agreed that Senegal could increase her production of groundnut oil for export to North Africa to avoid the necessity of transporting groundnuts to France for processing and then carrying the oil to North Africa. The British blockade of Dakar, and the destruction of Lesieur's Dunkirk factory, persuaded the administration to permit an increase in output from 12,000 tons in 1940 to 45,000 in 1941. And though French groundnut-oil interests kept a close rein on the expansion of the Senegalese groundnut-oil industry, lest it should eliminate the metropolitan industry after the war, French West Africa gained her first major industry. This, together with a number of small industries set up to produce what could no longer be imported, were the foundation of Dakar's industrialisation after the war.

## 5 Returns for aid

Chapter XI of the United Nations Charter promulgated at the end of the war was of vital importance to the colonial peoples of the world. Those members of the United Nations who were responsible for the administration of non-self-governing countries recognised solemnly an obligation to ensure the political, social and economic advancement of their inhabitants. They agreed that self-government (the French text read 'self-administration') should be the goal of their policies in their colonies.[74] The non-colonial members of the United Nations now had a forum in which they could legitimately criticise the conduct of the colonial powers in the administration of subject peoples, for France and Britain had supported the entrenchment in the Charter of the United Nations itself the declaration that the main task of a colonial power in its colonies was to develop them and to prepare their inhabitants for greater participation in the administration of their own affairs. In subscribing to this, both France and Britain were recognising the debt they had incurred with their colonies for their successful prosecution of the war.

As far as the French were concerned 'during the four years when fighting, France had been colonial France', as René Pleven put it.[75] De Gaulle declared at the Brazzaville Conference that it was in the colonies that Free France 'found her refuge and the starting point for her liberation . . . as a result of this there is henceforth a permanent bond between the Mother Country and the Empire'.[76]

Though the Second World War was to mark the end of the old colonial system in French West Africa and to inaugurate a series of reforms which with hindsight we can see were the prelude to its end, under the Vichy régime the colonial system was entrenched. The liberal reforms of the Popular Front Government, and the promises made on the outbreak of war by Colonial Minister Mandel and Deputy Diouf that there would be increased participation of Africans in their own affairs,[77] were followed under Vichy by a suspension, as in metropolitan France, of all consultative institutions. Even the Committees on Public Works, Railways and Colonial Ports were axed.[78] Decrees were passed that increased the authority of administrators to inflict summary punishments on Africans and abolished the exemption from the *indigénat* granted to certain categories of *sujets* by a decree of 1939.[79] Senegalese *citoyens* were the hardest hit, for they were now reduced to the position of *sujets*. For the majority of French West Africans, however, these changes made little difference. The *Conseils d' Administration* of the other territories, though they had more influence on the Governors' decision than is usually supposed,[80] never aroused the public interest the Legislative Councils of British West Africa did, and certainly never produced from their elected African members any politicians, let alone men of the calibre of a Bankole-Bright, a Casely-Hayford or an Adeniyi-Jones.

Despite the political setbacks suffered by Africans under Vichy, Governor-General Boisson seems clearly to have felt the need to offer them a brighter future in the reconstructed France of Marshal Pétain. 'I have often said—so strong is my conviction—that Africa will play a role of the first order in French recovery . . . Africa is the white man and the coloured man in association. May the young people of both learn to appreciate each other, learn to love each other. May they learn to aid each other, to combine their efforts. France desires to create for the young Negro people an important place in African France.'[81]

It was left to the Free French to give Africans this place. Though their régime incurred grave economic hardships for the African, right from the start the Free French made it clear that they intended to reform the colonial system in tropical Africa. The new Governor-General of French West Africa, Pierre Cournarie, spoke to the resuscitated *Conseil du Gouvernement* in December 1943 of France's mission, 'as if it were sacred', to increase the material and moral well-being of its African subjects.[82] A month later he attended the French African Conference at Brazzaville, better known as the Brazzaville Conference, at which the Free French committed themselves to a series of political, social and economic reforms which were to end the old colonial system in French Black Africa.

The Brazzaville Conference was essentially a meeting of French Colonial administrators under the direction of representatives of the Provisional Government of Algiers to discuss the role of the African colonies in post-war France. The only African voice heard there was that of Fily Dabo Sissoko, a Sudanese teacher and *chef de canton* through the medium of two papers he laid before the participants. The recommendations made by the Conference, all of which were in substance realised during the next five years, fall into three groups: social, economic and political.[83]

The social reforms proposed by the Conference affected immediately the greatest number of Africans. The hated *indigénat* was to be abolished and a new, uniform native penal code introduced. Forced labour was to be eliminated over a period of five years. Arbitrary *corvées* and taxation in kind were to be suppressed. On the positive side Labour inspectorates were to be established with a view to the regulation of conditions of work for Africans. Trade unionism was to be given official encouragement. Medical services were to be expanded and improved. Educational opportunities for Africans were to be greatly increased. At the conference on education held in Dakar in the following July, an educational plan was drawn up for French West Africa which envisaged that over a period of twenty years seventy-five *écoles normales* capable of producing 50,000 new teachers would be established, so that the 50,000 proposed new primary schools and 200 upper primary schools could be properly staffed. Despite the pleas of Governor-General Éboué, a confirmed anti-assimilationist,[84] Brazzaville recommended that the educational system be basically French in character. Finally it recommended that greater opportunities be given the educated African for participation in the administration.

In the economic sphere the Conference recommended that a definite plan of development of the colonies be drawn up. It laid particular emphasis on industrial development. The social and economic recommendations of Brazzaville were eventually embodied in F.I.D.E.S., or the *Fonds d'Investissement pour le Développement Économique et Social* which, in the fifteen years between the end of the war and the independence of the West African states, did much to transform this colonial slum into an area with the basic infra-structure of a modern developing economy. Where before 1945 almost no aid had been given by France to the West African colonies, in this period probably over £400 million was provided by her for their development.

In the political sphere Brazzaville made timid but, as it trans-pired, far-reaching recommendations. The Conference was quite explicit that there should be no question of eventual self-government or independence. The future of the colonies lay with France, and France alone. On the other hand there was to be decentralisation of the administration from Paris to the colonies themselves. Most important of all the colonies should be represented in the Constituent Assembly that would establish the constitution of the Fourth Republic. However, rather than the colonies being represented in the metropolitan legislature, they should be represented in a new Federal Assembly for France and its Empire. In addition assemblies, similar to the Conseil-Colonial of Senegal, should be set up in each territory, with as wide a franchise as possible for Africans. How-ever, there were to be two electoral colleges, one for Africans, one for Europeans, so that the latter could gain representation. Africans would not be given citizenship of France itself but of the Empire, exercising it through the proposed Federal Assembly. Politics were no more to be the monopoly of the Senegalese *citoyens*.

Many of the reforms proposed by Brazzaville were put into effect by decree during the following months or enacted by the constituent assemblies, where some of the future leaders of French West Africa like Léopold Sédar Senghor and Félix Houphouët-Boigny made their début. Together these two men represented the new departure in French West Africa's political history: Senghor represented the hitherto unenfranchised *sujets* of Senegal, while Houphouët-Boigny along with six other African deputies represented the voices of West Africans outside Senegal, hitherto unheard.

Although for Britain the West African context was less dramatic than for France, the implications of the war for her as a colonial power were the same. The myth of imperial impregnability was shattered. She had lost her Far Eastern colonies to a 'coloured' enemy, the Japanese, in humiliating circumstances: defeat had been swift and her Asian subjects appeared indifferent to her departure. To regain Burma, for instance, she had to depend in no small way on African troops. In Europe the Germans were masters. The great British Empire seemed to be falling part. No longer could Britain rely on the automatic loyalty of her colonial subjects. To gain India's support Churchill, who had once described Gandhi as a 'naked fakir', now had to promise its people independence. In West Africa there was no question of cajoling the people into the 'war effort'. They had to be courted assiduously through the radio, pamphlets, films and public address systems which explained to them the nature of the crisis,[85] and held out the promise of a brighter world for them, as well as the British, if the war were won. But as *The Times* warned: 'The white man will be judged, as never before, by the proved quality of his leadership, not by the lure of his promises.'[86] Nevertheless the very generous support given by Africans to the war effort had to be recompensed by the social, economic and political reforms which had been demanded by the élite over the past twenty years. And, during the war, more plans were made for development in all three spheres than in the preceding two decades.

The motivation for the most significant change in government policy in this period, the Colonial Development and Welfare Act, was, as it happened, not the war. Rather, riots in the West Indies the year before war broke out were its inspiration. The Royal Commission investigating them attributed their cause to the backward economic state of the islands. The British Government therefore established a special development fund for the West Indies and, realising that if such situations were to be avoided elsewhere in the colonial empire, made available funds for development for all her colonies. The Colonial Welfare and Development Act set aside £5 million a year for development projects and £500,000 for research. Britain had now accepted unequivocally her obligation to supply funds for the development of her colonies. The significance of this new departure in economic and social policy was put succinctly at a meeting of the West African Students' Union in honour of the Governor of Nigeria, Sir Bernard Bourdillon: 'The outstanding fact is the abandonment of the principle of self-sufficiency for the Colonies. Nigeria cannot balance her budget and make all the progress required.'[87]

The timing of the C.D. & W. Act was particularly fortunate. Passed on the outbreak of war, it seemed a marvellously generous gesture designed to secure the loyalty of colonial subjects. The *Gold Coast Spectator* reacted warmly: 'When Britain grows old, she shall not die for we, the growing sons, will keep the flag flying.'[88] The *Sierra Leone Weekly News* echoed these sentiments, while African members of Legislative Council expressed their gratitude officially. As it was, lack of staff made it difficult to spend the small sums actually available, which were anyway more than covered by the grants and loans made by the West African colonies to Britain for the war effort. But the principle had been established. As Julian Huxley wrote in 1944: 'Many responsible people are convinced that the £5,000,000 annually available under the Colonial Development and Welfare Act is quite inadequate. Parliament (and the British Taxpayer) will have to give the most serious consideration to their responsibility in this matter of raising the colonies' standard of life.'[89]

The responsibility was taken seriously. Development plans were drawn up for each colony. Nigeria's ten-year plan, promulgated in 1946, amounted to the astronomical sum by pre-war standards of £55 million to which C.D. & W. was to contribute £23 million.[90]

These development plans were concerned not only with economic problems but also with social ones, in particular education. Africans were appointed to a Commission on Higher Education in West Africa under the chairmanship of Walter Elliott, M.P. It was this Commission that recommended the establishment of University Colleges in Ibadan and Legon (Ghana). Nigeria was represented by Rev. Ransome-Kuti, Gold Coast by Mr. Arku Korsah, and Sierra Leone by Dr. E. H. Taylor-Cummings. Individual territories put forward their own plans for the expansion of primary and secondary education.[91] The Gold Coast Commission on education, which had parity of African and European representation, reported that 'even in the less prosperous areas, chiefs and communities are becoming more and more willing to pay for the establishment of schools and to support teachers',[92] while in 1944 the Advisory Committee on African Education, accepting self-government as the goal of colonial policy, advised that 'general well-being and prosperity can only be secured and maintained if the whole mass of people have a real share in education and have some understanding of the meaning of its purpose... without such understanding true democracy cannot function and the rising hope of self-government will suffer inevitable frustration'.[93]

The British Government promised West Africa an increase in its medical services and the number of African doctors appointed to them.[94] It introduced far-reaching labour legislation, setting up arbitration boards, conciliation boards, and wage boards overseeing the operation of new minimum wage laws. The British trade unionists appointed as labour advisers to the West African governments had the task of ensuring that workers had the possibility of expressing their opinions and were properly represented, and of bringing 'labour standards to a level comparable, so far as local conditions will allow, to those attained in Great Britain'.[95]

These economic and social reforms were supplemented by political reforms which, though they only went a small way to meet the demands of the nationalists, marked the beginning of the era of decolonisation. First, Africans were appointed to the Executive Councils of Nigeria, Sierra Leone and the Gold Coast, thus breaking the European monopoly of executive power. What was more, these Africans were unofficial members.[96] Second, Africans were admitted for the first time to the inner sanctum of colonialism: the Administrative Service. K. A. Busia and A. L. Adu in the Gold Coast were appointed Assistant District Officers, thus breaking the rule that Africans should never be allowed to administer their fellow men. Plans were also made to increase the rate of Africanisation in all four colonies, though this was only partly altruistic. Many places in the colonial service were vacant because their expatriate incumbents had been called up. Finally the colonial governors introduced proposals for new constitutions which would take effect after the war. Whilst these constitutions, especially those of the Gold Coast and Nigeria, far from satisfied the nationalists, they did make one major concession: the introduction of an African unofficial majority. This meant that for the first time Africans could out-vote white officials. On the other hand the unofficial majority was not wholly elected. Nevertheless these constitutions proved to be the prelude to a rapid series of constitutional reforms which brought Ghana self-government within six years, and independence within twelve, and Nigeria independence within fifteen years.

## 6 New horizons

For West Africans new horizons were opened up by the war and the reforms introduced during it. They had seen their colonial masters with their backs to the wall. French Africans had seen the metropolis over-run and the French themselves become 'subjects'. They had seen Frenchmen divided among themselves. The viciousness with which Free French turned on Vichy supporters in Dakar was paraded daily in the press. *Clarté* and later *Réveil* denounced colonial officials and dignitaries such as the Vicar Apostolic and the Comte de Bréteuil, publisher of *Paris-Dakar*, whom hitherto Africans had been taught to respect unquestioningly. *Clarté*, in the first issue, demanded: 'A rapid purge and the punishment of traitors. Let all those who received positions of responsibility, either from the Vichy Government or from that of Boisson, be at once dismissed and that without prejudicing any later penalties they may incur.'[97] These quarrels were of vital significance to the French who participated in them: to the Africans they merely revealed idols with feet of clay. What were they to make of a people who in 1940 under Vichy dismissed Governor Geismar because he was a Jew and brought him back in 1943 under the Free French to give him the second highest post in the Federation? What could they think of a people who bombed each other as when de Gaulle's Free French and the British attacked Dakar? The French had fallen from the pedestal on which all sensible colonial rulers place themselves, and it was impossible for them to climb back. Not only did they reduce their standing in the eyes of the Africans but they also alienated them by their senseless handling of the mutiny of African veterans at Tiaroye in December 1944. After release from internment in German prisoner-of-war camps these veterans demanded to be paid their back pay at the French rather than African rates. Frustrated in their demand, they mutinied and some forty were shot by French officers.

For British West Africans the myth of the white man's superiority was dispelled for ever. Africans had fought alongside white men, killed white men, seen brave Africans and white cowards, slept with white women, met white soldiers who treated them as equals, or who were, like themselves, hardly educated. They had visited new countries, seen people like the Indians living in squalor and poverty such as they had never seen at home. Above all, 'having fought in the defence of freedom, they considered it their right that they should have some share in the government of their own land'.[98] The myth of white aristocracy could only be preserved by keeping Africans at home. As Paul Catrice observed of the French African soldiers sent to France for their military service before the war: 'These native soldiers are in direct contact with Frenchmen, they penetrate their habits, their little ways and above all their vices; they quickly begin to doubt the superiority of colonisation, while through them the peaceful citizen discovers new horizons and new worlds.'[99] It is hardly surprising, then, that ex-soldiers in both French and British West Africa were to play a leading role in the ranks of the political parties which were formed to take advantage of the constitutional reforms made at the end of the war.

The war led to a great expansion of population in the coastal towns, and major centres in the interior like Kano and Kumasi. A whole new range of jobs became available as a result of the strategic role assumed by these towns or the creation of industries to produce goods that could not be imported. Living conditions were poor; many people had to live in hastily erected shacks. Goods were in short supply and prices were high. There was as a result considerable discontent in these towns on which politicians were able to draw for support.

Above all the war brought forth a new group of politicians who were no longer content to accept the pace of political change laid down by the colonial governments. Thus Sourou Migan Apithy told the Second Constituent Assembly: 'Our ideal is not to be French citizens. All we desire is to enjoy in our country the same rights and the same liberties as the French who dwell among us. I would like to say also that our ideal is also not to have a seat in an assembly on the banks of the Seine, nor to concern ourselves with matters that are essentially those of metropolitan France, but we wish to settle the affairs of our own country, on the banks of the Congo or the Niger, and to be free to discuss with the people of France those matters which concern the whole community which we form with that people.'[100] Similarly the constitution of the newly formed National Council of Nigeria and the Cameroons (N.C.N.C.) published in 1945 described its aims as the achievement of 'internal self-government for Nigeria and the Cameroon [*sic*] under British Mandate shall exercise executive, legislative and judicial powers'.[101] West Africans were no longer content to take the back seat in the running of their own affairs. Whether as in British West Africa their demand was for self-government, or in French West Africa for an equal place in the French Community with metropolitan Frenchmen, the effect was the same. Africans wanted to be masters in their own house. As Lord Hailey said as early as 1942, the colonial powers would now have to exchange the old concept of trusteeship of colonial peoples for one of partnership with them.[102]

# Notes

1 *The Times*, 16th August 1941.
2 *West Africa*, 29th June 1940.
3 Henri Laurentie, 'Pros and Cons of Colonialism: The French Colonies in the Modern World', *Renaissance*, October 1945, Mimeographed (Rhodes House Library).
4 *Ibid.*
5 Cited in Hailey, *African Survey* (Revised, 1956), p. 245.
6 René Pleven, *The Evolution of the Empire towards the French Union*. Address to the Annual Meeting of the Anti-Slavery Society, 21st July 1949, p. 6.
7 *Ibid.*, p. 6.
8 *The Times*, 23rd June 1942.
9 Kilson, *Sierra Leone*, p. 152.
10 Bye-laws of the G.E.C. of Dakar cited in Schachter-Morgenthau, *Political Parties in French-Speaking West Africa*, pp. 23-4.
11 *Ibid.*, p. 25.
12 Ly Abdoullaye, *Mercénaires Noires*, pp. 63-4.
13 Catrice, 'L'emploi de troupes indigènes', pp. 398-400.
14 Richard-Molard, *Afrique Occidentale Française*, p. 165.
15 *Paris-Dakar*, 4th June 1940.
16 Delavignette, *L'Afrique noire française et son destin*, p. 87.
17 *Paris-Dakar*, 19th June 1940.
18 *Ibid.*, 20th and 21st June 1940.
19 *The Times*, 27th June 1940.
20 Suret-Canale, *Afrique Noire II*, p. 571.
21 *Paris-Dakar*, 30th August 1940.
22 E. Louveau, '*Au Bagne*': *Entre les griffes de Vichy et de la milice*, Bamako, March 1947.
23 See Daniel Chenex, *Qui a sauve l'Afrique?*, Paris, n.d.; 'French West Africa', in *The Times*, 29th January 1943; and Paul M. Atkins, 'Dakar and the Strategy of West Africa', *Foreign Affairs*, January 1942, XX, 2, pp. 359-60.
24 *The Times*, 10th January 1925.
25 *Paris-Dakar*, 24th September 1940.
26 *Ibid.*, 25th September 1942.
27 *Ibid.*, 1st July 1942.
28 Atkins, 'Dakar and the Strategy of West Africa', p. 363.
29 Brochure of the *Légion française des Combattants de l'Afrique Noire*, 31st August 1941.
30 *Clarté*, February 1945.
31 *Journal Officiel*, 21st December 1941, pp. 1,053-4.
32 Abdel-Kader Diagne, *La résistance française au Sénégal et en A.O.F. pendant la guerre 1939-45*, Mimeographed, n.d., but preface dated 16th August 1949.

33 *Paris-Dakar*, 19th December 1942.
34 *Ibid.*, 4th January 1943.
35 *Ibid.*, 23rd April 1943.
36 *Ibid.*, 21st April 1943.
37 *The Colonial Empire (1939–47)*, Cmd. 7167, p. 116.
38 *The Times*, 6th April 1945.
39 *Colonial Empire (1939–47)*, p. 9.
40 Sir Ahmadu Bello, *My Life*, London, 1962, p. 53.
41 *Colonial Empire (1939–47)*, p. 115: Gambia £11,478; Gold Coast £361,696; Nigeria £409,255; Sierra Leone £148,698.
42 *Lagos Calling for Nigerian Savings Certificates*, Lagos, 1941.
43 *The Times*, 3rd November 1942.
44 *Ibid*, 19th August 1941.
45 *Ibid.*, 25th March 1940.
46 *West Africa*, 6th April 1940.
47 *The Times*, 7th October 1940.
48 The above account is based on Mars, 'Extra-Territorial Enterprises' (Section 6: War-time Operations), in Perham, ed., *Mining, Commerce and Finance in Nigeria*; and P. T. Bauer, *West African Trade* (Re-issue), London, 1963.
49 *Ibid.*, p. 109.
50 *Ibid.*, p. 109.
51 Bauer, *West African Trade*, p. 151.
52 *Ibid.*, p. 247.
53 *Ibid.*, p. 152.
54 Dr. Julian Huxley, 'West African Survey: I', *The Times*, 6th June 1944.
55 See Bauer, *West African Trade*, pp. 315–16.
56 Mars, 'Extra-Territorial Enterprises', p. 113.
57 *The Times*, 18th June 1942.
58 Lord Swinton, Minister Resident in West Africa in interview with *The Times*, 14th August 1943.
59 *The Times*, 23rd June 1942.
60 *West Africa*, 30th March 1940.
61 Governor-General Cayla in speech at the opening of the Conseil du Gouvernement of French West Africa reported in *West Africa*, 27th January 1940.
62 Discours prononcé par M. Hubert Deschamps, Gouverneur du Sénégal à l'ouverture de la séssion ordinaire du Conseil Colonial, 23rd August 1943, p. 22.
63 Amon d'Aby, *La Côte d'Ivoire*, p. 77.
64 *Ibid.*, p. 88.
65 *Ibid.*, p. 74; and Edward Mortimer, *France and the Africans*, forthcoming.
66 Suret-Canale, *Afrique Noire II*, p. 589.
67 Richard-Molard, *Afrique Occidentale Française*, p. 167.

68  See Suret-Canale, *Afrique Noire II*, pp. 588–91.

69  *Ibid.*, p. 588.

70  See Richard-Molard, *Afrique Occidentale Française*, p. 168. 'Under harsh threats, followed if thought necessary, by the immediate execution of them, the most exorbitant demands are made.' Also Suret-Canale, *La fin de la chefferie en Guinee*, pp. 472 ff., for the impact of Free French demands on Guinea.

71  *Discours du Gouverneur Deschamps*, 23rd August 1943, pp. 21–2.

72  *Discours du Gouverneur Charles Dagain, Gouverneur du Sénégal à l'ouverture de la session ordinaire du Conseil Colonial*, 3rd October 1944, pp. 4–5.

73  Suret-Canale, *Afrique Noire II*, p. 592.

74  *The Colonial Empire*, p. 19.

75  Pleven, *The Evolution of the French Empire*, p. 5.

76  Opening address to the *Conference Africaine Française*, Brazzaville, 30th January–8th February 1944, Commissariat aux Colonies, Algiers, 1944.

77  'Déclaration' of M. Robert Delmas, Vice-President of the Colonial Council of Senegal (cyclostyled), Dakar, November 1939.

78  *Journal Officiel de l'A.O.F.*, 1941.

79  *Ibid.*, 8th March 1941.

80  See Kenneth Robinson, 'Political Developments in French West Africa' in Stillman, ed., *Africa in the Modern World*, p. 148.

81  *Dakar-Jeunes*, I, 1941.

82  *Discours prononcé par le Gouverneur-Général de l'A.O.F. a l'ouverture de la séssion du Conseil du Gouvernement*, Rufisque, December 1943.

83  *La Conférence Africaine Française.*

84  See his *Circulaire-générale sur la politique indigène en Afrique Equatoriale Française*, Brazzaville, 8th November 1941.

85  Stanley Milburn, *Methods and Techniques of Community Development in the United Kingdom Dependent Territories*, United Nations Series on Community Organisation and Development, New York, 1954, p. 10, cited in Wilson, *Education and Changing West African Culture*, p. 74.

86  *The Times*, 19th August 1946.

87  *West Africa*, 25th May 1940.

88  *Ibid.*, 2nd March 1940.

89  *The Times*, 6th July 1941.

90  See *A Ten Year Plan of Development and Welfare*, Lagos, 1946.

91  See for example, *Nigeria: Ten Year Educational Plan (1942)*, Lagos, 1944.

92  *The Times*, 2nd January 1943.

93  *Mass Education in African Society*, Col. no. 186, 1944, p. 4.

94  Oliver Stanley, Secretary of State for the Colonies, quoted in *The Times*, 22nd March 1943.

95  *The Times*, 29th October 1941.

96 Nigeria: S. B. Rhodes and A. A. Alakija; Gold Coast: K. A. Korsah and Nana Sir Ofori Atta; Sierra Leone: Sowell Boston and Paramount Chief A. C. Caulker.

97 *Clarté*, I, January 1944.

98 *Report to His Excellency the Governor by the Committee on Constitutional Reform*, Gold Coast, Annual No. 24, London 1949.

99 Catrice, 'L'emploi de troupes indigènes', p. 401.

100 *Assemblée Nationale Constituante*, 2ᵉ Séance du 18th Septembre 1946, p. 3,802.

101 Nigeria, West Coast of Africa, *The Constitution of the National Council of Nigeria and the Cameroons*, Lagos, 1945, p. 1, para. 5.

102 *The Times*, 23rd June 1942.

## Governors-General of French West Africa, 1895–1946

| | |
|---|---|
| 1895 | J. B. Chaudié |
| 1900 | N. V. Ballay |
| 1902 | Ernest Roume |
| 1908 | William Merlaud-Ponty |
| 1916 | François Clozel |
| 1917 | Joost Van Vollenhoven |
| 1918 | G. Angoulvant |
| 1919 | Martial Merlin |
| 1923 | Jules G. Carde |
| 1930 | Jules Brévié |
| 1936 | Jules de Coppet |
| 1940 | Leon Henri Cayla |
| 1940 | Pierre Boisson |
| 1943–6 | Pierre Courmarie |

# British Governors of Nigeria, 1900–48

| *Colony of Lagos* | *Protectorate of Southern Nigeria* |
|---|---|
| *Governor* | *High Commissioner* |
| 1899–1904 | 1900–4 |
| Sir William Macgregor | Sir Ralph Moor |
| 1904–6 | 1904–6 |
| Sir Walter Egerton | Sir Walter Egerton |

| *Colony and Protectorate of Southern Nigeria* | *Protectorate of Northern Nigeria* |
|---|---|
| | *High Commissioner or* |
| *Governor* | *Governor* |
| 1906–12 | 1900–7 |
| Sir Walter Egerton | Sir Fredrick Lugard |
| 1912–14 | 1907–9 |
| Sir Fredrick Lugard | Sir Percy Girouard* |
| | 1909–12 |
| | Sir Hesketh Bell |
| | 1912–14 |
| | Sir Fredrick Lugard |

*Colony and Protectorate*
*of Nigeria*
*Governor-General*
1914–19
Sir Fredrick Lugard
*Governor*
1919–25
Sir Hugh Clifford
1925–31
Sir Graeme Thompson
1931–5
Sir Donald Cameron
1935–43
Sir Bernard Bourdillon
1943–8
Sir Arthur Richards

* Girouard's title was changed from High Commissioner to Governor in 1908.

## Governors of the Gold Coast (Ghana), 1885—1948

1885    William Brandford Griffith (knighted 1886)

1895    Sir William Edward Maxwell

1897    Sir Frederic Mitchell Hodgson

1900    Major Sir Matthew Nathan

1904    Sir John P. Rodger

1910    J. J. Tharburn

1912    Sir Hugh C. Clifford

1919    Brig.-Gen. Sir F. Gordon Guggisberg

1927    Sir Alexander Ransford Slater

1932    Sir Thomas Shenton W. Thomas

1934    Sir A. W. Hodson

1941–7  Sir A. C. M. Burns

1948    Sir Gerald H. Creasy

# Governors of Sierra Leone, 1885—1948

| | |
|---|---|
| 1885–88 | Surgeon-Major Sir Samuel Rowe |
| 1888–91 | Capt. Sir J. S. Hay |
| 1892–94 | Sir Francis Fleming |
| 1894–1900 | Col. Frederick Cardew |
| 1900 | Sir Charles Anthony King-Harman |
| 1904–11 | Sir Leslie Probyn |
| 1911–16 | Sir Edward Merewether |
| 1916–22 | R. J. Wilkinson |
| 1922 | Sir Ransford Slater |
| 1927 | Brig.-Gen. Sir J. A. Byrne |
| 1931 | Sir Arnold Hodson |
| 1934 | Sir Henry Moore |
| 1937 | Sir Douglas Jardine |
| 1941 | Sir Hubert Stevenson |
| 1948 | Sir George Beresford-Stooke |

# Governors of the Gambia, 1884—1947

| | |
|---|---|
| 1884 | Sir C. A. Moloney |
| 1886 | Sir J. S. Hay |
| 1888 | Sir G. T. Carter |
| 1891 | Sir R. B. Llewellyn |
| 1901 | Sir G. C. Denton |
| 1911 | Lt.-Col. Sir Henry Gallwey |
| 1914 | Sir Edward Cameron |
| 1920 | Capt. Sir Cecil Armitage |
| 1927 | Sir John Middleton |
| 1928 | Sir Edward Denham |
| 1930 | Sir Richmond Palmer |
| 1933 | Sir Arthur Richards (later Lord Milverton) |
| 1936 | Sir Thomas Southorn |
| 1942 | Sir Hilary Blood |
| 1947 | Sir Andrew Wright |

## The Nigerian Economy, 1900–45

| Year | Imports | Exports |
|------|---------|---------|
|      | £       | £       |
| 1900 | 1,735,244 | 1,886,883 |
| 1901 | 1,812,131 | 2,018,775 |
| 1902 | 1,977,615 | 2,512,380 |
| 1903 | 2,128,146 | 2,356,617 |
| 1904 | 2,422,716 | 2,781,113 |
| 1905 | 2,592,405 | 2,552,110 |
| 1906 | 2,847,317 | 2,950,391 |
| 1907 | 3,839,340 | 3,863,332 |
| 1908 | 4,046,572 | 3,335,911 |
| 1909 | 4,529,604 | 4,114,237 |
| 1910 | 5,122,370 | 5,258,452 |
| 1911 | 5,234,874 | 5,354,101 |
| 1912 | 5,951,883 | 5,773,488 |
| 1913 | 6,331,751 | 7,097,646 |
| 1914 | 6,276,956 | 6,420,461 |
| 1915 | 4,983,729 | 4,946,228 |
| 1916 | 5,174,474 | 6,029,546 |
| 1917 | 5,808,592 | 8,602,486 |
| 1918 | 7,423,158 | 9,511,971 |
| 1919 | 10,798,671 | 14,675,789 |
| 1920 | 20,763,382 | 16,956,270 |
| 1921 | 10,237,117 | 8,258,500 |
| 1922 | 10,303,688 | 8,936,302 |
| 1923 | 11,761,852 | 11,705,012 |
| 1924 | 12,921,337 | 15,038,077 |
| 1925 | 16,278,349 | 17,370,161 |
| 1926 | 13,597,480 | 17,339,618 |
| 1927 | 15,664,637 | 16,340,957 |
| 1928 | 16,663,525 | 17,206,933 |
| 1929 | 13,404,447 | 17,922,501 |
| 1930 | 12,700,037 | 15,174,315 |
| 1931 | 6,744,199 | 10,644,519 |
| 1932 | 7,243,143 | 9,628,944 |
| 1933 | 6,645,268 | 9,067,143 |
| 1934 | 5,435,054 | 10,078,226 |
| 1935 | 8,299,297 | 12,049,643 |
| 1936 | 12,665,772 | 15,557,256 |
| 1937 | 18,567,675 | 19,575,665 |
| 1938 | 11,567,104 | 14,390,662 |

| Year | Imports | Exports |
|------|---------|---------|
|      | £       | £       |
| 1939 | 8,626,112  | 14,150,510 |
| 1940 | 10,822,261 | 13,052,916 |
| 1941 | 7,025,099  | 14,582,594 |
| 1942 | 15,373,879 | 15,164,858 |
| 1943 | 18,567,694 | 15,436,949 |
| 1944 | 18,504,070 | 17,929,384 |
| 1945 | 15,917,862 | 19,251,836 |

## Nigeria: Revenue and Expenditure in the Twenties and Thirties

| Year | Revenue | Expenditure |
|---|---|---|
| | £ | £ |
| 1st Apr. 1922 | — | — |
| 1922–23 | 5,505,465 | 5,410,983 |
| 1923–24 | 6,260,561 | 5,501,242 |
| 1924–25 | 6,944,220 | 5,768,715 |
| 1925–26 | 8,268,928 | 6,583,167 |
| 1926–27 | 7,734,429 | 7,584,692 |
| 1927–28* | 6,304,636 | 6,723,715 |
| 1928–29 | 5,894,658 | 6,861,099 |
| 1929–30 | 6,045,359 | 6,289,901 |
| 1930–31 | 5,622,200 | 6,329,668 |
| 1931–32 | 4,857,612 | 6,188,301 |
| 1932–33 | 4,984,505 | 4,983,739 |
| 1933–34 | 4,889,152 | 5,035,562 |
| 1934–35 | 4,960,765 | 4,836,666 |
| 1935–36 | 5,995,921 | 5,757,180 |
| 1936–37 | 6,259,547 | 6,061,348 |
| 1937–38 | 7,342,450 | 7,375,570 |
| 1938–39 | 5,811,088 | 6,867,408 |
| 1939–40 | 6,113,126 | 6,498,566 |
| 1940–41 | 7,273,157 | 7,254,325 |
| 1941–42 | 7,975,054 | 7,026,894 |
| 1942–43 | 9,034,000 | 8,999,000 |
| 1943–44 | 10,913,000 | 9,977,000 |
| 1944–45 | 11,445,000 | 10,133,000 |

\* From 1927–8 onward the above figures exclude Railway Revenue and Expenditure, but include the net profit or loss on Railway working.

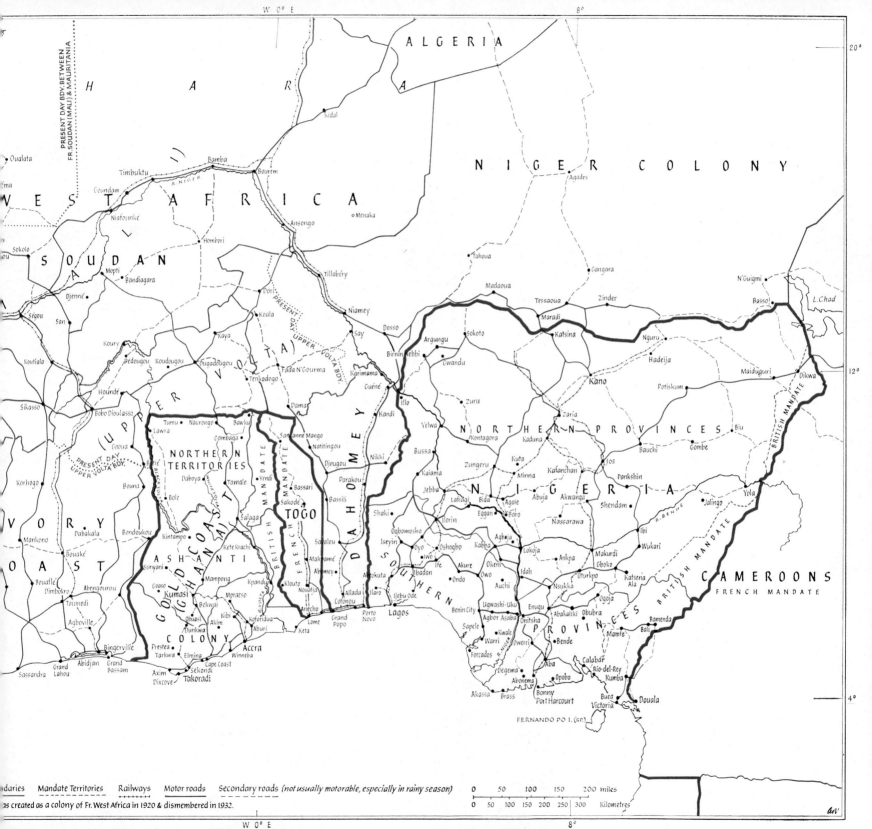

ALGERIA

NIGER COLONY

PRESENT DAY BDY BETWEEN
FR. SOUDAN (MALI) & MAURITANIA.

WEST AFRICA

H A R

A

Oualata

Kidal

Ema

Bamba
Timbuktu
R. NIGER
Goundam

Bourem

Agades

N'Guigmi

Sokolo
ou

Niafounké

SOUDAN

Hombori

Menaka

Ansongo

Tahoua

Gangara

L. Chad

Basso!

Ségou San
Djenné

Mopti
Bandiagara

Dori
PRESENT DAY (UPPER

Tillabéry

Madaoua

Tessaoua

Zinder

Niamey

Koutiala

Koury

Kaya

Koala

VOLTA) BDY.

Niamey

Say

Dosso

Argungu

Sokoto

Maradi

Katsina

Nguru

Hadeija

Maiduguri

12°

Sikasso

Houndé

Ouagadougou

Koudougou

Bédougou

Tenkodogo

Fada N'Gourma

Karimama

Guéné

Birnin Kebbi

Gwandu

Kano

Potiskum

Dikwa

BRITISH MANDATE

Boho Dioulasso

(UPPER

Tumu

Navrongo

Bawku

Pama

Illo

Zuru

Zaria

Bauchi

Gombe

Biu

Gaoua

Lawra

Santanne Mango

Kandi

Yelwa

Kontagora

Kaduna

NORTHERN PROVINCES

PRESENT DAY

Bitié

NORTHERN
TERRITORIES

Gambaga

Natitingou

Nikki

Bussa

Jos

Pankshin

Korhogo

UPPER VOLTA BDY.

BLACK VOLTA

Dahoya

Yendi

Bassari

Djougou

Parakou

Kaiama

Zungeru

Kuta

Minna

Kafanchan

Shendam

Yola

Jalingo

V O R Y

Bouma

Bole

Tamale

WHITE VOLTA

Bassili

Shaki

Jebba

Lafiagi

Bida

Agaie

Abuja

Akwanga

Nassarawa

R. BENUE

Mankono

Dabakala

Bondoukou

Kintampo

Salaga

TOGO

Saalou

Iseyin

Oyo

Oshogbo

Kabba

Eggan

Baro

Lokoja

Ankpa

Makurdi

Wukari

Ibi

C O A S T

Bouaké

ASHANTI

Sunyani

Kete Krachi

Atakpamé

Ogbomosho

Iwo

Ife

Akure

Okene

Owo

Ondo

Idah

Oturkpo

Gboko

Katsina Ala

CAMEROONS

FRENCH MANDATE

Bouaflé
Dimbokro

Goaso

Mampong

Mpraeso

Kpandu

Klouto

Nouatja

Abeokuta

Ibadan

Auchi

Nsukka

Ogoja

Obubra

BRITISH MANDATE

Toumodi

Abengourou

Kumasi

Bekwai

Allada

Cotonou

Benin City

Ugwashi-Uku

Enugu

Abakaliki

Bamenda

Bali

Agboville

GOLD COAST
(GHANA)

Obuasi

Akim

Koforidua

Aburi

Anecho

Lomé

Grand
Popo

Porto
Novo

Lagos

Agbor Asaba

Onitsha

Mamfe

Bingerville

COLONY

Prestea

Kibi

Dunkwa

Accra

Keta

Ilaro

Ijebu Ode

Sapele

Kwale

Bende

Sassandra

Grand
Lahou

Abidjan

Grand
Bassam

Tarkwa

Elmina

Winneba

Warri

Owerri

Aba

Calabar

Rio-del-Rey

Kumba

Axim
Dixcove

Sekondi

Cape Coast

Forcados

Degema

Opobo

Buea

Victoria

Douala

Takoradi

R. NIGER

Abonema

Bonny

Port Harcourt

Akassa

Brass

FERNANDO PO I. (SP.)

daries    Mandate Territories    Railways    Motor roads    Secondary roads (not usually motorable, especially in rainy season)

0    50    100    150    200 miles

0   50  100  150  200  250  300   Kilometres

as created as a colony of Fr. West Africa in 1920 & dismembered in 1932.

W 0° E

8°

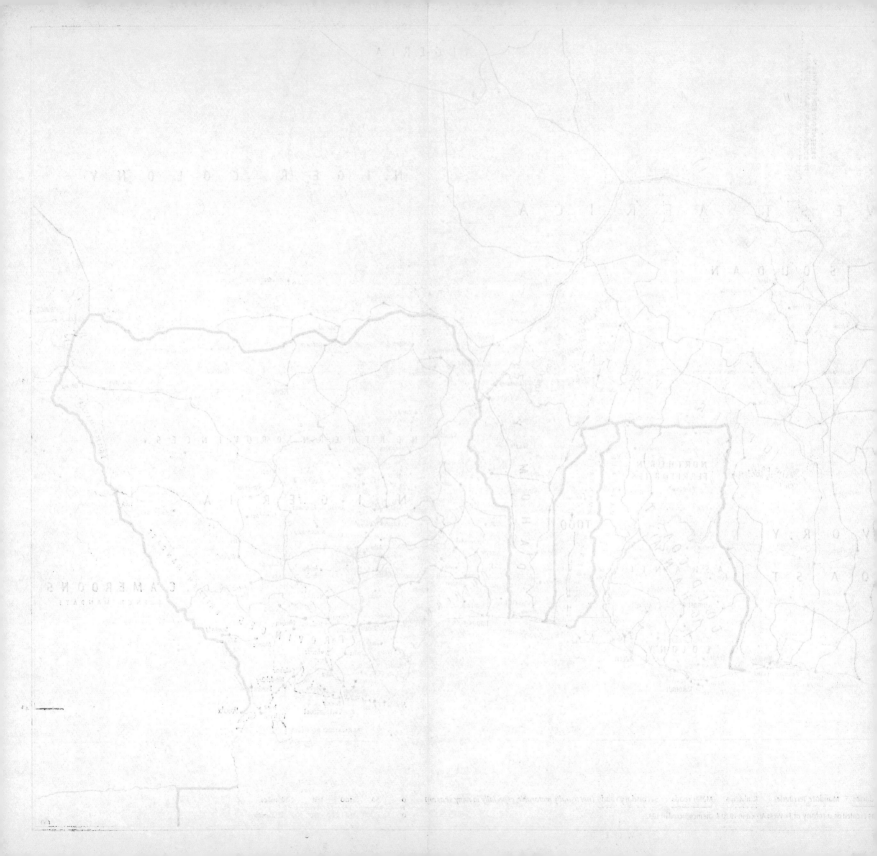

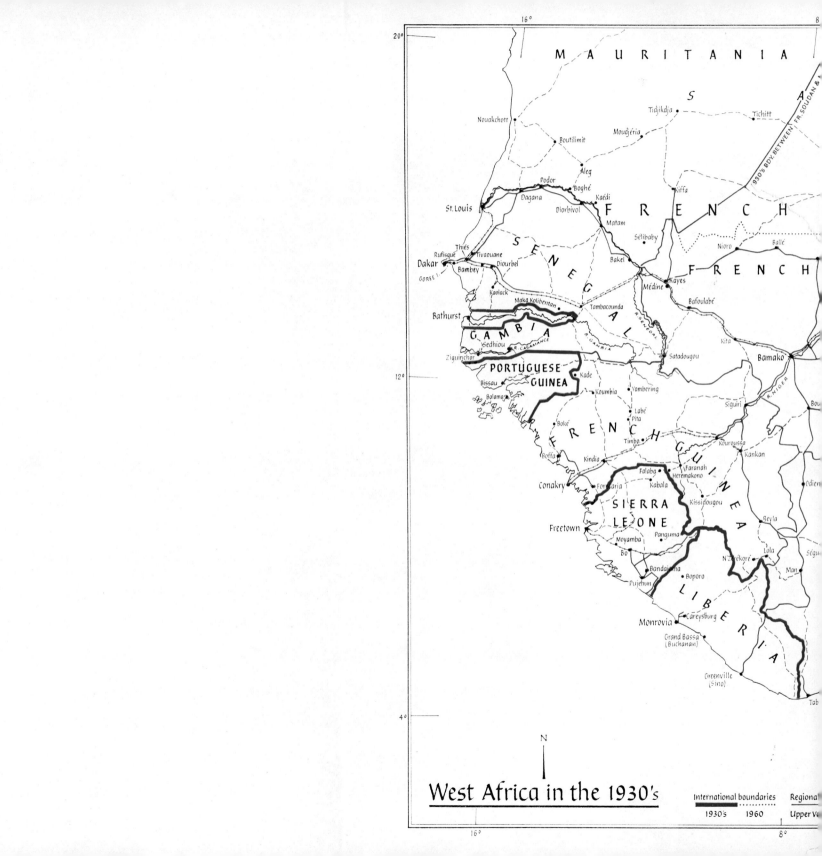

# West Africa in the 1930's

MAURITANIA

S A

Nouakchott · Tidjikdja · Tichitt

Boutilimit · Moudjéria

Aleg · Kiffa

Podor · Boghé
Dagana · Kaédi
St.Louis · Diorbivol · Matam · Sélibaby · Nioro · Ballé

Thiés · Tivaouane · Bakel
Rufisque · Diourbel · F R E N C H
Dakar · Bambey · Kayes
GOREE I. · Kaolack · Médine · Bafoulabé

S E N E G A L

Maka Kolibantan · Tambacounda · Kita

Bathurst · Bamako
G A M B I A · Satadougou

Sedhiou · R.CASAMANCE · R. SENEGAL · R.GAMBIA
Ziguinchor · PORTUGUESE · R. NIGER

GUINEA · Kade
Bissau · Koumbia · Yambering · Siguiri · Bou
Bolama · Labé · Pita
Boké · Timbo · Keuroussa
F R E N C H · Kankan
Boffa · Kindia · Faranah · Odien

Conakry · Forecaria · Kabala · Kissidougou
Falaba · Heremakono

S I E R R A · Beyla
L E O N E · Kissidougou

Freetown · Moyamba · Panguma · N'Zérékoré · Lola · Ségu
Bo · Man
Bandajuma · Boporo
Pujehun · L I B E R I A

Monrovia · Careysburg

Grand Bassa
(Buchanan)

Greenville
(Sino) · Tab

N

International boundaries  Regiona

1930's   1960        Upper V

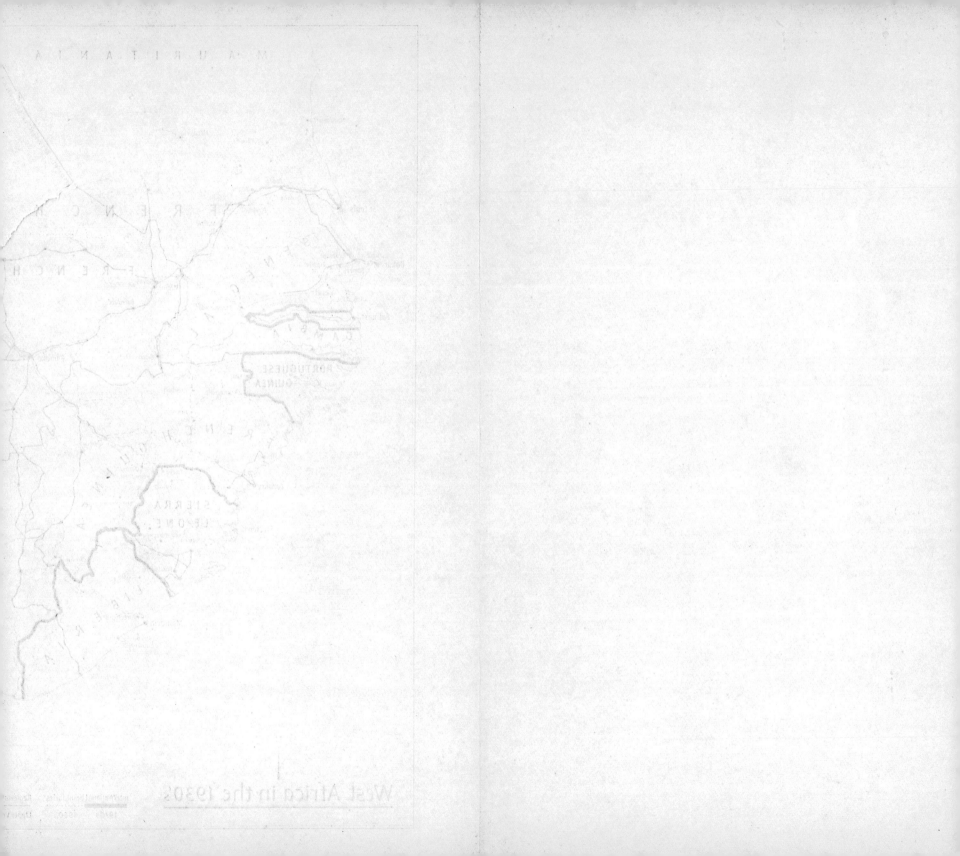

# Index